Blackstone's Statutes on

Public Law & Human Rights

Blackstone's Statutes Series

The original and best for 25 years

25 years

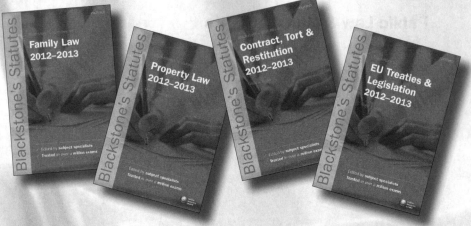

Books in the series:

Commercial and Consumer Law
  Francis Rose

Company Law
  Derek French

Contract, Tort and Restitution
  Francis Rose

Criminal Justice and Sentencing
  Barry Mitchell and Salim Farrar

Criminal Law
  Peter Glazebrook

EU Treaties and Legislation
  Nigel Foster

Employment Law
  Richard Kidner

Environmental Legislation
  Donald McGillivray

Evidence
  Phil Huxley

Family Law
  Mika Oldham

Intellectual Property
  Andrew Christie and Stephen Gare

International Human Rights Documents
  Sandy Ghandhi

International Law Documents
  Malcolm D. Evans

IT and e-Commerce
  Steve Hedley and Tanya Aplin

Media Law
  Richard Caddell and Howard Johnson

Medical Law
  Anne E. Morris and Michael A. Jones

Property Law
  Meryl Thomas

Public Law and Human Rights
  Robert G. Lee

UK and EU Competition Documents
  Kirsty Middleton

A rock-solid reputation for accuracy, reliability, and authority since 1987

www.oxfordtextbooks.co.uk/orc/statutes

Blackstone's Statutes on

Public Law & Human Rights

2012–2013

22nd edition

edited by

Robert G. Lee

LLB, LLD

*Professor of Law, Cardiff Law School, ESRC Centre for Business
Relationships, Accountability, Sustainability and Society,
Cardiff University*

Earlier editions of this book were produced jointly between Robert Lee and

Peter Wallington QC

11 KBW Chambers

OXFORD
UNIVERSITY PRESS

OXFORD
UNIVERSITY PRESS

Great Clarendon Street, Oxford, OX2 6DP,
United Kingdom

Oxford University Press is a department of the University of Oxford.
It furthers the University's objective of excellence in research, scholarship,
and education by publishing worldwide. Oxford is a registered trade mark of
Oxford University Press in the UK and in certain other countries

This selection © Robert G. Lee 2012

The moral rights of the author have been asserted

First published by Blackstone Press 1988
Nineteenth edition 2009
Twentieth edition 2010
Twenty-first edition 2011
Twenty-second edition 2012

Impression: 1

Public sector information reproduced under Open Government Licence v1.0
(http://www.nationalarchives.gov.uk/doc/open-government-licence/
open-government-licence.htm)

Crown Copyright material reproduced with the permission of the
Controller, HMSO (under the terms of the Click Use licence)

British Library Cataloguing in Publication Data

Data available

ISBN 978–0–19–965629–5

Printed in Great Britain by
MPG Books Group, Bodmin and King's Lynn

Links to third party websites are provided by Oxford in good faith and
for information only. Oxford disclaims any responsibility for the materials
contained in any third party website referenced in this work.

Contents

Part III   PACE Codes   515

Alphabetical contents

Editor's preface

The adage that Britain has no written constitution, while still technically true, is an increasingly un-helpful and unreal starting point for the study of Constitutional Law. As in many other areas of the law, statute has assumed an increasingly pervasive role. In addition, the incorporation of the European Convention on Human Rights into domestic law provides a significant constitutional yardstick against which laws must be measured. Other international sources play an increasing part in the regulation of power in the UK, making it important to look for comparison at the constitutional approach of some other jurisdictions. The volume of statutory and analogous material to which students in the field of Public Law need to refer is such that a set of materials is a necessary guide. Here a collection of statutes on all aspects of Constitutional and Administrative Law and Human Rights has been assembled. It is not intended to replace textbooks or cases and materials books, but to complement them and to pro-vide necessary and quick reference to essential texts. Since it contains no commentary it is suitable—and will hopefully be adopted—for reference in examinations in these subjects (but do check with your faculty or department whether this is so). The hope is that it will also encourage students to become more accustomed to reading and unravelling the language of Parliament—one of the most basic skills of a lawyer.

The selection of materials for a collection of statutes is a matter of sometimes arbitrary editorial judgement. This selection is based on the knowledge that courses vary in content and an attempt to meet the major needs of a fairly broad range of undergraduate courses. This means that the book will contain some material irrelevant to your particular course—but much that is central, or a valu-able supplement, to any course in the Public Law area (including important parts of Legal System courses). The book is designed to be used by English, Welsh and Scottish students. It includes the le-gislation allowing significant devolution of power within the United Kingdom. The Northern Ireland Act 1998 which makes provision for the Northern Ireland Assembly has been included given the grow-ing interest in devolution on public law courses. The territorial extent of the Act is indicated for each statute. It should be noted that one consequence of increasing devolution is that statutes extending to one jurisdiction may take a different form in relation to another of the jurisdictions; for simplicity the version applicable in England in such cases has been adopted here.

This most recent edition contains interesting new material. In the area of police powers and gov-ernance, this includes the Police Reform and Social Responsibility Act 2011 and wider powers to in-vestigate and seek to prevent terrorism under the Terrorism Prevention and Investigation Measures Act 2011. Certain reforms of local government are included following the passage of the Localism Act 2011. Also of great constitutional interest are the European Union Act 2011 (mandating greater Parliamentary scrutiny of EU legislation), the Fixed-term Parliaments Act 2011(governing the dis-solution of Parliament) and the Public Bodies Act 2011 (the cull of the quangos). The timescale for production of this book has allowed coverage of the significant provisions of public law up to the end of April 2012.

Part II of the book contains a range of non-UK material including constitutional material from elsewhere, relevant EU provisions and other relevant Treaties to which the UK is a party. This edition of the book now contains consolidated versions of the Treaty on European Union and the Treaty on the Functioning of the European Union. There is also some domestic non-statutory material, in the form of the most important PACE Codes of Practice in Part III. This edition contains recent revisions to the Codes.

The amount of new material in this edition has required, once again, some editing of the previous text. It is hoped, however, that nothing vital has been lost. As always comments are gratefully received concerning the editorial judgements exercised. Because this is a text for students rather than practi-tioners, it has been possible to be more selective in cutting material down to a manageable length. Omissions are indicated by a row of asterisks. Provisions as to commencement, etc. have also been omitted. The text is printed, where appropriate, as subsequently amended; new materials are shown by square brackets and repeals by dots. Statutes are printed in chronological order (in alphabetical order within each year); other material is gathered together in Part II.

This edition is accompanied by a website which contains, inter alia, a list of useful websites for further research. You can access any of these websites by hyperlinks from the Online Resource Centre (www.oxfordtextbooks.co.uk/orc/statutes/) which will also give you updates on important developments affecting the materials in this book.

The major acknowledgement of assistance must go to Peter Wallington QC who co-edited the text for so many years.

Grateful acknowledgement for help received goes to Clive Lewis, who advised on content and carefully checked the manuscript of the first edition. Gratitude is also owed to Jeremy McBride, both for suggestions as to inclusion and for the benefit of collaboration in the internal production of statutory materials for students at Cambridge, Birmingham, Lancaster and Cardiff. The research assistance of Clare and Cameron Pike, who worked on this edition, is greatly appreciated. Finally, thanks are due to the publishers for their speed and efficiency in production. The responsibility for errors is that of the editor alone.

Robert G. Lee
May 2012

New to this edition

The twenty-second edition of *Blackstone's Statutes on Public Law & Human Rights* has been fully revised and updated to include all relevant legislation through to April 2012.

- Police Reform and Social Responsibility Act 2011
- Terrorism Prevention and Investigation Measures Act 2011
- Localism Act 2011
- Fixed-term Parliaments Act 2011
- European Union Act 2011
- Public Bodies Act 2011

Legislation of the UK Parliament and other legislatures within the UK

Magna Carta

(Statute 25 Edw. 1, 1297)

Territorial extent: England and Wales, Northern Ireland

The Great Charter of the Liberties of England, and of the Liberties of the Forest; confirmed by King Edward, in the Twenty-fifth Year of his Reign.

Edward by the grace of God King of England, Lord of Ireland, and Duke of Guyan, to all archbishops, bishops, &c. We have seen the Great Charter of the Lord Henry sometimes King of England, our father, of the liberties of England in these words:

Henry by the grace of God King of England, Lord of Ireland, Duke of Normandy and Guyan, and Earl of Anjou, to all archbishops, bishops, abbots, priors, earls, barons, sheriffs, provosts, officers, and to all bailiffs, and other our faithful subjects, which shall see this present charter, greeting: Know ye, that we, unto the honour of Almighty God, and for the salvation of the souls of our progenitors and successors Kings of England, to the advancement of holy church and amendment of our realm, of our meer and free will, have given and granted to all archbishops, bishops, abbots, priors, earls, barons, and to all freemen of this our realm, these liberties following, to be kept in our kingdom of England for ever.

Chapter 1   Confirmation of liberties

First, we have granted to God, and by this our present charter have confirmed, for us and our heirs for ever, that the church of England shall be free, and shall have all her whole rights and liberties inviolable. We have granted also, and given to all the freemen of our realm, for us and our heirs for ever, these liberties underwritten, to have and to hold to them and their heirs, of us and our heirs for ever.

Chapters 2–8   ...

Chapter 9   *****

Chapters 10–28   ...

Chapter 29   Imprisonment, etc. contrary to law

No freeman shall be taken or imprisoned, or be disseised of his freehold, or liberties, or free customs, or be outlawed, or exiled, or any other wise destroyed; nor will we not pass upon him, nor condemn him, but by lawful judgment of his peers, or by the law of the land. We will sell to no man, we will not deny or defer to any man either justice or right.

Chapters 30–36   ...
*****

The Bill of Rights (1688)

(1 Will. & Mar. sess 2, c. 2)

An Act declaring the Rights and Liberties of the Subject and Setleing the Succession of the Crowne.

Territorial extent: England and Wales, Northern Ireland (for Scotland see the equivalent Act of the Scottish Parliament, the Claim of Right 1689)

Whereas the lords spirituall and temporall and comons assembled at Westminster lawfully fully and freely representing all estates of the people of this realme did upon the thirteenth day of February in the yeare of our Lord one thousand six hundred eighty eight present unto their Majesties then called and known by the names and stile of William and Mary Prince and Princesse of Orange being present in their proper persons a certaine declaration in writeing made by the said lords and comons in the words following viz

The heads of declaration of lords and commons, recited—Whereas the late King James the Second by the assistance of diverse evill councillors judges and ministers imployed by him did endeavour to subvert and extirpate the Protestant religion and the lawes and liberties of this kingdome.

Dispensing and suspending power—By assumeing and exerciseing a power of dispensing with and suspending of lawes and the execution of lawes without consent of Parlyament.

Committing prelates—By committing and prosecuting diverse worthy prelates for humbly petitioning to be excused from concurring to the said assumed power.

Ecclesiastical commission—By issueing and causeing to be executed a commission under the great seale for erecting a court called the court of commissioners for ecclesiasticall causes.

Levying money—By levying money for and to the use of the Crowne by pretence of prerogative for other time and in other manner then the same was granted by Parlyament.

Standing army—By raising and keeping a standing army within this kingdome in time of peace without consent of Parlyament and quartering soldiers contrary to law.

Disarming Protestants, etc.—By causing severall good subjects being protestants to be disarmed at the same time when papists were both armed and imployed contrary to law.

Violating elections—By violating the freedome of election of members to serve in Parlyament.

Illegal prosecutions—By prosecutions in the Court of King's Bench for matters and causes cognizable onely in Parlyament and by diverse other arbitrary and illegall courses.

Juries—And whereas of late yeares partiall corrupt and unqualifyed persons have beene returned and served on juryes in tryalls and particularly diverse jurors in tryalls for high treason which were not freeholders.

Excessive bail—And excessive baile hath beene required of persons committed in criminall cases to elude the benefitt of the lawes made for the liberty of the subjects.

Fines—And excessive fines have beene imposed.

Punishments—And illegall and cruell punishments inflicted.

Grants of fines, etc., before conviction, etc.—And severall grants and promises made of fines and forfeitures before any conviction or judgement against the persons upon whome the same were to be levyed.

All which are uterly and directly contrary to the knowne lawes and statutes and freedome of the realme.

And whereas the said late King James the Second haveing abdicated the government and the throne being thereby vacant his Highnesse the Prince of Orange (whome it hath pleased Almighty God to make the glorious instrument of delivering this kingdome from popery and arbitrary power) did (by the advice of the lords spirituall and temporall and diverse principall persons of the commons) cause letters to be written to the lords spirituall and temporall being protestants and other letters to the severall countyes cityes universities boroughss and cinque ports for the choosing of such persons to represent them as were of right to be sent to Parlyament to meete and sitt at Westminster upon the two and twentyeth day of January in this yeare one thousand six hundred eighty and eight in order to such an establishment as that their religion lawes and liberties might not againe be in danger of being subverted, upon which letters elections haveing beene accordingly made.

The subject's Rights—And thereupon the said lords spirituall and temporall and commons pursuant to their respective letters and elections being now assembled in a full and free representative of this nation takeing into their most serious consideration the best meanes for attaining the ends aforesaid doe in the first place (as their auncestors in like case have usually done) for the vindicating and asserting their auntient rights and liberties, declare

[1] **Suspending power**—That the pretended power of suspending of laws or the execution of laws by regall authority without consent of Parlyament is illegall.

Late dispensing power—That the pretended power of dispensing with laws or the execution of laws by regall authoritie as it hath beene assumed and exercised of late is illegall.

Ecclesiastical courts illegal—That the commission for erecting the late court of commissioners for ecclesiasticall causes and all other commissions and courts of like nature are illegal and pernicious.

Levying money—That levying money for or to the use of the Crowne by pretence of prerogative without grant of Parlyament for longer time or in other manner than the same is or shall be granted is illegal.

Right to petition—That it is the right of the subjects to petition the King and all commitments and prosecutions for such petitioning are illegal.

Standing army—That the raising or keeping a standing army within the kingdome in time of peace unlesse it be with consent of Parlyament is against law.

Subject's arms—That the subjects which are protestants may have arms for their defence suitable to their conditions and as allowed by law.

Freedom of election—That election of members of Parlyament ought to be free.

Freedom of speech—That the freedome of speech and debates or proceedings in Parlyament ought not to be impeached or questioned in any court or place out of Parlyament.

Excessive bail—That excessive baile ought not to be required nor excessive fines imposed nor cruell and unusuall punishments inflicted.

Juries—That jurors ought to be duly impannelled and returned . . .

Grants of forfeitures—That all grants and promises of fines and forfeitures of particular persons before conviction are illegal and void.

Frequent Parliaments—And that for redresse of all grievances and for the amending strengthening and preserving of the lawes Parlyaments ought to be held frequently.

The said right claimed, tender of the crown, regal power exercised, limitation of the crown, new oaths of allegiance, etc.—And they doe claime demand and insist upon all and singular the premises as their undoubted rights and liberties and that noe declarations judgements doeings or proceedings to the prejudice of the people in any of the said premises ought in any wise to be drawne hereafter into consequence or example. To which demand of their rights they are particularly encouraged by the declaration of his Highnesse the Prince of Orange as being the only meanes for obtaining a full redresse and remedy therein. Haveing therefore an intire confidence that his said Highnesse the Prince of Orange will perfect the deliverance soe farr advanced by him and will still preserve them from the violation of their rights which they have here asserted and from all other attempts upon their religion rights and liberties. The said lords spirituall and temporall and commons assembled at Westminster doe resolve that William and Mary Prince and Princesse of Orange be and be declared King and Queene of England France and Ireland and the dominions thereunto belonging to hold the crowne and royall dignity of the said kingdomes and dominions to them the said prince and princesse dureing their lives and the life of the survivour of them. And that the sole and full exercise of the regall power be onely in and executed by the said Prince of Orange in the names of the said prince and princesse dureing their joynt lives and after their deceases the said crowne and royall dignitie of the said kingdoms and dominions to be to the heires of the body of the said princesse and for default of such issue to the Princesse Anne of Denmarke and the heires of her body and for default of such issue to the heires of the body of the said Prince of Orange. And the lords spirituall and temporall and commons doe pray the said prince and princesse to accept the same accordingly. And that the oathes hereafter mentioned be taken by all persons of whome the oathes of allegiance and supremacy might be required by law instead of them and that the said oathes of allegiance and supremacy be abrogated.

I A B doe sincerely promise and sweare that I will be faithfull and beare true allegiance to their Majestyes King William and Queen Mary

Soe helpe me God

I A B doe sweare that I doe from my heart abhorr, detest and abjure as impious and hereticall this damnable doctrine and position that princes excommunicated or deprived by the Pope or any authority of the see of Rome may be deposed or murdered by their subjects or any other whatsoever. And I doe declare that noe forreigne prince person prelate, state or potentate hath or ought to have any jurisdiction power superiority preeminence or authoritie ecclesiasticall or spirituall within this realme.

Soe help me God

[**Note:** For the modern version of this effectively obsolete oath see the Accession Declaration Act 1910, Sch.]

Acceptance of the crown, the two Houses to sit, subjects' liberties to be allowed, and ministers hereafter to serve according to the same, William and Mary declared King and Queen, limitation of the crown, papists debarred the crown, every King, etc, shall make the declaration of 30 Car 2, if under 12 years old, to be done after attainment thereof, King's and Queen's assent. Upon which their said Majestyes did accept the crowne and royall dignitie of the kingdoms of England France and Ireland and the dominions thereunto belonging according to the resolution and desire of the said lords and commons contained in the said declaration. And thereupon their Majestyes were pleased that the said lords spirituall and temporall and commons being the two Houses of Parlyament should continue to sitt and with their Majesties royall concurrence make effectuall provision for the settlement of the religion lawes and liberties of this kingdome soe that the same for the future might not be in danger againe of being subverted, to which the said lords spirituall and temporall and commons did agree and proceede to act accordingly. Now in pursuance of the premises the said lords spirituall and temporall and commons in Parlyament assembled for the ratifying confirming and establishing the said declaration and the articles clauses matters and things therein contained by the force of a law made in due forme by authority of Parlyament doe pray that it may be declared and enacted that all and singular the rights and liberties asserted and claimed in the said declaration are the true auntient and indubitable rights and liberties of the people of this kingdome and soe shall be esteemed allowed adjudged deemed and taken to be and that all and every the particulars aforesaid shall be firmly and strictly holden and observed as they are expressed in the said declaration. And all officers and ministers whatsoever shall serve their Majestyes and their successors according to the same in all times to come. And the said lords spirituall and temporall and commons seriously considering how it hath pleased Almighty God in his marvellous providence and mercifull goodness to this nation to provide and preserve their said Majestyes royall persons most happily to raigne over us upon the throne of their auncestors for which they render unto him from the bottome of their hearts their humblest thanks and praises doe truely firmely assuredly and in the sincerity of their hearts thinke and doe hereby recognize acknowledge and declare that King James the Second haveing abdicated the government and their Majestyes having accepted the crowne and royall dignity as aforesaid their said Majestyes did become were are and of right ought to be by the lawes of the realme our soveraigne liege lord and lady King and Queene of England France and Ireland and the dominions thereunto belonging in and to whose princely persons the royall state crowne and dignity of the said realmes with all honours stiles titles regalities prerogatives powers jurisdictions and authorities to the same belonging and appertaining are most fully and rightfully and intirely invested and incorporated united and annexed. And for preventing all questions and divisions in this realme by reason of any pretended titles to the crowne and for preserveing a certainty in the succession thereof in and upon which the unity peace tranquillity and safety of this nation doth under God wholly consist and depend the said lords spirituall and temporall and commons doe beseech their Majestyes that it may be enacted established and declared that the crowne and regall government of the said kingdoms and dominions with all and singular the premisses thereunto belonging and appertaining shall bee and continue to their said Majestyes and the survivour of them dureing their lives and the life of the survivour of them and that the entire perfect and full exercise of the regall power and government be onely in and executed by his Majestie in the names of both their Majestyes dureing their joynt lives and after their deceases the said crowne and premisses shall be and remaine to the heires of the body of her Majestie and for default of such issue to her royall Highnesse the Princess Anne of Denmarke and the heires of her body and for default of such issue to the heires of the body of his said Majestie And thereunto the said lords spirituall and temporall and commons doe in the name of all the people aforesaid most humbly and faithfully submitt themselves their heires and posterities for ever and doe faithfully promise that they will stand to maintaine and defend their said Majesties and alsoe the limitation and succession of the crowne herein specified and contained to the utmost of their powers with their lives and estates against all persons whatsoever that shall attempt any thing to the contrary. And whereas it hath beene found by experience that it is inconsistent with the safety and welfaire of this protestant kingdome to be governed by a popish prince or by any King or Queene marrying a papist the said lords spirtuall and temporall and commons doe further pray that it may be enacted that all and every person and persons that is are or shall be reconciled to or shall hold communion with the see or church of Rome or shall professe the popish religion or shall marry a papist shall be excluded and be for ever uncapeable to inherit possesse or enjoy the crowne and government of this realme and Ireland and the dominions thereunto belonging or any part of the same or to have use or exercise any regall power authoritie or jurisdiction within the same And in all and every such case or cases the people of these realmes shall be and are hereby absolved of their allegiance and the said crowne and government shall from time to time descend to and be enjoyed by such person or persons being protestants as should have inherited and enjoyed the same in case the said person or persons soe reconciled holding communion or professing or marrying as aforesaid were naturally dead And that every King and Queene of this realme who at any time hereafter shall come to and succeede in the imperiall crowne of this kingdome shall on the first day of the meeting of the first Parlyament next after his or her comeing to the crowne sitting in his or her throne in the House of Peeres in the presence of the lords and commons therein assembled or at his or her coronation before such person or persons who shall administer the coronation oath to him or her at the time of his or her takeing the said oath (which shall first happen) make subscribe and audibly repeate the declaration mentioned in the Statute made in the thirtyeth yeare of the raigne of King Charles the Second entituled An Act for the more effectuall preserveing the Kings person and government by disableing papists from sitting in either House of Parlyament But if it shall happen that such King or Queene upon his or her succession to the crowne of this realme shall be under the age of twelve yeares then every such King or Queene shall make subscribe and audibly repeate the said declaration at his or her coronation or the first day of the meeting of the first Parlyament as aforesaid which shall first happen after such King or Queene shall have attained the said age of twelve years. All which their Majestyes are contented and pleased shall be declared enacted and established by authoritie of this present Parliament and shall stand remaine and be the law of this realme for ever And the same are by their said Majesties by and with the advice and consent of the lords spirituall and temporall and commons in Parlyament assembled and by the authoritie of the same declared enacted and established accordingly

2   Non obstantes made void

... noe dispensation by non obstante of or to any statute or any part thereof shall be allowed but ... the same shall be held void and of noe effect except a dispensation be allowed of in such statutes ...

3   ...

Crown and Parliament Recognition Act 1689

(2 Will. & Mar., c. 1)

An Act for Recognizing King William and Queene Mary and for avoiding all Questions touching the Acts made in the Parliament assembled at Westminster the thirteenth day of February one thousand six hundred eighty eight

Territorial extent: England and Wales, Northern Ireland (effectively extended to Scotland by the Union with Scotland Act 1706, below)

Wee your Majestyes most humble and loyall subjects the lords spirituall and temporall and commons in this present Parlyament assembled doe beseech your most excellent Majestyes that it may be publisehd and declared in this High Court of Parlyament and enacted by authoritie of the same that we doe recognize and acknowledge your Majestyes were are and of right ought to be by the laws of this realme our soveraigne liege lord and lady King and Queene of England France and Ireland and the dominions thereunto belonging in and to whose princely persons the royall state crowne and dignity of the said realms with all honours stiles tiles regalities prerogatives powers jurisdictions and authorities to the same belonging and appertaining are most fully rightfully and intirely invested and incorporated united and annexed. And for the avoiding of all disputes and questions concerning the being and authority of the late Parliament assembled at Westminster the thirteenth day of February one thousand six hundred eighty eight wee doe most humbly beseech your Majestyes that it may be enacted and bee it enacted by the King and Queenes most excellent Majestyes by and with the advice and consent of the lords spirituall and temporall and commons in this present Parlyament assembled and by authoritie of the same that all and singular the Acts made and enacted in the said Parlyament were and are laws and statutes of this kingdome and as such ought to be reputed taken and obeyed by all the people of this kingdome.

The Act of Settlement (1700)

(12 & 13 Will. 3, c. 2)

An Act for the further Limitation of the Crown and better securing the Rights and Liberties of the Subject.

Territorial extent: England and Wales, Northern Ireland; effectively extended to Scotland by the Union with Scotland Act 1706

1   The Princess Sophia, Electress and Duchess dowager of Hanover, daughter of the late Queen of Bohemia, daughter of King James the First, to inherit after the King and the Princess Anne, in default of issue of the said princess and his Majesty, respectively; and the heirs of her body, being Protestants

Whereas in the first year of the reign of your Majesty and of our late most gracious soverign lady Queen Mary (of blessed memory) an Act of Parliament was made intituled (An Act for declaring the rights and liberties of the subject and for setling the succession of the crown) wherein it was (amongst other things) enacted established and declared that the crown and regall government of the kingdoms of England France and Ireland and the dominions thereunto belonging should be and continue to your Majestie and the said late Queen during the joynt lives of your Majesty and the said Queen and to the survivor and that after the decease of your Majesty and of the said Queen the said crown and regall government should be and remain to the heirs of the body of the said late Queen and for default of such issue to her royall Highness the Princess Ann of Denmark and the heirs of her body and for default of such issue to the heirs of the body of your Majesty And it was thereby further enacted that all and every person and persons that then were or afterwards should be reconciled to or shall hold communion with the see or church of Rome or should professe the popish religion or marry a papist should be excluded and are by that Act made for ever incapable to inherit possess or enjoy the crown and government of this realm and Ireland and the dominions thereunto belonging or any part of the same or to have use or exercise any regall power authority or jurisdiction within the same and in all and every such case and cases the people of these realms shall be and are thereby absolved of their allegiance and that the said crown and government shall from time to time descend to and be enjoyed by such person or persons being protestants as should have inherited and enjoyed the same in case the said person or persons so reconciled holding communion professing or marrying as aforesaid were naturally dead After the making of which Statute and the settlement therein contained your Majesties good subjects who were restored to the full and free possession and enjoyment of their religion rights and liberties by the providence of God giving success to your Majesties just undertakings and unwearied endeavours for that purpose had no greater temporall felicity to hope or wish for than to see a royall progeny descending from your Majesty to whom (under God) they owe their tranquility and whose ancestors have for many years been principall assertors of the reformed religion and the liberties of Europe and from our said most gracious sovereign lady whose memory will always be precious to the subjects of these realms And it having since pleased Almighty God to take away our said sovereign lady and also the most hopefull Prince William Duke of Gloucester (the only surviving issue of her royall Highness the Princess Ann of Denmark) to the unspeakable grief and sorrow of your Majesty and your said good subjects who under such losses being sensibly put in mind that it standeth wholly in the pleasure of Almighty God to prolong the lives of your Majesty and of her royall Highness and to grant to your Majesty or to her royall Highness such issue as may be inheritable to the crown and regall government aforesaid by the respective limitations in the said recited Act contained doe constantly implore the divine mercy for those blessings And your Majesties said subjects having daily experience of your royall care and concern for the present and future welfare of these kingdoms and particularly recommending from your throne a further provision to be made for the succession of the crown in the protestant line for the happiness of the nation and the security of our religion and it being absolutely necessary for the safety peace and quiet of this realm to obviate all doubts and contentions in the same by reason of any pretended titles to the crown and to maintain a certainty in the succession thereof to which your subjects may safely have recourse for their protection in case the limitations in the said recited Act should determine Therefore for a further provision of the succession of the crown in the protestant line we your Majesties most dutifull and loyal subjects the lords spirituall and temporall and commons in this present Parliament assembled do beseech your Majesty that it may be enacted and declared and be it enacted and declared by the Kings most excellent Majesty by and with the advice and consent of the lords spirituall and temporall and commons in this present Parliament assembled and by the authority of the same that the most excellent Princess Sophia Electress and Dutchess dowager of Hanover daughter of the most excellent Princess Elizabeth late Queen of Bohemia daughter of our late sovereign lord King James the First of happy memory be and is hereby declared to be the next in succession in the protestant line to the imperiall crown and dignity of the [said] realms of England France and Ireland with the dominions and territories thereunto belonging after his Majesty and the Princess Ann of Denmark and in default of issue of the said Princess Ann and of his Majesty respectively and that from and after the deceases of his said Majesty our own soveriegn lord and of her royall Highness the Princess Ann of Denmark and for default of issue of the said Princess Ann and of his Majesty respectively the crown and regall government of the said kingdoms of England France and Ireland and of the dominions thereunto belonging with the royall state and dignity of the said realms and all honours stiles titles regalities prerogatives powers jurisdictions and authorities to the same belonging and appertaining shall be remain and continue to the said most excellent Princess Sophia and the heirs of her body being protestants And thereunto the said lords spirituall and temporall and commons shall and will in the name of all the people of this realm most humbly and faithfully submit themselves their heirs and posterities and do faithfully promise that after the deceases of his Majesty and her royall Highness and the failure of the heirs of their respective bodies to stand to maintain and defend the said Princess Sophia and the heirs of her body being protestants according to the limitation and succession of the crown in this Act specified and contained to the utmost of their powers with their lives and estates against all persons whatsoever that shall attempt any thing to the contrary.

2   The persons inheritable by this Act, holding communion with the church of Rome, incapacitated as by the former Act; to take the oath at their coronation, according to Stat 1 W & M c. 6

Provided always and it is hereby enacted that all and every person and persons who shall or may take or inherit the said crown by vertue of the limitation of this present Act and is are or shall be reconciled to or shall hold communion with the see or church of Rome or shall profess the popish religion or shall marry a papist shall be subject to such incapacities as in such case or cases are by the said recited Act provided enacted and established. And that every King and Queen of this realm who shall come to and succeed in the imperiall crown of this kingdom by vertue of this Act shall have the coronation oath administered to him her or them at their respective coronations according to the Act of Parliament made in the first year of the reign of his Majesty and the said late Queen Mary intituled An Act for establishing the coronation oath and shall make subscribe and repeat the declaration in the Act first above recited mentioned or referred to in the manner and form thereby prescribed.

3   Further provisions for securing the religions, laws, and liberties of these realms

And whereas it is requisite and necessary that some further provision be made for securing our religion laws and liberties from and after the death of his Majesty and the Princess Ann of Denmark and in default of issue of the body of the said princess and of his Majesty respectively Be it enacted by the Kings most excellent Majesty by and with the advice and consent of the lords spirituall and temporall and commons in Parliament and by the authority of the same

   That whosoever shall hereafter come to the possession of this crown shall joyn in communion with the Church of England as by law established

   That in case the crown and imperiall dignity of this realm shall hereafter come to any person not being a native of this kingdom of England this nation be not obliged to ingage in any warr for the defence of any dominions or territories which do not belong to the crown of England without the consent of Parliament

. . .

That after the said limitation shall take effect as aforesaid no person born out of the kingdoms of England Scotland or Ireland or the dominions thereunto belonging (although he be. . .made a denizen (except such as are born of English parents)) shall be capable to be of the privy councill or a member of either House of Parliament or to enjoy any office or place of trust either civill or military or to have any grant of lands tenements or hereditaments from the Crown to himself or to any other or others in trust for him.

. . .

   That no pardon under the great seal of England be pleadable to an impeachment by the commons in Parliament.

4   The laws and statutes of the realm confirmed

And whereas the laws of England are the birthright of the people thereof and all the Kings and Queens who shall ascend the throne of this realm ought to administer the government of the same according to the said laws and all their officers and ministers ought to serve them respectively according to the same The said lords spirituall and temporall and commons do therefore further humbly pray that all the laws and statutes of this realm for securing the established religion and the rights and liberties of the people thereof and all other laws and statutes of the same now in force may be ratified and confirmed And the same are by his Majesty by and with the advice and consent of the said lords spirituall and temporall and commons and by authority of the same ratified and confirmed accordingly.

Union with Scotland Act 1706

(6 Anne, c. 11)

An Act for an Union of the Two Kingdoms of England and Scotland.

Territorial extent: England, Wales and Scotland (by the combined effect of this Act and the equivalent Act of the Parliament of Scotland (APS, XI, 406)); subsequently applied to Northern Ireland

   Most Gracious Sovereign
Whereas articles of union were agreed on the twenty second day of July in the fifth year of your Majesties reign by the commissioners nominated on behalf of the kingdom of England under your Majesties great seal of England bearing date at Westminster the tenth day of April then last past in pursuance of an Act of Parliament made in England in the third year of your Majesties reign and the commissioners nominated on the behalf of the kingdom of Scotland under your Majesties great seal of Scotland bearing date the twenty-seventh day of February in the fourth year of your Majesties reign in pursuance of the fourth Act of the third session of the present Parliament of Scotland to treat of and concerning an union of the said kingdoms And whereas an Act hath passed in the Parliament of Scotland at Edinburgh the sixteenth day of January in the fifth year of your Majesties reign wherein 'tis mentioned that the estates of Parliament considering the said articles of union of the two kingdoms had agreed to and approved of the said articles of union with some additions and explanations and that your Majesty with advice and consent of the estates of Parliament for establishing the Protestant religion and Presbyterian Church government within the kingdom of Scotland had passed in the same session of Parliament an Act intituled Act for securing of the Protestant religion and Presbyterian Church government which by the tenor thereof was appointed to be inserted in any Act ratifying the treaty and expresly declared to be a fundamental and essential condition of the said treaty or union in all times coming the tenor of which articles as ratified and approved of with additions and explanations by the said Act of Parliament of Scotland follows.

Article I   The kingdoms united; ensigns armorial
That the two kingdoms of England and Scotland shall upon the first day of May which shall be in the year one thousand seven hundred and seven and for ever after be united into one kingdom by the name of Great Britain and that the ensigns armorial of the said United Kingdom be such as her Majesty shall appoint and the crosses of St. George and St. Andrew be conjoyned in such manner as Her Majesty shall think fit and used in all flags banners standards and ensigns both at sea and land.

Article II   Succession to the monarchy
That the succession to the monarchy of the United Kingdom of Great Britain and of the dominions thereto belonging after her most sacred Majesty and in default of issue of her Majesty be remain and continue to the most excellent Princess Sophia Electoress and Dutchess dowager of Hanover and the heirs of her body being protestants upon whom the crown of England is settled by an Act of Parliament made in England in the twelfth year of the reign of his late Majesty King William the Third intituled An Act for the further limitation of the crown and better securing the right and liberties of the subject And that all papists and persons marrying papists shall be excluded from and for ever incapable to inherit possess or enjoy the imperial crown of Great Britain and the dominions thereunto belonging or any part thereof and in every such case the crown and government shall from time to time descend to and be enjoyed by such person being a protestant as should have inherited and enjoyed the same in case such papist or person marrying a papist was naturally dead according to the provision for the descent of the crown of England made by another Act of Parliament in England in the first year of the reign of their late Majesties King William and Queen Mary intituled An Act declaring the rights and liberties of the subject and settling the succession of the crown.

Article III Parliament

That the United Kingdom of Great Britain be represented by one and the same Parliament to be stiled the Parliament of Great Britain.

Article IIII Trade and navigation and other rights

That all the subjects of the United Kingdom of Great Britain shall from and after the union have full freedom and intercourse of trade and navigation to and from any port or place within the said United Kingdom and the dominions and plantations thereunto belonging and that there be a communication of all other rights privileges and advantages which do or may belong to the subjects of either kingdom except where it is otherwise expressly agreed in these articles.

Article V ...

Article VI Regulations of trade, duties, etc.

That all parts of the United Kingdom for ever from and after the union shall have the same allowances encouragements and drawbacks and be under the same prohibitions restrictions and regulations of trade and liable to the same customs and duties on import and export and that the allowances encouragements and drawbacks prohibitions restrictions and regulations of trade and the customs and duties on import and export settled in England when the union commences shall from and after the union take place throughout the whole United Kingdom...

Articles VII, XVI *****

Articles VIII–XV, XVII ...

Article XVIII Laws concerning public rights; private rights

That the laws concerning regulation of trade customs and such excises to which Scotland is by virtue of this treaty to be liable be the same in Scotland from and after the union as in England and that all other laws in use within the kingdom of Scotland do after the union and notwithstanding thereof remain in the same force as before (except such as are contrary to or inconsistent with this treaty) but alterable by the Parliament of Great Britain with this difference betwixt the laws concerning publick right policy and civil government and those which concern private right that the laws which concern publick right policy and civil government may be made the same throughout the whole United Kingdom. But that no alteration be made in laws which concern private right except for evident utility of the subjects within Scotland. E + W

Article XIX Court of Session etc.

That the Court of Session or Colledge of Justice do after the Union and notwithstanding thereof remain in all time coming within Scotland as it is now constituted by the Laws of that Kingdom and with the same authority and privileges as before the Union Subject nevertheless to such regulations for the better Administration of Justice as shall be made by the Parliament of Great Britain and that hereafter none shall be named by Her Majesty or Her Royal Successors to be ordinary Lords of Session but such who have served in the Colledge of Justice as Advocates or Principal Clerks of Session for the Space of Five years or as Writers to the Signet for the Space of ten years with this provision that no Writer to the Signet be capable to be admitted a Lord of the Session unless he undergo a private and publick Tryal on the Civil Law before the Faculty of Advocates and be found by them qualified for the said Office two years before he be named to be a Lord of the Session yet so as the Qualifications made or to be made for capacitating persons to be named ordinary Lords of Session may be altered by the Parliament of Great Britain And that the Court of Justiciary do also after the Union and notwithstanding thereof remain in all time coming within Scotland as it is now constituted by the Laws of that Kingdom and with the same authority and privileges as before the Union Subject nevertheless to such regulations as shall be made by the Parliament of Great Britain and without prejudice of other rights of Justiciary ... And that the heretable rights of Admiralty and Vice Admiralties in Scotland be reserved to the respective proprietors as rights of property Subject nevertheless as to the manner of exercising such heretable rights to such regulations and alterations as shall be thought proper to be made by the Parliament of Great Britain And that all other Courts now in being within the Kingdom of Scotland do remain but Subject to alterations by the Parliament of Great Britain And that all inferior Courts within the said limits do remain Subordinate as they are now to the supreme Courts of Justice within the same in all time coming And that no Causes in Scotland be cognoscible by the Courts of Chancery Queen's Bench Common Pleas or any other Court in Westminster Hall and that the said Courts or any other of the like nature after the Union shall have no Power to cognosce review or alter the Acts or Sentences of the Judicatures within Scotland or stop the Execution of the same . . .

Articles XX–XXIV   *****

Article XXV   Laws inconsistent with the articles, void
That all laws and statutes in either kingdom so far as they are contrary to or inconsistent with the terms of these articles or any of them shall from and after the union cease and become void and shall be so declared to be by the respective Parliaments of the said kingdoms.

As by the said articles of union ratified and approved by the said Act of Parliament of Scotland relation being thereunto had may appear.
*****

5   Cap 8 ante, and the said Act of Parliament of Scotland to be observed as fundamental conditions of the said union; and the said articles and Acts of Parliament to continue the union
And it is hereby further enacted by the authority aforesaid that the said Act passed in this present session of Parliament intituled An Act for securing the Church of England as by law established and all and every the matters and things therein contained and also the said Act of Parliament of Scotland intituled Act for securing the Protestant religion and Presbyterian Church government with the establishment in the said Act contained be and shall for ever be held and adjudged to be and observed as fundamental and essential conditions of the said union and shall in all times coming be taken to be and are hereby declared to be essential and fundamental parts of the said articles and union and the said articles of union so as aforesaid ratified approved and confirmed by Act of Parliament of Scotland and by this present Act and the said Act passed in this present session of Parliament intituled an Act for securing the Church of England as by law established and also the said Act passed in the Parliament of Scotland intituled Act for securing the Protestant religion and Presbyterian Church government are hereby enacted and ordained to be and continue in all times coming the complete and intire union of the two kingdoms of England and Scotland.
*****

Official Secrets Act 1911

(1 & 2 Geo. 5, c. 28)

An Act to re-enact the Official Secrets Act 1889, with Amendments.

Territorial extent: United Kingdom. See also s. 10(1)

1   Penalties for spying
(1) If any person for any purpose prejudicial to the safety or interests of the State—
   (a) approaches [inspects, passes over] or is in the neighbourhood of, or enters any prohibited place within the meaning of this Act; or
   (b) makes any sketch, plan, model, or note which is calculated to be or might be or is intended to be directly or indirectly useful to an enemy; or
   (c) obtains, [collects, records, or publishes,] or communicates to any other person [any secret official code word or pass word, or] any sketch, plan, model, article, or note, or other

document or information which is calculated to be or might be or is intended to be directly or indirectly useful to an enemy;

he shall be guilty of felony ...

(2) On a prosecution under this section, it shall not be necessary to show that the accused person was guilty of any particular act tending to show a purpose prejudicial to the safety or interests of the State, and, notwithstanding that no such act is proved against him, he may be convicted if, from the circumstances of the case, or his conduct, or his known character as proved, it appears that his purpose was a purpose prejudicial to the safety or interests of the State; and if any sketch, plan, model, article, note, document, or information relating to or used in any prohibited place within the meaning of this Act, or anything in such a place [or any secret official code word or pass word], is made, obtained, [collected, recorded, published], or communicated by any person other than a person acting under lawful authority, it shall be deemed to have been made, obtained, [collected, recorded, published] or communicated for a purpose prejudicial to the safety or interests of the State unless the contrary is proved.

2   ...

[**Note:** Printed as amended by the Official Secrets Act 1920; s. 2 was repealed by the Official Secrets Act 1989 (below).]

3   Definition of prohibited place

For the purposes of this Act, the expression 'prohibited place' means—

[(a)   any work of defence, arsenal, naval or air force establishment or station, factory, dock-yard, mine, minefield, camp, ship, or aircraft belonging to or occupied by or on behalf of His Majesty, or any telegraph, telephone, wireless or signal station, or office so belonging or occupied, and any place belonging to or occupied by or on behalf of His Majesty and used for the purpose of building, repairing, making, or storing any munitions of war, or any sketches, plans, models, or documents relating thereto, or for the purpose of getting any metals, oil, or minerals of use in time of war];

(b)   any place not belonging to His Majesty where any [munitions of war], or any [sketches, models, plans] or documents relating thereto, are being made, repaired, [gotten] or stored under contract with, or with any person on behalf of, His Majesty, or otherwise on behalf of His Majesty; and

(c)   any place belonging to [or used for the purposes of] His Majesty which is for the time being declared [by order of a Secretary of State] to be a prohibited place for the purposes of this section on the ground that information with respect thereto, or damage thereto, would be useful to an enemy; and

(d)   any railway, road, way, or channel, or other means of communication by land or water (including any works or structures being part thereof or connected therewith), or any place used for gas, water, or electricity works or other works for purposes of a public character, or any place where any [munitions of war], or any [sketches, models, plans] or documents relating thereto, are being made, repaired, or stored otherwise than on behalf of His Majesty, which is for the time being declared [by order or a Secretary of State] to be a prohibited place for the purposes of this section, on the ground that information with respect thereto, or the destruction or obstruction thereof, or interference therewith, would be useful to an enemy.

4–6   ...

7   *****

8   Restriction on prosecution

A prosecution for an offence under this Act shall not be instituted except by or with the consent of the Attorney-General:

...

9   Search warrants

(1) If a justice of the peace is satisfied by information on oath that there is reasonable ground for suspecting that an offence under this Act has been or is about to be committed, he may grant a search warrant authorising any constable... to enter at any time any premises or place named in the warrant, if necessary, by force, and to search the premises or place and every person found therein, and to seize any sketch, plan, model, article, note, or document, or anything of a like nature or anything which is evidence of an offence under this Act having been or being about to be committed, which he may find on the premises or place or on any such person, and with regard to or in connexion with which he has reasonable ground for suspecting that an offence under this Act has been or is about to be committed.

(2) Where it appears to a superintendent of police that the case is one of great emergency and that in the interests of the State immediate action is necessary, he may by a written order under his hand give to any constable the like authority as may be given by the warrant of a justice under the section.

10   Extent of Act and place of trial of offence

(1) This Act shall apply to all acts which are offences under this Act when committed in any part of His Majesty's dominions, or when committed by British officers or subjects elsewhere.

*****

Parliament Act 1911

(1 & 2 Geo. 5, c. 13)

An Act to make provision with respect to the powers of the House of Lords in relation of the House of Commons, and to limit the duration of Parliament.

Territorial extent: United Kingdom

Preamble

Whereas it is expedient that provision should be made for regulating the relations between the two Houses of Parliament:

And whereas it is intended to substitute for the House of Lords as it at present exists a Second Chamber constituted on a popular instead of hereditary basis, but such substitution cannot be immediately brought into operation:

And whereas provision will require hereafter to be made by Parliament in a measure effecting such substitution for limiting and defining the powers of the new Second Chamber, but it is expedient to make such provision as in this Act appears for restricting the existing powers of the House of Lords:

1   Powers of House of Lords as to Money Bills

(1) If a Money Bill, having been passed by the House of Commons, and sent up to the House of Lords at least one month before the end of the session, is not passed by the House of Lords without amendment within one month after it is so sent up to that House, the Bill shall, unless the House of Commons direct to the contrary, be presented to His Majesty and become an Act of Parliament on the Royal Assent being signified, notwithstanding that the House of Lords have not consented to the Bill.

(2) A Money Bill means a Public Bill which in the opinion of the Speaker of the House of Commons contains only provisions dealing with all or any of the following subjects, namely, the imposition, repeal, remission, alteration, or regulation of taxation; the imposition for the payment of debt or other financial purposes of charges on the Consolidated Fund, [the National Loans Fund] or on money provided by Parliament, or the variation or repeal of any such charges; supply; the appropriation, receipt, custody, issue or audit of accounts of public money; the raising or guarantee of any loan or the repayment thereof; or subordinate matters incidental to those subjects or any of them. In this

subsection the expressions 'taxation', 'public money' and 'loan' respectively do not include any taxation, money, or loan raised by local authorities or bodies for local purposes.

(3) There shall be endorsed on every Money Bill when it is sent up to the House of Lords and when it is presented to His Majesty for assent the certificate of the Speaker of the House of Commons signed by him that it is a Money Bill. Before giving his certificate, the Speaker shall consult, if practicable, two members to be appointed from the Chairmen's Panel at the beginning of each Session by the Committee of Selection.

2   Restriction of the powers of the House of Lords as to Bills other than Money Bills

(1) If any Public Bill (other than a Money Bill or a Bill containing any provision to extend the maximum duration of Parliament beyond five years) is passed by the House of Commons [in two successive sessions] (whether of the same Parliament or not), and, having been sent up to the House of Lords at least one month before the end of the session, is rejected by the House of Lords in each of those sessions, that Bill shall, on its rejection [for the second time] by the House of Lords, unless the House of Commons direct to the contrary, be presented to His Majesty and become an Act of Parliament on the Royal Assent being signified thereto, notwithstanding that the House of Lords have not consented to the Bill:

Provided that this provision shall not take effect unless [one year has elapsed] between the date of the second reading in the first of those sessions of the Bill in the House of Commons and the date on which it passes the House of Commons [in the second of those sessions].

(2) When a Bill is presented to His Majesty for assent in pursuance of the provisions of this section, there shall be endorsed on the Bill the certificate of the Speaker of the House of Commons signed by him that the provisions of this section have been duly complied with.

(3) A Bill shall be deemed to be rejected by the House of Lords if it is not passed by the House of Lords either without amendment or with such amendments only as may be agreed to by both Houses.

(4) A Bill shall be deemed to be the same Bill as a former Bill sent up to the House of Lords in the preceding session if, when it is sent up to the House of Lords, it is identical with the former Bill or contains only such alterations as are certified by the Speaker of the House of Commons to be necessary owing to the time which has elapsed since the date of the former Bill, or to represent any amendments which have been made by the House of Lords in the former Bill in the preceding sesion, and any amendments which are certified by the Speaker to have been made by the House of Lords [in the second session] and agreed to by the House of Commons shall be inserted in the Bill as presented for Royal Assent in pursuance of this section:

Provided that the House of Commons may, if they think fit, on the passage of such a Bill through the House [in the second session], suggest any further amendments without inserting the amendments in the Bill, and any such suggested amendments shall be considered by the House of Lords, and, if agreed to by that House, shall be treated as amendments made by the House of Lords and agreed to by the House of Commons; but the exercise of this power by the House of Commons shall not affect the operation of this section in the event of the Bill being rejected by the House of Lords.

[**Note:** The words in square brackets in s. 2 were substituted by the Parliament Act 1949.]

3   Certificate of Speaker

Any certificate of the Speaker of the House of Commons given under this Act shall be conclusive for all purposes, and shall not be questioned in any court of law.

4   Enacting words

(1) In every Bill presented to His Majesty under the preceding provisions of this Act, the words of enactment shall be as follows, that is to say:–

'Be it enacted by the King's most Excellent Majesty, by and with the advice and consent of the Commons in this present Parliament assembled, in accordance with the provisions of [the Parliament Acts 1911 and 1949], and by authority of the same, as follows.'

(2) Any alteration of a Bill necessary to give effect to this section shall not be deemed to be an amendment of the Bill.

5 Provisional Order Bills excluded
In this Act the expression 'Public Bill' does not include any Bill for confirming a Provisional Order.

6 Saving for existing rights and privileges of the House of Commons
Nothing in this Act shall diminish or qualify the existing rights and privileges of the House of Commons.

7 ...

Official Secrets Act 1920

(10 & 11 Geo. 5, c. 75)

An Act to amend the Official Secrets Act 1911.

Territorial extent: United Kingdom

1 Unauthorised use of uniforms; falsification of reports, forgery, personation, and false documents

(1) If any person for the purpose of gaining admission, or of assisting any other person to gain admission, to a prohibited place, within the meaning of the Official Secrets Act 1911 (hereinafter referred to as 'the principal Act'), or for any other purpose prejudicial to the safety or interests of the State within the meaning of the said Act—

(a) uses or wears, without lawful authority, any naval, military, air-force, police, or other official uniform, or any uniform so nearly resembling the same as to be calculated to deceive, or falsely represents himself to be a person who is or has been entitled to use or wear any such uniform; or

(b) orally, or in writing in any declaration or application, or in any document signed by him or on his behalf, knowingly makes or connives at the making of any false statement or any omission; or

(c) ... tampers with any passport or any naval, military, air-force, police, or official pass, permit, certificate, licence, or other document of a similar character (hereinafter in this section referred to as an official document), ... or has in his possession any ... forged, altered, or irregular official document; or

(d) personates, or falsely represents himself to be a person holding, or in the employment of a person holding office under His Majesty, or to be or not to be a person to whom an official document or secret official code word or pass word has been duly issued or communicated, or with intent to obtain an official document, secret official code word or pass word, whether for himself or any other person, knowingly makes any false statement; or

(e) uses, or has in his possession or under his control, without the authority of the Government Department or the authority concerned, any die, seal, or stamp of or belonging to, or used, made or provided by any Government Department, or by any diplomatic, naval, military, or air force authority appointed by or acting under the authority of His Majesty, or any die, seal or stamp so nearly resembling any such die, seal or stamp as to be calculated to deceive, or counterfeits any such die, seal or stamp, or uses, or has in his possession, or under his control, any such counterfeited die, seal or stamp;

he shall be guilty of a misdemeanour.

(2) If any person—

(a) retains for any purpose prejudicial to the safety or interests of the State any official document, whether or not completed or issued for use, when he has no right to retain it, or when it is contrary to his duty to retain it, or fails to comply with any directions issued by any Government Department or any person authorised by such department with regard to the return or disposal thereof; or

(b) allows any other person to have possession of any official document issued for his use alone, or communicates any secret official code word or pass word so issued, or, without lawful authority or excuse, has in his possession any official document or secret official code word or pass word issued for the use of some person other than himself, or on obtaining possession of any official document by finding or otherwise, neglects or fails to restore it to the person or authority by whom or for whose use it was issued, or to a police constable; or

(c) without lawful authority or excuse, manufactures or sells, or has in his possession for sale any such die, seal or stamp as aforesaid;

he shall be guilty of a misdemeanour.

(3) In the case of any prosecution under this section involving the proof of a purpose prejudicial to the safety or interests of the State, subsection (2) of section one of the principal Act shall apply in like manner as it applies to prosecutions under that section.

2, 3 *****

4, 5 ...

6   Duty of giving information as to commission of offences

[(1) Where a chief officer of police is satisfied that there is reasonable ground for suspecting that an offence under section one of the principal Act has been committed and for believing that any person is able to furnish information as to the offence or suspected offence, he may apply to a Secretary of State for permission to exercise the powers conferred by this subsection and, if such permission is granted, he may authorise a superintendent of police, or any police officer not below the rank of inspector, to require the person believed to be able to furnish information to give any information in his power relating to the offence or suspected offence, and, if so required and on tender of his reasonable expenses, to attend at such reasonable time and place as may be specified by the superintendent or other officer; and if a person required in pursuance of such an authorisation to give information, or to attend as aforesaid, fails to comply with any such requirement or knowingly gives false information, he shall be guilty of a misdemeanour.

(2)   Where a chief officer of police has reasonable grounds to believe that the case is one of great emergency and that in the interest of the State immediate action is necessary, he may exercise the powers conferred by the last foregoing subsection without applying for or being granted the permission of a Secretary of State, but if he does so shall forthwith report the circumstances to the Secretary of State.

(3)   References in this section to a chief officer of police shall be construed as including references to any other officer of police expressly authorised by a chief officer of police to act on his behalf for the purposes of this section when by reason of illness, absence or other cause he is unable to do so.]
*****

The Statute of Westminster 1931

(22 & 23 Geo. 5, c. 4)

An Act to give effect to certain resolutions passed by Imperial Conferences held in the years 1926 and 1930.

Territorial extent: As indicated in the Act (and see note to s. 4)

Whereas the delegates of His Majesty's Governments in the United Kingdom, the Dominion of Canada, the Commonwealth of Australia, the Dominion of New Zealand, the Union of South Africa, the Irish Free State and Newfoundland, at Imperial Conferences holden at Westminster in the years of our

Lord nineteen hundred and twenty-six and nineteen hundred and thirty did concur in making the declarations and resolutions set forth in the Reports of the said Conferences:

And whereas it is meet and proper to set out by way of preamble to this Act that, inasmuch as the Crown is the symbol of the free association of the members of the British Commonwealth of Nations, and as they are united by a common allegiance to the Crown, it would be in accord with the established constitutional position of all the members of the Commonwealth in relation to one another that any alteration in the law touching the Succession to the Throne or the Royal Style and Titles shall hereafter require the assent as well of the Parliaments of all the Dominions as of the Parliament of the United Kingdom:

And whereas it is in accord with the established constitutional position that no law hereafter made by the Parliament of the United Kingdom shall extend to any of the said Dominions as part of the law of that Dominion otherwise than at the request and with the consent of that Dominion:

And whereas it is necessary for the ratifying, confirming and establishing of certain of the said declarations and resolutions of the said Conferences that a law be made and enacted in due form by authority of the Parliament of the United Kingdom:

And whereas the Dominion of Canada, the Commonwealth of Australia, the Dominion of New Zealand, the Union of South Africa, the Irish Free State and Newfoundland have severally requested and consented to the submission of a measure to the Parliament of the United Kingdom for making such provision with regard to the matters aforesaid as is hereafter in this Act contained:

1 Meaning of 'Dominion' in this Act
In this Act the expression 'Dominion' means any of the following Dominions, that is to say, the Dominion of Canada, the Commonwealth of Australia, the Dominion of New Zealand, . . . the Irish Free State and Newfoundland.

2 Validity of laws made by Parliament of a Dominion
(1) The Colonial Laws Validity Act 1865 shall not apply to any law made after the commencement of this Act by the Parliament of a Dominion.

(2) No law and no provision of any law made after the commencement of this Act by the Parliament of a Dominion shall be void or inoperative on the ground that it is repugnant to the law of England, or to the provisions of any existing or future Act of Parliament of the United Kingdom, or to any order, rule or regulation made under any such Act, and the powers of the Parliament of a Dominion shall include the power to repeal or amend any such Act, order, rule or regulation in so far as the same is part of the law of the Dominion.

3 Power of Parliament of Dominion to legislate extra-territorially
It is hereby declared and enacted that the Parliament of a Dominion has full power to make laws having extra-territorial operation.

4 Parliament of United Kingdom not to legislate for Dominion except by consent
No Act of Parliament of the United Kingdom passed after the commencement of this Act shall extend, or be deemed to extend, to a Dominion as part of the law of that Dominion unless it is expressly declared in that Act that that Dominion has requested, and consented to, the enactment thereof.

[**Note:** This section has been repealed in relation to Canada by the Canada Act 1982 s. 1, Sch. B and in relation to Australia by the Australia Act 1986 s. 12.]
*****

Public Order Act 1936

(1 Edw. 8 & 1 Geo. 6, c. 6)

An Act to prohibit the wearing of uniforms in connection with political objects and the maintenance by private persons of associations of military or similar character; and to make further provision for the preservation of public order on the occasion of public processions and meetings and in public places.

Territorial extent: England and Wales, Scotland (s. 8: Scotland only). The amendment to s. 2(5) substituting 'three months' for 'one month' does not apply to Scotland.

1   Prohibition of uniforms in connection with political objects

(1) Subject as hereinafter provided, any person who in any public place or at any public meeting wears uniform signifying his association with any political organisation or with the promotion of any political object shall be guilty of an offence:

Provided that, if the chief officer of police is satisfied that the wearing of any such uniform as aforesaid on any ceremonial, anniversary, or other special occasion will not be likely to involve risk of public disorder, he may, with the consent of a Secretary of State, by order permit the wearing of such uniform on that occasion either absolutely or subject to such conditions as may be specified in the order.

(2) Where any person is charged before any court with an offence under this section, no further proceedings in respect thereof shall be taken against him without the consent of the Attorney-General [except such as are authorised by [section 6 of the Prosecution of Offences Act 1979]] so, however, that if that person is remanded in custody he shall, after the expiration of a period of eight days from the date on which he was so remanded, be entitled to be [released on bail] without sureties unless within that period the Attorney-General has consented to such further proceedings as aforesaid.

2   Prohibition of quasi-military organisations

(1) If the members or adherents of any association of persons, whether incorporated or not, are—

(a) organised or trained or equipped for the purpose of enabling them to be employed in usurping the functions of the police or of the armed forces of the Crown; or

(b) organised and trained or organised and equipped either for the purpose of enabling them to be employed for the use or display of physical force in promoting any political object, or in such manner as to arouse reasonable apprehension that they are organised and either trained or equipped for that purpose;

then any person who takes part in the control or management of the association, or in so organising or training as aforesaid any members or adherents thereof, shall be guilty of an offence under this section:

Provided that in any proceedings against a person charged with the offence of taking part in the control or management of such an association as aforesaid it shall be a defence to that charge to prove that he neither consented to nor connived at the organisation, training, or equipment of members or adherents of the association in contravention of the provisions of this section.

(2) No prosecution shall be instituted under this section without the consent of the Attorney-General.

(3), (4) *****

(5) If a judge of the High Court is satisfied by information on oath that there is reasonable ground for suspecting that an offence under this section has been committed, and that evidence of the commission thereof is to be found at any premises or place specified in the information, he may, on an application made by an officer of police of a rank not lower than that of inspector, grant a search warrant authorising any such officer as aforesaid named in the warrant together with any other persons named in the warrant and any other officers of police to enter the premises or place at any time within [three months] from the date of the warrant, if necessary by force, and to search the premises or place and every person found therein, and to seize anything found on the premises or place or on any such person which the officer has reasonable ground for suspecting to be evidence of the commission of such an offence as aforesaid:

Provided that no woman shall, in pursuance of a warrant issued under this subsection, be searched except by a woman.

(6) Nothing in this section shall be construed as prohibiting the employment of a reasonable number of persons as stewards to assist in the preservation of order at any public meeting held upon private premises, or the making of arrangements for that purpose or the instruction of the persons to be so employed in their lawful duties as such stewards, or their being furnished with badges or other distinguishing signs.

3–5A ...

6 (Amends the Public Meeting Act 1908, printed above as amended)

7   Enforcement

(1) Any person who commits an offence under section two of this Act shall be liable on summary conviction to imprisonment for a term not exceeding six months or to a fine not exceeding [the prescribed sum], or to both such imprisonment and fine, or, on conviction on indictment, to imprisonment for a term not exceeding two years or to a fine [of any amount] or to both such imprisonment and fine.

(2) Any person guilty of [any offence under this Act other than an offence under section 2...] shall be liable on summary conviction to imprisonment for a term not exceeding three months or to a fine not exceeding [level 4 on the standard scale], or to both such imprisonment and fine.

(3) ...

8   Application to Scotland

This Act shall apply to Scotland subject to the following modifications:—

(1) Subsection (2) of section one and subsection (2) of section two of this Act shall not apply.

(2) In subsection (3) of section two the Lord Advocate shall be substituted for the Attorney-General and the Court of Session shall be substituted for the High Court.

(3) Subsection (5) of section two shall have effect as if for any reference to a judge of the High Court there were substituted a reference to the Sheriff and any application for a search warrant under the said subsection shall be made by the procurator fiscal instead of such officer as is therein mentioned.

(4) The power conferred on the sheriff by subsection (5) of section two, as modified by the last foregoing paragraph, shall not be exercisable by an [honorary sheriff].

(5), (6) ...

9   Interpretation, etc.

(1) In this Act the following expressions have the meanings hereby respectively assigned to them, that is to say:—

...

'Meeting' means a meeting held for the purpose of the discussion of matters of public interest or for the purpose of the expression of views on such matters;

'Private premises' means premises to which the public have access (whether on payment or otherwise) only by permission of the owner, occupier, or lessee of the premises;

'Public meeting' includes any meeting in a public place and any meeting which the public or any section thereof are permitted to attend, whether on payment or otherwise;

['Public place' includes any highway and any other premises or place to which at the material time the public have or are permitted to have access, whether on payment or otherwise;]

...

(2) ...

(3), (4) *****

10 *****
*****

Statutory Instruments Act 1946

(9 & 10 Geo. 6, c. 36)

An Act to repeal the Rules Publication Act, 1893, and to make further provision as to the instruments by which statutory powers to make orders, rules, regulations and other subordinate legislation are exercised.

[26th March 1946]

Territorial extent: United Kingdom

[**Note:** By virtue of the Scotland Act (Transitory and Transitional Provisions) (Statutory Instruments) Order 1999 any reference in s. 1 below to an Act includes a reference to an Act of the Scottish Parliament and later sections are to be read to apply to the Scottish Parliament. Similarly references to powers exercisable by Ministers of the Crown shall include the Scottish Ministers in accordance with the Order.]

1   Definition of 'statutory instrument'

(1) Where by this Act or any Act passed after the commencement of this Act power to make, confirm or approve orders, rules, regulations or other subordinate legislation is conferred on His Majesty in Council or on any Minister of the Crown then, if the power is expressed—

(a) in the case of a power conferred on His Majesty, to be exercisable by Order in Council;

(b) in the case of a power conferred on a Minister of the Crown, to be exercisable by statutory instrument,

any document by which that power is exercised shall be known as a 'statutory instrument' and the provisions of this Act shall apply thereto accordingly.

[(1A) Where by any Act power to make, confirm or approve orders, rules, regulations or other subordinate legislation is conferred on the Welsh Ministers and the power is expressed to be exercisable by statutory instrument, any document by which that power is exercised shall be known as a 'statutory instrument' and the provisions of this Act shall apply to it accordingly.]

(2) Where by any Act passed before the commencement of this Act power to make statutory rules within the meaning of the Rules Publication Act, 1893, was conferred on any rule-making authority within the meaning of that Act, any document by which that power is exercised after the commencement of this Act shall, save as is otherwise provided by regulations made under this Act, be known as a 'statutory instrument' and the provisions of this Act shall apply thereto accordingly.

2   Numbering, printing, publication and citation

(1) Immediately after the making of any statutory instrument, it shall be sent to the King's printer of Acts of Parliament and numbered in accordance with regulations made under this Act, and except in such cases as may be provided by any Act passed after the commencement of this Act or prescribed by regulations made under this Act, copies thereof shall as soon as possible be printed and sold by [or under the authority of] the King's printer of Acts of Parliament.

(2) Any statutory instrument may, without prejudice to any other mode of citation, be cited by the number given to it in accordance with the provisions of this section, and the calendar year.

3   Supplementary provisions as to publication

(1) Regulations made for the purposes of this Act shall make provision for the publication by His Majesty's Stationery Office of lists showing the date upon which every statutory instrument printed and sold by [or under the authority of] the King's printer of Acts of Parliament was first issued by [or under the authority of] that office; and in any legal proceedings a copy of any list so published . . . shall be received in evidence as a true copy, and an entry therein shall be conclusive evidence of the date on which any statutory instrument was first issued by [or under the authority of] His Majesty's Stationery Office.

(2) In any proceedings against any person for an offence consisting of a contravention of any such statutory instrument, it shall be a defence to prove that the instrument had not been issued by [or under the authority of] His Majesty's Stationery Office at the date of the alleged contravention

unless it is proved that at that date reasonable steps had been taken for the purpose of bringing the purport of the instrument to the notice of the public, or of persons likely to be affected by it, or of the person charged.

(3) Save as therein otherwise expressly provided, nothing in this section shall affect any enactment or rule of law relating to the time at which any statutory instrument comes into operation.

4   Statutory instruments which are required to be laid before Parliament

(1) Where by this Act or any Act passed after the commencement of this Act any statutory instrument is required to be laid before Parliament after being made, a copy of the instrument shall be laid before each House of Parliament and, subject as hereinafter provided, shall be so laid before the instrument comes into operation:

Provided that if it is essential that any such instrument should come into operation before copies thereof can be so laid as aforesaid, the instrument may be made so as to come into operation before it has been so laid; and where any statutory instrument comes into operation before it is laid before Parliament, notification shall forthwith be sent to [the Speaker of the House of Commons and the Speaker of the House of Lords] drawing attention to the fact that copies of the instrument have yet to be laid before Parliament and explaining why such copies were not so laid before the instrument came into operation.

(2) Every copy of any such statutory instrument sold by [or under the authority of] the King's printer of Acts of Parliament shall bear on the face thereof—

(a) a statement showing the date on which the statutory instrument came or will come into operation; and

(b) either a statement showing the date on which copies thereof were laid before Parliament or a statement that such copies are to be laid before Parliament.

(3) *****

5   Statutory instruments which are subject to annulment by resolution of either House of Parliament

(1) Where by this Act or any Act passed after the commencement of this Act, it is provided that any statutory instrument shall be subject to annulment in pursuance of resolution of either House of Parliament, the instrument shall be laid before Parliament after being made and the provisions of the last foregoing section shall apply thereto accordingly, and if either House, within the period of forty days beginning with the day on which a copy thereof is laid before it, resolves that an Address be presented to His Majesty praying that the instrument be annulled, no further proceedings shall be taken thereunder after the date of the resolution, and His Majesty may by Order in Council revoke the instrument, so, however, that any such resolution and revocation shall be without prejudice to the validity of anything previously done under the instrument or to the making of a new statutory instrument.

(2) *****

6   Statutory instruments of which drafts are to be laid before Parliament

(1) Where by this Act or any Act passed after the commencement of this Act it is provided that a draft of any statutory instrument shall be laid before Parliament, but the Act does not prohibit the making of the instrument without the approval of Parliament, then, in the case of an Order in Council the draft shall not be submitted to His Majesty in Council, and in any other case the statutory instrument shall not be made, until after the expiration of a period of forty days beginning with the day on which a copy of the draft is laid before each House of Parliament, or, if such copies are laid on different days, with the later of the two days, and if within that period either House resolves that the draft be not submitted to His Majesty or that the statutory instrument be not made, as the case may be, no further proceedings shall be taken thereon, but without prejudice to the laying before Parliament of a new draft.

(2) *****

*****

Crown Proceedings Act 1947

(10 & 11 Geo. 6, c. 44)

An Act to amend the law relating to the civil liabilities and rights of the Crown and to civil proceedings by and against the Crown, to amend the law relating to the civil liabilities of persons other than the Crown in certain cases involving the affairs or property of the Crown, and for purposes connected with the matters aforesaid.   [31st July 1947]

Territorial extent: United Kingdom (ss. 2, 4, 11, 21, 40), England and Wales, Northern Ireland (ss. 1, 17)

PART I SUBSTANTIVE LAW

1   Right to sue the Crown

Where any person has a claim against the Crown after the commencement of this Act, and, if this Act had not been passed, the claim might have been enforced, subject to the grant of His Majesty's fiat, by petition of right, or might have been enforced by a proceeding provided by any stautory provision repealed by this Act, then, subject to the provisions of this Act, the claim may be enforced as of right, and without the fiat of His Majesty, by proceedings taken against the Crown for that purpose in accordance with the provisions of this Act.

2   Liability of the Crown in tort

(1) Subject to the provisions of this Act, the Crown shall be subject to all those liabilities in tort to which, if it were a private person of full age and capacity, it would be subject—

    (a) in respect of torts committed by its servants or agents;

    (b) in respect of any breach of those duties which a person owes to his servants or agents at common law by reason of being their employer; and

    (c) in respect of any breach of the duties attaching at common law to the ownership, occupation, possession or control of property:

Provided that no proceedings shall lie against the Crown by virtue of paragraph (a) of this subsection in respect of any act or omission of a servant or agent of the Crown unless the act or omission would apart from the provisions of this Act have given rise to a cause of action in tort against that servant or agent or his estate.

(2) Where the Crown is bound by a statutory duty which is binding also upon persons other than the Crown and its officers, then, subject to the provisions of this Act, the Crown shall, in respect of a failure to comply with that duty, be subject to all those liabilities in tort (if any) to which it would be so subject if it were a private person of full age and capacity.

(3) Where any functions are conferred or imposed upon an officer of the Crown as such either by any rule of the common law or by statute, and that officer commits a tort while performing or purporting to perform those functions, the liabilities of the Crown in respect of the tort shall be such as they would have been if those functions had been conferred or imposed solely by virtue of instructions lawfully given by the Crown.

(4) *****

(5) No proceedings shall lie against the Crown by virtue of this section in respect of anything done or omitted to be done by any person while discharging or purporting to discharge any responsibilities of a judicial nature vested in him, or any responsibilities which he has in connection with the execution of judicial process.

(6) No proceedings shall lie against the Crown by virtue of this section in respect of any act, neglect or default of any officer of the Crown, unless that officer has been directly or indirectly appointed by the Crown and was at the material time paid in respect of his duties as an officer of the Crown wholly out of the Consolidated Fund of the United Kingdom, moneys provided by Parliament,

[the Scottish Consolidated Fund] ..., or any other Fund certified by the Treasury for the purposes of this subsection or was at the material time holding an office in respect of which the Treasury certify that the holder thereof would normally be so paid.

3   *****

4   Application of law as to indemnity, contribution, joint and several tort-feasors, and contributory negligence

(1) Where the Crown is subject to any liability by virtue of this Part of this Act, the law relating to indemnity and contribution shall be enforceable by or against the Crown in respect of the liability to which it is so subject as if the Crown were a private person of full age and capacity.

(2) ...

(3) Without prejudice to the general effect of section one of this Act, the Law Reform (Contributory Negligence) Act 1945 (which amends the law relating to contributory negligence) shall bind the Crown.

5–10   ...

11   Saving in respect of acts done under prerogative and statutory powers

(1) Nothing in Part I of this Act shall extinguish or abridge any powers or authorities which, if this Act had not been passed, would have been exercisable by virtue of the prerogative of the Crown, or any powers or authorities conferred on the Crown by any statute, and, in particular, nothing in the said Part I shall extinguish or abridge any powers or authorities exercisable by the Crown, whether in time of peace or of war, for the purpose of the defence of the realm or of training, or maintaining the efficiency of, any of the armed forces of the Crown.

(2) Where in any proceedings under this Act it is material to determine whether anything was properly done or omitted to be done in the exercise of the prerogative of the Crown, . . .a Secretary of State may, if satisfied that the act or omission was necessary for any such purpose as is mentioned in the last preceding subsection, issue a certificate to the effect that the act or omission was necessary for that purpose; and the certificate shall, in those precedings, be conclusive as to the matter so certified.

12–16   *****

PART II JURISDICTION AND PROCEDURE

17   Parties to proceedings

(1) [The Minister for the Civil Service] shall publish a list specifying the several Government departments which are authorised departments for the purposes of this Act, and the name and address for service of the person who is, or is acting for the purposes of this Act as, the solicitor for each such department, and may from time to time amend or vary the said list.

Any document purporting to be a copy of a list published under this section and purporting to be printed under the superintendence or the authority of His Majesty's Stationery Office shall in any legal proceedings be received as evidence for the purpose of establishing what departments are authorised departments for the purposes of this Act, and what person is, or is acting for the purposes of this Act as, the solicitor for any such department.

(2) Civil proceedings by the Crown may be instituted either by an authorised Government department in its own name, whether that department was or was not at the commencement of this Act authorised to sue, or by the Attorney General.

(3) Civil proceedings against the Crown shall be instituted against the appropriate authorised Government department, or, if none of the authorised Government departments is appropriate or the person instituting the proceedings has any reasonable doubt whether any and if so which of those departments is appropriate, against the Attorney General.

(4), (5) *****

18 *****

19 ...

20 *****

21   Nature of relief

(1) In any civil proceedings by or against the Crown the court shall, subject to the provisions of this Act, have power to make all such orders as it has power to make in proceedings between subjects, and otherwise to give such appropriate relief as the case may require:

Provided that:—

    (a) where in any proceedings against the Crown any such relief is sought as might in proceedings between subjects be granted by way of injunction or specific performance, the court shall not grant an injunction or make an order for specific performance, but may in lieu thereof make an order declaratory of the rights of the parties; and

    (b) in any proceedings against the Crown for the recovery of land or other property the court shall not make an order for the recovery of the land or the delivery of the property, but may in lieu thereof make an order declaring that the plaintiff is entitled as against the Crown to the land or property or to the possession thereof.

(2) The court shall not in any civil proceedings grant any injunction or make any order against an officer of the Crown if the effect of granting the injunction or making the order would be to give any relief against the Crown which could not have been obtained in proceedings against the Crown.

22–27 *****

PART IV   MISCELLANEOUS AND SUPPLEMENTAL

28, 29, 31–33, 35, 37–38 *****

30, 34, 36, 39 ...

40   Savings

(1) Nothing in this Act shall apply to proceedings by or against, or authorise proceedings in tort to be brought against, His Majesty in His private capacity.

(2)–(5) *****

*****

Obscene Publications Act 1959

(7 & 8 Eliz. 2, c. 66)

An Act to amend the law relating to the publication of obscene matter; to provide for the protection of literature; and to strengthen the law concerning pornography. [29th July 1959]

Territorial extent: England and Wales

1   Test of obscenity

(1) For the purposes of this Act an article shall be deemed to be obscene if its effect or (where the article comprises two or more distinct items) the effect of any one of its items is, if taken as a whole, such as to tend to deprave and corrupt persons who are likely, having regard to all relevant circumstances, to read, see or hear the matter contained or embodied in it.

(2) In this Act 'article' means any description of article containing or embodying matter to be read or looked at or both, any sound record, and any film or other record of a picture or pictures.

(3) For the purposes of this Act a person publishes an article who—
  (a) distributes, circulates, sells, lets on hire, gives, or lends it, or who offers it for sale or for letting on hire; or
  (b) in the case of an article containing or embodying matter to be looked at or a record, shows, plays or projects it [, or, where the matter is data stored electronically, transmits that data.]

...

  [(4) For the purposes of this Act a person also publishes an article to the extent that any matter recorded on it is included by him in a programme included in a programme service.

  (5) Where the inclusion of any matter in a programme so included would, if that matter were recorded matter, constitute the publication of an obscene article for the purposes of this Act by virtue of subsection (4) above, this Act shall have effect in relation to the inclusion of that matter in that programme as if it were recorded matter.

  (6) In this section 'programme' and 'programme service' have the same meaning as in the Broadcasting Act 1990.]

2 Prohibition of publication of obscene matter

  (1) Subject as hereinafter provided, any person who, whether for gain or not, publishes an obscene article [or who has an obscene article for publication for gain (whether gain to himself or gain to another)] shall be liable—
  (a) on summary conviction to a fine not exceeding [the prescribed sum] or to imprisonment for a term not exceeding six months;
  (b) on conviction on indictment to a fine or to imprisonment for a term not exceeding [five years] or both.

  (2) ...

  (3) A prosecution ... for an offence against this section shall not be commenced more than two years after the commission of the offence.

  [(3A) Proceedings for an offence under this section shall not be instituted except by or with the consent of the Director of Public Prosecutions in any case where the article in question is a moving picture film of a width of not less than sixteen millimetres and the relevant publication or the only other publication which followed or could reasonably have been expected to follow from the relevant publication took place or (as the case may be) was to take place in the course of [an exhibition of a film]; and in this subsection 'the relevant publication' means—
  (a) in the case any proceedings under this section for publishing an obscene article, the publication in respect of which the defendant would be charged if the proceedings were brought; and
  (b) in the case of any proceedings under this section for having an obscene article for publication for gain, the publication which, if the proceedings were brought, the defendant would be alleged to have had in contemplation.]

  (4) A person publishing an article shall not be proceeded against for an offence at common law consisting of the publication of any matter contained or embodied in the article where it is of the essence of the offence that the matter is obscene.

  [(4A) Without prejudice to subsection (4) above, a person shall not be proceeded against for an offence at common law—
  (a) in respect of [an exhibition of a film] or anything said or done in the course of [an exhibition of a film], where it is of the essence of the common law offence that the exhibition or, as the case may be, what was said or done was obscene, indecent, offensive, disgusting or injurious to morality; or
  (b) in respect of an agreement to give [an exhibition of a film] or to cause anything to be said or done in the course of such an exhibition where the common law offence consists of conspiring to corrupt public morals or to do any act contrary to public morals or decency.]

(5) A person shall not be convicted of an offence against this section if he proves that he had not examined the article in respect of which he is charged and had no reasonable cause to suspect that it was such that his publication of it would make him liable to be convicted of an offence against this section.

(6) In any proceedings against a person under this section the question whether an article is obscene shall be determined without regard to any publication by another person unless it could reasonably have been expected that the publication by the other person would follow from publication by the person charged.

(7) In this section ['exhibition of a film'] has the [meaning given in paragraph 15 of Schedule 1 to the Licensing Act 2003].

3 *****

4   Defence of public good

(1) [Subject to subsection (1A) of this section] a person shall not be convicted of an offence against section two of this Act, and an order for forfeiture shall not be made under the foregoing section, if it is proved that publication of the article in question is justified as being for the public good on the ground that it is in the interests of science, literature, art or learning, or of other objects of general concern.

[(1A) Subsection (1) of this section shall not apply where the article in question is a moving picture film or soundtrack, but—

    (a) a person shall not be convicted of an offence against section 2 of this Act in relation to any such film or soundtrack, and

    (b) an order for forfeiture of any such film or soundtrack shall not be made under section 3 of this Act,

if it is proved that publication of the film or soundtrack is justified as being for the public good on the ground that it is in the interests of drama, opera, ballet or any other art, or of literature or learning.]

(2) It is hereby declared that the opinion of experts as to the literary, artistic, scientific or other merits of an article may be admitted in any proceedings under this Act either to establish or to negative the said ground.

[(3) In this section 'moving picture soundtrack' means any sound record designed for playing with a moving picture film, whether incorporated with the film or not.]

*****

Criminal Law Act 1967

(1967, c. 58)

An Act to amend the law of England and Wales by abolishing the division of crimes into felonies and misdemeanours and to amend and simplify the law in respect of matters arising from or related to that division or the abolition of it; to do away (within or without England and Wales) with certain obsolete crimes together with the torts of maintenance and champerty; and for purposes connected therewith.   [21st July 1967]

Territorial extent: England and Wales

PART I FELONY AND MISDEMEANOUR

1 *****

2 ...

3   Use of force in making arrest, etc.

(1) A person may use such force as is reasonable in the circumstances in the prevention of crime, or in effecting or assisting in the lawful arrest of offenders or suspected offenders or of persons unlawfully at large.

(2) Subsection (1) above shall replace the rules of the common law on the question when force used for a purpose mentioned in the subsection is justified by that purpose.
*****

Parliamentary Commissioner Act 1967

(1967, c. 13)

An Act to make provision for the appointment and functions of a Parliamentary Commissioner for the investigation of administrative action taken on behalf of the Crown, and for purposes connected therewith.

[22nd March 1967]

Territorial extent: United Kingdom

[**Note:** This Act is printed as extensively amended by the Parliamentary and Health Service Commissioners Act 1987.]

The Parliamentary Commissioner for Administration

1 Appointment and tenure of office

(1) For the purpose of conducting investigations in accordance with the following provisions of this Act there shall be appointed a Commissioner, to be known as the Parliamentary Commissioner for Administration.

(2) Her Majesty may by Letters Patent from time to time appoint a person to be the Commissioner. ...

[(2A) A person appointed to be the Commissioner shall hold office until the end of the period for which he is appointed.

(2B) That period must be not more than seven years.

(2C) Subsection (2A) is subject to subsections (3) and (3A).]

[(3) A person appointed to be the Commissioner may be—

   (a) relieved of office by Her Majesty at his own request, or

   (b) removed from office by Her Majesty, on the ground of misbehaviour, in consequence of Addresses from both Houses of Parliament.]

[(3A) Her Majesty may declare the office of Commissioner to have been vacated if satisfied that the person appointed to be the Commissioner is incapable for medical reasons—

   (a) of performing duties of his office; and

   (b) of requesting to be relieved of it.]

[(3B) A person appointed to be the Commissioner is not eligible for re-appointment.]

(4), (5) ...

2 *****

3 Administrative provisions

(1) The Commissioner may appoint such officers as he may determine with the approval of the Treasury as to numbers and conditions of service.

[(1A) The Commissioner may appoint and pay a mediator or other appropriate person to assist him in the conduct of an investigation under this Act.]

(2), (2A), (3) *****

3A *****

[4 Departments etc. subject to investigation

(1) Subject to the provisions of this section and to the notes contained in Schedule 2 to this Act, this Act applies to the government departments, corporations and unincorporated bodies listed in that Schedule; and references in this Act to an authority to which this Act applies are references to any such corporation or body.

(2) Her Majesty may by Order in Council amend Schedule 2 to this Act by the alteration of any entry or note, the removal of any entry or note or the insertion of any additional entry or note.

(3) An Order in Council may only insert an entry if—

    (a) it relates—

        (i) to a government department; or

        (ii) to a corporation or body whose functions are exercised on behalf of the Crown; or

    (b) it relates to a corporation or body—

        (i) which is established by virtue of Her Majesty's prerogative or by an Act of Parliament or an Order in Council or order made under an Act of Parliament or which is established in any other way by a Minister of the Crown in his capacity as a Minister or by a government department;

        (ii) at least half of whose revenues derive directly from money provided by Parliament, a levy authorised by an enactment, a fee or charge of any other description so authorised or more than one of those sources; and

        (iii) which is wholly or partly constituted by appointment made by Her Majesty or a Minister of the Crown or government department.

[(3A) No entry shall be made if the result of making it would be that the Parliamentary Commissioner could investigate action which can be investigated [by the Public Services Ombudsman for Wales under the Public Services Ombudsman (Wales) Act 2005].]

[(3B) No entry shall be made in respect of—

    (a) the Scottish Administration or any part of it;

    (b) any Scottish public authority with mixed functions or no reserved functions within the meaning of the Scotland Act 1998; or

    (c) the Scottish Parliamentary Corporate Body.]

(4) No entry shall be made in respect of a corporation or body whose sole activity is, or whose main activities are, included among the activities specified in subsection (5) below.

(5) The activities mentioned in subsection (4) above are—

    (a) the provision of education, or the provision of training otherwise than under the Industrial Training Act 1982;

    (b) the development of curricula, the conduct of examinations or the validation of educational courses;

    (c) the control of entry to any profession or the regulation of the conduct of members of any profession;

    (d) the investigation of complaints by members of the public regarding the actions of any person or body, or the supervision or review of such investigations or of steps taken following them.

(6) No entry shall be made in respect of a corporation or body operating in an exclusively or predominantly commercial manner or a corporation carrying on under national ownership an industry or undertaking or part of an industry or undertaking.

(7) Any statutory instrument made by virtue of this section shall be subject to annulment in pursuance of a resolution of either House of Parliament.]

(8) *****

5 Matters subject to investigation

(1) Subject to the provisions of this section, the Commissioner may investigate any action taken by or on behalf of a government department or other authority to which this Act applies, being action taken in the exercise of administrative functions of that department or authority, in any case where—

    (a) a written complaint is duly made to a member of the House of Commons by a member of the public who claims to have sustained injustice in consequence of maladministration in connection with the action so taken; and

    (b) the complaint is referred to the Commissioner, with the consent of the person who made it, by a member of that House with a request to conduct an investigation thereon.

(1A)–(1C) *****

(2) Except as hereinafter provided, the Commissioner shall not conduct an investigation under this Act in respect of any of the following matters, that is to say—

    (a) any action in respect of which the person aggrieved has or had a right of appeal, reference or review to or before a tribunal constituted by or under any enactment or by virtue of Her Majesty's prerogative;

    (b) any action in respect of which the person aggrieved has or had a remedy by way of proceedings in any court of law:

Provided that the Commissioner may conduct an investigation notwithstanding that the person aggrieved has or had such a right or remedy if satisfied that in the particular circumstances it is not reasonable to expect him to resort or have resorted to it.

    (2A) *****

(3) Without prejudice to subsection (2) of this section, the Commissioner shall not conduct [an investigation under subsection (1) of this section] in respect of any such action or matter as is described in Schedule 3 to this Act.

(4) Her Majesty may by Order in Council amend the said Schedule 3 so as to exclude from the provisions of that Schedule such actions or matters as may be described in the Order; and any statutory instrument made by virtue of this subsection shall be subject to annulment in pursuance of a resolution of either House of Parliament.

    (4A)–(4C) *****

(5) In determining whether to initiate, continue or discontinue an investigation under this Act, the Commissioner shall, subject to the foregoing provisions of this section, act in accordance with his own discretion; and any question whether a complaint is duly made under this Act shall be determined by the Commissioner.

    (5A)–(9A) *****

6 Provisions relating to complaints

(1) A complaint under this Act may be made by any individual, or by any body of persons whether incorporated or not, not being—

    (a) a local authority or other authority or body constituted for purposes of the public service or of local government or for the purposes of carrying on under national ownership any industry or undertaking or part of an industry or undertaking;

    [(b) any other authority or body within subsection (1A) below.

(1A) An authority or body is within this subsection if—

    (a) its members are appointed by—

        (i) Her Majesty;

        (ii) any Minister of the Crown;

        (iii) any government department;

        (iv) the Scottish Ministers;

        (v) the First Minister; or

        (vi) the Lord Advocate, or

    (b) its revenues consist wholly or mainly of—

        (i) money provided by Parliament; or

        (ii) sums payable out of the Scottish Consolidated Fund (directly or indirectly).]

(2) Where the person by whom a complaint might have been made under the foregoing provisions of this Act has died or is for any reason unable to act for himself, the complaint may be made by his personal representative or by a member of his family or other individual suitable to represent him; but except as aforesaid a complaint shall not be entertained under this Act unless made by the person aggrieved himself.

(3) A complaint shall not be entertained under this Act unless it is made to a member of the House of Commons not later than twelve months from the day on which the person aggrieved first had notice of the matters alleged in the complaint; but the Commissioner may conduct an investigation

pursuant to a complaint not made within that period if he considers that there are special circumstances which make it proper to do so.

(4) [Except as provided in subsection (5) below] a complaint shall not be entertained under this Act unless the person aggrieved is resident in the United Kingdom (or, if he is dead, was so resident at the time of his death) or the complaint relates to action taken in relation to him while he was present in the United Kingdom or on an installation in a designated area within the meaning of the Continental Shelf Act 1964 or on a ship registered in the United Kingdom or an aircraft so registered, or in relation to rights or obligations which accrued or arose in the United Kingdom or on such an installation, ship or aircraft.

(5) *****

7   Procedure in respect of investigations

(1) Where the Commissioner proposes to conduct an investigation pursuant to a complaint under [section 5(1) of] this Act, he shall afford to the principal officer of the department or authority concerned, and to any person who is alleged in the complaint to have taken or authorised the action complained of, an opportunity to comment on any allegations contained in the complaint.

(1A) *****

(2) Every [investigation under this Act] shall be conducted in private, but except as aforesaid the procedure for conducting an investigation shall be such as the Commissioner considers appropriate in the circumstances of the case; and without prejudice to the generality of the foregoing provision the Commissioner may obtain information from such persons and in such manner, and make such inquiries, as he thinks fit, and may determine whether any person may be represented, by counsel or solicitor or otherwise, in the investigation.

(3), (4) *****

8   Evidence

(1) For the purposes of an investigation under [section 5(1) of] this Act the Commissioner may require any Minister, officer or member of the department or authority concerned or any other person who in his opinion is able to furnish information or produce documents relevant to the investigation to furnish any such information or produce any such document.

(1A) *****

(2) For the purposes of any [investigation under this Act] the Commissioner shall have the same powers as the Court in respect of the attendance and examination of witnesses (including the administration of oaths or affirmations and the examination of witnesses abroad) and in respect of the production of documents.

(3) No obligation to maintain secrecy or other restriction upon the disclosure of information obtained by or furnished to persons in Her Majesty's service, whether imposed by any enactment or by any rule of law, shall apply to the disclosure of information for the purposes of an investigation under this Act; and the Crown shall not be entitled in relation to any such investigation to any such privilege in respect of the production of documents or the giving of evidence as is allowed by law in legal proceedings.

(4) No person shall be required or authorised by virtue of this Act to furnish any information or answer any question relating to proceedings of the Cabinet or of any committee of the Cabinet or to produce so much of any document as relates to such proceedings; and for the purposes of this subsection a certificate issued by the Secretary of the Cabinet with the approval of the Prime Minister and certifying that any information, question, document or part of a document so relates shall be conclusive.

(5) *****

9   Obstruction and contempt

(1) If any person without lawful excuse obstructs the Commissioner or any officer of the Commissioner in the performance of his functions under this Act, or is guilty of any act or omission in relation to any investigation under this Act which, if that investigation were a proceeding

in the Court, would constitute contempt of court, the Commissioner may certify the offence to the Court.

(2) Where an offence is certified under this section, the Court may inquire into the matter and, after hearing any witnesses who may be produced against or on behalf of the person charged with the offence, and after hearing any statement that may be offered in defence, deal with him in any manner in which the court could deal with him if he had committed the like offence in relation to the Court.

(3) *****

10   Reports by Commissioner

(1) In any case where the Commissioner conducts an investigation under this Act or decides not to conduct such an investigation, he shall send to the member of the House of Commons by whom the request for investigation was made (or if he is no longer a member of that House, to such member of that House as the Commissioner thinks appropriate) a report of the results of the investigation or, as the case may be, a statement of his reasons for not conducting an investigation.

(2) In any case where the Commissioner conducts an investigation under [section 5(1) of] this Act, he shall also send a report of the results of the investigation to the principal officer of the department or authority concerned and to any other person who is alleged in the relevant complaint to have taken or authorised the action complained of.

(2A) *****

(3) If, after conducting an investigation under [section 5(1) of] this Act, it appears to the Commissioner that injustice has been caused to the person aggrieved in consequence of maladministration and that the injustice has not been, or will not be, remedied, he may, if he thinks fit, lay before each House of Parliament a special report upon the case.

(3A), (3B) *****

(4) The Commissioner shall annually lay before each House of Parliament a general report on the performance of his functions under this Act and may from time to time lay before each House of Parliament such other reports with respect to those functions as he thinks fit.

(5) For the purposes of the law of defamation, any such publication as is hereinafter mentioned shall be absolutely privileged, that is to say—

  (a) the publication of any matter by the Commissioner in making a report to either House of Parliament for the purposes of this Act;
  (b) the publication of any matter by a member of the House of Commons in communicating with the Commissioner or his officers for those purposes or by the Commissioner or his officers in communicating with such a member for those purposes;
  (c) the publication by such a member to the person by whom a complaint was made under this Act of a report or statement sent to the member in respect of the complaint in pursuance of section (1) of this section;
  (d) the publication by the Commissioner to such a person as is mentioned in subsection (2) [or (2A)] of this section of a report to that person in pursuance of that subsection.

11, 11A, 11AA, 11ZAA, 11B, 11C *****

Supplemental

12   Interpretation

(1), (2) *****

(3) It is hereby declared that nothing in this Act authorises or requires the Commissioner to question the merits of a decision taken without maladministration by a government department or other authority in the exercise of a discretion vested in that department or authority.

13, 14 *****

*****

Section 5   **SCHEDULE 3**

MATTERS NOT SUBJECT TO INVESTIGATION

1. Action taken in matters certified by a Secretary of State or other Minister of the Crown to affect relations or dealings between the Government of the United Kingdom and any other Government or any international organisation of States or Governments.

2. [(1) Action taken, in any country or territory outside the United Kingdom, by or on behalf of any officer representing or acting under the authority of Her Majesty in respect of the United Kingdom, or any other officer of the Government of the United Kingdom other than,

  (a) action which is taken by an officer (not being an honorary consular officer) in the exercise of a consular function on behalf of the Government of the United Kingdom;

  (b) action which is taken by an officer within a control zone or a supplementary control zone; or

  (c) action which is taken by a British sea-fishery officer.]

(2) *****

3. Action taken in connection with the administration of the government of any country or territory outside the United Kingdom which forms part of Her Majesty's dominions or in which Her Majesty has jurisdiction.

[4. Action taken by the Secretary of State under the Extradition Act 2003].

5. Action taken by or with the authority of the Secretary of State for the purposes of investigating crime or of protecting the security of the State, including action so taken with respect to passports.

6. The commencement or conduct of civil or criminal proceedings before any court of law in the United Kingdom, of [service law proceedings (as defined by section 324(5) of the Armed Forces Act 2006) (anywhere)], or of proceedings before any international court or tribunal.

[6A. Action taken by any person appointed by the Lord Chancellor as a member of the administrative staff of any court or tribunal, so far as that action is taken at the direction, or on the authority (whether express or implied) of any person acting in a judicial capacity or as a member of the tribunal.]

[6B. (1) Action taken by any member of the administrative staff of a relevant tribunal so far as that action is taken at the direction, or on the authority (whether express or implied), of any person acting in his capacity as a member of the tribunal.

(2) In this paragraph, 'relevant tribunal' has the meaning given by section 5(8) of this Act.]

[6C ...]

7. Any exercise of the prerogative of mercy or of the power of a Secretary of State to make a reference in respect of any person to... the High Court of Justiciary or the [Court Martial Appeal Court.]

8. [(1)] Action taken on behalf of...the Secretary of State by [a local authority, the National Health Service Commissioning Board, a clinical commissioning group]...

[(2) For the purposes of this paragraph, action taken by [a local authority, the National Health Service Commissioning Board, a clinical commissioning group or...Special Health Authority...in the exercise of functions of the Secretary of State shall be regarded as action taken on his behalf.]

9. Action taken in matters relating to contractual or other commercial transactions, whether within the United Kingdom or elsewhere, being transactions of a government department or authority to which this Act applies or of any such authority or body as is mentioned in paragraph (a) or (b) of subsection (1) of section 6 of this Act and not being transactions for or relating to—

  (a) the acquisition of land compulsorily or in circumstances in which it could be acquired compulsorily;

  (b) the disposal as surplus of land acquired compulsorily or in such circumstances as aforesaid.

10. [(1)] Action taken in respect of appointments or removals, pay, discipline, superannuation or other personnel matters, in relation to—

(a) service in any of the armed forces of the Crown, including reserve and auxiliary and cadet forces;

(b) service in any office or employment under the Crown or under any authority [(to which this Act applies)]; or

(c) service in any office or employment, or under any contract for services, in respect of which power to take action, or to determine or approve the action to be taken, in such matters is vested in Her Majesty, any Minister of the Crown or any such authority as aforesaid.

[(2) Sub-paragraph (1)(c) above shall not apply to any action (not otherwise excluded from investigation by this Schedule) which is taken by the Secretary of State in connection with—

(a) the provision of information relating to the terms and conditions of any employment covered by an agreement entered into by him under section 12(1) of the Overseas Development and Cooperation Act 1980 [or pursuant to the exercise of his powers under Part 1 of the International Development Act 2002] or

(b) the provision of any allowance, grant or supplement or any benefit (other than those relating to superannuation) arising from the designation of any person in accordance with such an agreement.]

11. The grant of honours, awards or privileges within the gift of the Crown, including the grant of Royal Charters.

*****

Immigration Act 1971

(1971, c. 77)

An Act to amend and replace the present immigration laws, to make certain related changes in the citizenship law and enable help to be given to those wishing to return abroad, and for purposes connected therewith.   [28th October 1971]

Territorial extent: United Kingdom

PART I REGULATION OF ENTRY INTO AND STAY IN UNITED KINGDOM

1 General principles

(1) All those who are in this Act expressed to have the right of abode in the United Kingdom shall be free to live in, and to come and go into and from, the United Kingdom without let or hindrance except such as may be required under and in accordance with this Act to enable their right to be established or as may be otherwise lawfully imposed on any person.

(2) Those not having that right may live, work and settle in the United Kingdom by permission and subject to such regulation and control of their entry into, stay in and departure from the United Kingdom as is imposed by this Act; and indefinite leave to enter or remain in the United Kingdom shall, by virtue of this provision, be treated as having been given under this Act to those in the United Kingdom at its coming into force, if they are then settled there (and not exempt under this Act from the provisions relating to leave to enter or remain).

(3) Arrival in and departure from the United Kingdom on a local journey from or to any of the Islands (that is to say, the Channel Islands and Isle of Man) or the Republic of Ireland shall not be subject to control under this Act, nor shall a person require leave to enter the United Kingdom on so arriving, except in so far as any of those places is for any purpose excluded from this subsection under the powers conferred by this Act; and in this Act the United Kingdom and those places, or such of them as are not so excluded, are collectively referred to as 'the common travel area'.

(4) The rules laid down by the Secretary of State as to the practice to be followed in the administration of this Act for regulating the entry into and stay in the United Kingdom of persons not having the right of abode shall include provision for admitting (in such cases and subject to such restrictions as may be provided by the rules, and subject or not to conditions as to length of stay or otherwise) persons coming for the purpose of taking employment, or for purposes of study, or as visitors, or as dependants of persons lawfully in or entering the United Kingdom.

(5) ...

[2   Statement of right of abode in United Kingdom

(1) A person is under this Act to have the right of abode in the United Kingdom if—

(a) he is a British citizen; or

(b) he is a Commonwealth citizen who—

    (i)   immediately before the commencement of the British Nationality Act 1981 was a Commonwealth citizen having the right of abode in the United Kingdom by virtue of section 2(1)(d) or section 2(2) of this Act as then in force; and

    (ii)   has not ceased to be a Commonwealth citizen in the meanwhile.

(2) In relation to Commonwealth citizens who have the right of abode in the United Kingdom by virtue of subsection (1)(b) above, this Act, except this section and section [(5(2)] shall apply as if they were British citizens; and in this Act (except as aforesaid) 'British citizen' shall be construed accordingly.]

[2A   Deprivation of right of abode

(1) The Secretary of State may by order remove from a specified person a right of abode in the United Kingdom which he has under section 2(1)(b).

(2) The Secretary of State may make an order under subsection (1) in respect of a person only if the Secretary of State thinks that it would be conducive to the public good for the person to be excluded or removed from the United Kingdom.

(3) An order under subsection (1) may be revoked by order of the Secretary of State.

(4) While an order under subsection (1) has effect in relation to a person—

(a) section 2(2) shall not apply to him, and

(b) any certificate of entitlement granted to him shall have no effect.]

3   General provisions for regulation and control

(1) Except as otherwise provided by or under this Act, where a person is not [a British citizen]—

(a)   he shall not enter the United Kingdom unless given leave to do so in accordance with [the provisions of, or made under] this Act;

(b)   he may be given leave to enter the United Kingdom (or, when already there, leave to remain in the United Kingdom) either for a limited or for an indefinite period;

[(c)   if he is given limited leave to enter or remain in the United Kingdom, it may be given subject to any or all of the following conditions, namely—

    (i)   a condition restricting his employment or occupation in the United Kingdom;

    [(ia) a condition restricting his studies in the United Kingdom;]

    (ii)   a condition requiring him to maintain and accommodate himself, and any dependants of his, without recourse to public funds; ...

    (iii)   a condition requiring him to register with the police;

    [(iv) a condition requiring him to report to an immigration officer or the Secretary of State; and

    (v)   a condition about residence].]

(2) The Secretary of State shall from time to time (and as soon as may be) lay before Parliament statements of the rules, or of any changes in the rules, laid down by him as to the practice to be followed in the administration of this Act for regulating the entry into and stay in the United Kingdom of persons required by this Act to have leave to enter, including any rules as to the period for which leave is to be given and the conditions to be attached in different circumstances; and section 1(4) above shall not be taken to require uniform provision to be made by the

rules as regards admission of persons for a purpose or in a capacity specified in section 1(4) (and in particular, for this as well as other purposes of this Act, account may be taken of citizenship or nationality).

If a statement laid before either House of Parliament under this subsection is disapproved by a resolution of that House passed within the period of forty days beginning with the date of laying (and exclusive of any period during which Parliament is dissolved or prorogued or during which both Houses are adjourned for more than four days), then the Secretary of State shall as soon as may be make such changes or further changes in the rules as appear to him to be required in the circumstances, so that the statement of those changes be laid before Parliament at latest by the end of the period of forty days beginning with the date of the resolution (but exclusive as aforesaid).

(3) In the case of a limited leave to enter or remain in the United Kingdom,—

(a) a person's leave may be varied, whether by restricting, enlarging or removing the limit on its duration, or by adding, varying or revoking conditions, but if the limit on its duration is removed, any conditions attached to the leave shall cease to apply; and

(b) the limitation on and any conditions attached to a person's leave [(whether imposed originally or on a variation) shall], if not superseded, apply also to any subsequent leave he may obtain after an absence from the United Kingdom within the period limited for the duration of the earlier leave.

(4) A person's leave to enter or remain in the United Kingdom shall lapse on his going to a country or territory outside the common travel area (whether or not he lands there), unless within the period for which he had leave he returns to the United Kingdom in circumstances in which he is not required to obtain leave to enter; but, if he does so return, his previous leave (and any limitation on it or conditions attached to it) shall continue to apply.

[(5) A person who is not a British citizen is liable to deportation from the United Kingdom if—

(a) the Secretary of State deems his deportation to be conducive to the public good; or

(b) another person to whose family he belongs is or has been ordered to be deported.]

(6) Without prejudice to the operation of subsection (5) above, a person who is not [a British citizen] shall also be liable to deportation from the United Kingdom if, after he has attained the age of seventeen, he is convicted of an offence for which he is punishable with imprisonment and on his conviction is recommended for deportation by a court empowered by this Act to do so.

(7) Where it appears to Her Majesty proper so to do by reason of restrictions or conditions imposed on [British citizens, [British overseas territories citizens] or British Overseas citizens] when leaving or seeking to leave any country or the territory subject to the government of any country, Her Majesty may by Order in Council make provision for prohibiting persons who are nationals or citizens of the country and are not [British citizens] from embarking in the United Kingdom, or from doing so elsewhere than at a port of exit, or for imposing restrictions or conditions on them when embarking or about to embark in the United Kingdom; and Her Majesty may also make provision by Order in Council to enable those who are not [British citizens] to be, in such cases as may be prescribed by the Order, prohibited in the interests of safety from so embarking on a ship or aircraft specified or indicated in the prohibition.

Any Order in Council under this subsection shall be subject to annulment in pursuance of a resolution of either House of Parliament.

(8) When any question arises under this Act whether or not a person is [a British citizen], or is entitled to any exemption under this Act, it shall lie on the person asserting it to prove that he is.

[(9) A person seeking to enter the United Kingdom and claiming to have the right of abode there shall prove it by means of—

(a) a United Kingdom passport describing him as a British citizen,

(b) a United Kingdom passport describing him as a British subject with the right of abode in the United Kingdom, [or]

(c) ...

(d) ...

(e) a certificate of entitlement.]

3A–3D, 4, 5   *****

6   Recommendations by court for deportation

(1) Where under section 3(6) above a person convicted of an offence is liable to deportation on the recommendation of a court, he may be recommended for deportation by any court having power to sentence him for the offence unless the court commits him to be sentenced or further dealt with for that offence by another court:
*****

(2)–(4) *****

(5) Where a court recommends or purports to recommend a person for deportation, the validity of the recommendation shall not be called in question except on an appeal against the recommendation or against the conviction on which it is made; but—

    (a) . . . the recommendation shall be treated as a sentence for the purpose of any enactment providing an appeal against sentence; . . .

    (b) . . .

(6), (7) *****

7   Exemption from deportation for certain existing residents

(1) Notwithstanding anything in section 3(5) or (6) above but subject to the provisions of this section, a Commonwealth citizen or citizen of the Republic of Ireland who was such a citizen at the coming into force of this Act and was then ordinarily resident in the United Kingdom—

    (a) . . .

    (b) [shall not be liable to deportation under section 3(5) if at the time of the Secretary of State's decision he had for the last five years been ordinarily resident in the United Kingdom and Islands]; and

    (c) shall not on conviction of an offence be recommended for deportation under section 3(6) if at the time of the conviction he had for the last five years been ordinarily resident in the United Kingdom and Islands.

(2) A person who has at any time become ordinarily resident in the United Kingdom or in any of the Islands shall not be treated for the purposes of this section as having ceased to be so by reason only of his having remained there in breach of the immigration laws.

(3)–(5) *****

8–11   *****

12–21, 23   . . .

22   *****

PART III CRIMINAL PROCEEDINGS

24   Illegal entry and similar offences

(1) A person who is not [a British citizen] shall be guilty of an offence punishable on summary conviction with a fine of not more than [[level 5] on the standard scale] or with imprisonment for not more than six months, or with both, in any of the following cases:—

    (a) if contrary to this Act he knowingly enters the United Kingdom in breach of a deportation order or without leave;

    [(aa) . . .]

    (b) if, having only a limited leave to enter or remain in the United Kingdom, he knowingly either—

       (i)   remains beyond the time limited by the leave; or

       (ii) fails to observe a condition of the leave;

    (c) if, having lawfully entered the United Kingdom without leave by virtue of section 8(1) above, he remains without leave beyond the time allowed by section 8(1);

(d) if, without reasonable excuse, he fails to comply with any requirement imposed on him under Schedule 2 to this Act to report to a medical officer of health, or to attend, or submit to a test or examination, as required by such an officer;

(e) if, without reasonable excuse, he fails to observe any restriction imposed on him under Schedule 2 or 3 to this Act as to residence [, as to his employment or occupation] or as to reporting to the police [, to an immigration officer or to the Secretary of State];

(f) if he disembarks in the United Kingdom from a ship or aircraft after being placed on board under Schedule 2 or 3 to this Act with a view to his removal from the United Kingdom;

(g) if he embarks in contravention of a restriction imposed by or under an Order in Council under section 3(7) of this Act.

[(1A) A person commits an offence under subsection (1)(b)(i) above on the day when he first knows that the time limited by his leave has expired and continues to commit it throughout any period during which he is in the United Kingdom thereafter; but a person shall not be prosecuted under that provision more than once in respect of the same limited leave.]

(2) ...

(3), (4) *****

24A, 25–32 *****

PART IV SUPPLEMENTARY

33 Interpretation

(1) For purposes of this Act, except in so far as the context otherwise requires—
*****

['certificate of entitlement' means a certificate under section 10 of the Nationality, Immigration and Asylum Act 2002 that a person has the right of abode in the United Kingdom;]
*****

['entrant' means a person entering or seeking to enter the United Kingdom, and 'illegal entrant' means a person—

[(a) unlawfully entering or seeking to enter in breach of a deportation order or of the immigration laws, or

(b) entering or seeking to enter by means which include deception by another person, and includes also a person who has entered as mentioned in paragraph (a) or (b) above;]

'entry clearance' means a visa, entry certificate or other document which, in accordance with the immigration rules, is to be taken as evidence [or the requisite evidence] of a person's eligibility, though not [a British citizen], for entry into the United Kingdom (but does not include a work permit);

'immigration laws' means this Act and any law for purposes similar to this Act which is for the time being or has (before or after the passing of this Act) been in force in any part of the United Kingdom and Islands;

'immigration rules' means the rules for the time being laid down as mentioned in section 3(2) above;
*****

'limited leave' and 'indefinite leave' mean respectively leave under this Act to enter or remain in the United Kingdom which is, and one which is not, limited as to duration;

'settled' shall be construed in accordance [with subsection (2A) below];
*****

'work permit' means a permit indicating, in accordance with the immigration rules, that a person named in it is eligible, though not [a British citizen], for entry into the United Kingdom for the purpose of taking employment.

(1A) *****

(2) It is hereby declared that, except as otherwise provided in this Act, a person is not to be treated for the purposes of any provision of this Act as ordinarily resident in the United Kingdom or in any of the Islands at a time when he is there in breach of the immigration laws.

[(2A) Subject to section 8(5) above, references to a person being settled in the United Kingdom are references to his being ordinarily resident there without being subject under the immigration laws to any restriction on the period for which he may remain.]

(3), (4) *****

(5) This Act shall not be taken to supersede or impair any power exercisable by Her Majesty in relation to aliens by virtue of Her prerogative.

*****

Misuse of Drugs Act 1971

(1971, c. 38)

An Act to make new provision with respect to dangerous or otherwise harmful drugs and related matters, and for purposes connected therewith.   [27th May 1971]

Territorial extent: United Kingdom
*****

Law enforcement and punishment of offences

23   Powers to search and obtain evidence

(1) A constable or other person authorised in that behalf by a general or special order of the Secretary of State ... shall, for the purposes of the execution of this Act, have power to enter the premises of a person carrying on business as a producer or supplier of any controlled drugs and to demand the production of, and to inspect, any books or documents relating to dealings in any such drugs and to inspect any stocks of any such drugs.

(2) If a constable has reasonable grounds to suspect that any person is in possession of a controlled drug in contravention of this Act or of any regulations made thereunder, the constable may—

(a) search that person, and detain him for the purpose of searching him;

(b) search any vehicle or vessel in which the constable suspects that the drug may be found, and for that purpose require the person in control of the vehicle or vessel to stop it;

(c) seize and detain, for the purposes of proceedings under this Act, anything found in the course of the search which appears to the constable to be evidence of an offence under this Act.

In this subsection 'vessel' includes a hovercraft within the meaning of the Hovercraft Act 1968; and nothing in this subsection shall prejudice any power of search or any power to seize or detain property which is exercisable by a constable apart from this subsection.

(3) If a justice of the peace (or in Scotland a justice of the peace, a magistrate or a sheriff) is satisfied by information on oath that there is reasonable ground for suspecting—

(a) that any controlled drugs are, in contravention of this Act or of any regulations made thereunder, in the possession of a person on any premises; or

(b) that a document directly or indirectly relating to, or connected with, a transaction or dealing which was, or an intended transaction or dealing which would if carried out be, an offence under this Act, or in the case of a transaction or dealing carried out or intended to be carried out in a place outside the United Kingdom, an offence against the provision of a corresponding law in force in that place, is in the possession of a person on any premises,

he may grant a warrant authorising any constable acting for the police area in which the premises are situated at any time or times within one month from the date of the warrant, to enter, if need be by force, the premises named in the warrant, and to search the premises and any person found therein and, if there is reasonable ground for suspecting that an offence under this Act has been committed in relation to any controlled drugs found on the premises or in the possession of any such persons, or that a document so found is such a document as is mentioned in paragraph (b) above, to seize and detain those drugs or that document, as the case may be.

(3A) *****

(4) A person commits an offence if he—

 (a) intentionally obstructs a person in the exercise of his powers under this section; or

 (b) conceals from a person acting in the exercise of his powers under subsection (1) above any such books, documents, stocks or drugs as are mentioned in that subsection; or

 (c) without reasonable excuse (proof of which shall lie on him) fails to produce any such books or documents as are so mentioned where their production is demanded by a person in the exercise of his powers under that subsection.

(5) *****

*****

European Communities Act 1972

(1972, c. 68)

An Act to make provision in connection with the enlargement of the European Communities to include the United Kingdom, together with (for certain purposes) the Channel Islands, the Isle of Man and Gibraltar.   [17th October 1972]

Territorial extent: United Kingdom

PART I GENERAL PROVISIONS

1 Short title and interpretation

(1) This Act may be cited as the European Communities Act 1972.

(2) In this Act...

['the EU' means the European Union, being the Union established by the Treaty on European Union signed at Maastricht on 7th February 1992 (as amended by any later Treaty);]

'the Communities' means the European Economic Community, the European Coal and Steel Community and the European Atomic Energy Community;

'the Treaties' or ['the EU Treaties'] means, subject to subsection (3) below, the pre-accession treaties, that is to say, those described in Part I of Schedule 1 to this Act, taken with—

***** [list omitted]

and any expression defined in Schedule 1 to this Act has the meaning there given to it.

(3) If Her Majesty by Order in Council declares that a treaty specified in the Order is to be regarded as one of [the EU Treaties] as herein defined, the Order shall be conclusive that it is to be so regarded; but a treaty entered into by the United Kingdom after the 22nd January 1972, other than a pre-accession treaty to which the United Kingdom accedes on terms settled on or before that date, shall not be so regarded unless it is so specified, nor be so specified unless a draft of the Order in Council has been approved by resolution of each House of Parliament.

(4) For purposes of subsections (2) and (3) above, 'treaty' includes any international agreement, and any protocol or annex to a treaty or international agreement.

[**Note:** The full list of Treaties in s. 1(2) includes those adopted and ratified by the UK since 1972 as well as the original treaties, so that major constitutional changes such as the incorporation of the Single European Act of 1986, the Maastricht Treaty 1992 and the Lisbon Treaty are achieved by amendments to the subsection.]

2 General implementation of Treaties

(1) All such rights, powers, liabilities, obligations and restrictions from time to time created or arising by or under the Treaties, and all such remedies and procedures from time to time provided for by or under the Treaties, as in accordance with the Treaties are without further enactment to be given legal effect or used in the United Kingdom shall be recognised and available in law, and be enforced, allowed and followed accordingly; and the expression ['enforceable EU right'] and similar expressions shall be read as referring to one to which this subsection applies.

(2) Subject to Schedule 2 to this Act, at any time after its passing Her Majesty may by Order in Council, and any designated Minister or department may by [order, rules, regulations or schemes], make provision—

(a) for the purpose of implementing any [EU obligation] of the United Kingdom, or enabling any such obligation to be implemented, or of enabling any rights enjoyed or to be enjoyed by the United Kingdom under or by virtue of the Treaties to be exercised; or

(b) for the purpose of dealing with matters arising out of or related to any such obligation or rights or the coming into force, or the operation from time to time, of subsection (1) above;

and in the exercise of any statutory power or duty, including any power to give directions or to legislate by means of orders, rules, regulations or other subordinate instrument, the person entrusted with the power or duty may have regard to the [objects of the EU] and to any such obligation or rights as aforesaid.

In this subsection 'designated Minister or Department' means such Minister of the Crown or government department as may from time to time be designated by Order in Council in relation to any matter or for any purpose, but subject to such restrictions or conditions (if any) as may be specified by the Order in Council.

(3) There shall be charged on and issued out of the Consolidated Fund or, if so determined by the Treasury, the National Loans Fund the amounts required to meet any [EU obligation] to make payments to [the EU or a member State], or any [EU obligation] in respect of contributions to the capital or reserves of the European Investment Bank or in respect of loans to the Bank, or to redeem any notes or obligations issued or created in respect of any such [EU obligation]; and, except as otherwise provided by or under any enactment,—

(a) any other expenses incurred under or by virtue of the Treaties or this Act by any Minister of the Crown or government department may be paid out of moneys provided by Parliament; and

(b) any sums received under or by virtue of the Treaties or this Act by any Minister of the Crown or government department, save for such sums as may be required for disbursements permitted by any other enactment, shall be paid into the Consolidated Fund or, if so determined by the Treasury, the National Loans Fund.

(4) The provision that may be made under subsection (2) above includes, subject to Schedule 2 to this Act, any such provision (of any such extent) as might be made by Act of Parliament, and any enactment passed or to be passed, other than one contained in this Part of this Act, shall be construed and have effect subject to the foregoing provisions of this section; but, except as may be provided by any Act passed after this Act, Schedule 2 shall have effect in connection with the powers conferred by this and the following sections of this Act to make Orders in Council [or orders, rules, regulations or schemes].

(5), (6) *****

[**Note:** In s. 2, references to a statutory power or duty include a power or duty conferred by an Act of the Scottish Parliament or an instrument made thereunder, and s. 2(2) is to be read as applying to regulations made by Scottish Ministers: see the Scotland Act 1998, Sch. 8, para. 5.]

3 Decisions on, and proof of, Treaties and [EU instruments], etc.

(1) For the purposes of all legal proceedings any question as to the meaning or effect of any of the Treaties, or as to the validity, meaning or effect of any [EU instrument], shall be treated as a question

of law (and, if not referred to the European Court, be for determination as such in accordance with the principles laid down by and any relevant decision of [the European Court]).

(2) Judicial notice shall be taken of the Treaties, of the [Official Journal of the European Union] and of any decision of, or expression of opinion by [the European Court] on any such question as aforesaid; and the Official Journal shall be admissible as evidence of any instrument or other act thereby communicated of [the EU] or of any [EU institution].

(3), (4), (5) *****

*****

Section 2   **SCHEDULE 2**

PROVISIONS AS TO SUBORDINATE LEGISLATION

1.—(1) The powers conferred by section 2(2) of this Act to make provision for the purposes mentioned in section 2(2)(a) and (b) shall not include power—

(a) to make any provision imposing or increasing taxation; or

(b) to make any provision taking effect from a date earlier than that of the making of the instrument containing the provision; or

(c) to confer any power to legislate by means of orders, rules regulations or other subordinate instrument, other than rules of procedure for any court or tribunal; or

(d) to create any new criminal offence punishable with imprisonment for more than two years or punishable on summary conviction with imprisonment for more than [the prescribed term] or with a fine of more than [level 5 on the standard scale] (if not calculated on a daily basis) or with a fine of more than [£100 a day].

(2) Sub-paragraph (1)(c) above shall not be taken to preclude the modification of a power to legislate conferred otherwise than under section 2(2), or the extension of any such power to purposes of the like nature as those for which it was conferred; and a power to give directions as to matters of administration is not to be regarded as a power to legislate within the meaning of sub-paragraph (1)(c).

[(3) In sub-paragraph (1)(d), 'the prescribed term' means—

(a) in relation to England and Wales, where the offence is a summary offence, 51 weeks;

(b) in relation to England and Wales, where the offence is triable either way, twelve months;

(c) in relation to Scotland and Northern Ireland, three months.]

[1A.—(1) Where—

(a) subordinate legislation makes provision for a purpose mentioned in section 2(2) of this Act,

(b) the legislation contains a reference to a [EU instrument] or any provision of a [EU instrument], and

(c) it appears to the person making the legislation that it is necessary or expedient for the reference to be construed as a reference to that instrument or that provision as amended from time to time,

the subordinate legislation may make express provision to that effect.

(2) In this paragraph 'subordinate legislation' means any Order in Council, order, rules, regulations, scheme, warrant, byelaws or other instrument made after the coming into force of this paragraph under any Act, Act of the Scottish Parliament [, Measure or Act of the National Assembly for Wales] or Northern Ireland legislation passed or made before or after the coming into force of this paragraph.]

2.—(1) Subject to paragraph 3 below, where a provision contained in any section of this Act confers power to make [any order, rules, regulations or scheme] (otherwise than by modification or extension of an existing power), the power shall be exercisable by statutory instrument.

(2) Any statutory instrument containing an Order in Council or [any order, rules, regulations or scheme] made in the exercise of a power so conferred, if made without a draft having been approved by resolution of each House of Parliament, shall be subject to annulment in pursuance of a resolution of either House.

[2A.—(1) This paragraph applies where, pursuant to paragraph 2(2) above, a draft of a statutory instrument containing provision made in exercise of the power conferred by section 2(2) of this Act is laid before Parliament for approval by resolution of each House of Parliament and—

    (a) the instrument also contains provision made in exercise of a power conferred by any other enactment; and

    (b) apart from this paragraph, any of the conditions in sub-paragraph (2) below applies in relation to the instrument so far as containing that provision.

(2) The conditions referred to in sub-paragraph (1)(b) above are that—

    (a) the instrument, so far as containing the provision referred to in sub-paragraph (1) (a) above, is by virtue of any enactment subject to annulment in pursuance of a resolution of either House of Parliament;

    (b) the instrument so far as containing that provision is by virtue of any enactment required to be laid before Parliament after being made and to be approved by resolution of each House of Parliament in order to come into or remain in force;

    (c) in a case not falling within paragraph (a) or (b) above, the instrument so far as containing that provision is by virtue of any enactment required to be laid before Parliament after being made;

    (d) the instrument or a draft of the instrument so far as containing that provision is not by virtue of any enactment required at any time to be laid before Parliament.

(3) Where this paragraph applies in relation to the draft of a statutory instrument—

    (a) the instrument, so far as containing the provision referred to in sub-paragraph (1) (a) above, may not be made unless the draft is approved by a resolution of each House of Parliament;

    (b) in a case where the condition in sub-paragraph (2)(a) above is satisfied, the instrument so far as containing that provision is not subject to annulment in pursuance of a resolution of either House of Parliament;

    (c) in a case where the condition in sub-paragraph (2)(b) above is satisfied, the instrument is not required to be laid before Parliament after being made (and accordingly any requirement that the instrument be approved by each House of Parliament in order for it to come into or remain in force does not apply); and

    (d) in a case where the condition in sub-paragraph (2)(c) above is satisfied, the instrument so far as containing that provision is not required to be laid before Parliament after being made.

(4) In this paragraph, references to an enactment are to an enactment passed or made before or after the coming into force of this paragraph.

2B.—(1) This paragraph applies where, pursuant to paragraph 2(2) above, a statutory instrument containing provision made in exercise of the power conferred by section 2(2) of this Act is laid before Parliament under section 5 of the Statutory Instruments Act 1946 (instruments subject to annulment) and—

    (a) the instrument also contains provision made in exercise of a power conferred by any other enactment; and

    (b) apart from this paragraph, either of the conditions in sub-paragraph (2) below applies in relation to the instrument so far as containing that provision.

(2) The conditions referred to in sub-paragraph (1)(b) above are that—

    (a) the instrument so far as containing the provision referred to in sub-paragraph (1) (a) above is by virtue of any enactment required to be laid before Parliament after being made but—

        (i) is not subject to annulment in pursuance of a resolution of either House of Parliament; and

(ii) is not by virtue of any enactment required to be approved by resolution of each House of Parliament in order to come into or remain in force;

(b) the instrument or a draft of the instrument so far as containing that provision is not by virtue of any enactment required at any time to be laid before Parliament.

(3) Where this paragraph applies in relation to a statutory instrument, the instrument, so far as containing the provision referred to in sub-paragraph (1)(a) above, is subject to annulment in pursuance of a resolution of either House of Parliament.

(4) In this paragraph, references to an enactment are to an enactment passed or made before or after the coming into force of this paragraph.

2C. Paragraphs 2A and 2B above apply to a Scottish statutory instrument containing provision made in the exercise of the power conferred by section 2(2) of this Act (and a draft of any such instrument) as they apply to any other statutory instrument containing such provision (or, as the case may be, any draft of such an instrument), but subject to the following modifications—

(a) references to Parliament and to each or either House of Parliament are to be read as references to the Scottish Parliament;

(b) references to an enactment include an enactment comprised in, or in an instrument made under, an Act of the Scottish Parliament; and

(c) the reference in paragraph 2B(1) to section 5 of the Statutory Instruments Act 1946 is to be read as a reference to article 11 of the Scotland Act 1998 (Transitory and Transitional Provisions) (Statutory Instruments) Order 1999 (SI 1999/1096).]

Local Government Act 1972

(1972, c. 70)

An Act to make provision with respect to local government and the functions of local authorities in England and Wales; to amend Part II of the Transport Act 1968; to confer rights of appeal in respect of decisions relating to licences under the Home Counties (Music and Dancing) Licensing Act 1926; to make further provision with respect to magistrates' courts committees; to abolish certain inferior courts of record; and for connected purposes.   [26th October 1972]

Territorial extent: England and Wales
*****

[PART VA ACCESS TO MEETINGS AND DOCUMENTS OF CERTAIN AUTHORITIES, COMMITTEES AND SUB-COMMITTEES

[100A   Admission to meetings of principal councils

(1) A meeting of a principal council shall be open to the public except to the extent that they are excluded (whether during the whole or part of the proceedings) under subsection (2) below or by resolution under subsection (4) below.

(2) The public shall be excluded from a meeting of a principal council during an item of business whenever it is likely, in view of the nature of the business to be transacted or the nature of the proceedings, that, if members of the public were present during that item, confidential information would be disclosed to them in breach of the obligation of confidence; and nothing in this Part shall be taken to authorise or require the disclosure of confidential information in breach of the obligation of confidence.

(3) For the purposes of subsection (2) above, 'confidential information' means—

(a) information furnished to the council by a Government department upon terms (however expressed) which forbid the disclosure of the information to the public; and

(b) information the disclosure of which to the public is prohibited by or under any enactment or by the order of a court;

and, in either case, the reference to the obligation of confidence is to be construed accordingly.

(4) A principal council may by resolution exclude the public from a meeting during an item of business whenever it is likely, in view of the nature of the business to be transacted or the nature of the proceedings, that if members of the public were present during that item there would be disclosure to them of exempt information, as defined in section 100I below.

(5), (6) *****

(7) Nothing in this section shall require a principal council to permit the taking of photographs of any proceedings, or the use of any means to enable persons not present to see or hear any proceedings (whether at the time or later), or the making of any oral report on any proceedings as they take place.

(8) This section is without prejudice to any power of exclusion to suppress or prevent disorderly conduct or other misbehaviour at a meeting.

100B   Access to agenda and connected reports

(1) Copies of the agenda for a meeting of a principal council and, subject to subsection (2) below, copies of any report for the meeting shall be open to inspection by members of the public at the offices of the council in accordance with subsection (3) below.

(2) If the proper officer thinks fit, there may be excluded from the copies of reports provided in pursuance of subsection (1) above the whole of any report which, or any part which, relates only to items during which, in his opinion, the meeting is likely not to be open to the public.

(3) Any document which is required by subsection (1) above to be open to inspection shall be so open at least [five] clear days before the meeting, except that—

(a) where the meeting is convened at shorter notice, the copies of the agenda and reports shall be open to inspection from the time the meeting is convened, and

(b) where an item is added to an agenda copies of which are open to inspection by the public, copies of the item (or of the revised agenda), and the copies of any report for the meeting relating to the item, shall be open to inspection from the time the item is added to the agenda;

but nothing in this subsection requires copies of any agenda, item or report to be open to inspection by the public until copies are available to members of the council.

(4) An item of business may not be considered at a meeting of a principal council unless either—

(a) a copy of the agenda including the item (or a copy of the item) is open to inspection by members of the public in pursuance of subsection (1) above for at least [five] clear days before the meeting or, where the meeting is convened at shorter notice, from the time the meeting is convened; or

(b) by reason of special circumstances, which shall be specified in the minutes, the chairman of the meeting is of the opinion that the item should be considered at the meeting as a matter of urgency.

(5)–(8) *****

[Note: The amendments in subsections (2) and (4) only apply to England; in Wales the original provision (three clear days) remains in force.]

100C   Inspection of minutes and other documents after meetings

(1) After a meeting of a principal council the following documents shall be open to inspection by members of the public at the offices of the council until the expiration of the period of six years beginning with the date of the meeting, namely—

(a) the minutes, or a copy of the minutes, of the meeting, excluding so much of the minutes of proceedings during which the meeting was not open to the public as discloses exempt information;

(b) where applicable, a summary under subsection (2) below;

(c) a copy of the agenda for the meeting; and

(d) a copy of so much of any report for the meeting as relates to any item during which the meeting was open to the public.

(2) *****

100D   Inspection of background papers

[(1) Subject, in the case of section 100C(1), to subsection (2) below, if and so long as copies of the whole or part of a report for a meeting of a principal council are required by section 100B(1) or 100C(1) above to be open to inspection by members of the public—

(a) those copies shall each include a copy of a list compiled by the proper officer, of the background papers for the report or the part of the report; and

(b) at least one copy of each of the documents included in that list shall also be open to inspection at the offices of the council.]

(2) Subsection (1) above does not require a copy . . . of any document included in the list, to be open to inspection after the expiration of the period of four years beginning with the date of the meeting.

(3)–(5) *****

100E   Application to committees and sub-committees

(1) Sections 100A to 100D above shall apply in relation to a committee or sub-committee of a principal council as they apply in relation to a principal council.]

(2)–(4) *****

[100EA   Inspection of records relating to functions exercisable by members]

[(1) The Secretary of State may by regulations make provision for written records of decisions made or action taken by a member of a local authority, in exercise of a function of the authority by virtue of arrangements made under section 236 of the Local Government and Public Involvement in Health Act 2007, to be made and provided to the authority by the member.

(2) Any written record provided to the authority under regulations under subsection (1) shall be open to inspection by members of the public at the offices of the authority for the period of six years beginning with the date on which the decision was made or action was taken.

(3) A statutory instrument containing regulations under subsection (1) shall be subject to annulment in pursuance of a resolution of either House of Parliament.]

100F–100K   *****

PART VI DISCHARGE OF FUNCTIONS

101   Arrangements for discharge of functions by local authorities

(1) Subject to any express provision contained in this Act or any Act passed after this Act, a local authority may arrange for the discharge of any of their functions—

(a) by a committee, a sub-committee or an officer of the authority; or

(b) by any other local authority.

(1A), (1B), (1C) *****

(2) Where by virtue of this section any functions of a local authority may be discharged by a committee of theirs, then, unless the local authority otherwise direct, the committee may arrange for the discharge of any of those functions by a sub-committee or an officer of the authority and where by virtue of this section any functions of a local authority may be discharged by a sub-committee of the authority, then, unless the local authority or the committee otherwise direct, the sub-committee may arrange for the discharge of any of those functions by an officer of the authority.

(3) Where arrangements are in force under this section for the discharge of any functions of a local authority by another local authority, then, subject to the terms of the arrangements, that other authority may arrange for the discharge of those functions by a committee, sub-committee or officer of theirs and subsection (2) above shall apply in relation to those functions as it applies in relation to the functions of that other authority.

(4)–(5B) *****

(6) A local authority's functions with respect to levying, or issuing a precept for, a rate … shall be discharged only by the authority.

(6A)–(15) *****

102–109 *****

110 …

PART VII MISCELLANEOUS POWERS OF LOCAL AUTHORITIES

111   Subsidiary powers of local authorities

(1) Without prejudice to any powers exercisable apart from this section but subject to the provisions of this Act and any other enactment passed before or after this Act, a local authority shall have power to do anything (whether or not involving the expenditure, borrowing or lending of money or the acquisition or disposal of any property or rights) which is calculated to facilitate, or is conducive or incidental to, the discharge of any of their functions.

(2) For the purposes of this section, transacting the business of a parish or community meeting or any other parish or community business shall be treated as a function of the parish or community council.

(3) A local authority shall not by virtue of this section raise money, whether by means of rates, precepts or borrowing, or lend money except in accordance with the enactments relating to those matters respectively.

(4) In this section 'local authority' includes the Common Council.

112   Appointment of staff

(1) Without prejudice to section 111 above but subject to the provisions of this Act, a local authority shall appoint such officers as they think necessary for the proper discharge by the authority of such of their or another authority's functions as fall to be discharged by them and the carrying out of any obligations incurred by them in connection with an agreement made by them in pursuance of section 113 below.

(2) An officer appointed under subsection (1) above shall hold office on such reasonable terms and conditions, including conditions as to remuneration, as the authority appointing him think fit.

[(2A) A local authority's power to appoint officers on such reasonable terms and conditions as the authority thinks fit is subject to section 41 of the Localism Act 2011 (requirement for determinations relating to terms and conditions of chief officers to comply with pay policy statement).]

(3) Subject to subsection (4) below, any enactment or instrument made under an enactment which requires or empowers all local authorities or local authorities of any description or committees of local authorities to appoint a specified officer shall, to the extent that it makes any such provision, cease to have effect.

The reference in this section to committees of local authorities does not include a reference to any committee of which some members are required to be appointed by a body or person other than a local authority.

(4)–(6) *****
*****

PART XI GENERAL PROVISIONS AS TO LOCAL AUTHORITIES

Legal proceedings

222   Power of local authorities to prosecute or defend legal proceedings

(1) Where a local authority consider it expedient for the promotion or protection of the interests of the inhabitants of their area—

(a) they may prosecute or defend or appear in any legal proceedings and, in the case of civil proceedings, may institute them in their own name, and

(b) they may, in their own name, make representations in the interests of the inhabitants at any public inquiry held by or on behalf of any Minister or public body under any enactment.

(2) In this section 'local authority' includes the Common Council [and the London Fire and Emergency Planning Authority.]

*****

Byelaws

235   Power of councils to make byelaws for good rule and government and suppression of nuisances

(1) The council of a district [the council of a principal area in Wales] and the council of a London borough may make byelaws for the good rule and government of the whole or any part of the district [principal area] or borough, as the case may be, and for the prevention and suppression of nuisances therein.

(2) The confirming authority in relation to byelaws made under this section shall be the Secretary of State.

(3) Byelaws shall not be made under this section for any purpose as respects any area if provision for that purpose as respects that area is made by, or is or may be made under, any other enactment.

*****

[SCHEDULE 12A ACCESS TO INFORMATION: EXEMPT INFORMATION]

[PART 1 DESCRIPTIONS OF EXEMPT INFORMATION: ENGLAND]

[1. Information relating to any individual.]

[2. Information which is likely to reveal the identity of an individual.]

2A. [. . .]

[3. Information relating to the financial or business affairs of any particular person (including the authority holding that information).]

[4. Information relating to any consultations or negotiations, or contemplated consultations or negotiations, in connection with any labour relations matter arising between the authority or a Minister of the Crown and employees of, or office holders under, the authority.]

[5. Information in respect of which a claim to legal professional privilege could be maintained in legal proceedings.]

[6. Information which reveals that the authority proposes—

(a) to give under any enactment a notice under or by virtue of which requirements are imposed on a person; or

(b) to make an order or direction under any enactment.]

[7. Information relating to any action taken or to be taken in connection with the prevention, investigation or prosecution of crime.]

[PART 2 QUALIFICATIONS: ENGLAND]

[8. Information falling within paragraph 3 above is not exempt information by virtue of that paragraph if it is required to be registered under—

(a) [the Companies Acts (as defined in section 2 of the Companies Act 2006)];

(b) the Friendly Societies Act 1974;

(c) the Friendly Societies Act 1992;

     (d) the [Co-operative and Community Benefit Societies and Credit Unions] Acts 1965 to 1978;

     (e) the Building Societies Act 1986; or

     (f) the Charities Act 2011.]

    [9. Information is not exempt information if it relates to proposed development for which the local planning authority may grant itself planning permission pursuant to regulation 3 of the Town and Country Planning General Regulations 1992.]

    [10. Information which—

     (a) falls within any of paragraphs 1 to 7 above; and

     (b) is not prevented from being exempt by virtue of paragraph 8 or 9 above,

is exempt information if and so long, as in all the circumstances of the case, the public interest in maintaining the exemption outweighs the public interest in disclosing the information.]

[PART 3 INTERPRETATION: ENGLAND]

    [11.—(1) In Parts 1 and 2 and this Part of this Schedule—

'employee' means a person employed under a contract of service;

'financial or business affairs' includes contemplated, as well as past or current, activities;

'labour relations matter' means—

     (a) any of the matters specified in paragraphs (a) to (g) of section 218(1) of the Trade Union and Labour Relations (Consolidation) Act 1992 (matters which may be the subject of a trade dispute, within the meaning of that Act); or

     (b) any dispute about a matter falling within paragraph (a) above;

and for the purposes of this definition the enactments mentioned in paragraph (a) above, with the necessary modifications, shall apply in relation to office-holders under the authority as they apply in relation to employees of the authority;

'office-holder', in relation to the authority, means the holder of any paid office appointments to which are or may be made or confirmed by the authority or by any joint board on which the authority is represented or by any person who holds any such office or is an employee of the authority;

'registered' in relation to information required to be registered under the Building Societies Act 1986, means recorded in the public file of any building society (within the meaning of that Act).]

    (2) *****

*****

Local Government Act 1974

(1974, c. 7)

An Act to make further provision, in relation to England and Wales, with respect to the payment of grants to local authorities, rating and valuation, borrowing and lending by local authorities and the classification of highways; to extend the powers of the Countryside Commission to give financial assistance; to provide for the establishment of Commissions for the investigation of administrative action taken by or on behalf of local and other authorities; to restrict certain grants under the Transport Act 1968; to provide for the removal or relaxation of certain statutory controls affecting local government activities; to make provision in relation to the collection of sums by local authorities on behalf of water authorities; to amend section 259(3) of the Local Government Act 1972 and to make certain minor amendments of or consequential on that Act; and for connected purposes.   [8th February 1974]

Territorial extent: England and Wales

*****

PART III LOCAL GOVERNMENT ADMINISTRATION

23 The Commissions for Local Administration

    (1) For the purpose of conducting investigations in accordance with this Part [and Part 3A] of this Act, there shall be—

   (a) a body of commissioners to be known as the Commission for Local Administration in
      England, ...
   (b) ...
[but [the Commission] may include persons appointed to act as advisers, not exceeding the number
appointed to conduct investigations.]
   (2) The Parliamentary Commissioner shall be a member of [the Commission].
   [(2A) ...]
   (3) In the following provisions of this Part of this Act the expression 'Local Commissioner'
means a person, other than the Parliamentary Commissioner, [...] [or an advisory member] who is a
member of [the Commission].
   [(3A) ...]
   (4) Appointments to the office of ... Commissioner shall be made by Her Majesty on the recommendation of the Secretary of State ...
   [(4A) Subject to subsections (5) to (6), a Commissioner shall hold and vacate office in accordance
with the terms of his appointment.]
   [(5) A Commissioner's appointment may be a full-time or part-time appointment and, with the
Commissioner's consent, the terms of the appointment may be varied as to whether it is full-time or
part-time.
   (5A) A Commissioner must be appointed for a period of not more than 7 years.
   (5B) A Commissioner shall, subject to subsection (6), hold office until the end of the period for
which he is appointed.]
   (6) A ... Commissioner may be relieved of office by Her Majesty at his own request or may be
removed from office by Her Majesty on grounds of incapacity or misbehaviour...
   [(6A) A person appointed to be a Commissioner is not eligible for re-appointment.]
   (7) The Secretary of State shall designate two of the Local Commissioners for England as chairman and vice-chairman respectively of the Commission for Local Administration in England...
   (8) ...
   (8A)–(13) *****

23A *****

24 ...

[24A   Power to investigate]
   [(1) Under this Part of this Act, a Local Commissioner may investigate a matter—
      (a) which relates to action taken by or on behalf of an authority to which this Part of this Act
         applies,
      (b) which is subject to investigation under this Part of this Act by virtue of section 26, and
      (c) in relation to which subsection (2), (3) or (5) is satisfied.
   (2) This subsection is satisfied if, in relation to the matter, a complaint which satisfies sections
26A and 26B has been made to a Local Commissioner.
   (3) This subsection is satisfied if, in relation to the matter—
      (a) a complaint which satisfies sections 26A and 26B has been made to a member of an author-
         ity to which this Part of this Act applies, and
      (b) the complaint has been referred, or is treated as having been referred, to a Local
         Commissioner under section 26C.
   (4) Any question whether subsection (2) or (3) is satisfied in relation to a matter shall be determined by a Local Commissioner.
   (5) This subsection is satisfied if—
      (a) the matter has come to the attention of a Local Commissioner, and
      (b) section 26D applies to the matter.
   (6) In determining whether to initiate, continue or discontinue an investigation, a Local
Commissioner shall, subject to the provisions of this section and sections 26 to 26D, act in accordance
with his own discretion.

(7) Without prejudice to the discretion conferred by subsection (6), a Local Commissioner may in particular decide—

    (a) not to investigate a matter, or

    (b) to discontinue an investigation of a matter,

if he is satisfied with action which the authority concerned have taken or propose to take.]

25　Authorities subject to investigation

(1) This Part of this Act applies to [the following authorities]—

(a)	any local authority,
[(aaa)	the Greater London Authority,]
[(aa)	...],
[(ab)	a National Park Authority [for a National Park in England],]
(b)	any joint board the constituent authorities of which are all local authorities,
[(ba)	...
(bb)	any development corporation established for the purposes of a new town,
(bbb)	...]
(bc)	...
(bd)	any urban development corporation established by an order under section 135 of the Local Government, Planning and Land Act 1980 [for an urban development area in England],]
[(bda)	a Mayoral development corporation,]
[(be)	any housing action trust established under Part III of the Housing Act 1988 [for a designated area in England]],
[(bf)	the [Homes and Communities] Agency,]
[(bg)	[a fire and rescue authority [in England] constituted by a scheme under section 2 of the Fire and Rescue Services Act 2004 or a scheme to which section 4 of that Act applies;]
[(c)	any joint authority established by Part IV of the Local Government Act 1985;
[(cza)	the London Fire and Emergency Planning Authority;]
[(ca)	any police and crime commissioner;]
[(caa)	any Mayor's Office for Policing and Crime;]
(cb)	...
[(cc)	Transport for London ...]
[(cd)	an authority established for an area in England by an order under section 207 of the Local Government and Public Involvement in Health Act 2007 (joint waste authorities);]
[(ce)	any economic prosperity board established under section 88 of the Local Democracy, Economic Development and Construction Act 2009;
(cf)	any combined authority established under section 103 of that Act;]
[(d)	in relation to the flood defence functions of the Environment Agency, within the meaning of the Water Resources Act 1991, the Environment Agency and any regional flood defence committee [for an area wholly or partly in England]] [; and
(e)	The London Transport Users' Committee.]

(2) Her Majesty may by Order in Council provide that this Part of this Act shall also apply, subject to any modifications or exceptions specified in the Order, to any authority specified in the Order, being an authority which is established by or under an Act of Parliament, and which has power to levy a rate, or to issue a precept.

(3)–(8) *****

26　Matters subject to investigation

[(1) For the purpose of section 24A(1)(b), in relation to an authority to which this Part of this Act applies, the following matters are subject to investigation by a Local Commissioner under this Part of this Act—

(a) alleged or apparent maladministration in connection with the exercise of the authority's administrative functions;

(b) an alleged or apparent failure in a service which it was the authority's function to provide;

(c) an alleged or apparent failure to provide such a service.

[(d) an alleged or apparent failure in a service provided by the authority in oursuance of arrangements under section 7A of the National Health Service Act 2006;

(e) an alleged or apparent failure to provide a service in pursuance of such arrangements.]

(1A) Subsection (1) is subject to the following provisions of this section.]

(2)–(4) ...

[(5) Before proceeding to investigate [a matter], a Local Commissioner shall satisfy himself that—

[(a) [the matter has] been brought, by or on behalf of [the person affected] to the notice of the authority to which [it relates] and that that authority has been afforded a reasonable opportunity [to investigate the matter and to respond]; or

(b) in the particular circumstances, it is not reasonable to expect [the matter to be] brought to the notice of that authority or for that authority to be afforded a reasonable opportunity [to investigate the matter and to respond]].

(6) A Local Commissioner shall not conduct an investigation under this Part of this Act in respect of any of the following matters, that is to say,—

(a) any action in respect of which the [person affected] has or had a right of appeal, reference or review to or before a tribunal constituted by or under any enactment;

(b) any action in respect of which the [person affected] has or had a right of appeal to a Minister of the Crown [. . .]; or

(c) any action in respect of which the [person affected] has or had a remedy by way of proceedings in any court of law:

Provided that a Local Commissioner may conduct an investigation notwithstanding the existence of such a right or remedy if satisfied that in the particular circumstances it is not reasonable to expect the [person affected] to resort or have resorted to it.

[(6A) A Local Commissioner shall not conduct an investigation under this Part of this Act in respect of [any action taken by or on behalf of an authority in the exercise] of any of the authority's functions otherwise than in relation to England.]

(7)–(9) *****

(10) ...

(11), (12), (13) *****

[26A   Who can complain

(1) Under this Part of this Act, a complaint about a matter may only be made—

(a) by a member of the public who claims to have sustained injustice in consequence of the matter,

(b) by a person authorised in writing by such a member of the public to act on his behalf, or

(c) in accordance with subsection (2).

(2) Where a member of the public by whom a complaint about a matter might have been made under this Part of this Act has died or is otherwise unable to authorise a person to act on his behalf, the complaint may be made—

(a) by his personal representative (if any), or

(b) by a person who appears to a Local Commissioner to be suitable to represent him.

26B   Procedure for making complaints

(1) Subject to subsection (3), a complaint about a matter under this Part of this Act must be made—

(a) in writing, and

(b) before the end of the permitted period.

(2) In subsection (1)(b), "the permitted period" means the period of 12 months beginning with —

    (a) the day on which the person affected first had notice of the matter, or

    (b) if the person affected has died without having notice of the matter—

        (i) the day on which the personal representatives of the person affected first had notice of the matter, or

        (ii) if earlier, the day on which the complainant first had notice of the matter.

(3) A Local Commissioner may disapply either or both of the requirements in subsection (1)(a) and (b) in relation to a particular complaint.

26C Referral of complaints by authorities

(1) This section applies where a complaint about a matter is made to a member of an authority to which this Part of this Act applies.

(2) If the complainant consents, the complaint may be referred to a Local Commissioner by—

    (a) the member of the authority to whom the complaint was made,

    (b) any other member of that authority, or

    (c) a member of any other authority to which this Part of this Act applies which is alleged in the complaint to have taken or authorised the action complained of.

(3) Subject to subsection (4), a referral under this section must be made in writing.

(4) A Local Commissioner may disapply the requirement in subsection (3) in relation to a particular referral.

    (5)–(8) *****

26D Matters coming to attention of Local Commissioner

(1) This section applies to a matter which has come to the attention of a Local Commissioner if—

    (a) the matter came to his attention during the course of an investigation under this Part [or Part 3A] of this Act,

    (b) (subject to subsection (3)) the matter came to his attention—

        (i) before the person affected or his personal representatives had notice of the matter, or

        (ii) in any other case, before the end of the permitted period, and

    (c) it appears to the Local Commissioner that a member of the public has, or may have, suffered injustice in consequence of the matter.

(2) In subsection (1)(b)(ii), "the permitted period" means the period of 12 months beginning with—

    (a) the day on which the person affected first had notice of the matter, or

    (b) if the person affected has died without having notice of the matter, the day on which the personal representatives of the person affected first had notice of the matter.

(3) A Local Commissioner may disapply the requirement in subsection (1)(b) in relation to a particular matter.]

27 [Members of the public]

(1) [In this Part of this Act, "member of the public" means an individual or a body of persons, whether incorporated or not, other than—]

    (a) a local authority or other authority or body constituted for purposes of the public service or of local government, [(including [the Welsh Ministers, the National Assembly for Wales Commission or the] the National Assembly for Wales)], or for the purposes of carrying on under national ownership any industry or undertaking or part of an industry or undertaking;

    (b) any other authority or body whose members are appointed by Her Majesty or any Minister of the Crown or government department [or by the [Welsh Ministers]], or whose revenues consist wholly or mainly of moneys provided by Parliament [or the [Welsh Ministers]].

    (2) . . .

28 Procedure in respect of investigations

(1) Where a Local Commissioner proposes to [investigate a matter under this Part of this Act], he shall afford to the authority concerned, and to any person who is alleged in the complaint [(if any), or who otherwise appears to the Local Commissioner,] to have taken or authorised [the action which would be the subject of the investigation], an opportunity to comment on [the matter].

(2) Every [investigation under this Part of the Act] shall be conducted in private, but except as aforesaid the procedure for conducting an investigation shall be such as the Local Commissioner considers appropriate in the circumstances of the case; and without prejudice to the generality of the preceding provision the Local Commissioner may obtain information from such persons and in such manner, and make such inquiries as he thinks fit, and may determine whether any person may be represented (by counsel or solicitor or otherwise) in the investigation.

(3) *****

(4) The conduct of an investigation under this Part of this Act shall not affect any action taken by the authority concerned [or any other person], or any power or duty of [the authority concerned or any other person] to take further action with respect to any matters subject to the investigation.

29 Investigations: further provisions

(1) For the purposes of an investigation [under this Part of this Act] a Local Commissioner may require any member or officer of the authority concerned, or any other person who in his opinion is able to furnish information or produce documents relevant to the investigation, to furnish any such information or produce any such documents.

(2) For the purposes of any such investigation a Local Commissioner shall have the same powers as the High Court in respect of the attendance and examination of witnesses, and in respect of the production of documents.

(3)–(10) *****

30 Reports on investigations

[(1) If a Local Commissioner completes an investigation of a matter, [under this Part of this Act], he shall prepare a report of the results of the investigation and send a copy to each of the persons concerned (subject to subsection (1B)).

(1A) A Local Commissioner may include in a report on a matter under subsection (1) any recommendations that he could include in a further report on the matter by virtue of section 31(2A) to (2BA).

(1B) If, after the investigation of a matter is completed, the Local Commissioner decides—

(a) that he is satisfied with action which the authority concerned have taken or propose to take, and

(b) that it is not appropriate to prepare and send a copy of a report under subsection (1),

he may instead prepare a statement of his reasons for the decision and send a copy to each of the persons concerned.

(1C) If a Local Commissioner decides—

(a) not to investigate a matter, or

(b) to discontinue an investigation of a matter,

he shall prepare a statement of his reasons for the decision and send a copy to each of the persons concerned.

(1D) For the purposes of subsections (1) to (1C), the persons concerned are—

(a) the complainant (if any),

(b) any person who referred the matter under section 26C(2),

(c) the authority concerned, and

(d) any other authority or person who is alleged in the complaint, or who otherwise appears to the Local Commissioner, to have taken or authorised the action which is or would be the subject of the investigation.]

(2), (2AA), (2AB) *****

(2A) ...

[(2B) Subsections (3) to (8) apply in the case of a report under subsection (1)].

(3) Apart from identifying the authority or authorities concerned the report shall not ...—

(a) mention the name of any person, or

(b) contain any particulars which, in the opinion of the Local Commissioner, are likely to identify any person and can be omitted without impairing the effectiveness of the report,

unless, after taking into account the public interest as well as [the interests of the complainant (if any) and of other persons], the Local Commissioner considers it necessary to mention the name of that person or to include in the report any such particulars.

[(3AA) Nothing in subsection (3) above prevents a report—

(a) mentioning the name of, or

(b) containing particulars likely to identify,

the Mayor of London or any member of the London Assembly.]

(3A) ...

(4) Subject to the provisions of subsection (7) below, the authority concerned shall for a period of three weeks make copies of the report available for inspection by the public without charge at all reasonable hours at one or more of their offices; and any person shall be entitled to take copies of, or extracts from, the report when so made available.

[(4A) Subject to subsection (7) below, the authority concerned shall supply a copy of the report to any person on request if he pays such charge as the authority may reasonably require.]

(5) Not later than [two weeks] after the report is received by the authority concerned, the proper officer of the authority shall give public notice, by advertisement in the newspapers and such other ways as appear to him appropriate, that [copies of the report will be available as provided by subsections (4) and (4A)] above, and shall specify the date, being a date [not more than one week after the public notice is first given] from which the period of three weeks will begin.

(6) *****

(7) The Local Commissioner may, if he thinks fit after taking into account the public interest as well as [the interests of the complainant (if any) and of other persons], direct that a report specified in the direction shall not be subject to the provisions of subsections (4) [,(4A) and (5) above.]

(8) *****

31   Reports on investigations: further provisions

[(1) This section applies where a Local Commissioner reports that there has been—

(a) maladministration in connection with the exercise of the authority's administrative functions,

(b) a failure in a service which it was the function of an authority to provide, or

(c) a failure to provide such a service.]

(2) The report shall be laid before the authority concerned and it shall be the duty of that authority to consider the report and, within the period of three months beginning with the date on which they received the report, or such longer period as the Local Commissioner may agree in writing, to notify the Local Commissioner of the action which the authority have taken or propose to take.

[(2A) If the Local Commissioner—

(a) does not receive the notification required by subsection (2) above within the period allowed by or under that subsection, or

(b) is not satisfied with the action which the authority concerned have taken or propose to take, or

(c) does not within a period of three months beginning with the end of the period so allowed, or such longer period as the Local Commissioner may agree in writing, receive confirmation from the authority concerned that they have taken action, as proposed, to the satisfaction of the Local Commissioner,

he shall make a further report setting out those facts and making recommendations.

[(2B) Where the report relates to maladministration, those recommendations are recommen-dations with respect to action which, in the Local Commissioner's opinion, the authority concerned should take—

    (a) to remedy any injustice sustained by the person affected in consequence of the maladmin-istration, and

    (b) to prevent injustice being caused in the future in consequence of similar maladministra-tion in connection with the exercise of the authority's administrative functions.

(2BA) Where the report relates to a failure in, or to provide, a service which it was the function of the authority to provide, those recommendations are recommendations with respect to action which, in the Local Commissioner's opinion, the authority concerned should take—

    (a) to remedy any injustice sustained by the person affected in consequence of the failure, and

    (b) to prevent injustice being caused in the future in consequence of a similar failure in, or to provide, a service which it is the function of the authority to provide.]

(2C) Section 30 above, with any necessary modifications, and subsection (2) above shall apply to a report under subsection (2A) above as they apply to a report under that section.

(2D) If the Local Commissioner—

    (a) does not receive the notification required by subsection (2) above as applied by subsection (2C) above within the period allowed by or under that subsection or is satisfied before the period allowed by that subsection has expired that the authority concerned have decided to take no action, or

    (b) is not satisfied with the action which the authority concerned have taken or propose to take, or

    (c) does not within a period of three months beginning with the end of the period allowed by or under subsection (2) above as applied by subsection (2C) above, or such longer period as the Local Commissioner may agree in writing, receive confirmation from the author-ity concerned that they have taken action, as proposed, to the satisfaction of the Local Commissioner,

he may, by notice to the authority, require them to arrange for a statement to be published in accord-ance with subsections (2E) and (2F) below.

(2E) The statement referred to in subsection (2D) above is a statement, in such form as the authority concerned and the Local Commissioner may agree, consisting of—

    (a) details of any action recommended by the Local Commissioner in his further report which the authority have not taken;

    (b) such supporting material as the Local Commissioner may require; and

    (c) if the authority so require, a statement of the reasons for their having taken no action on, or not the action recommended in, the report.]

(2F)–(2H) *****

[(3) In any case where—

    (a) a report is laid before an authority under subsection [(2) or (2C)] above, and

    (b) on consideration of the report, it appears to the authority that a payment should be made to, or some other benefit should be provided for, a person who has suffered injustice in consequence of [the maladministration or failure] [to which the report relates],

the authority may incur such expenditure as appears to them to be appropriate in making such a pay-ment or providing such a benefit.]

(4) *****

31A–33A   *****

34   Interpretation of Part III

(1), (2) *****

(3) It is hereby declared that nothing in this Part of this Act authorises or requires a Local Commissioner to question the merits of a decision taken without maladministration by an authority in the exercise of a discretion vested in that authority.

*****

Section 26   **SCHEDULE 5**

MATTERS NOT SUBJECT TO INVESTIGATION

1. The commencement or conduct of civil or criminal proceedings before any court of law.

2. Action taken by [or on behalf of] any [local policing body] in connection with the investigation or prevention of crime.

[3.—(1) Action taken in matters relating to contractual or other commercial transactions of any authority to which Part 3 of this Act Applies relating to—

    (a) the operation of public passenger transport;

    (b) the carrying on of a dock or harbour undertaking;

    (c) the provision of entertainment;

    (d) the provision and operation of industrial establishments;

    (e) the provision and operation of markets.

(2) Sub-paragraph (1) does not include transactions for or relating to—

    (a) the acquisition or disposal of land;

    (b) the acquisition or disposal of moorings which are not moorings provided in connection with a dock or harbour undertaking.

(3) Sub-paragraph (1)(a) does not include action taken by or on behalf of the London Transport Users Committee in operating a procedure for examining complaints or reviewing decisions.

(4) Sub-paragraph (1)(e) does not include transactions relating to—

    (a) the grant, renewal or revocation of a licence to occupy a pitch or stall in a fair or market, or

    (b) the attachment of any condition to such a licence.]

4. Action taken in respect of appointments or removals, pay, discipline, superannuation or other personnel matters.

5.–8. *****

House of Commons Disqualification Act 1975

(1975, c. 24)

An Act to consolidate certain enactments relating to disqualification for membership of the House of Commons.   [8th May 1975]

Territorial extent: United Kingdom

1   Disqualification of holders of certain offices and places

(1) Subject to the provisions of this Act, a person is disqualified for membership of the House of Commons who for the time being—

    [(za) is a Lord Spiritual;]

    (a)   holds any of the judicial offices specified in Part I of Schedule 1 to this Act;

    (b)   is employed in the civil service of the Crown, whether in an established capacity or not, and whether for the whole or part of his time;

(c)   is a member of any of the regular armed forces of the Crown...

(d)   is a member of any police force maintained by [a local policing body or] a police authority;

[(da) ...]

(e)   is a member of the legislature of any country or territory outside the Commonwealth [other than Ireland]; or

(f)   holds any office described in Part II or Part III of Schedule 1.

(2), (3) *****

(4) Except as provided by this Act, a person shall not be disqualified for membership of the House of Commons by reason of his holding an office or place of profit under the Crown or any other office or place; and a person shall not be disqualified for appointment to or for holding any office or place by reason of his being a member of that House.

2   Ministerial offices

(1) Not more than ninety-five persons being the holders of offices specified in Schedule 2 to this Act (in this section referred to as Ministerial offices) shall be entitled to sit and vote in the House of Commons at any one time.

(2) If at any time the number of members of the House of Commons who are holders of Ministerial offices exceeds the number entitled to sit and vote in that House under subsection (1) above, none except any who were both members of that House and holders of Ministerial offices before the excess occurred shall sit or vote therein until the number has been reduced, by death, resignation or otherwise, to the number entitled to sit and vote as aforesaid.

(3) A person holding a Ministerial office is not disqualified by this Act by reason of any office held by him ex officio as the holder of that Ministerial office.

3   *****

4   Stewardship of Chiltern Hundreds, etc.

For the purposes of the provisions of this Act relating to the vacation of the seat of a member of the House of Commons who becomes disqualified by this Act for membership of that House, the office of steward or bailiff of Her Majesty's three Chiltern Hundreds of Stoke, Desborough and Burnham, or of the Manor of Northstead, shall be treated as included among the offices described in Part III of Schedule 1 to this Act.

5   Power to amend Schedule 1

(1) If at any time it is resolved by the House of Commons that Schedule 1 to this Act be amended, whether by the addition or omission of any office or the removal of any office from one Part of the Schedule to another, or by altering the description of any office specified therein, Her Majesty may by Order in Council amend that Schedule accordingly.

(2) *****

6   Effects of disqualification and provision for relief

(1) Subject to any order made by the House of Commons under this section,—

(a) if any person disqualified by this Act for membership of that House, or for membership for a particular constituency, is elected as a member of that House, or as a member for that constituency, as the case may be, his election shall be void; and

(b) if any person being a member of that House becomes disqualified by this Act for membership for the constituency for which he is sitting, his seat shall be vacated.

(2) If, in a case falling or alleged to fall within subsection (1) above, it appears to the House of Commons that the grounds of disqualification or alleged disqualification under this Act which subsisted or arose at the material time have been removed, and that it is otherwise proper so to do, that House may by order direct that any such disqualification incurred on those grounds at that time shall be disregarded for the purposes of this section.

(3), (4) *****

7   Jurisdiction of Privy Council as to disqualification

(1) Any person who claims that a person purporting to be a member of the House of Commons is disqualified by this Act, or has been so disqualified at any time since his election, may apply to Her Majesty in Council, in accordance with such rules as Her Majesty in Council may prescribe, for a declaration to that effect.

(2) Section 3 of the Judicial Committee Act 1833 (reference to the Judicial Committee of the Privy Council of appeals to Her Majesty in Council) shall apply to any application under this section as it applies to an appeal to Her Majesty in Council from a court.

(3)–(5) *****

8, 9   *****

10   ...

*****

Section 2   **SCHEDULE 2**

MINISTERIAL OFFICE

Prime Minister and First Lord of the Treasury.
Lord President of the Council.
Lord Privy Seal.
Chancellor of the Duchy of Lancaster.
Paymaster General.
Secretary of State.
Chancellor of the Exchequer.
...
President of the Board of Trade.
Minister of State.
Chief Secretary to the Treasury.
Minister in charge of a public department of Her Majesty's Government in the United Kingdom (if not within the other provisions of this Schedule).
Attorney General.
...
Solicitor General.
[Advocate General for Scotland.]
...
Parliamentary Secretary to the Treasury.
Financial Secretary to the Treasury.
Parliamentary Secretary in a Government Department other than the Treasury, or not in a department.
Junior Lord of the Treasury.
Treasurer of Her Majesty's Household.
Comptroller of Her Majesty's Household.
Vice-Chamberlain of Her Majesty's Household.
Assistant Government Whip.

Ministerial and Other Salaries Act 1975

(1975, c. 27)

An Act to consolidate the enactments relating to the salaries of Ministers and Opposition Leaders and Chief Whips and to other matters connected therewith.   [8th May 1975]

Territorial extent: United Kingdom

1   Salaries

    (1) Subject to the provisions of this Act—

        (a) there shall be paid to the holder of any Ministerial office specified in Schedule 1 to this Act such salary as is provided for by that Schedule; and

        (b) there shall be paid to the Leaders and Whips of the Opposition such salaries as are provided for by Schedule 2 to this Act.

    (2) There shall be paid to the Lord Chancellor a salary (which shall be charged on and paid out of the Consolidated Fund of the United Kingdom) at such rate as [together with any salary payable to him as Speaker of the House of Lords] will amount to [[£2,500] a year more than the salary payable to the Lord Chief Justice] ...

    (3) There shall be paid to the Speaker of the House of Commons a salary (which shall be charged on and paid out of the Consolidated Fund of the United Kingdom) of [£75,766] a year; and on a dissolution of Parliament the Speaker of the House of Commons at the time of the dissolution shall for this purpose be deemed to remain Speaker until a Speaker is chosen by the New Parliament.

    [(3A) There shall be paid to the Speaker of the House of Lords a salary (which shall be paid out of money provided by Parliament) of £101,038 a year.]

    (4) ...

    (5) *****

1A, 1B   *****

2   Opposition Leaders and Whips

    (1) In this Act 'Leader of the Opposition' means, in relation to either House of Parliament, that Member of that House who is for the time being the Leader in that House of the party in opposition to Her Majesty's Government having the greatest numerical strength in the House of Commons; and 'Chief Opposition Whip' means, in relation to either House of Parliament, the person for the time being nominated as such by the Leader of the Opposition in that House; and 'Assistant Opposition Whip', in relation to the House of Commons, means a person for the time being nominated as such, and to be paid as such, by the Leader of the Opposition in the House of Commons.

    (2) If any doubt arises as to which is or was at any material time the party in opposition to Her Majesty's Government having the greatest numerical strength in the House of Commons, or as to who is or was at any material time the leader in that House of such a party, the question shall be decided for the purposes of this Act by the Speaker of the House of Commons, and his decision, certified in writing under his hand, shall be final and conclusive.

    (3) If any doubt arises as to who is or was at any material time the Leader in the House of Lords of the said party, the question shall be decided for the purposes of this Act by [the Speaker of the House of Lords] and his decision, certified in writing under his hand, shall be final and conclusive.

3   *****

4   Interpretation

    (1) In this Act—

'Junior Lord of the Treasury' means any Lord Commissioner of the Treasury other than the First Lord and the Chancellor of the Exchequer;

'Minister of State' and 'Parliamentary Secretary' have the same meanings as in the House of Commons Disqualification Act 1975.

    (2) *****

British Nationality Act 1981

(1981, c. 61)

An Act to make fresh provision about citizenship and nationality, and to amend the Immigration Act 1971 as regards the right of abode in the United Kingdom.   [30th October 1981]

Territorial extent: United Kingdom

PART I BRITISH CITIZENSHIP

Acquisition after commencement

1   Acquisition by birth or adoption

(1) A person born in the United Kingdom after commencement [, or in a qualifying territory on or after the appointed day] shall be a British citizen if at the time of the birth his father or mother is—

    (a) a British citizen; or

    (b) settled in the United Kingdom [or that territory].

[(1A) A person born in the United Kingdom or a qualifying territory on or after the relevant day shall be a British citizen if at the time of the birth his father or mother is a member of the armed forces.]

(2) A new-born infant who, after commencement, is found abandoned in the United Kingdom [, or on or after the appointed day is found abandoned in a qualifying territory] shall, unless the contrary is shown, be deemed for the purposes of subsection (1)—

    (a) to have been born in the United Kingdom after commencement [or in that territory on or after the appointed day]; and

    (b) to have been born to a parent who at the time of the birth was a British citizen or settled in the United Kingdom [or that territory].

(3) A person born in the United Kingdom after commencement who is not a British citizen by virtue of subsection (1), [1A] or (2) shall be entitled to be registered as a British citizen if, while he is a minor—

    (a) his father or mother becomes a British citizen or becomes settled in the United Kingdom; and

    (b) an application is made for his registration as a British citizen.

[(3A) A person born in the United Kingdom on or after the relevant day who is not a British citizen by virtue of subsection (1), (1A) or (2) shall be entitled to be registered as a British citizen if, while he is a minor—

    (a) his father or mother becomes a member of the armed forces; and

    (b) an application is made for his registration as a British citizen].

(4) A person born in the United Kingdom after commencement who is not a British citizen by virtue of subsection (1), [1A] or (2) shall be entitled, on an application for his registration as a British citizen made at any time after he has attained the age of ten years, to be registered as such a citizen if, as regards each of the first ten years of that person's life, the number of days on which he was absent from the United Kingdom in that year does not exceed 90.

(5)–(9) *****

2   Acquisition by descent

(1) A person born outside the United Kingdom [and the qualifying territories] after commencement shall be a British citizen if at the time of the birth his father or mother—

    (a) is a British citizen otherwise than by descent; or

   (b) is a British citizen and is serving outside the United Kingdom [and the qualifying terri-
        tories] in service to which this paragraph applies, his or her recruitment for that service
        having taken place in the United Kingdom [or a qualifying territory]; or
   (c) is a British citizen and is serving outside the United Kingdom [and the qualifying
        territories] in service under [an] [EU] institution, his or her recruitment for that service
        having taken place in a country which at the time of the recruitment was a member of the
        [European Union].
   (2) Paragraph (b) of subsection (1) applies to—
   (a) Crown service under the government of the United Kingdom [or of a qualifying territory];
        and
   (b) service of any description for the time being designated under subsection (3).
   (3) For the purposes of this section the Secretary of State may by order made by statutory instrument designate any description of service which he considers to be closely associated with the activities outside the United Kingdom [and the qualifying territories] of Her Majesty's government in the
United Kingdom [or in a qualifying territory].
   (4) Any order made under subsection (3) shall be subject to annulment in pursuance of a resolution of either House of Parliament.

3 Acquisition by registration: minors

   (1) If while a person is a minor an application is made for his registration as a British citizen, the
Secretary of State may, if he thinks fit, cause him to be registered as such a citizen.
   (2) A person born outside the United Kingdom [and the qualifying territories] shall be entitled,
on an application for his registration as a British citizen made [while he is a minor], to be registered as
such a citizen if the requirements specified in subsection (3) or, in the case of a person born stateless,
the requirements specified in paragraphs (a) and (b) of that subsection, are fulfilled in the case of either
that person's father or his mother ('the parent in question').
   (3) The requirements referred to in subsection (2) are—
   (a) that the parent in question was a British citizen by descent at the time of the birth; and
   (b) that the father or mother of the parent in question—
        (i)   was a British citizen otherwise than by descent at the time of the birth of the parent
              in question; or
        (ii) became a British citizen otherwise than by descent at commencement, or would have
              become such a citizen otherwise than by descent at commencement but for his or her
              death; and
   (c) that, as regards some period of three years ending with a date not later than that date of
        the birth—
        (i)   the parent in question was in the United Kingdom [or a qualifying territory] at the
              beginning of that period; and
        (ii) the number of days on which the parent in question was absent from the United
              Kingdom [and the qualifying territories] in the period does not exceed 270.
   (4) ...
   (5) A person born outside the United Kingdom [and the qualifying territories] shall be entitled,
on an application for his registration as a British citizen made while he is a minor, to be registered as
such a citizen if the following requirements are satisfied, namely—
   (a) that at the time of that person's birth his father or mother was a British citizen by descent;
        and
   (b) subject to subsection (6), that that person and his father and mother were in the United
        Kingdom [or a qualifying territory] at the beginning of the period of three years ending
        with the date of the application and that, in the case of each of them, the number of days
        on which the person in question was absent from the United Kingdom [and the qualifying
        territories] in that period does not exceed 270; and

      (c) subject to subsection (6), that the consent of his father and mother to the registration has been signified in the prescribed manner.

    (6) In the case of an application under subsection (5) of the registration of a person as a British citizen—

      (a) if his father or mother died, or their marriage [or civil partnership] was terminated, on or before the date of the application, or his father and mother were legally separated on that date, the references to his father and mother in paragraph (b) of that subsection shall be read either as references to his father or as references to his mother; [and]

      (b) if his father or mother died on or before that date, the reference to his father and mother in paragraph (c) of that subsection shall be read as a reference to either of them. . . .

4, 4A–D *****

5 Acquisition by registration: nationals for purposes of the Community treaties

A [British overseas territories citizen] who falls to be treated as a national of the United Kingdom for the purposes of the Community Treaties shall be entitled to be registered as a British citizen if an application is made for his registration as such a citizen.

6 Acquisition by naturalisation

    (1) If, on an application for naturalisation as a British citizen made by a person of full age and capacity, the Secretary of State is satisfied that the applicant fulfils the requirements of Schedule 1 for naturalisation as such a citizen under this subsection, he may, if he thinks fit, grant to him a certificate of naturalisation as such a citizen.

    (2) If, on an application for naturalisation as a British citizen made by a person of full age and capacity who on the date of the application [has a relevant family association], the Secretary of State is satisfied that the applicant fulfils the requirements of Schedule 1 for naturalisation as such a citizen under this subsection, he may, if he thinks fit, grant to him a certificate of naturalisation as such a citizen.

    (3), (4) *****

7–9 . . .

10 *****

Acquisition at commencement

11 Citizens of UK and Colonies who are to become British citizens at commencement

    (1) Subject to subsection (2), a person who immediately before commencement—

      (a) was a citizen of the United Kingdom and Colonies; and

      (b) had the right of abode in the United Kingdom under the Immigration Act 1971 as then in force,

shall at commencement become a British citizen.

    (2) A person who was registered as a citizen of the United Kingdom and Colonies under section 1 of the British Nationality (No 2) Act 1964 (stateless persons) on the ground mentioned in subsection (1)(a) of that section (namely that his mother was a citizen of the United Kingdom and Colonies at the time when he was born) shall not become a British citizen under subsection (1) unless—

      (a) his mother becomes a British citizen under subsection (1) or would have done so but for her death; or

      (b) immediately before commencement he had the right of abode in the United Kingdom by virtue of section 2(1)(c) of the Immigration Act 1971 as then in force (settlement in United Kingdom, combined with five or more years' ordinary residence there as a citizen of the United Kingdom and Colonies).

(3) A person who—

    (a) immediately before commencement was a citizen of the United Kingdom and Colonies by virtue of having been registered under subsection (6) of section 12 of the 1948 Act (British subjects before commencement of 1948 Act becoming citizens of United Kingdom and Colonies) under arrangements made by virtue of subsection (7) of that section (registration in independent Commonwealth country by United Kingdom High Commissioner); and

    (b) was so registered on an application under the said subsection (6) based on the applicant's descent in the male line from a person ("the relevant person") possessing one of the qualifications specified in subsection (1)(a) and (b) of that section (birth or naturalisation in the United Kingdom and Colonies),

shall at commencement become a British citizen if the relevant person was born or naturalised in the United Kingdom.

12 Renunciation

(1) If any British citizen of full age and capacity makes in the prescribed manner a declaration of renunciation of British citizenship, then, subject to subsections (3) and (4), the Secretary of State shall cause the declaration to be registered.

(2) On the registration of a declaration made in pursuance of this section the person who made it shall cease to be a British citizen.

(3) A declaration made by a person in pursuance of this section shall not be registered unless the Secretary of State is satisfied that the person who made it will after the registration have or acquire some citizenship or nationality other than British citizenship; and if that person does not have any such citizenship or nationality on the date of registration and does not acquire some such citizenship or nationality within six months from that date, he shall be, and be deemed to have remained, a British citizen notwithstanding the registration.

(4) The Secretary of State may withhold registration of any declaration made in pursuance of this section if it is made during any war in which Her Majesty may be engaged in right of Her Majesty's government in the United Kingdom.

(5) For the purposes of this section any person who has been married [, or has formed a civil partnership,] shall be deemed to be of full age.

13, 14 *****

PART II BRITISH [OVERSEAS TERRITORIES] CITIZENSHIP

Acquisition after commencement

15 Acquisition by birth or adoption

(1) A person born in a [British overseas territory] after commencement shall be a [British overseas territories citizen] if at the time of the birth his father or mother is—

    (a) a [British overseas territories citizen]; or

    (b) settled in a [British overseas territory].

(2)–(7) *****

16 Acquisition by descent

(1) A person born outside the [British overseas territories] after commencement shall be a [British overseas territories citizen] if at the time of the birth his father or mother—

    (a) is such a citizen otherwise than by descent; or

    (b) is such a citizen and is serving outside the [British overseas territories] in service to which this paragraph applies, his or her recruitment for that service having taken place in a [British overseas territory].

(2) Paragraph (b) of subsection (1) applies to—

(a) Crown service under the government of a [British overseas territory]; and

(b) service of any description for the time being designated under subsection (3).

(3), (4) *****

17, 18, 22–25 *****

19–21 ...

PART III BRITISH OVERSEAS CITIZENSHIP

26   Citizens of UK and Colonies who are to become British Overseas citizens at commencement

Any person who was a citizen of the United Kingdom and Colonies immediately before commencement and who does not at commencement become either a British citizen or a [British overseas territories citizen] shall at commencement become a British Overseas citizen.

27–35 *****

PART V MISCELLANEOUS AND SUPPLEMENTARY

36 *****

37   Commonwealth citizenship

(1) Every person who—

(a) under [the British Nationality Acts 1981 and 1983] [or the British Overseas Territories Act 2002] is a British citizen, a [British overseas territories citizen], [a British National (Overseas),] a British Overseas citizen or a British subject; or

(b) under any enactment for the time being in force in any country mentioned in Schedule 3 is a citizen of that country,

shall have the status of a Commonwealth citizen.

(2) Her Majesty may by Order in Council amend Schedule 3 by the alteration of any entry, the removal of any entry, or the insertion of any additional entry.

(3) Any Order in Council made under this section shall be subject to annulment in pursuance of a resolution of either House of Parliament.

(4) After commencement no person shall have the status of a Commonwealth citizen or the status of a British subject otherwise than under this Act.

[**Note:** Schedule 3 (not printed) lists those countries currently members of the Commonwealth.]

38, 39 *****

[40   Deprivation of citizenship

(1) In this section a reference to a person's 'citizenship status' is a reference to his status as—

(a) a British citizen,

(b) a British overseas territories citizen,

(c) a British Overseas citizen,

(d) a British National (Overseas),

(e) a British protected person, or

(f) a British subject.

[(2) The Secretary of State may by order deprive a person of a citizenship status if the Secretary of State is satisfied that deprivation is conducive to the public good.]

(3) The Secretary of State may by order deprive a person of a citizenship status which results from his registration or naturalisation if the Secretary of State is satisfied that the registration or naturalisation was obtained by means of—

    (a) fraud,

    (b) false representation, or

    (c) concealment of a material fact.

(4) The Secretary of State may not make an order under subsection (2) if he is satisfied that the order would make a person stateless.

(5) Before making an order under this section in respect of a person the Secretary of State must give the person written notice specifying—

    (a) that the Secretary of State has decided to make an order,

    (b) the reasons for the order, and

    (c) the person's right of appeal under section 40A(1) or under section 2B of the Special Immigration Appeals Commission Act 1997].

(6) *****

[40A   Deprivation of citizenship: appeal

(1) A person who is given notice under section 40(5) of a decision to make an order in respect of him under section 40 may appeal against the decision to [the First-tier Tribunal].

(2) Subsection (1) shall not apply to a decision if the Secretary of State certifies that it was taken wholly or partly in reliance on information which in his opinion should not be made public—

    (a) in the interests of national security,

    (b) in the interests of the relationship between the United Kingdom and another country, or

    (c) otherwise in the public interest.]

(3) *****

(4)–(8) ...

41–41A   *****

[42   Registration and naturalisation: citizenship ceremony, oath and pledge

(1) A person of full age shall not be registered under this Act as a British citizen unless he has made the relevant citizenship oath and pledge specified in Schedule 5 at a citizenship ceremony.

(2) A certificate of naturalisation as a British citizen shall not be granted under this Act to a person of full age unless he has made the relevant citizenship oath and pledge specified in Schedule 5 at a citizenship ceremony.

(3) A person of full age shall not be registered under this Act as a British overseas territories citizen unless he has made the relevant citizenship oath and pledge specified in Schedule 5.

(4) A certificate of naturalisation as a British overseas territories citizen shall not be granted under this Act to a person of full age unless he has made the relevant citizenship oath and pledge specified in Schedule 5.

(5) A person of full age shall not be registered under this Act as a British Overseas citizen or a British subject unless he has made the relevant citizenship oath specified in Schedule 5.

(6) Where the Secretary of State thinks it appropriate because of the special circumstances of a case he may—

    (a) disapply any of subsections (1) to (5), or

    (b) modify the effect of any of those subsections.

(7) Sections 5 and 6 of the Oaths Act 1978 (c. 19) (affirmation) apply to a citizenship oath; and a reference in this Act to a citizenship oath includes a reference to a citizenship affirmation.]

42A   ...

42B, 43   *****

44   Decisions involving exercise of discretion

(1) Any discretion vested by or under this Act in the Secretary of State, a Governor or a Lieutenant-Governor shall be exercised without regard to the race, colour or religion of any person who may be affected by its exercise.

(2), (3) . . .

44A–48 *****

49 . . .

50   Interpretation

(1) In this Act, unless the context otherwise requires—

'the 1948 Act' means the British Nationality Act 1948:

'alien' means a person who is neither a Commonwealth citizen nor a British protected person nor a citizen of the Republic of Ireland;

*****

['British National (Overseas)' means a person who is a British National (Overseas) under the Hong Kong (British Nationality) Order 1986, and 'status of a British National (Overseas)' shall be construed accordingly;

'British Overseas citizen' includes a person who is a British Overseas citizen under the Hong Kong (British Nationality) Order 1986;]

['British overseas territory' means a territory mentioned in Schedule 6;]

'British protected person' means a person who is a member of any class of person declared to be British protected persons by an Order in Council for the time being in force under section 38 or is a British protected person by virtue of the Solomon Islands Act 1978;

*****

'foreign country' means a country other than the United Kingdom, a [British overseas territory], a country mentioned in Schedule 3 and the Republic of Ireland;

*****

'immigration laws'—

(a) in relation to the United Kingdom, means the Immigration Act 1971 and any law for purposes similar to that Act which is for the time being or has at any time been in force in any part of the United Kingdom;

(b) in relation to a [British overseas territory], means any law for purposes similar to the Immigration Act 1971 which is for the time being or has at any time been in force in that territory;

*****

(1A), (1B) *****

(2) Subject to subsection (3), references in this Act to a person being settled in the United Kingdom or in a [British overseas territory] are references to his being ordinarily resident in the United Kingdom or, as the case may be, in that territory without being subject under the immigration laws to any restriction on the period for which he may remain.

(3), (4) *****

(5) It is hereby declared that a person is not to be treated for the purpose of any provision of this Act as ordinarily resident in the United Kingdom or in a [British overseas territory] at a time when he is in the United Kingdom or, as the case may be, in that territory in breach of the immigration laws.

(6)–(14) *****

50A–53 *****

SCHEDULE 1

REQUIREMENTS FOR NATURALISATION

Naturalisation as a British citizen under section 6(1)

1.—(1) Subject to paragraph 2, the requirements for naturalisation as a British citizen under section 6(1) are, in the case of any person who applies for it—

    (a) the requirements specified in sub-paragraph (2) of this paragraph, ...; and

    (b) that he is of good character; and

    (c) that he has a sufficient knowledge of the English, Welsh or Scottish Gaelic language; and

  [(ca) that he has sufficient knowledge about life in the United Kingdom; and]

    (d) that either—

        (i) his intentions are such that, in the event of a certificate of naturalisation as a British citizen being granted to him, his home or (if he has more than one) his principal home will be in the United Kingdom; or

        (ii) he intends, in the event of such a certificate being granted to him, to enter into, or continue in, Crown service under the government of the United Kingdom, or service under an international organisation of which the United Kingdom or Her Majesty's government therein is a member, or service in the employment of a company or association established in the United Kingdom.

  [(2) The requirements referred to in sub-paragraph (1)(a) of this paragraph are—

    (a) that the applicant ("A") was in the United Kingdom at the beginning of the qualifying period;

    (b) that the number of days on which A was absent from the United Kingdom in each year of the qualifying period does not exceed 90;

    (c) that A had a qualifying immigration status for the whole of the qualifying period;

    (d) that on the date of the application A has probationary citizenship leave, permanent residence leave, a qualifying CTA entitlement, a Commonwealth right of abode or a permanent EEA entitlement;

    (e) that, where on the date of the application A has probationary citizenship leave granted for the purpose of taking employment in the United Kingdom, A has been in continuous employment since the date of the grant of that leave; and

    (f) that A was not at any time in the qualifying period in the United Kingdom in breach of the immigration laws.]

  (3) ...

2., 2A. *****

Naturalisation as a British citizen under section 6(2)

3.—(1) Subject to paragraph 4, the requirements for naturalisation as a British citizen under section 6(2) are, in the case of any person ("A") who applies for it—

    (a) the requirements specified in sub-paragraph (2) of this paragraph;

    (b) the requirement specified in sub-paragraph (3) of this paragraph;

    (c) that A is of good character;

    (d) that A has a sufficient knowledge of the English, Welsh or Scottish Gaelic language; and

    (e) that A has sufficient knowledge about life in the United Kingdom.

  (2) The requirements referred to in sub-paragraph (1)(a) are—

    (a) that A was in the United Kingdom at the beginning of the qualifying period;

    (b) that the number of days on which A was absent from the United Kingdom in each year of the qualifying period does not exceed 90;

(c) that, subject to sub-paragraph (5)—

    (i) A had a relevant family association for the whole of the qualifying period, and

    (ii) A had a qualifying immigration status for the whole of that period;

(d) that on the date of the application—

    (i) A has probationary citizenship leave, or permanent residence leave, based on A's having the relevant family association referred to in section 6(2), or

    (ii) A has a qualifying CTA entitlement or a Commonwealth right of abode; and

(e) that A was not at any time in the qualifying period in the United Kingdom in breach of the immigration laws.

(3) The requirement referred to in sub-paragraph (1)(b) is—

(a) that A's intentions are such that, in the event of a certificate of naturalisation as a British citizen being granted to A, A's home or (if A has more than one) A's principal home will be in the United Kingdom;

(b) that A intends, in the event of such a certificate being granted to A, to enter into, or continue in, service of a description mentioned in sub-paragraph (4); or

(c) that, in the event of such a certificate being granted to A—

    (i) the person with whom A has the relevant family association referred to in section 6(2) ("B") intends to enter into, or continue in, service of a description mentioned in sub-paragraph (4); and

    (ii) A intends to reside with B for the period during which B is in the service in question.

*****

[SCHEDULE 5 CITIZENSHIP OATH AND PLEDGE

1. The form of citizenship oath and pledge is as follows for registration of or naturalisation as a British citizen—

Oath

'I, *[name]*, swear by Almighty God that, on becoming a British citizen, I will be faithful and bear true allegiance to Her Majesty Queen Elizabeth the Second, Her Heirs and Successors according to law.'

Pledge

'I will give my loyalty to the United Kingdom and respect its rights and freedoms. I will uphold its democratic values. I will observe its laws faithfully and fulfil my duties and obligations as a British citizen.']

*****

Contempt of Court Act 1981

(1981, c. 49)

An Act to amend the law relating to contempt of court and related matters.   [27th July 1981]

Territorial extent: United Kingdom (ss. 1–6, 8–11, Sch. 1); England and Wales (ss. 12–14); Scotland (s. 15); England, Wales and Northern Ireland (s. 7). For additional provisions applying to Northern Ireland see Sch. 4.

Strict liability

1 The strict liability rule

In this Act 'the strict liability rule' means the rule of law whereby conduct may be treated as a contempt of court as tending to interfere with the course of justice in particular legal proceedings regardless of intent to do so.

2 Limitation of scope of strict liability

(1) The strict liability rule applies only in relation to publications, and for this purpose 'publication' includes any speech, writing, [programme included in a programme service] or other communication in whatever form, which is addressed to the public at large or any section of the public.

(2) The strict liability rule applies only to a publication which creates a substantial risk that the course of justice in the proceedings in question will be seriously impeded or prejudiced.

(3) The strict liability rule applies to a publication only if the proceedings in question are active within the meaning of this section at the time of the publication.

(4) Schedule 1 applies for determining the times at which proceedings are to be treated as active within the meaning of this section.

[(5) In this section, 'programme service' has the same meaning as in the Broadcasting Act 1990.]

3 Defence of innocent publication or distribution

(1) A person is not guilty of contempt of court under the strict liability rule as the publisher of any matter to which that rule applies if at the time of publication (having taken all reasonable care) he does not know and has no reason to suspect that relevant proceedings are active.

(2) A person is not guilty of contempt of court under the strict liability rule as the distributor of a publication containing any such matter if at the time of distribution (having taken all reasonable care) he does not know that it contains such matter and has no reason to suspect that it is likely to do so.

(3) The burden of proof of any fact tending to establish a defence afforded by this section to any person lies upon that person.

(4) . . .

4 Contemporary reports of proceedings

(1) Subject to this section a person is not guilty of contempt of court under the strict liability rule in respect of a fair and accurate report of legal proceedings held in public, published contemporaneously and in good faith.

(2) In any such proceedings the court may, where it appears to be necessary for avoiding a substantial risk of prejudice to the administration of justice in those proceedings, or in any other proceedings pending or imminent, order that the publication of any report of the proceedings, or any part of the proceedings, be postponed for such period as the court thinks necessary for that purpose.

(2A), (3) *****

(4) . . .

5 Discussion of public affairs

A publication made as or as part of a discussion in good faith of public affairs or other matters of general public interest is not to be treated as a contempt of court under the strict liability rule if the risk of impediment or prejudice to particular legal proceedings is merely incidental to the discussion.

6 Savings

Nothing in the foregoing provisions of this Act—

(a) prejudices any defence available at common law to a charge of contempt of court under the strict liability rule;

(b) implies that any publication is punishable as contempt of court under that rule which would not be so punishable apart from those provisions;

(c) restricts liability for contempt of court in respect of conduct intended to impede or prejudice the administration of justice.

7 Consent required for institution of proceedings

Proceedings for a contempt of court under the strict liability rule (other than Scottish proceedings) shall not be instituted except by or with the consent of the Attorney General or on the motion of a court having jurisdiction to deal with it.

Other aspects of law and procedure

8 Confidentiality of jury's deliberations

(1) Subject to subsection (2) below, it is a contempt of court to obtain, disclose or solicit any particulars of statements made, opinions expressed, arguments advanced or votes cast by members of a jury in the course of their deliberations in any legal proceedings.

(2) This section does not apply to any disclosure of any particulars—

    (a) in the proceedings in question for the purpose of enabling the jury to arrive at their verdict, or in connection with the delivery of that verdict, or

    (b) in evidence in any subsequent proceedings for an offence alleged to have been committed in relation to the jury in the first mentioned proceedings, or to the publication of any particulars so disclosed.

(3) Proceedings for a contempt of court under this section (other than Scottish proceedings) shall not be instituted except by or with the consent of the attorney general or on the motion of a court having jurisdiction to deal with it.

9 Use of tape recorders

(1) Subject to subsection (4) below, it is a contempt of court—

    (a) to use in court, or bring into court for use, any tape recorder or other instrument for recording sound, except with the leave of the court;

    (b) to publish a recording of legal proceedings made by means of any such instrument, or any recording derived directly or indirectly from it, by playing it in the hearing of the public or any section of the public, or to dispose of it or any recording so derived, with a view to such publication;

    (c) to use any such recording in contravention of any conditions of leave granted under paragraph (a).

(2) Leave under paragraph (a) of subsection (1) may be granted or refused at the discretion of the court, and if granted may be granted subject to such conditions as the court thinks proper with respect to the use of any recording made pursuant to the leave; and where leave has been granted the court may at the like discretion withdraw or amend it either generally or in relation to any particular part of the proceedings.

(3), (4) *****

10 Sources of information

No court may require a person to disclose, nor is any person guilty of contempt of court for refusing to disclose, the source of information contained in a publication for which he is responsible, unless it be established to the satisfaction of the court that disclosure is necessary in the interests of justice or national security or for the prevention of disorder or crime.

11 Publication of matters exempted from disclosure in court

In any case where a court (having power to do so) allows a name or other matter to be withheld from the public in proceedings before the court, the court may give such directions prohibiting the publication of that name or matter in connection with the proceedings as appear to the court to be necessary for the purpose of which it was so withheld.

12 Offences of contempt of magistrates' courts

(1) A magistrates' court has jurisdiction under this section to deal with any person who—

    (a) wilfully insults the justice or justices, any witness before or officer of the court or any solicitor or counsel having business in the court, during his or their sitting or attendance in court or in going to or returning from the court; or

    (b) wilfully interrupts the proceedings of the court or otherwise misbehaves in court.

(2) In any such case the court may order any officer of the court, or any constable, to take the offender into custody and detain him until the rising of the court; and the court may, if it thinks fit,

commit the offender to custody for a specified period not exceeding one month or impose on him a fine not exceeding [£2,500], or both.

(2A), (4), (5) *****

(3) ...

13 ...

Penalties for contempt and kindred offences

14 Proceedings in England and Wales

(1) In any case where a court has power to commit a person to prison for contempt of court and (apart from this provision) no limitation applies to the period of committal, the committal shall (without prejudice to the power of the court to order his earlier discharge) be for a fixed term, and that term shall not on any occasion exceed two years in the case of committal by a superior court, or one month in the case of committal by an inferior court.

(2) In any case where an inferior court has power to fine a person for contempt of court and (apart from the provision) no limit applies to the amount of the fine, the fine shall not on any occasion exceed [£2,500].

(2A)–(4), (4A) *****

[(4A) For the purposes of the preceding provisions of this section a county court shall be treated as a superior court and not as an inferior court.]

(5) *****

[**Note:** This section, as amended, contains two subsections both (4A).]

15 Penalties for contempt of court in Scottish proceedings

(1) In Scottish proceedings, when a person is committed to prison for contempt of court the committal shall (without prejudice to the power of the court to order his earlier discharge) be for a fixed term.

(2) The maximum penalty which may be imposed by way of imprisonment or fine for contempt of court in Scottish proceedings shall be two years' imprisonment or a fine or both, except that—

(a) where the contempt is dealt with by the sheriff in the course of or in connection with proceedings other than criminal proceedings on indictment, such penalty shall not exceed three months' imprisonment or a fine [of level 4 on the standard scale] or both; and

(b) where the contempt is dealt with by the district court, such penalty shall not exceed sixty days' imprisonment or a fine of [level 4 on the standard scale] or both.

(3)–(5) *****

(6) ...

16–21 *****

Section 2   **SCHEDULE 1**

TIMES WHEN PROCEEDINGS ARE ACTIVE FOR PURPOSES OF SECTION 2

Preliminary

1. In this Schedule 'criminal proceedings' means proceedings against a person in respect of an offence, not being appellate proceedings or proceedings commenced by motion for committal or attachment in England and Wales or Northern Ireland; and 'appellate proceedings' means proceedings on appeal from or for the review of the decision of a court in any proceedings.

[1A. In paragraph 1 the reference to an offence includes a service offence within the meaning of the Armed Forces Act 2006.]

2. Criminal, appellate and other proceedings are active within the meaning of section 2 at the times respectively prescribed by the following paragraphs of this Schedule; and in relation to proceedings in which more than one of the steps described in any of those paragraphs is taken, the reference in that paragraph is a reference to the first of those steps.

Criminal proceedings

3. Subject to the following provisions of this Schedule, criminal proceedings are active from the relevant initial step specified in paragraph 4 [or 4A] until concluded as described in paragraph 5.

4. The initial steps of criminal proceedings are:—

   (a) arrest without warrant;

   (b) the issue, or in Scotland the grant, of a warrant for arrest;

   (c) the issue of a summons to appear, or in Scotland the grant of a warrant to cite;

   (d) the service of an indictment or other document specifying the charge;

   (e) except in Scotland, oral charge.

[4A. Where as a result of an order under section 54 of the Criminal Procedure and Investigations Act 1996 (acquittal tainted by administration of justice offence) proceedings are brought against a person for an offence of which he has previously been acquitted, the initial step of the proceedings is a certification under subsection (2) of that section; and paragraph 4 has effect subject to this.]

5. Criminal proceedings are concluded—

   (a) by acquittal or, as the case may be, by sentence;

   (b) by any other verdict, finding, order or decision which puts an end to the proceedings;

   (c) by discontinuance or by operation of law.

6. The reference in paragraph 5(a) to sentence includes any order or decision consequent on conviction or finding of guilt which disposes of the case, either absolutely or subject to future events, and a deferment of sentence under [section 1 of the Powers of Criminal Courts (Sentencing) Act 2000], section 219 or 432 of the Criminal Procedure (Scotland) Act 1975 or Article 14 of the Treatment of Offenders (Northern Ireland) Order 1976.

7. Proceedings are discontinued within the meaning of paragraph 5(c)—

   (a)   in England and Wales or Northern Ireland, if the charge or summons is withdrawn or a *nolle prosequi* entered;

   [(aa) in England and Wales, if they are discontinued by virtue of section 23 of the Prosecution of Offences Act 1985;]

   (b)   in Scotland, if the proceedings are expressly abandoned by the prosecutor or are deserted *simpliciter*;

   (c)   in the case of proceedings in England and Wales or Northern Ireland commenced by arrest without warrant, if the person arrested is released, otherwise than on bail, without having been charged.

8.–10. *****

11. Criminal proceedings against a person which become active on the issue or the grant of a warrant for his arrest cease to be active at the end of the period of twelve months beginning with the date of the warrant unless he has been arrested within that period, but become active again if he is subsequently arrested.

Other proceedings at first instance

12. Proceedings other than criminal proceedings and appellate proceedings are active from the time when arrangements for the hearing are made or, if no such arrangements are previously made, from the time the hearing begins, until the proceedings are disposed of or discontinued or withdrawn; and for the purposes of this paragraph any motion or application made in or for the purposes of any proceedings, and any pre-trial review in the county court, is to be treated as a distinct proceeding.

13. In England and Wales or Northern Ireland arrangements for the hearing of proceedings to which paragraph 12 applies are made within the meaning of that paragraph—

(a) in the case of proceedings in the High Court for which provision is made by rules of court for setting down for trial, when the case is set down;

(b) in the case of any proceedings, when a date for the trial or hearing is fixed.

14. In Scotland arrangements for the hearing of proceedings to which paragraph 12 applies are made within the meaning of that paragraph—

(a) in the case of an ordinary action in the Court of Session or in the sheriff court, when the record is closed;

(b) in the case of a motion or application, when it is enrolled or made;

(c) in any other case, when the date for a hearing is fixed or a hearing is allowed.

Appellate proceedings

15. Appellate proceedings are active from the time when they are commenced—

(a) by application for leave to appeal or apply for review, or by notice of such an application;

(b) by notice of appeal or of application for review;

(c) by other originating process,

until disposed of or abandoned, discontinued or withdrawn.

16. Where, in appellate proceedings relating to criminal proceedings, the court—

(a) remits the case to the court below; or

(b) orders a new trial or a *venire de novo*, or in Scotland grants authority to bring a new prosecution,

any further or new proceedings which result shall be treated as active from the conclusion of the appellate proceedings.

*****

[Senior Courts Act 1981]

(1981, c. 54)

An Act to consolidate with amendments the Supreme Court of Judicature (Consolidation) Act 1925 and other enactments relating to the [Senior Courts] in England and Wales and the administration of justice therein; to repeal certain obsolete or unnecessary enactments so relating; to amend Part VIII of the Mental Health Act 1959, the Courts-Martial (Appeals) Act 1968, the Arbitration Act 1979 and the law relating to county courts; and for connected purposes. [28 July 1981]

Territorial extent: England and Wales

1–3   *****

The High Court

4   The High Court

(1) The High Court shall consist of—

(a)   . . .

(b)   the Lord Chief Justice;

[(ba)   the President of the Queen's Bench Division;

(c)   the President of the Family Division;

(d)   the Chancellor of the High Court;]

[(dd)   the Senior Presiding Judge;]

[(ddd) the vice-president of the Queen's Bench Division;] and

(e)   not more than [108] puisne judges of that court.

(2) The puisne judges of the High Court shall be styled 'Justices of the High Court'.

(3) All the judges of the High Court shall, except where this Act expressly provides otherwise, have in all respects equal power, authority and jurisdiction.

(4)–(6) *****

5–9   *****

10   Appointment of judges of [Senior Courts]

(1) Whenever the office of Lord Chief Justice, Master of the Rolls, [President of the Queen's Bench Division, President of the Family Division or Chancellor of the High Court] is vacant, Her Majesty may [on the recommendation of the Lord Chancellor] by letters patent appoint a qualified person to that office.

(2) Subject to the limits on numbers for the time being imposed by sections 2(1) and 4(1), Her Majesty may [on the recommendation of the Lord Chancellor] from time to time by letters patent appoint qualified persons as Lords Justices of Appeal or as puisne judges of the High Court.

(3) No person shall be qualified for appointment—

   (a) as Lord Chief Justice, Master of the Rolls, [President of the Queen's Bench Division, President of the Family Division or Chancellor of High Court], unless he is qualified for appointment as a Lord Justice of Appeal or is a judge of the Court of Appeal;

   (b) as a Lord Justice of Appeal, [unless—

      (i) [he satisfies the judicial-appointment eligibility condition on a 7 year basis]; or

      (ii) he is a judge of the High Court;] or

   (c) as a puisne judge of the High Court, [unless—

      (i) [he satisfies the judicial-appointment eligibility condition on a 7 year basis]; or

      (ii) he is a Circuit Judge who has held that office for at least 2 years.]

(4)–(8) *****

11   Tenure of office of judges of [Senior Courts]

(1) This section applies to the office of any judge of the [Senior Courts] . . .

(2) A person appointed to an office to which this section applies shall vacate it on the day on which he attains the age of [seventy] years unless by virtue of this section he has ceased to hold it before then.

(3) A person appointed to an office to which this section applies shall hold that office during good behaviour, subject to a power of removal by Her Majesty on an address presented to Her by both Houses of Parliament.

[(3A) It is for the Lord Chancellor to recommend to Her Majesty the exercise of the power of removal under subsection (3).]

(4)–(6) *****

(7) A person who holds an office to which this section applies may at any time resign it by giving the Lord Chancellor notice in writing to that effect.

(8) The Lord Chancellor, if satisfied by means of a medical certificate that a person holding an office to which this section applies—

   (a) is disabled by permanent infirmity from the performance of the duties of his office; and

   (b) is for the time being incapacitated from resigning his office,

may, subject to subsection (9), by instrument under his hand declare that person's office to have been vacated; and the instrument shall have the like effect for all purposes as if that person had on the date of the instrument resigned his office.

(9) A declaration under subsection (8) with respect to a person shall be of no effect unless it is made—

   (a) in the case of any of the Lord Chief Justice, the Master of the Rolls, [the President of the Queen's Bench Division, the President of the Family Division and the Chancellor of the High Court], with the concurrence of two others of them;

   (b) in the case of a Lord Justice of Appeal, with the concurrence of the Master of the Rolls;

   (c) in the case of a puisne judge of any Division of the High Court, with the concurrence of the senior judge of that Division.

(10) . . .

12   Salaries etc. of judges of [Senior Courts]

(1) Subject to subsections (2) and (3), there shall be paid to judges of the [Senior Courts] . . . such salaries as may be determined by the Lord Chancellor with the concurrence of the Minister for the Civil Service.

(2) Until otherwise determined under this section, there shall be paid to the judges mentioned in subsection (1) the same salaries as at the commencement of this Act.

(3) Any salary payable under this section may be increased, but not reduced, by a determination or further determination under this section.

(4) ...

(5)–(7) *****

13–18 *****

PART II JURISDICTION

The High Court

General jurisdiction

19   General jurisdiction

(1) The High Court shall be a superior court of record.

(2) Subject to the provisions of this Act, there shall be exercisable by the High Court—

(a) all such jurisdiction (whether civil or criminal) as is conferred on it by this or any other Act; and

(b) all such other jurisdiction (whether civil or criminal) as was exercisable by it immediately before the commencement of this Act (including jurisdiction conferred on a judge of the High Court by any statutory provision).

(3), (4) *****

*****

Other particular fields of jurisdiction

29   [Mandatory, prohibiting and quashing orders]

[(1) The orders of mandamus, prohibition and certiorari shall be known instead as mandatory, prohibiting and quashing orders respectively.

(1A) The High Court shall have jurisdiction to make mandatory, prohibiting and quashing orders in those classes of case in which, immediately before 1st May 2004, it had jurisdiction to make orders of mandamus, prohibition and certiorari respectively.]

(2) Every such order shall be final, subject to any right of appeal therefrom.

(3) In relation to the jurisdiction of the Crown Court, other than its jurisdiction in matters relating to trial on indictment, the High Court shall have all such jurisdiction to make [mandatory, prohibiting or quashing orders] as the High Court possesses in relation to the jurisdiction of an inferior court.

(3A) *****

(4) The power of the High Court under any enactment to require justices of the peace or a judge or officer of a county court to do any act relating to the duties of their respective offices, or to require a magistrates' court to state a case for the opinion of the High Court, in any case where the High Court formerly had by virtue of any enactment jurisdiction to make a rule absolute, or an order, for any of those purposes, shall be exercisable by [mandatory order].

[(5) In any statutory provision—

(a) references to mandamus or to a writ or order of mandamus shall be read as references to a mandatory order;

(b) references to prohibition or to a writ or order of prohibition shall be read as references to a prohibiting order;

(c) references to certiorari or to a writ or order of certiorari shall be read as references to a quashing order; and

(d) references to the issue or award of a writ of mandamus, prohibition or certiorari shall be read as references to the making of the corresponding mandatory, prohibiting or quashing order.]

(6) *****

30 *****

31 Application for judicial review

(1) An application to the High court for one or more of the following forms of relief, namely—

[(a) a mandatory, prohibiting or quashing order;]

(b) a declaration or injunction under subsection (2); or

(c) an injunction under section 30 restraining a person not entitled to do so from acting in an office to which that section applies,

shall be made in accordance with rules of court by a procedure to be known as an application for judicial review.

(2) A declaration may be made or an injunction granted under this subsection in any case where an application for judicial review, seeking that relief, has been made and the High Court considers that, having regard to—

(a) the nature of the matters in respect of which relief may be granted by [mandatory, prohibiting or quashing orders;]

(b) the nature of the persons and bodies against whom relief may be granted by such orders; and

(c) all the circumstances of the case,

it would be just and convenient for the declaration to be made or for the injunction to be granted, as the case may be.

(3) No application for judicial review shall be made unless the leave of the High Court has been obtained in accordance with rules of court; and the court shall not grant leave to make such an application unless it considers that the applicant has a sufficient interest in the matter to which the application relates.

[(4) On an application for judicial review the High Court may award to the applicant damages, restitution or the recovery of a sum due if—

(a) the application includes a claim for such an award arising from any matter to which the application relates; and

(b) the court is satisfied that such an award would have been made if the claim had been made in an action begun by the applicant at the time of making the application.]

[(5) If, on an application for judicial review, the High Court quashes the decision to which the application relates, it may in addition—

(a) remit the matter to the court, tribunal or authority which made the decision, with a direction to reconsider the matter and reach a decision in accordance with the findings of the High Court, or

(b) substitute its own decision for the decision in question.

(5A) But the power conferred by subsection (5)(b) is exercisable only if—

(a) the decision in question was made by a court or tribunal,

(b) the decision is quashed on the ground that there has been an error of law, and

(c) without the error, there would have been only one decision which the court or tribunal could have reached.

(5B) Unless the High Court otherwise directs, a decision substituted by it under subsection (5)(b) has effect as if it were a decision of the relevant court or tribunal.]

(6) Where the High Court considers that there has been undue delay in making an application for judicial review, the court may refuse to grant—

(a) leave for the making of the application; or

(b) any relief sought on the application,

if it considers that the granting of the relief sought would be likely to cause substantial hardship to, or substantially prejudice the rights of, any person or would be detrimental to good administration.

(7) Subsection (6) is without prejudice to any enactment or rule of court which has the effect of limiting the time within which an application for judicial review may be made.

*****

Canada Act 1982

(1982, c. 11)

An Act to give effect to a request by the Senate and House of Commons of Canada.   [29th March 1982]

Territorial extent: Canada

Whereas Canada has requested and consented to the enactment of an Act of the Parliament of the United Kingdom to give effect to the provisions hereinafter set forth and the Senate and the House of Commons of Canada in Parliament assembled have submitted an address to Her Majesty requesting that Her Majesty may graciously be pleased to cause a Bill to be laid before the Parliament of the United Kingdom for that purpose:

Be it therefore enacted by the Queen's Most Excellent Majesty, by and with the advice and consent of the Lords Spiritual and Temporal, and Commons, in this present Parliament assembled, and by the authority of the same, as follows:

1   Constitution Act 1982 enacted
The Constitution Act 1982 set out in Schedule B to this Act is hereby enacted for and shall have the force of law in Canada and shall come into force as provided in that Act.

2   Termination of power to legislate for Canada
No Act of the Parliament of the United Kingdom passed after the Constitution Act 1982 comes into force shall extend to Canada as part of its law.

3   French version
So far as it is not contained in Schedule B, the French version of this Act is set out in Schedule A to this Act and has the same authority in Canada as the English version thereof.

4   Short title
This Act may be cited as the Canada Act 1982.

*****

SCHEDULE B CONSTITUTION ACT 1982

PART I CANADIAN CHARTER OF RIGHTS AND FREEDOMS

Whereas Canada is founded upon principles that recognize the supremacy of God and the rule of law:

Guarantee of rights and freedoms

1   Rights and freedoms in Canada
The *Canadian Charter of Rights and Freedoms* guarantees the rights and freedoms set out in it subject only to such reasonable limits prescribed by law as can be demonstrably justified in a free and democratic society.

Fundamental freedoms

2   Fundamental freedoms

Everyone has the following fundamental freedoms:

- (a) freedom of conscience and religion;
- (b) freedom of thought, belief, opinion and expression, including freedom of the press and other media of communication;
- (c) freedom of peaceful assembly; and
- (d) freedom of association.

Democratic rights

3   Democratic rights of citizens

Every citizen of Canada has the right to vote in an election of members of the House of Commons or of a legislative assembly and to be qualified for membership therein.

4   Maximum duration of legislative bodies

(1) No House of Commons and no legislative assembly shall continue for longer than five years from the date fixed for the return of the writs at a general election of its members.

Continuation in special circumstances

(2) In time of real or apprehended war, invasion or insurrection, a House of Commons may be continued by Parliament and a legislative assembly may be continued by the legislature beyond five years if such continuation is not opposed by the votes of more than one-third of the members of the House of Commons or the legislative assembly, as the case may be.

5   Annual sitting of legislative bodies

There shall be a sitting of Parliament and of each legislature at least once every twelve months.

Mobility rights

6   Mobility of citizens

(1) Every citizen of Canada has the right to enter, remain in and leave Canada.

Rights to move and gain livelihood

(2) Every citizen of Canada and every person who has the status of a permanent resident of Canada has the right

- (a) to move to and take up residence in any province; and
- (b) to pursue the gaining of a livelihood in any province.

Limitation

(3) The rights specified in subsection (2) are subject to

- (a) any laws or practices of general application in force in a province other than those that discriminate among persons primarily on the basis of province of present or previous residence; and
- (b) any laws providing for reasonable residency requirements as a qualification for the receipt of publicly provided social services.

Affirmative action programs

(4) Subsections (2) and (3) do not preclude any law, program or activity that has as its object the amelioration in a province of conditions of individuals in that province who are socially or economically disadvantaged if the rate of employment in that province is below the rate of employment in Canada.

Legal rights

7   Life, liberty and security of person

Everyone has the right to life, liberty and security of the person and the right not to be deprived thereof except in accordance with the principles of fundamental justice.

8 Search or seizure

Everyone has the right to be secure against unreasonable search or seizure.

9 Detention or imprisonment

Everyone has the right not to be arbitrarily detained or imprisoned.

10 Arrest or detention

Everyone has the right on arrest or detention

(a) to be informed promptly of the reasons therefor;

(b) to retain and instruct counsel without delay and to be informed of that right; and

(c) to have the validity of the detention determined by way of *habeas corpus* and to be released if the detention is not lawful.

11 Proceedings in criminal and penal matters

Any person charged with an offence has the right

(a) to be informed without unreasonable delay of the specific offence;

(b) to be tried within a reasonable time;

(c) not to be compelled to be a witness in proceedings against that person in respect of the offence;

(d) to be presumed innocent until proven guilty according to law in a fair and public hearing by an independent and impartial tribunal;

(e) not to be denied reasonable bail without just cause;

(f) except in the case of an offence under military law tried before a military tribunal, to the benefit of trial by jury where the maximum punishment for the offence is imprisonment for five years or a more severe punishment;

(g) not to be found guilty on account of any act or omission unless, at the time of the act or omission, it constituted an offence under Canadian or international law or was criminal according to the general principles of law recognized by the community of nations;

(h) if finally acquitted of the offence, not to be tried for it again and, if finally found guilty and punished for the offence, not to be tried or punished for it again; and

(i) if found guilty of the offence and if the punishment for the offence has been varied between the time of commission and the time of sentencing, to the benefit of the lesser punishment.

12 Treatment or punishment

Everyone has the right not to be subjected to any cruel and unusual treatment or punishment.

13 Self-crimination

A witness who testifies in any proceedings has the right not to have any incriminating evidence so given used to incriminate that witness in any other proceedings, except in a prosecution for perjury or for the giving of contradictory evidence.

14 Interpreter

A party or witness in any proceedings who does not understand or speak the language in which the proceedings are conducted or who is deaf has the right to the assistance of an interpreter.

Equality rights

15 Equality before and under law and equal protection and benefit of law

(1) Every individual is equal before and under the law and has the right to the equal protection and equal benefit of the law without discrimination and, in particular, without discrimination based on race, national or ethnic origin, colour, religion, sex, age or mental or physical disability.

Affirmative action programs

(2) Subsection (1) does not preclude any law, program or activity that has as its object the amelioration of conditions of disadvantaged individuals or groups including those that are disadvantaged because of race, national or ethnic origin, colour, religion, sex, age or mental or physical disability.

Official languages of Canada

16   Official languages of Canada

(1) English and French are the official languages of Canada and have equality of status and equal rights and privileges as to their use in all institutions of the Parliament and government of Canada.

(2), (3) *****

17–23   *****

Enforcement

24   Enforcement of guaranteed rights and freedoms

(1) Anyone whose rights or freedoms, as guaranteed by this Charter, have been infringed or denied may apply to a court of competent jurisdiction to obtain such remedy as the court considers appropriate and just in the circumstances.

Exclusion of evidence bringing administration of justice into disrepute

(2) Where, in proceedings under subsection (1), a court concludes that evidence was obtained in a manner that infringed or denied any rights or freedoms guaranteed by this Charter, the evidence shall be excluded if it is established that, having regard to all the circumstances, the admission of it in the proceedings would bring the administration of justice into disrepute.

General

25   Aboriginal rights and freedoms not affected by Charter

The guarantee in this Charter of certain rights and freedoms shall not be construed so as to abrogate or derogate from any aboriginal, treaty or other rights or freedoms that pertain to the aboriginal peoples of Canada including

    (a) any rights or freedoms that have been recognised by the Royal Proclamation of October 7, 1763; and

    (b) any rights or freedoms that may be acquired by the aboriginal peoples of Canada by way of land claims settlement.

26   Other rights and freedoms not affected by Charter

The guarantee in this Charter of certain rights and freedoms shall not be construed as denying the existence of any other rights or freedoms that exist in Canada.

27   Multicultural heritage

This Charter shall be interpreted in a manner consistent with the preservation and enhancement of the multicultural heritage of Canadians.

28   Rights guaranteed equally to both sexes

Notwithstanding anything in this Charter, the rights and freedoms referred to in it are guaranteed equally to male and female persons.

29   Rights respecting certain schools preserved

Nothing in this Charter abrogates or derogates from any rights or privileges guaranteed by or under the Constitution of Canada in respect of denominational, separate or dissentient schools.

30   *****

31   Legislative powers not extended

Nothing in this Charter extends the legislative powers of any body or authority.

Application of Charter

32   Application of Charter

(1) This Charter applies

(a) to the Parliament and government of Canada in respect of all matters within the authority of Parliament including all matters relating to the Yukon Territory and Northwest Territories; and

(b) to the legislature and government of each province in respect of all matters within the authority of the legislature of each province.

Exception

(2) Notwithstanding subsection (1), section 15 shall not have effect until three years after this section comes into force.

33 Exceptions where express declaration

(1) Parliament or the legislature of a province may expressly declare in an Act of Parliament or of the legislature, as the case may be, that the Act or a provision thereof shall operate notwithstanding a provision included in section 2 or sections 7 to 15 of this Charter.

Operation of exception

(2) An Act or a provision of an Act in respect of which a declaration made under this section is in effect shall have such operation as it would have but for the provision of this Charter referred to in the declaration.

Five year limitation

(3) A declaration made under subsection (1) shall cease to have effect five years after it comes into force or on such earlier date as may be specified in the declaration.

Re-enactment

(4) Parliament or the legislature of a province may re-enact a declaration made under subsection (1).

Five year limitation

(5) Subsection (3) applies in respect of a re-enactment made under subsection (4).

Citation

34 Citation

This Part may be cited as the *Canadian Charter of Rights and Freedoms.*
*****

[Note: Schedule A to this Act is a French language version of the Act, and Sch. B is also printed in English and French. Both texts have equal status.]

Representation of the People Act 1983

(1983, c. 2)

An Act to consolidate the Representation of the People Acts of 1949, 1969, 1977, 1978 and 1980, The Electoral Registers Acts of 1949 and 1953, the Elections (Welsh Forms) Act 1964, Part III of the Local Government Act 1972, sections 6 to 10 of the Local Government (Scotland) Act 1973, the Representation of the People (Armed Forces) Act 1976, the Returning Officers (Scotland) Act 1977, section 3 of the Representation of the People Act 1981, section 62 of and Schedule 2 to the Mental Health (Amendment) Act 1982, and connected provisions; and to repeal as obsolete the Representation of the People Act 1979 and other enactments related to the Representation of the People Acts.   [8th February 1983]

Territorial extent: United Kingdom

PART I PARLIAMENTARY AND LOCAL GOVERNMENT FRANCHISE AND ITS EXERCISE

Parliamentary and local government franchise

[1   Parliamentary electors

(1) A person is entitled to vote as an elector at a parliamentary election in any constituency if on the date of the poll he—

(a) is registered in the register of parliamentary electors for that constituency;

(b) is not subject to any legal incapacity to vote (age apart);

(c) is either a Commonwealth citizen or a citizen of the Republic of Ireland; and

(d) is of voting age (that is, 18 years or over).

(2) A person is not entitled to vote as an elector—

(a) more than once in the same constituency at any parliamentary election; or

(b) in more than one constituency at a general election.]

*****

PART II THE ELECTION CAMPAIGN

75   Prohibition of expenses not authorised by election agent

[(1) No expenses shall, with a view to promoting or procuring the election of a candidate [(or, in the case of an election of the London members of the London Assembly at an ordinary election, a registered political party or candidates of that party)] at an election, be incurred [after he becomes a candidate at that election] by any person other than the candidate, his election agent and persons authorised in writing by the election agent on account—

(a) of holding public meetings or organising any public display; or

(b) of issuing advertisements, circulars or publications; or

(c) of otherwise presenting to the electors the candidate or his views or the extent or nature of his backing or disparaging another candidate; [or

(d) in the case of an election of the London members of the London Assembly at an ordinary election, of otherwise presenting to the electors the candidate's registered political party (if any) or the views of that party or the extent or nature of that party's backing or disparaging any other registered political party],

. . .

[(1ZZA) Paragraph (c) or (d) of subsection (1) above does not restrict the publication of any matter relating to the election in—

(a) a newspaper or other periodical,

(b) a broadcast made by the British Broadcasting Corporation or by Sianel Pedwar Cymru, or

(c) a programme included in any service licensed under Part 1 or 3 of the Broadcasting Act 1990 or Part 1 or 2 of the Broadcasting Act 1996.

(1ZZB) Subsection (1) above does not apply to any expenses incurred by any person—

(a) which do not exceed in the aggregate the permitted sum (and are not incurred by that person as part of a concerted plan of action), or

(b) in travelling or in living away from home or similar personal expenses.]

[(1ZA) For the purposes of [subsection (1ZZB)(a)] above, 'the permitted sum' means—

(a) in respect of a candidate at a parliamentary election, £500;

(b) in respect of a candidate at a local government election, £50 together with an additional 0.5p for every entry in the register of local government electors for the electoral area in question as it has effect on the last day for publication of notice of the election;

and expenses shall be regarded as incurred by a person 'as part of a concerted plan of action' if they are incurred by that person in pursuance of any plan or other arrangement whereby that person and one or more other persons are to incur, with a view to promoting or procuring the election of the same candidate, expenses which (disregarding [subsection (1ZZB)(a)]) fall within subsection (1) above.]

    [(1A)] *****

    [(1B), (1C) ...]

    (2)–(4C) *****

    (5) If a person—

        (a) incurs, or aids, abets, counsels or procures any other person to incur, any expenses in contravention of this section, or

        (b) knowingly makes the declaration required by subsection (2) falsely,

he shall be guilty of a corrupt practice; and if a person fails to [deliver or] send any declaration or return or a copy of it as required by this section he shall be guilty of an illegal practice, but—

        (i)   the court before whom a person is convicted under this subsection may, if they think it just in the special circumstances of the case, mitigate or entirely remit any incapacity imposed by virtue of section 173 below; and

        (ii) a candidate shall not be liable, nor shall his election be avoided, for a corrupt or illegal practice under this subsection committed by an agent without his consent or connivance.

*****

92   Broadcasting from outside United Kingdom

    [(1) No person shall, with intent to influence persons to give or refrain from giving their votes at a parliamentary or local government election, include, or aid, abet, counsel or procure the inclusion of, any matter relating to the election in any programme service (within the meaning of the Broadcasting Act 1990) provided from a place outside the United Kingdom otherwise than in pursuance of arrangements made with—

        (a) the British Broadcasting Corporation;

        (b) Sianel Pedwar Cymru; or

        (c) the holder of any licence granted by [the Office of Communications].

for the reception and re-transmission of that matter by that body or the holder of that licence.]

    (2) An offence under this section shall be an illegal practice, but the court before whom a person is convicted of an offence under this section may, if they think it just in the special circumstances of the case, mitigate or entirely remit any incapacity imposed by virtue of section 173 below.

    (3) *****

[93   Broadcasting of local items during election period

    (1) Each broadcasting authority shall adopt a code of practice with respect to the participation of candidates at a parliamentary or local government election in items about the constituency or electoral area in question which are included in relevant services during the election period.

    (2) The code for the time being adopted by a broadcasting authority under this section shall be either—

        (a) a code drawn up by that authority, whether on their own or jointly with one or more other broadcasting authorities, or

        (b) a code drawn up by one or more other such authorities;

and a broadcasting authority shall from time to time consider whether the code for the time being so adopted by them should be replaced by a further code falling within paragraph (a) or (b).

    (3) Before drawing up a code under this section a broadcasting authority shall have regard to any views expressed by the Electoral Commission for the purposes of this subsection; and any such code may make different provision for different cases.

    (4) The [Office of Communications shall] do all that they can to secure that the code for the time being adopted by them under this section is observed in the provision of relevant services; and the British Broadcasting Corporation and Sianel Pedwar Cymru shall each observe in the provision of relevant services the code so adopted by them.

(5) For the purposes of subsection (1) 'the election period', in relation to an election, means the period beginning—

(a) (if a parliamentary general election) with the date of the dissolution of Parliament ...

(b) (if a parliamentary by-election) with the date of the issue of the writ for the election or any earlier date on which a certificate of the vacancy is notified in the London Gazette in accordance with the Recess Elections Act 1975, or

(c) (if a local government election) with the last date for publication of notice of the election, and ending with the close of the poll.]

(6) *****

94–96 *****

97 Disturbances at election meetings

(1) A person who at a lawful public meeting to which this section applies acts, or incites others to act, in a disorderly manner for the purpose of preventing the transaction of the business for which the meeting was called together shall be guilty of an illegal practice.

(2) *****

(3) If a constable reasonably suspects any person of committing an offence under subsection (1) above, he may if requested so to do by the chairman of the meeting require that person to declare to him immediately his name and address and, if that person refuses or fails so to declare his name and address or gives a false name and address, he shall be liable on summary conviction to a fine not exceeding [level 1 on the standard scale,] ...

This subsection does not apply in Northern Ireland.

98 ...

99 *****

100 Illegal canvassing by police officers

(1) No member of a police force shall by word, message, writing or in any other manner, endeavour to persuade any person to give, or dissuade any person from giving, his vote, whether as an elector or as proxy—

(a) at any parliamentary election for a constituency, or

(b) at any local government election for any electoral area, wholly or partly within the police area.

(2) A person acting in contravention of subsection (1) above shall be liable [on summary conviction to a fine not exceeding level 3 on the standard scale, but] nothing in that subsection shall subject a member of a police force to any penalty for anything done in the discharge of his duty as a member of the force.

(3) In this section references to a member of a police force and to a police area are to be taken in relation to Northern Ireland as references to a member of the [Police Service of Northern Ireland] and to Northern Ireland.
*****

Police and Criminal Evidence Act 1984

(1984, c. 60)

An Act to make further provision in relation to the powers and duties of the police, persons in police detention, criminal evidence, police discipline and complaints against the police; to provide for arrangements for obtaining the views of the community on policing and for a rank of deputy chief constable; to amend the law relating to the Police Federations and Police Forces and Police Cadets in Scotland; and for connected purposes.   [31st October 1984]

Territorial extent: England and Wales

PART I POWERS TO STOP AND SEARCH

1 Power of constable to stop and search persons, vehicles etc.

(1) A constable may exercise any power conferred by this section—

    (a) in any place to which at the time when he proposes to exercise the power the public or any section of the public has access, on payment or otherwise, as of right or by virtue of express or implied permission; or

    (b) in any other place to which people have ready access at the time when he proposes to exercise the power but which is not a dwelling.

(2) Subject to subsection (3) to (5) below, a constable—

    (a) may search—

        (i) any person or vehicle;

        (ii) anything which is in or on a vehicle,

        for stolen or prohibited articles [any article to which subsection (8A) below applies or any firework to which subsection (8B) below applies]; and

    (b) may detain a person or vehicle for the purpose of such a search.

(3) This section does not give a constable power to search a person or vehicle or anything in or on a vehicle unless he has reasonable grounds for suspecting that he will find stolen or prohibited articles [any article to which subsection (8A) below applies or any firework to which subsection (8B) below applies].

(4), (5) *****

(6) If in the course of such a search a constable discovers an article which he has reasonable grounds for suspecting to be a stolen or prohibited article [, an article to which subsection (8A) applies or a firework to which subsection (8B) applies], he may seize it.

(7) An article is prohibited for the purposes of this Part of this Act if it is—

    (a) an offensive weapon; or

    (b) an article—

        (i) made or adapted for use in the course of or in connection with an offence to which this sub-paragraph applies; or

        (ii) intended by the person having it with him for such use by him or by some other person.

(8) The offences to which subsection (7)(b)(i) above applies are—

    (a) burglary;

    (b) theft;

    (c) offences under section 12 of the Theft Act 1968 (taking motor vehicle or other conveyance without authority); . . .

    [(d) fraud (contrary to section 1 of the Fraud Act 2006)] [; and

    (e) offences under section 1 of the Criminal Damage Act 1971 (destroying or damaging property).]

[(8A) This subsection applies to any article in relation to which a person has committed, or is committing or is going to commit an offence under section 139 of the Criminal Justice Act 1988.]

(8B), (8C) *****

(9) In this Part of this Act 'offensive weapon' means any article—

    (a) made or adapted for use for causing injury to persons; or

    (b) intended by the person having it with him for such use by him or by some other person.

2 Provisions relating to search under section 1 and other powers

(1) A constable who detains a person or vehicle in the exercise—

    (a) of the power conferred by section 1 above; or

    (b) of any other power—

        (i) to search a person without first arresting him; or

        (ii) to search a vehicle without making an arrest,

need not conduct a search if it appears to him subsequently—

    (i)   that no search is required; or

    (ii) that a search is impracticable.

(2) If a constable contemplates a search, other than a search of an unattended vehicle, in the exercise—

    (a) of the power conferred by section 1 above; or

    (b) of any other power, except the power conferred by section 6 below and the power conferred by section 27(2) of the Aviation Security Act 1982—

        (i)   to search a person without first arresting him; or

        (ii) to search a vehicle without making an arrest,

it shall be his duty, subject to subsection (4) below, to take reasonable steps before he commences the search to bring to the attention of the appropriate person—

    (i)   if the constable is not in uniform, documentary evidence that he is a constable; and

    (ii) whether he is in uniform or not, the matters specified in subsection (3) below;

and the constable shall not commence the search until he has performed that duty.

(3) The matters referred to in subsection (2)(ii) above are—

    (a) the constable's name and the name of the police station to which he is attached;

    (b) the object of the proposed search;

    (c) the constable's grounds for proposing to make it; and

    (d) the effect of section 3(7) or (8) below, as may be appropriate.

(4) A constable need not bring the effect of section 3(7) or (8) below to the attention of the appropriate person if it appears to the constable that it will not be practicable to make the record in section 3(1) below.

(5) In this section 'the appropriate person' means—

    (a) if the constable proposes to search a person, that person; and

    (b) if he proposes to search a vehicle, or anything in or on a vehicle, the person in charge of the vehicle.

(6) On completing a search of an unattended vehicle or anything in or on such a vehicle in the exercise of any such power as is mentioned in subsection (2) above a constable shall leave a notice—

    (a) stating that he has searched it;

    (b) giving the name of the police station to which he is attached;

    (c) stating that an application for compensation for any damage caused by the search may be made to that police station; and

    (d) stating the effect of section 3(8) below.

(7) *****

(8) The time for which a person or vehicle may be detained for the purposes of such a search is such time as is reasonably required to permit a search to be carried out either at the place where the person or vehicle was first detained or nearby.

(9) Neither the power conferred by section 1 above nor any other power to detain and search a person without first arresting him or to detain and search a vehicle without making an arrest is to be construed—

    (a) as authorising a constable to require a person to remove any of his clothing in public other than an outer coat, jacket or gloves; or

    (b) as authorising a constable not in uniform to stop a vehicle.

(10) *****

3   Duty to make records concerning searches

(1) Where a constable has carried out a search in the exercise of any such power as is mentioned in section 2(1) above, other than a search—

    (a) under section 6 below; or

    (b) under section 27(2) of the Aviation Security Act 1982, [a record of the search shall be made] in writing unless it is not practicable to do so.

[(2) If a record of a search is required to be made by subsection (1) above—

   (a) in a case where the search results in a person being arrested and taken to a police station, the constable shall secure that the record is made as part of the person's custody record;

   (b) in any other case, the constable shall make the record on the spot, or, if that is not practicable, as soon as practicable after the completion of the search.]

(3)–(5) ...

(6) The record of a search of a person or a vehicle—

   (a) shall state—

      (i)   the object of the search;

      (ii)   the grounds for making it;

      (iii) the date and time when it was made;

      (iv)   the place where it was made;

      [(v)   except in the case of a search of an unattended vehicle, the ethnic origins of the person searched or the person in charge of the vehicle searched (as the case may be; and;]

      (vi) ...

   (b) shall identify the constable [who carried out the search].

(6A) The requirement in subsection (6)(a)(v) above for a record to state a person's ethnic origins is a requirement to state—

   (a) the ethnic origins of the person as described by the person, and

   (b) if different, the ethnic origins of the person as perceived by the constable.]

(7) [If a record of a search of a person has been made under this section,] the person who was searched shall be entitled to a copy of the record if he asks for one before the end of the period specified in subsection (9) below.

(8) If—

   (a) the owner of a vehicle which has been searched or the person who was in charge of the vehicle at the time when it was searched asks for a copy of the record of the search before the end of the period specified in subsection (9) below; and

   [(b) a record of the search of the vehicle has been made under this section,]

the person who made the request shall be entitled to a copy.

(9) The period mentioned in subsections (7) and (8) above is the period of [3 months] beginning with the date on which the search was made.

(10) *****

4 Road checks

(1) This section shall have effect in relation to the conduct of road checks by police officers for the purpose of ascertaining whether a vehicle is carrying—

   (a) a person who has committed an offence other than a road traffic offence or a [vehicle] excise offence;

   (b) a person who is a witness to such an offence;

   (c) a person intending to commit such an offence; or

   (d) a person who is unlawfully at large.

(2) For the purposes of this section a road check consists of the exercise in a locality of the power conferred by section [163 of the Road Traffic Act 1988] in such a way as to stop during the period for which its exercise in that way in that locality continues all vehicles or vehicles selected by any criterion.

(3) Subject to subsection (5) below, there may only be such a road check if a police officer of the rank of superintendent or above authorises it in writing.

(4) An officer may only authorise a road check under subsection (3) above—

   (a) for the purpose specified in subsection (1)(a) above, if he has reasonable grounds—

      (i)   for believing that the offence is [an indictable offence]; and

      (ii)   for suspecting that the person is, or is about to be, in the locality in which vehicles would be stopped if the road check were authorised;

(b) for the purpose specified in subsection (1)(b) above, if he has reasonable grounds for believing that the offence is [an indictable offence];

(c) for the purpose specified in subsection (1)(c) above, if he has reasonable grounds—

    (i)   for believing that the offence would be [an indictable offence]; and

    (ii) for suspecting that the person is, or is about to be, in the locality in which vehicles would be stopped if the road check were authorised;

(d) for the purpose specified in subsection (1)(d) above, if he has reasonable grounds for suspecting that the person is, or is about to be, in that locality.

(5) An officer below the rank of superintendent may authorise such a road check if it appears to him that it is required as a matter of urgency for one of the purposes specified in subsection (1) above.

(6)–(14) *****

(15) Where a vehicle is stopped in a road check, the person in charge of the vehicle at the time when it is stopped shall be entitled to obtain a written statement of the purpose of the road check if he applies for such a statement not later than the end of the period of twelve months from the day on which the vehicle was stopped.

(16) Nothing in this section affects the exercise by police officers of any power to stop vehicles for purposes other than those specified in subsection (1) above.

5–7 *****

PART II POWERS OF ENTRY, SEARCH AND SEIZURE

Search warrants

8 Power of justice of the peace to authorise entry and search of premises

(1) If on an application made by a constable a justice of the peace is satisfied that there are reasonable grounds for believing—

(a) that [an indictable offence] has been committed; and

(b) that there is material on premises [mentioned in subsection (1A) below] which is likely to be of substantial value (whether by itself or together with other material) to the investigation of the offence; and

(c) that the material is likely to be relevant evidence; and

(d) that it does not consist of or include items subject to legal privilege, excluded material or special procedure material; and

(e) that any of the conditions specified in subsection (3) below applies, [in relation to each set of premises specified in the application,]

he may issue a warrant authorising a constable to enter and search the premises.

[(1A) The premises referred to in subsection (1)(b) above are—

(a) one or more sets of premises specified in the application (in which case the application is for a 'specific premises warrant'); or

(b) any premises occupied or controlled by a person specified in the application, including such sets of premises as are so specified (in which case the application is for an 'all premises warrant').

(1B) If the application is for an all premises warrant, the justice of the peace must also be satisfied—

(a) that because of the particulars of the offence referred to in paragraph (a) of subsection (1) above, there are reasonable grounds for believing that it is necessary to search premises occupied or controlled by the person in question which are not specified in the application in order to find the material referred to in paragraph (b) of that subsection; and

(b) that it is not reasonably practicable to specify in the application all the premises which he occupies or controls and which might need to be searched.]

[(1C) The warrant may authorise entry to and search of premises on more than one occasion if, on the application, the justice of the peace is satisfied that it is necessary to authorise multiple entries in order to achieve the purpose for which he issues the warrant.

(1D) If it authorises multiple entries, the number of entries authorised may be unlimited, or limited to a maximum.]

(2) A constable may seize and retain anything for which a search has been authorised under subsection (1) above.

(3) The conditions mentioned in subsection (1)(e) above are—

    (a) that it is not practicable to communicate with any person entitled to grant entry to the premises;

    (b) that it is practicable to communicate with a person entitled to grant entry to the premises but it is not practicable to communicate with any person entitled to grant access to the evidence;

    (c) that entry to the premises will not be granted unless a warrant is produced;

    (d) that the purpose of a search may be frustrated or seriously prejudiced unless a constable arriving at the premises can secure immediate entry to them.

(4) In this Act 'relevant evidence', in relation to an offence, means anything that would be admissible in evidence at a trial for the offence.

(5) The power to issue a warrant conferred by this section is in addition to any such power otherwise conferred.

(6), (7) *****

9 Special provisions as to access

(1) A constable may obtain access to excluded material or special procedure material for the purposes of a criminal investigation by making an application under Schedule 1 below and in accordance with that Schedule.

(2), (2A) *****

10 Meaning of 'items subject to legal privilege'

(1) Subject to subsection (2) below, in this Act 'items subject to legal privilege' means—

    (a) communications between a professional legal adviser and his client or any person representing his client made in connection with the giving of legal advice to the client;

    (b) communications between a professional legal adviser and his client or any person representing his client or between such an adviser or his client or any such representative and any other person made in connection with or in contemplation of legal proceedings and for the purposes of such proceedings; and

    (c) items enclosed with or referred to in such communications and made—

        (i) in connection with the giving of legal advice; or

        (ii) in connection with or in contemplation of legal proceedings and for the purposes of such proceedings,

when they are in the possession of a person who is entitled to possession of them.

(2) Items held with the intention of furthering a criminal purpose are not items subject to legal privilege.

11 Meaning of 'excluded material'

(1) Subject to the following provisions of this section, in this Act 'excluded material' means—

    (a) personal records which a person has acquired or created in the course of any trade, business, profession or other occupation or for the purposes of any paid or unpaid office and which he holds in confidence;

    (b) human tissue or tissue fluid which has been taken for the purposes of diagnosis or medical treatment and which a person holds in confidence;

    (c) journalistic material which a person holds in confidence and which consists—

        (i) of documents; or

        (ii) of records other than documents.

(2), (3) *****

12   Meaning of 'personal records'

In this Part of this Act 'personal records' means documentary and other records concerning an individual (whether living or dead) who can be identified from them and relating—

    (a) to his physical or mental health;

    (b) to spiritual counselling or assistance given or to be given to him; or

    (c) to counselling or assistance given or to be given to him, for the purposes of his personal welfare, by any voluntary organisation or by any individual who—

        (i) by reason of his office or occupation has responsibilities for his personal welfare; or

        (ii) by reason of an order of a court has responsibilities for his supervision.

13   Meaning of 'journalistic material'

(1) Subject to subsection (2) below, in this Act 'journalistic material' means material acquired or created for the purposes of journalism.

(2) Material is only journalistic material for the purposes of this Act if it is in the possession of a person who acquired or created it for the purposes of journalism.

(3) A person who receives material from someone who intends that the recipient shall use it for the purposes of journalism is to be taken to have acquired it for those purposes.

14   Meaning of 'special procedure material'

(1) In this Act 'special procedure material' means—

    (a) material to which subsection (2) below applies; and

    (b) journalistic material, other than excluded material.

(2) Subject to the following provisions of this section, this subsection applies to material, other than items subject to legal privilege and excluded material, in the possession of a person who—

    (a) acquired or created it in the course of any trade, business, profession or other occupation or for the purposes of any paid or unpaid office; and

    (b) holds it subject—

        (i) to an express or implied undertaking to hold it in confidence; or

        (ii) to a restriction or obligation such as is mentioned in section 11(2)(b) above.

(3)–(6) *****

15   Search warrants—safeguards

(1) This section and section 16 below have effect in relation to the issue to constables under any enactment, including an enactment contained in an Act passed after this Act, of warrants to enter and search premises; and an entry on or search of premises under a warrant is unlawful unless it complies with this section and section 16 below.

(2) Where a constable applies for any such warrant, it shall be his duty—

    (a) to state—

        (i) the ground on which he makes the application; . . .

        (ii) the enactment under which the warrant would be issued; [and]

      [(iii) if the application is for a warrant authorising entry and search on more than one occasion, the ground on which he applies for such a warrant, and whether he seeks a warrant authorising an unlimited number of entries, or (if not) the maximum number of entries desired;]

    [(b) to specify the matters set out in subsection (2A) below; and]

    (c) to identify, so far as is practicable, the articles or persons to be sought.

(2A) *****

(3) An application for such a warrant shall be made ex parte and supported by an information in writing.

(4) The constable shall answer on oath any question that the justice of the peace or judge hearing the application asks him.

(5) A warrant shall authorise an entry on one occasion only [unless it specifies that it authorises multiple entries].

[(5A) If it specifies that it authorises multiple entries, it must also specify whether the number of entries authorised is unlimited, or limited to a specified maximum.]

(6) A warrant—
  (a) shall specify—
    (i)   the name of the person who applies for it;
    (ii)   the date on which it is issued;
    (iii) the enactment under which it is issued; and
    [(iv) each set of premises to be searched, or (in the case of an all premises warrant) the person who is in occupation or control of premises to be searched, together with any premises under his occupation or control which can be specified and which are to be searched; and]
  (b) shall identify, so far as is practicable, the articles or persons to be sought.
(7), (8) *****

[**Note:** This section, and ss. 16, 21 and 22, are modified in relation to confiscation and money laundering investigations under the Proceeds of Crime Act 2002, by SI 2003/174, Arts 2–5 respectively.]

16 Execution of warrants

(1) A warrant to enter and search premises may be executed by any constable.

(2) Such a warrant may authorise persons to accompany any constable who is executing it.

[(2A) A person so authorised has the same powers as the constable whom he accompanies in respect of—
  (a) the execution of the warrant, and
  (b) the seizure of anything to which the warrant relates.

(2B) But he may exercise those powers only in the company, and under the supervision, of a constable.]

(3) Entry and search under a warrant must be within [three months] from the date of its issue.

(3A), (3B) *****

(4) Entry and search under a warrant must be at a reasonable hour unless it appears to the constable executing it that the purpose of a search may be frustrated on an entry at a reasonable hour.

(5) Where the occupier of premises which are to be entered and searched is present at the time when a constable seeks to execute a warrant to enter and search them, the constable—
  (a) shall identify himself to the occupier and, if not in uniform, shall produce to him documentary evidence that he is a constable;
  (b) shall produce the warrant to him; and
  (c) shall supply him with a copy of it.

(6) Where—
  (a) the occupier of such premises is not present at the time when a constable seeks to execute such a warrant; but
  (b) some other person who appears to the constable to be in charge of the premises is present,
subsection (5) above shall have effect as if any reference to the occupier were a reference to that other person.

(7) If there is no person present who appears to the constable to be in charge of the premises, he shall leave a copy of the warrant in a prominent place on the premises.

(8) A search under a warrant may only be a search to the extent required for the purpose for which the warrant was issued.

(9) A constable executing a warrant shall make an endorsement on it stating—
  (a) whether the articles or persons sought were found; and
  (b) whether any articles were seized, other than articles which were sought [and,

unless the warrant is a...warrant specifying one set of premises only, he shall do so separately in respect of each set of premises entered and searched which he shall in each case stated in the endorsement.]

(10)–(12) *****

Entry and search without search warrant

17   Entry for purpose of arrest etc.

(1) Subject to the following provisions of this section, and without prejudice to any other enactment, a constable may enter and search any premises for the purpose—

(a) of executing—

(i)   a warrant of arrest issued in connection with or arising out of criminal proceedings; or

(ii)   a warrant of commitment issued under section 76 of the Magistrates' Courts Act 1980;

(b) of arresting a person for an [indictable] offence;

*****

(d) of recapturing [any person whatever] who is unlawfully at large and whom he is pursuing; or

(e) of saving life or limb or preventing serious damage to property.

(2) Except for the purpose specified in paragraph (e) of subsection (1) above, the powers of entry and search conferred by this section—

(a) are only exercisable if the constable has reasonable grounds for believing that the person whom he is seeking is on the premises; and

(b) are limited, in relation to premises consisting of two or more separate dwellings, to powers to enter and search—

(i)   any parts of the premises which the occupiers of any dwelling comprised in the premises use in common with the occupiers of any other such dwelling; and

(ii)   any such dwelling in which the constable has reasonable grounds for believing that the person whom he is seeking may be.

(3) The powers of entry and search conferred by this section are only exercisable for the purposes specified in subsection (1)(c)(ii) [or (iv)] above by a constable in uniform.

(4) The power of search conferred by this section is only a power to search to the extent that is reasonably required for the purpose for which the power of entry is exercised.

(5) Subject to subsection (6) below, all the rules of common law under which a constable has power to enter premises without a warrant are hereby abolished.

(6) Nothing in subsection (5) above affects any power of entry to deal with or prevent a breach of the peace.

18   Entry and search after arrest

(1) Subject to the following provisions of this section, a constable may enter and search any premises occupied or controlled by a person who is under arrest for an [indictable] offence, if he has reasonable grounds for suspecting that there is on the premises evidence, other than items subject to legal privilege, that relates—

(a) to that offence; or

(b) to some other [indictable] offence which is connected with or similar to that offence.

(2) A constable may seize and retain anything for which he may search under subsection (1) above.

(3) The power to search conferred by subsection (1) above is only a power to search to the extent that is reasonably required for the purpose of discovering such evidence.

(4)–(8) *****

Seizure etc.

19 General power of seizure etc.

(1) The powers conferred by subsections (2), (3) and (4) below are exercisable by a constable who is lawfully on any premises.

(2) The constable may seize anything which is on the premises if he has reasonable grounds for believing—

(a) that it has been obtained in consequence of the commission of an offence; and

(b) that it is necessary to seize it in order to prevent it being concealed, lost, damaged, altered or destroyed.

(3) The constable may seize anything which is on the premises if he has reasonable grounds for believing—

(a) that it is evidence in relation to an offence which he is investigating or any other offence; and

(b) that it is necessary to seize it in order to prevent the evidence being concealed, lost, altered or destroyed.

(4)–(6) *****

20 Extension of powers of seizure to computerised information

(1) Every power of seizure which is conferred by an enactment to which this section applies on a constable who has entered premises in the exercise of a power conferred by an enactment shall be construed as including a power to require any information [stored in any electronic form] and accessible from the premises to be produced in a form in which it can be taken away and in which it is visible and legible [or from which it can readily be produced in a visible and legible form].

(2) This section applies—

(a) to any enactment contained in an Act passed before this Act;

(b) to sections 8 and 18 above;

(c) to paragraph 13 of Schedule 1 to this Act; and

(d) to any enactment contained in an Act passed after this Act.

21 Access and copying

(1) A constable who seizes anything in the exercise of a power conferred by any enactment, including an enactment contained in an Act passed after this Act, shall, if so requested by a person showing himself—

(a) to be the occupier of premises on which it was seized; or

(b) to have had custody or control of it immediately before the seizure, provide that person with a record of what he seized.

(2) The officer shall provide the record within a reasonable time from the making of the request for it.

(3) Subject to subsection (8) below, if a request for permission to be granted access to anything which—

(a) has been seized by a constable; and

(b) is retained by the police for the purpose of investigating an offence,

is made to the officer in charge of the investigation by a person who had custody or control of the thing immediately before it was so seized or by someone acting on behalf of such a person the officer shall allow the person who made the request access to it under the supervision of a constable.

(4) Subject to subsection (8) below, if a request for a photograph or copy of any such thing is made to the officer in charge of the investigation by a person who had custody or control of the thing immediately before it was so seized, or by someone acting on behalf of such a person, the officer shall—

(a) allow the person who made the request access to it under the supervision of a constable for the purpose of photographing or copying it; or

(b) photograph or copy it, or cause it to be photographed or copied.

(5)–(7) *****

(8) There is no duty under this section to grant access to, or to supply a photograph or copy of, anything if the officer in charge of the investigation for the purposes of which it was seized has reasonable grounds for believing that to do so would prejudice—

    (a) that investigation;

    (b) the investigation of an offence other than the offence for the purposes of investigating which the thing was seized; or

    (c) any criminal proceedings which may be brought as a result of—

        (i)   the investigation of which he is in charge; or

        (ii) any such investigation as is mentioned in paragraph (b) above.

[(9) The references to a constable in subsections (1), (2), (3)(a) and (5) include a person authorised under section 16(2) to accompany a constable executing a warrant.]

22   Retention

(1) Subject to subsection (4) below, anything which has been seized by a constable or taken away by a constable following a requirement made by virtue of section 19 or 20 above may be retained so long as is necessary in all the circumstances.

(2) Without prejudice to the generality of subsection (1) above—

    (a) anything seized for the purposes of a criminal investigation may be retained, except as provided by subsection (4) below—

        (i)   for use as evidence at a trial for an offence; or

        (ii) for forensic examination or for investigation in connection with an offence; and

    (b) anything may be retained in order to establish its lawful owner, where there are reasonable grounds for believing that it has been obtained in consequence of the commission of an offence.

(3) *****

(4) Nothing may be retained for either of the purposes mentioned in subsection (2)(a) above if a photograph or copy would be sufficient for that purpose.

(5)–(7) *****

23   *****

PART III   ARREST

[24   Arrest without warrant: constables

(1) A constable may arrest without a warrant—

    (a) anyone who is about to commit an offence;

    (b) anyone who is in the act of committing an offence;

    (c) anyone whom he has reasonable grounds for suspecting to be about to commit an offence;

    (d) anyone whom he has reasonable grounds for suspecting to be committing an offence.

(2) If a constable has reasonable grounds for suspecting that an offence has been committed, he may arrest without a warrant anyone whom he has reasonable grounds to suspect of being guilty of it.

(3) If an offence has been committed, a constable may arrest without a warrant—

    (a) anyone who is guilty of the offence;

    (b) anyone whom he has reasonable grounds for suspecting to be guilty of it.

(4) But the power of summary arrest conferred by subsection (1), (2) or (3) is exercisable only if the constable has reasonable grounds for believing that for any of the reasons mentioned in subsection (5) it is necessary to arrest the person in question.

(5) The reasons are—

    (a) to enable the name of the person in question to be ascertained (in the case where the constable does not know, and cannot readily ascertain, the person's name, or has reasonable grounds for doubting whether a name given by the person as his name is his real name);

    (b) correspondingly as regards the person's address;
    (c) to prevent the person in question—
        (i) causing physical injury to himself or any other person;
        (ii) suffering physical injury;
        (iii) causing loss of or damage to property;
        (iv) committing an offence against public decency (subject to subsection (6)); or
        (v) causing an unlawful obstruction of the highway;
    (d) to protect a child or other vulnerable person from the person in question;
    (e) to allow the prompt and effective investigation of the offence or of the conduct of the person in question;
    (f) to prevent any prosecution for the offence from being hindered by the disappearance of the person in question.

(6) Subsection (5)(c)(iv) applies only where members of the public going about their normal business cannot reasonably be expected to avoid the person in question.

24A Arrest without warrant: other persons

(1) A person other than a constable may arrest without a warrant—
    (a) anyone who is in the act of committing an indictable offence;
    (b) anyone whom he has reasonable grounds for suspecting to be committing an indictable offence.

(2) Where an indictable offence has been committed, a person other than a constable may arrest without a warrant—
    (a) anyone who is guilty of the offence;
    (b) anyone whom he has reasonable grounds for suspecting to be guilty of it.

(3) But the power of summary arrest conferred by subsection (1) or (2) is exercisable only if—
    (a) the person making the arrest has reasonable grounds for believing that for any of the reasons mentioned in subsection (4) it is necessary to arrest the person in question; and
    (b) it appears to the person making the arrest that it is not reasonably practicable for a constable to make it instead.

(4) The reasons are to prevent the person in question—
    (a) causing physical injury to himself or any other person;
    (b) suffering physical injury;
    (c) causing loss of or damage to property; or
    (d) making off before a constable can assume responsibility for him.]

[(5) This section does not apply in relation to an offence under Part 3 or 3A of the Public Order Act 1986.]

25 . . .

26, 27 *****

28 Information to be given on arrest

(1) Subject to subsection (5) below, where a person is arrested, otherwise than by being informed that he is under arrest, the arrest is not lawful unless the person arrested is informed that he is under arrest as soon as is practicable after his arrest.

(2) Where a person is arrested by a constable, subsection (1) above applies regardless of whether the fact of the arrest is obvious.

(3) Subject to subsection (5) below, no arrest is lawful unless the person arrested is informed of the ground for the arrest at the time of, or as soon as is practicable after, the arrest.

(4) Where a person is arrested by a constable, subsection (3) above applies regardless of whether the ground for the arrest is obvious.

(5) Nothing in this section is to be taken to require a person to be informed—
    (a) that he is under arrest; or
    (b) of the ground for the arrest,

if it was not reasonably practicable for him to be so informed by reason of his having escaped from arrest before the information could be given.

29   Voluntary attendance at police station etc.
Where for the purpose of assisting with an investigation a person attends voluntarily at a police station or at any other place where a constable is present or accompanies a constable to a police station or any such other place without having been arrested—

>   (a) he shall be entitled to leave at will unless he is placed under arrest;
>   (b) he shall be informed at once that he is under arrest if a decision is taken by a constable to prevent him from leaving at will.

30   Arrest elsewhere than at police station
[(1) Subsection (1A) applies where a person is, at any place other than a police station—

>   (a) arrested by a constable for an offence, or
>   (b) taken into custody by a constable after being arrested for an offence by a person other than a constable.

(1A) The person must be taken by a constable to a police station as soon as practicable after the arrest.

(1B) Subsection (1A) has effect subject to section 30A (release on bail) and subsection (7) (release without bail).]

(2)–(6) *****

[(7) A person arrested by a constable at any place other than a police station must be released without bail if the condition in subsection (7A) is satisfied.

(7A) The condition is that, at any time before the person arrested reaches a police station, a constable is satisfied that there are no grounds for keeping him under arrest or releasing him on bail under section 30A.]

(8), (9) *****

[(10) Nothing in subsection (1A) or in section 30A prevents a constable delaying taking a person to a police station or releasing him on bail if the condition in subsection (10A) is satisfied.

(10A) The condition is that the presence of the person at a place (other than a police station) is necessary in order to carry out such investigations as it is reasonable to carry out immediately.

(11) Where there is any such delay the reasons for the delay must be recorded when the person first arrives at the police station or (as the case may be) is released on bail.]

(12), (13) *****

[30A   Bail elsewhere than at police station
(1) A constable may release on bail a person who is arrested or taken into custody in the circumstances mentioned in section 30(1).

(2) A person may be released on bail under subsection (1) at any time before he arrives at a police station.

(3) A person released on bail under subsection (1) must be required to attend a police station.

[(3A) Where a constable releases a person on bail under subsection (1)—

>   (a) no recognizance for the person's surrender to custody shall be taken from the person,
>   (b) no security for the person's surrender to custody shall be taken from the person or from anyone else on the person's behalf,
>   (c) the person shall not be required to provide a surety or sureties for his surrender to custody, and
>   (d) no requirement to reside in a bail hostel may be imposed as a condition of bail.

(3B) Subject to subsection (3A), where a constable releases a person on bail under subsection (1) the constable may impose, as conditions of the bail, such requirements as appear to the constable to be necessary—

>   (a) to secure that the person surrenders to custody,
>   (b) to secure that the person does not commit an offence while on bail,

(c) to secure that the person does not interfere with witnesses or otherwise obstruct the course of justice, whether in relation to himself or any other person, or

(d) for the person's own protection or, if the person is under the age of 17, for the person's own welfare or in the person's own interests.

(4) Where a person is released on bail under subsection (1), a requirement may be imposed on the person as a condition of bail only under the preceding provisions of this section.]

(5) The police station which the person is required to attend may be any police station.]

[30B Bail under section 30A: notices

[(1) Where a constable grants bail to a person under section 30A, he must give that person a notice in writing before he is released.

(2) The notice must state—

(a) the offence for which he was arrested, and

(b) the ground on which he was arrested.

(3) The notice must inform him that he is required to attend a police station.

(4) It may also specify the police station which he is required to attend and the time when he is required to attend.

[(4A) If the person is granted bail subject to conditions under section 30A(3B), the notice also—

(a) must specify the requirements imposed by those conditions,

(b) must explain the opportunities under sections 30CA(1) and 30CB(1) for variation of those conditions, and

(c) if it does not specify the police station at which the person is required to attend, must specify a police station at which the person may make a request under section 30CA(1) (b).]

(5) If the notice does not include the information mentioned in subsection (4), the person must subsequently be given a further notice in writing which contains that information.]

(6), (7) *****

[30C–30CB *****

30D Failure to answer to bail under section 30A

(1) A constable may arrest without a warrant a person who—

(a) has been released on bail under section 30A subject to a requirement to attend a specified police station, but

(b) fails to attend the police station at the specified time.]

(2) A person arrested under subsection (1) must be taken to a police station (which may be the specified police station or any other police station) as soon as practicable after the arrest.

[(2A) A person who has been released on bail under section 30A may be arrested without a warrant by a constable if the constable has reasonable grounds for suspecting that the person has broken any of the conditions of bail.

(2B) A person arrested under subsection (2A) must be taken to a police station (which may be the specified police station mentioned in subsection (1) or any other police station) as soon as practicable after the arrest.]

(3), (4) *****

31 *****

32 Search upon arrest

(1) A constable may search an arrested person, in any case where the person to be searched has been arrested at a place other than a police station, if the constable has reasonable grounds for believing that the arrested person may present a danger to himself or others.

(2) Subject to subsections (3) to (5) below, a constable shall also have power in any such case—

(a) to search the arrested person for anything—

(i)   which he might use to assist him to escape from lawful custody; or

(ii) which might be evidence relating to an offence; and

(b) [if the offence for which he has been arrested is an indictable offence, to enter and search any premises in which he was when arrested or immediately before he was arrested for evidence relating to the offence].

(3) The power to search conferred by subsection (2) above is only a power to search to the extent that is reasonably required for the purpose of discovering any such thing or any such evidence.

(4) The powers conferred by this section to search a person are not to be construed as authorising a constable to require a person to remove any of his clothing in public other than an outer coat, jacket or gloves [but they do authorise a search of a person's mouth].

(5) A constable may not search a person in the exercise of the power conferred by subsection (2)(a) above unless he has reasonable grounds for believing that the person to be searched may have concealed on him anything for which a search is permitted under that paragraph.

(6) A constable may not search premises in the exercise of the power conferred by subsection (2)(b) above unless he has reasonable grounds for believing that there is evidence for which a search is permitted under that paragraph on the premises.

(7)–(10) *****

33 . . .

PART IV DETENTION

Detention—conditions and duration

34   Limitations on police detention

(1) A person arrested for an offence shall not be kept in police detention except in accordance with the provisions of this Part of this Act.

(2) Subject to subsection (3) below, if at any time a custody officer—

    (a) becomes aware, in relation to any person in police detention, that the grounds for the detention of that person have ceased to apply; and

    (b) is not aware of any other grounds on which the continued detention of that person could be justified under the provisions of this Part of this Act,

it shall be the duty of the custody officer, subject to subsection (4) below, to order his immediate release from custody.

(3) No person in police detention shall be released except on the authority of a custody officer at the police station where his detention was authorised or, if it was authorised at more than one station, a custody officer at the station where it was last authorised.

(4) A person who appears to the custody officer to have been unlawfully at large when he was arrested is not to be released under subsection (2) above.

(5)–(8) *****

35   Designated police stations

(1) The chief officer of police for each police area shall designate the police stations in his area which, subject to [sections 30(3) and (5), 30A(5) and 30D(2)] above, are to be the stations in that area to be used for the purpose of detention arrested persons.

(2) A chief officer's duty under subsection (1) above is to designate police stations appearing to him to provide enough accommodation for that purpose.

(2A), (3), (4) *****

36   Custody officers at police stations

(1) One or more custody officers shall be appointed for each designated police station.

(2), [(2A)] *****

[(3) No officer may be appointed a custody officer unless the officer is at least of the rank of sergeant.]

(4) An officer of any rank may perform the functions of a custody officer at a designated police station if a custody officer is not readily available to perform them.

(5)–(10) *****

(11) ...

37 Duties of custody officer before charge

(1) Where—

    (a) a person is arrested for an offence—

        (i) without a warrant; or

        (ii) under a warrant not endorsed for bail, ...

    (b) ...

the custody officer at each police station where he is detained after his arrest shall determine whether he has before him sufficient evidence to charge that person with the offence for which he was arrested and may detain him at the police station for such period as is necessary to enable him to do so.

(2) If the custody officer determines that he does not have such evidence before him, the person arrested shall be released either on bail or without bail, unless the custody officer has reasonable grounds for believing that his detention without being charged is necessary to secure or preserve evidence relating to an offence for which he is under arrest or to obtain such evidence by questioning him.

(3) If the custody officer has reasonable grounds for so believing, he may authorise the person arrested to be kept in police detention.

(4) Where a custody officer authorises a person who has not been charged to be kept in police detention, he shall, as soon as is practicable, make a written record of the grounds for the detention.

(5) Subject to subsection (6) below, the written record shall be made in the presence of the person arrested who shall at that time be informed by the custody officer of the grounds for his detention.

(6) Subsection (5) above shall not apply where the person arrested is, at the time when the written record is made—

    (a) incapable of understanding what is said to him;

    (b) violent or likely to become violent; or

    (c) in urgent need of medical attention.

(7)–(10), (15) *****

(11)–(14) ...

37A–37D *****

38 Duties of custody officer after charge

(1) Where a person arrested for an offence otherwise than under a warrant endorsed for bail is charged with an offence, the custody officer shall[, subject to section 25 of the Criminal Justice and Public Order Act 1994,] order his release from police detention, either on bail or without bail, unless—

    (a) if the person arrested is not an arrested juvenile—

        (i) his name or address cannot be ascertained or the custody officer has reasonable grounds for doubting whether a name or address furnished by him as his name or address is his real name or address;

        [(ii) the custody officer has reasonable grounds for believing that the person arrested will fail to appear in court to answer to bail;

        (iii) in the case of a person arrested for an imprisonable offence, the custody officer has reasonable grounds for believing that the detention of the person arrested is necessary to prevent him from committing an offence;

        [(iiia) in a case where a sample may be taken from the person under section 63B below, the custody officer has reasonable grounds for believing that the detention of the person is necessary to enable a sample to be taken from him;]

        (iv) in the case of a person arrested for an offence which is not an imprisonable offence, the custody officer has reasonable grounds for believing that the detention of the person arrested is necessary to prevent him from causing physical injury to any other person or from causing loss of or damage to property;

> > (v)   the custody officer has reasonable grounds for believing that the detention of the person arrested is necessary to prevent him from interfering with the administration of justice or with the investigation of offences or of a particular offence; or
> > (vi)   the custody officer has reasonable grounds for believing that the detention of the person arrested is necessary for his own protection;]
> (b) if he is an arrested juvenile—
> > (i)   any of the requirements of paragraph (a) above is satisfied [(but, in the case of paragraph (a)(iiia) above only if the arrested juvenile has attained the minimum age)]; or
> > (ii)   the custody officer has reasonable grounds for believing that he ought to be detained in his own interests.
> [(c) the offence with which the person is charged is murder].

(2) If the release of a person arrested is not required by subsection (1) above, the custody officer may authorise him to be kept in police detention [but may not authorise a person to be kept in police detention by virtue of subsection (1)(a)(iiia) after the end of the period of six hours beginning when he was charged with the offence.].

(2A) *****

(3) Where a custody officer authorises a person who has been charged to be kept in police detention, he shall, as soon as practicable, make a written record of the grounds for the detention.

(4) Subject to subsection (5) below, the written record shall be made in the presence of the person charged who shall at that time be informed by the custody officer of the grounds for his detention.

(5) Subsection (4) above shall not apply where the person charged is, at the time when the written record is made—

> (a) incapable of understanding what is said to him;
> (b) violent or likely to become violent; or
> (c) in urgent need of medical attention.

(6)–(8) *****

[**Note:** The 'minimum age' is 14 (subs. (6A)).]

39   Responsibilities in relation to persons detained

(1) Subject to subsection (2) and (4) below, it shall be the duty of the custody officer at a police station to ensure—

> (a) that all persons in police detention at that station are treated in accordance with this Act and any code of practice issued under it and relating to the treatment of persons in police detention; and
> (b) that all matters relating to such persons which are required by this Act or by such codes of practice to be recorded are recorded in the custody records relating to such persons.

(2)–(6) *****

(7) . . .

40   Review of police detention

(1) Reviews of the detention of each person in police detention in connection with the investigation of an offence shall be carried out periodically in accordance with the following provisions of this section—

> (a) in the case of a person who has been arrested and charged, by the custody officer; and
> (b) in the case of a person who has been arrested but not charged, by an officer of at least the rank of inspector who has not been directly involved in the investigation.

(2) The officer to whom it falls to carry out a review is referred to in this section as a 'review officer'.

(3) Subject to subsection (4) below—

> (a) the first review shall be not later than six hours after the detention was first authorised;

(b) the second review shall be not later than nine hours after the first;

(c) subsequent reviews shall be at intervals of not more than nine hours.

(4) A review may be postponed—

(a) if, having regard to all the circumstances prevailing at the latest time for it specified in subsection (3) above, it is not practicable to carry out the review at that time;

(b) without prejudice to the generality of paragraph (a) above—

(i) if at that time the person in detention is being questioned by a police officer and the review officer is satisfied that an interruption of the questioning for the purpose of carrying out the review would prejudice the investigation in connection with which he is being questioned; or

(ii) if at that time no review officer is readily available.

(5) If a review is postponed under subsection (4) above it shall be carried out as soon as practicable after the latest time specified for it in subsection (3) above.

(6) If a review is carried out after postponement under subsection (4) above, the fact that it was so carried out shall not affect any requirement of this section as to the time at which any subsequent review is to be carried out.

(7) The review officer shall record the reasons for any postponement of a review in the custody record.

(8)–(14) *****

40A *****

41   Limits on period of detention without charge

(1) Subject to the following provisions of this section and to sections 42 and 43 below, a person shall not be kept in police detention for more than 24 hours without being charged.

(2) The time from which the period of detention of a person is to be calculated (in this Act referred to as 'the relevant time')—

(a) in the case of a person to whom this paragraph applies, shall be—

(i) the time at which that person arrives at the relevant police station; or

(ii) the time 24 hours after the time of that person's arrest, whichever is the earlier;

(b) in the case of a person arrested outside England and Wales, shall be—

(i) the time at which that person arrives at the first police station to which he is taken in the police area in England or Wales in which the offence for which he was arrested is being investigated; or

(ii) the time 24 hours after the time of that person's entry into England and Wales, whichever is the earlier;

(c) in the case of a person who—

(i) attends voluntarily at a police station; or

(ii) accompanies a constable to a police station without having been arrested, and is arrested at the police station, the time of his arrest;

[(ca) in the case of a person who attends a police station to answer bail granted under section 30A, the time when he arrives at the police station;]

(d) in any other case, except where subsection (5) below applies, shall be the time at which the person arrested arrives at the first police station to which he is taken after his arrest.

(3)–(6) *****

(7) Subject to subsection (8) below, a person who at the expiry of 24 hours after the relevant time is in police detention and has not been charged shall be released at that time either on bail or without bail.

(8) Subsection (7) above does not apply to a person whose detention for more than 24 hours after the relevant time has been authorised or is otherwise permitted in accordance with section 42 or 43 below.

(9) *****

42   Authorisation of continued detention

(1) Where a police officer of the rank of superintendent or above who is responsible for the police station at which a person is detained has reasonable grounds for believing that—

(a)   the detention of that person without charge is necessary to secure or preserve evidence relating to an offence for which he is under arrest or to obtain such evidence by questioning him;

[(b)   an offence for which he is under arrest is an [indictable] offence; and]

(c)   the investigation is being conducted diligently and expeditiously,

he may authorise the keeping of that person in police detention for a period expiring at or before 36 hours after the relevant time.

(2) Where an officer such as is mentioned in subsection (1) above has authorised the keeping of a person in police detention for a period expiring less than 36 hours after the relevant time, such an officer may authorise the keeping of that person in police detention for a further period expiring not more than 36 hours after that time if the conditions specified in subsection (1) above are still satisfied when he gives the authorisation.

(3) If it is proposed to transfer a person in police detention to another police area, the officer determining whether or not to authorise keeping him in detention under subsection (1) above shall have regard to the distance and the time the journey would take.

(4)–(5) *****

(6) Before determining whether to authorise the keeping of a person in detention under subsection (1) or (2) above, an officer shall give—

(a) that person; or

(b) any solicitor representing him who is available at the time when it falls to the officer to determine whether to give the authorisation,

an opportunity to make representations to him about the detention.

(7)–(9) *****

(10) Where an officer has authorised the keeping of a person who has not been charged in detention under subsection (1) or (2) above, he shall be released from detention, either on bail or without bail, not later than 36 hours after the relevant time, unless—

(a) he has been charged with an offence; or

(b) his continued detention is authorised or otherwise permitted in accordance with section 43 below.

(11) *****

43   Warrants of further detention

(1) Where, on an application on oath made by a constable and supported by an information, a magistrate's court is satisfied that there are reasonable grounds for believing that the further detention of the person to whom the application relates is justified, it may issue a warrant of further detention authorising the keeping of that person in police detention.

(2) A court may not hear an application for a warrant of further detention unless the person to whom the application relates—

(a)   has been furnished with a copy of the information; and

(b)   has been brought before the court for the hearing.

(3) The person to whom the application relates shall be entitled to be legally represented at the hearing and, if he is not so represented but wishes to be so represented—

(a)   the court shall adjourn the hearing to enable him to obtain representation; and

(b)   he may be kept in police detention during the adjournment.

(4) A person's further detention is only justified for the purposes of this section or section 44 below if—

(a)   his detention without charge is necessary to secure or preserve evidence relating to an offence for which he is under arrest or to obtain such evidence by questioning him;

(b)   an offence for which he is under arrest is [an indictable offence]; and

(c) the investigation is being conducted diligently and expeditiously.

(5)–(7) *****

(8) Where on an application such as is mentioned in subsection (1) above a magistrates' court is not satisfied that there are reasonable grounds for believing that the further detention of the person to whom the application relates is justified, it shall be its duty—

(a) to refuse the application; or

(b) to adjourn the hearing of it until a time not later than 36 hours after the relevant time.

(9) The person to whom the application relates may be kept in police detention during the adjournment.

(10) A warrant of further detention shall—

(a) state the time at which it is issued;

(b) authorise the keeping in police detention of the person to whom it relates for the period stated in it.

(11) Subject to subsection (12) below, the period stated in a warrant of further detention shall be such period as the magistrates' court thinks fit, having regard to the evidence before it.

(12) The period shall not be longer than 36 hours.

(13), (14) *****

(15) Where an application under this section is refused, the person to whom the application relates shall forthwith be charged or, subject to subsection (16) below, released, either on bail or without bail.

(16) A person need not be released under subsection (15) above—

(a) before the expiry of 24 hours after the relevant time; or

(b) before the expiry of any longer period for which his continued detention is or has been authorised under section 42 above.

(17) Where an application under this section is refused, no further application shall be made under this section in respect of the person to whom the refusal relates, unless supported by evidence which has come to light since the refusal.

(18), (19) *****

44 Extension of warrants of further detention

(1) On an application on oath made by a constable and supported by an information a magistrates' court may extend a warrant of further detention issued under section 43 above if it is satisfied that there are reasonable grounds for believing that the further detention of the person to whom the application relates is justified.

(2) Subject to subsection (3) below, the period for which a warrant of further detention may be extended shall be such period as the court thinks fit, having regard to the evidence before it.

(3) The period shall not—

(a) be longer than 36 hours; or

(b) end later than 96 hours after the relevant time.

(4)–(8) *****

45 Detention before charge—supplementary

(1) In sections 43 and 44 of this Act 'magistrates' court' means a court consisting of two or more justices of the peace sitting otherwise than in open court.

(2) Any reference in this Part of this Act to a period of time or a time of day is to be treated as approximate only.

45A *****

Detention—miscellaneous

46 Detention after charge

(1) Where a person—

(a) is charged with an offence; and

(b) after being charged—
  (i) is kept in police detention; or
  (ii) is detained by a local authority in pursuance of arrangements made under section 38(6) above,

he shall be brought before a magistrates' court in accordance with the provisions of this section.

(2) If he is to be brought before a magistrates' court [in the local justice] area in which the police station at which he was charged is situated, he shall be brought before such a court as soon as is practicable and in any event not later than the first sitting after he is charged with the offence.

(3) If no magistrates' court [in that area] is due to sit either on the day on which he is charged or on the next day, the custody officer for the police station at which he was charged shall inform the [designated officer] for the area that there is a person in the area to whom subsection (2) above applies.

(4) If the person charged is to be brought before a magistrates' court [in a local justice] area other than that in which the police station at which he was charged is situated, he shall be removed to that area as soon as is practicable and brought before such a court as soon as is practicable after this arrival in the area and in any event not later than the first sitting of a magistrates' court [in that area] after this arrival in the area.

(5)–(9) *****

46ZA–51 *****

52 ...

[**Note:** Section 46ZA is not reproduced above but relates to persons granted live link bail.]

PART V QUESTIONING AND TREATMENT OF PERSONS BY POLICE

53   Abolition of certain powers of constables to search persons

(1) Subject to subsection (2) below, there shall cease to have effect any Act (including a local Act) passed before this Act in so far as it authorises—
  (a) any search by a constable of a person in police detention at a police station; or
  (b) an intimate search of a person by a constable; and any rule of common law which authorises a search such as is mentioned in paragraph (a) or (b) above is abolished.

(2) ...

54   Search of detained persons

(1) The custody officer at a police station shall ascertain ... everything which a person has with him when he is—
  (a) brought to the station after being arrested elsewhere or after being committed to custody by an order or sentence of a court; or
  [(b) arrested at the station or detained there[, as a person falling within section 34(7), under section 37 above] [or as a person to whom section 46ZA(4) or (5) applies]].

[(2) The custody officer may record or cause to be recorded all or any of the things which he ascertains under subsection (1).

(2A) In the case of an arrested person, any such record may be made as part of his custody record.]

(3) Subject to subsection (4) below, a custody officer may seize and retain any such thing or cause any such thing to be seized and retained.

(4) Clothes and personal effects may only be seized if the custody officer—
  (a) believes that the person from whom they are seized may use them—
    (i) to cause physical injury to himself or any other person;

(ii)　to damage property;

(iii)　to interfere with evidence; or

(iv)　to assist him to escape; or

(b)　has reasonable grounds for believing that they may be evidence relating to an offence.

(5)　Where anything is seized, the person from whom it is seized shall be told the reason for the seizure unless he is—

(a)　violent or likely to become violent; or

(b)　incapable of understanding what is said to him.

(6)　Subject to subsection (7) below, a person may be searched if the custody officer considers it necessary to enable him to carry out his duty under subsection (1) above and to the extent that the custody officer considers necessary for that purpose.

[(6A)　A person who is in custody at a police station or is in police detention otherwise than at a police station may at any time be searched in order to ascertain whether he has with him anything which he could use for any of the purposes specified in subsection (4)(a) above.

(6B)　Subject to subsection (6C) below, a constable may seize and retain, or cause to be seized and retained, anything found on such a search.

(6C)　A constable may only seize clothes and personal effects in the circumstances specified in subsection (4) above.]

(7)　An intimate search may not be conducted under this section.

(8)　A search under this section shall be carried out by a constable.

(9)　The constable carrying out a search shall be of the same sex as the person searched.

[54A　Searches and examination to ascertain identity

(1)　If an officer of at least the rank of inspector authorises it, a person who is detained in a police station may be searched or examined, or both—

(a)　for the purpose of ascertaining whether he has any mark that would tend to identify him as a person involved in the commission of an offence; or

(b)　for the purpose of facilitating the ascertainment of his identity.

(2)　An officer may only give an authorisation under subsection (1) for the purpose mentioned in paragraph (a) of that subsection if—

(a)　the appropriate consent to a search or examination that would reveal whether the mark in question exists has been withheld; or

(b)　it is not practicable to obtain such consent.

(3)　An officer may only give an authorisation under subsection (1) in a case in which subsection (2) does not apply if—

(a)　the person in question has refused to identify himself; or

(b)　the officer has reasonable grounds for suspecting that that person is not who he claims to be.

(4)　An officer may give an authorisation under subsection (1) orally or in writing but, if he gives it orally, he shall confirm it in writing as soon as is practicable.

(5)　Any identifying mark found on a search or examination under this section may be photographed—

(a)　with the appropriate consent; or

(b)　if the appropriate consent is withheld or it is not practicable to obtain it, without it.

(6)　Where a search or examination may be carried out under this section, or a photograph may be taken under this section, the only persons entitled to carry out the search or examination, or to take the photograph, are [constables].

(7)　A person may not under this section carry out a search or examination of a person of the opposite sex or take a photograph of any part of the body of a person of the opposite sex.

(8)　An intimate search may not be carried out under this section.

(9)　A photograph taken under this section—

(a)　may be used by, or disclosed to, any person for any purpose related to the prevention or detection of crime, the investigation of an offence or the conduct of a prosecution; and

(b) after being so used or disclosed, may be retained but may not be used or disclosed except for a purpose so related.]

(10)–(13) *****

54B, 54C *****

55 Intimate searches

(1) Subject to the following provisions of this section, if an officer of at least the rank of [inspector] has reasonable grounds for believing—

    (a) that a person who has been arrested and is in police detention may have concealed on him anything which—

      (i) he could use to cause physical injury to himself or others; and

      (ii) he might so use while he is in police detention or in the custody of a court; or

    (b) that such a person—

      (i) may have a Class A drug concealed on him; and

      (ii) was in possession of it with the appropriate criminal intention before his arrest, he may authorise [an intimate] search of that person.

(2) An officer may not authorise an intimate search of a person for anything unless he has reasonable grounds for believing that it cannot be found without his being intimately searched.

(3)–(3B) *****

(4) An intimate search which is only a drug offence search shall be by way of examination by a suitably qualified person.

(5) Except as provided by subsection (4) above, an intimate search shall be by way of examination by a suitably qualified person unless an officer of at least the rank of [inspector] considers that this is not practicable.

(6) An intimate search which is not carried out as mentioned in subsection (5) above shall be carried out by a constable.

(7) A constable may not carry out an intimate search of a person of the opposite sex.

(8) No intimate search may be carried out except—

    (a) at a police station;

    (b) at a hospital;

    (c) at a registered medical practitioner's surgery; or

    (d) at some other place used for medical purposes.

(9) An intimate search which is only a drug offence search may not be carried out at a police station.

(10) If an intimate search of a person is carried out, the custody record relating to him shall state—

    (a) which parts of his body were searched; and

    (b) why they were searched.

(10A), (11) *****

(12) The custody officer at a police station may seize and retain anything which is found on an intimate search of a person, or cause any such thing to be seized and retained—

    (a) if he believes that the person from whom it is seized may use it—

      (i) to cause physical injury to himself or any other person;

      (ii) to damage property;

      (iii) to interfere with evidence; or

      (iv) to assist him to escape; or

    (b) if he has reasonable grounds for believing that it may be evidence relating to an offence.

(13) Where anything is seized under this section, the person from whom it is seized shall be told the reason for the seizure unless he is—

    (a) violent or likely to become violent; or

    (b) incapable of understanding what is said to him.

(13A)–(16) *****

(17) In this section—

*****

'Class A drug' has the meaning assigned to it by section 2(1)(b) of the Misuse of Drugs Act 1971;

'drug offence search' means an intimate search for a Class A drug which an officer has authorised by virtue of subsection (1)(b) above; and

'suitably qualified person' means—

(a) a registered medical practitioner; or

(b) a registered nurse.

[55A X-rays and ultrasound scans

(1) If an officer of at least the rank of inspector has reasonable grounds for believing that a person who has been arrested for an offence and is in police detention—

(a) may have swallowed a Class A drug, and

(b) was in possession of it with the appropriate criminal intent before his arrest,

the officer may authorise that an x-ray is taken of the person or an ultrasound scan is carried out on the person (or both).

(2) An x-ray must not be taken of a person and an ultrasound scan must not be carried out on him unless the appropriate consent has been given in writing.

(3) If it is proposed that an x-ray is taken or an ultrasound scan is carried out, an appropriate officer must inform the person who is to be subject to it—

(a) of the giving of the authorisation for it, and

(b) of the grounds for giving the authorisation.

(4) An x-ray may be taken or an ultrasound scan carried out only by a suitably qualified person and only at—

(a) a hospital,

(b) a registered medical practitioner's surgery, or

(c) some other place used for medical purposes.]

(5)–(10) *****

56 Right to have someone informed when arrested

(1) Where a person has been arrested and is being held in custody in a police station or other premises, he shall be entitled, if he so requests, to have one friend or relative or other person who is known to him or who is likely to take an interest in his welfare told, as soon as is practicable except to the extent that delay is permitted by this section, that he has been arrested and is being detained there.

(2) Delay is only permitted—

(a) in the case of a person who is in police detention for [an indictable offence]; and

(b) if an officer of at least the rank of [inspector] authorises it.

(3) In any case the person in custody must be permitted to exercise the right conferred by subsection (1) above within 36 hours from the relevant time as defined in section 41(2) above.

(4)–(5B) *****

(6) If a delay is authorised—

(a) the detained person shall be told the reason for it; and

(b) the reason shall be noted on his custody record.

(7)–(10) *****

57 ***

58 Access to legal advice

(1) A person arrested and held in custody in a police station or other premises shall be entitled, if he so requests, to consult a solicitor privately at any time.

(2) Subject to subsection (3) below, a request under subsection (1) above and the time at which it was made shall be recorded in the custody record.

(3) Such a request need not be recorded in the custody record of a person who makes it at a time while he is at a court after being charged with an offence.

(4) If a person makes such a request, he must be permitted to consult a solicitor as soon as is practicable except to the extent that delay is permitted by this section.

(5) In any case he must be permitted to consult a solicitor within 36 hours from the relevant time, as defined in section 41(2) above.

(6) Delay in compliance with a request is only permitted—

    (a) in the case of a person who is in police detention for [an indictable offence]; and

    (b) if an officer of at least the rank of superintendent authorises it.

(7)–(8B) *****

(9) If delay is authorised—

    (a) the detained person shall be told the reason for it; and

    (b) the reason shall be noted on his custody record.

(10) The duties imposed by subsection (9) above shall be performed as soon as is practicable.

(11) There may be no further delay in permitting the exercise of the right conferred by subsection (1) above once the reason for authorising delay ceases to subsist.

[(12) Nothing in this section applies to a person arrested or detained under the terrorism provisions.]

59 . . .

60   Tape-recording of interviews

(1) It shall be the duty of the Secretary of State—

    (a) to issue a code of practice in connection with the tape-recording of interviews of persons suspected of the commission of criminal offences which are held by police officers at police stations; and

    (b) to make an order requiring the tape-recording of interviews of persons suspected of the commission of criminal offences, or of such descriptions of criminal offences as may be specified in the order, which are so held, in accordance with the code as it has effect for the time being.

(2) An order under subsection (1) above shall be made by statutory instrument and shall be subject to annulment in pursuance of a resolution of either House of Parliament.

[60A   Visual recording of interviews

(1) The Secretary of State shall have power—

    (a) to issue a code of practice for the visual recording of interviews held by police officers at police stations; and

    (b) to make an order requiring the visual recording of interviews so held, and requiring the visual recording to be in accordance with the code for the time being in force under this section.]

(2)–(4) *****

61   Fingerprinting

(1) Except as provided by this section no person's fingerprints may be taken without the appropriate consent.

(2) Consent to the taking of a person's fingerprints must be in writing if it is given at a time when he is at a police station.

[(3) The fingerprints of a person detained at a police station may be taken without the appropriate consent if—

    (a) he is detained in consequence of his arrest for a recordable offence; and

    (b) he has not had his fingerprints taken in the course of the investigation of the offence by the police.]

(3A) *****

[(4) The fingerprints of a person detained at a police station may be taken without the appropriate consent if—

    (a) he has been charged with a recordable offence or informed that he will be reported for such an offence; and

    (b) he has not had his fingerprints taken in the course of the investigation of the offence by the police.]

(4A)–(10) *****

61A–63C *****

[64 Retention of samples and fingerprints, etc generally]

[(1) This section applies to the following material—

    (a) fingerprints, samples or impressions of footwear—

        (i)   taken from a person under any power conferred by this Part of this Act, or

        (ii) taken in connection with the investigation of an offence with the consent of the person from whom they were taken, and

    (b) a DNA profile derived from a DNA sample falling within paragraph (a).

(2) Material to which this section applies may be retained after it has fulfilled the purpose for which it was taken or derived.

(3) This section is subject to sections 64ZA to 64ZJ.

(4) This section and sections 64ZA to 64ZH do not apply to material to which paragraph 14 of Schedule 8 to the Terrorism Act 2000 applies.

(5), (6) *****

[64ZA Destruction of samples]

[(1) A DNA sample to which section 64 applies must be destroyed—

    (a) as soon as a DNA profile has been derived from the sample, or

    (b) if sooner, before the end of the period of 6 months beginning with the date on which the sample was taken.

(2) Any other sample to which section 64 applies must be destroyed before the end of the period of 6 months beginning with the date on which it was taken.]

[64ZB Destruction of data given voluntarily]

[(1) This section applies to—

    (a) fingerprints or impressions of footwear taken in connection with the investigation of an offence with the consent of the person from whom they were taken, and

    (b) a DNA profile derived from a DNA sample taken in connection with the investigation of an offence with the consent of the person from whom the sample was taken.

(2) Material to which this section applies must be destroyed as soon as it has fulfilled the purpose for which it was taken or derived, unless it is—

    (a) material relating to a person who is convicted of the offence,

    (b) material relating to a person who has previously been convicted of a recordable offence, other than a person who has only one exempt conviction,

    (c) material in relation to which any of sections 64ZC to 64ZH applies, or

    (d) material which is not required to be destroyed by virtue of consent given under section 64ZL.

(3) If material to which this section applies leads to the person to whom the material relates being arrested for or charged with an offence other than the offence under investigation—

    (a) the material is not required to be destroyed by virtue of this section, and

    (b) sections 64ZD to 64ZH have effect in relation to the material as if the material was taken (or, in the case of a DNA profile, was derived from material taken) in connection with the investigation of the offence in respect of which the person is arrested or charged.]

64ZC–64ZI *****

[64ZJ   Destruction of fingerprints taken under section 61(6A)]

[Fingerprints taken from a person by virtue of section 61(6A) (taking fingerprints for the purposes of identification) must be destroyed as soon as they have fulfilled the purpose for which they were taken.]

[64ZK   Retention for purposes of national security]

[(1) Subsection (2) applies if the responsible chief officer of police determines that it is necessary for—

    (a) a DNA profile to which section 64 applies, or

    (b) fingerprints to which section 64 applies, other than fingerprints taken under section 61(6A),

to be retained for the purposes of national security.

(2) Where this subsection applies—

    (a) the material is not required to be destroyed in accordance with sections 64ZB to 64ZH, and

    (b) section 64ZN(2) does not apply to the material,

for as long as the determination has effect.

(3) A determination under subsection (1) has effect for a maximum of 2 years beginning with the date on which the material would otherwise be required to be destroyed, but a determination may be renewed.

(4) "Responsible chief officer of police" means the chief officer of police for the police area—

    (a) in which the fingerprints were taken, or

    (b) in the case of a DNA profile, in which the sample from which the DNA profile was derived was taken.]

64ZL   ***

[64ZM   Destruction of copies, and notification of destruction]

[(1) If fingerprints or impressions of footwear are required to be destroyed by virtue of any of sections 64ZB to 64ZJ, any copies of the fingerprints or impressions of footwear must also be destroyed.

(2) If a DNA profile is required to be destroyed by virtue of any of those sections, no copy may be kept except in a form which does not include information which identifies the person to whom the DNA profile relates.

(3) If a person makes a request to the responsible chief officer of police to be notified when anything relating to the person is destroyed under any of sections 64ZA to 64ZJ, the responsible chief officer of police or a person authorised by the chief officer or on the chief officer's behalf must within three months of the request issue the person with a certificate recording the destruction.

(4) "Responsible chief officer of police" means the chief officer of police for the police area—

    (a) in which the samples, fingerprints or impressions of footwear which have been destroyed were taken, or

    (b) in the case of a DNA profile which has been destroyed, in which the samples from which the DNA profile was derived were taken.]

[64ZN   Use of retained material]

[(1) Any material to which section 64 applies which is retained after it has fulfilled the purpose for which it was taken or derived must not be used other than—

    (a) in the interests of national security,

    (b) for the purposes of a terrorist investigation,

    (c) for purposes related to the prevention or detection of crime, the investigation of an offence or the conduct of a prosecution, or

    (d) for purposes related to the identification of a deceased person or of the person to whom the material relates.

(2) Material which is required to be destroyed by virtue of any of sections 64ZA to 64ZJ, or of section 64ZM, must not at any time after it is required to be destroyed be used—

(a) in evidence against the person to whom the material relates, or

(b) for the purposes of the investigation of any offence.

(3) In this section—

(a) the reference to using material includes a reference to allowing any check to be made against it and to disclosing it to any person,

(b) the reference to crime includes a reference to any conduct which—

(i) constitutes one or more criminal offences (whether under the law of a part of the United Kingdom or of a country or territory outside the United Kingdom), or

(ii) is, or corresponds to, any conduct which, if it all took place in any one part of the United Kingdom, would constitute one or more criminal offences, and

(c) the references to an investigation and to a prosecution include references, respectively, to any investigation outside the United Kingdom of any crime or suspected crime and to a prosecution brought in respect of any crime in a country or territory outside the United Kingdom.]

[64A   Photographing of suspects etc.

(1) A person who is detained at a police station may be photographed—

(a) with the appropriate consent; or

(b) if the appropriate consent is withheld or it is not practicable to obtain it, without it.

(1A), (1B) *****

(2) A person proposing to take a photograph of any person under this section—

(a) may, for the purpose of doing so, require the removal of any item or substance worn on or over the whole or any part of the head or face of the person to be photo graphed; and

(b) if the requirement is not complied with, may remove the item or substance himself.

(3) Where a photograph may be taken under this section, the only persons entitled to take the photograph are [constables].

(4) A photograph taken under this section—

(a) may be used by, or disclosed to, any person for any purpose related to the prevention or detection of crime, the investigation of an offence or the conduct of a prosecution [or to the enforcement of a sentence]; and

(b) after being so used or disclosed, may be retained but may not be used or disclosed except for a purpose so related.]

(5)–(7) *****

65   Part V—supplementary

(1) In this Part of this Act—

['analysis', in relation to a skin impression, includes comparison and matching;]

'appropriate consent' means—

(a) in relation to a person who has attained the age of 17 years, the consent of that person;

(b) in relation to a person who has not attained that age but has attained the age of 14 years, the consent of that person and his parent or guardian; and

(c) in relation to a person who has not attained the age of 14 years, the consent of his parent or guardian;

*****

['fingerprints', in relation to any person, means a record (in any form and produced by any method) of the skin pattern and other physical characteristics or features of—

(a) any of that person's fingers; or

(b) either of his palms;];

['intimate sample' means—

(a) a sample of blood, semen or any other tissue fluid, urine or pubic hair;

(b) a dental impression;

(c) [a swab taken from any part of a person's genitals (including pubic hair) or from a person's body orifice other than the mouth];]

'intimate search' means a search which consists of the physical examination of a person's body orifices other than the mouth;

'non-intimate sample' means—

(a) a sample of hair other than pubic hair;

(b) a sample taken from a nail or from under a nail;

(c) [a swab taken from any part of a person's body other than a part from which a swab taken would be an intimate sample;]

(d) saliva;

[(e) a skin impression;]]

*****

. . .

(1A), (1B), (2), (2A), (3) *****

65A *****

PART VI CODES OF PRACTICE—GENERAL

66 Codes of practice

(1) The Secretary of State shall issue codes of practice in connection with—

(a) the exercise by police officers of statutory powers—

(i)   to search a person without first arresting him; . . .

(ii)   to search a vehicle without making an arrest; [or

(iii) to arrest a person;]

(b) the detention, treatment, questioning and indication of persons by police officers;

(c) searches of premises by police officers; and

(d) the seizure of property found by police officers on persons or premises.

[(2) Codes shall (in particular) include provisions in connection with the exercise by police officers of powers under section 63B, above.]

67 Codes of practice—supplementary

[(1) In this section, 'code' means a code of practice under section 60, 60A or 66.

(2) The Secretary of State may at any time revise the whole or any part of a code.

(3) A code may be made, or revised, so as to—

(a) apply only in relation to one or more specified areas,

(b) have effect only for a specified period,

(c) apply only in relation to specified offences or descriptions of offender.

(4) Before issuing a code, or any revision of a code, the Secretary of State must consult—

[(a) such persons as appear to the Secretary of State to represent the views of police and crime commissioners,

(aa) the Mayor's Office for Policing and Crime,

(ab) the Common Council of the City of London,]

(b) the Association of Chief Police Officers of England, Wales and Northern Ireland,

(c) the General Council of the Bar,

(d) the Law Society of England and Wales,

(e) the Institute of Legal Executives, and

(f) such other persons as he thinks fit.

(5) A code, or a revision of a code, does not come into operation until the Secretary of State by order so provides.

(6) The power conferred by subsection (5) is exercisable by statutory instrument.

(7) An order bringing a code into operation may not be made unless a draft of the order has been laid before Parliament and approved by a resolution of each House.]

(7A)–(7D) *****

(8) ...

(9) Persons other than police officers who are charged with the duty of investigating offences or charging offenders shall in the discharge of that duty have regard to any relevant provision of ... a code.

[(9A) Persons on whom powers are conferred by—

    (a) any designation under section 38 or 39 of the Police Reform Act 2002 (c 30) (police powers for [civilian staff]), or

    (b) any accreditation under section 41 of that Act (accreditation under community safety accreditation schemes),

shall have regard to any relevant provision of a code ... in the exercise or performance of the powers and duties conferred or imposed on them by that designation or accreditation.]

(10) A failure on the part—

    (a) of a police officer to comply with any provision of ... a code; ...

    (b) of any person other than a police officer who is charged with the duty of investigating offences or charging offenders to have regard to any relevant provision of ... a code in the discharge of the duty; [or

    (c) of a person designated under section 38 or 39 or accredited under section 41 of the Police Reform Act 2002 to have regard to any relevant provision of ... a code in the exercise or performance of the powers and duties conferred or imposed on him by that designation or accreditation,]

shall not of itself render him liable to any criminal or civil proceedings.

(11) In all criminal and civil proceedings any ... code shall be admissible in evidence; and if any provision of ... a code appears to the court or tribunal conducting the proceedings to be relevant to any question arising in the proceedings it shall be taken into account in determining that question.

[(12), (13)] *****

[**Note:** Extracts from the Codes of Practice issued under this section (as revised) are printed at the end of Part II.]

68 ...

69–72 *****

PART VIII EVIDENCE IN CRIMINAL PROCEEDINGS—GENERAL

*****

Confessions

76 Confessions

(1) In any proceedings a confession made by an accused person may be given in evidence against him in so far as it is relevant to any matter in issue in the proceedings and is not excluded by the court in pursuance of this section.

(2) If, in any proceedings where the prosecution proposes to give in evidence a confession made by an accused person, it is represented to the court that the confession was or may have been obtained—

    (a) by oppression of the person who made it; or

    (b) in consequence of anything said or done which was likely, in the circumstances existing at the time, to render unreliable any confession which might be made by him in consequence thereof,

the court shall not allow the confession to be given in evidence against him except in so far as the prosecution proves to the court beyond reasonable doubt that the confession (notwithstanding that it may be true) was not obtained as aforesaid.

(3) In any proceedings where the prosecution proposes to give in evidence a confession made by an accused person, the court may of its own motion require the prosecution, as a condition of allowing it to do so, to prove that the confession was not obtained as mentioned in subsection (2) above.

(4) The fact that a confession is wholly or partly excluded in pursuance of this section shall not affect the admissibility in evidence—

　　(a) of any facts discovered as a result of the confession; or

　　(b) where the confession is relevant as showing that the accused speaks, writes or expresses himself in a particular way, of so much of the confession as is necessary to show that he does so.

(5) Evidence that a fact to which this subsection applies was discovered as a result of a statement made by an accused person shall not be admissible unless evidence of how it was discovered is given by him or on his behalf.

(6) Subsection (5) above applies—

　　(a) to any fact discovered as a result of a confession which is wholly excluded in pursuance of this section; and

　　(b) to any fact discovered as a result of a confession which is partly so excluded, if that fact is discovered as a result of the excluded part of the confession.

(7) Nothing in Part VII of this Act shall prejudice the admissibility of a confession made by an accused person.

(8) In this section 'oppression' includes torture, inhuman or degrading treatment, and the use or threat of violence (whether or not amounting to torture).

(9) …

[76A   Confessions may be given in evidence for co-accused

(1) In any proceedings a confession made by an accused person may be given in evidence for another person charged in the same proceedings (a co-accused) in so far as it is relevant to any matter in issue in the proceedings and is not excluded by the court in pursuance of this section.

(2) If, in any proceedings where a co-accused proposes to give in evidence a confession made by an accused person, it is represented to the court that the confession was or may have been obtained—

　　(a) by oppression of the person who made it; or

　　(b) in consequence of anything said or done which was likely, in the circumstances existing at the time, to render unreliable any confession which might be made by him in consequence thereof,

the court shall not allow the confession to be given in evidence for the co-accused except in so far as it is proved to the court on the balance of probabilities that the confession (notwithstanding that it may be true) was not so obtained.

(3) Before allowing a confession made by an accused person to be given in evidence for a co-accused in any proceedings, the court may of its own motion require the fact that the confession was not obtained as mentioned in subsection (2) above to be proved in the proceedings on the balance of probabilities.

(4) The fact that a confession is wholly or partly excluded in pursuance of this section shall not affect the admissibility in evidence—

　　(a) of any facts discovered as a result of the confession; or

　　(b) where the confession is relevant as showing that the accused speaks, writes or expresses himself in a particular way, of so much of the confession as is necessary to show that he does so.]

(5)–(7) *****

77   Confessions by mentally handicapped persons

(1) Without prejudice to the general duty of the court at a trial on indictment [with a jury] to direct the jury on any matter on which it appears to the court appropriate to do so, where at such a trial—

　　(a) the case against the accused depends wholly or substantially on a confession by him; and

    (b) the court is satisfied—

        (i)   that he is mentally handicapped; and

        (ii) that the confession was not made in the presence of an independent person,

the court shall warn the jury that there is special need for caution before convicting the accused in reliance on the confession, and shall explain that the need arises because of the circumstances mentioned in paragraphs (a) and (b) above.

    (2) In any case where at the summary trial of a person for an offence it appears to the court that a warning under subsection (1) above would be required if the trial were on indictment [with a jury], the court shall treat the case as one in which there is a special need for caution before convicting the accused on his confession.

    (2A), (3) *****

Miscellaneous

78 Exclusion of unfair evidence

    (1) In any proceedings the court may refuse to allow evidence on which the prosecution proposes to rely to be given if it appears to the court that, having regard to all the circumstances, including the circumstances in which the evidence was obtained, the admission of the evidence would have such an adverse effect on the fairness of the proceedings that the court ought not to admit it.

    (2) Nothing in this section shall prejudice any rule of law requiring a court to exclude evidence.

    (3) ...

79–81 *****

PART VIII SUPPLEMENTARY

82 Part VIII—interpretation

    (1) In this Part of this Act—

  'confession' includes any statement wholly or partly adverse to the person who made it, whether made to a person in authority or not and whether made in words or otherwise;

  *****

    (2) ...

    (3) Nothing in this Part of this Act shall prejudice any power of a court to exclude evidence (whether by preventing questions from being put or otherwise) at its discretion.

83–106 ...

PART XI MISCELLANEOUS AND SUPPLEMENTARY

107, 111, 113–115 *****

108–110, 112, 116 ...

117 Power of constable to use reasonable force

Where any provision of this Act—

    (a) confers a power on a constable; and

    (b) does not provide that the power may only be exercised with the consent of some person, other than a police officer,

the officer may use reasonable force, if necessary, in the exercise of the power.

118 General interpretation

    (1) *****

(2) [Subject to subsection (2A)] a person is in police detention for the purposes of this Act if—

    (a) he has been taken to a police station after being arrested for an offence or after being arrested under section 41 of the Terrorism Act 2000]]; or

    (b) he is arrested at a police station after attending voluntarily at the station or accompanying a constable to it,

and is detained there or is detained elsewhere in the charge of a constable, except that a person who is at a court after being charged is not in police detention for those purposes.

[(2A) Where a person is in another's lawful custody by virtue of paragraph 22, 34(1) or 35(3) of Schedule 4 to the Police Reform Act 2002, he shall be treated as in police detention.]

*****

Section 9

SCHEDULE 1

SPECIAL PROCEDURE

Making of orders by circuit judge

1. If on an application made by a constable a [judge] is satisfied that one or other of the sets of access conditions is fulfilled, he may make an order under paragraph 4 below.

2. The first set of access conditions is fulfilled if—

    (a) there are reasonable grounds for believing—

        (i)   that [an indictable offence] has been committed;

        (ii) that there is material which consists of special procedure material or includes special procedure material and does not also include excluded material on premises specified in the application [, or on premises occupied or controlled by a person specified in the application (including all such premises on which there are reasonable grounds for believing that there is such material as it is reasonably practicable so to specify);];

        (iii) that the material is likely to be of substantial value (whether by itself or together with other material) to the investigation in connection with which the application is made; and

        (iv) that the material is likely to be relevant evidence;

    (b) other methods of obtaining the material—

        (i)   have been tried without success; or

        (ii) have not been tried because it appeared that they were bound to fail; and

    (c) it is in the public interest, having regard—

        (i)   to the benefit likely to accrue to the investigation if the material is obtained; and

        (ii) to the circumstances under which the person in possession of the material holds it,

that the material should be produced or that access to it should be given.

3. The second set of access conditions is fulfilled if—

    (a) there are reasonable grounds for believing that there is material which consists of or includes excluded material or special procedure material on premises specified in the application [, or on premises occupied or controlled by a person specified in the application (including all such premises on which there are reasonable grounds for believing that there is such material as it is reasonably practicable so to specify)];

    (b) but for section 9(2) above a search of [such premises] for that material could have been authorised by the issue of a warrant to a constable under an enactment other than this Schedule; and

    (c) the issue of such a warrant would have been appropriate.

4. An order under this paragraph is an order that the person who appears to the [judge] to be in possession of the material to which the application relates shall—

    [(a) produce it to a constable for him to take away; or]

(b)   give a constable access to it,

not later than the end of the period of seven days from the date of the order or the end of such longer period as the order may specify.

5. Where the material consists of information [stored in any electronic form]—

(a) an order under paragraph 4(a) above shall have effect as an order to produce the material in a form in which it can be taken away and in which it is visible and legible [or from which it can readily be produced in a visible and legible form]; and

(b) an order under paragraph 4(b) above shall have effect as an order to give a constable access to the material in a form in which it is visible and legible.

6. For the purposes of sections 21 and 22 above material produced in pursuance of an order under paragraph 4(a) above shall be treated as if it were material seized by a constable.

Notices of applications for orders

7. An application for an order under paragraph 4 above shall be made inter partes.

8. Notice of an application for such an order may be served on a person either by delivering it to him or by leaving it at his proper address or by sending it by post to him in a registered letter or by the recorded delivery service.

9.–11. *****

Issue of warrants by [a judge]

12. If on an application made by a constable a [judge]—

(a) is satisfied—

(i)   that either set of access conditions is fulfilled; and

(ii) that any of the further conditions set out in paragraph 14 below is also fulfilled [in relation to each set of premises specified in the application]; or

(b) is satisfied—

(i)   that the second set of access conditions is fulfilled; and

(ii) that an order under paragraph 4 above relating to the material has not been complied with,

he may issue a warrant authorising a constable to enter and search the premises [or (as the case may be) all premises occupied or controlled by the person referred to in paragraph 2(a)(ii) or 3(a), including such sets of premises as are specified in the application (an 'all premises warrant')].

12A *****

13. A constable may seize and retain anything for which a search has been authorised under paragraph 12 above.

14. The further conditions mentioned in paragraph 12(a)(ii) above are—

(a) that it is not practicable to communicate with any person entitled to grant entry to the premises . . . ;

(b) that it is practicable to communicate with a person entitled to grant entry to the premises but it is not practicable to communicate with any person entitled to grant access to the material;

(c) that the material contains information which—

(i)   is subject to a restriction or obligation such as is mentioned in section 11(2)(b) above; and

(ii) is likely to be disclosed in breach of it if a warrant is not issued;

(d) that service of notice of an application for an order under paragraph 4 above may seriously prejudice the investigation.

15.—(1) If a person fails to comply with an order under paragraph 4 above, a [judge] may deal with him as if he had committed a contempt of the Crown Court.

(2) Any enactment relating to contempt of the Crown Court shall have effect in relation to such a failure as if it were such a contempt.

16.–17. *****

*****

Prosecution of Offences Act 1985

(1985, c. 23)

An Act to provide for the establishment of a Crown Prosecution Service for England and Wales; to make provision as to costs in criminal cases; to provide for the imposition of time limits in relation to preliminary stages of criminal proceedings; to amend section 42 of the Supreme Court Act 1981 and section 3 of the Children and Young Persons Act 1969; to make provision with respect to consents to prosecutions; to repeal section 9 of the Perjury Act 1911; and for connected purposes.   [23rd May 1985]

Territorial extent: England and Wales

PART I THE CROWN PROSECUTION SERVICE

Constitution and functions of Service

1   The Crown Prosecution Service

(1) There shall be a prosecuting service for England and Wales (to be known as the 'Crown Prosecution Service') consisting of—

   (a) the Director of Public Prosecutions, who shall be head of the Service;

   (b) the Chief Crown Prosecutors, designated under subsection (4) below, each of whom shall be the member of the Service responsible to the Director for supervising the operation of the service in his area; and

   (c) the other staff appointed by the Director under this section.

(2) The Director shall appoint such staff for the Service as, with the approval of the Treasury as to numbers, remuneration and other terms and conditions of service, he considers necessary for the discharge of his functions.

(3) The Director may designate any member of the Service [who has a general qualification (within the meaning of section 71 of the Courts and Legal Services Act 1990)] for the purposes of this subsection, and any person so designated shall be known as a Crown Prosecutor.

(4) The Director shall divide England and Wales into areas and, for each of those areas, designate a Crown Prosecutor for the purposes of this subsection and any person so designated shall be known as a Chief Crown Prosecutor.

(5) The Director may, from time to time, vary the division of England and Wales made for the purpose of subsection (4) above.

(6) Without prejudice to any functions which may have been assigned to him in his capacity as a member of the Service, every Crown Prosecutor shall have all the powers of the Director as to the institution and conduct of proceedings but shall exercise those powers under the direction of the Director.

(7) There any enactment (whenever passed)—

   (a) prevents any step from being taken without the consent of the Director or without his consent or the consent of another; or

   (b) requires any step to be taken by or in relation to the Director; any consent given by or, as the case may be, step taken by or in relation to, a Crown Prosecutor shall be treated, for the purposes of that enactment, as given by or, as the case may be, taken by or in relation to the Director.

2   The Director of Public Prosecutions

(1) The Director of Public Prosecutions shall be appointed by the Attorney General.

(2) The Director must be a [person who has a 10 year general qualification, within the meaning of section 71 of the Courts and Legal Services Act 1990.]

   (3) *****

3   Functions of the Director

(1) The Director shall discharge his functions under this or any other enactment under the superintendence of the Attorney General.

(2) It shall be the duty of the Director [, subject to any provisions contained in the Criminal Justice Act 1987]—

    (a)   to take over the conduct of all criminal proceedings, other than specified proceedings, instituted on behalf of a police force (whether by a member of that force or by any other person);

    [(aa) to take over the conduct of any criminal proceedings instituted by an immigration officer (as defined for the purposes of the Immigration Act 1971) acting in his capacity as such an officer;]

    (b)   to institute and have the conduct of criminal proceedings in any case where it appears to him that—

        (i) the importance or difficulty of the case makes it appropriate that proceedings should be instituted by him; or

        (ii) it is otherwise appropriate for proceedings to be instituted by him;

    [(ba) to institute and have the conduct of any criminal proceedings in any case where the proceedings relate to the subject matter of a report a copy of which has been sent to him under paragraph 23 or 24 of Schedule 3 to the Police Reform Act 2002 (reports or investigations into conduct of persons serving with the police);]

    (c)   to take over the conduct of all binding over proceedings instituted on behalf of a police force (whether by a member of that force or by any other person);

    *****

    (g)   to discharge such other functions as may from time to time be assigned to him by the Attorney General in pursuance of this paragraph.

(2A), (3), (4) *****

4, 5   *****

6   Prosecutions instituted and conducted otherwise than by the Service

(1) Subject to subsection (2) below, nothing in this Part shall preclude any person from instituting any criminal proceedings or conducting any criminal proceedings to which the Director's duty to take over the conduct of proceedings does not apply.

(2) Where criminal proceedings are instituted in circumstances in which the Director is not under a duty to take over their conduct, he may nevertheless do so at any stage.

7–9   *****

Guidelines

10   Guidelines for Crown Prosecutors

(1) The Director shall issue a Code for Crown Prosecutors giving guidance on general principles to be applied by them—

    (a) in determining, in any case—

        (i)   whether proceedings for an offence should be instituted or, where proceedings have been instituted, whether they should be discontinued; or

        (ii) what charges should be preferred; and

    (b) in considering, in any case, representations to be made by them to any magistrates' court about the mode of trial suitable for that case.

(2) The Director may from time to time make alterations in the Code.

(3) The provisions of the Code shall be set out in the Director's report under section 9 of this Act for the year in which the Code is issued; and any alteration in the Code shall be set out in his report under that section for the year in which the alteration is made.
*****

Public Order Act 1986

(1986, c. 64)

An Act to abolish the common law offences of riot, rout, unlawful assembly and affray and certain statu-tory offences relating to public order; to create new offences relating to public order; to control public processions and assemblies; to control the stirring up of racial hatred; to provide for the exclusion of certain offenders from sporting events; to create a new offence relating to the contamination of or inter-ference with goods; to confer power to direct certain trespassers to leave land; to amend section 7 of the Conspiracy and Protection of Property Act 1875, section 1 of the Prevention of Crime Act 1953, Part V of the Criminal Justice (Scotland) Act 1980 and the Sporting Events (Control of Alcohol etc.) Act 1985; to repeal certain obsolete or unnecessary enactments; and for connected purposes. [7th November 1986]

Territorial extent: England and Wales (ss. 1–9, 13, 29A–N, 39, 40(4)); England and Wales, Scotland (remainder)

PART I NEW OFFENCES

1 Riot

(1) Where 12 or more persons who are present together use or threaten unlawful violence for a common purpose and the conduct of them (taken together) is such as would cause a person of reason-able firmness present at the scene to fear for his personal safety, each of the persons using unlawful violence for the common purpose is guilty of riot.

(2) It is immaterial whether or not the 12 or more use or threaten unlawful violence simultaneously.

(3) The common purpose may be inferred from conduct.

(4) No person of reasonable firmness need actually be, or be likely to be, present at the scene.

(5) Riot may be committed in private as well as in public places.

(6) A person guilty of riot is liable on conviction on indictment to imprisonment for a term not exceeding ten years or a fine or both.

2 Violent disorder

(1) Where 3 or more persons who are present together use or threaten unlawful violence and the conduct of them (taken together) is such as would cause a person of reasonable firmness present at the scene to fear for his personal safety, each of the persons using or threatening unlawful violence is guilty of violent disorder.

(2) It is immaterial whether or not the 3 or more use or threaten unlawful violence simultaneously.

(3) No person of reasonable firmness need actually be, or be likely to be, present at the scene.

(4) Violent disorder may be committed in private as well as in public places.

(5) A person guilty of violent disorder is liable on conviction on indictment to imprisonment for a term not exceeding 5 years or a fine or both, or on summary conviction to imprisonment for a term not exceeding 6 months or a fine not exceeding the statutory maximum or both.

3 Affray

(1) A person is guilty of affray if he uses or threatens unlawful violence towards another and his conduct is such as would cause a person of reasonable firmness present at the scene to fear for his personal safety.

(2) Where 2 or more persons use or threaten the unlawful violence, it is the conduct of them taken together that must be considered for the purposes of subsection (1).

(3) For the purposes of this section a threat cannot be made by the use of words alone.

(4) No person of reasonable firmness need actually be, or be likely to be, present at the scene.

(5) Affray may be committed in private as well as in public places.

(6) ...

(7) A person guilty of affray is liable on conviction on indictment to imprisonment for a term not exceeding 3 years or a fine or both, or on summary conviction to imprisonment for a term not exceeding 6 months or a fine not exceeding the statutory maximum or both.

4 Fear or provocation of violence

(1) A person is guilty of an offence if he—

(a) uses towards another person threatening, abusive or insulting words or behaviour, or

(b) distributes or displays to another person any writing, sign or other visible representation which is threatening, abusive or insulting,

with intent to cause that person to believe that immediate unlawful violence will be used against him or another by any person, or to provoke the immediate use of unlawful violence by that person or another, or whereby that person is likely to believe that such violence will be used or it is likely that such violence will be provoked.

(2) An offence under this section may be committed in a public or a private place, except that no offence is committed where the words or behaviour are used, or the writing, sign or other visible representation is distributed or displayed, by a person inside a dwelling and the other person is also inside that or another dwelling.

(3) ...

(4) A person guilty of an offence under this section is liable on summary conviction to imprisonment for a term not exceeding 6 months or a fine not exceeding level 5 on the standard scale or both.

[4A Intentional harassment, alarm or distress

(1) A person is guilty of an offence if, with intent to cause a person harassment, alarm or distress, he—

(a) uses threatening, abusive or insulting words or behaviour, or disorderly behaviour, or

(b) displays any writing, sign or other visible representation which is threatening, abusive or insulting,

thereby causing that or another person harassment, alarm or distress.

(2) An offence under this section may be committed in a public or a private place, except that no offence is committed where the words or behaviour are used, or the writing, sign or other visible representation is displayed, by a person inside a dwelling and the person who is harassed, alarmed or distressed is also inside that or another dwelling.

(3) It is a defence for the accused to prove—

(a) that he was inside a dwelling and had no reason to believe that the words or behaviour used, or the writing, sign or other visible representation displayed, would be heard or seen by a person outside that or any other dwelling, or

(b) that his conduct was reasonable.

(4) ...

(5) A person guilty of an offence under this section is liable on summary conviction to imprisonment for a term not exceeding 6 months or a fine not exceeding level 5 on the standard scale or both.]

5 Harassment, alarm or distress

(1) A person is guilty of an offence if he—

(a) uses threatening, abusive or insulting words or behaviour, or disorderly behaviour, or

(b) displays any writing, sign or other visible representation which is threatening, abusive or insulting,

within the hearing or sight of a person likely to be caused harassment, alarm or distress thereby.

(2) An offence under this section may be committed in a public or a private place, except that no offence is committed where the words or behaviour are used, or the writing, sign or other visible

representation is displayed, by a person inside a dwelling and the other person is also inside that or another dwelling.

(3) It is a defence for the accused to prove—

(a) that he had no reason to believe that there was any person within hearing or sight who was likely to be caused harassment, alarm or distress, or

(b) that he was inside a dwelling and had no reason to believe that the words or behaviour used, or the writing, sign or other visible representation displayed, would be heard or seen by a person outside that or any other dwelling, or

(c) that his conduct was reasonable.

(4), (5) ...

(6) A person guilty of an offence under this section is liable on summary conviction to a fine not exceeding level 3 on the standard scale.

6 Mental element: miscellaneous

(1) A person is guilty of riot only if he intends to use violence or is aware that his conduct may be violent.

(2) A person is guilty of violent disorder or affray only if he intends to use or threaten violence or is aware that his conduct may be violent or threaten violence.

(3) A person is guilty of an offence under section 4 only if he intends his words or behaviour, or the writing, sign or other visible representation, to be threatening, abusive or insulting, or is aware that it may be threatening, abusive or insulting.

(4) A person is guilty of an offence under section 5 only if he intends his words or behaviour, or the writing, sign or other visible representation, to be threatening, abusive or insulting, or is aware that it may be threatening, abusive or insulting or (as the case may be) he intends his behaviour to be or is aware that it may be disorderly.

(5) For the purposes of this section a person whose awareness is impaired by intoxication shall be taken to be aware of that of which he would be aware if not intoxicated, unless he shows either that his intoxication was not self-induced or that it was caused solely by the taking or administration of a substance in the course of medical treatment.

(6) In subsection (5) 'intoxication' means any intoxication, whether caused by drink, drugs or other means, or by a combination of means.

(7) Subsections (1) and (2) do not affect the determination for the purposes of riot or violent disorder of the number of persons who use or threaten violence.

7 Procedure: miscellaneous

(1) No prosecution for an offence of riot or incitement to riot may be instituted except by or with the consent of the Director of Public Prosecutions.

(2)–(4) *****

8 Interpretation

In this Part—

'dwelling' means any structure or part of a structure occupied as a person's home or as other living accommodation (whether the occupation is separate or shared with others) but does not include any part not so occupied, and for this purpose 'structure' includes a tent, caravan, vehicle, vessel or other temporary or movable structure;

'violence' means any violent conduct, so that—

(a) except in the context of affray, it includes violent conduct towards property as well as violent conduct towards persons, and

(b) it is not restricted to conduct causing or intended to cause injury or damage but includes any other violent conduct (for example, throwing at or towards a person a missile of a kind capable of causing injury which does not hit or falls short).

9 Offences abolished

(1) The Common Law offences of riot, rout, unlawful assembly and affray are abolished.

(2) ...

10   *****

PART II   PROCESSIONS AND ASSEMBLIES

11 Advance notice of public processions

(1) Written notice shall be given in accordance with this section of any proposal to hold a public procession intended—

    (a) to demonstrate support for or opposition to the views or actions of any person or body of persons,

    (b) to publicise a cause or campaign, or

    (c) to mark or commemorate an event, unless it is not reasonably practicable to give any advance notice of the procession.

(2) Subsection (1) does not apply where the procession is one commonly or customarily held in the police area (or areas) in which it is proposed to be held or is a funeral procession organised by a funeral director acting in the normal course of his business.

(3) The notice must specify the date when it is intended to hold the procession, the time when it is intended to start it, its proposed route, and the name and address of the person (or of one of the persons) proposing to organise it.

(4) Notice must be delivered to a police station—

    (a) in the police area in which it is proposed the procession will start, or

    (b) where it is proposed the procession will start in Scotland and cross into England, in the first police area in England on the proposed route.

(5), (6) *****

(7) Where a public procession is held, each of the persons organising it is guilty of an offence if—

    (a) the requirements of this section as to notice have not been satisfied, or

    (b) the date when it is held, the time when it starts, or its route, differs from the date, time or route specified in the notice.

(8) It is a defence for the accused to prove that he did not know of, and neither suspected nor had reason to suspect, the failure to satisfy the requirements or (as the case may be) the difference of date, time or route.

(9) To the extent that an alleged offence turns on a difference of date, time or route, it is a defence for the accused to prove that the difference arose from circumstances beyond his control or from something done with the agreement of a police officer or by his direction.

(10) A person guilty of an offence under subsection (7) is liable on summary conviction to a fine not exceeding level 3 on the standard scale.

12 Imposing conditions on public processions

(1) If the senior police officer, having regard to the time or place at which and the circumstances in which any public procession is being held or is intended to be held and to its route or proposed route, reasonably believes that—

    (a) it may result in serious public disorder, serious damage to property or serious disruption to the life of the community, or

    (b) the purpose of the persons organising it is the intimidation of others with a view to compelling them not to do an act they have a right to do, or to do an act they have a right not to do,

he may give directions imposing on the persons organising or taking part in the procession such conditions as appear to him necessary to prevent such disorder, damage, disruption or intimidation, including conditions as to the route of the procession or prohibiting it from entering any public place specified in the directions.

(2) In subsection (1) 'the senior police officer' means—

(a) in relation to a procession being held, or to a procession intended to be held in a case where persons are assembling with a view to taking part in it, the most senior in rank of the police officers present at the scene, and

(b) in relation to a procession intended to be held in a case where paragraph (a) does not apply, the chief officer of police.

(3) A direction given by a chief officer of police by virtue of subsection (2)(b) shall be given in writing.

(4) A person who organises a public procession and knowingly fails to comply with a condition imposed under this section is guilty of an offence, but it is a defence for him to prove that the failure arose from circumstances beyond his control.

(5) A person who takes part in a public procession and knowingly fails to comply with a condition imposed under this section is guilty of an offence, but it is a defence for him to prove that the failure arose from circumstances beyond his control.

(6) A person who incites another to commit an offence under subsection (5) is guilty of an offence.

(7) ...

(8) A person guilty of an offence under subsection (4) is liable on summary conviction to imprisonment for a term not exceeding 3 months or a fine not exceeding level 4 on the standard scale or both...

(9) A person guilty of an offence under subsection (5) is liable on summary conviction to a fine not exceeding level 3 on the standard scale.

(10) A person guilty of an offence under subsection (6) is liable on summary conviction to imprisonment for a term not exceeding 3 months or a fine not exceeding level 4 on the standard scale or both...

(11) In Scotland this section applies only in relation to a procession being held, and to a procession intended to be held in a case where persons are assembling with a view to taking part in it.

[**Note:** The maximum sentence of 3 months' imprisonment for certain offences under this section and ss. 13 and 14 will be increased to 51 weeks' imprisonment when the Criminal Justice Act 2003, Sch. 26, para. 37, is brought into force.]

13   Prohibiting public processions

(1) If at any time the chief officer of police reasonably believes that, because of particular circumstances existing in any district or part of a district, the powers under section 12 will not be sufficient to prevent the holding of public processions in that district or part from resulting in serious public disorder, he shall apply to the council of the district for an order prohibiting for such period not exceeding 3 months as may be specified in the application the holding of all public processions (or of any class of public procession so specified) in the district or part concerned.

(2) On receiving such an application, a council may with the consent of the Secretary of State make an order either in the terms of the application or with such modifications as may be approved by the Secretary of State.

(3) Subsection (1) does not apply in the City of London or the metropolitan police district.

(4) If at any time the Commissioner of Police for the City of London or the Commissioner of Police of the Metropolis reasonably believes that, because of particular circumstances existing in his police area or part of it, the powers under section 12 will not be sufficient to prevent the holding of public processions in that area or part from resulting in serious public disorder, he may with the consent of the Secretary of State make an order prohibiting for such period not exceeding 3 months as may be specified in the order the holding of all public processions (or of any class of public procession so specified) in the area or part concerned.

(5) An order made under this section may be revoked or varied by a subsequent order made in the same way, that is, in accordance with subsections (1) and (2) or subsection (4), as the case may be.

(6) An order under this section shall, if not made in writing, be recorded in writing as soon as practicable after being made.

(7) A person who organises a public procession the holding of which he knows is prohibited by virtue of an order under this section is guilty of an offence.

(8) A person who takes part in a public procession the holding of which he knows is prohibited by virtue of an order under this section is guilty of an offence.

(9) A person who incites another to commit an offence under subsection (8) is guilty of an offence.

(10) ...

(11) A person guilty of an offence under subsection (7) is liable on summary conviction to imprisonment for a term not exceeding 3 months or a fine not exceeding level 4 on the standard scale or both.

(12) A person guilty of an offence under subsection (8) is liable on summary conviction to a fine not exceeding level 3 on the standard scale.

(13) A person guilty of an offence under subsection (9) is liable on summary conviction to imprisonment for a term not exceeding 3 months or a fine not exceeding level 4 on the standard scale or both...

14   Imposing conditions on public assemblies

(1) If the senior police officer, having regard to the time or place at which and the circumstances in which any public assembly is being held or is intended to be held, reasonably believes that—

(a) it may result in serious public disorder, serious damage to property or serious disruption to the life of the community, or

(b) the purpose of the persons organising it is the intimidation of others with a view to compelling them not to do an act they have a right to do, or to do an act they have a right not to do,

he may give directions imposing on the persons organising or taking part in the assembly such conditions as to the place at which the assembly may be (or continue to be) held, its maximum duration, or the maximum number of persons who may constitute it, as appear to him necessary to prevent such disorder, damage, disruption or intimidation.

(2) An subsection (1) 'the senior police officer' means—

(a) in relation to an assembly being held, the most senior in rank of the police officers present at the scene, and

(b) in relation to an assembly intended to be held, the chief officer of police.

(3) A direction given by a chief officer of police by virtue of subsection (2)(b) shall be given in writing.

(4) A person who organises a public assembly and knowingly fails to comply with a condition imposed under this section is guilty of an offence, but it is a defence for him to prove that the failure arose from circumstances beyond his control.

(5) A person who takes part in a public assembly and knowingly fails to comply with a condition imposed under this section is guilty of an offence, but it is a defence for him to prove that the failure arose from circumstances beyond his control.

(6) A person who incites another to commit an offence under subsection (5) is guilty of an offence.

(7) ...

(8) A person guilty of an offence under subsection (4) is liable on summary conviction to imprisonment for a term not exceeding 3 months or a fine not exceeding level 4 on the standard scale or both.

(9) A person guilty of an offence under subsection (5) is liable on summary conviction to a fine not exceeding level 3 on the standard scale.

(10) A person guilty of an offence under subsection (6) is liable on summary conviction to imprisonment for a term not exceeding 3 months or a fine not exceeding level 4 on the standard scale or both, ...

[14A   Prohibiting trespassory assemblies

(1) If at any time the chief officer of police reasonably believes that an assembly is intended to be held in any district at a place on land to which the public has no right of access or only a limited right of access and that the assembly—

(a) is likely to be held without the permission of the occupier of the land or to conduct itself in such a way as to exceed the limits of any permission of his or the limits of the public's right of access, and

(b) may result—

  (i)   in serious disruption to the life of the community, or

  (ii) where the land, or a building or monument on it, is of historical, architectural, archaeological or scientific importance, in significant damage to the land, building or monument,

he may apply to the council of the district for an order prohibiting for a specified period the holding of all trespassory assemblies in the district or a part of it, as specified.

(2) On receiving such an application, a council may—

(a) in England and Wales, with the consent of the Secretary of State make an order either in the terms of the application or with such modifications as may be approved by the Secretary of State; or

(b) in Scotland, make an order in the terms of the application.

(3), (4) *****

(5) An order prohibiting the holding of trespassory assemblies operates to prohibit any assembly which—

(a) is held on land to which the public has no right of access or only a limited right of access, and

(b) takes place in the prohibited circumstances, that is to say, without the permission of the occupier of the land or so as to exceed the limits of any permission of his or the limits of the public as right of access.

(6) No order under this section shall prohibit the holding of assemblies for a period exceeding 4 days or in an area exceeding an area represented by a circle with a radius of 5 miles from a specified centre.

(7) An order made under this section may be revoked or varied by a subsequent order made in the same way, that is, in accordance with subsection (1) and (2) or subsection (4), as the case may be.

(8) Any order under this section shall, if not made in writing, be recorded in writing as soon as practicable after being made.

(9) In this section and sections 14B and 14C—

'assembly' means an assembly of 20 or more persons;

'land', means land in the open air;

*****

(9A), (10), (11) *****

14B   Offences in connection with trespassory assemblies and arrest therefor

(1) A person who organises an assembly the holding of which he knows is prohibited by an order under section 14A is guilty of an offence.

(2) A person who takes part in an assembly which he knows is prohibited by an order under section 14A is guilty of an offence.

(3) In England and Wales, a person who incites another to commit an offence under subsection (2) is guilty of an offence.

(4) . . .

(5)–(8) *****

14C   Stopping persons from proceeding to trespassory assemblies

(1) If a constable in uniform reasonably believes that a person is on his way to an assembly within the area to which an order under section 14A applies which the constable reasonably believes is likely to be an assembly which is prohibited by that order, he may, subject to subsection (2) below—

(a) stop that person, and

(b) direct him not to proceed in the direction of the assembly.

(2) The power conferred by subsection (1) may only be exercised within the area to which the order applies.

(3) A person who fails to comply with a direction under subsection (1) which he knows has been given to him is guilty of an offence.

(4) ...

(5) A person guilty of an offence under subsection (3) is liable on summary conviction to a fine not exceeding level 3 on the standard scale.]

15   *****

16   Interpretation

In this Part—
    *****

'public assembly' means an assembly of [2] or more persons in a public place which is wholly or partly open to the air;

'public place' means—

(a) any highway, or in Scotland any road within the meaning of the Roads (Scotland) Act 1984, and

(b) any place to which at the material time the public or any section of the public has access, on payment or otherwise, as of right or by virtue of express or implied permission;

'public procession' means a procession in a public place.

[**Note:** The amendment to the definition of 'public assembly' applies only to England and Wales; in Scotland the minimum number of persons remains 20: see the Anti-social Behaviour Act 2003, s. 57.]

PART III RACIAL HATRED

Meaning of 'racial hatred'

17   Meaning of 'racial hatred'

In this Part 'racial hatred' means hatred against a group of persons . . . defined by reference to colour, race, nationality (including citizenship) or ethnic or national origins.

Acts intended or likely to stir up racial hatred

18   Use of words or behaviour or display of written material

(1) A person who uses threatening, abusive or insulting words or behaviour, or displays any written material which is threatening, abusive or insulting, is guilty of an offence if—

(a) he intends thereby to stir up racial hatred, or

(b) having regard to all the circumstances racial hatred is likely to be stirred up thereby.

(2) An offence under this section may be committed in a public or a private place, except that no offence is committed where the words or behaviour are used, or the written material is displayed, by a person inside a dwelling and are not heard or seen except by other persons in that or another dwelling.

(3) ...

(4) In proceedings for an offence under this section it is a defence for the accused to prove that he was inside a dwelling and had no reason to believe that the words or behaviour used, or the written material displayed, would be heard or seen by a person outside that or any other dwelling.

(5) A person who is not shown to have intended to stir up racial hatred is not guilty of an offence under this section if he did not intend his words or behaviour, or the written material, to be, and was not aware that it might be, threatening, abusive or insulting.

(6) This section does not apply to words or behaviour used, or written material displayed, solely for the purpose of being [included in a programme service].

19 Publishing or distributing written material

(1) A person who publishes or distributes written material which is threatening, abusive or insulting is guilty of an offence if—

(a) he intends thereby to stir up racial hatred, or

(b) having regard to all the circumstances racial hatred is likely to be stirred up thereby.

(2) In proceedings for an offence under this section it is a defence for an accused who is not shown to have intended to stir up racial hatred to prove that he was not aware of the content of the material and did not suspect, and had no reason to suspect, that it was threatening, abusive or insulting.

(3) References in this Part to the publication or distribution of written material are to its publication or distribution to the public or a section of the public.

20 Public performance of play

(1) If a public performance of a play is given which involves the use of threatening, abusive or insulting words or behaviour, any person who presents or directs the performance is guilty of an offence if—

(a) he intends thereby to stir up racial hatred, or

(b) having regard to all the circumstances (and, in particular, taking the performance as a whole) racial hatred is likely to be stirred up thereby.

(2)–(6) *****

21, 22 *****

Racially inflammatory material

23 Possession of racially inflammatory material

(1) A person who has in his possession written material which is threatening, abusive or insulting, or a recording of visual images or sounds which are threatening, abusive or insulting, with a view to—

(a) in the case of written material, its being displayed, published, distributed, [or included in a programme service], whether by himself or another, or

(b) in the case of a recording, its being distributed, shown, played, [or included in a programme service], whether by himself or another,

is guilty of an offence if he intends racial hatred to be stirred up thereby or, having regard to all the circumstances, racial hatred is likely to be stirred up thereby.

(2) For this purpose regard shall be had to such display, publication, distribution, showing, playing, [or inclusion in a programme service] as he has, or it may reasonably be inferred that he has, in view.

(3) In proceedings for an offence under this section it is a defence for an accused who is not shown to have intended to stir up racial hatred to prove that he was not aware of the content of the written material or recording and did not suspect, and had no reason to suspect, that it was threatening, abusive or insulting.

(4) ...

24, 25 *****

Supplementary provisions

26 Savings for reports of parliamentary or judicial proceedings

(1) Nothing in this Part applies to a fair and accurate report of proceedings in Parliament [or in the Scottish Parliament] [or in the National Assembly for Wales].

(2) Nothing in this Part applies to a fair and accurate report of proceedings publicly heard before a court or tribunal exercising judicial authority where the report is published contemporaneously with the proceedings or, if it is not reasonably practicable or would be unlawful to publish a report of them contemporaneously, as soon as publication is reasonably practicable and lawful.

27 Procedure and punishment

(1) No proceedings for an offence under this Part may be instituted in England and Wales except by or with the consent of the Attorney General.

(2) For the purposes of the rules in England and Wales against charging more than one offence in the same count or information, each of sections 18 to 23 creates one offence.

(3) A person guilty of an offence under this Part is liable—

    (a) on conviction on indictment to imprisonment for a term not exceeding [seven] years or a fine or both;

    (b) on summary conviction to imprisonment for a term not exceeding six months or a fine not exceeding the statutory maximum or both.

28, 29 *****

[PART IIIA HATRED AGAINST PERSONS ON RELIGIOUS GROUNDS [OR GROUNDS OF SEXUAL ORIENTATION]]

Meaning of 'religious hatred' [and 'hatred on the grounds of sexual orientation']

[29A Meaning of 'religious hatred'

In this Part 'religious hatred' means hatred against a group of persons defined by reference to religious belief or lack of religious belief.

[29AB Meaning of 'hatred on the grounds of sexual orientation']

[In this Part 'hatred on the grounds of sexual orientation' means hatred against a group of persons defined by reference to sexual orientation (whether towards persons of the same sex, the opposite sex or both).]

Acts intended to stir up religious hatred [or hatred on the grounds of sexual orientation]

29B Use of words or behaviour or display of written material

(1) A person who uses threatening words or behaviour, or displays any written material which is threatening, is guilty of an offence if he intends thereby to stir up religious hatred [or hatred on the grounds of sexual orientation].

(2) An offence under this section may be committed in a public or a private place, except that no offence is committed where the words or behaviour are used, or the written material is displayed, by a person inside a dwelling and are not heard or seen except by other persons in that or another dwelling.

(3) ...

(4) In proceedings for an offence under this section it is a defence for the accused to prove that he was inside a dwelling and had no reason to believe that the words or behaviour used, or the written material displayed, would be heard or seen by a person outside that or any other dwelling.

(5) This section does not apply to words or behaviour used, or written material displayed, solely for the purpose of being included in a programme service.

29C Publishing or distributing written material

(1) A person who publishes or distributes written material which is threatening is guilty of an offence if he intends thereby to stir up religious hatred [or hatred on the grounds of sexual orientation].

(2) References in this Part to the publication or distribution of written material are to its publication or distribution to the public or a section of the public.

29D   Public performance of play

(1) If a public performance of a play is given which involves the use of threatening words or behaviour, any person who presents or directs the performance is guilty of an offence if he intends thereby to stir up religious hatred [or hatred on the grounds of sexual orientation].

(2) This section does not apply to a performance given solely or primarily for one or more of the following purposes—

(a) rehearsal,

(b) making a recording of the performance, or

(c) enabling the performance to be included in a programme service;

but if it is proved that the performance was attended by persons other than those directly connected with the giving of the performance or the doing in relation to it of the things mentioned in paragraph (b) or (c), the performance shall, unless the contrary is shown, be taken not to have been given solely or primarily for the purpose mentioned above.

(3) For the purposes of this section—

(a) a person shall not be treated as presenting a performance of a play by reason only of his taking part in it as a performer,

(b) a person taking part as a performer in a performance directed by another shall be treated as a person who directed the performance if without reasonable excuse he performs otherwise than in accordance with that person's direction, and

(c) a person shall be taken to have directed a performance of a play given under his direction notwithstanding that he was not present during the performance;

and a person shall not be treated as aiding or abetting the commission of an offence under this section by reason only of his taking part in a performance as a performer.

(4), (5) *****

29E   Distributing, showing or playing a recording

(1) A person who distributes, or shows or plays, a recording of visual images or sounds which are threatening is guilty of an offence if he intends thereby to stir up religious hatred [or hatred on the grounds of sexual orientation].

(2) In this Part 'recording' means any record from which visual images or sounds may, by any means, be reproduced; and references to the distribution, showing or playing of a recording are to its distribution, showing or playing to the public or a section of the public.

(3) This section does not apply to the showing or playing of a recording solely for the purpose of enabling the recording to be included in a programme service.

29F   Broadcasting or including programme in programme service

(1) If a programme involving threatening visual images or sounds is included in a programme service, each of the persons mentioned in subsection (2) is guilty of an offence if he intends thereby to stir up religious hatred [or hatred on the grounds of sexual orientation].

(2) The persons are—

(a) the person providing the programme service,

(b) any person by whom the programme is produced or directed, and

(c) any person by whom offending words or behaviour are used.

Inflammatory material

29G   Possession of inflammatory material

(1) A person who has in his possession written material which is threatening, or a recording of visual images or sounds which are threatening, with a view to—

(a) in the case of written material, its being displayed, published, distributed, or included in a programme service whether by himself or another, or

(b) in the case of a recording, its being distributed, shown, played, or included in a programme service, whether by himself or another,

is guilty of an offence if he intends [thereby to stir up religious hatred or hatred on the grounds of sexual orientation].

(2) For this purpose regard shall be had to such display, publication, distribution, showing, playing, or inclusion in a programme service as he has, or it may be reasonably be inferred that he has, in view.

29H, 29I *****

29J Protection of freedom of expression
Nothing in this Part shall be read or given effect in a way which prohibits or restricts discussion, criticism or expressions of antipathy, dislike, ridicule, insult or abuse of particular religions or the beliefs or practices of their adherents, or of any other belief system or the beliefs or practices of its adherents, or proselytising or urging adherents of a different religion or belief system to cease practising their religion or belief system.

[29JA Protection of freedom of expression (sexual orientation)]
[In this Part, for the avoidance of doubt, the discussion or criticism of sexual conduct or practices or the urging of persons to refrain from or modify such conduct or practices shall not be taken of itself to be threatening or intended to stir up hatred.]

Supplementary provisions

29K Savings for reports of parliamentary or judicial proceedings
(1) Nothing in this Part applies to a fair and accurate report of proceedings in Parliament or in the Scottish Parliament [, in the Scottish Parliament or in the National Assembly for Wales].

(2) Nothing in this Part applies to a fair and accurate report of proceedings publicly heard before a court or tribunal exercising judicial authority where the report is published contemporaneously with the proceedings or, if it is not reasonably practicable or would be unlawful to publish a report of them contemporaneously, as soon as publication is reasonably practicable and lawful.

29L Procedure and punishment
(1) No proceedings for an offence under this Part may be instituted . . . except by or with the consent of the Attorney General.

(2)–(4) *****

29M Offences by corporations
(1) Where a body corporate is guilty of an offence under this Part and it is shown that the offence was committed with the consent or connivance of a director, manager, secretary or other similar officer of the body, or a person purporting to act in any such capacity, he as well as the body corporate is guilty of the offence and liable to be proceeded against and punished accordingly.

(2) Where the affairs of a body corporate are managed by its members, subsection (1) applies in relation to the acts and defaults of a member in connection with his functions of management as it applies to a director.

29N Interpretation
In this Part—

'distribute', and related expressions, shall be construed in accordance with section 29C(2) (written material) and section 29E(2) (recordings);

'dwelling' means any structure or part of a structure occupied as a person's home or other living accommodation (whether the occupation is separate or shared with others) but does not include any part not so occupied, and for this purpose 'structure' includes a tent, caravan, vehicle, vessel or other temporary or movable structure;

['hatred on the grounds of sexual orientation' has the meaning given by section 29AB;]

'programme' means any item which [is included in a programme service];

['programme service' has the same meaning as in the Broadcasting Act 1990];

'publish', and related expressions, in relation to written material, shall be construed in accordance with section 29C(2);

'religious hatred' has the meaning given by section 29A;

'recording' has the meaning given by section 29E(2), and 'play' and 'show', and related expressions, in relation to a recording, shall be construed in accordance with that provision;

'written material' includes any sign or other visible representation.]

30–34, 36, 39 ...

35, 37, 38 *****

40   Amendments repeals and savings

(1)–(3) *****

(4) Nothing in this Act affects the common law powers in England and Wales to deal with or prevent a breach of the peace.

(5) As respects Scotland, nothing in this Act affects any power of a constable under any rule of law.

*****

Criminal Justice Act 1988

(1988, c. 33)

An Act to make fresh provision for extradition; to amend the rules of evidence in criminal proceedings; to provide for the reference by the Attorney General of certain questions relating to sentencing to the Court of Appeal; to amend the law with regard to the jurisdiction and powers of criminal courts, the collection, enforcement and remission of fines imposed by coroners, juries, supervision orders, the detention of children and young persons, probation and the probation service, criminal appeals, anonymity in cases of rape and similar cases, orders under sections 4 and 11 of the Contempt of Court Act 1981 relating to trials on indictment, orders restricting the access of the public to the whole or any part of a trial on indictment or to any proceedings ancillary to such a trial and orders restricting the publication of any report of the whole or any part of a trial on indictment or any such ancillary proceedings, the alteration of names of petty sessions areas, officers of inner London magistrates' courts and the costs and expenses of prosecution witnesses and certain other persons; to make fresh provision for the payment of compensation by the Criminal Injuries Compensation Board; to make provision for the payment of compensation for a miscarriage of justice which has resulted in a wrongful conviction; to create an offence of torture and an offence of having an article with a blade or point in a public place; to create further offences relating to weapons; to create a summary offence of possession of an indecent photograph of a child; to amend the Police and Criminal Evidence Act 1984 in relation to searches, computer data about fingerprints and bail for persons in customs detention; to make provision in relation to the taking of body samples by the police in Northern Ireland; to amend the Bail Act 1976; to give a justice of the peace power to authorise entry and search of premises for offensive weapons; to provide for the enforcement of the Video Recordings Act 1984 by officers of a weights and measures authority and in Northern Ireland by Officers of the Department of Economic Development; to extend to the purchase of easements and other rights over land the power to purchase land conferred on the Secretary of State by section 36 of the Prison Act 1952; and for connected purposes.   [29th July 1988]

Territorial extent: United Kingdom (sections printed)

*****

PART XI MISCELLANEOUS

Miscarriages of justice

133   Compensation for miscarriages of justice

(1) Subject to subsection (2) below, when a person has been convicted of a criminal offence and when subsequently his conviction has been reversed or he has been pardoned on the ground that a new or newly discovered fact shows beyond reasonable doubt that there has been a miscarriage of justice,

the Secretary of State shall pay compensation for the miscarriage of justice to the person who has suffered punishment as a result of such conviction or, if he is dead, to his personal representatives, unless the non-disclosure of the unknown fact was wholly or partly attributable to the person convicted.

[1A] *****

(2) No payment of compensation under this section shall be made unless an application for such compensation has been made to the Secretary of State [before the end of the period of 2 years beginning with the date on which the conviction of the person concerned is reversed or he is pardoned.

[(2AA) Such an application requires to be made within the period of 3 years starting with—

    (a) in the case of compensation under subsection (1), the date on which the conviction is reversed or (as the case may be) the person is pardoned,

    (b) in the case of compensation under subsection (1A), whichever is relevant of—

        (i)   that date, or

        (ii) the date on which the person is acquitted or the relevant decision is made known to the person.

(2AB) The Scottish Ministers may accept such an application outwith that time limit if they think it is appropriate in exceptional circumstances to do so.]

(2A) But the Secretary of State may direct that an application for compensation made after the end of that period is to be treated as if it had been made within that period if the Secretary of State considers that there are exceptional circumstances which justify doing so.]

(3) The question whether there is a right to compensation under this section shall be determined by the Secretary of State.

(4) If the Secretary of State determines that there is a right to such compensation, the amount of the compensation shall be assessed by an assessor appointed by the Secretary of State.

[(4A) Section 133A applies in relation to the assessment of the amount of the compensation.]

[(4B)]–(9) *****

[133A   Miscarriages of justice: amount of compensation]

[(1) This section applies where an assessor is required to assess the amount of compensation payable to or in respect of a person under section 133 for a miscarriage of justice.

(2) In assessing so much of any compensation payable under section 133 as is attributable to suffering, harm to reputation or similar damage, the assessor must have regard in particular to—

    (a) the seriousness of the offence of which the person was convicted and the severity of the punishment suffered as a result of the conviction, and

    (b) the conduct of the investigation and prosecution of the offence.

(3) The assessor may make from the total amount of compensation that the assessor would otherwise have assessed as payable under section 133 any deduction or deductions that the assessor considers appropriate by reason of either or both of the following—

    (a) any conduct of the person appearing to the assessor to have directly or indirectly caused, or contributed to, the conviction concerned; and

    (b) any other convictions of the person and any punishment suffered as a result of them.

(4) If, having had regard to any matters falling within subsection (3)(a) or (b), the assessor considers that there are exceptional circumstances which justify doing so, the assessor may determine that the amount of compensation payable under section 133 is to be a nominal amount only.

(5) The total amount of compensation payable to or in respect of a person under section 133 for a particular miscarriage of justice must not exceed the overall compensation limit.

That limit is—

    (a) £1 million in a case to which section 133B applies, and

    (b) £500,000 in any other case.

(6) The total amount of compensation payable under section 133 for a person's loss of earnings or earnings capacity in respect of any one year must not exceed the earnings compensation limit.

That limit is an amount equal to 1.5 times the median annual gross earnings according to the latest figures published by the Office of National Statistics at the time of the assessment.

(7) The Secretary of State may by order made by statutory instrument amend subsection (5) or (6) so as to alter any amount for the time being specified as the overall compensation limit or the earnings compensation limit.

(8) No order may be made under subsection (7) unless a draft of the order has been laid before and approved by a resolution of each House of Parliament.]

[133B Cases where person has been detained for at least 10 years]

[(1) For the purposes of section 133A(5) this section applies to any case where the person concerned ("P") has been in qualifying detention for a period (or total period) of at least 10 years by the time when—

(a) the conviction is reversed, or

(b) the pardon is given,

as mentioned in section 133(1).

(2) P was "in qualifying detention" at any time when P was detained in a prison, a hospital or at any other place, if P was so detained—

(a) by virtue of a sentence passed in respect of the relevant offence,

(b) under mental health legislation by reason of P's conviction of that offence (disregarding any conditions other than the fact of the conviction that had to be fulfilled in order for P to be so detained), or

(c) as a result of P's having been remanded in custody in connection with the relevant offence or with any other offence the charge for which was founded on the same facts or evidence as that for the relevant offence.

(3) In calculating the period (or total period) during which P has been in qualifying detention as mentioned in subsection (1), no account is to be taken of any period of time during which P was both—

(a) in qualifying detention, and

(b) in excluded concurrent detention.

(4) P was "in excluded concurrent detention" at any time when P was detained in a prison, a hospital or at any other place, if P was so detained—

(a) during the term of a sentence passed in respect of an offence other than the relevant offence,

(b) under mental health legislation by reason of P's conviction of any such other offence (disregarding any conditions other than the fact of the conviction that had to be fulfilled in order for P to be so detained), or

(c) as a result of P's having been remanded in custody in connection with an offence for which P was subsequently convicted other than—

(i)   the relevant offence, or

(ii) any other offence the charge for which was founded on the same facts or evidence as that for the relevant offence.

(5) But P was not "in excluded concurrent detention" at any time by virtue of subsection (4)(a), (b) or (c) if P's conviction of the other offence mentioned in that provision was quashed on appeal, or a pardon was given in respect of it.

(6) In this section—

"mental health legislation" means—

(a) Part 3 of the Mental Health Act 1983,

(b) Part 3 of the Mental Health (Northern Ireland) Order 1986, or

(c) the provisions of any earlier enactment corresponding to Part 3 of that Act or Part 3 of that Order;

"the relevant offence" means the offence in respect of which the conviction is quashed or the pardon is given (but see subsection (7));

"remanded in custody" is to be read in accordance with subsections (8) and (9);

"reversed" has the same meaning as in section 133 of this Act.

(7) If, as a result of the miscarriage of justice—

(a) two or more convictions are reversed, or

(b) a pardon is given in respect of two or more offences,

"the relevant offence" means any of the offences concerned.

(8) In relation to England and Wales, "remanded in custody" has the meaning given by section 242(2) of the Criminal Justice Act 2003, but that subsection applies for the purposes of this section as if any reference there to a provision of the Mental Health Act 1983 included a reference to any corresponding provision of any earlier enactment.

(9) In relation to Northern Ireland, "remanded in custody" means—

(a) remanded in or committed to custody by an order of a court, or

(b) remanded, admitted or removed to hospital under Article 42, 43, 45 or 54 of the Mental Health (Northern Ireland) Order 1986 or under any corresponding provision of any earlier enactment.]

Torture

134   Torture

(1) A public official or person acting in an official capacity, whatever his nationality, commits the offence of torture if in the United Kingdom or elsewhere he intentionally inflicts severe pain or suffering on another in the performance or purported performance of his official duties.

(2) A person not falling within subsection (1) above commits the offence of torture, whatever his nationality, if—

(a) in the United Kingdom or elsewhere he intentionally inflicts severe pain or suffering on another at the instigation or with the consent or acquiescence—

(i)   of a public official; or

(ii) of a person acting in an official capacity; and

(b) the official or other person is performing or purporting to perform his official duties when he instigates the commission of the offence or consents to or acquiesces in it.

(3) It is immaterial whether the pain or suffering is physical or mental and whether it is caused by an act or an omission.

(4) It shall be a defence for a person charged with an offence under this section in respect of any conduct of his to prove that he had lawful authority, justification or excuse for that conduct.

(5), (6) *****

135   Requirement of Attorney General's consent for prosecutions

Proceedings for an offence under section 134 above shall not be begun—

(a) in England and Wales, except by, or with the consent of, the Attorney General; or

(b) in Northern Ireland, except by, or with the consent of, the Attorney General for Northern Ireland.

136–158   *****

159   Crown Court proceedings—orders restricting or preventing reports or restricting public access

(1) A person aggrieved may appeal to the Court of Appeal, if that court grants leave, against—

(a)   an order under section 4 or 11 of the Contempt of Court Act 1981 made in relation to a trial on indictment;

[(aa) an order made by the Crown Court under section 58(7) or (8) of the Criminal Procedure and Investigations Act 1996 in a case where the court has convicted a person on a trial on indictment;]

(b)   any order restricting the access of the public to the whole or any part of a trial on indictment or to any proceedings ancillary to such a trial; and

(c)   any order restricting the publication of any report of the whole or any part of a trial on indictment or any such ancillary proceedings;

and the decision of the Court of Appeal shall be final.

(2)–(7) *****

*****

Official Secrets Act 1989

(1989, c. 6)

An Act to replace section 2 of the Official Secrets Act 1911 by provisions protecting more limited classes of official information.   [11th May 1989]

Territorial extent: United Kingdom

1   Security and intelligence

(1) A person who is or has been—

(a) a member of the security and intelligence services; or

(b) a person notified that he is subject to the provisions of this subsection,

is guilty of an offence if without lawful authority he discloses any information, document or other article relating to security or intelligence which is or has been in his possession by virtue of his position as a member of any of those services or in the course of his work while the notification is or was in force.

(2) The reference in subsection (1) above to disclosing information relating to security or intelligence includes a reference to making any statement which purports to be a disclosure of such information or is intended to be taken by those to whom it is addressed as being such a disclosure.

(3) A person who is or has been a Crown Servant or government contractor is guilty of an offence if without lawful authority he makes a damaging disclosure of any information, document or other article relating to security or intelligence which is or has been in his possession by virtue of his position as such but otherwise than as mentioned in subsection (1) above.

(4) For the purposes of subsection (3) above a disclosure is damaging if—

(a) it causes damage to the work of, or of any part of, the security and intelligence service; or

(b) it is of information or a document or other article which is such that its unauthorised disclosure would be likely to cause such damage or which falls within a class or description of information, documents or articles the unauthorised disclosure of which would be likely to have that effect.

(5) It is a defence for a person charged with an offence under this section to prove that at the time of the alleged offence he did not know, and had no reasonable cause to believe, that the information, document or article in question related to security or intelligence or, in the case of an offence under subsection (3), that the disclosure would be damaging within the meaning of that subsection.

(6)–(8) *****

(9) In this section 'security or intelligence' means the work of, or in support of, the security and intelligence services or any part of them, and references to information relating to security or intelligence include references to information held or transmitted by those services or by persons in support of, or of any part of, them.

2   Defence

(1) A person who is or has been a Crown servant or government contractor is guilty of an offence if without lawful authority he makes a damaging disclosure of any information, document or other article relating to defence which is or has been in his possession by virtue of his position as such.

(2) For the purposes of subsection (1) above a disclosure is damaging if—

(a) it damages the capability of, or of any part of, the armed forces of the Crown to carry out their tasks or leads to loss of life or injury to members of those forces or serious damage to the equipment or installations of those forces; or

(b) otherwise than as mentioned in paragraph (a) above, it endangers the interests of the United Kingdom abroad, seriously obstructs the promotion or protection by the United Kingdom of those interests or endangers the safety of British citizens abroad; or

(c) it is of information or of a document or article which is such that its unauthorised disclosure would be likely to have any of those effects.

(3) It is a defence for a person charged with an offence under this section to prove that at the time of the alleged offence he did not know, and had no reasonable cause to believe, that the information, document or article in question related to defence or that its disclosure would be damaging within the meaning of subsection (1) above.

(4) ******

3   International relations

(1) A person who is or has been a Crown servant or government contractor is guilty of an offence if without lawful authority he makes a damaging disclosure of—

(a) any information, document or other article relating to international relations; or

(b) any confidential information, document or other article which was obtained from a State other than the United Kingdom or an international organisation,

being information or a document or article which is or has been in his possession by virtue of his position as a Crown servant or government contractor.

(2) For the purposes of subsection (1) above a disclosure is damaging if—

(a) it endangers the interests of the United Kingdom abroad, seriously obstructs the promotion or protection by the United Kingdom of those interests or endangers the safety of British citizens abroad; or

(b) it is of information or of a document or article which is such that its unauthorised disclosure would be likely to have any of those effects.

(3) In the case of information or a document or article within subsection (1)(b) above—

(a) the fact that it is confidential, or

(b) its nature or contents,

may be sufficient to establish for the purposes of subsection (2)(b) above that the information, document or article is such that its unauthorised disclosure would be likely to have any of the effects there mentioned.

(4) It is a defence for a person charged with an offence under this section to prove that at the time of the alleged offence he did not know, and had no reasonable cause to believe, that the information, document or article in question was such as is mentioned in subsection (1) above or that its disclosure would be damaging within the meaning of that subsection.

(5), (6) *****

4   Crime and special investigation powers

(1) A person who is or has been a Crown servant or government contractor is guilty of an offence if without lawful authority he discloses any information, document or other article to which this section applies and which is or has been in his possession by virtue of his position as such.

(2) This section applies to any information, document or other article—

(a) the disclosure of which—

(i) results in the commission of an offence; or

(ii) facilitates an escape from legal custody or the doing of any other act prejudicial to the safekeeping of persons in legal custody; or

(iii) impedes the prevention or detection of offences or the apprehension or prosecution of suspected offenders; or

(b) which is such that its unauthorised disclosure would be likely to have any of those effects.

(3) This section also applies to—

(a) any information obtained by reason of the interception of any communication in obedience to a warrant issued under section 2 of the Interception of Communications Act 1985 [or under the authority of an interception warrant under section 5 of the Regulation of Investigatory Powers Act 2000], any information relating to the obtaining of information by reason of any such interception and any document or other article which is or has been used or held for use in, or has been obtained by reason of, any such interception; and

(b) any information obtained by reason of action authorised by a warrant issued under section 3 of the Security Service Act 1989 [or under section 5 of the Intelligence Services Act 1994 or by an authorisation given under section 7 of that Act], any information relating to the obtaining of information by reason of any such action and any document or other article which is or has been used or held for use in, or has been obtained by reason of, any such action.

(4) It is a defence for a person charged with an offence under this section in respect of a disclosure falling within subsection (2)(a) above to prove that at the time of the alleged offence he did not know, and had no reasonable cause to believe, that the disclosure would have any of the effects there mentioned.

(5) It is a defence for a person charged with an offence under this section in respect of any other disclosure to prove that at the time of the alleged offence he did not know, and had no reasonable cause to believe, that the information, document or article in question was information or a document or article to which this section applies.

(6) In this section "legal custody" includes detention in pursuance of any enactment or any instrument made under an enactment.

5 Information resulting from unauthorised disclosures or entrusted in confidence

(1) Subsection (2) below applies where—

(a) any information, document or other article protected against disclosure by the foregoing provisions of this Act has come into a person's possession as a result of having been—
  (i)   disclosed (whether to him or another) by a Crown servant or government contractor without lawful authority; or
  (ii) entrusted to him by a Crown servant or government contractor on terms requiring it to be held in confidence or in circumstances in which the Crown servant or government contractor could reasonably expect that it would be so held; or
  (iii) disclosed (whether to him or another) without lawful authority by a person to whom it was entrusted as mentioned in sub-paragraph (ii) above; and
(b) the disclosure without lawful authority of the information, document or article by the person into whose possession it has come is not an offence under any of those provisions.

(2) Subject to subsections (3) and (4) below, the person into whose possession the information, document or article has come is guilty of an offence if he discloses it without lawful authority knowing, or having reasonable cause to believe, that it is protected against disclosure by the foregoing provisions of this Act and that it has come into his possession as mentioned in subsection (1) above.

(3) In the case of information or a document or article protected against disclosure by sections 1 to 3 above, a person does not commit an offence under subsection (2) above unless—

(a) the disclosure by him is damaging; and
(b) he makes it knowing, or having reasonable cause to believe, that it would be damaging;
and the question whether a disclosure is damaging shall be determined for the purposes of this subsection as it would be in relation to a disclosure of that information, document or article by a Crown servant in contravention of section 1(3), 2(1) or 3(1) above.

(4) A person does not commit an offence under subsection (2) above in respect of information or a document or other article which has come into his possession as a result of having been disclosed—

(a) as mentioned in subsection (1)(a)(i) above by a government contractor; or
(b) as mentioned in subsection (1)(a)(iii) above,
unless that disclosure was by a British citizen or took place in the United Kingdom, in any of the Channel Islands or in the Isle of Man or a colony.

(5) For the purposes of this section information or a document or article is protected against disclosure by the foregoing provisions of this Act if—

    (a) it relates to security or intelligence, defence or international relations within the meaning of section 1, 2 or 3 above or is such as is mentioned in section 3(1)(b) above; or

    (b) it is information or a document or article to which section 4 above applies;

and information or a document or article is protected against disclosure by sections 1 to 3 above if it falls within paragraph (a) above.

(6) A person is guilty of an offence if without lawful authority he discloses any information, document or other article which he knows, or has reasonable cause to believe, to have come into his possession as a result of a contravention of section 1 of the Official Secrets Act 1911.

6 *****

7 Authorised disclosures

(1) For the purposes of this Act a disclosure by—

    (a) a Crown servant; or

    (b) a person, not being a Crown servant or government contractor, in whose case a notification for the purposes of section 1(1) above is in force,

is made with lawful authority if, and only if, it is made in accordance with his official duty.

(2) For the purposes of this Act a disclosure by a government contractor is made with lawful authority if, and only if, it is made—

    (a) in accordance with an official authorisation; or

    (b) for the purposes of the functions by virtue of which he is a government contractor and without contravening an official restriction.

(3) or the purposes of this Act a disclosure made by any other person is made with lawful authority if, and only if, it is made—

    (a) to a Crown servant for the purposes of his functions as such; or

    (b) in accordance with an official authorisation.

(4) It is a defence for a person charged with an offence under any of the foregoing provisions of this Act to prove that at the time of the alleged offence he believed that he had lawful authority to make the disclosure in question and had no reasonable cause to believe otherwise.

(5), (6) *****

8 Safeguarding of information

(1) Where a Crown servant or government contractor, by virtue of his position as such, has in his possession or under his control any document or other article which it would be an offence under any of the foregoing provisions of this Act for him to disclose without lawful authority he is guilty of an offence if—

    (a) being a Crown servant, he retains the document or article contrary to his official duty; or

    (b) being a government contractor, he fails to comply with an official direction for the return or disposal of the document or article,

or if he fails to take such care to prevent the unauthorised disclosure of the document or article as a person in his position may reasonably be expected to take.

(2) It is a defence for a Crown servant charged with an offence under subsection (1)(a) above to prove that at the time of the alleged offence he believed that he was acting in accordance with his official duty and had no reasonable cause to believe otherwise.

(3)–(9) *****

9 Prosecutions

(1) Subject to subsection (2) below, no prosecution for an offence under this Act shall be instituted in England and Wales or in Northern Ireland except by or with the consent of the Attorney General or, as the case may be, the Attorney General for Northern Ireland.

(2) *****

10　Penalties

(1)　A person guilty of an offence under any provision of this Act other than section 8(1), (4) or (5) shall be liable—

   (a)　on conviction on indictment, to imprisonment for a term not exceeding two years or a fine or both;

   (b)　on summary conviction, to imprisonment for a term not exceeding six months or a fine not exceeding the statutory maximum or both.

(2)　A person guilty of an offence under section 8(1), (4) or (5) above shall be liable on summary conviction to imprisonment for a term not exceeding three months or a fine not exceeding level 5 on the standard scale or both.

11　Arrest, search and trial

(1)　...

(2)　*****

(3)　Section 9(1) of the Official Secrets Act 1911 (search warrants) shall have effect as if references to offences under that Act included references to offences under any provision of this Act other than section 8(1), (4) or (5); and the following provisions of the Police and Criminal Evidence Act 1984, that is to say—

   (a)　section 9(2) (which excludes items subject to legal privilege and certain other material from powers of search conferred by previous enactments); and

   (b)　paragraph 3(b) of Schedule 1 (which prescribes access conditions for the special procedure laid down in that Schedule),

shall apply to section 9(1) of the said Act of 1911 as extended by this subsection as they apply to that section as originally enacted.

(4)　Section 8(4) of the Official Secrets Act 1920 (exclusion of public from hearing on grounds of national safety) shall have effect as if references to offences under that Act included references to offences under any provision of this Act other than section 8(1), (4) or (5).

(5)　Proceedings for an offence under this Act may be taken in any place in the United Kingdom.

12　'Crown servant' and 'government contractor'

(1)　In this Act 'Crown servant' means—

   (a)　　a Minister of the Crown;

   [(aa)　a member of the Scottish Executive or a Junior Scottish Minister;]

   (ab)　the First Minister for Wales, a Welsh Minister appointed under section 48 of the Government of Wales Act 2006, the Counsel General to the Welsh Assembly Government or a Deputy Welsh Minister;]

   (b)　　...

   (c)　　any person employed in the civil service of the Crown, including Her Majesty's Diplomatic Service, Her Majesty's Overseas Civil Service, the civil service of Northern Ireland and the Northern Ireland Court Service;

   (d)　　any member of the naval, military or air forces of the Crown, including any person employed by an association established for the purposes of [Part XI of the Reserve Forces Act 1996];

   (e)　　any constable and any other person employed or appointed in or for the purposes of any police force [(including the Police Service of Northern Ireland and the Police Service of Northern Ireland Reserve)] [or of the Serious Organised Crime Agency];

   (f)　　any person who is a member or employee of a prescribed body or a body of a prescribed class and either is prescribed for the purposes of this paragraph or belongs to a prescribed class of members or employees of any such body;

   (g)　　any person who is the holder of a prescribed office or who is an employee of such a holder and either is prescribed for the purposes of this paragraph or belongs to a prescribed class of such employees.

(2) In this Act 'government contractor' means, subject to subsection (3) below, any person who is not a Crown servant but who provides, or is employed in the provision of, goods or services—

(a)   For the purposes of any Minister or person mentioned in paragraph (a)[, (ab)] or (b) of subsection (1) above, [of any office-holder in the Scottish Administration,] of any of the services, forces or bodies mentioned in that subsection or of the holder of any office prescribed under that subsection;

[(aa) ...] or

(b)   under any agreement or arrangement certified by the Secretary of State as being one to which the government of a State other than the United Kingdom or an international organisation is a party or which is subordinate to, or made for the purposes of implementing, any such agreement or arrangement.

(3)–(5) *****

13 Other interpretation provisions

(1) In this Act—

'disclose' and 'disclosure', in relation to a document or other article, include parting with possession of it;

'international organisation' means, subject to subsections (2) and (3) below, an organisation of which only States are members and includes a reference to any organ of such an organisation;

'prescribed' means prescribed by an order made by the Secretary of State;

'State' includes the government of a State and any organ of its government and references to a State other than the United Kingdom include references to any territory outside the United Kingdom.

(2) In section 12(2)(b) above the reference to an international organisation includes a reference to any such organisation whether or not one of which only States are members and includes a commercial organisation.

(3) In determining for the purposes of subsection (1) above whether only States are members of an organisation, any member which is itself an organisation of which only States are members, or which is an organ of such an organisation, shall be treated as a State.

*****

Security Service Act 1989

(1989, c. 5)

An Act to place the Security Service on a statutory basis; to enable certain actions to be taken on the authority of warrants issued by the Secretary of State, with provision for the issue of such warrants to be kept under review by a Commissioner; to establish a procedure for the investigation by a Tribunal or, in some cases, by the Commissioner of complaints about the Service; and for connected purposes.

[27th April 1989]

Territorial extent: United Kingdom

1 The Security Service

(1) There shall continue to be a Security Service (in this Act referred to as 'the Service') under the authority of the Secretary of State.

(2) The function of the Service shall be the protection of national security and, in particular, its protection against threats from espionage, terrorism and sabotage, from the activities of agents of foreign powers and from actions intended to overthrow or undermine parliamentary democracy by political, industrial or violent means.

(3) It shall also be the function of the Service to safeguard the economic well-being of the United Kingdom against threats posed by the actions or intentions of persons outside the British Islands.

[(4) It shall also be the function of the Service to act in support of the activities of police forces [, the Serious Organised Crime Agency,] and other law enforcement agencies in the prevention and detection of serious crime.]

(5) *****

2　The Director-General

(1) The operations of the Service shall continue to be under the control of a Director-General appointed by the Secretary of State.

(2) The Director-General shall be responsible for the efficiency of the Service and it shall be his duty to ensure—

(a) that there are arrangements for securing that no information is obtained by the Service except so far as necessary for the proper discharge of its functions or disclosed by it except so far as necessary for that purpose or for the purpose of [the prevention or detection of] serious crime [or for the purpose of any criminal proceedings]; and

(b) that the Service does not take any action to further the interests of any political party; [and

(c) that there are arrangements, agreed with [the Director General of the Serious Organised Crime Agency], for co-ordinating the activities of the Service in pursuance of section 1(4) of this Act with the activities of police forces [, the Serious Organised Crime Agency] and other law enforcement agencies.]

(3) The arrangements mentioned in subsection (2)(a) above shall be such as to ensure that information in the possession of the Service is not disclosed for use in determining whether a person should be employed, or continue to be employed, by any person, or in any office or capacity, except in accordance with provisions in that behalf approved by the Secretary of State.

(3A) *****

(3B) ...

(4) The Director-General shall make an annual report on the work of the Service to the Prime Minister and the Secretary of State and may at any time report to either of them on any matter relating to its work.

3–5 ...

*****

Criminal Justice and Public Order Act 1994

(1994, c. 33)

An Act to make further provision in relation to criminal justice (including employment in the prison service); to amend or extend the criminal law and powers for preventing crime and enforcing that law; to amend the Video Recordings Act 1984; and for purposes connected with those purposes.　　[3rd November 1994]

Territorial extent: England and Wales, Scotland (ss. 61–66, 163), United Kingdom (ss. 68, 69), England and Wales (remaining provisions printed here). Sections 34–37 (below) have been applied, with modifications, to the armed forces by the Criminal Justice and Public Order Act 1994 (Application to the Armed Forces) Order 2009 (SI 2009/990)

*****

Inferences from accused's silence

34　Effect of accused's failure to mention facts when questioned or charged

(1) Where, in any proceedings against a person for an offence, evidence is given that the accused—

(a) at any time before he was charged with the offence, on being questioned under caution by a constable trying to discover whether or by whom the offence had been committed, failed to mention any fact relied on in his defence in those proceedings; or

    (b) on being charged with the offence or officially informed that he might be prosecuted for it, failed to mention any such fact,

being a fact which in the circumstances existing at the time the accused could reasonably have been expected to mention when so questioned, charged or informed, as the case may be, subsection (2) below applies.

    (2) Where this subsection applies—

      *****

    (c) the court, in determining whether there is a case to answer; and

    (d) the court or jury, in determining whether the accused is guilty of the offence charged,

may draw such inferences from the failure as appear proper.

    [(2A) Where the accused was at an authorised place of detention at the time of the failure, subsections (1) and (2) above do not apply if he had not been allowed an opportunity to consult a solicitor prior to being questioned, charged or informed as mentioned in subsection (1) above.]

    (3) Subject to any directions by the court, evidence tending to establish the failure may be given before or after evidence tending to establish the fact which the accused is alleged to have failed to mention.

    (4) This section applies in relation to questioning by persons (other than constables) charged with the duty of investigating offences or charging offenders as it applies in relation to questioning by constables; and in subsection (1) above 'officially informed' means informed by a constable or any such person.

    (5) This section does not—

    (a) prejudice the admissibility in evidence of the silence or other reaction of the accused in the face of anything said in his presence relating to the conduct in respect of which he is charged, in so far as evidence thereof would be admissible apart from this section; or

    (b) preclude the drawing of any inference from any such silence or other reaction of the accused which could properly be drawn apart from this section.

    (6) *****

    (7) ...

35   Effect of accused's silence at trial

    (1) At the trial of any person . . . for an offence, subsections (2) and (3) below apply unless—

    (a) the accused's guilt is not in issue; or

    (b) it appears to the court that the physical or mental condition of the accused makes it undesirable for him to give evidence;

but subsection (2) below does not apply if, at the conclusion of the evidence for the prosecution, his legal representative informs the court that the accused will give evidence or, where he is unrepresented, the court ascertains from him that he will give evidence.

    (2) Where this subsection applies, the court shall, at the conclusion of the evidence for the prosecution, satisfy itself (in the case of proceedings on indictment [with a jury], in the presence of the jury) that the accused is aware that the stage has been reached at which evidence can be given for the defence and that he can, if he wishes, give evidence and that, if he chooses not to give evidence, or having been sworn, without good cause refuses to answer any question, it will be permissible for the court or jury to draw such inferences as appear proper from his failure to give evidence or his refusal, without good cause, to answer any question.

    (3) Where this subsection applies, the court or jury, in determining whether the accused is guilty of the offence charged, may draw such inferences as appear proper from the failure of the accused to give evidence or his refusal, without good cause, to answer any question.

    (4) This section does not render the accused compellable to give evidence on his own behalf, and he shall accordingly not be guilty of contempt of court by reason of a failure to do so.

    (5) For the purposes of this section a person who, having been sworn, refuses to answer any question shall be taken to do so without good cause unless—

(a) he is entitled to refuse to answer the question by virtue of any enactment, whenever passed or made, or on the ground of privilege; or

(b) the court in the exercise of its general discretion excuses him from answering it.

(6) ...

(7) *****

36   Effect of accused's failure or refusal to account for objects, substances or marks

(1) Where—

(a) a person is arrested by a constable, and there is—

(i)   on his person; or

(ii)   in or on his clothing or footwear; or

(iii) otherwise in his possession; or

(iv)   in any place in which he is at the time of his arrest,

any object, substance or mark, or there is any mark on any such object; and

(b) that or another constable investigating the case reasonably believes that the presence of the object, substance or mark may be attributable to the participation of the person arrested in the commission of an offence specified by the constable; and

(c) the constable informs the person arrested that he so believes, and requests him to account for the presence of the object, substance or mark; and

(d) the person fails or refuses to do so, then if, in any proceedings against the person for the offence so specified, evidence of those matters is given,

subsection (2) below applies.

(2) Where this subsection applies—

*****

(c) the court, in determining whether there is a case to answer, and

(d) the court or jury, in determining whether the accused is guilty of the offence charged, may draw such inferences from the failure or refusal as appear proper.

(3) Subsections (1) and (2) above apply to the condition of clothing or footwear as they apply to a substance or mark thereon.

(4) Subsections (1) and (2) above do not apply unless the accused was told in ordinary language by the constable when making the request mentioned in subsection (1)(c) above what the effect of this section would be if he failed or refused to comply with the request.

(4A)–(7) *****

(8) ...

37   Effect of accused's failure or refusal to account for presence at a particular place

(1) Where—

(a) a person arrested by a constable was found by him at a place at or about the time the offence for which he was arrested is alleged to have been committed; and

(b) that or another constable investigating the offence reasonably believes that the presence of the person at that place and at that time may be attributable to his participation in the commission of the offence; and

(c) the constable informs the person that he so believes, and requests him to account for that presence; and

(d) the person fails or refuses to do so,

then if, in any proceedings against the person for the offence, evidence of those matters is given, subsection (2) below applies.

(2) Where this subsection applies—

*****

(c) the court, in determining whether there is a case to answer; and

(d) the court or jury, in determining whether the accused is guilty of the offence charged,
may draw such inferences from the failure or refusal as appear proper.

(3) Subsections (1) and (2) do not apply unless the accused was told in ordinary language by
the constable when making the request mentioned in subsection (1)(c) above what the effect of this
section would be if he failed or refused to comply with the request.

(3A)–(6) *****

(7) ...

38–59 *****

Powers of police to stop and search

60 Powers to stop and search in anticipation of [, or after,] violence

[(1) If a police officer of or above the rank of inspector reasonably believes—

(a) that incidents involving serious violence may take place in any locality in his police
area, and that it is expedient to give an authorisation under this section to prevent their
occurrence,

[(aa) that—

(i) an incident involving serious violence has taken place in England and Wales in his
police area;

(ii) a dangerous instrument or offensive weapon used in the incident is being carried
in any locality in his police area by a person; and

(iii) it is expedient to give an authorisation under this section to find the instrument or
weapon;] or

(b) that persons are carrying dangerous instruments or offensive weapons in any locality in
his police area without good reason,

he may give an authorisation that the powers conferred by this section are to be exercisable at any
place within that locality for a specified period not exceeding 24 hours.]

(2) ...

(3) If it appears to [an officer of or above the rank of] superintendent that it is expedient to do so,
having regard to offences which have, or are reasonably suspected to have, been committed in connection with any [activity] falling within the authorisation, he may direct that the authorisation shall
continue in being for a further [24] hours.

(3A) *****

(4) This section confers on any constable in uniform power—

(a) to stop any pedestrian and search him or anything carried by him for offensive weapons or
dangerous instruments,

(b) to stop any vehicle and search the vehicle, its driver and any passenger for offensive weapons or dangerous instruments.

(4A) ... (not repealed in Scotland)

(5) A constable may, in the exercise of [the powers conferred by subsection (4) above], stop any
person or vehicle and make any search he thinks fit whether or not he has any grounds for suspecting
that the person or vehicle is carrying weapons or articles of that kind.

(6) If in the course of a search under this section a constable discovers a dangerous instrument
or an article which he has reasonable grounds for suspecting to be an offensive weapon, he may
seize it.

(7)–(10A) *****

(11) In this section—
*****

'dangerous instruments' means instruments which have a blade or are sharply pointed;

'offensive weapon' has the meaning given by section 1(9) of the Police and Criminal Evidence Act
1984 [or, in relation to Scotland, section 47(4) of the Criminal Law (Consolidation) (Scotland) Act
1995]; [but in subsections (1)(aa), (4), (5) and (6) above and subsection (11A) below includes, in

the case of an incident of the kind mentioned in subsection (1)(aa)(i) above, any article used in the incident to cause or threaten injury to any person or otherwise to intimidate]; . . . and

'vehicle' includes a caravan as defined in section 29(1) of the Caravan Sites and Control of Development Act 1960.

[(11A) For the purposes of this section, a person carries a dangerous instrument or an offensive weapon if he has it in his possession.]

(12) The powers conferred by this section are in addition to, and not in derogation of, any power otherwise conferred.

[60AA Powers to require removal of disguises
(1) Where—
- (a) an authorisation under section 60 is for the time being in force in relation to any locality for any period, or
- (b) an authorisation under subsection (3) that the powers conferred by subsection (2) shall be exercisable at any place in a locality is in force for any period,

those powers shall be exercisable at any place in that locality at any time in that period.

(2) This subsection confers power on any constable in uniform—
- (a) to require any person to remove any item which the constable reasonably believes that person is wearing wholly or mainly for the purpose of concealing his identity;
- (b) to seize any item which the constable reasonably believes any person intends to wear wholly or mainly for that purpose.

(3) If a police officer of or above the rank of inspector reasonably believes—
- (a) that activities may take place in any locality in his police area that are likely (if they take place) to involve the commission of offences, and
- (b) that it is expedient, in order to prevent or control the activities, to give an authorisation under this subsection,

he may give an authorisation that the powers conferred by this section shall be exercisable at any place within that locality for a specified period not exceeding twenty-four hours.

(4)–(6) *****

(7) A person who fails to remove an item worn by him when required to do so by a constable in the exercise of his power under this section shall be liable, on summary conviction, to imprisonment for a term not exceeding one month or to a fine not exceeding level 3 on the standard scale or both.

(8), (9) *****

(10) The powers conferred by this section are in addition to, and not in derogation of, any power otherwise conferred.

(11) This section does not extend to Scotland.]

60A, 60B   *****

PART V PUBLIC ORDER: COLLECTIVE TRESPASS OR NUISANCE ON LAND

Powers to remove trespassers on land

61   Power to remove trespassers on land
(1) If the senior police officer present at the scene reasonably believes that two or more persons are trespassing on land and are present there with the common purpose of residing there for any period, that reasonable steps have been taken by or on behalf of the occupier to ask them to leave and—
- (a) that any of those persons has caused damage to the land or to property on the land or used threatening, abusive or insulting words or behaviour towards the occupier, a member of his family or an employee or agent of his, or
- (b) that those persons have between them six or more vehicles on the land,

he may direct those persons, or any of them, to leave the land and to remove any vehicles or other property they have with them on the land.

(2) Where the persons in question are reasonably believed by the senior police officer to be persons who were not originally trespassers but have become trespassers on the land, the officer must reasonably believe that the other conditions specified in subsection (1) are satisfied after those persons become trespassers before he can exercise the power conferred by that subsection.

(3) A direction under subsection (1) above, if not communicated to the persons referred to in subsection (1) by the police officer giving the direction, may be communicated to them by any constable at the scene.

(4) If a person knowing that a direction under subsection (1) above has been given which applies to him—

    (a) fails to leave the land as soon as reasonably practicable, or

    (b) having left again enters the land as a trespasser within the period of [51 weeks] beginning with the day on which the direction was given,

he commits an offence and is liable on summary conviction to imprisonment for a term not exceeding three months or a fine not exceeding level 4 on the standard scale, or both.

(4A), (4B) *****

(5) ...

(6) In proceedings for an offence under this section it is a defence for the accused to show—

    (a) that he was not trespassing on the land, or

    (b) that he had a reasonable excuse for failing to leave the land as soon as reasonably practicable or, as the case may be, for again entering the land as a trespasser.

(7)–(9) *****

62 Supplementary powers of seizure

(1) If a direction has been given under section 61 and a constable reasonably suspects that any person to whom the direction applies has, without reasonable excuse—

    (a) failed to remove any vehicle on the land which appears to the constable to belong to him or to be in his possession or under his control; or

    (b) entered the land as a trespasser with a vehicle within the period of three months beginning with the day on which the direction was given,

the constable may seize and remove that vehicle.

(2) *****

[62A Power to remove trespassers: alternative site available

(1) If the senior police officer present at a scene reasonably believes that the conditions in subsection (2) are satisfied in relation to a person and land, he may direct the person—

    (a) to leave the land;

    (b) to remove any vehicle and other property he has with him on the land.

(2) The conditions are—

    (a) that the person and one or more others ('the trespassers') are trespassing on the land;

    (b) that the trespassers have between them at least one vehicle on the land;

    (c) that the trespassers are present on the land with the common purpose of residing there for any period;

    (d) if it appears to the officer that the person has one or more caravans in his possession or under his control on the land, that there is a suitable pitch on a relevant caravan site for that caravan or each of those caravans;

    (e) that the occupier of the land or a person acting on his behalf has asked the police to remove the trespassers from the land.

(3) A direction under subsection (1) may be communicated to the person to whom it applies by any constable at the scene

(4)–(8) *****

62B   Failure to comply with direction under section 62A: offences

(1) A person commits an offence if he knows that a direction under section 62A(1) has been given which applies to him and—

(a) he fails to leave the relevant land as soon as reasonably practicable, or

(b) he enters any land in the area of the relevant local authority as a trespasser before the end of the relevant period with the intention of residing there.

(2) The relevant period is the period of 3 months starting with the day on which the direction is given.

(3) A person guilty of an offence under this section is liable on summary conviction to imprisonment for a term not exceeding three months or a fine not exceeding level 4 on the standard scale or both.

(4) ...

(5) In proceedings for an offence under this section it is a defence for the accused to show—

(a) that he was not trespassing on the land in respect of which he is alleged to have committed the offence, or

(b) that he had a reasonable excuse—

(i)   for failing to leave the relevant land as soon as reasonably practicable, or

(ii) for entering land in the area of the relevant local authority as a trespasser with the intention of residing there, or

(c) that, at the time the direction was given, he was under the age of 18 years and was residing with his parent or guardian.

62C   Failure to comply with direction under section 62A: seizure

(1) This section applies if a direction has been given under section 62A(1) and a constable reasonably suspects that a person to whom the direction applies has, without reasonable excuse—

(a) failed to remove any vehicle on the relevant land which appears to the constable to belong to him or to be in his possession or under his control; or

(b) entered any land in the area of the relevant local authority as a trespasser with a vehicle before the end of the relevant period with the intention of residing there.

(2) The relevant period is the period of 3 months starting with the day on which the direction is given.

(3) The constable may seize and remove the vehicle.]

62D–67   *****

68   Offence of aggravated trespass

(1) A person commits the offence of aggravated trespass if he trespasses on land. . . and, in relation to any lawful activity which persons are engaging in or are about to engage in on that or adjoining land . . . , does there anything which is intended by him to have the effect—

(a) of intimidating those persons or any of them so as to deter them or any of them from engaging in that activity,

(b) of obstructing that activity, or

(c) of disrupting that activity.

(1A) *****

(2) Activity on any occasion on the part of a person or persons on land is 'lawful' for the purposes of this section if he or they may engage in the activity on the land on that occasion without committing an offence or trespassing on the land.

(3) A person guilty of an offence under this section is liable on summary conviction to imprisonment for a term not exceeding the three months or a fine not exceeding level 4 on the standard scale, or both.

(4) ...

(5) *****

69   Powers to remove persons committing or participating in aggravated trespass

(1) If the senior police officer present at the scene reasonably believes—

   (a) that a person is committing, has committed or intends to commit the offence of aggravated trespass on land . . . ; or

   (b) that two or more persons are trespassing on land . . . and are present there with the common purpose of intimidating persons so as to deter them from engaging in a lawful activity or of obstructing or disrupting a lawful activity,

   he may direct that person or (as the case may be) those persons (or any of them) to leave the land.

(2) A direction under subsection (1) above, if not communicated to the persons referred to in subsection (1) by the police officer giving the direction, may be communicated to them by any constable at the scene.

(3) If a person knowing that a direction under subsection (1) above has been given which applies to him—

   (a) fails to leave the land as soon as practicable, or

   (b) having left again enters the land as a trespasser within the period of three months beginning with the day on which the direction was given,

   he commits an offence and is liable on summary conviction to imprisonment for a term not exceeding three months or a fine not exceeding level 4 on the standard scale, or both.

(4) In proceedings for an offence under subsection (3) it is a defence for the accused to show—

   (a) that he was not trespassing on the land, or

   (b) that he had a reasonable excuse for failing to leave the land as soon as practicable or, as the case may be, for again entering the land as a trespasser.

(5) . . .

(6) In this section 'lawful activity' and 'land' have the same meaning as in section 68.

*****

Intelligence Services Act 1994

(1994, c. 13)

An Act to make provision about the Secret Intelligence Service and the Government Communications Headquarters, including provision for the issue of warrants and authorisations enabling certain actions to be taken and for the issue of such warrants and authorisations to be kept under review; to make further provision about warrants issued on applications by the Security Service; to establish a procedure for the investigation of complaints about the Secret Intelligence Service and the Government Communications Headquarters; to make provision for the establishment of an Intelligence and Security Committee to scrutinise all three of those bodies; and for connected purposes.   [26th May 1994]

Territorial extent: United Kingdom. Sections 5(1) and 11(1) also apply to the Colonies listed in the Intelligence Services Act 1994 (Dependent Territories) Order 1995 (SI 1995/752)

The Secret Intelligence Service

1   The Secret Intelligence Service

(1) There shall continue to be a Secret Intelligence Service (in this Act referred to as 'the Intelligence Service') under the authority of the Secretary of State; and, subject to subsection (2) below, its functions shall be—

   (a) to obtain and provide information relating to the actions or intentions of persons outside the British Islands; and

   (b) to perform other tasks relating to the actions or intentions of such persons.

(2) The functions of the Intelligence Service shall be exercisable only—

    (a) in the interests of national security, with particular reference to the defence and foreign policies of Her Majesty's Government in the United Kingdom; or

    (b) in the interests of the economic well-being of the United Kingdom; or

    (c) in support of the prevention or detection of serious crime.

2 The Chief of the Intelligence Service

(1) The operations of the Intelligence Service shall continue to be under the control of a Chief of that Service appointed by the Secretary of State.

(2) The Chief of the Intelligence Service shall be responsible for the efficiency of that Service and it shall be his duty to ensure—

    (a) that there are arrangements for securing that no information is obtained by the Intelligence Service except so far as necessary for the proper discharge of its functions and that no information is disclosed by it except so far as necessary—

        (i)   for that purpose;

        (ii)   in the interests of national security;

        (iii) for the purpose of the prevention or detection of serious crime; or

        (iv)   for the purpose of any criminal proceedings; and

    (b) that the Intelligence Service does not take any action to further the interests of any United Kingdom political party.

(3), (4) *****

GCHQ

3 The Government Communications Headquarters

(1) There shall continue to be a Government Communications Headquarters under the authority of the Secretary of State; and, subject to subsection (2) below, its functions shall be—

    (a) to monitor or interfere with electromagnetic, acoustic and other emissions and any equipment producing such emissions and to obtain and provide information derived from or related to such emissions or equipment and from encrypted material; and

    (b) to provide advice and assistance about—

        (i)   languages, including terminology used for technical matters, and

        (ii) cryptography and other matters relating to the protection of information and other material, to the armed forces of the Crown,

to Her Majesty's Government in the United Kingdom or to a Northern Ireland Department or to any other organisation which is determined for the purposes of this section in such manner as may be specified by the Prime Minister.

(2) The functions referred to in subsection (1)(a) above shall be exercisable only—

    (a) in the interests of national security, with particular reference to the defence and foreign policies of Her Majesty's Government in the United Kingdom; or

    (b) in the interests of the economic well-being of the United Kingdom in relation to the actions or intentions of persons outside the British Islands; or

    (c) in support of the prevention or detection of serious crime.

(3) In this Act the expression 'GCHQ' refers to the Government Communications Headquarters and to any unit or part of a unit of the armed forces of the Crown which is for the time being required by the Secretary of State to assist the Government Communications Headquarters in carrying out its functions.

4 The Director of GCHQ

(1) The operations of GCHQ shall continue to be under the control of a Director appointed by the Secretary of State.

(2) The Director shall be responsible for the efficiency of GCHQ and it shall be his duty to ensure—

    (a) that there are arrangements for securing that no information is obtained by GCHQ except so far as necessary for the proper discharge of its functions and that no information is disclosed by it except so far as necessary for that purpose or for the purpose of any criminal proceedings; and

(b) that GCHQ does not take any action to further the interests of any United Kingdom political party.

(3), (4) *****

Authorisation of certain actions

5   Warrants: general

(1) No entry on or interference with property or with wireless telegraphy shall be unlawful if it is authorised by a warrant issued by the Secretary of State under this section.

(2) The Secretary of State may, on an application made by the Security Service, the Intelligence Service or GCHQ, issue a warrant under this section authorising the taking, subject to subsection (3) below, of such action as is specified in the warrant in respect of any property so specified or in respect of wireless telegraphy so specified if the Secretary of State—

(a) thinks it necessary for the action to be taken [for the purpose of] assisting, as the case may be,—

   (i)   the Security Service in carrying out any of its functions under the 1989 Act; or

   (ii) the Intelligence Service in carrying out any of its functions under section 1 above; or

   (iii) GCHQ in carrying out any function which falls within section 3(1)(a) above; and

[(b) is satisfied that the taking of the action is proportionate to what the action seeks to achieve;] and

(c) is satisfied that satisfactory arrangements are in force under section 2(2)(a) of the 1989 Act (duties of the Director-General of the Security Service), section 2(2)(a) above or section 4(2)(a) above with respect to the disclosure of information obtained by virtue of this section and that any information obtained under the warrant will be subject to those arrangements.

[(2A) The matters to be taken into account in considering whether the requirements of subsection (2)(a) and (b) and satisfied in the case of any warrant shall include whether what it is thought necessary to achieve by the conduct authorised by the warrant could reasonably be achieved by other means.]

[(3) A warrant issued on the application of the Intelligence Service or GCHQ for the purposes of the exercise of their functions by virtue of section 1(2)(c) or 3(2)(c) above may not relate to property in the British Islands.

(3A) A warrant issued on the application of the Security Service for the purposes of the exercise of their function under section 1(4) of the Security Service Act 1989 may not relate to property in the British Islands unless it authorises the taking of action in relation to conduct within subsection (3B) below.

(3B) Conduct is within this subsection if it constitutes (or, if it took place in the United Kingdom, would constitute) one or more offences, and either—

(a) it involves the use of violence, results in substantial financial gain or is conduct by a large number of persons in pursuit of a common purpose; or

(b) the offence or one of the offences is an offence for which a person who has attained the age of twenty-one and has no previous convictions could reasonably be expected to be sentenced to imprisonment for a term of three years or more.]

(4), (5) *****

6   *****

7   Authorisation of acts outside the British Islands

(1) If, apart from this section, a person would be liable in the United Kingdom for any act done outside the British Islands, he shall not be so liable if the act is one which is authorised to be done by virtue of an authorisation given by the Secretary of State under this section.

(2) In subsection (1) above 'liable in the United Kingdom' means liable under the criminal or civil law of any part of the United Kingdom.

(3) The Secretary of State shall not give an authorisation under this section unless he is satisfied—

>   (a) that any acts which may be done in reliance on the authorisation or, as the case may be, the operation in the course of which the acts may be done will be necessary for the proper discharge of a function of the Intelligence Service [or GCHQ]; and
>
>   (b) that there are satisfactory arrangements in force to secure—
>
>>   (i)   that nothing will be done in reliance on the authorisation beyond what is necessary for the proper discharge of a function of the Intelligence Service [or GCHQ]; and
>>
>>   (ii) that, in so far as any act may be done in reliance on the authorisation, their nature and likely consequences will be reasonable, having regard to the purposes for which they are carried out; and
>
>   (c) that there are satisfactory arrangements in force under section 2(2)(a) [or 4(2)(a)] above with respect to the disclosure of information obtained by virtue of this section and that any information obtained by virtue of anything done in reliance on the authorisation will be subject to those arrangements.

(4)–(14) *****

8, 9 ...

10   The Intelligence and Security Committee

(1) There shall be a Committee, to be known as the Intelligence and Security Committee and in this section referred to as 'the Committee', to examine the expenditure, administration and policy of—

>   (a) the Security Service;
>   (b) the Intelligence Service; and
>   (c) GCHQ.

(2) The Committee shall consist of nine members—

>   (a) who shall be drawn both from the members of the House of Commons and from the members of the House of Lords; and
>   (b) none of whom shall be a Minister of the Crown.

(3) The members of the Committee shall be appointed by the Prime Minister after consultation with the Leader of the Opposition, within the meaning of the Ministerial and other Salaries Act 1975; and one of those members shall be so appointed as Chairman of the Committee.

(4)–(7) *****

*****

Criminal Appeal Act 1995

An Act to amend provisions relating to appeals and references to the Court of Appeal in criminal cases; to establish a Criminal Cases Review Commission and confer functions on, and make other provision in relation to, the Commission; to amend section 142 of the Magistrates' Courts Act 1980 and introduce in Northern Ireland provision similar to those of that section; to amend section 133 of the Criminal Justice Act 1988; and for connected purposes. [19th July 1995]

Territorial extent: England and Wales, Northern Ireland (except ss. 9, 11)

[**Note:** The '1968 Act' refers to the Criminal Appeal Act 1968 and the '1980 Act' refers to the Criminal Appeal (Northern Ireland) Act 1980.]

PART II THE CRIMINAL CASES REVIEW COMMISSION

The Commission

8 The Commission

(1) There shall be a body corporate to be known as the Criminal Cases Review Commission.

(2) The Commission shall not be regarded as the servant or agent of the Crown or as enjoying any status, immunity or privilege of the Crown; and the Commission's property shall not be regarded as property of, or held on behalf of, the Crown.

(3) The Commission shall consist of not fewer than eleven members.

(4) The members of the Commission shall be appointed by Her Majesty on the recommendation of the Prime Minister.

(5) At least one third of the members of the Commission shall be persons who are legally qualified; and for this purpose a person is legally qualified if—

   (a) The has a ten year general qualification, within the meaning of section 71 of the Courts and Legal Services Act 1990, or

   (b) The is a member of the Bar of Northern Ireland, or solicitor of the [Court of Judicature of Northern Ireland] of at least ten years' standing.

(6) At least two thirds of the members of the Commission shall be persons who appear to the Prime Minister to have knowledge or experience of any aspect of the criminal justice system and of them at least one shall be a person who appears to him to have knowledge or experience of any aspect of the criminal justice system in Northern Ireland; and for the purposes of this subsection the criminal justice system includes, in particular, the investigation of offences and the treatment of offenders.

(7) *****

References to court

9 Cases dealt with on indictment in England and Wales

(1) Where a person has been convicted of an offence on indictment in England and Wales, the Commission—

   (a) may at any time refer the conviction to the Court of Appeal, and

   (b) (whether or not they refer the conviction) may at any time refer to the Court of Appeal any sentence (not being a sentence fixed by law) imposed on, or in subsequent proceedings relating to, the conviction.

(2) A reference under subsection (1) of a person's conviction shall be treated for all purposes as an appeal by the person under section 1 of the 1968 Act against the conviction.

(3) A reference under subsection (1) of a sentence imposed on, or in subsequent proceedings relating to, a person's conviction on an indictment shall be treated for all purposes as an appeal by the person under section 9 of the 1968 Act against—

   (a) the sentence, and

   (b) any other sentence (not being a sentence fixed by law) imposed on, or in subsequent proceedings relating to, the conviction or any other conviction on the indictment.

(4) On a reference under subsection (1) of a person's conviction on an indictment the Commission may give notice to the Court of Appeal that any other conviction on the indictment which is specified in the notice is to be treated as referred to the Court of Appeal under subsection (1).

(5), (6) *****

10 *****

11 Cases dealt with summarily in England and Wales

(1) Where a person has been convicted of an offence by a magistrates' court in England and Wales, the Commission—

   (a) may at any time refer the conviction to the Crown Court, and

   (b) (whether or not they refer the conviction) may at any time refer to the Crown Court any sentence imposed on, or in subsequent proceedings relating to, the conviction.

(2) A reference under subsection (1) of a person's conviction shall be treated for all purposes as an appeal by the person under section 108(1) of the Magistrates' Courts Act 1980 against the conviction (whether or not he pleaded guilty).

(3) A reference under subsection (1) of a sentence imposed on, or in subsequent proceedings relating to, a person's conviction shall be treated for all purposes as an appeal by the person under section 108(1) of the Magistrates' Courts Act 1980 against—

(a) the sentence, and

(b) any other sentence imposed on, or in subsequent proceedings relating to, the conviction or any related conviction.

(4)–(7) *****

12–12B *****

13   Conditions for making of references

(1) A reference of a conviction, verdict, finding or sentence shall not be made under any of sections 9 to [12B] unless—

(a) the Commission consider that there is a real possibility that the conviction, verdict, finding or sentence would not be upheld were the reference to be made,

(b) the Commission so consider—

(i) in the case of a conviction, verdict or finding, because of an argument, or evidence, not raised in the proceedings which led to it or on any appeal or application for leave to appeal against it, or

(ii) in the case of a sentence, because of an argument on a point of law, or information, not so raised, and

(c) an appeal against the conviction, verdict, finding or sentence has been determined or leave to appeal against it has been refused.

(2) Nothing in subsection (1)(b)(i) or (c) shall prevent the making of a reference if it appears to the Commission that there are exceptional circumstances which justify making it.

14, 15 *****

16   Assistance in connection with prerogative of mercy

(1) Where the Secretary of State refers to the Commission any matter which arises in the consideration of whether to recommend the exercise of Her Majesty's prerogative of mercy in relation to a conviction and on which he desires their assistance, the Commission shall—

(a) consider the matter referred, and

(b) give to the Secretary of State a statement of their conclusions on it; and the Secretary of State shall, in considering whether so to recommend, treat the Commission's statement as conclusive of the matter referred.

(2) Where in any case the Commission are of the opinion that the Secretary of State should consider whether to recommend the exercise of Her Majesty's prerogative of mercy in relation to the case they shall give him the reasons for their opinion.

(3) *****

Defamation Act 1996

(1996, c. 31)

An Act to amend the law of defamation and to amend the law of limitation with respect to actions for defamation or malicious falsehood.   [4th July 1996]

Territorial extent: United Kingdom

*****

Evidence concerning proceedings in Parliament

13 Evidence concerning proceedings in Parliament

(1) Where the conduct of a person in or in relation to proceedings in Parliament is in issue in defamation proceedings, he may waive for the purposes of those proceedings, so far as concerns him, the protection of any enactment or rule of law which prevents proceedings in Parliament being impeached or questioned in any court or place out of Parliament.

(2) Where a person waives that protection—

(a) any such enactment or rule of law shall not apply to prevent evidence being given, questions being asked or statements, submissions, comments or findings being made about his conduct, and

(b) none of those things shall be regarded as infringing the privilege of either House of Parliament.

(3) The waiver by one person of that protection does not affect its operation in relation to another person who has not waived it.

(4) Nothing in this section affects any enactment or rule of law so far as it protects a person (including a person who has waived the protection referred to above) from legal liability for words spoken or things done in the course of, or for the purposes of or incidental to, any proceedings in Parliament.

(5) Without prejudice to the generality of subsection (4), that subsection applies to—

(a) the giving of evidence before either House or a committee;

(b) the presentation or submission of a document to either House or a committee;

(c) the preparation of a document for the purposes of or incidental to the transacting of any such business;

(d) the formulation, making or publication of a document, including a report, by or pursuant to an order of either House or a committee; and

(e) any communication with the Parliamentary Commissioner for Standards or any person having functions in connection with the registration of Members' interests.

In this subsection 'a committee' means a committee of either House or a joint committee of both Houses of Parliament.

Statutory privilege

14 Reports of court proceedings absolutely privileged

(1) A fair and accurate report of proceedings in public before a court to which this section applies, if published contemporaneously with the proceedings, is absolutely privileged.

(2) A report of proceedings which by an order of the court, or as a consequence of any statutory provision, is required to be postponed shall be treated as published contemporaneously if it is published as soon as practicable after publication is permitted.

(3) This section applies to—

(a) any court in the United Kingdom,

(b) the European Court of Justice or any court attached to that court,

(c) the European Court of Human Rights, and

(d) any international criminal tribunal established by the Security Council of the United Nations or by an international agreement to which the United Kingdom is a party.

In paragraph (a) 'court' includes any tribunal or body exercising the judicial power of the State.

(4) . . .

15 Reports, &c. protected by qualified privilege

(1) The publication of any report or other statement mentioned in Schedule 1 to this Act is privileged unless the publication is shown to be made with malice, subject as follows.

(2) In defamation proceedings in respect of the publication of a report or other statement mentioned in Part II of that Schedule, there is no defence under this section if the plaintiff shows that the defendant—

(a) was requested by him to publish in a suitable manner a reasonable letter or statement by way of explanation or contradiction, and

(b) refused or neglected to do so.

For this purpose 'in a suitable manner' means in the same manner as the publication complained of or in a manner that is adequate and reasonable in the circumstances.

(3) This section does not apply to the publication to the public, or a section of the public, of matter which is not of public concern and the publication of which is not for the public benefit.

(4) Nothing in this section shall be construed—

(a) as protecting the publication of matter the publication of which is prohibited by law, or

(b) as limiting or abridging any privilege subsisting apart from this section.

16–20 *****

Section 15   **SCHEDULE 1   QUALIFIED PRIVILEGE**

PART I STATEMENTS HAVING QUALIFIED PRIVILEGE WITHOUT EXPLANATION OR CONTRADICTION

1. A fair and accurate report of proceedings in public of a legislature anywhere in the world.

2. A fair and accurate report of proceedings in public before a court anywhere in the world.

3. A fair and accurate report of proceedings in public of a person appointed to hold a public inquiry by a government or legislature anywhere in the world.

4. A fair and accurate report of proceedings in public anywhere in the world of an international organisation or an international conference.

5. A fair and accurate copy of or extract from any register or other document required by law to be open to public inspection.

6. A notice or advertisement published by or on the authority of a court, or of a judge or officer of a court, anywhere in the world.

7. A fair and accurate copy of or extract from matter published by or on the authority of a government or legislature anywhere in the world.

8. A fair and accurate copy of or extract from matter published anywhere in the world by an international organisation or an international conference.

PART II STATEMENTS PRIVILEGED SUBJECT TO EXPLANATION OR CONTRADICTION

9.—(1) A fair and accurate copy of or extract from a notice or other matter issued for the information of the public by or on behalf of—

(a) a legislature in any member State or the European parliament;

(b) the government of any member State, or any authority performing governmental functions in any member State or part of a member State, or the European Commission;

(c) an international organisation or international conference.

(2) In this paragraph 'governmental functions' includes police functions.

10. A fair and accurate copy of or extract from a document made available by a court in any member State or the European Court of Justice (or any court attached to that court), or by a judge or officer of any such court.

11.—(1) A fair and accurate report of proceedings at any public meeting or sitting in the United Kingdom of—

(a)   a local authority or local authority committee;

[(aa) in the case of a local authority which are operating executive arrangements, the executive of that authority or a committee of that executive];

    (b)   a justice or justices of the peace acting otherwise than as a court exercising judicial authority;

    (c)   a commission, tribunal, committee or person appointed for the purposes of any inquiry by any statutory provision, by Her Majesty or by a Minister of the Crown [a member of the Scottish Executive] [, the Welsh Ministers or the Counsel General to the Welsh Assembly Government] or a Northern Ireland Department;

    (d)   a person appointed by a local authority to hold a local inquiry in pursuance of any statutory provision;

    (e)   any other tribunal, board, committee or body constituted by or under, and exercising functions under, any statutory provision.

(1A)–(3) *****

*****

Police Act 1996

(1996, c. 16)

An Act to consolidate the Police Act 1964, Part IX of the Police and Criminal Evidence Act 1984, Chapter I of Part I of the Police and Magistrates' Courts Act 1994 and certain other enactments relating to the police.   [22nd May 1996]

Territorial extent: England and Wales (and in the case of Part III (ss. 59–64) Scotland)

PART I ORGANISATION OF POLICE FORCES

Police areas [and police forces]

1 Police areas

(1) England and Wales shall be divided into police areas.

(2) The police areas referred to in subsection (1) shall be—

    (a) those listed in Schedule 1 (subject to any amendment made to that Schedule by an order under section 32 below, section 58 of the Local Government Act 1972, or [section 17 of the Local Government Act 1992 or Part 1 of the Local Government and Public Involvement in Health Act 2007]),

    (b) the metropolitan police district, and

    (c) the City of London police area.

(3) References in Schedule 1 to any local government area are to that area as it is for the time being . . .

2 Maintenance of police forces

[(1)] A police force shall be maintained for every police area for the time being listed in Schedule 1.

[(2) For further provision about the maintenance of those police forces, see Chapter 1 of Part 1 of the Police Reform and Social Responsibility Act 2011.]

3–5 . . .

[The metropolitan police force]

5A Maintenance of the metropolitan police force

[(1)] A police force shall be maintained for the metropolitan police district.

[(2) For further provision about the maintenance of the metropolitan police force, see Chapter 2 of Part 1 of the Police Reform and Social Responsibility Act 2011.]

5B–6 . . .

[The City of London]

[6AZA   Common Council to remain police authority for City]

[The Common Council of the City of London is to continue to be the police authority for the City of London police area.]

[6ZA   Power to confer particular functions on [the Common Council]]

[(1) The Secretary of State may by order confer particular functions on [the Common Council].

(2) Without prejudice to the generality of subsection (1), an order under this section may contain provision requiring [the Common Council]—

    (a) to monitor the performance of [the City of London Police Force] in—

        (i) complying with any duty imposed on the force by or under this Act, the Human Rights Act 1998 or any other enactment;

        (ii) carrying out any plan issued by virtue of section 6ZB;

    (b) to secure that arrangements are made for that force to co-operate with other police forces whenever necessary or expedient;

    (c) to promote diversity within that force and within [the Common Council].

(3) Before making an order under this section the Secretary of State must consult—

    (a) [the Common Council,

    (b) Commissioner of Police for the City of London, and]

    (c) such other persons as he thinks fit.

(4) ...

(5) A statutory instrument containing an order under this section shall be subject to annulment in pursuance of a resolution of either House of Parliament.]

[6ZB   Plans by [the Common Council]

[(1) Before the beginning of each financial year [the Common Council] shall issue a plan (a 'policing plan') setting out—

    (a) [the Common Council's] objectives ('policing objectives') for [the policing of the City of London police area, and for the discharge by the City of London Police of its national or international functions] during that year; and

    (b) the proposed arrangements for the policing of that area for the period of three years beginning with that year.

[(2) In issuing a policing plan, the Common Council must have regard to the strategic policing requirement issued under section 37A.]

(3) Before determining policing objectives, [the Common Council] shall—

    (a) consult the [Commissioner of Police for the City of London], and

    (b) consider any views obtained by the [Common Council] in accordance with arrangements made under section 96.

(4) A draft of a policing plan required to be issued by [the Common Council] under this section shall be prepared by the [Commissioner of Police for the City of London] and submitted by him to the [Common Council] for it to consider.

The [the Common Council] shall consult the [Commissioner of Police for the City of London] before issuing a policing plan which differs from the draft submitted by him under this subsection.

(5)–(11) *****

[6ZC   Reports by [the Common Council]]

[(1) The Secretary of State may by order require [the Common Council] to issue reports concerning the [discharge of the Common Council's functions].

(2) An order under this section may contain provision as to—

    (a) the periods to be covered by reports, and, as regards each period, the date by which reports are to be issued;

    (b) the matters to be dealt with in reports;

    (c) persons to whom copies of reports are to be sent.

(3)–(5) *****

6A–9G ...

9H Other members of the metropolitan police force

(1) The ranks that may be held in the metropolitan police force shall be such as may be prescribed by regulations under section 50.

(2) The ranks so prescribed in the case of the metropolitan police force shall include, in addition to the ranks of—

(a) Commissioner of Police of the Metropolis,

(b) Deputy Commissioner of Police of the Metropolis,

(c) Assistant Commissioner of Police of the Metropolis,

[(ca) Deputy Assistant Commissioner of Police of the Metropolis, and]

(d) Commander,

those of [chief superintendent,] superintendent, chief inspector, inspector, sergeant and constable.

(3) In the metropolitan police force, appointments and promotions to any rank below that of Commander shall be made in accordance with regulations under section 50 by the Commissioner of Police of the Metropolis.]

10–12A *****

13 Other members of police forces

(1) The ranks that may be held in a police force maintained under section 2 shall be such as may be prescribed by regulations under section 50 and the ranks so prescribed shall include, in addition to chief constable [, deputy chief constable] and assistant chief constable, the ranks of [chief superintendent], superintendent, chief inspector, inspector, sergeant and constable.

(2) ...

(3) Appointments and promotions to any rank below that of assistant chief constable in any police force maintained under section 2 shall be made, in accordance with regulations under section 50, by the chief constable.

14–17 ...

18–21 *****

General provisions

22 Reports by chief constables to police authorities

(1) [The Commissioner of Police for the City of London] shall, as soon as possible after the end of each financial year, submit to the [Common Council] a general report on the policing during that year of [the City of London Police area].

(2) [The Chief Constable] shall arrange for a report submitted by him under subsection (1) to be published in such manner as appears to him to be appropriate.

(3) [The Commissioner of Police for the City of London] shall, whenever so required by the [Common Council], submit to [the Common Council] a report on such matters as may be specified in the requirement, being matters connected with [the policing of the City of London Police area].

(4) A report submitted under subsection (3) shall be in such form as the [Common Council] may specify.

(5) If it appears to [the Commissioner of Police for the City of London] that a report in compliance with subsection (3) would contain information which in the public interest ought not to be disclosed, or is not needed for the discharge of the functions of the [Common Council], he may request [the Common Council] to refer the requirement to submit the report to the Secretary of State; and in any such case the requirement shall be of no effect unless it is confirmed by the Secretary of State.

(6) The [Common Council] may arrange, or require the [chief officer] to arrange, for a report submitted under subsection (3) to be published in such manner as appears to the [Common Council] to be appropriate.

(7) ...

[22A   Collaboration agreements]

[(1) A collaboration agreement may be made by—

(a) two or more policing bodies; or

(b) the chief officers of police of one or more police forces and two or more policing bodies.

(2) A collaboration agreement is an agreement containing one or more of the following—

(a) provision about the discharge of functions of members of a police force ("force collaboration provision");

(b) provision about support by a policing body for another policing body ("policing body collaboration provision");

(c) provision about support by a policing body for the police force which another policing body is responsible for maintaining ("policing body & force collaboration provision").

(3) A collaboration agreement may not contain force collaboration provision unless the parties to the agreement consist of, or include,—

(a) the chief officer of police of each police force to which the provision relates, and

(b) the policing body that is responsible for maintaining each such police force.

(4) A collaboration agreement may not contain policing body collaboration provision unless the parties to the agreement consist of, or include, each policing body to which the provision relates.

(5) A collaboration agreement may not contain policing body & force collaboration provision unless the parties to the agreement consist of, or include—

(a) the policing body, or each policing body, to which the provision relates;

(b) the chief officer of police of the police force, or each police force, to which the provision relates; and

(c) the policing body that is responsible for maintaining each such police force.

(6) Subsection (1) does not prevent other persons from being parties to collaboration agreements.

(7) Subsection (2) does not prevent a collaboration agreement from including other kinds of provision.

(8) For the purposes of subsections (3) and (5), the circumstances in which force collaboration provision, or policing body & force collaboration provision, is to be taken to relate to a police force include the cases where provision relates—

(a) to functions of a kind which are or may be exercisable by members of that police force, or

(b) to the police area for which that police force is established.

(9) For the purposes of subsections (4) and (5), the circumstances in which policing body collaboration provision, or policing body & force collaboration provision, is to be taken to relate to a policing body include the cases where provision relates—

(a) to functions of a kind which are or may be exercisable by that policing body or members of the staff of that body, or

(b) to the police area for which that policing body is established.]

[22B   Duty of chief officers to keep collaboration agreements under review]

[(1) The chief officer of police of a police force must keep under consideration the ways in which the collaboration functions could be exercised by the chief officer and by one or more other persons to improve the efficiency or effectiveness of—

(a) that police force, and

(b) one or more other police forces.

(2) If the chief officer considers that there is a particular way in which the collaboration functions could be so exercised by the chief officer and by one or more other particular persons ("the proposed collaboration"), the chief officer must notify those other persons (the "proposed partners") of the proposed collaboration.

(3) The chief officer, and the proposed partners notified under subsection (2) (the "notified proposed partners"), must consider whether to exercise the collaboration functions to give effect to the proposed collaboration.

(4) In considering whether to so exercise the collaboration functions, the chief officer and the notified proposed partners must consider whether the proposed collaboration would be in the interests of the efficiency or effectiveness of one or more police forces.

(5) Subsection (6) applies if all, or two or more, of—

(a) the chief officer, and

(b) the notified proposed partners,

(the "agreeing parties") are of the view that the proposed collaboration would be in the interests of the efficiency or effectiveness of one or more police forces (if the agreeing parties were to exercise the collaboration functions to give effect to the proposed collaboration, or to give effect to it so far as it relates to them).

(6) The agreeing parties must exercise the collaboration functions so as to give effect to the proposed collaboration or to give effect to it so far as it relates to them.

(7) In this section "collaboration functions" means functions of chief officers of police or policing bodies under any of sections 22A to 23I (apart from this section).]

[22C   Duty of policing bodies to keep collaboration agreements under review]

[(1) A policing body must keep under consideration the ways in which the collaboration functions could be exercised by the policing body and by one or more other persons to improve—

(a) the efficiency or effectiveness of—

(i)   that policing body,

(ii)   the police force which that policing body is responsible for maintaining, or

(iii)   that body and that force, and

(b) the efficiency or effectiveness of one or more other policing bodies and police forces.

(2) If the policing body considers that there is a particular way in which the collaboration functions could be so exercised by the policing body and by one or more other particular persons ("the proposed collaboration"), the policing body must notify those other persons (the "proposed partners") of the proposed collaboration.

(3) The policing body, and the proposed partners notified under subsection (2) (the "notified proposed partners"), must consider whether to exercise the collaboration functions to give effect to the proposed collaboration.

(4) In considering whether to so exercise the collaboration functions, the policing body and the notified proposed partners must consider whether the proposed collaboration would be in the interests of the efficiency or effectiveness of one or more policing bodies or police forces.

(5) Subsection (6) applies if all, or two or more, of—

(a) the policing body, and

(b) the notified proposed partners,

(the "agreeing parties") are of the view that the proposed collaboration would be in the interests of the efficiency or effectiveness of one or more policing bodies or police forces (if the agreeing parties were to exercise the collaboration functions to give effect to the proposed collaboration, or to give effect to it so far as it relates to them).

(6) The agreeing parties must exercise the collaboration functions so as to give effect to the proposed collaboration, or to give effect to it so far as it relates to them.

(7) In this section "collaboration functions" means functions of policing bodies or chief officers of police under any of sections 22A to 23I (apart from this section).]

23   *****

24   Aid of one police force by another

(1) The chief officer of police of any police force may, on the application of the chief officer of police of any other police force, provide constables or other assistance for the purpose of enabling the other force to meet any special demand on its resources.

(2) If it appears to the Secretary of State to be expedient in the interests of public safety or order that any police force should be reinforced or should receive other assistance for the purpose

of enabling it to meet any special demand on its resources, and that satisfactory arrangements under subsection (1) cannot be made, or cannot be made in time, he may direct the chief officer of police of any police force to provide such constables or other assistance for that purpose as may be specified in the direction.

(3) While a constable is provided under this section for the assistance of another police force he shall, notwithstanding [sections 2 and 4 of the Police Reform and Social Responsibility Act 2011 ("the 2011 Act")], be under the direction and control of the chief officer of police of that other force.

[(3A) While a member of the civilian staff of a police force maintained under section 2, or a member of the civilian staff of the metropolitan police force, is provided under this section for the assistance of another police force, that member of staff is, notwithstanding section 2 or 4 of the 2011 Act, under the direction and control of the chief officer of police of that other force.]

(4) The [local policing body] maintaining a police force for which assistance is provided under this section shall pay to the [local policing body] maintaining the force from which that assistance is provided such contribution as may be agreed upon between [those bodies] or, in the absence of any such agreement, as may be provided by any agreement subsisting at the time between all [local policing bodies] generally, or, in the absence of such general agreement, as may be determined by the Secretary of State.

[(4A) This section shall apply in relation to the British Transport Police Authority, the British Transport Police Force and the Chief Constable of that Force as it applies to a [local policing body], a police force and a chief officer of police respectively; and for that purpose the reference in subsection (3) to [sections 2 and 4 of the 2011 Act] shall be construed as including a reference to section 24(2) of the Railways and Transport Safety Act 2003.]

[(5) ...]

25   Provision of special services

(1) The chief officer of police of a police force may provide, at the request of any person, special police services at any premises or in any locality in the police area for which the force is maintained, subject to the payment to the [local policing body] of charges on such scales as may be determined by [that body].

(1A) *****

(2) ...

26   Provision of advice and assistance to international organisations etc

(1) Subject to the provisions of this section, a [local policing body] may provide advice and assistance—

>   (a) to an international organisation or institution, or
>   (b) to any other person or body which is engaged outside the United Kingdom in the carrying on of activities similar to any carried on by [the body] or the chief officer of police for its area.

(2) The power conferred on a [local policing body] by subsection (1) includes a power to make arrangements under which a member of the police force maintained by [the body] is engaged for a period of temporary service with a person or body within paragraph (a) or (b) of that subsection.

(3) The power conferred by subsection (1) shall not be exercised except with the consent of the Secretary of State or in accordance with a general authorisation given by him.

(4) A consent or authorisation under subsection (3) may be given subject to such conditions as appear to the Secretary of State to be appropriate.

(5) Nothing in this section authorises a [local policing body] to provide any financial assistance by—

>   (a) making a grant or loan,
>   (b) giving a guarantee or indemnity, or
>   (c) investing by acquiring share or loan capital.

(6) A [local policing body] may make charges for advice or assistance provided by it under this section.

(7) ...

(8) The provisions of this section are without prejudice to the Police (Overseas Service) Act 1945...

27–28 *****

29   Attestation of constables

Every member of a police force maintained for a police area and every special constable appointed for a police area shall, on appointment, be attested as a constable by making a declaration in the form set out in Schedule 4—

    (a) ...

    (b) ... before a justice of the peace having jurisdiction within the police area.

30   Jurisdiction of constables

    (1) A member of a police force shall have all the powers and privileges of a constable throughout England and Wales and the adjacent United Kingdom waters.

    [(2) A special constable shall have all the powers and privileges of a constable throughout England and Wales and the adjacent United Kingdom waters.]

    (3) ...

    [(3A) A member of the British Transport Police Force who is for the time being required by virtue of [section 22A] to serve with a police force maintained by a [local policing body] shall have all the powers and privileges of a member of that police force.]

    [(3B) Where a member of the British Transport Police Force is for the time being under the direction and control of the chief officer of another police force by virtue of a [collaboration agreement under section 22A], the member shall have all the powers and privileges of a member of that other force.]

    [(3C) In subsection (3B), "police force" and "chief officer" have the meanings given by section 23I.]

    (4) ...

    (5), (6) *****

31 *****

32   Power to alter police areas by order

    (1) The Secretary of State may by order make alterations in police areas in England and Wales other than the City of London police area.

    (2) The alterations that may be made by an order under this section include alterations that result in a reduction or an increase in the number of police areas, but not alterations that result in the abolition of the metropolitan police district.

    (3) The Secretary of State shall not exercise his power under this section to make alterations unless either—

        (a) he has received a request to make the alterations from the [local policing body] for each of the areas ... affected by them, or

        (b) it appears to him to be expedient to make the alterations in the interests of efficiency or effectiveness.

    (4) The Secretary of State shall exercise his power to make orders under this section in such a way as to ensure that [no police area falls partly in England and partly in Wales and that] none of the following areas—

        (a) a county in which there are no district councils,

        (b) a district in any other county,

        (c) a county borough in Wales, and

        (d) a London borough,

is divided between two or more police areas.

    (5) ...

33–35 *****

PART II CENTRAL SUPERVISION, DIRECTION AND FACILITIES

Functions of Secretary of State

36   General duty of Secretary of State

(1) The Secretary of State shall exercise his powers under the provisions of this Act referred to in subsection (2) in such manner and to such extent as appears to him to be best calculated to promote the efficiency and effectiveness of the police.

(2) The provisions of this Act mentioned in subsection (1) are—

(a) Part I;

(b) this Part;

(c) Part III (other than sections 61 and 62);

(d) in Chapter II of Part IV, [sections 84 and 85] and Schedule 6; and

(e) in Part V, section 95.

36A, 37 ...

[37A   The strategic policing requirement]

[(1) The Secretary of State must, from time to time, issue a document (the "strategic policing requirement") which sets out what, in the Secretary of State's view, are—

(a) national threats at the time the document is issued, and

(b) appropriate national policing capabilities to counter those national threats.

(2) A chief officer of police must, in exercising the functions of chief officer, have regard to the strategic policing requirement.

(3) Before issuing the strategic policing requirement, the Secretary of State—

(a) must obtain the advice of—

(i) such persons as appear to the Secretary of State to represent the views of chief officers of police, and

(ii) such persons as appear to the Secretary of State to represent the views of local policing bodies, and

(b) must consult such other persons as the Secretary of State thinks fit.

(4)–(6) *****

38   Setting of performance targets

(1) Where [a strategic priority has been determined under section 37A], the Secretary of State may direct police authorities to establish levels of performance ('performance targets') to be aimed at in seeking [to give effect to that priority].

(2) A direction under this section may be given to all police authorities [to which [section 37A] applies] or to one or more particular authorities.

(3) A direction given under this section may impose conditions with which the performance targets must conform, and different conditions may be imposed for different authorities.

(4) The Secretary of State shall arrange for any direction given under this section to be published in such manner as appears to him to be appropriate.

[(5) A [local policing body] that is given a direction under this section shall comply with it.

39 ...

39A *****

[40   Power to give directions in relation to police force]

[(1) Where the Secretary of State is satisfied that the whole or any part of a police force is failing to discharge any of its functions in an effective manner, whether generally or in particular respects, he may direct the [local policing body] responsible for maintaining the force to take specified measures for the purpose of remedying the failure.

(2) Where the Secretary of State is satisfied that the whole or a part of a police force will fail to discharge any of its functions in an effective manner, whether generally or in particular respects, unless remedial measures are taken, he may direct the [local policing body] responsible for maintaining the force to take specified measures in order to prevent such a failure occurring.

(3) The measures that may be specified in a direction under subsection (1) or (2) include the submission to the Secretary of State of an action plan setting out the measures which the person or persons submitting the plan propose to take for the purpose of remedying the failure in question or (as the case may be) preventing such a failure occurring.

(4) The Secretary of State shall not give a direction under this section in relation to any police force unless—

    (a) the [local policing body] responsible for maintaining the force and the chief officer of police of that force have each been given such information about the Secretary of State's grounds for proposing to give that direction as he considers appropriate for enabling them to make representations or proposals under the following paragraphs of this subsection;

    (b) that [local policing body] and chief officer have each been given an opportunity of making representations about those grounds;

    (c) that [local policing body] and chief officer have each had an opportunity of making proposals for the taking of remedial measures that would make the giving of the direction unnecessary; and

    (d) the Secretary of State has considered any such representations and any such proposals.

(5) Subsection (4) does not apply if the Secretary of State is satisfied that—

    (a) the [local policing body] responsible for maintaining the force and the chief officer of police of that force have already been made aware of the matters constituting the Secretary of State's grounds for proposing to give a direction under this section;

    (b) the information they had about those matters was sufficient to enable them to identify remedial measures that would have made the giving of the direction unnecessary; and

    (c) they have each had a reasonable opportunity to take such measures.

(6) The Secretary of State shall not give a direction under this section unless Her Majesty's Chief Inspector of Constabulary has been given—

    (a) the same information about the grounds for proposing to give that direction as is required to be given under subsection (4)(a) (or would be so required but for subsection (5)); and

    (b) an opportunity of making written observations about those grounds.

The Secretary of State shall publish any such observations in such manner as appears to him to be appropriate.

(7) A [local policing body] that is given a direction under this section shall comply with it.

[40A Power to give directions in relation to police authority]

[(1) Where the Secretary of State is satisfied that a [local policing body] is failing to discharge any of its functions in an effective manner, whether generally or in particular respects, he may direct the [local policing body] to take specified measures for the purpose of remedying the failure.

(2) Where the Secretary of State is satisfied that a [local policing body] will fail to discharge any of its functions in an effective manner, whether generally or in particular respects, unless remedial measures are taken, he may direct the [local policing body] to take specified measures in order to prevent such a failure occurring.

(3)–(7) *****

(8) Nothing in this section or in section 40 prevents the Secretary of State from exercising (whether in relation to the same matter or different matters or at the same time or at different times) both his powers under this section and his powers under section 40.]

[40B Procedure for directions under section 40 or 40A]

[(1) The Secretary of State may by regulations make further provision as to the procedure to be followed in cases where—

    (a) a proposal is made for the giving of a direction under section 40;

     (b) a proposal is made for the giving of a direction under section 40A.

  (2) Before making any regulations under this section, the Secretary of State shall consult with—

     [(a) such persons as appear to the Secretary of State to represent the views of police and crime commissioners;

     (aa) the Mayor's Office for Policing & Crime;

     (ab) the Common Council;]

     (b) the Association of Chief Police Officers; and

     (c) such other persons as he thinks fit.

  (3) Regulations under this section may make different provision for different cases and circumstances.

  (4) A statutory instrument containing regulations under this section shall not be made unless a draft of the regulations has been laid before Parliament and approved by a resolution of each House.

  (5) On giving a direction under section 40 or section 40A to a [local policing body], the Secretary of State shall notify the chief officer of police of the force in question that he has given that direction.

  (6) Where the Secretary of State gives a direction under section 40 or section 40A he shall lay before Parliament—

     (a) a copy of the direction; and

     (b) a report about it.

  (7) A report under subsection (6)—

     (a) shall be prepared at such time as the Secretary of State considers appropriate; and

     (b) may relate to more than one direction.]

41   *****

41A, 41B ...

42   Removal of chief constables etc.

  [(1) The Secretary of State may—

     (a) require the Mayor's Office for Policing & Crime to exercise its power under section 48 of the Police Reform and Social Responsibility Act 2011 to call upon the Commissioner of Police of the Metropolis or Deputy Commissioner of Police of the Metropolis, to retire or to resign.

  (1A) The Secretary of State may also require the Mayor's Office of Policing & Crime to exercise the power under section 48 of the 2011 Act to suspend the Commissioner of Police of the Metropolis, or the Deputy Commissioner of the Police of the Metropolis, if the Secretary of State considers that it is necessary for the maintenance of public confidence in the metropolitan police force for that police officer to be suspended.]

  (2) [Before requiring the Mayor's Office of Policing & Crime to exercise its power to call upon the Commissioner of Police of the Metropolis or Deputy Commissioner of Police of the Metropolis to retire or to resign, the Secretary of State shall—]

     (a) give the officer concerned a notice in writing—

       (i) informing him of the Secretary of State's intention to require the exercise of that power; and

       (ii) explaining the Secretary of State's grounds for requiring the exercise of that power; and

     (b) give that officer an opportunity to make representations to the Secretary of State.

  (2A) Where the Secretary of State gives a notice under subsection (2)(a), he shall send a copy of the notice to the [Mayor's Office of Policing & Crime.]

  (2B) The Secretary of State shall consider any representations made to him under subsection (2).]

  (3) [Where the Secretary of State proposes to require the exercise of a power mentioned in subsection (1), he] shall, appoint one or more persons (one at least of whom shall be a person who is not an officer of police or of a Government department) to hold an inquiry and report to him and shall consider any report made under this subsection.

[(3A) At an inquiry held under subsection (3)—

    (a) the Commissioner [or Deputy Commissioner] shall be entitled, in accordance with any regulations under section 42A, to make representations to the inquiry;

    (b) the [Mayor's Office of Policing & Crime] shall be entitled, in accordance with any regulations made under section 42A, to make representations to the inquiry.

(3B) The entitlement of the Commissioner [or Deputy Commissioner] to make representations shall include the entitlement to make them in person.]

(4) The costs incurred by the Commissioner [or Deputy Commissioner] in respect of an inquiry under this section, taxed in such manner as the Secretary of State may direct, shall be defrayed out of the police fund.

(4A)–(4C) *****

(5) ...

42A–45 *****

46 Police grant

(1) Subject to the following provisions of this section, the Secretary of State shall for each financial year make grants for police purposes to—

    (a)   [police and crime commissioners]

    [(aa) the Common Council;]

    (b)   [the Greater London Authority];

[and in those provisions a reference to a grant recipient is a reference to a police and crime commissioner, the Common Council or the Greater London Authority].

(2) For each financial year the Secretary of State shall with the approval of the Treasury determine—

    (a) the aggregate amount of grants to be made under this section, and

    (b) the amount of the grant to be made to each [grant recipient];

and any determination may be varied by further determinations under this subsection.

(3) The Secretary of State shall prepare a report setting out any determination under subsection (2), and stating the considerations which he took into account in making the determination.

(4) In determining the allocation among [grant recipients] of the whole or any part of the aggregate amount of grants, the Secretary of State may exercise his discretion by applying such formulae or other rules as he considers appropriate.

(5) The considerations which the Secretary of State takes into account in making a determination under subsection (2), and the formulae and other rules referred to in subsection (4), may be different for different authorities or different [grant recipients or different classes of grant recipient].

(6)–(9) *****

47, 48 *****

49 ...

50 Regulations for police forces

(1) Subject to the provisions of this section, the Secretary of State may make regulations as to the government, administration and conditions or service of police forces.

(2) Without prejudice to the generality of subsection (1), regulations under this section may make provision with respect to—

    (a) the ranks to be held by members of police forces;

    (b) the qualifications for appointment and promotion of members of police forces;

    (c) periods of service on probation;

    (d) voluntary retirement of members of police forces;

    (e) the conduct, efficiency and effectiveness of members of police forces and the maintenance of discipline;

    (f) the suspension of members of a police force from membership of that force and from their office as constable;

    (g) the maintenance of personal records of members of police forces;

    (h) the duties which are or are not to be performed by members of police forces;

    (i) the treatment as occasions of police duty of attendance at meetings of the Police Federations and of any body recognised by the Secretary of State for the purposes of section 64;

    (j) the hours of duty, leave, pay and allowances of members of police forces; and

    (k) the issue, use and return of police clothing, personal equipment and accoutrements.

(2A), (2B) *****

[(3) Without prejudice to the powers conferred by this section, regulations under this section shall—

    (a) establish, or

    (b) make provision for the establishment of,

procedures for the taking of disciplinary proceedings in respect of the conduct, efficiency and effectiveness of members of police forces, including procedures for cases in which such persons may be dealt with by dismissal.]

    For the purposes of this subsection 'senior officer' means a member of a police force holding a rank above that of [chief] superintendent.

(4), (5) *****

(6) Regulations under this section as to conditions of service shall secure that appointments for fixed terms are not made except where the person appointed holds the rank of superintendent or a higher rank.

(6A)–(8) *****

51–[53D] *****

Inspectors of constabulary

54 Appointment and functions of inspectors of constabulary

(1) Her Majesty may appoint such number of inspectors (to be known as 'Her Majesty's Inspectors of Constabulary') as the Secretary of State may with the consent of the Treasury determine, and of the persons so appointed one may be appointed as chief inspector of constabulary.

(2) The inspectors of constabulary shall inspect, and report . . . on the efficiency and effectiveness of, every police force maintained for a police area [. . .]

(2A)–(6) *****

55–58 *****

PART III POLICE REPRESENTATIVE INSTITUTIONS

59 Police Federations

(1) There shall continue to be a Police Federation for England and Wales and a Police Federation of Scotland for the purpose of representing members of the police forces in those countries respectively in all matters affecting their welfare and efficiency, except for—

    (a) questions of promotion affecting individuals, and

    (b) (subject to subsection (2)) questions of discipline affecting individuals.

(2) A Police Federation may represent a member of a police force at any proceedings brought under regulations made in accordance with section 50(3) above or section 26(2A) of the Police (Scotland) Act 1967 or on an appeal from any such proceedings.

(3) Except on an appeal to a police appeals tribunal or as [provided in regulations made in accordance with] section 84, a member of a police force may only be represented under subsection (2) by another member of a police force.

(4) The Police Federations shall act through local and central representative bodies.

(5) The Police Federations and every branch of a Federation shall be entirely independent of, and subject to subsection (6) unassociated with, any body or person outside the police service, but may employ persons outside the police service in an administrative or advisory capacity.

(6) The Secretary of State—

    (a) may authorise a Police Federation or a branch of a Federation to be associated with a person or body outside the police service in such cases and manner, and subject to such conditions and restrictions, as he may specify, and

    (b) may vary or withdraw an authorisation previously given; and anything for the time being so authorised shall not be precluded by subsection (5).

(7) This section applies to police cadets as it applies to members of police forces, and references to the police service shall be construed accordingly.

[(7A) For the purposes of subsection (1), a member of the staff of the National Policing Improvement Agency who is—

    (a) a constable, and

    (b) an employee of the Agency,

shall be treated as a member of a police force in England and Wales, and references in this section to police service shall be construed accordingly.]

[(8) . . .]

60   Regulations for Police Federations

(1) The Secretary of State may by regulations—

    (a) prescribe the constitution and proceedings of the Police Federations, or

    (b) authorise the Federations to make rules concerning such matters relating to their constitution and proceedings as may be specified in the regulations.

(2) Without prejudice to the generality of subsection (1), regulations under this section may make provision—

    (a) with respect to the membership of the Federations;

    (b) with respect to the raising of funds by the Federations by voluntary subscription and the use and management of funds derived from such subscriptions;

    (c) with respect to the manner in which representations may be made by committees or bodies of the Federations to [local policing bodies,] chief officers of police and the Secretary of State;

    (d) for the payment by the Secretary of State of expenses incurred in connection with the Federations and for the use by the Federations of premises provided by [local policing bodies or] police authorities for police purposes; and

    (e) for modifying any regulations under the Police Pensions Act 1976, section 50 above or section 26 of the Police (Scotland) Act 1967 in relation to any member of a police force who is the secretary or an officer of a Police Federation and for requiring the appropriate Federation to make contributions in respect of the pay, pension or allowances payable to or in respect of any such person.

(2A) . . .

(3)–(6) *****

[60A] *****

61   The Police Negotiating Board for the United Kingdom

(1) There shall continue to be a Police Negotiation Board for the United Kingdom for the consideration by persons representing the interests of—

    (a)   the [persons and bodies] who between them maintain the police forces in Great Britain and the [Police Service of Northern Ireland],

    [(aa) . . .]

    (b)   the persons who are members of those police forces or of [the Police Service] or are police cadets,

    [(ba) . . .]

    [(bb) the members of the staff of the National Policing Improvement Agency who are constables,]

    (c)   the Commissioner of Police of the Metropolis, . . .

[(ca) the Scottish Police Services Authority,

(cb) constables seconded to that Authority under paragraph 10(2) of schedule 1 to the Police, Public Order and Criminal Justice (Scotland) Act 2006 but not appointed to be police members of the Scottish Crime and Drug Enforcement Agency in accordance with paragraph 7 of schedule 2 to that Act,

(cc) persons seconded to that Authority under paragraph 10(3) of schedule 1 to that Act but not appointed as mentioned in paragraph (cb),

(cd) persons appointed as police members of the Scottish Crime and Drug Enforcement Agency in accordance with paragraph 7 of schedule 2 to that Act,]

(d) the Secretary of State [and

(e) the Scottish Ministers],

of questions relating to hours of duty, leave, pay and allowances, pensions or the issue, use and return of police clothing, personal equipment and accoutrements.

(2) The Chairman and any deputy chairman or chairmen of the Board shall be appointed by the Prime Minister [after consultation with the Scottish Ministers].

(3)–(6) *****

62, 63 *****

64 Membership of trade unions

(1) Subject to the following provisions of this section, a member of a police force shall not be a member of any trade union, or of any association having for its objects, or one of its objects, to control or influence the pay, pensions or conditions of service of any police force.

(2) Where a person was a member of a trade union before becoming a member of a police force, he may, with the consent of the chief officer of police, continue to be a member of that union during the time of his service in the police force.

(3), (4A), (4B) ...

(4), (4C)–(4F), (5) *****

PART IV COMPLAINTS, DISCIPLINARY PROCEEDINGS ETC.

65–83 ...

Chapter II Disciplinary and other proceedings

84 Representation etc. at disciplinary and other proceedings

[(1) The Secretary of State shall by regulations make provision for or in connection with—

(a) enabling the officer concerned or a relevant authority to be represented in proceedings conducted under regulations made in pursuance of section 50(3) or section 51(2A);

(b) enabling the panel conducting such proceedings to receive advice from a relevant lawyer or another person falling within any prescribed description of persons.

(2) Regulations under this section may in particular make provision—

(a) specifying the circumstances in which the officer concerned or a relevant authority is entitled to be legally represented (by a relevant lawyer);

(b) specifying the circumstances in which the officer concerned or a relevant authority is entitled to be represented by a person (other than a relevant lawyer) who falls within any prescribed description of persons;

(c) for securing that—

(i) a relevant authority may be legally represented, and

(ii) the panel conducting the proceedings may receive advice from a relevant lawyer,

whether or not the officer concerned is legally represented.

(3) Without prejudice to the powers conferred by this section, regulations under this section shall, in relation to cases where the officer concerned is entitled to legal or other representation, make provision—

    (a) for securing that the officer is notified of his right to such representation;

    (b) specifying when the officer is to be so notified;

    (c) for securing that proceedings at which the officer may be dismissed are not to take place unless the officer has been notified of his right to such representation].

    (4)–(9) *****

85 Appeals against dismissal etc.

[(1) The Secretary of State shall by rules make provision specifying the cases in which a member of a police force or a special constable may appeal to a police appeals tribunal.

(2) A police appeals tribunal may, on the determination of an appeal under this section, make an order dealing with the appellant in any way in which he could have been dealt with by the person who made the decision appealed against.]

(3) The Secretary of State may make rules as to the procedure on appeals to police appeals tribunals under this section.

    (4)–(6) *****

86 ...

87 *****

88 Liability for wrongful acts of constables

(1) The chief officer of police for a police area shall be liable in respect of [any unlawful conduct of] constables under his direction and control in the performance or purported performance of their functions in like manner as a master is liable in respect of [any unlawful conduct of] his servants in the course of their employment, and accordingly shall [, in the case of a tort,] be treated for all purposes as a joint tortfeasor.

(2) There shall be paid out of the police fund—

    (a) any damages or costs awarded against the chief officer of police in any proceedings brought against him by virtue of this section and any costs incurred by him in any such proceedings so far as not recovered by him in the proceedings; and

    (b) any sum required in connection with the settlement of any claim made against the chief officer of police by virtue of this section, if the settlement is approved by the [local policing body].

(3) Any proceedings in respect of a claim made by virtue of this section shall be brought against the chief officer of police for the time being or, in the case of a vacancy in that office, against the person for the time being performing the functions of the chief officer of police; and references in subsections (1) and (2) to the chief officer of police shall be construed accordingly.

(4) A [local policing body] may, in such cases and to such extent as appear to it to be appropriate, pay out of the police fund—

    (a) any damages or costs awarded against a person to whom this subsection applies in proceedings for [any lawful conduct of] that person,

    (b) any costs incurred and not recovered by such a person in such proceedings, and

    (c) any sum required in connection with the settlement of a claim that has or might have given rise to such proceedings.

(5) Subsection (4) applies to a person who is—

    (a) a member of the police force maintained by the [local policing body],

    (b) a constable for the time being required to serve with that force by virtue of section 24 or 98 [of this Act . . .], or

    (c) a special constable appointed for the [local policing body's] police area.

    (5A)–(8) *****

PART V MISCELLANEOUS AND GENERAL

Offences

89 Assaults on constables

(1) Any person who assaults a constable in the execution of his duty, or a person assisting a constable in the execution of his duty, shall be guilty of an offence and liable on summary conviction to imprisonment for a term not exceeding six months or to a fine not exceeding level 5 on the standard scale, or to both.

(2) Any person who resists or wilfully obstructs a constable in the execution of his duty, or a person assisting a constable in the execution of his duty, shall be guilty of an offence and liable on summary conviction to imprisonment for a term not exceeding one month or to a fine not exceeding level 3 on the standard scale, or to both.

(3)–(6) *****

90 Impersonation, etc.

(1) Any person who with intent to deceive impersonates a member of a police force or special constable, or makes any statement or does any act calculated falsely to suggest that he is such a member or constable, shall be guilty of an offence and liable on summary conviction to imprisonment for a term not exceeding six months or to a fine not exceeding level 5 on the standard scale, or to both.

(2) Any person who, not being a constable, wears any article of police uniform in circumstances where it gives him an appearance so nearly resembling that of a member of a police force as to be calculated to deceive shall be guilty of an offence and liable on summary conviction to a fine not exceeding level 3 on the standard scale.

(3) Any person who, not being a member of a police force or special constable, has in his possession any article of police uniform shall, unless he proves that he obtained possession of that article lawfully and has possession of it for a lawful purpose, be guilty of an offence and liable on summary conviction to a fine not exceeding level 1 on the standard scale.

(4) *****

91 Causing disaffection

(1) Any person who causes, or attempts to cause, or does any act calculated to cause, disaffection amongst the members of any police force, or induces or attempts to induce, or does any act calculated to induce, any member of a police force to withhold his services, [or to commit breaches of discipline], shall be guilty of an offence and liable—

    (a) on summary conviction, to imprisonment for a term not exceeding six months or to a fine not exceeding the statutory maximum, or to both;

    (b) on conviction on indictment, to imprisonment for a term not exceeding two years or to a fine, or to both.

[(2) This section applies in the case of—

    (a)   special constables appointed for a police area,

    [(aa) members of the staff of the National Policing Improvement Agency who are constables,]

    (b)   members of the Civil Nuclear Constabulary, and

    (c)   members of the British Transport Police Force,

as it applies in the case of members of a police force.]

[(3) Liability under subsection (1) for any behaviour is in addition to any civil liability for that behaviour.]

92 *****

93 Acceptance of gifts and loans

(1) A [local policing body] may, in connection with the discharge of any of its functions, accept gifts of money, and gifts or loans of other property, on such terms as appear to the [body] to be appropriate.

(2) The terms on which gifts or loans are accepted under subsection (1) may include terms providing for the commercial sponsorship of any activity of the [local policing body] or of the police force maintained by it.

(3) ...

SCHEDULE 4 FORM OF DECLARATION

[*I, ... of .... do solemnly and sincerely declare and affirm that I will well and truly serve the Queen in the office of constable, with fairness, integrity, diligence and impartiality, upholding fundamental human rights and according equal respect to all people; and that I will, to the best of my power, cause the peace to be kept and preserved, and prevent all offences against people and property; and that while I continue to hold the said office I will to the best of my skill and knowledge discharge all the duties thereof faithfully according to law.*]

*****

Police Act 1997

(1997, c. 50)

An Act to make provision for the National Criminal Intelligence Service and the National Crime Squad; to make provision about entry on and interference with property and with wireless telegraphy in the course of the prevention or detection of serious crime; to make provision for the Police Information Technology Organisation; to provide for the issue of certificates about criminal records; to make provision about the administration and organisation of the police; to repeal certain enactments about rehabilitation of offenders; and for connected purposes.   [21st March 1997]

Territorial extent: United Kingdom (sections printed)

1–87, 89, 90 ...

88   *****

PART III AUTHORISATION OF ACTION IN RESPECT OF PROPERTY

The Commissioners

91 The Commissioners

(1) The Prime Minister [, after consultation with the Scottish Ministers] shall appoint for the purposes of this Part—

(a) a Chief Commissioner, and

(b) such number of other Commissioners as the Prime Minister thinks fit.

(2) The persons appointed under subsection (1) shall be persons who hold or have held high judicial office within the meaning of [Part 3 of the Constitutional Reform Act 2005 or are or have been members of the Judicial Committee of the Privy Council].

(3) Subject to subsections (4) to (7), each Commissioner shall hold and vacate office in accordance with the terms of his appointment.

(4) Each Commissioner shall be appointed for a term of three years.

(5) A person who ceases to be a Commissioner (otherwise than under subsection (7)) may be reappointed under this section.

(6) Subject to subsection (7), a Commissioner shall not be removed from office before the end of the term for which he is appointed unless [—

(a) a resolution approving his removal has been passed by each House of Parliament; and

(b) a resolution approving his removal has been passed by the Scottish Parliament.]

(7)–(9A) *****

(10) The decisions of the Chief Commissioner or, subject to sections 104 and 106, any other Commissioner (including decisions as to his jurisdiction) shall not be subject to appeal or liable to be questioned in any court.

Authorisations

92   Effect of authorisation under Part III

No entry on or interference with property or with wireless telegraphy shall be unlawful if it is authorised by an authorisation having effect under this Part.

93   Authorisations to interfere with property etc.

(1) Where subsection (2) applies, an authorising officer may authorise—

    (a)   the taking of such action, in respect of such property in the relevant area, as he may specify,

    [(ab) the taking of such action falling within subsection (1A) in respect of property outside the relevant area, as he may specify, or]

    (b)   the taking of such action in the relevant area as he may specify, in respect of wireless telegraphy.

[(1A) The action falling within this subsection is action for maintaining or retrieving any equipment, apparatus or device the placing or use of which in the relevant area has been authorised under this Part or Part II of the Regulation of Investigatory Powers Act 2000 or under any enactment contained in or made under an Act of the Scottish Parliament which makes provision equivalent to that made by Part II of that Act of 2000.

(1B) Subsection (1) applies where the authorising officer is a [member of the staff of the Serious Organised Crime Agency,] [an officer of Revenue and Customs] [or an officer of the Office of Fair Trading] with the omission of—

    (a)   the words 'in the relevant area' in each place where they occur; and

    (b)   paragraph (ab).]

(2) This subsection applies where the authorising officer believes—

    (a)   that it is necessary for the action specified to be taken [for the purpose of preventing or detecting] serious crime, and

    (b)   [that the taking of the action is proportionate to what the action seeks to achieve.]

[(2A)–(2B)], (3), [(3A)–(3E)] *****

(4) For the purposes of subsection (2), conduct which constitutes one or more offences shall be regarded as serious crime if, and only if,—

    (a)   it involves the use of violence, results in substantial financial gain or is conduct by a large number of persons in pursuit of a common purpose, or

    (b)   the offence or one of the offences is an offence for which a person who has attained the age of twenty-one [(eighteen in relation to England and Wales)] and has no previous convictions could reasonably be expected to be sentenced to imprisonment for a term of three years or more,

and, where the authorising officer is within subsection (5)(h), it relates to an assigned matter within the meaning of section 1(1) of the Customs and Excise Management Act 1979.

(5) In this section 'authorising officer' means—

    (a)   the chief constable of a police force maintained under section 2 of the Police Act 1996 (maintenance of police forces for areas in England and Wales except London);

    (b)   the Commissioner, or an Assistant Commissioner, of Police of the Metropolis;

    (c)   the Commissioner of Police for the City of London;

    (d)   the chief constable of a police force maintained under or by virtue of section 1 of the Police (Scotland) Act 1967 (maintenance of police forces for areas in Scotland);

    (e)   the Chief Constable or a Deputy Chief Constable of the [Police Service of Northern Ireland];

[(ea) the Chief Constable of the Ministry of Defence Police;

[(eb) the Provost Marshal of the [Royal Navy Police];

[(ec) the Provost Marshal of the Royal Military Police;

[(ed) the Provost Marshal of the Royal Air Force Police;

[(ee) the Chief Constable of the British Transport Police;]

[(f) the Director General of the Serious Organised Crime Agency, or any member of the staff of that Agency who is designated for the purposes of this paragraph by that Director General;]

(h) [an officer of Revenue and Customs who is a senior official within the meaning of the Regulation of Investigatory Powers Act 2000 and who is designated for the purposes of this paragraph by the Commissioners of Her Majesty's Revenue and Customs] [; or

(i) the chairman of the Office of Fair Trading];

[(j) the Director General of the Scottish Crime and Drug Enforcement Agency].

(6), (6A), (6B) *****

(7) The powers conferred by, or by virtue of, this section are additional to any other powers which a person has as a constable either at common law or under or by virtue of any other enactment and are not to be taken to affect any of those other powers.

94 *****

95 Authorisations: form and duration etc.

(1) An authorisation shall be in writing, except that in an urgent case an authorisation (other than one given by virtue of section 94) may be given orally.

(2) An authorisation shall, unless renewed under subsection (3), cease to have effect—

(a) if given orally or by virtue of section 94, at the end of the period of 72 hours beginning with the time when it took effect;

(b) in any other case, at the end of the period of three months beginning with the day on which it took effect.

(3) If at any time before an authorisation would cease to have effect the authorising officer who gave the authorisation, or in whose absence it was given, considers it necessary for the authorisation to continue to have effect for the purpose for which it was issued, he may, in writing, renew it for a period of three months beginning with the day on which it would cease to have effect.

(4) A person shall cancel an authorisation given by him if satisfied that [the authorisation is one in relation to which the requirement of paragraphs (a) to (b) of section 93(2) are no longer satisfied.]

(5)–(7) *****

96 *****

Authorisations requiring approval

97 Authorisations requiring approval

(1) An authorisation to which this section applies shall not take effect until—

(a) it has been approved in accordance with this section by a Commissioner appointed under section 91(1)(b), and

(b) the person who gave the authorisation has been notified under subsection (4).

(2) Subject to subsection (3), this section applies to an authorisation if, at the time it is given, the person who gives it believes—

(a) that any of the property specified in the authorisation—

(i) is used wholly or mainly as a dwelling or as a bedroom in a hotel, or

(ii) constitutes office premises, or

(b) that the action authorised by it is likely to result in any person acquiring knowledge of—

(i) matters subject to legal privilege,

(ii) confidential personal information, or

(iii) confidential journalistic material.

(3) This section does not apply to an authorisation where the person who gives it believes that the case is one of urgency.

(4) Where a Commissioner receives a notice under section 96 which specifies that this section applies to the authorisation, he shall as soon as is reasonably practicable—

(a) decide whether to approve the authorisation or refuse approval, and

(b) give written notice of his decision to the person who gave the authorisation.

(5) A Commissioner shall approve an authorisation if, and only if, he is satisfied that there are reasonable grounds for believing the matters specified in section 93(2).

(6)–(8) *****

98 Matters subject to legal privilege

(1) Subject to subsection (5) below, in section 97 'matters subject to legal privilege' means matters to which subsection (2), (3) or (4) below applies.

(2) This subsection applies to communications between a professional legal adviser and—

(a) his client, or

(b) any person representing his client, which are made in connection with the giving of legal advice to the client.

(3) This subsection applies to communications—

(a) between a professional legal adviser and his client or any person representing his client, or

(b) between a professional legal adviser or his client or any such representative and any other person,

which are made in connection with or in contemplation of legal proceedings and for the purposes of such proceedings.

(4) This subsection applies to items enclosed with or referred to in communications of the kind mentioned in subsection (2) or (3) and made—

(a) in connection with the giving of legal advice, or

(b) in connection with or in contemplation of legal proceedings and for the purposes of such proceedings.

(5) For the purposes of section 97—

(a) communications and items are not matters subject to legal privilege when they are in the possession of a person who is not entitled to possession of them, and

(b) communications and items held, or oral communications made, with the intention of furthering a criminal purpose are not matters subject to legal privilege.

99 Confidential personal information

(1) In section 97 'confidential personal information' means—

(a) personal information which a person has acquired or created in the course of any trade, business, profession or other occupation or for the purposes of any paid or unpaid office, and which he holds in confidence, and

(b) communications as a result of which personal information—

(i) is acquired or created as mentioned in paragraph (a), and

(ii) is held in confidence.

(2) For the purposes of this section 'personal information' means information concerning an individual (whether living or dead) who can be identified from it and relating—

(a) to his physical or mental health, or

(b) to spiritual counselling or assistance given or to be given to him.

(3) A person holds information in confidence for the purposes of this section if he holds it subject—

(a) to an express or implied undertaking to hold it in confidence, or

(b) to a restriction on disclosure or an obligation of secrecy contained in any enactment (including an enactment contained in an Act passed after this Act).

100   Confidential journalistic material

(1) In section 97 'confidential journalistic material' means—

(a) material acquired or created for the purposes of journalism which—

    (i)   is in the possession of persons who acquired or created it for those purposes,

    (ii) is held subject to an undertaking, restriction or obligation of the kind mentioned in section 99(3), and

    (iii) has been continuously held (by one or more persons) subject to such an undertaking, restriction or obligation since it was first acquired or created for the purposes of journalism, and

(b) communications as a result of which information is acquired for the purposes of journalism and held as mentioned in paragraph (a)(ii).

(2) For the purposes of subsection (1), a person who receives material, or acquires information, from someone who intends that the recipient shall use it for the purposes of journalism is to be taken to have acquired it for those purposes.

101, 102   ...

103   Quashing of authorisations etc.

(1) Where, at any time, a Commissioner appointed under section 91(1)(b) is satisfied that, at the time an authorisation was given or renewed, there were no reasonable grounds for believing the matters specified in section 93(2), he may quash the authorisation or, as the case may be, renewal.

(2) Where, in the case of an authorisation or renewal to which section 97 does not apply, a Commissioner appointed under section 91(1)(b) is at any time satisfied that, at the time the authorisation was given or, as the case may be, renewed,—

(a) there were reasonable grounds for believing any of the matters specified in subsection (2) of section 97, and

(b) there were no reasonable grounds for believing the case to be one of urgency for the purposes of subsection (3) of that section,

he may quash the authorisation or, as the case may be, renewal.

(3) Where a Commissioner quashes an authorisation or renewal under subsection (1) or (2), he may order the destruction of any records relating to information obtained by virtue of the authorisation (or, in the case of a renewal, relating wholly or partly to information so obtained after the renewal) other than records required for pending criminal or civil proceedings.

(4)–(9) *****

*****

Special Immigration Appeals Commission Act 1997

(1997, c. 68)

An Act to establish the Special Immigration Appeals Commission; to make provision with respect to its jurisdiction; and for connected purposes.   [17th December 1997]

Territorial extent: United Kingdom

1   Establishment of the Commission

(1) There shall be a commission, known as the Special Immigration Appeals Commission, for the purpose of exercising the jurisdiction conferred by this Act.

(2) Schedule 1 to this Act shall have effect in relation to the Commission.

[(3) The Commission shall be a superior court of record.

(4) A decision of the Commission shall be questioned in legal proceedings only in accordance with—

(a) section 7 ...]

(b) ...

2   Jurisdiction: appeals

[(1) A person may appeal to the Special Immigration Appeals Commission against a decision if—

   (a) he would be able to appeal against the decision under section 82(1) [, 83(2) or 83 (2A)] of the Nationality, Immigration and Asylum Act 2002 but for a certificate of the Secretary of State under section 97 of that Act (national security, &c), or

   (b) an appeal against the decision under section 82(1) [, 83(2) or 83(2A)] of that Act lapsed under section 99 of that Act by virtue of a certificate of the Secretary of State under section 97 of that Act.

(2), (3) *****

(4) An appeal against the rejection of a claim for asylum under this section shall be treated as abandoned if the appellant leaves the United Kingdom.

(5) A person may bring or continue an appeal against an immigration decision under this section while he is in the United Kingdom only if he would be able to bring or continue the appeal while he was in the United Kingdom if it were an appeal under section 82(1) of that Act.

(6) In this section 'immigration decision' has the meaning given by section 82(2) of the Nationality, Immigration and Asylum Act 2002.]

2A ...

[2B
A person may appeal to the Special Immigration Appeals Commission against a decision to make an order under section 40 of the British Nationality Act 1981 (deprivation of citizenship) if he is not entitled to appeal under section 40A(1) of that Act because of a certificate under section 40A(2) [(and section 40A(3)(a) shall have effect in relation to appeals under this section)].]

3 *****

4 ...

5   Procedure in relation to jurisdiction under sections 2 and 3

(1) The Lord Chancellor may make rules—

   (a) for regulating the exercise of the rights of appeal conferred by section 2 ... [or 2B] above,

   (b) for prescribing the practice and procedure to be followed on or in connection with appeals under [section 2 ... [or 2B] above], including the mode and burden of proof and admissibility of evidence on such appeals, and

   (c) for other matters preliminary or incidental to or arising out of such appeals, including proof of the decisions of the Special Immigration Appeals Commission.

(2) Rules under this section shall provide that an appellant has the right to be legally represented in any proceedings before the Commission on an appeal under section 2. ... [or 2B] above, subject to any power conferred on the Commission by such rules.

[(2A) Rules under this section may, in particular, do anything which may be done by [Tribunal Procedure Rules].]

(3) Rules under this section may, in particular—

   (a) make provision enabling proceedings before the Commission to take place without the appellant being given full particulars of the reasons for the decision which is the subject of the appeal,

   (b) make provision enabling the Commission to hold proceedings in the absence of any person, including the appellant and any legal representative appointed by him,

   (c) make provision about the functions in proceedings before the Commission of persons appointed under section 6 below, and

   (d) make provision enabling the Commission to give the appellant a summary of any evidence taken in his absence.

(4)–(9) *****

6   Appointment of person to represent the appellant's interests

(1) The relevant law officer may appoint a person to represent the interests of an appellant in any proceedings before the Special Immigration Appeals Commission from which the appellant and any legal representative of his are excluded.

(2) For the purposes of subsection (1) above, the relevant law officer is—

   (a) in relation to proceedings before the Commission in England and Wales, the Attorney General,

   (b) in relation to proceedings before the Commission in Scotland, the Lord Advocate, and

   (c) in relation to proceedings before the Commission in Northern Ireland, the Attorney General for Northern Ireland.

(3) A person appointed under subsection (1) above—

   (a) if appointed for the purposes of proceedings in England and Wales, shall have a general qualification for the purposes of section 71 of the Courts and Legal Services Act 1990,

   (b) if appointed for the purposes of proceedings in Scotland, shall be—

      (i)   an advocate, or

      (ii) a solicitor who has by virtue of section 25A of the Solicitors (Scotland) Act 1980 rights of audience in the Court of Session and the High Court of Justiciary, and

   (c) if appointed for the purposes of proceedings in Northern Ireland, shall be a member of the Bar of Northern Ireland.

(4) A person appointed under subsection (1) above shall not be responsible to the person whose interests he is appointed to represent.

7   Appeals from the Commission

(1) Where the Special Immigration Appeals Commission has made a final determination of an appeal, any party to the appeal may bring a further appeal to the appropriate appeal court on any question of law material to that determination.

(2) An appeal under this section may be brought only with the leave of the Commission or, if such leave is refused, with the leave of the appropriate appeal court.

(3) In this section 'the appropriate appeal court' means—

   (a) in relation to a determination made by the Commission in England and Wales, the Court of Appeal,

   (b) in relation to a determination made by the Commission in Scotland, the Court of Session, and

   (c) in relation to a determination made by the Commission in Northern Ireland, the Court of Appeal in Northern Ireland.

(4) ...

*****

Civil Procedure Rules 1998

*****

PART 54   JUDICIAL REVIEW AND STATUTORY REVIEW

54.1   Scope and interpretation

(1) This [section of this] Part contains rules about judicial review.

(2) In this [section]—

   (a) a 'claim for judicial review' means a claim to review the lawfulness of—

      (i)   an enactment; or

      (ii) a decision, action or failure to act in relation to the exercise of a public function;

   (b)–(d) ...

   (e) 'the judicial review procedure' means the Part 8 procedure as modified by this [section];

(f) 'interested party' means any person (other than the claimant and defendant) who is directly affected by the claim; and

(g) 'court' means the High Court, unless otherwise stated.

(Rule 8.1(6)(b) provides that a rule or practice direction may, in relation to a specified type of proceedings, disapply or modify any of the rules set out in Part 8 as they apply to those proceedings)

54.2   When this [section] must be used

The judicial review procedure must be used in a claim for judicial review where the claimant is seeking—

(a) a mandatory order;

(b) a prohibiting order;

(c) a quashing order; or

(d) an injunction under section 30 of the [Senior Courts Act 1981] (restraining a person from acting in any office in which he is not entitled to act).

54.3   When this [section] may be used

(1) The judicial review procedure may be used in a claim for judicial review where the claimant is seeking—

(a) a declaration; or

(b) an injunction.

(Section 31(2) of the [Senior Courts Act 1981] sets out the circumstances in which the court may grant a declaration or injunction in a claim for judicial review)

(Where the claimant is seeking a declaration or injunction in addition to one of the remedies listed in rule 54.2, the judicial review procedure must be used)

(2) A claim for judicial review may include a claim for damages [, restitution or the recovery of a sum due] but may not seek [such a remedy] alone.

(Section 31(4) of the [Senior Courts Act 1981] sets out the circumstances in which the court may award damages [, restitution or a sum due] on a claim for judicial review)

54.4   Permission required

The court's permission to proceed is required in a claim for judicial review whether started under this [section] or transferred to the Administrative Court.

54.5   Time limit for filing claim form

(1) The claim form must be filed—

(a) promptly; and

(b) in any event not later than 3 months after the grounds to make the claim first arose.

(2) The time limit in this rule may not be extended by agreement between the parties.

(3) This rule does not apply when any other enactment specifies a shorter time limit for making the claim for judicial review.

54.6   Claim form

(1) In addition to the matters set out in rule 8.2 (contents of the claim form) the claimant must also state—

(a) the name and address of any person he considers to be an interested party;

(b) that he is requesting permission to proceed with a claim for judicial review;

(c) any remedy (including any interim remedy) he is claiming.

(Part 25 sets out how to apply for an interim remedy)

(2) The claim form must be accompanied by the documents required by [Practice Direction 54A].

54.7   Service of claim form

The claim form must be served on—

(a) the defendant; and

(b) unless the court otherwise directs, any person the claimant considers to be an interested party,

within 7 days after the date of issue.

54.8 Acknowledgment of service

(1) Any person served with the claim form who wishes to take part in the judicial review must file an acknowledgment of service in the relevant practice form in accordance with the following provisions of this rule.

(2) Any acknowledgment of service must be—

(a) filed not more than 21 days after service of the claim form; and

(b) served on—

(i) the claimant; and

(ii) subject to any direction under rule 54.7(b), any other person named in the claim form, as soon as practicable and, in any event, not later than 7 days after it is filed.

(3) The time limits under this rule may not be extended by agreement between the parties.

(4) The acknowledgment of service—

(a) must—

(i) where the person filing it intends to contest the claim, set out a summary of his grounds for doing so; and

(ii) state the name and address of any person the person filing it considers to be an interested party; and

(b) may include or be accompanied by an application for directions.

(5) Rule 10.3(2) does not apply.

54.9–54.16 *****

54.17 Court's powers to hear any person

(1) Any person may apply for permission—

(a) to file evidence; or

(b) make representations at the hearing of the judicial review.

(2) An application under paragraph (1) should be made promptly.

54.18 Judicial review may be decided without a hearing

The court may decide the claim for judicial review without a hearing where all the parties agree.

54.19 Court's powers in respect of quashing orders

(1) This rule applies where the court makes a quashing order in respect of the decision to which the claim relates.

[(2) The court may—

(a)

(i) remit the matter to the decision-maker; and

(ii) direct it to reconsider the matter and reach a decision in accordance with the judgment of the court; or

(b) in so far as any enactment permits, substitute its own decision for the decision to which the claim relates.

(Section 31 of the Supreme Court Act 1981 enables the High Court, subject to certain conditions, to substitute its own decision for the decision in question.)]

(3) ...

54.20 Transfer

The court may—

(a) order a claim to continue as if it had not been started under this [section] and

(b) where it does so, give directions about the future management of the claim.

(Part 30 (transfer) applies to transfers to and from the Administrative Court.)

*****

Crime and Disorder Act 1998

(1998, c. 37)

An Act to make provision for preventing crime and disorder; to create certain racially-aggravated offences; to abolish the rebuttable presumption that a child is doli incapax and to make provision as to the effect of a child's failure to give evidence at his trial; to abolish the death penalty for treason and piracy; to make changes to the criminal justice system; to make further provision for dealing with offenders; to make further provision with respect to remands and committals for trial and the release and recall of prisoners; to amend Chapter I of Part II of the Crime (Sentences) Act 1997 and to repeal Chapter I of Part III of the Crime and Punishment (Scotland) Act 1997; to make amendments designed to facilitate, or otherwise desirable in connection with, the consolidation of certain enactments; and for connected purposes. [31st July 1998]

Territorial extent: England and Wales; ss. 12 and following, and 33, make equivalent provisions for Scotland to those reproduced. Certain provisions (not reproduced here) concerning the abolition of the death penalty for treason and piracy apply to Scotland and Northern Ireland.

PART I PREVENTION OF CRIME AND DISORDER

Crime and disorder: general

1 Anti-social behaviour orders

(1) An application for an order under this section may be made by a relevant authority if it appears to the authority that the following conditions are fulfilled with respect to any person aged 10 or over, namely—

    (a)   that the person has acted, since the commencement date, in an anti-social manner, that is to say, in a manner that caused or was likely to cause harassment, alarm or distress to one or more persons not of the same household as himself; and

    [(b) that such an order is necessary to protect relevant persons from further anti-social acts by him.]

    ...

(1A), (1B), [(1C)] *****

(2) ...

(3) Such an application shall be made by complaint to [a magistrates' court].

(4) If, on such an application, it is proved that the conditions mentioned in subsection (1) above are fulfilled, the magistrates' court may make an order under this section (an 'anti-social behaviour order') which prohibits the defendant from doing anything described in the order.

(5) For the purpose of determining whether the condition mentioned in subsection (1)(a) above is fulfilled, the court shall disregard any act of the defendant which he shows was reasonable in the circumstances.

(5A) *****

[(6) The prohibitions that may be imposed by an anti-social behaviour order are those necessary for the purpose of protecting persons (whether relevant persons or persons elsewhere in England and Wales) from further anti-social acts by the defendant.]

(7) An anti-social behaviour order shall have effect for a period (not less than two years) specified in the order or until further order.

(8) Subject to subsection (9) below, the applicant or the defendant may apply by complaint to the court which made an anti-social behaviour order for it to be varied or discharged by a further order.

(9) Except with the consent of both parties, no anti-social behaviour order shall be discharged before the end of the period of two years beginning with the date of service of the order.

(10) If without reasonable excuse a person does anything which he is prohibited from doing by an anti-social behaviour order, he [is guilty of an offence and] liable—

(a) on summary conviction, to imprisonment for a term not exceeding six months or to a fine not exceeding the statutory maximum, or to both; or

(b) on conviction on indictment, to imprisonment for a term not exceeding five years or to a fine, or to both.

(10A)–(12) *****

1A–1B   *****

[1C   Orders on conviction in criminal proceedings

(1) This section applies where a person (the 'offender') is convicted of a relevant offence.

(2) If the court considers—

(a) that the offender has acted, at any time since the commencement date, in an anti-social manner, that is to say in a manner that caused or was likely to cause harassment, alarm or distress to one or more persons not of the same household as himself, and

(b) that an order under this section is necessary to protect persons in any place in England and Wales from further anti-social acts by him,

it may make an order which prohibits the offender from doing anything described in the order.

(3) The court may make an order under this section—

[(a) if the prosecutor asks it to do so, or

(b) if the court thinks it is appropriate to do so.]

[(3A) For the purpose of deciding whether to make an order under this section the court may consider evidence led by the prosecution and the defence.

(3B) It is immaterial whether evidence led in pursuance of subsection (3A) would have been admissible in the proceedings in which the offender was convicted.]

(4) An order under this section shall not be made except—

(a) in addition to a sentence imposed in respect of the relevant offence; or

(b) in addition to an order discharging him conditionally.]

(4A)–(4C), (5) *****

(6)–(8) ...

(9)–(10) *****

1CA–10   *****

11   Child safety orders

(1) Subject to subsection (2) below, if a magistrates' court, on the application of a local authority, is satisfied that one or more of the conditions specified in subsection (3) below are fulfilled with respect to a child under the age of 10, it may make an order (a 'child safety order') which—

(a) places the child, for a period (not exceeding the permitted maximum) specified in the order, under the supervision of the responsible officer; and

(b) requires the child to comply with such requirements as are so specified.

(2) A court shall not make a child safety order unless it has been notified by the Secretary of State that arrangements for implementing such orders are available in the area in which it appears that the child resides or will reside and the notice has not been withdrawn.

(3) The conditions are—

(a) that the child has committed an act which, if he had been aged 10 or over, would have constituted an offence;

(b) that a child safety order is necessary for the purpose of preventing the commission by the child of such an act as is mentioned in paragraph (a) above;

(c) ...; and

(d) that the child has acted in a manner that caused or was likely to cause harassment, alarm or distress to one or more persons not of the same household as himself.

(4) The maximum period permitted for the purposes of subsection (1)(a) above is [twelve months].

(5) The requirements that may be specified under subsection (1)(b) above are those which the court considers desirable in the interests of—

(a) securing that the child receives appropriate care, protection and support and is subject to proper control; or

(b) preventing any repetition of the kind of behaviour which led to the child safety order being made.

(6) Proceedings under this section or section 12 below shall be family proceedings for the purposes of the 1989 Act or section 65 of the Magistrates' Courts Act 1980 ('the 1980 Act'); and the standard of proof applicable to such proceedings shall be that applicable to civil proceedings.

(7), (8) *****

12–27 *****

PART II CRIMINAL LAW

Racially [or religiously] aggravated offences: England and Wales

28   Meaning of 'racially [or religiously] aggravated'

(1) An offence is racially [or religiously] aggravated for the purposes of sections 29 to 32 below if—

(a) at the time of committing the offence, or immediately before or after doing so, the offender demonstrates towards the victim of the offence hostility based on the victim's membership (or presumed membership) of a racial [or religious] group; or

(b) the offence is motivated (wholly or partly) by hostility towards members of a racial [or religious] group based on their membership of that group.

(2) In subsection (1)(a) above—

'membership', in relation to a racial [or religious] group, includes association with members of that group;

'presumed' means presumed by the offender.

(3) It is immaterial for the purposes of paragraph (a) or (b) of subsection (1) above whether or not the offender's hostility is also based, to any extent, on [any other factor not mentioned in that paragraph.]

(4) In this section 'racial group' means a group of persons defined by reference to race, colour, nationality (including citizenship) or ethnic or national origins.

[(5) In this section 'religious group' means a group of persons defined by reference to religious belief or lack of religious belief.]

29   Racially [or religiously] aggravated assaults

(1) A person is guilty of an offence under this section if he commits—

(a) an offence under section 20 of the Offences Against the Person Act 1861 (malicious wounding or grievous bodily harm);

(b) an offence under section 47 of that Act (actual bodily harm); or

(c) common assault,

which is racially [or religiously] aggravated for the purposes of this section.

(2) A person guilty of an offence falling within subsection (1)(a) or (b) above shall be liable—

(a) on summary conviction, to imprisonment for a term not exceeding six months or to a fine not exceeding the statutory maximum, or to both;

(b) on conviction on indictment, to imprisonment for a term not exceeding seven years or to a fine, or to both.

(3) A person guilty of an offence falling within subsection (1)(c) above shall be liable—

(a) on summary conviction, to imprisonment for a term not exceeding six months or to a fine not exceeding the statutory maximum, or to both;

(b) on conviction on indictment, to imprisonment for a term not exceeding two years or to a fine, or to both.

30 Racially [or religiously] aggravated criminal damage

(1) A person is guilty of an offence under this section if he commits an offence under section 1(1) of the Criminal Damage Act 1971 (destroying or damaging property belonging to another) which is racially [or religiously] aggravated for the purposes of this section.

(2) A person guilty of an offence under this section shall be liable—

   (a) on summary conviction, to imprisonment for a term not exceeding six months or to a fine not exceeding the statutory maximum, or to both;

   (b) on conviction on indictment, to imprisonment for a term not exceeding fourteen years or to a fine, or to both.

(3) *****

31 Racially [or religiously] aggravated public order offences

(1) A person is guilty of an offence under this section if he commits—

   (a) an offence under section 4 of the Public Order Act 1986 (fear or provocation of violence);

   (b) an offence under section 4A of that Act (intentional harassment, alarm or distress); or

   (c) an offence under section 5 of that Act (harassment, alarm or distress),

which is racially [or religiously] aggravated for the purposes of this section.

(2), (3) ...

(4) A person guilty of an offence falling within subsection (1)(a) or (b) above shall be liable—

   (a) on summary conviction, to imprisonment for a term not exceeding six months or to a fine not exceeding the statutory maximum, or to both;

   (b) on conviction on indictment, to imprisonment for a term not exceeding two years or to a fine, or to both.

(5) A person guilty of an offence falling within subsection (1)(c) above shall be liable on summary conviction to a fine not exceeding level 4 on the standard scale.

(6), (7) *****

32 Racially [or religiously] aggravated harassment etc.

(1) A person is guilty of an offence under this section if he commits—

   (a) an offence under section 2 of the Protection from Harassment Act 1997 (offence of harassment); or

   (b) an offence under section 4 of that Act (putting people in fear of violence),

which is racially [or religiously] aggravated for the purposes of this section.

(2) ...

(3) A person guilty of an offence falling within subsection (1)(a) above shall be liable—

   (a) on summary conviction, to imprisonment for a term not exceeding six months or to a fine not exceeding the statutory maximum, or to both;

   (b) on conviction on indictment, to imprisonment for a term not exceeding two years or to a fine, or to both.

(4) A person guilty of an offence falling within subsection (1)(b) above shall be liable—

   (a) on summary conviction, to imprisonment for a term not exceeding six months or to a fine not exceeding the statutory maximum, or to both;

   (b) on conviction on indictment, to imprisonment for a term not exceeding seven years or to a fine, or to both.

(5)–(6) *****

(7) ...

*****

Human Rights Act 1998

(1998, c. 42)

An Act to give further effect to rights and freedoms guaranteed under the European Convention on Human Rights; to make provision with respect to holders of certain judicial offices who become judges of the European Court of Human Rights; and for connected purposes. [9th November 1998]

Territorial extent: United Kingdom

Introduction

1 The Convention Rights

(1) In this Act 'the Convention rights' means the rights and fundamental freedoms set out in—

(a) Articles 2 to 12 and 14 of the Convention,

(b) Articles 1 to 3 of the First Protocol, and

(c) [Article 1 of the Thirteenth Protocol,]

as read with Articles 16 to 18 of the Convention.

(2) Those Articles are to have effect for the purposes of this Act subject to any designated derogation or reservation (as to which see sections 14 and 15).

(3) The Articles are set out in Schedule 1.

(4) The [Secretary of State] may by order make such amendments to this act as he considers appropriate to reflect the effect, in relation to the United Kingdom, of a protocol.

(5) In subsection (4) 'protocol' means a protocol to the Convention—

(a) which the United Kingdom has ratified; or

(b) which the United Kingdom has signed with a view to ratification.

(6) No amendment may be made by an order under subsection (4) so as to come into force before the protocol concerned is in force in relation to the United Kingdom.

[Note: Schedule 1 is omitted, as the relevant Articles of and Protocols to the Convention are printed as part of the Convention in Part II. Note that Article 13 of the Convention (effective remedy) is not incorporated by s. 1.]

2 Interpretation of Convention rights

(1) A court or tribunal determining a question which has arisen in connection with a Convention right must take into account any—

(a) judgment, decision, declaration or advisory opinion of the European Court of Human Rights,

(b) opinion of the Commission given in a report adopted under Article 31 of the Convention,

(c) decision of the Commission in connection with Article 26 or 27(2) of the convention, or

(d) decision of the Committee of Ministers taken under Article 46 of the Convention,

whenever made or given, so far as, in the opinion of the court or tribunal, it is relevant to the proceedings in which that question has arisen.

(2), (3) *****

Legislation

3 Interpretation of legislation

(1) So far as it is possible to do so, primary legislation and subordinate legislation must be read and given effect in a way which is compatible with Convention rights.

(2) This section—

(a) applies to primary legislation and subordinate legislation whenever enacted;

(b) does not affect the validity, continuing operation or enforcement of any incompatible primary legislation; and

(c) does not affect the validity, continuing operation or enforcement of any incompatible subordinate legislation if (disregarding any possibility of revocation) primary legislation prevents removal of the incompatibility.

4   Declaration of incompatibility

(1) Subsection (2) applies in any proceedings in which a court determines whether a provision of primary legislation is compatible with a Convention right.

(2) If the court is satisfied that the provision is incompatible with a Convention right, it may make a declaration of that incompatibility.

(3) Subsection (4) applies in any proceedings in which a court determines whether a provision of subordinate legislation, made in the exercise of a power conferred by primary legislation, is compatible with a Convention right.

(4) If the court is satisfied—

(a) that the provision is incompatible with a Convention right, and

(b) that (disregarding any possibility of revocation) the primary legislation concerned prevents removal of the incompatibility,

it may make a declaration of that incompatibility.

(5) In this section 'court' means—

[(a) the Supreme Court;]

(b) the Judicial Committee of the Privy Council;

(c) the [Court-Martial Appeal Court];

(d) in Scotland, the High Court of Justiciary sitting otherwise than as a trial court or the Court of Session;

(e) in England and Wales or Northern Ireland, the High Court or the Court of Appeal;

[(f) the Court of Protection, in any matter being dealt with by the President of the Family Division, the Vice Chancellor or a puisne judge of the High Court.]

(6) A declaration under this section ('a declaration of incompatibility')—

(a) does not affect the validity, continuing operation or enforcement of the provision in respect of which it is given; and

(b) is not binding on the parties to the proceedings in which it is made.

5   *****

Public authorities

6   Acts of public authorities

(1) It is unlawful for a public authority to act in a way which is incompatible with a Convention right.

(2) Subsection (1) does not apply to an act if—

(a) as the result of one or more provisions of primary legislation, the authority could not have acted differently; or

(b) in the case of one or more provisions of, or made under, primary legislation which cannot be read or given effect in a way which is compatible with the Convention rights, the authority was acting so as to give effect to or enforce those provisions.

(3) In this section 'public authority' includes—

(a) a court or tribunal, and

(b) any person certain of whose functions are functions of a public nature,

but does not include either House of Parliament or a person exercising functions in connection with proceedings in Parliament.

(4) ...

(5) In relation to a particular act, a person is not a public authority by virtue only of subsection (3)(b) if the nature of the act is private.

(6) 'An act' includes a failure to act but does not include a failure to—

    (a) introduce in, or lay before, Parliament a proposal for legislation; or

    (b) make any primary legislation or remedial order.

7 Proceedings

(1) A person who claims that a public authority has acted (or proposes to act) in a way which is made unlawful by section 6(1) may—

    (a) bring proceedings against the authority under this Act in the appropriate court or tribunal, or

    (b) rely on the convention right or rights concerned in any legal proceedings,

but only if he is (or would be) a victim of the unlawful act.

(2) In subsection (1)(a) 'appropriate court or tribunal' means such court or tribunal as may be determined in accordance with rules; and proceedings against an authority include a counterclaim or similar proceedings.

(3) If the proceedings are brought on an application for judicial review, the applicant is to be taken to have a sufficient interest in relation to the unlawful act only if he is, or would be, a victim of that act.

(4) If the proceedings are made by way of a petition for judicial review in Scotland, the applicant shall be taken to have title and interest to sue in relation to the unlawful act only if he is, or would be, a victim of that act.

(5) Proceedings under subsection (1)(a) must be brought before the end of—

    (a) the period of one year beginning with the date on which the act complained of took place; or

    (b) such longer period as the court or tribunal considers equitable having regard to all the circumstances,

but that is subject to any rule imposing a stricter time limit in relation to the procedure in question.

(6) In subsection (1)(b) 'legal proceedings' includes—

    (a) proceedings brought by or at the instigation of a public authority; and

    (b) an appeal against the decision of a court or tribunal.

(7) For the purposes of this section, a person is a victim of an unlawful act only if he would be a victim for the purposes of Article 34 of the Convention if proceedings were brought in the European Court of Human Rights in respect of that act.

(8) Nothing in this Act creates a criminal offence.

(9)–(13) *****

8 Judicial remedies

(1) In relation to any act (or proposed act) of a public authority which the court finds is (or would be) unlawful, it may grant such relief or remedy, or make such order, within its powers as it considers just and appropriate.

(2) But damages may be awarded only by a court which has power to award damages, or to order the payment of compensation, in civil proceedings.

(3) No award of damages is to be made unless, taking account of all the circumstances of the case, including—

    (a) any other relief or remedy granted, or order made, in relation to the act in question (by that or any other court), and

    (b) the consequences of any decision (of that or any other court) in respect of that act,

the court is satisfied that the award is necessary to afford just satisfaction to the person in whose favour it is made.

(4) In determining—

    (a) whether to award damages, or

    (b) the amount of an award,

the court must take into account the principles applied by the European Court of Human Rights in relation to the award of compensation under Article 41 of the Convention.

(5), (6) *****

9 Judicial acts

(1) Proceedings under section 7(1)(a) in respect of a judicial act may be brought only—

    (a) by exercising a right of appeal;

    (b) on an application (in Scotland a petition) for a judicial review; or

    (c) in such other forum as may be prescribed by rules.

(2) That does not affect any rule of law which prevents a court from being the subject of judicial review.

(3) In proceedings under this Act in respect of a judicial act done in good faith, damages may not be awarded otherwise than to compensate a person to the extent required by Article 5(5) of the Convention.

(4) An award of damages permitted by subsection (3) is to be made against the Crown; but no award may be made unless the appropriate person, if not a party to the proceedings, is joined.

(5) In this section—

'appropriate person' means the minister responsible for the court concerned or a person or government department nominated by him;

'court' includes a tribunal;

'judge' includes a member of a tribunal, a justice of the peace [(or, in Northern Ireland, a lay magistrate)] and a clerk or other officer entitled to exercise the jurisdiction of a court;

'judicial act' means a judicial act of a court and includes an act done on the instructions, or on behalf, of a judge; and

'rules' has the same meaning as in section 7(9).

Remedial action

10 Power to take remedial action

(1) This section applies if—

    (a) a provision of legislation has been declared under section 4 to be incompatible with a Convention right and, if an appeal lies—

        (i)   all persons who may appeal have stated in writing that they do not intend to do so;

        (ii) the time for bringing an appeal has expired and no appeal has been brought within that time; or

        (iii) an appeal brought within that time has been determined or abandoned; or

    (b) it appears to a Minister of the Crown or Her Majesty in Council that, having regard to a finding of the European Court of Human Rights made after the coming into force of this section in proceedings against the United Kingdom, a provision of legislation is incompatible with an obligation of the United Kingdom arising from the Convention.

(2) If a Minister of the Crown considers that there are compelling reasons for proceedings under this section, he may by order make such amendments to the legislation as he considers necessary to remove the incompatibility.

(3) If, in the case of subordinate legislation, a Minister of the Crown considers—

    (a) that it is necessary to amend the primary legislation under which the subordinate legislation in question was made, in order to enable the incompatibility to be removed, and

    (b) that there are compelling reasons for proceeding under this section,

he may by order make such amendments to the primary legislation as he considers necessary.

(4)–(7) *****

Other rights and proceedings

11   Safeguard for existing human rights

A person's reliance on a Convention right does not restrict—

  (a) any other right or freedom conferred on him by or under any law having effect in any part of the United Kingdom; or

  (b) his right to make any claim or bring any proceedings which he could make or bring apart from sections 7 to 9.

12   Freedom of expression

(1) This section applies if a court is considering whether to grant any relief which, if granted, might affect the exercise of the Convention right to freedom of expression.

(2) If the person against whom the application for relief is made ('the respondent') is neither present nor represented, no such relief is to be granted unless the court is satisfied—

  (a) that the applicant has taken all practicable steps to notify the respondent; or

  (b) that there are compelling reasons why the respondent should not be notified.

(3) No such relief is to be granted so as to restrain publication before trial unless the court is satisfied that the applicant is likely to establish that publication should not be allowed.

(4) The court must have particular regard to the importance of the Convention right to freedom of expression and, where the proceedings relate to material which the respondent claims, or which appears to the court, to be journalistic, literary or artistic material (or to conduct connected with such material), to—

  (a) the extent to which—

    (i)   the material has, or is about to, become available to the public; or

    (ii) it is, or would be, in the public interest for the material to be published;

  (b) any relevant privacy code.

(5) In this section—

'court' includes a tribunal; and

'relief' includes any remedy or order (other than in criminal proceedings).

13   Freedom of thought, conscience and religion

(1) If a court's determination of any question arising under this Act might affect the exercise by a religious organisation (itself or its members collectively) of the Convention right to freedom of thought, conscience and religion, it must have particular regard to the importance of that right.

(2) In this section 'court' includes a tribunal.

14   Derogations

(1) In this Act 'designated derogation' means. .. any derogation by the United Kingdom from an Article of the Convention, or of any protocol to the Convention, which is designated for the purposes of this Act in an order made by the [Secretary of State].

(2) . . .

(3)–(6) *****

15–18   *****

19   Statements of compatibility

(1) A Minister of the Crown in charge of a Bill in either House of Parliament must, before Second Reading of the Bill—

  (a) make a statement to the effect that in his view the provisions of the Bill are compatible with the Convention rights ('a statement of compatibility'); or

  (b) make a statement to the effect that although he is unable to make a statement of compatibility the government nevertheless wishes the House to proceed with the Bill.

(2) The statement must be in writing and be published in such manner as the Minister making it considers appropriate.

*****

Northern Ireland Act 1998

(1998, c. 47)

An Act to make new provision for the government of Northern Ireland for the purpose of implementing the agreement reached at multi-party talks on Northern Ireland set out in Command Paper 3883.   [19th November 1998]

Territorial extent: Northern Ireland

[**Note:** Section 4 and Schedules 2 and 3 list the matters excepted, reserved and transferred to the Assembly but are not included in this text.]

PART I   PRELIMINARY

1   Status of Northern Ireland

(1) It is hereby declared that Northern Ireland in its entirety remains part of the United Kingdom and shall not cease to be so without the consent of a majority of the people of Northern Ireland voting in a poll held for the purposes of this section in accordance with Schedule 1.

(2) But if the wish expressed by a majority in such a poll is that Northern Ireland should cease to be part of the United Kingdom and form part of a united Ireland, the Secretary of State shall lay before Parliament such proposals to give effect to that wish as may be agreed between Her Majesty's Government in the United Kingdom and the Government of Ireland.

2–4 *****

PART II   LEGISLATIVE POWERS

General

5   Acts of the Northern Ireland Assembly

(1) Subject to sections 6 to 8, the Assembly may make laws, to be known as Acts.

(2) A Bill shall become an Act when it has been passed by the Assembly and has received Royal Assent.

(3) A Bill receives Royal Assent at the beginning of the day on which Letters Patent under the Great Seal of Northern Ireland signed with Her Majesty's own hand signifying Her Assent are notified to the Presiding Officer.

(4) The date of Royal Assent shall be written on the Act by the Presiding Officer, and shall form part of the Act.

(5) The validity of any proceedings leading to the enactment of an Act of the Assembly shall not be called into question in any legal proceedings.

(6) This section does not affect the power of the Parliament of the United Kingdom to make laws for Northern Ireland, but an Act of the Assembly may modify any provision made by or under an Act of Parliament in so far as it is part of the law of Northern Ireland.

6   Legislative competence

(1) A provision of an Act is not law if it is outside the legislative competence of the Assembly.

(2) A provision is outside that competence if any of the following paragraphs apply—

    (a) it would form part of the law of a country or territory other than Northern Ireland, or confer or remove functions exercisable otherwise than in or as regards Northern Ireland;

    (b) it deals with an excepted matter and is not ancillary to other provisions (whether in the Act or previously enacted) dealing with reserved or transferred matters;

    (c) it is incompatible with any of the Convention rights;

    (d) it is incompatible with [EU] law;

    (e) it discriminates against any person or class of person on the ground of religious belief or political opinion;

    (f) it modifies an enactment in breach of section 7.

(3)–(5) *****

7   Entrenched enactments

(1) Subject to subsection (2), the following enactments shall not be modified by an Act of the Assembly or subordinate legislation made, confirmed or approved by a Minister or Northern Ireland department—

    (a) the European Communities Act 1972;

    (b) the Human Rights Act 1998;...

    (c) section 43(1) to (6) and (8), section 67, sections 84 to [86B], section 95(3) and (4) and section 98; [and

    (d) section 1 and section 84 of the Justice (Northern Ireland) Act 2002].

(2) Subsection (1) does not prevent an Act of the Assembly or subordinate legislation modifying section 3(3) or (4) or 11(1) of the European Communities Act 1972.

(3) In this Act "Minister", unless the context otherwise requires, means the First Minister, the deputy First Minister or a Northern Ireland Minister.

8–15 *****

PART III   EXECUTIVE AUTHORITIES

Authorities

16 ...

[16A   Appointment of First Minister, deputy First Minister and Northern Ireland Ministers following Assembly election]

[(1) This section applies where an Assembly is elected under section 31 or 32.

(2) All Northern Ireland Ministers shall cease to hold office.

(3) Within a period of seven days beginning with the first meeting of the Assembly—

    (a) the offices of First Minister and deputy First Minister shall be filled by applying subsections (4) to (7); and

    (b) the Ministerial offices to be held by Northern Ireland Ministers shall be filled by applying section 18(2) to (6).

(4) The nominating officer of the largest political party of the largest political designation shall nominate a member of the Assembly to be the First Minister.

(5) The nominating officer of the largest political party of the second largest political designation shall nominate a member of the Assembly to be the deputy First Minister.

(6) If the persons nominated do not take up office within a period specified in standing orders, further nominations shall be made under subsections (4) and (5).

(7) Subsections (4) to (6) shall be applied as many times as may be necessary to secure that the offices of First Minister and deputy First Minister are filled.

(8) But no person may take up office as First Minister, deputy First Minister or Northern Ireland Minister by virtue of this section after the end of the period mentioned in subsection (3) (see further section 32(3)).

(9) The persons nominated under subsections (4) and (5) shall not take up office until each of them has affirmed the terms of the pledge of office.

(10) Subject to the provisions of this Part, the First Minister and the deputy First Minister shall hold office until immediately before those offices are next filled by virtue of this section.

(11) The holder of the office of First Minister or deputy First Minister may by notice in writing to the Presiding Officer designate a Northern Ireland Minister to exercise the functions of that office—

    (a) during any absence or incapacity of the holder; or

    (b) during any vacancy in that office arising otherwise than under section 16B(2),

but a person shall not have power to act by virtue of paragraph (a) for a continuous period exceeding six weeks.

(12) This section shall be construed in accordance with, and is subject to, section 16C.]

[16B   Vacancies in the office of First Minister or deputy First Minister]

[(1) The First Minister or the deputy First Minister—

    (a) may at any time resign by notice in writing to the Presiding Officer; and

    (b) shall cease to hold office if he ceases to be a member of the Assembly otherwise than by virtue of a dissolution.

(2) If either the First Minister or the deputy First Minister ceases to hold office at any time, whether by resignation or otherwise, the other—

    (a) shall also cease to hold office at that time; but

    (b) may continue to exercise the functions of his office until immediately before those offices are filled in accordance with this section.

(3) Where the offices of the First Minister and the deputy First Minister become vacant at any time, they shall be filled by applying subsections (4) to (7) within a period of seven days beginning with that time.

(4) The nominating officer of the largest political party of the largest political designation shall nominate a member of the Assembly to be the First Minister.

(5) The nominating officer of the largest political party of the second largest political designation shall nominate a member of the Assembly to be the deputy First Minister.

(6) If the persons nominated do not take up office within a period specified in standing orders, further nominations shall be made under subsections (4) and (5).

(7) Subsections (4) to (6) shall be applied as many times as may be necessary to secure that the offices of First Minister and deputy First Minister are filled.

(8) But no person may take up office as First Minister or deputy First Minister under this section after the end of the period mentioned in subsection (3) (see further section 32(3)).

(9) The persons nominated under subsections (4) and (5) shall not take up office until each of them has affirmed the terms of the pledge of office.

(10) This section shall be construed in accordance with, and is subject to, section 16C.]

[16C   Sections 16A and 16B: supplementary]

[(1) In sections 16A and 16B and this section "nominating officer", in relation to a party, means—

    (a) the person registered under Part 2 of the Political Parties, Elections and Referendums Act 2000 as the party's nominating officer; or

    (b) a member of the Assembly nominated by him for the purposes of this section.

(2) For the purposes of sections 16A and 16B and this section—

    (a) the size of a political party is to be determined by reference to the number of seats in the Assembly which were held by members of the party on the day on which the Assembly first met following its election; but

    (b) if two or more parties are taken by virtue of paragraph (a) to be of the same size, the respective sizes of those parties is to be determined by reference to the number of first preference votes cast for the parties at the last general election of members of the Assembly;

(this is subject to subsections (7) and (8)).

(3) For the purposes of sections 16A and 16B and this section, a political party to which one or more members of the Assembly belong is to be taken—

   (a) to be of the political designation "Nationalist" if, at the relevant time (see subsection (11)), more than half of the members of the Assembly who belonged to the party were designated Nationalists;

   (b) to be of the political designation "Unionist" if, at the relevant time, more than half of the members of the Assembly who belonged to the party were designated Unionists;

   (c) otherwise, to be of the political designation "Other".

(4) For the purposes of sections 16A and 16B and this section—

   (a) the size of the political designation "Nationalist" is to be taken to be equal to the number of members of the Assembly who, at the relevant time, were designated Nationalists;

   (b) the size of the political designation "Unionist" is to be taken to be equal to the number of members of the Assembly who, at the relevant time, were designated Unionists;

   (c) the size of the political designation "Other" is to be taken to be equal to the number of members of the Assembly who, at the relevant time, were neither designated Nationalists nor designated Unionists.

(5) But if two or more political designations are taken by virtue of subsection (4) to be of the same size, the respective sizes of those designations is to be determined by reference to the aggregate number of first preference votes cast, at the last general election of members of the Assembly, for members of the Assembly who, at the relevant time, were—

   (a) designated Nationalists (in the case of the political designation "Nationalist");

   (b) designated Unionists (in the case of the political designation "Unionist"); or

   (c) neither designated Nationalists nor designated Unionists (in the case of the political designation "Other").

(6) If at any time the party which is the largest political party of the largest political designation is not the largest political party—

   (a) any nomination to be made at that time under section 16A(4) or 16B(4) shall instead be made by the nominating officer of the largest political party; and

   (b) any nomination to be made at that time under section 16A(5) or 16B(5) shall instead be made by the nominating officer of the largest political party of the largest political designation.

(7) Where—

   (a) the Assembly has resolved under section 30(2) that a political party does not enjoy its confidence; and

   (b) the party's period of exclusion (see subsection (12)) under that provision has not come to an end,

subsection (2)(a) above shall have effect as if the number of seats in the Assembly which were held by members of the party on the day on which the Assembly first met following its election was nil.

(8) ...

(9) Where—

   (a) a person nominated by the nominating officer of a political party ceased to hold office as First Minister or deputy First Minister as a result of a resolution of the Assembly under section 30(2)...; and

   (b) the party's period of exclusion under section 30(2)...subsequently comes to an end otherwise than by virtue of the dissolution of the Assembly,

the First Minister and the deputy First Minister shall cease to hold office when the party's period of exclusion under that provision comes to an end...

(10) ...

(11) In this section "the relevant time" means the end of the day on which the Assembly first met following its election.

(12) In this section, a reference to a period of exclusion...is, in the case of a period of exclusion...which has been extended, a reference to that period as extended.

(13) Standing orders may make further provision in connection with the making of nominations under sections 16A and 16B.

(14) In this Act "the pledge of office" means the pledge of office which, together with the code of conduct to which it refers, is set out in Schedule 4.]

17   Ministerial offices

(1) The First Minister and the deputy First Minister acting jointly may at any time, and shall where subsection (2) applies, determine—

   (a) the number of Ministerial offices to be held by Northern Ireland Ministers; and
   (b) the functions to be exercisable by the holder of each such office.

(2) This subsection applies where provision is made by an Act of the Assembly for establishing a new Northern Ireland department or dissolving an existing one.

(3) In making a determination under subsection (1), the First Minister and the deputy First Minister shall ensure that the functions exercisable by those in charge of the different Northern Ireland departments existing at the date of the determination are exercisable by the holders of different Ministerial offices.

(4) The number of Ministerial offices shall not exceed 10 or such greater number as the Secretary of State may by order provide.

(5) A determination under subsection (1) shall not have effect unless it is approved by a resolution of the Assembly passed with cross-community support.

18–19A   *****

20   The Executive Committee

(1) There shall be an Executive Committee of each Assembly consisting of the First Minister, the deputy First Minister and the Northern Ireland Ministers.

(2) The First Minister and the deputy First Minister shall be chairmen of the Committee.

(3) The Committee shall have the functions set out in paragraphs 19 and 20 of Strand One of the Belfast Agreement.

[(4) The Committee shall also have the function of discussing and agreeing upon—

   (a) significant or controversial matters that are clearly outside the scope of the agreed programme referred to in paragraph 20 of Strand One of that Agreement;
   (b) significant or controversial matters that the First Minister and deputy First Minister acting jointly have determined to be matters that should be considered by the Executive Committee.]

[(5) Subsections (3) and (4) are subject to subsection (6).

(6) Quasi-judicial decisions may be made by the Department of Justice or the Minister in charge of that Department without recourse to the Executive Committee.]

21–[21C]   *****

Functions

22   Statutory functions

(1) An Act of the Assembly or other enactment may confer functions on a Minister (but not a junior Minister) or a Northern Ireland department by name.

(2) Functions conferred on a Northern Ireland department by an enactment passed or made before the appointed day shall, except as provided by an Act of the Assembly or other subsequent enactment, continue to be exercisable by that department.

23   Prerogative and executive powers

(1) The executive power in Northern Ireland shall continue to be vested in Her Majesty.

(2) As respects transferred matters, the prerogative and other executive powers of Her Majesty in relation to Northern Ireland shall, subject to [subsections (2A) and (3)], be exercisable on Her Majesty's behalf by any Minister or Northern Ireland department.

[(2A) So far as the Royal prerogative of mercy is exercisable on Her Majesty's behalf under subsection (2), it is exercisable only by the Minister in charge of the Department of Justice.]

(3) As respects the Northern Ireland Civil Service and the Commissioner for Public Appointments for Northern Ireland, the prerogative and other executive powers of Her Majesty in relation to Northern Ireland shall be exercisable on Her Majesty's behalf by the First Minister and the deputy First Minister acting jointly.

(4) The First Minister and deputy First Minister acting jointly may by prerogative order under subsection (3) direct that such of the powers mentioned in that subsection as are specified in the order shall be exercisable on Her Majesty's behalf by a Northern Ireland Minister or Northern Ireland department so specified.

24   [EU] law, Convention rights etc

(1) A Minister or Northern Ireland department has no power to make, confirm or approve any subordinate legislation, or to do any act, so far as the legislation or act—

   (a) is incompatible with any of the Convention rights;
   (b) is incompatible with [EU] law;
   (c) discriminates against a person or class of person on the ground of religious belief or political opinion;
   (d) in the case of an act, aids or incites another person to discriminate against a person or class of person on that ground; or
   (e) in the case of legislation, modifies an enactment in breach of section 7.

(2) Subsection (1)(c) and (d) does not apply in relation to any act which is unlawful by virtue of the [Fair Employment and Treatment (Northern Ireland) Order 1998], or would be unlawful but for some exception made by virtue of [Part VIII of that Order].

25   Excepted and reserved matters

(1) If any subordinate legislation made, confirmed or approved by a Minister or Northern Ireland department contains a provision dealing with an excepted or reserved matter, the Secretary of State may by order revoke the legislation.

(2) An order made under subsection (1) shall recite the reasons for revoking the legislation and may make provision having retrospective effect.

26   International obligations

(1) If the Secretary of State considers that any action proposed to be taken by a Minister or Northern Ireland department would be incompatible with any international obligations, with the interests of defence or national security or with the protection of public safety or public order, he may by order direct that the proposed action shall not be taken.

(2) If the Secretary of State considers that any action capable of being taken by a Minister or Northern Ireland department is required for the purpose of giving effect to any international obligations, of safeguarding the interests of defence or national security or of protecting public safety or public order, he may by order direct that the action shall be taken.

(3) In subsections (1) and (2), "action" includes making, confirming or approving subordinate legislation and, in subsection (2), includes introducing a Bill in the Assembly.

(4)–(5) *****

27–38   *****

Presiding Officer and Commission

39 Presiding Officer

(1) Each Assembly shall as its first business elect from among its members a Presiding Officer and deputies.

(2)–(6) *****

(7) A person shall not be elected under subsections (1) to (3) without cross-community support.

40 *****

Proceedings etc

41 Standing orders

(1) The proceedings of the Assembly shall be regulated by standing orders.

(2) Standing orders shall not be made, amended or repealed without cross-community support.

(3) *****

42 Petitions of concern

(1) If 30 members petition the Assembly expressing their concern about a matter which is to be voted on by the Assembly, the vote on that matter shall require cross-community support.

(2) Standing orders shall make provision with respect to the procedure to be followed in petition-ing the Assembly under this section, including provision with respect to the period of notice required.

(3) Standing orders shall provide that the matter to which a petition under this section relates may be referred, in accordance with paragraphs 11 and 13 of Strand One of the Belfast Agreement, to the committee established under section 13(3)(a).

43 Members' interests

(1) Standing orders shall include provision for a register of interests of members of the Assembly, and for—

(a) registrable interests (as defined in standing orders) to be registered in it; and

(b) the register to be published and made available for public inspection.

(2)–(8) *****

44–49 *****

50 Privilege

(1) For the purposes of the law of defamation, absolute privilege shall attach to—

(a) the making of a statement in proceedings of the Assembly; and

(b) the publication of a statement under the Assembly's authority.

(2), (3) *****

51–[51D] *****

PART V   NSMC, BIC, BIIC ETC

[52A North-South Ministerial Council and British-Irish Council]

[(1) The First Minister and the deputy First Minister acting jointly shall, as far in advance of each meeting of the North-South Ministerial Council or the British-Irish Council as is reasonably practica-ble, give to the Executive Committee and to the Assembly the following information in relation to the meeting—

(a) the date;

(b) the agenda; and

(c) (once determined under this section) the names of the Ministers or junior Ministers who are to attend the meeting.

(2) Each Minister or junior Minister who has responsibility (whether or not with another Minister or junior Minister) in relation to any matter included in the agenda for a meeting of either Council ("appropriate Minister") shall be entitled—

      (a) to attend the meeting; and

      (b) to participate (see section 52C) in the meeting so far as it relates to that matter.

(3)–(10) *****

[52B]–67 *****

PART VII   HUMAN RIGHTS AND EQUAL OPPORTUNITIES

Human rights

68   The Northern Ireland Human Rights Commission

(1) There shall be a body corporate to be known as the Northern Ireland Human Rights Commission.

(2) The Commission shall consist of a Chief Commissioner and other Commissioners appointed by the Secretary of State.

(3) In making appointments under this section, the Secretary of State shall as far as practicable secure that the Commissioners, as a group, are representative of the community in Northern Ireland.

(4) Schedule 7 (which makes supplementary provision about the Commission) shall have effect.

69   The Commission's functions

(1) The Commission shall keep under review the adequacy and effectiveness in Northern Ireland of law and practice relating to the protection of human rights.

(2) The Commission shall, before the end of the period of two years beginning with the commencement of this section, make to the Secretary of State such recommendations as it thinks fit for improving—

      (a) its effectiveness;

      (b) the adequacy and effectiveness of the functions conferred on it by this Part; and

      (c) the adequacy and effectiveness of the provisions of this Part relating to it.

(3) The Commission shall advise the Secretary of State and the Executive Committee of the Assembly of legislative and other measures which ought to be taken to protect human rights—

      (a) as soon as reasonably practicable after receipt of a general or specific request for advice; and

      (b) on such other occasions as the Commission thinks appropriate.

(4) The Commission shall advise the Assembly whether a Bill is compatible with human rights—

      (a) as soon as reasonably practicable after receipt of a request for advice; and

      (b) on such other occasions as the Commission thinks appropriate.

(5) The Commission may—

      (a) give assistance to individuals in accordance with section 70; and

      (b) bring proceedings involving law or practice relating to the protection of human rights.

(6)   The Commission shall promote understanding and awareness of the importance of human rights in Northern Ireland; and for this purpose it may undertake, commission or provide financial or other assistance for—

      (a) research; and

      (b) educational activities.

(7)–(11) *****

[69A]–79 *****

80   Legislative power to remedy ultra vires acts

(1) The Secretary of State may by order make such provision as he considers necessary or expedient in consequence of—

    (a) any provision of an Act of the Assembly which is not, or may not be, within the legislative competence of the Assembly; or

    (b) any purported exercise by a Minister or Northern Ireland department of his or its functions which is not, or may not be, a valid exercise of those functions.

(2) An order under this section may—

    (a) make provision having retrospective effect;

    (b) make consequential or supplementary provision, including provision amending or repealing any Northern Ireland legislation, or any instrument made under such legislation;

    (c) make transitional or saving provision.

81   Powers of courts or tribunals to vary retrospective decisions

(1) This section applies where any court or tribunal decides that—

    (a) any provision of an Act of the Assembly is not within the legislative competence of the Assembly; or

    (b) a Minister or Northern Ireland department does not have the power to make, confirm or approve a provision of subordinate legislation that he or it has purported to make, confirm or approve.

(2) The court or tribunal may make an order—

    (a) removing or limiting any retrospective effect of the decision; or

    (b) suspending the effect of the decision for any period and on any conditions to allow the defect to be corrected.

(3) In deciding whether to make an order under this section, the court or tribunal shall (among other things) have regard to the extent to which persons who are not parties to the proceedings would otherwise be adversely affected.

(4)–(7) *****

82   ...

83   Interpretation of Acts of the Assembly etc

(1) This section applies where—

    (a) any provision of an Act of the Assembly, or of a Bill for such an Act, could be read either—

        (i)   in such a way as to be within the legislative competence of the Assembly; or

        (ii) in such a way as to be outside that competence; or

    (b) any provision of subordinate legislation made, confirmed or approved, or purporting to be made, confirmed or approved, by a Northern Ireland authority could be read either—

        (i)   in such a way as not to be invalid by reason of section 24 or, as the case may be, section 76; or

        (ii) in such a way as to be invalid by reason of that section.

(2) The provision shall be read in the way which makes it within that competence or, as the case may be, does not make it invalid by reason of that section, and shall have effect accordingly.

(3) In this section "Northern Ireland authority" means a Minister, a Northern Ireland department or a public authority (within the meaning of section 76) carrying out functions relating to Northern Ireland.

*****

Scotland Act 1998

(1998, c. 46)

An Act to provide for the establishment of a Scottish Parliament and Administration and other changes in the government of Scotland; to provide for changes in the constitution and functions of certain public authorities; to provide for the variation of the basic rate of income tax in relation to income of Scottish taxpayers in accordance with a resolution of the Scottish Parliament; to amend the law about parliamentary constituencies in Scotland; and for connected purposes.   [19th November 1998]

Territorial extent: United Kingdom (although many of the provisions apply only in Scotland) except for s. 25 which extends to Scotland alone

PART I

THE SCOTTISH PARLIAMENT

The Scottish Parliament

1   The Scottish Parliament

(1) There shall be a Scottish Parliament.

(2) One member of the Parliament shall be returned for each constituency (under the simple majority system) at an election held in the constituency.

(3) Members of the Parliament for each region shall be returned at a general election under the additional member system of proportional representation provided for in this part and vacancies among such members shall be filled in accordance with this Part.

(4) The validity of any proceedings of the Parliament is not affected by any vacancy in its membership.

(5) Schedule 1 (which makes provision for the constituencies and regions for the purposes of this Act and the number of regional members) shall have effect.

General elections

2   Ordinary general elections

(1) The day on which the poll at the first ordinary general election for membership of the Parliament shall be held, and the day, time and place for the meeting of the Parliament following that poll, shall be appointed by order made by the Secretary of State.

(2) The poll at subsequent ordinary general elections shall be held on the first Thursday in May in the fourth calendar year following that in which the previous ordinary general election was held, unless the day of the poll is determined by a proclamation under subsection (5).

(3)–(6) *****

3   Extraordinary general elections

(1) The Presiding Officer shall propose a day for the holding of a poll if—

    (a) the Parliament resolves that it should be dissolved and, if the resolution is passed on a division, the number of members voting in favour of it is not less than two-thirds of the total number of seats for members of the Parliament, or

    (b) any period during which the Parliament is required under section 46 to nominate one of its members for appointment as First Minister ends without such a nomination being made.

(2) If the Presiding Officer makes such a proposal, Her Majesty may by proclamation under the Scottish Seal—

    (a) dissolve the Parliament and require an extraordinary general election to be held,

(b) require the poll at the election to be held on the day proposed, and

(c) require the Parliament to meet within the period of seven days beginning immediately after the day of the poll.

(3) If a poll is held under this section within the period of six months ending with the day on which the poll at the next ordinary general election would be held (disregarding section 2(5)), that ordinary general election shall not be held.

(4) Subsection (3) does not affect the year in which the subsequent ordinary general election is to be held.

4 *****

5 Candidates

(1) At a general election, the candidates may stand for return as constituency members or regional members.

(2) A person may not be a candidate to be a constituency member for more than one constituency.

(3) The candidates to be regional members shall be those included in a list submitted under sub-section (4) or individual candidates.

(4) Any registered political party may submit to the regional returning officer a list of candidates to be regional members for a particular region (referred to in this Act, in relation to the region, as the party's 'regional list').

(5) A registered political party's regional list has effect in relation to the general election and any vacancy occurring among the regional members after that election and before the next general election.

(6) Not more than twelve persons may be included in the list (but the list may include only one person).

(7)–(9) *****

6 Poll for regional members

(1) This section and sections 7 and 8 are about the return of regional members at a general election.

(2) In each of the constituencies for the Parliament, a poll shall be held at which each person entitled to vote as elector may give a vote (referred to in this Act as a 'regional vote') for—

(a) a registered political party which has submitted a regional list, or

(b) an individual candidate to be a regional member for the region.

(3) The right conferred on a person by subsection (2) is in addition to any right the person may have to vote in any poll for the return of a constituency member.

7 Calculation of regional figures

(1) The persons who are to be returned as constituency members for constituencies included in the region must be determined before the persons who are to be returned as the regional members for the region.

(2) For each registered political party which has submitted a regional list, the regional figure for the purposes of section 8 is—

(a) the total number of regional votes given for the party in all the constituencies included in the region, divided by

(b) the aggregate of one plus the number of candidates of the party returned as constituency members for any of those constituencies.

(3) Each time a seat is allocated to the party under section 8, that figure shall be recalculated by increasing (or further increasing) the aggregate in subsection (2)(b) by one.

(4) For each individual candidate to be a regional member for the region, the regional figure for the purposes of section 8 is the total number of regional votes given for him in all the constituencies included in the region.

8   Allocation of seats to regional members

(1) The first regional member seat shall be allocated to the registered political party or individual candidate with the highest regional figure.

(2) The second and subsequent regional member seats shall be allocated to the registered political party or individual candidate with the highest regional figure, after any recalculation required by section 7(3) has been carried out.

(3) An individual candidate already returned as a constituency or regional member shall be disregarded.

(4) Seats for the region which are allocated to a registered political party shall be filled by the persons in the party's regional list in the order in which they appear in the list.

(5) For the purposes of this section and section 10, a person in a registered political party's regional list who is returned as a member of the Parliament shall be treated as ceasing to be in the list (even if his return is void).

(6) Once a party's regional list has been exhausted (by the return of persons included in it as constituency members or by the previous application of subsection (1) or (2)) the party shall be disregarded.

(7)–(9) *****

Vacancies

9   Constituency vacancies

(1) Where the seat of a constituency member is vacant, an election shall be held to fill the vacancy (subject to subsection (4)).

(2) The date of the poll shall be fixed by the Presiding Officer.

(3) The date shall fall within the period of three months—
    (a) beginning with the occurrence of the vacancy, or
    (b) if the vacancy does not come to the notice of the Presiding Officer within the period of one month beginning with its occurrence, beginning when it does come to his notice.

(4) The election shall not be held if the latest date for holding the poll would fall within the period of three months ending with the day on which the poll at the next ordinary general election would be held (disregarding section 2(5)).

(5), (6) *****

10   Regional vacancies

(1) This section applies where the seat of a regional member is vacant.

(2) If the regional member was returned as an individual candidate, or the vacancy is not filled in accordance with the following provisions, the seat shall remain vacant until the next general election.

(3) If the regional member was returned (under section 8 or this section) from a registered political party's regional list, the regional returning officer shall notify the Presiding Officer of the name of the person who is to fill the vacancy.

(4)–(7) *****

Franchise and conduct of elections

11   Electors

(1) The persons entitled to vote as electors at an election for membership of the parliament held in any constituency are those who on the day of the poll—
    (a) would be entitled to vote as electors at a local government election in an electoral area falling wholly or partly within the constituency, and
    (b) are registered in the register of local government electors at an address within the constituency.

(2) A person is not entitled to vote as elector in any constituency—
    (a) more than once at a poll for the return of a constituency member, or

(b) more than once at a poll for the return of regional members,

or to vote as elector in more than one constituency at a general election.

12–18   *****

Presiding Officer and administration

19   Presiding Officer

(1) The Parliament shall, at its first meeting following a general election, elect from among its members a Presiding Officer and two deputies.

(2) A person elected Presiding Officer or deputy shall hold office until the conclusion of the next election for Presiding Officer under subsection (1) unless he previously resigns, ceases to be a member of the Parliament otherwise than by virtue of a dissolution or is removed from office by resolution of the Parliament.

(3) If the Presiding Officer or a deputy ceases to hold office before the Parliament is dissolved, the Parliament shall elect another from among its members to fill his place.

(4)–(7) *****

20   Clerk of the Parliament

(1) There shall be a Clerk of the Parliament.

(2) The Clerk shall be appointed by the Scottish Parliamentary Corporate Body (established under section 21).

(3), (4) *****

21   Scottish Parliamentary Corporate Body

(1) There shall be a body corporate to be known as 'the Scottish Parliamentary Corporate Body' (referred to in this Act as the Parliamentary corporation) to perform the functions conferred on the corporation by virtue of this Act or any other enactment.

(2) The members of the corporation shall be—

(a) the Presiding Officer, and

(b) four members of the Parliament appointed in accordance with standing orders.

(3) The corporation shall provide the Parliament, or ensure that the Parliament is provided, with the property, staff and services required for the Parliament's purposes.

(4) The Parliament may give special or general directions to the corporation for the purpose of or in connection with the exercise of the corporation's functions.

(5)–(8) *****

Proceedings etc.

22   Standing orders

(1) The proceedings of the Parliament shall be regulated by standing orders.

(2) *****

23–27   *****

Legislation

28   Acts of the Scottish Parliament

(1) Subject to section 29, the Parliament may make laws, to be known as Acts of the Scottish Parliament.

(2) Proposed Acts of the Scottish Parliament shall be known as Bills; and a Bill shall become an Act of the Scottish Parliament when it has been passed by the Parliament and has received Royal Assent.

(3) A Bill receives Royal Assent at the beginning of the day on which Letters Patent under the Scottish Seal signed with Her Majesty's own hand signifying Her Assent are recorded in the Register of the Great Seal.

(4) The date of Royal Assent shall be written on the Act of the Scottish Parliament by the Clerk, and shall form part of the Act.

(5) The validity of an Act of the Scottish Parliament is not affected by any invalidity in the proceedings of the Parliament leading to its enactment.

(6) Every Act of the Scottish Parliament shall be judicially noticed.

(7) This section does not affect the power of the Parliament of the United Kingdom to make laws for Scotland.

29   Legislative competence

(1) An Act of the Scottish Parliament is not law so far as any provision of the Act is outside the legislative competence of the Parliament.

(2) A provision is outside the competence so far as any of the following paragraphs apply—

    (a) it would form part of the law of a country or territory other than Scotland, or confer or remove functions exercisable otherwise than in or as regards Scotland,

    (b) it relates to reserved matters,

    (c) it is in breach of the restrictions in Schedule 4.

    (d) it is incompatible with any of the Convention rights or with Community law,

    (e) it would remove the Lord Advocate from his position as head of the systems of criminal prosecution and investigation of deaths in Scotland.

(3) For the purposes of this section, the question whether a provision of an Act of the Scottish Parliament relates to a reserved matter is to be determined, subject to subsection (4), by reference to the purpose of the provision, having regard (among other things) to its effect in all the circumstances.

(4) *****

30   Legislative competence: supplementary

(1) Schedule 5 (which defines reserved matters) shall have effect.

(2)–(4) *****

31   Scrutiny of Bills before introduction

(1) A member of the Scottish Executive in charge of a Bill shall, on or before introduction of the Bill in the Parliament state that in his view the provisions of the Bill would be within the legislative competence of the Parliament.

(2) The Presiding Officer shall, on or before the introduction of a Bill in the Parliament, decide whether or not in his view the provisions of the Bill would be within the legislative competence of the Parliament and state his decision.

(3) The form of any statement, and the manner in which it is to be made, shall be determined under standing orders, and standing orders may provide for any statement to be published.

32   Submission of Bills for Royal Assent

(1) It is for the Presiding Officer to submit Bills for Royal Assent.

(2) The Presiding Officer shall not submit a Bill for Royal Assent at any time when—

    (a) the Advocate General, the Lord Advocate or the Attorney General is entitled to make a reference in relation to the Bill under section 33,

    (b) any such reference has been made but has not been decided or otherwise disposed of by the [Supreme Court], or

    (c) an order may be made in relation to the Bill under section 35.

(3) The Presiding Officer shall not submit a Bill in its unamended form for Royal Assent if—

    (a) the [Supreme Court has] decided that the Bill or any provision of it would not be within the legislative competence of the Parliament, or

    (b) a reference made in relation to the Bill under section 33 has been withdrawn following a request for withdrawal of the reference under section 34(2)(b).

(4) *****

33   Scrutiny of Bills by the [Supreme Court]

(1) The Advocate General, the Lord Advocate or the Attorney General may refer the question of whether a Bill or any provision of a Bill would be within the legislative competence of the Parliament to the [Supreme Court] for decision.

(2), (3) *****

34   ECJ references

(1) This section applies where—

    (a) a reference has been made in relation to a Bill under section 33,

    (b) a reference for a preliminary ruling has been made by the [Supreme Court] in connection with that reference, and

    (c) neither of those references has been decided or otherwise disposed of.

(2) If the Parliament resolves that it wishes to reconsider the Bill—

    (a) the Presiding Officer shall notify the Advocate General, the Lord Advocate and the Attorney General of that fact, and

    (b) the person who made the reference in relation to the Bill under section 33 shall request the withdrawal of the reference.

(3) In this section 'a reference for a preliminary ruling' means a reference of a question to the European Court under Article 177 of the Treaty establishing the European Community, Article 41 of the Treaty establishing the European Coal and Steel Community or Article 150 of the Treaty establishing the European Atomic Energy Community.

35   Power to intervene in certain cases

(1) If a Bill contains provisions—

    (a) which the Secretary of State has reasonable grounds to believe would be incompatible with any international obligations or the interests of defence or national security, or

    (b) which make modifications of the law as it applies to reserved matters and which the Secretary of State has reasonable grounds to believe would have an adverse effect on the operation of the law as it applies to reserved matters,

he may make an order prohibiting the Presiding Officer from submitting the Bill for Royal Assent.

(2)–(5) *****

36   *****

Other provisions

37   Acts of Union

The Union with Scotland Act 1706 and the Union with England Act 1707 have effect subject to this Act.

38   *****

39   Members' interests

(1) Provision shall be made for a register of interests of members of the Parliament and for the register to be published and made available for public inspection.

(2) Provision shall be made—

    (a) requiring members of the Parliament to register in that register financial interests (including benefits in kind), as defined for the purposes of this paragraph,

    (b) requiring that any member of the Parliament who has a financial interest (including benefits in kind), as defined for the purposes of this paragraph, in any matter declares that interest before taking part in any proceedings of the Parliament relating to that matter.

(3) Provision made in pursuance of subsection (2) shall include any provision which the Parliament considers appropriate for preventing or restricting the participation in proceedings of the

Parliament of a member with an interest defined for the purposes of subsection (2)(a) or (b) in a matter to which the proceedings relate.

    (4) Provision shall be made prohibiting a member of the Parliament from—

        (a) advocating or initiating any cause or matter on behalf of any person, by any means specified in the provision, in consideration of any payment or benefit in kind of a description so specified, or

        (b) urging, in consideration of any such payment or benefit in kind, any other member on behalf of any person by any such means.

    (5) Provision made in pursuance of subsections (2) to (4) shall include any provision which the Parliament considers appropriate for excluding from proceedings of the Parliament any member who fails to comply with, or contravenes, any provision made in pursuance of those subsections.

    (6)–(8) *****

Legal issues

40 *****

41 Defamatory statements

    (1) For the purposes of the law of defamation—

        (a) any statement made in proceedings of the Parliament, and

        (b) the publication under the authority of the Parliament of any statement, shall be absolutely privileged.

    (2) In subsection (1), 'statement' has the same meaning as in the Defamation Act 1996.

42 Contempt of court

    (1) The strict liability rule shall not apply in relation to any publication—

        (a) made in proceedings of the Parliament in relation to a Bill or subordinate legislation, or

        (b) to the extent that it consists of a fair and accurate report of such proceedings made in good faith.

    (2) In subsection (1), 'the strict liability rule' and 'publication' have the same meanings as in the Contempt of Court Act 1981.

43 ...

PART II

THE SCOTTISH ADMINISTRATION

Ministers and their staff

44 The Scottish Executive

    (1) There shall be a Scottish Executive, whose members shall be—

        (a) the First Minister,

        (b) such Ministers as the First Minister may appoint under section 47, and

        (c) the Lord Advocate and the Solicitor General for Scotland.

    (2) The members of the Scottish Executive are referred to collectively as the Scottish Ministers.

    (3) A person who holds a Ministerial office may not be appointed a member of the Scottish Executive; and if a member of the Scottish Executive is appointed to a Ministerial office he shall cease to hold office as a member the Scottish Executive.

    (4) In subsection (3), references to a member of the Scottish Executive include a junior Scottish Minister and 'Ministerial office' has the same meaning as in section 2 of the House of Commons Disqualification Act 1975.

45 The First Minister

(1) The First Minister shall be appointed by Her Majesty from among the members of the Parliament and shall hold office at Her Majesty's pleasure.

(2) The First Minister may at any time tender his resignation to Her Majesty and shall do so if the Parliament resolves that the Scottish Executive no longer enjoys the confidence of the Parliament.

(3) The First Minister shall cease to hold office if a person is appointed in his place.

(4) If the office of First Minister is vacant or he is for any reason unable to act, the functions exercisable by him shall be exercisable by a person designated by the Presiding Officer.

(5)–(7) *****

46 Choice of the First Minister

(1) If one of the following events occurs, the Parliament shall within the period allowed nominate one of its members for appointment as First Minister.

(2) The events are—

(a) the holding of a poll at a general election,

(b) the First Minister tendering his resignation to Her Majesty,

(c) the office of First Minister becoming vacant (otherwise than in consequence of his so tendering his resignation),

(d) the First Minister ceasing to be a member of the Parliament otherwise than by virtue of a dissolution.

(3) The period allowed is the period of 28 days which begins with the day on which the event in question occurs; but—

(a) if another of those events occurs within the period allowed, that period shall be extended (subject to paragraph (b)) so that it ends with the period of 28 days beginning with the day on which that other event occurred, and

(b) the period shall end if the Parliament passes a resolution under section 3(1)(a) or when Her Majesty appoints a person as First Minister.

(4) The Presiding Officer shall recommend to Her Majesty the appointment of any member of the Parliament who is nominated by the Parliament under this section.

47 Ministers

(1) The First Minister may, with the approval of Her Majesty, appoint Ministers from among the members of the Parliament.

(2) The First Minister shall not seek Her Majesty's approval for any appointment under this section without the agreement of the Parliament.

(3) A Minister appointed under this section—

(a) shall hold office at her Majesty's pleasure,

(b) may be removed from office by the First Minister,

(c) may at any time resign and shall do so if the Parliament resolves that the Scottish Executive no longer enjoys the confidence of the Parliament,

(d) if he resigns, shall cease to hold office immediately, and

(e) shall cease to hold office if he ceases to be a member of the Parliament otherwise than by virtue of a dissolution.

48–50 *****

51 The Civil Service

(1) The Scottish Ministers may appoint persons to be members of the staff of the Scottish Administration.

(2) Service as—

(a) the holder of any office in the Scottish Administration which is not a ministerial office, or

(b) a member of the staff of the Scottish Administration,

shall be service in the [civil service of the State].

(3)–(8) *****

(9) ...

Ministerial functions

52   *****

53   General transfer of functions

(1) The functions mentioned in subsection (2) shall, so far as they are exercisable within devolved competence, be exercisable by the Scottish Ministers instead of by a Minister of the Crown.

(2) Those functions are—

    (a) those of Her Majesty's prerogative and other executive functions which are exercisable on behalf of Her Majesty by a Minister of the Crown,

    (b) other functions conferred on a Minister of the Crown by a prerogative instrument, and

    (c) functions conferred on a Minister of the Crown by any pre-commencement enactment,

but do not include any retained functions of the Lord Advocate.

(3), (4) *****

54–56   *****

57   Community law and Convention rights

(1) Despite the transfer to the Scottish Ministers by virtue of section 53 of functions in relation to observing and implementing obligations under Community law, any function of a Minister of the Crown in relation to any matter shall continue to be exercisable by him as regards Scotland for the purposes specified in section 2(2) of the European Communities Act 1972.

(2) A member of the Scottish Executive has no power to make any subordinate legislation, or to do any other act, so far as the legislation or act is incompatible with any of the Convention rights or with Community law.

(3) Subsection (2) does not apply to an act of the Lord Advocate—

    (a) in prosecuting any offence, or

    (b) in his capacity as head of the systems of criminal prosecution and investigation of deaths in Scotland,

which, because of subsection (2) of section 6 of the Human Rights Act 1998, is not unlawful under subsection (1) of that section.

58   Power to prevent or require action

(1) If the Secretary of State has reasonable grounds to believe that any action proposed to be taken by a member of the Scottish Executive would be incompatible with any international obligations, he may by order direct that the proposed action shall not be taken.

(2) If the Secretary of State has reasonable grounds to believe that any action capable of being taken by a member of the Scottish Executive is required for the purpose of giving effect to any such obligations, he may by order direct that the action shall be taken.

(3) In subsections (1) and (2), 'action' includes making, confirming or approving subordinate legislation and, in subsection (2), includes introducing a Bill in the Parliament.

(4) If any subordinate legislation made or which could be revoked by a member of the Scottish Executive contains provisions—

    (a) which the Secretary of State has reasonable grounds to believe to be incompatible with any international obligations or the interests of defence or national security, or

    (b) which make modifications of the law as it applies to reserved matters and which the Secretary of State has reasonable grounds to believe to have an adverse effect on the operation of the law as it applies to reserved matters,

the Secretary of State may by order revoke the legislation.

(5) An order under this section must state the reasons for making the order.

59–72 *****

73 Power to fix basic rate for Scottish taxpayers

(1) Subject to section 74, this section applies for any year of assessment for which income tax is charged if—

    (a) the Parliament has passed a resolution providing for the percentage determined to be the basic rate for that year to be increased or reduced for Scottish taxpayers in accordance with the resolution,

    (b) the increase or reduction provided for is confined to an increase or reduction by a number not exceeding three which is specified in the resolution and is either a whole number or half of a whole number, and

    (c) the resolution has not been cancelled by a subsequent resolution of the Parliament.

(2) Where this section applies for any year of assessment the Income Tax Acts (excluding this Part) shall have effect in relation to the income of Scottish taxpayers as if any rate determined by the Parliament of the United Kingdom to be the basic rate for that year were increased or reduced in accordance with the resolution of the Scottish Parliament.

(3)–(5) *****

74–90 *****

Miscellaneous

91 Maladministration

(1) The Parliament shall make provision for the investigation of relevant complaints made to its members in respect of any action taken by or on behalf of—

    (a) a member of the Scottish Executive in the exercise of functions conferred on the Scottish Ministers, or

    (b) any other office-holder in the Scottish Administration.

(2) For the purposes of subsection (1), a complaint is a relevant complaint if it is a complaint of a kind which could be investigated under the Parliamentary Commissioner Act 1967 if it were made to a member of the House of Commons in respect of a government department or other authority to which that Act applies.

(3)–(6) *****

92–94 *****

95 Appointment and removal of judges

(1) It shall continue to be for the Prime Minister to recommend to Her Majesty the appointment of a person as Lord President of the Court of Session or Lord Justice Clerk.

(2) The Prime Minister shall not recommend to Her Majesty the appointment of any person who has not been nominated by the First Minister for such appointment.

(3) Before nominating persons for such appointment the First Minister shall consult the Lord President and the Lord Justice Clerk (unless, in either case, the office is vacant).

(4) It is for the First Minister, after consulting the Lord President, to recommend to Her Majesty the appointment of a person as—

    (a) a judge of the Court of Session (other than the Lord President or the Lord Justice Clerk), or

    (b) a sheriff principal or a sheriff.

(5) The First Minister shall comply with any requirement in relation to—

    (a) a nomination under subsection (2), or

    (b) a recommendation under subsection (4),

imposed by virtue of any enactment.

(6) A judge of the Court of Session and the Chairman of the Scottish Land Court may be removed from office only by Her Majesty; and any recommendation to Her Majesty for such removal shall be made by the First Minister.

(7) The First Minister shall make such a recommendation if (and only if) the Parliament, on a motion made by the First Minister, resolves that such a recommendation should be made.

(8) Provision shall be made for a tribunal constituted by the First Minister to investigate and report on whether a judge of the Court of Session or the Chairman of the Scottish Land Court is unfit for office by reason of inability, neglect of duty or misbehaviour and for the report to be laid before the Parliament.

(9)–(11) *****

96–99 *****

100 Human rights

(1) This Act does not enable a person—

(a) to bring any proceedings in a court or tribunal on the ground that an act is incompatible with the Convention rights, or

(b) to rely on any of the Convention rights in any such proceedings,

unless he would be a victim for the purposes of Article 34 of the Convention (within the meaning of the Human Rights Act 1998) if proceedings in respect of the act were brought in the European Court of Human Rights.

(2) Subsection (1) does not apply to the Lord Advocate, the Advocate General, or the Attorney General or the Attorney General for Northern Ireland.

(3) This Act does not enable a court or tribunal to award any damages in respect of an act which is incompatible with any of the Convention rights which it could not award if section 8(3) and (4) of the Human Rights Act 1998 applied.

[(3A)–(3E)] *****

(4) [Subject to subsection (3D),] in this section 'act' means—

(a) making any legislation,

(b) any other act or failure to act, if it is the act or failure of a member of the Scottish Executive.

101 Interpretation of Acts of the Scottish Parliament etc.

(1) This section applies to—

(a) any provision of an Act of the Scottish Parliament, or of a Bill for such an Act, and

(b) any provision of subordinate legislation made, confirmed or approved, or purporting to be made, confirmed or approved, by a member of the Scottish Executive,

which could be read in such a way as to be outside competence.

(2) Such a provision is to be read as narrowly as is required for it to be within competence, if such a reading is possible, and is to have effect accordingly.

(3) In this section 'competence'—

(a) in relation to an Act of the Scottish Parliament, or a Bill for such an Act, means the legislative competence of the Parliament, and

(b) in relation to subordinate legislation, means the powers conferred by virtue of this Act.

102 Powers of courts or tribunals to vary retrospective decisions

(1) This section applies where any court or tribunal decides that—

(a) an Act of the Scottish Parliament or any provision of such an Act is not within the legislative competence of the Parliament, or

(b) a member of the Scottish Executive does not have the power to make, confirm or approve a provision of subordinate legislation that he has purported to make, confirm or approve.

(2) The court or tribunal may make an order—

(a) removing or limiting any retrospective effect of the decision, or

(b) suspending the effect of the decision for any period and on any conditions to allow the defect to be corrected.

(3) In deciding whether to make an order under this section, the court or tribunal shall (among other things) have regard to the extent to which persons who are not parties to the proceedings would otherwise be adversely affected.

(4)–(7) *****

*****

Sections 29 and 53(4)   **SCHEDULE 4**

ENACTMENTS ETC. PROTECTED FROM MODIFICATION

PART I THE PROTECTED PROVISIONS

Particular enactments

1.—(1) An Act of the Scottish Parliament cannot modify, or confer power by subordinate legislation to modify, any of the following provisions.

(2) The provisions are—

(a) Articles 4 and 6 of the Union with Scotland Act 1706 and of the Union with England Act 1707 so far as they relate to freedom of trade,

(b) the Private Legislation Procedure (Scotland) Act 1936,

(c) the following provisions of the European Communities Act 1972—

Section 1 and Schedule 1,

Section 2, other than subsection (2), the words following 'such Community obligation' in subsection (3) and the words 'subject to Schedule 2 to this Act' in subsection (4),

Section 3(1) and (2),

Section 11(2),

(d) paragraphs 5(3)(b) and 15(4)(b) of Schedule 32 to the Local Government, Planning and Land Act 1980 (designation of enterprise zones),

(e) sections 140A to 140G of the Social Security Administration Act 1992 (rent rebate and rent allowance subsidy and council tax benefit),

(f) the Human Rights Act 1998.

The law on reserved matters

2.—(1) An Act of the Scottish Parliament cannot modify, or confer power by subordinate legislation to modify, the law on reserved matters.

(2) In this paragraph, 'the law on reserved matters' means—

(a) any enactment the subject-matter of which is a reserved matter and which is comprised in an Act of Parliament or subordinate legislation under an Act of Parliament, and

(b) any rule of law which is not contained in an enactment and the subject-matter of which is a reserved matter,

and in this sub-paragraph 'Act of Parliament' does not include this Act.

(3), (4) *****

3.—(1) Paragraph 2 does not apply to modifications which—

(a) are incidental to, or consequential on, provision made (whether by virtue of the Act in question or another enactment) which does not relate to reserved matters, and

(b) do not have a greater effect on reserved matters than is necessary to give effect to the purpose of the provision.

(2) In determining for the purposes of sub-paragraph (1)(b) what is necessary to give effect to the purpose of a provision, any power to make laws other than the power of the Parliament is to be disregarded.

This Act

4.—(1) An Act of the Scottish Parliament cannot modify, or confer power by subordinate legislation to modify, this Act.

(2) This paragraph does not apply to modifying sections 1(4), 17(5), 19(7), 21(5), 24(2), 28 (5), 39(7), 40 to 43, 50, 69(3), 85, [93 and 97] and paragraphs 4(1) to (3) and 6(1) of Schedule 2.

(3)–(5) *****

[4A]–14. *****

Section 30   ## SCHEDULE 5

RESERVED MATTERS

PART I   GENERAL RESERVATIONS

The Constitution

1. The following aspects of the constitution are reserved matters, that is—
   (a) the Crown, including succession to the Crown and a regency,
   (b) the Union of the Kingdoms of Scotland and England,
   (c) the Parliament of the United Kingdom,
   (d) the continued existence of the High Court of Justiciary as a criminal court of first instance and of appeal,
   (e) the continued existence of the Court of Session as a civil court of first instance and of appeal.

2.–5. *****

Political parties

6. The registration and funding of political parties is a reserved matter [but this paragraph does not reserve making payments to any political party for the purpose of assisting members of the Parliament who are connected with the party to perform their Parliamentary duties].

Foreign affairs etc.

7.—(1) International relations, including relations with territories outside the United Kingdom, the European Communities (and their institutions) and other international organisations, regulation of international trade, and international development assistance and co-operation are reserved matters.

(2) Sub-paragraph (1) does not reserve—
   (a) observing and implementing international obligations, obligations under the Human Rights Convention and obligations under Community law,
   (b) assisting Ministers of the Crown in relation to any matter to which that sub-paragraph applies.

Public service

8.—(1) The Civil Service of the State is a reserved matter.

(2) Sub-paragraph (1) does not reserve the subject-matter of—
   (a) Part I of the Sheriff Courts and Legal Officers (Scotland) Act 1927 (appointment of sheriff clerks and procurators fiscal etc.),

(b) Part III of the Administration of Justice (Scotland) Act 1933 (officers of the High Court of Justiciary and of the Court of Session).

Defence

9.—(1) The following are reserved matters—
    (a) the defence of the realm,
    (b) the naval, military or air forces of the Crown, including reserve forces,
    (c) visiting forces,
    (d) international headquarters and defence organisations,
    (e) trading with the enemy and enemy property.
(2) Sub-paragraph (1) does not reserve—
    (a) the exercise of civil defence functions by any person otherwise than as a member of any force or organisation referred to in sub-paragraph (1)(b) to (d) or any other force or organisation reserved by virtue of sub-paragraph (1)(a),
    (b) the conferral of enforcement powers in relation to sea fishing.

Treason

10. Treason (including constructive treason), treason felony and misprision of treason are reserved matters.

PART II SPECIFIC RESERVATIONS

Preliminary

1. The matters to which any of the Sections in this Part apply are reserved matters for the purposes of this Act.

2. A Section applies to any matter described or referred to in it when read with any illustrations, exceptions or interpretation provisions in that Section.

3. Any illustrations, exceptions or interpretation provisions in a Section relate only to that Section (so that an entry under the heading 'exceptions' does not affect any other Section).

Reservations

Head A—Financial and Economic Matters

Section A1

A1. Fiscal, economic and monetary policy
Fiscal, economic and monetary policy, including the issue and circulation of money, taxes and excise duties, government borrowing and lending, control over United Kingdom public expenditure, the exchange rate and the Bank of England.

Exception

Local taxes to fund local authority expenditure (for example, council tax and non-domestic rates).

Section A2

A2. The currency
Coinage, legal tender and bank notes.

Section A3

A3. Financial services
Financial services, including investment business, banking and deposit-taking, collective investment schemes and insurance.

Exception

The subject-matter of section 1 of the Banking and Financial Dealings Act 1971 (bank holidays).

Section A4

A4. Financial markets
Financial markets, including listing and public offers of securities and investments, transfer of securities and insider dealing.

Section A5

A5. Money laundering
The subject-matter of the Money Laundering Regulations 1993, but in relation to any type of business.
*****

[**Note:** The text of remaining headings is omitted for reasons of space. The other headings are categorised as follows:

Head B – Home Affairs
Head C – Trade and Industry
Head D – Energy
Head E – Transport
Head F – Social Security
Head G – Regulation of the Professions
Head H – Employment
Head J – Health and Medicines
Head K – Media and Culture
Head L – Miscellaneous]

Section 98   # SCHEDULE 6

DEVOLUTION ISSUES

PART I PRELIMINARY

1. In this Schedule 'devolution issue' means—
    (a) a question whether an Act of the Scottish Parliament or any provision of an Act of the Scottish Parliament is within the legislative competence of the Parliament,
    (b) a question whether any function (being a function which any person has purported, or is proposing, to exercise) is a function of the Scottish Ministers, the First Minister or the Lord Advocate,
    (c) a question whether the purported or proposed exercise of a function by a member of the Scottish Executive is, or would be, within devolved competence,
    (d) a question whether a purported or proposed exercise of a function by a member of the Scottish Executive is, or would be incompatible with any of the Convention rights or with Community law,
    (e) a question whether a failure to act by a member of the Scottish Executive is incompatible with any of the Convention rights or with Community law,
    (f) any other question about whether a function is exercisable within devolved competence or in or as regards Scotland and any other question arising by virtue of this Act about reserved matters.
    2. A devolution issue shall not be taken to arise in any proceedings merely because of any contention of a party to the proceedings which appears to the court or tribunal before which the proceedings take place to be frivolous or vexatious.

PART II PROCEEDINGS IN SCOTLAND

Application of Part II

3. This Part of this Schedule applies in relation to devolution issues in proceedings in Scotland.

Institution of proceedings

4.—(1) Proceedings for the determination of a devolution issue may be instituted by the Advocate General or the Lord Advocate.

(2) The Lord Advocate may defend any such proceedings instituted by the Advocate General.

(3) This paragraph is without prejudice to any power to institute or defend proceedings exercisable apart from this paragraph by any person.

Intimation of devolution issue

5. Intimation of any devolution issue which arises in any proceedings before a court or tribunal shall be given to the Advocate General and the Lord Advocate (unless the person to whom the intimation would be given is a party to the proceedings).

6. A person to whom intimation is given in pursuance of paragraph 5 may take part as a party in the proceedings, so far as they relate to a devolution issue.

Reference of devolution issue to higher court

7. A court, other than the [Supreme Court] or any court consisting of three or more judges of the Court of Session, may refer any devolution issue which arises in proceedings (other than criminal proceedings) before it to the Inner House of the Court of Session.

8. A tribunal from which there is no appeal shall refer any devolution issue which arises in proceedings before it to the Inner House of the Court of Session; and any other tribunal may make such a reference.

9. A court, other than any court consisting of two or more judges of the High Court of Justiciary, may refer any devolution issue which arises in criminal proceedings before it to the High Court of Justiciary.

References from superior courts to [Supreme Court]

10. Any court consisting of three or more judges of the Court of Session may refer any devolution issue which arises in proceedings before it (otherwise than on a reference under paragraph 7 or 8) to the [Supreme Court].

11. Any court consisting of two or more judges of the High Court of Justiciary may refer any devolution issue which arises in proceedings before it (otherwise than on a reference under paragraph 9) to the [Supreme Court].

Appeals from superior courts to [Supreme Court]

12. An appeal against a determination of a devolution issue by the Inner House of the Court of Session on a reference under paragraph 7 or 8 shall lie to the [Supreme Court].

13. An appeal against a determination of a devolution issue by—

    (a) a court of two or more judges of the High Court of Justiciary (whether in the ordinary course of proceedings or on a reference under paragraph 9), or

    (b) a court of three or more judges of the Court of Session from which there is no appeal to the [Supreme Court apart from this paragraph],

shall lie to the [Supreme Court], but only with [permission] of the court [from which the appeal lies] or, failing such [permission], with [permission] of the [Supreme Court].

PART III PROCEEDINGS IN ENGLAND AND WALES

Application of Part III

14. This Part of this Schedule applies in relation to devolution issues in proceedings in England and Wales.

Institution of proceedings

15.—(1) Proceedings for the determination of a devolution issue may be instituted by the Attorney General.

(2) The Lord Advocate may defend any such proceedings.

(3) This paragraph is without prejudice to any power to institute or defend proceedings exercisable apart from this paragraph by any person.

Notice of devolution issue

16. A court or tribunal shall order notice of any devolution issue which arises in any proceedings before it to be given to the Attorney General and the Lord Advocate (unless the person to whom the notice would be given is a party to the proceedings).

17. A person to whom notice is given in pursuance of paragraph 16 may take part as a party in the proceedings, so far as they relate to a devolution issue.

Reference of devolution issue to High Court or Court of Appeal

18. A magistrates' court may refer any devolution issue which arises in proceedings (other than criminal proceedings) before it to the High Court.

19.—(1) A court may refer any devolution issue which arises in proceedings (other than criminal proceedings) before it to the Court of Appeal.

(2) Sub-paragraph (1) does not apply to—

    (a) a magistrates' court, the Court of Appeal or the [Supreme Court], or

    (b) the High Court if the devolution issue arises in proceedings on a reference under paragraph 18.

20. A tribunal from which there is no appeal shall refer any devolution issue which arises in proceedings before it to the Court of Appeal; and any other tribunal may make such a reference.

21. A court, other than the [Supreme Court] or the Court of Appeal, may refer any devolution issue which arises in criminal proceedings before it to—

    (a) the High Court (if the proceedings are summary proceedings), or

    (b) the Court of Appeal (if the proceedings are proceedings on indictment).

References from Court of Appeal to [Supreme Court]

22. The Court of Appeal may refer any devolution issue which arises in proceedings before it (otherwise than on a reference under paragraph 19, 20 or 21) to the [Supreme Court].

Appeals from superior courts to [Supreme Court]

23. An appeal against a determination of a devolution issue by the High Court or the Court of Appeal on a reference under paragraph 18, 19, 20 or 21 shall lie to the [Supreme Court] but only with [permission] of the High Court or (as the case may be) the Court of Appeal or, failing such [permission], with [permission] of the [Supreme Court].

24.–31. *****

(Equivalent provisions for issues arising in Northern Ireland)

PART V GENERAL

32. ...

Direct references to [Supreme Court]

33. The Lord Advocate, the Advocate General, the Attorney General or the Attorney General for Northern Ireland may require any court or tribunal to refer to the [Supreme Court] any devolution issue which has arisen in proceedings before it to which he is a party.

34. The Lord Advocate, the Attorney General, the Advocate General or the Attorney General for Northern Ireland may refer to the [Supreme Court] any devolution issue which is not the subject of proceedings.

35.–38. *****

*****

Greater London Authority Act 1999

(1999, c. 29)

An Act to establish and make provision about the Greater London Authority, the Mayor of London and the London Assembly; to make provision in relation to London borough councils and the Common Council of the City of London with respect to matters consequential or the establishment of the Greater London Authority; to make provision with respect to the functions of other local authorities and statutory bodies exercising functions in Greater London; to make provision about transport and road traffic in and around Greater London; to make provision about policing in Greater London and to make an adjustment of the metropolitan police district; and for connected purposes. [11th November 1999]

Territorial extent: England, Scotland and Wales (but necessarily the substantive provisions apply only to London)

PART I THE GREATER LONDON AUTHORITY

The Authority

1   The Authority

(1) There shall be an authority for Greater London, to be known as the Greater London Authority.

(2) The Authority shall be a body corporate.

(3) The Authority shall have the functions which are transferred to, or conferred or imposed on, the Authority by or under this Act or any other Act.

Membership

2   Membership of the Authority and the Assembly

(1) The Authority shall consist of—

(a) the Mayor of London; and

(b) an Assembly for London, to be known as the London Assembly.

(2) The Assembly shall consist of twenty five members, of whom—

(a) fourteen shall be members of Assembly constituencies ('constituency members'); and

(b) eleven shall be members for the whole of Greater London ('London Members').

(3) There shall be one constituency member for each Assembly constituency.

(4) The Assembly constituencies shall be the areas, and shall be known by the names, specified in an order made by [statutory instrument by [the Local Government Boundary Commission for England]].

(5)–(11) *****

3–19 *****

Qualifications and disqualifications

20   Qualification to be the Mayor or an Assembly member

(1) Subject to any disqualification by virtue of this Act or any other enactment, a person is qualified to be elected and to be the Mayor or an Assembly member if he satisfies the requirements of subsections (2) to (4) below.

(2) The person must be—

    (a) a [qualifying] Commonwealth citizen;

    (b) a citizen of the Republic of Ireland; or

    (c) a relevant citizen of the Union.

(3) On the relevant day, the person must have attained the age of [18] years.

(4) The person must satisfy at least one of the following conditions—

    (a) on the relevant day he is, and from that day continues to be, a local government elector for Greater London;

    (b) he has, during the whole of the twelve months preceding that day, occupied as owner or tenant any land or other premises in Greater London;

    (c) his principal or only place of work during that twelve months has been in Greater London;

    (d) he has during the whole of that twelve months resided in Greater London.

(5)–(8) *****

21–29 *****

PART II GENERAL FUNCTIONS AND PROCEDURE

The general and subsidiary powers of the Authority

30   The general power of the Authority

(1) The Authority shall have power to do anything which it considers will further any one or more of its principal purposes.

(2) Any reference in this Act to the principal purposes of the Authority is a reference to the purposes of—

    (a) promoting economic development and wealth creation in Greater London;

    (b) promoting social development in Greater London; and

    (c) promoting the improvement of the environment in Greater London.

(3) In determining whether or how to exercise the power conferred by subsection (1) above to further any one or more of its principal purposes, the Authority shall have regard to the desirability of so exercising that power as to—

    (a) further the remaining principal purpose or purposes, so far as reasonably practicable to do so; and

    (b) secure, over a period of time, a reasonable balance between furthering each of its principal purposes.

(4) In determining whether or how to exercise the power conferred by subsection (1) above, the Authority shall have regard to the effect which the proposed exercise of the power would have on [each of the following]—

    (a)   the health of persons in Greater London;

    [(aa) health inequalities between persons living in Greater London;]

    (b)   the achievement of sustainable development in the United Kingdom;

    [(c) climate change and the consequences of climate change.]

(5) Where the Authority exercises the power conferred by subsection (1) above, it shall do so in the way which it considers best calculated—

    (a)   to promote improvements in the health of persons in Greater London,

    [(aa) to promote the reduction of health inequalities between persons living in Greater London . . .]

    (b)   to contribute towards the achievement of sustainable development in the United Kingdom, [and

    [(c)   to contribute towards the mitigation of, or adaptation to, climate change in the United Kingdom,] except to the extent that the Authority considers that any action that would need to be taken by virtue of paragraph (a)[, (aa),] (b) [or (c)] above is not reasonably practicable in all the circumstances of the case.

(6) In subsection (5)(a) above, the reference to promoting improvements in health includes a reference to mitigating any detriment to health which would otherwise be occasioned by the exercise of the power.

[(6A) In subsection 5(aa) above, the reference to promoting the reduction of health inequalities includes a reference to mitigating any increase in health inequalities which would otherwise be occasioned by the exercise of the power.]

(7)–(11) *****

31–51 *****

Meetings and procedure of the Assembly

52   Meetings of the whole Assembly

(1) The Assembly may hold, in addition to any meetings required to be held by or under this section or any other enactment, such other meetings as it may determine.

(2) Before the expiration of the period of ten days following the day of the poll at an ordinary election, there shall be a meeting of the Assembly to elect—

(a) the Chair of the Assembly; and

(b) the Deputy Chair of the Assembly.

(3) On such ten occasions in each calendar year as the Assembly may determine, there shall be a meeting of the Assembly—

(a) to consider the written report submitted for the meeting by the Mayor under section 45 above,

(b) to enable Assembly members to put—

(i)   oral or written questions to the Mayor, and

(ii)   oral questions to any employees of the Authority who are required to attend such meetings and answer questions put to them by Assembly members; and

(c) to transact any other business on the agenda for the meeting.

(4)–(6) *****

(7) …

(8) An extraordinary meeting of the Assembly may be called at any time by the Chair of the Assembly.

(9), (10) *****

53   ** ***

54   Discharge of functions by committees or single members

(1) The Assembly may arrange for any of the functions exercisable by it to be discharged on its behalf—

(a) by a committee or sub-committee of the Assembly; or

(b) by a single member of the Assembly.

(2) …

(3) Where by virtue of this section any functions exercisable by the Assembly may be discharged by a committee of the Assembly, then, unless the Assembly otherwise directs, the committee may arrange for the discharge of any of those functions by a sub-committee or by a single member of the Assembly.

(4) Where by virtue of this section any functions exercisable by the Assembly may be discharged by a sub-committee of the Assembly, then, unless the Assembly or the committee concerned otherwise directs, the sub-committee may arrange for the discharge of any of those functions by a single member of the Assembly.

(5)–(8) *****

*****

House of Lords Act 1999

(1999, c. 34)

An Act to restrict membership of the House of Lords by virtue of a hereditary peerage; to make related provision about disqualifications for voting at elections to and for membership of the House of Commons; and for connected purposes.   [11th November 1999]

Territorial extent: United Kingdom

1   Exclusion of hereditary peers

No-one shall be a member of the House of Lords by virtue of a hereditary peerage.

2   Exception from section 1

(1) Section 1 shall not apply in relation to anyone excepted from it by or in accordance with Standing Orders of the House.

(2) At any time 90 people shall be excepted from section 1; but anyone excepted as holder of the office of Earl Marshal, or as performing the office of Lord Great Chamberlain, shall not count towards that limit.

(3) Once excepted from section 1, a person shall continue to be so throughout his life (until an Act of Parliament provides to the contrary).

(4) Standing Orders shall make provision for filling vacancies among the people excepted from section 1; and in any case where—

    (a) the vacancy arises on a death occurring after the end of the first Session of the next Parliament after that in which this Act is passed, and

    (b) the deceased person was excepted in consequence of an election, that provision shall require the holding of a by-election.

(5) A person may be excepted from section 1 by or in accordance with Standing Orders made in anticipation of the enactment or commencement of this section.

(6) Any question whether a person is excepted from section 1 shall be decided by the Clerk of the Parliaments, whose certificate shall be conclusive.

3   Removal of disqualifications in relation to the House of Commons

(1) The holder of a hereditary peerage shall not be disqualified by virtue of that peerage for—

    (a) voting at elections to the House of Commons, or

    (b) being, or being elected as, a member of that House.

(2) Subsection (1) shall not apply in relation to anyone excepted from section 1 by virtue of section 2.

4   *****

5   Commencement and transitional provision

(1) Sections 1 to 4 (including Schedules 1 and 2) shall come into force at the end of the Session of Parliament in which this Act is passed.

(2) Accordingly, any writ of summons issued for the present Parliament in right of a hereditary peerage shall not have effect after that Session unless it has been issued to a person who, at the end of the Session, is excepted from section 1 by virtue of section 2.

(3), (4) *****

6   Interpretation and short title

(1) In this Act 'hereditary peerage' includes the principality of Wales and the earldom of Chester.

(2) This Act may be cited as the House of Lords Act 1999.

*****

Immigration and Asylum Act 1999

(1999, c. 33)

An Act to make provision about immigration and asylum; to make provision about procedures in connection with marriage on superintendent registrar's certificate; and for connected purposes. [11th November 1999]

Territorial extent: United Kingdom

*****

10   Removal of certain persons unlawfully in the United Kingdom

(1) A person who is not a British citizen may be removed from the United Kingdom, in accordance with directions given by an immigration officer, if—

(a)   having only a limited leave to enter or remain, he does not observe a condition attached to the leave or remains beyond the time limited by the leave;

[(b)   he uses deception in seeking (whether successfully or not) leave to remain]; or

[(ba) his indefinite leave to enter or remain has been revoked under section 76(3) of the Nationality, Immigration and Asylum Act 2002 (person ceasing to be refugee)]; or

(c)   directions ... have been given for the removal, under this section, of a person ... to whose family he belongs.

(2) Directions may not be given under subsection (1)(a) if the person concerned has made an application for leave to remain in accordance with regulations made under section 9.

[(3) Directions for the removal of a person may not be given under subsection (1)(c) unless the Secretary of State has given the person concerned written notice of the intention to remove him.]

(4)–(10) *****

11, 12, 15   ...

13, 14, 16–31   *****

PART II CARRIERS' LIABILITY

[**Note:** Sections 32–36 are printed as amended by the Nationality, Asylum and Immigration Act 2002. The amendments so made came into force in December 2002 in relation to clandestine entrants by rail or road vehicles but are not yet (April 2012) in force for clandestine entrants by ship or aircraft.]

Clandestine entrants

32   Penalty for carrying clandestine entrants

(1) A person is a clandestine entrant if—

(a)   he arrives in the United Kingdom concealed in a vehicle, ship or aircraft,

[(aa) he arrives in the United Kingdom concealed in a rail freight wagon,]

(b)   he passes, or attempts to pass, through immigration control concealed in a vehicle, or

(c)   he arrives in the United Kingdom on a ship or aircraft, having embarked—

(i) concealed in a vehicle; and

(ii) at a time when the ship or aircraft was outside the United Kingdom,

and claims, or indicates that he intends to seek, asylum in the United Kingdom or evades, or attempts to evade, immigration control.

[(2) The Secretary of State may require a person who is responsible for a clandestine entrant to pay—

(a) a penalty in respect of the clandestine entrant;

(b) a penalty in respect of any person who was concealed with the clandestine entrant in the same transporter.

(2A) In imposing a penalty under subsection (2) the Secretary of State—
  (a) must specify an amount which does not exceed the maximum prescribed for the purpose of this paragraph,
  (b) may, in respect of a clandestine entrant or a concealed person, impose separate penalties on more than one of the persons responsible for the clandestine entrant, and
  (c) may not impose penalties in respect of a clandestine entrant or a concealed person which amount in aggregate to more than the maximum prescribed for the purpose of this paragraph.]

(3) A penalty imposed under this section must be paid to the Secretary of State before the end of the prescribed period.

(4)–(10) *****

[32A   Level of penalty: code of practice

(1) The Secretary of State shall issue a code of practice specifying matters to be considered in determining the amount of a penalty under section 32.

(2) The Secretary of State shall have regard to the code (in addition to any other matters he thinks relevant)—
  (a) when imposing a penalty under section 32, and
  (b) when considering a notice of objection under section 35(4).

(3) Before issuing the code the Secretary of State shall lay a draft before Parliament.

(4) After laying the draft code before Parliament the Secretary of State may bring the code into operation by order.

(5) The Secretary of State may from time to time revise the whole or any part of the code and issue the code as revised.

(6) Subsections (3) and (4) also apply to a revision or proposed revision of the code.]

33   *****

34   Defences to claim that penalty is due under section 32

[(1) A person ('the carrier') shall not be liable to the imposition of a penalty under section 32(2) if he has a defence under this section.]

(2) It is a defence for the carrier to show that he, or an employee of his who was directly responsible for allowing the clandestine entrant to be concealed, was acting under duress.

(3) It is also a defence for the carrier to show that—
  (a) he did not know, and had no reasonable grounds for suspecting, that a clandestine entrant was, or might be, concealed in the transporter;
  (b) an effective system for preventing the carriage of clandestine entrants was in operation in relation to the transporter; and
  (c) ... on the occasion in question the person or persons responsible for operating that system did so properly.

(3A), (4) *****

(5) ...

[(6) Where a person has a defence under subsection (2) in respect of a clandestine entrant, every other responsible person in respect of the clandestine entrant is also entitled to the benefit of the defence.]

35   Procedure

(1) If the Secretary of State decides that a person ('P') is liable to one or more penalties under section 32, he must notify P of his decision.

(2) A notice under subsection (1) (a 'penalty notice') must—
  (a) state the Secretary of State's reasons for deciding that P is liable to the penalty (or penalties);
  (b) state the amount of the penalty (or penalties) to which P is liable;

    (c) specify the date before which, and the manner in which, the penalty (or penalties) must be paid; and

    (d) include an explanation of the steps—

        (i)   that P [may] take if he objects to the penalty;

        (ii) that the Secretary of State may take under this Part to recover any unpaid penalty.

[(3) Subsection (4) applies where a person to whom a penalty notice is issued objects on the ground that—

    (a) he is not liable to the imposition of a penalty, or

    (b) the amount of the penalty is too high.

(4) The person may give a notice of objection to the Secretary of State.

(5) A notice of objection must—

    (a) be in writing,

    (b) give the objector's reasons, and

    (c) be given before the end of such period as may be prescribed.

(6) Where the Secretary of State receives a notice of objection to a penalty in accordance with this section he shall consider it and—

    (a) cancel the penalty,

    (b) reduce the penalty,

    (c) increase the penalty, or

    (d) determine to take no action under paragraphs (a) to (c).

(7) Where the Secretary of State considers a notice of objection under subsection (6) he shall—

    (a) inform the objector of his decision before the end of such period as may be prescribed or such longer period as he may agree with the objector,

    (b) if he increases the penalty, issue a new penalty notice under subsection (1), and

    (c) if he reduces the penalty, notify the objector of the reduced amount.]

(8) . . .

(9)–(13) *****

[35A Appeal

(1) A person may appeal to the court against a penalty imposed on him under section 32 on the ground that—

    (a) he is not liable to the imposition of a penalty, or

    (b) the amount of the penalty is too high.

(2) On an appeal under this section the court may—

    (a) allow the appeal and cancel the penalty,

    (b) allow the appeal and reduce the penalty, or

    (c) dismiss the appeal.

(3) An appeal under this section shall be a re-hearing of the Secretary of State's decision to impose a penalty and shall be determined having regard to—

    (a) any code of practice under section 32A which has effect at the time of the appeal,

    (b) the code of practice under section 33 which had effect at the time of the events to which the penalty relates, and

    (c) any other matters which the court thinks relevant (which may include matters of which the Secretary of State was unaware).]

(4), (5) *****

36 Power to detain vehicles etc in connection with penalties under section 32

(1) If a penalty notice has been [issued] under section 35, a senior officer may detain any relevant—

    (a) vehicle,

    (b) small ship, . . .

    (c) small aircraft, [or

    (d) rail freight wagon,]

until all penalties to which the notice relates, and any expenses reasonably incurred by the Secretary of State in connection with the detention, have been paid.

(2) That power—

(a) may be exercised only if, in the opinion of the senior officer concerned, there is a signifi-cant risk that the penalty (or one or more of the penalties) will not be paid before the end of the prescribed period if the transporter is not detained; and

(b) may not be exercised if alternative security which the Secretary of State considers is satis-factory, has been given.

(2A)–(5) *****

36A–38 *****

39 ...

Passengers without proper documents

[40   Charge in respect of passenger without proper documents

(1) This section applies if an individual requiring leave to enter the United Kingdom arrives in the United Kingdom by ship or aircraft and, on being required to do so by an immigration officer, fails to produce—

(a) an immigration document which is in force and which satisfactorily establishes his iden-tity and his nationality or citizenship, and

(b) if the individual requires a visa, a visa of the required kind.

(2) The Secretary of State may charge the owner of the ship or aircraft, in respect of the indi-vidual, the sum of £2,000.

(3) The charge shall be payable to the Secretary of State on demand.

(4) No charge shall be payable in respect of any individual who is shown by the owner to have produced the required document or documents to the owner or his employee or agent when embark-ing on the ship or aircraft for the voyage or flight to the United Kingdom.

(5) For the purpose of subsection (4) an owner shall be entitled to regard a document as—

(a) being what it purports to be unless its falsity is reasonably apparent, and

(b) relating to the individual producing it unless it is reasonably apparent that it does not relate to him.]

(6)–(10) *****

[40A   Notification and objection

(1) If the Secretary of State decides to charge a person under section 40, the Secretary of State must notify the person of his decision.

(2) A notice under subsection (1) (a 'charge notice') must—

(a) state the Secretary of State's reasons for deciding to charge the person,

(b) state the amount of the charge,

(c) specify the date before which, and the manner in which, the charge must be paid,

(d) include an explanation of the steps that the person may take if he objects to the charge, and

(e) include an explanation of the steps that the Secretary of State may take under this Part to recover any unpaid charge.

(3) Where a person on whom a charge notice is served objects to the imposition of the charge on him, he may give a notice of objection to the Secretary of State.

(4) A notice of objection must—

(a) be in writing,

(b) give the objector's reasons, and

(c) be given before the end of such period as may be prescribed.

(5) Where the Secretary of State receives a notice of objection to a charge in accordance with this section, he shall—

(a) consider it, and

(b) determine whether or not to cancel the charge.]

(6)–(9) *****

[**40B   Appeal**

(1) A person may appeal to the court against a decision to charge him under section 40.

(2) On an appeal under this section the court may—

(a) allow the appeal and cancel the charge, or

(b) dismiss the appeal.

(3) An appeal under this section—

(a) shall be a re-hearing of the Secretary of State's decision to impose a charge, and

(b) may be determined having regard to matters of which the Secretary of State was unaware.]

(4), (5) *****

*****

Freedom of Information Act 2000

(2000, c. 36)

An Act to make provision for the disclosure of information held by public authorities or by persons providing services for them and to amend the Data Protection Act 1998 and the Public Records Act 1958; and for connected purposes.   [30th November 2000]

Territorial extent: England and Wales, Northern Ireland. The Act applies also to a limited extent to public bodies which operate also in Scotland, but not to purely Scottish public authorities such as the Scottish Parliament or Executive (which are covered by the Freedom of Information (Scotland) Act 2002)

PART I   ACCESS TO INFORMATION HELD BY PUBLIC AUTHORITIES

Right to information

1   General right of access to information held by public authorities

(1) Any person making a request for information to a public authority is entitled—

(a) to be informed in writing by the public authority whether it holds information of the description specified in the request, and

(b) if that is the case, to have that information communicated to him.

(2) Subsection (1) has effect subject to the following provisions of this section and to the provisions of sections 2, 9, 12 and 14.

(3) Where a public authority—

(a) reasonably requires further information in order to identify and locate the information requested, and

(b) has informed the applicant of that requirement,

the authority is not obliged to comply with subsection (1) unless it is supplied with that further information.

(4) The information—

(a) in respect of which the applicant is to be informed under subsection (1)(a), or

(b) which is to be communicated under subsection (1)(b),

is the information in question held at the time when the request is received, except that account may be taken of any amendment or deletion made between that time and the time when the information is to be communicated under subsection (1)(b), being an amendment or deletion that would have been made regardless of the receipt of the request.

(5) A public authority is to be taken to have complied with subsection (1)(a) in relation to any information if it has communicated the information to the applicant in accordance with subsection (1)(b).

(6) In this Act, the duty of a public authority to comply with subsection (1)(a) is referred to as 'the duty to confirm or deny'.

2   Effect of the exemptions in Part II

(1) Where any provision of Part II states that the duty to confirm or deny does not arise in relation to any information, the effect of the provision is that where either—

   (a) the provision confers absolute exemption, or
   (b) in all the circumstances of the case, the public interest in maintaining the exclusion of the duty to confirm or deny outweighs the public interest in disclosing whether the public authority holds the information,

section 1(1)(a) does not apply.

(2) In respect of any information which is exempt information by virtue of any provision of Part II, section 1(1)(b) does not apply if or to the extent that—

   (a) the information is exempt information by virtue of a provision conferring absolute exemption, or
   (b) in all the circumstances of the case, the public interest in maintaining the exemption outweighs the public interest in disclosing the information.

(3) For the purposes of this section, the following provisions of Part II (and no others) are to be regarded as conferring absolute exemption—

   (a) section 21,
   (b) section 23,
   (c) section 32,
   (d) section 34,
   (e) section 36 so far as relating to information held by the House of Commons or the House of Lords,
   [(ea) in section 37, paragraphs (a) to (ab) of subsection (1), and subsection (2) so far as relating to those paragraphs,]
   (f) in section 40—
      (i) subsection (1), and
      (ii) subsection (2) so far as relating to cases where the first condition referred to in that subsection is satisfied by virtue of subsection (3)(a)(i) or (b) of that section,
   (g) section 41, and
   (h) section 44.

3   Public authorities

(1) In this Act 'public authority' means—

   (a) subject to section 4(4), any body which, any other person who, or the holder of any office which—
      (i) is listed in Schedule 1, or
      (ii) is designated by order under section 5, or
   (b) a publicly-owned company as defined by section 6.

(2) For the purposes of this Act, information is held by a public authority if—

   (a) it is held by the authority, otherwise than on behalf of another person, or
   (b) it is held by another person on behalf of the authority.

4, 5   *****

6   Publicly-owned companies

(1) A company is a 'publicly-owned company' for the purposes of section 3(1)(b) if—

   (a) it is wholly owned by the Crown, or

      (b) it is wholly owned by any public authority listed in Schedule 1 other than—

          (i)   a government department, or

          (ii) any authority which is listed only in relation to particular information.

    (2), (3) *****

7   *****

8 Request for information

    (1) In this Act any reference to a 'request for information' is a reference to such a request which—

      (a) is in writing,

      (b) states the name of the applicant and an address for correspondence, and

      (c) describes the information requested.

    (2) For the purposes of subsection (1)(a), a request is to be treated as made in writing where the text of the request—

      (a) is transmitted by electronic means,

      (b) is received in legible form, and

      (c) is capable of being used for subsequent reference.

9 Fees

    (1) A public authority to whom a request for information is made may, within the period for complying with section 1(1), give the applicant a notice in writing (in this Act referred to as a 'fees notice') stating that a fee of an amount specified in the notice is to be charged by the authority for complying with section 1(1).

    (2) Where a fees notice has been given to the applicant, the public authority is not obliged to comply with section 1(1) unless the fee is paid within the period of three months beginning with the day on which the fees notice is given to the applicant.

    (3) Subject to subsection (5), any fee under this section must be determined by the public authority in accordance with regulations made by the [Secretary of State].

    (4), (5) *****

10 Time for compliance with request

    (1) Subject to subsections (2) and (3), a public authority must comply with section 1(1) promptly and in any event not later than the twentieth working day following the date of receipt.

    (2) Where the authority has given a fees notice to the applicant and the fee is paid in accordance with section 9(2), the working days in the period beginning with the day on which the fees notice is given to the applicant and ending with the day on which the fee is received by the authority are to be disregarded in calculating for the purposes of subsection (1) the twentieth working day following the date of receipt.

    (3)–(6) *****

11 Means by which communication to be made

    (1) Where, on making his request for information, the applicant expresses a preference for communication by any one or more of the following means, namely—

      (a) the provision to the applicant of a copy of the information in permanent form or in another form acceptable to the applicant,

      (b) the provision to the applicant of a reasonable opportunity to inspect a record containing the information, and

      (c) the provision to the applicant of a digest or summary of the information in permanent form or in another form acceptable to the applicant,

the public authority shall so far as reasonably practicable give effect to that preference.

    (2) In determining for the purposes of this section whether it is reasonably practicable to communicate information by particular means, the public authority may have regard to all the circumstances, including the cost of doing so.

    (3) Where the public authority determines that it is not reasonably practicable to comply with any preference expressed by the applicant in making his request, the authority shall notify the applicant of the reasons for its determination.

(4) Subject to subsection (1), a public authority may comply with a request by communicating information by any means which are reasonable in the circumstances.

12   Exemption where cost of compliance exceeds appropriate limit

(1) Section 1(1) does not oblige a public authority to comply with a request for information if the authority estimates that the cost of complying with the request would exceed the appropriate limit.

(2) Subsection (1) does not exempt the public authority from its obligation to comply with paragraph (a) of section 1(1) unless the estimated cost of complying with that paragraph alone would exceed the appropriate limit.

(3) In subsections (1) and (2) 'the appropriate limit' means such amount as may be prescribed, and different amounts may be prescribed in relation to different cases.

(4) The [Secretary of State] may by regulations provide that, in such circumstances as may be prescribed, where two or more requests for information are made to a public authority—

    (a) by one person, or

    (b) by different persons who appear to the public authority to be acting in concert or in pursuance of a campaign,

the estimated cost of complying with any of the requests is to be taken to be the estimated total cost of complying with all of them.

(5) The [Secretary of State] may by regulations make provision for the purposes of this section as to the costs to be estimated and as to the manner in which they are to be estimated.

13–16   *****

Refusal of request

17   Refusal of request

(1) A public authority which, in relation to any request for information, is to any extent relying on a claim that any provision of Part II relating to the duty to confirm or deny is relevant to the request or on a claim that information is exempt information must, within the time for complying with section 1(1), give the applicant a notice which—

    (a) states that fact,

    (b) specifies the exemption in question, and

    (c) states (if that would not otherwise be apparent) why the exemption applies.

(2) *****

(3) A public authority which, in relation to any request for information, is to any extent relying on a claim that subsection (1)(b) or (2)(b) of section 2 applies must, either in the notice under subsection (1) or in a separate notice given within such time as is reasonable in the circumstances, state the reasons for claiming—

    (a) that, in all the circumstances of the case, the public interest in maintaining the exclusion of the duty to confirm or deny outweighs the public interest in disclosing whether the authority holds the information, or

    (b) that, in all the circumstances of the case, the public interest in maintaining the exemption outweighs the public interest in disclosing the information.

(4) A public authority is not obliged to make a statement under subsection (1)(c) or (3) if, or to the extent that, the statement would involve the disclosure of information which would itself be exempt information.

(5) A public authority which, in relation to any request for information, is relying on a claim that section 12 or 14 applies must, within the time for complying with section 1(1), give the applicant a notice stating that fact.

(6), (7)   *****

18   *****

Publication schemes

19 Publication schemes

(1) It shall be the duty of every public authority—

    (a) to adopt and maintain a scheme which relates to the publication of information by the authority and is approved by the Commissioner (in this Act referred to as a 'publication scheme'),

    (b) to publish information in accordance with its publication scheme, and

    (c) from time to time to review its publication scheme.

(2) A publication scheme must—

    (a) specify classes of information which the public authority publishes or intends to publish,

    (b) specify the manner in which information of each class is, or is intended to be, published, and

    (c) specify whether the material is, or is intended to be, available to the public free of charge or on payment.

(3) In adopting or reviewing a publication scheme, a public authority shall have regard to the public interest—

    (a) in allowing public access to information held by the authority, and

    (b) in the publication of reasons for decisions made by the authority.

(4) A public authority shall publish its publication scheme in such manner as it thinks fit.

(5)–(7) *****

20 *****

PART II EXEMPT INFORMATION

21 Information accessible to applicant by other means

(1) Information which is reasonably accessible to the applicant otherwise than under section 1 is exempt information.

(2) For the purposes of subsection (1)—

    (a) information may be reasonably accessible to the applicant even though it is accessible only on payment, and

    (b) information is to be taken to be reasonably accessible to the applicant if it is information which the public authority or any other person is obliged by or under any enactment to communicate (otherwise than by making the information available for inspection) to members of the public on request, whether free of charge or on payment.

(3) *****

22 *****

23 Information supplied by, or relating to, bodies dealing with security matters

(1) Information held by a public authority is exempt information if it was directly or indirectly supplied to the public authority by, or relates to, any of the bodies specified in subsection (3).

(2) A certificate signed by a Minister of the Crown certifying that the information to which it applies was directly or indirectly supplied by, or relates to, any of the bodies specified in subsection (3) shall, subject to section 60, be conclusive evidence of that fact.

(3) The bodies referred to in subsections (1) and (2) are—

    (a) the Security Service,

    (b) the Secret Intelligence Service,

    (c) the Government Communications Headquarters,

    (d) the special forces,

    (e) the Tribunal established under section 65 of the Regulation of Investigatory Powers Act 2000,

(f) the Tribunal established under section 7 of the Interception of Communications Act 1985,

(g) the Tribunal established under section 5 of the Security Service Act 1989,

(h) the Tribunal established under section 9 of the Intelligence Services Act 1994,

(i) the Security Vetting Appeals Panel,

(j) the Security Commission,

(k) the National Criminal Intelligence Service, ...

(l) the Service Authority for the National Criminal Intelligence Service [, and

(m) the Serious Organised Crime Agency.]

(4), (5) *****

24 National security

(1) Information which does not fall within section 23(1) is exempt information if exemption from section 1(1)(b) is required for the purpose of safeguarding national security.

(2) The duty to confirm or deny does not arise if, or to the extent that, exemption from section 1(1)(a) is required for the purpose of safeguarding national security.

(3) A certificate signed by a Minister of the Crown certifying that exemption from section 1(1)(b), or from section 1(1)(a) and (b), is, or at any time was, required for the purpose of safeguarding national security shall, subject to section 60, be conclusive evidence of that fact.

(4) A certificate under subsection (3) may identify the information to which it applies by means of a general description and may be expressed to have prospective effect.

25   *****

26   Defence

(1) Information is exempt information if its disclosure under this Act would, or would be likely to, prejudice—

(a) the defence of the British Islands or of any colony, or

(b) the capability, effectiveness or security of any relevant forces.

(2) In subsection (1)(b) 'relevant forces' means—

(a) the armed forces of the Crown, and

(b) any forces co-operating with those forces,

or any part of any of those forces.

(3) The duty to confirm or deny does not arise if, or to the extent that, compliance with section 1(1)(a) would, or would be likely to, prejudice any of the matters mentioned in subsection (1).

27   International relations

(1) Information is exempt information if its disclosure under this Act would, or would be likely to, prejudice—

(a) relations between the United Kingdom and any other State,

(b) relations between the United Kingdom and any international organisation or international court,

(c) the interests of the United Kingdom abroad, or

(d) the promotion or protection by the United Kingdom of its interests abroad.

(2) Information is also exempt information if it is confidential information obtained from a State other than the United Kingdom or from an international organisation or international court.

(3) For the purposes of this section, any information obtained from a State, organisation or court is confidential at any time while the terms on which it was obtained require it to be held in confidence or while the circumstances in which it was obtained make it reasonable for the State, organisation or court to expect that it will be so held.

(4) The duty to confirm or deny does not arise if, or to the extent that, compliance with section 1(1)(a)—

(a) would, or would be likely to, prejudice any of the matters mentioned in subsection (1), or

(b) would involve the disclosure of any information (whether or not already recorded) which is confidential information obtained from a State other than the United Kingdom or from an international organisation or international court.

(5) *****

28   Relations within the United Kingdom

(1) Information is exempt information if its disclosure under this Act would, or would be likely to, prejudice relations between any administration in the United Kingdom and any other such administration.

(2) In subsection (1) 'administration in the United Kingdom' means—

(a) the government of the United Kingdom,

(b) the Scottish Administration,

(c) the Executive Committee of the Northern Ireland Assembly, or

[(d) the Welsh Assembly Government].

(3) The duty to confirm or deny does not arise if, or to the extent that, compliance with section 1(1)(a) would, or would be likely to, prejudice any of the matters mentioned in subsection (1).

29   The economy

(1) Information is exempt information if its disclosure under this Act would, or would be likely to, prejudice—

(a) the economic interests of the United Kingdom or of any part of the United Kingdom, or

(b) the financial interests of any administration in the United Kingdom, as defined by section 28(2).

(2) The duty to confirm or deny does not arise if, or to the extent that, compliance with section 1(1)(a) would, or would be likely to, prejudice any of the matters mentioned in subsection (1).

30   Investigations and proceedings conducted by public authorities

(1) Information held by a public authority is exempt information if it has at any time been held by the authority for the purposes of—

(a) any investigation which the public authority has a duty to conduct with a view to it being ascertained—

(i)   whether a person should be charged with an offence, or

(ii)   whether a person charged with an offence is guilty of it,

(b) any investigation which is conducted by the authority and in the circumstances may lead to a decision by the authority to institute criminal proceedings which the authority has power to conduct, or

(c) any criminal proceedings which the authority has power to conduct.

(2) *****

(3) The duty to confirm or deny does not arise in relation to information which is (or if it were held by the public authority would be) exempt information by virtue of subsection (1) or (2).

(4)–(6) *****

31   Law enforcement

(1) Information which is not exempt information by virtue of section 30 is exempt information if its disclosure under this Act would, or would be likely to, prejudice—

(a) the prevention or detection of crime,

(b) the apprehension or prosecution of offenders,

(c) the administration of justice,

(d) the assessment or collection of any tax or duty or of any imposition of a similar nature,

(e) the operation of the immigration controls,

(f) the maintenance of security and good order in prisons or in other institutions where persons are lawfully detained,

(g) the exercise by any public authority of its functions for any of the purposes specified in subsection (2),

   (h) any civil proceedings which are brought by or on behalf of a public authority and arise
       out of an investigation conducted, for any of the purposes specified in subsection (2), by
       or on behalf of the authority by virtue of Her Majesty's prerogative or by virtue of powers
       conferred by or under an enactment, or
   (i) any inquiry held under the Fatal Accidents and Sudden Deaths Inquiries (Scotland)
       Act 1976 to the extent that the inquiry arises out of an investigation conducted, for
       any of the purposes specified in subsection(2), by or on behalf of the authority by
       virtue of Her Majesty's prerogative or by virtue of powers conferred by or under an
       enactment.
(2) The purposes referred to in subsection (1)(g) to (i) are—
   (a) the purpose of ascertaining whether any person has failed to comply with the law
   (b) the purpose of ascertaining whether any person is responsible for any conduct which is
       improper,
   (c) the purpose of ascertaining whether circumstances which would justify regulatory action
       in pursuance of any enactment exist or may arise,
   (d) the purpose of ascertaining a person's fitness or competence in relation to the manage-
       ment of bodies corporate or in relation to any profession or other activity which he is, or
       seeks to become, authorised to carry on,
   (e) the purpose of ascertaining the cause of an accident,
   (f) the purpose of protecting charities against misconduct or mismanagement (whether by
       trustees or other persons) in their administration,
   (g) the purpose of protecting the property of charities from loss or misapplication,
   (h) the purpose of recovering the property of charities,
   (i) the purpose of securing the health, safety and welfare of persons at work, and
   (j) the purpose of protecting persons other than persons at work against risk to health or
       safety arising out of or in connection with the actions of persons at work.
(3) The duty to confirm or deny does not arise if, or to the extent that, compliance with section
1(1)(a) would, or would be likely to, prejudice any of the matters mentioned in subsection (1).

32–33   *****

34 Parliamentary privilege

   (1) Information is exempt information if exemption from section 1(1)(b) is required for the purpose of avoiding an infringement of the privileges of either House of Parliament.
   (2) The duty to confirm or deny does not apply if, or to the extent that, exemption from section
1(1)(a) is required for the purpose of avoiding an infringement of the privileges of either House of
Parliament.
   (3) A certificate signed by the appropriate authority certifying that exemption from section
1(1)(b), or from section 1(1)(a) and (b), is, or at any time was, required for the purpose of avoiding
an infringement of the privileges of either House of Parliament shall be conclusive evidence of that
fact.
   (4) In subsection (3) 'the appropriate authority' means—
   (a) in relation to the House of Commons, the Speaker of that House, and
   (b) in relation to the House of Lords, the Clerk of the Parliaments.

35 Formulation of government policy, etc.

   (1) Information held by a government department or by the [Welsh Assembly Government] is
exempt information if it relates to—
   (a) the formulation or development of government policy,
   (b) Ministerial communications,
   (c) the provision of advice by any of the Law Officers or any request for the provision of such
       advice, or
   (d) the operation of any Ministerial private office.

(2) Once a decision as to government policy has been taken, any statistical information used to provide an informed background to the taking of the decision is not to be regarded—

    (a) for the purposes of subsection (1)(a), as relating to the formulation or development of government policy, or

    (b) for the purposes of subsection (1)(b), as relating to ministerial communications.

(3) The duty to confirm or deny does not arise in relation to information which is (or if it were held by the public authority would be) exempt information by virtue of subsection (1).

    (4), (5) *****

36 Prejudice to effective conduct of public affairs

(1) This section applies to—

    (a) information which is held by a government department or by the [Welsh Assembly Government] and is not exempt information by virtue of section 35, and

    (b) information which is held by any other public authority.

(2) Information to which this section applies is exempt information if, in the reasonable opinion of a qualified person, disclosure of the information under this Act—

    (a) would, or would be likely to, prejudice—

        (i)   the maintenance of the convention of the collective responsibility of Ministers of the Crown, or

        (ii) the work of the Executive Committee of the Northern Ireland Assembly, or

        [(iii) the work of the Cabinet of the Welsh Assembly Government],

    (b) would, or would be likely to, inhibit—

        (i)   the free and frank provision of advice, or

        (ii) the free and frank exchange of views for the purposes of deliberation, or

    (c) would otherwise prejudice, or would be likely otherwise to prejudice, the effective conduct of public affairs.

(3) The duty to confirm or deny does not arise in relation to information to which this section applies (or would apply if held by the public authority) if, or to the extent that, in the reasonable opinion of a qualified person, compliance with section 1(1)(a) would, or would be likely to, have any of the effects mentioned in subsection (2).

    (4)–(7) *****

37 Communications with Her Majesty, etc. and honours

(1) Information is exempt information if it relates to—

    [(a) communications with the Sovereign,

    (aa) communications with the heir to, or the person who is for the time being second in line of succession to, the Throne,

    (ab) communications with a person who has subsequently acceded to the Throne or become heir to, or second in line to, the Throne,

    (ac) communications with other members of the Royal Family (other than communications which fall within any of paragraphs (a) to (ab) because they are made or received on behalf of a person falling within any of those paragraphs), and

    (ad) communications with the Royal Household (other than communications which fall within any of paragraphs (a) to (ac) because they are made or received on behalf of a person falling within any of those paragraphs), or]

    (b) the conferring by the Crown of any honour or dignity.

(2) The duty to confirm or deny does not arise in relation to information which is (or if it were held by the public authority would be) exempt information by virtue of subsection (1).

38–41 *****

42 Legal professional privilege

(1) Information in respect of which a claim to legal professional privilege or, in Scotland, to confidentiality of communications could be maintained in legal proceedings is exempt information.

(2) The duty to confirm or deny does not arise if, or to the extent that, compliance with section 1(1)(a) would involve the disclosure of any information (whether or not already recorded) in respect of which such a claim could be maintained in legal proceedings.

43, 44 *****

PART III GENERAL FUNCTIONS OF . . . LORD CHANCELLOR AND INFORMATION COMMISSIONER

45   Issue of code of practice . . .

(1) The [Secretary of State] shall issue, and may from time to time revise, a code of practice providing guidance to public authorities as to the practice which it would, in his opinion, be desirable for them to follow in connection with the discharge of the authorities' functions under Part I.

(2), (3) *****

(4) Before issuing or revising any code under this section, the [Secretary of State] shall consult the Commissioner.

(5) The [Secretary of State] shall lay before each House of Parliament any code or revised code made under this section.

46–49 *****

PART IV ENFORCEMENT

50   Application for decision by Commissioner

(1) Any person (in this section referred to as 'the complainant') may apply to the Commissioner for a decision whether, in any specified respect, a request for information made by the complainant to a public authority has been dealt with in accordance with the requirements of Part I.

(2) In receiving an application under this section, the Commissioner shall make a decision unless it appears to him—

  (a) that the complainant has not exhausted any complaints procedure which is provided by the public authority in conformity with the code of practice under section 45,

  (b) that there has been undue delay in making the application,

  (c) that the application is frivolous or vexatious, or

  (d) that the application has been withdrawn or abandoned.

(3) Where the Commissioner has received an application under this section, he shall either—

  (a) notify the complainant that he has not made any decision under this section as a result of the application and of his grounds for not doing so, or

  (b) serve notice of his decision (in this Act referred to as a 'decision notice') on the complainant and the public authority.

(4) Where the Commissioner decides that a public authority—

  (a) has failed to communicate information, or to provide confirmation or denial, in a case where it is required to do so by section 1(1), or

  (b) has failed to comply with any of the requirements of sections 11 and 17,

the decision notice must specify the steps which must be taken by the authority for complying with that requirement and the period within which they must be taken.

(5) A decision notice must contain particulars of the right of appeal conferred by section 57.

(6), (7) *****

*****

Local Government Act 2000

(2000, c. 22)

An Act to make provision with respect to the functions and procedures of local authorities and provision with respect to local authority elections; to make provision with respect to grants and housing benefit in respect of certain welfare services; to amend section 29 of the Children Act 1989; and for connected purposes.   [28th July 2000]

Territorial extent: England and Wales

PART I PROMOTION OF ECONOMIC, SOCIAL OR ENVIRONMENTAL WELL-BEING ETC.

Interpretation

1 Meaning of 'local authority' in Part I

In this Part 'local authority' means—

    (a) in relation to England—

        (i)   a county council,

        (ii) a district council,

        (iii) a London borough council,

        (iv) the Common Council of the City of London in its capacity as a local authority,

        (v) the Council of the Isles of Scilly,

        [(vi) an eligible parish council,]

    (b) in relation to Wales, a county council or a county borough council [or a community council].

    [(2) A parish council is 'eligible' for the purposes of this Part if the council meets the conditions prescribed by the Secretary of State by order for the purposes of this section.]

Political Parties, Elections and Referendums Act 2000

(2000, c. 41)

An Act to establish an Electoral Commission; to make provision about the registration and finances of political parties; to make provision about donations and expenditure for political purposes; to make provision about election and referendum campaigns and the conduct of referendums; to make provision about election petitions and other legal proceedings in connection with elections; to reduce the qualifying periods set out in sections 1 and 3 of the Representation of the People Act 1985; to make pre-consolidation amendments relating to European Parliamentary Elections; and for connected purposes.

[30th November 2000]

Territorial extent: United Kingdom, except that ss. 50–69 do not apply to Northern Ireland (see SI 2001/446)

1 Establishment of the Electoral Commission

    (1) There shall be a body corporate to be known as the Electoral Commission or, in Welsh, Comisiwn Etholiadol (in this Act referred to as 'the Commission').

    (2) The Commission shall consist of members to be known as Electoral Commissioners.

    (3) There shall be [nine or ten] Electoral Commissioners.

    (4) The Electoral Commissioners shall be appointed by Her Majesty (in accordance with section 3).

    (5) Her Majesty shall (in accordance with section 3 [but subject to section 3A(6)]) appoint one of the Electoral Commissioners to be the chairman of the Commission.

(6) Schedule 1, which makes further provision in relation to the Commission, shall have effect.

2   Speaker's Committee

(1) There shall be a Committee (to be known as 'the Speaker's Committee') to perform the functions conferred on the Committee by this Act.

(2) The Speaker's Committee shall consist of the Speaker of the House of Commons, who shall be the chairman of the Committee, and the following other members, namely—

(a) the Member of the House of Commons who is for the time being the Chairman of the Home Affairs Select Committee of the House of Commons;

(b) the [Lord President of the Council;]

(c) a Member of the House of Commons who is a Minister of the Crown with responsibilities in relation to local government; and

(d) five Members of the House of Commons who are not Ministers of the Crown.

(3) The member of the Committee mentioned in subsection (2)(c) shall be appointed to membership of the Committee by the Prime Minister.

(4) The members of the Committee mentioned in subsection (2)(d) shall be appointed to membership of the Committee by the Speaker of the House of Commons.

(5), (6) *****

3–21   *****

22   Parties to be registered in order to field candidates at elections

(1) Subject to subsection (4), no nomination may be made in relation to a relevant election unless the nomination is in respect of—

(a) a person who stands for election in the name of a qualifying registered party; or

(b) a person who does not purport to represent any party; or

(c) a qualifying registered party, where the election is one for which registered parties may be nominated.

(2) For the purposes of subsection (1) a party (other than a minor party) is a 'qualifying registered party' in relation to a relevant election if—

(a) the constituency, local government area or electoral region in which the election is held—

(i)   is in England, Scotland or Wales, or

(ii)   is the electoral region of Scotland or Wales,

and the party was, [on the day ('the relevant day') which is two days before the last day for the delivery of nomination papers at that election], registered in respect of that part of Great Britain in the Great Britain register maintained by the Commission under section 23, or

(b) the constituency, district electoral area or electoral region in which the election is held—

(i)   is in Northern Ireland, or

(ii)   is the electoral region of Northern Ireland,

and the party was, [on the relevant day], registered in the Northern Ireland register maintained by the Commission under that section.

[(2A)] *****

(3) For the purposes of subsection (1) a person does not purport to represent any party if either—

(a) the description of the candidate given in his nomination paper, is—

(i)   'Independent', or

(ii)   where the candidate is the Speaker of the House of Commons seeking re-election, 'The Speaker seeking re-election'; or

(b) no description of the candidate is given in his nomination paper.

(4) Subsection (1) does not apply in relation to any parish or community election.

(5) The following elections are relevant elections for the purposes of this Part—

(a) parliamentary elections,

(b) elections to the European Parliament,

(c) elections to the Scottish Parliament,

(d) elections to the National Assembly for Wales,

(e) elections to the Northern Ireland Assembly,

(f) local government elections, and

(g) local elections in Northern Ireland.

(6) For the purposes of this Act a person stands for election in the name of a registered party if his nomination paper includes a description authorised by a certificate issued by or on behalf of the registered nominating officer of the party.

23   The new registers

(1) In place of the register of political parties maintained by the registrar of companies under the Registration of Political Parties Act 1998, there shall be the new registers of political parties mentioned in subsection (2) which—

(a) shall be maintained by the Commission, and

(b) (subject to the provisions of this section) shall be so maintained in such form as the Commission may determine.

(2) The new registers of political parties are—

(a) a register of parties that intend to contest relevant elections in one or more of England, Scotland and Wales (referred to in this Act as 'the Great Britain register'); and

(b) a register of parties that intend to contest relevant elections in Northern Ireland (referred to in this Act as 'the Northern Ireland register').

(3)–(6) *****

24–36   *****

37   Party political broadcasts

(1) A broadcaster shall not include in its broadcasting services any party political broadcast made on behalf of a party which is not a registered party.

(2) In this Act 'broadcaster' means—

(a) the holder of a licence under the Broadcasting Act 1990 or 1996,

(b) the British Broadcasting Corporation, or

(c) Sianel Pedwar Cymru.

(3) *****

38–53   *****

54   Permissible donors

(1) A donation received by a registered party must not be accepted by the party if—

(a) the person by whom the donation would be made is not, at the time of its receipt by the party, a permissible donor;

[(aa) any declaration required to be made in respect of the donation by section 54A or 54B has not been received by the party; or]

(b) the party is (whether because the donation is given anonymously or by reason of any deception or concealment or otherwise) unable to ascertain the identity of [the person offering the donation].

(2) For the purposes of this Part the following are permissible donors—

(a) an individual [who is registered in an electoral register and (subject to subsection (2ZB)) satisfies the condition set out in subsection (2ZA)];

(b) a company—

(i) [registered under the Companies Act 2006], and

(ii) incorporated within the United Kingdom or another member State, which carries on business in the United Kingdom;

(c) a registered party [,other than a Gibraltar party whose entry in the register includes a statement that it intends to contest one or more elections to the European Parliament in the combined region];

(d) a trade union entered in the list kept under the Trade Union and Labour Relations (Consolidation) Act 1992 or the Industrial Relations (Northern Ireland) Order 1992;

(e) a building society (within the meaning of the Building Societies Act 1986);

(f) a limited liability partnership registered under the Limited Liability Partnerships Act . . . which carries on business in the United Kingdom;

(g) a friendly society registered under the Friendly Societies Act 1974 or a society registered (or deemed to be registered) under the Industrial and Provident Societies Act 1965 or the Industrial and Provident Societies Act (Northern Ireland) 1969; and

(h) any unincorporated association of two or more persons which does not fall within any of the preceding paragraphs but which carries on business or other activities wholly or mainly in the United Kingdom and whose main office is there.

(2ZA)–(8) *****

[54A   Declaration as to source of donation]

[(1) Where a person (P) causes an amount exceeding £7,500 to be received by a registered party by way of a donation, a written declaration must be given to the party—

(a) by P, if P is an individual, or

(b) if not, by an individual authorised by P to make the declaration,

stating, to the best of the individual's knowledge and belief, whether or not subsection (2) applies to the donation.

(2) This subsection applies to the donation if—

(a) a person other than P has provided, or is expected to provide, money or any other benefit to P with a view to, or otherwise in connection with, the making of the donation, and

(b) the money, or the value of the benefit, is more than £7,500.]

(3)–(6) *****

54B, 55   *****

56   Acceptance or return of donations: general

(1) Where—

(a) a donation is received by a registered party, and

(b) it is not immediately decided that the party should (for whatever reason) refuse the donation,

all reasonable steps must be taken forthwith by or on behalf of the party to verify (or, so far as any of the following is not apparent, ascertain) the identity of the donor, whether he is a permissible donor, and (if that appears to be the case) all such details in respect of him as are required by virtue of paragraph 2 [or 2A] of Schedule 6 to be given in respect of the donor of a recordable donation.

[(1A) In so far as subsection (1) requires steps to be taken to verify or ascertain whether an individual satisfies the condition set out in section 54(2ZA), the requirement is treated as having being complied with if—

(a) the individual has given to the party a declaration under section 54B stating that the individual satisfies that condition, and

(b) the party had no reasonable grounds for thinking that the statement was incorrect.]

(2) if a registered party receives a donation which it is prohibited from accepting by virtue of section 54(1), or which it is decided that the party should for any other reason refuse, then—

(a) unless the donation falls within [section 54(1)(aa) or (b)], the donation, or a payment of an equivalent amount, must be sent back to the person who made the donation or any person appearing to be acting on his behalf,

[(aa) if the donation falls within section 54(1)(aa) (but not section 54(1)(b)), the donation, or a payment of an equivalent amount, must be sent back to the person appearing to be the donor,]

(b) if the donation falls within [section 54(1)(b)], the required steps (as defined by section 57 (1)) must be taken in relation to the donation,

within the period of 30 days beginning with the date when the donation is received by the party.

(3) Where—

(a) subsection (2)(a) applies in relation to a donation, and

(b) the donation is not dealt with in accordance with that provision,

the party and the treasurer of the party are each guilty of an offence.

[(3A) Where a party or its treasurer is charged with an offence under subsection (3), it shall be a defence to prove that—

(a) all reasonable steps were taken by or on behalf of the party to verify (or ascertain) whether the donor was a permissible donor, and

(b) as a result, the treasurer believed the donor to be a permissible donor.]

[(3B) Where—

(a) subsection (2)(aa) applies in relation to a donation, and

(b) the donation is not dealt with in accordance with that provision,

the party and the treasurer of the party are each guilty of an offence.]

(4) Where—

(a)   subsection (2)(b) applies in relation to a donation, and

(b)   the donation is not dealt with in accordance with that provision,

the treasurer of the party is guilty of an offence.

(5), (6) *****

57 Return of donations where donor unidentifiable

(1) For the purposes of section 56(2)(b) the required steps are as follows—

(a) if the donation mentioned in that provision was transmitted by a person other than the donor, and the identity of that person is apparent, to return the donation to that person;

(b) if paragraph (a) does not apply but it is apparent that the donor has, in connection with the donation, used any facility provided by an identifiable financial institution, to return the donation to that institution; and

(c) in any other case, to send the donation to the Commission.

(2) In subsection (1) any reference to returning or sending a donation to any person or body includes a reference to sending a payment of an equivalent amount to that person or body.

(3) Any amount sent to the Commission in pursuance of subsection (1)(c) shall be paid by them into the Consolidated Fund.

57A . . .

58 Forfeiture of donations made by impermissible or unidentifiable donors

(1) This section applies to any donation received by a registered party—

(a) which, by virtue of [section 54(1)(a) (aa) or (b)], the party are prohibited from accepting, but

(b) which has been accepted by the party.

(2) The court may, on an application made by the Commission, order the forfeiture by the party of an amount equal to the value of the donation.

(3) The standard of proof in proceedings on an application under this section shall be that applicable to civil proceedings.

(4) An order may be made under this section whether or not proceedings are brought against any person for an offence connected with the donation.

(5) *****

*****

Regulation of Investigatory Powers Act 2000

(2000, c. 23)

An Act to make provision for and about the interception of communications, the acquisition and disclosure of data relating to communications, the carrying out of surveillance, the use of covert human intelligence sources and the acquisition of the means by which electronic data protected by encryption or passwords may be decrypted or accessed; to provide for Commissioners and a tribunal with functions and jurisdiction in relation to those matters, to entries on and interferences with property or with wireless telegraphy and to the carrying out of their functions by the Security Service, the Secret Intelligence Service and the Government Communications Headquarters; and for connected purposes.   [28th July 2000]

Territorial extent: United Kingdom

1   Unlawful interception

(1) It shall be an offence for a person intentionally and without lawful authority to intercept, at any place in the United Kingdom, any communication in the course of its transmission by means of—

    (a) a public postal service; or

    (b) a public telecommunication system.

(2) It shall be an offence for a person—

    (a) intentionally and without lawful authority, and

    (b) otherwise than in circumstances in which his conduct is excluded by subsection (6) from criminal liability under this subsection,

    [(1A), (1B)] *****

to intercept, at any place in the United Kingdom, any communication in the course of its transmission by means of a private telecommunication system.

(3) Any interception of a communication which is carried out at any place in the United Kingdom by, or with the express or implied consent of, a person having the right to control the operation or the use of a private telecommunication system shall be actionable at the suit or instance of the sender or recipient, or intended recipient, of the communication if it is without lawful authority and is either—

    (a) an interception of that communication in the course of its transmission by means of that private system; or

    (b) an interception of that communication in the course of its transmission, by means of a public telecommunication system, to or from apparatus comprised in that private telecommunication system.

(4) *****

(5) Conduct has lawful authority for the purposes of this section if, and only if—

    (a) it is authorised by or under section 3 or 4;

    (b) it takes place in accordance with a warrant under section 5 ('an interception warrant'); or

    (c) it is in exercise, in relation to any stored communication, of any statutory power that is exercised (apart from this section) for the purpose of obtaining information or of taking possession of any document or other property;

and conduct (whether or not prohibited by this section) which has lawful authority for the purposes of this section by virtue of paragraph (a) or (b) shall also be taken to be lawful for all other purposes.

(6) The circumstances in which a person makes an interception of a communication in the course of its transmission by means of a private telecommunication system are such that his conduct is excluded from criminal liability under subsection (2) if—

    (a) he is a person with a right to control the operation or the use of the system, or

    (b) he has the express or implied consent of such a person to make the interception.

(7) A person who is guilty of an offence under subsection (1) or (2) shall be liable—

    (a) on conviction on indictment, to imprisonment for a term riot exceeding two years or to a fine, or to both;

(b) on summary conviction, to a fine not exceeding the statutory maximum.

(8) *****

2 *****

3 Lawful interception without an interception warrant

(1) Conduct by any person consisting in the interception of a communication is authorised by this section if the communication is one which . . . is both—

    (a) a communication sent by a person who has consented to the interception; and

    (b) a communication the intended recipient of which has so consented.

(2) Conduct by any person consisting in the interception of a communication is authorised by this section if—

    (a) the communication is one sent by, or intended for, a person who has consented to the interception; and

    (b) surveillance by means of that interception has been authorised under Part II.

(3) Conduct consisting in the interception of a communication is authorised by this section if—

    (a) it is conduct by or on behalf of a person who provides a postal service or a telecommunications service; and

    (b) it takes place for purposes connected with the provision or operation of that service or with the enforcement, in relation to that service, of any enactment relating to the use of postal services or telecommunications services.

(3A), (4), (5) *****

4 Power to provide for lawful interception

(1) Conduct by any person ('the interceptor') consisting in the interception of a communication in the course of its transmission by means of a telecommunication system is authorised by this section if—

    (a) the interception is carried out for the purpose of obtaining information about the communications of a person who, or who the interceptor has reasonable grounds for believing, is in a country or territory outside the United Kingdom;

    (b) the interception relates to the use of a telecommunications service provided to persons in that country or territory which is either—

      (i) a public telecommunications service; or

      (ii) a telecommunications service that would be a public telecommunications service if the persons to whom it is offered or provided were members of the public in a part of the United Kingdom;

    (c) the person who provides that service (whether the interceptor or another person) is required by the law of that country or territory to carry out, secure or facilitate the interception in question;

    (d) the situation is one in relation to which such further conditions as may be prescribed by regulations made by the Secretary of State are required to be satisfied before conduct may be treated as authorised by virtue of this subsection; and

    (e) the conditions so prescribed are satisfied in relation to that situation.

(2) Subject to subsection (3), the Secretary of State may by regulations authorise any such conduct described in the regulations as appears to him to constitute a legitimate practice reasonably required for the purpose, in connection with the carrying on of any business, of monitoring or keeping a record of—

    (a) communications by means of which transactions are entered into in the course of that business; or

    (b) other communications relating to that business or taking place in the course of its being carried on.

(3) Nothing in any regulations under subsection (2) shall authorise the interception of any communication except in the course of its transmission using apparatus or services provided by or to the person carrying on the business for use wholly or partly in connection with that business.

(4)–(9) *****

5   Interception with a warrant

(1) Subject to the following provisions of this Chapter, the Secretary of State may issue a warrant authorising or requiring the person to whom it is addressed, by any such conduct as may be described in the warrant, to secure any one or more of the following—

    (a) the interception in the course of their transmission by means of a postal service or telecommunication system of the communications described in the warrant,

    (b) the making, in accordance with an international mutual assistance agreement, of a request for the provision of such assistance in connection with, or in the form of, an interception of communications as may be so described;

    (c) the provision, in accordance with an international mutual assistance agreement, to the competent authorities of a country or territory outside the United Kingdom of any such assistance in connection with, or in the form of, an interception of communications as may be so described;

    (d) the disclosure, in such manner as may be so described, of intercepted material obtained by any interception authorised or required by the warrant, and of related communications data.

(2) The Secretary of State shall not issue an interception warrant unless he believes—

    (a) that the warrant is necessary on grounds falling within subsection (3); and

    (b) that the conduct authorised by the warrant is proportionate to what is sought to be achieved by that conduct.

(3) Subject to the following provisions of this section, a warrant is necessary on grounds falling within this subsection if it is necessary—

    (a) in the interests of national security;

    (b) for the purpose of preventing or detecting serious crime;

    (c) for the purpose of safeguarding the economic well-being of the United Kingdom; or

    (d) for the purpose, in circumstances appearing to the Secretary of State to be equivalent to those in which he would issue a warrant by virtue of paragraph (b), of giving effect to the provisions of any international mutual assistance agreement.

(4) The matters to be taken into account in considering whether the requirements of subsection (2) are satisfied in the case of any warrant shall include whether the information which it is thought necessary to obtain under the warrant could reasonably be obtained by other means.

(5), (6) *****

6–14   *****

15   General safeguards

(1) Subject to subsection (6), it shall be the duty of the Secretary of State to ensure, in relation to all interception warrants, that such arrangements are in force as he considers necessary for securing—

    (a) that the requirements of subsections (2) and (3) are satisfied in relation to the intercepted material and any related communications data; and

    (b) in the case of warrants in relation to which there are section 8(4) certificates, that the requirements of section 16 are also satisfied.

(2) The requirements of this subsection are satisfied in relation to the intercepted material and any related communications data if each of the following—

    (a) the number of persons to whom any of the material or data is disclosed or otherwise made available,

    (b) the extent to which any of the material or data is disclosed or otherwise made available,

    (c) the extent to which any of the material or data is copied, and

    (d) the number of copies that are made,

is limited to the minimum that is necessary for the authorised purposes.

(3) The requirements of this subsection are satisfied in relation to the intercepted material and any related communications data if each copy made of any of the material or data (if not destroyed earlier) is destroyed as soon as there are no longer any grounds for retaining it as necessary for any of the authorised purposes.

(4)–(8) *****

16–58 *****

59 Intelligence Services Commissioner

(1) The Prime Minister shall appoint a Commissioner to be known as the Intelligence Services Commissioner.

(2) Subject to subsection (4), the Intelligence Services Commissioner shall keep under review, so far as they are not required to be kept under review by the Interception of Communications Commissioner—

(a) the exercise by the Secretary of State of his powers under sections 5 to 7 of [, or the Scottish Ministers (by virtue of provision made under section 63 of the Scotland Act 1998) of their powers under sections 5 and 6(3) and (4) of] the Intelligence Services Act 1994 (warrants for interference with wireless telegraphy, entry and interference with property etc.);

(b) the exercise and performance by the Secretary of State, [or the Scottish Ministers (by virtue of provision made under section 63 of the Scotland Act 1998)] in connection with or in relation to—

(i) the activities of the intelligence services, and

(ii) the activities in places other than Northern Ireland of the officials of the Ministry of Defence and of members of Her Majesty's forces,

of the powers and duties conferred or imposed on him by Parts II and III of this Act [or on them by Part II of this Act];

(c) the exercise and performance by members of the intelligence services of the powers and duties conferred or imposed on them by or under Parts II and III of this Act;

(d) the exercise and performance in places other than Northern Ireland, by officials of the Ministry of Defence and by members of Her Majesty's forces, of the powers and duties conferred or imposed on such officials or members of Her Majesty's forces by or under Parts II and III; and

(e) the adequacy of the arrangements by virtue of which the duty imposed by section 55 is sought to be discharged—

(i) in relation to the members of the intelligence services; and

(ii) in connection with any of their activities in places other than Northern Ireland, in relation to officials of the Ministry of Defence and members of Her Majesty's forces.

(2A) ...

(3) The Intelligence Services Commissioner shall give the Tribunal all such assistance (including his opinion as to any issue falling to be determined by the Tribunal) as the Tribunal may require—

(a) in connection with the investigation of any matter by the Tribunal; or

(b) otherwise for the purposes of the Tribunal's consideration or determination of any matter.

(4) It shall not be the function of the Intelligence Services Commissioner to keep under review the exercise of any power of the Secretary of State to make, amend or revoke any subordinate legislation.

(5) A person shall not be appointed under this section as the Intelligence Services Commissioner unless he holds or has held a high judicial office (within the meaning of [Part 3 of the Constitutional Reform Act 2005) or is or has been a member of the Judicial Committee of the Privy Council]).

(6)–(10) *****

60   Co-operation with and reports by s. 59 Commissioner

(1) It shall be the duty of—

(a) every member of an intelligence service,

(b) every official of the department of the Secretary of State [and every member of staff of the Scottish Administration (by virtue of provision under section 63 of the Scotland Act 1998)], and

(c) every member of Her Majesty's forces,

to disclose or provide to the Intelligence Services Commissioner all such documents and information as he may require for the purpose of enabling him to carry out his functions under section 59.

(2) As soon as practicable after the end of each calendar year, the Intelligence Services Commissioner shall make a report to the Prime Minister with respect to the carrying out of that Commissioner's functions.

(3) The Intelligence Services Commissioner may also, at any time, make any such other report to the Prime Minister on any matter relating to the carrying out of the Commissioner's functions as the Commissioner thinks fit.

(3A) *****

(4) The Prime Minister shall lay before each House of Parliament a copy of every annual report made by the Intelligence Services Commissioner under subsection (2), together with a statement as to whether any matter has been excluded from that copy in pursuance of subsection (5).

(4A)–(6) *****

61–64   *****

65   The Tribunal

(1) There shall, for the purpose of exercising the jurisdiction conferred on them by this section, be a tribunal consisting of such number of members as Her Majesty may by Letters Patent appoint.

(2) The jurisdiction of the Tribunal shall be—

(a) to be the only appropriate tribunal for the purposes of section 7 of the Human Rights Act 1998 in relation to any proceedings under subsection (1)(a) of that section (proceedings for actions incompatible with Convention rights) which fall within subsection (3) of this section;

(b) to consider and determine any complaints made to them which, in accordance with subsection (4) [...], are complaints for which the Tribunal is the appropriate forum;

(c) to consider and determine any reference to them by any person that he has suffered detriment as a consequence of any prohibition or restriction, by virtue of section 17, on his relying in, or for the purposes of, any civil proceedings on any matter; and

(d) to hear and determine any other such proceedings falling within subsection (3) as may be allocated to them in accordance with provision made by the Secretary of State by order.

(3) Proceedings fall within this subsection if—

(a)   they are proceedings against any of the intelligence services;

(b)   they are proceedings against any other person in respect of any conduct, or proposed conduct, by or on behalf of any of those services;

(c)   they are proceedings brought by virtue of section 55(4); [or]

[(ca)...

(cb) ...]

(d)   they are proceedings relating to the taking place in any challengeable circumstances of any conduct falling within subsection (5).

(4) The Tribunal is the appropriate forum for any complaint if it is a complaint by a person who is aggrieved by any conduct falling within subsection (5) which he believes—

(a) to have taken place in relation to him, to any of his property, to any communications sent by or to him, or intended for him, or to his use of any postal service, telecommunications service or telecommunication system; and

(b) to have taken place in challengeable circumstances or to have been carried out by or on behalf of any of the intelligence services.

[(4A) ...]

(5) Subject to subsection (6), conduct falls within this subsection if (whenever it occurred)it is—

    (a)   conduct by or on behalf of any of the intelligence services;

    (b)   conduct for or in connection with the interception of communications in the course of their transmission by means of a postal service or telecommunication system;

    (c)   conduct to which Chapter II of Part I applies;

    [(ca) the carrying out of surveillance by a foreign police or customs officer (within the meaning of section 76A);]

    (d)   [other] conduct to which Part II applies;

    (e)   the giving of a notice under section 49 or any disclosure or use of a key to protected information;

    (f)   any entry on or interference with property or any interference with wireless telegraphy.

(6) For the purposes only of subsection (3), nothing mentioned in paragraph (d) or (f) of subsection (5) shall be treated as falling, within that subsection unless it is conduct by or on behalf of a person holding any office, rank or position with—

    (a)   any of the intelligence services;

    (b)   any of Her Majesty's forces;

    (c)   any police force;

    [(d)   the Serious Organised Crime Agency;]

    [(da) the Scottish Crime and Drug Enforcement Agency; or]

    [(f)   the Commissioners for Her Majesty's Revenue and Customs;]

and section 48(5) applies for the purposes of this subsection as it applies for the purposes of Part II.

(7) For the purposes of this section conduct takes place in challengeable circumstances if—

    (a) it takes place with the authority, or purported authority, of anything falling within subsection (8); or

    (b) the circumstances are such that (whether or not there is such authority) it would not have been appropriate for the conduct to take place without it, or at least without proper consideration having been given to whether such authority should be sought;

but conduct does not take place in challengeable circumstances to the extent that it is authorised by, or takes place with the permission of, a judicial authority.

(7A)–(11) *****

*****

Terrorism Act 2000

(2000, c. 11)

An Act to make provision about terrorism; and to make temporary provision for Northern Ireland about the prosecution and punishment of certain offences, the preservation of peace and the maintenance of order.   [20th July 2000]

Territorial extent: United Kingdom (with certain limited exceptions)

PART I INTRODUCTORY

1 Terrorism: interpretation

    (1) In this Act 'terrorism' means the use or threat of action where—

        (a) the action falls within subsection (2),

        (b) the use or threat is designed to influence the government [or an international governmental organisation] or to intimidate the public or a section of the public, and

        (c) the use or threat is made for the purpose of advancing a political, religious [, racial] or ideological cause.

(2) Action falls within this subsection if it—

    (a) involves serious violence against a person,

    (b) involves serious damage to property,

    (c) endangers a person's life, other than that of the person committing the action,

    (d) creates a serious risk to the health or safety of the public or a section of the public, or

    (e) is designed seriously to interfere with or seriously to disrupt an electronic system.

(3) The use or threat of action falling within subsection (2) which involves the use of firearms or explosives is terrorism whether or not subsection (1)(b) is satisfied.

(4) In this section—

    (a) 'action' includes action outside the United Kingdom,

    (b) a reference to any person or to property is a reference to any person, or to property, wherever situated,

    (c) a reference to the public includes a reference to the public of a country other than the United Kingdom, and

    (d) 'the government' means the government of the United Kingdom, of a Part of the United Kingdom or of a country other than the United Kingdom.

(5) In this Act a reference to action taken for the purposes of terrorism includes a reference to action taken for the benefit of a proscribed organisation.

2 *****

PART II PROSCRIBED ORGANISATIONS

Procedure

3 Proscription

(1) For the purposes of this Act an organisation is proscribed if—

    (a) it is listed in Schedule 2, or

    (b) it operates under the same name as an organisation listed in that Schedule.

(2) Subsection (1)(b) shall not apply in relation to an organisation listed in Schedule 2 if its entry is the subject of a note in that Schedule.

(3) The Secretary of State may by order—

    (a) add an organisation to Schedule 2;

    (b) remove an organisation from that Schedule,

    (c) amend that Schedule in some other way.

(4) The Secretary of State may exercise his power under subsection (3)(a) in respect of an organisation only if he believes that it is concerned in terrorism.

(5) For the purposes of subsection (4) an organisation is concerned in terrorism if it—

    (a) commits or participates in acts of terrorism,

    (b) prepares for terrorism,

    (c) promotes or encourages terrorism, or

    (d) is otherwise concerned in terrorism.

(5A)–(9) *****

4 Deproscription: application

(1) [An application may be made to the Secretary of State for an order under section 3(3) or (8)—

    (a) removing an organisation from Schedule 2, or

    (b) providing for a name to cease to be treated as a name for an organisation listed in that Schedule].

(2) An application may be made by—

    (a) the organisation, or

    (b) any person affected by the organisation's proscription [or by the treatment of the name as a name for the organisation].

(3) The Secretary of State shall make regulations prescribing the procedure for applications under this section.

(4) The regulations shall, in particular—

(a) require the Secretary of State to determine an application within a specified period of time, and

(b) require an application to state the grounds on which it is made.

5 Deproscription: appeal

(1) There shall be a commission, to be known as the Proscribed Organisations Appeal Commission.

(2) Where an application under section 4 has been refused, the applicant may appeal to the Commission.

(3) The Commission shall allow an appeal against a refusal to deproscribe an organisation [or to provide for a name to cease to be treated as a name for an organisation] if it considers that the decision to refuse was flawed when considered in the light of the principles applicable on an application for judicial review.

(4)–(6) *****

6 Further appeal

(1) A party to an appeal under section 5 which the, Proscribed Organisations Appeal Commission has determined may bring a further appeal on a question of law to—

(a) the Court of Appeal, if the first appeal was heard in England and Wales,

(b) the Court of Session, if the first appeal was heard in Scotland, or

(c) the Court of Appeal in Northern Ireland, if the first appeal was heard in Northern Ireland.

(2) An appeal under subsection (1) may be brought only with the permission—

(a) of the Commission, or

(b) where the Commission refuses permission, of the court to which the appeal would be brought.

(3) An order under section 5(4) shall not require the Secretary of State to take any action until the final determination or disposal of an appeal under this section (including any appeal to the [Supreme Court]).

7–10 *****

Offences

11 Membership

(1) A person commits an offence if he belongs or professes to belong to a proscribed organisation.

(2) It is a defence for a person charged with an offence under subsection (1) to prove—

(a) that the organisation was not proscribed on the last (or only) occasion on which he became a member or began to profess to be a member, and

(b) that he has not taken part in the activities of the organisation at any time while it was proscribed.

(3) A person guilty of an offence under this section shall be liable—

(a) on conviction on indictment, to imprisonment for a term not exceeding ten years, to a fine or to both, or

(b) on summary conviction, to imprisonment for a term not exceeding six months, to a fine not exceeding the statutory maximum or to both.

(4) *****

12 Support

(1) A person commits an offence if—

(a) he invites support for a proscribed organisation, and

(b) the support is not, or is not restricted to, the provision of money or other property (within the meaning of section 15).

(2) A person commits an offence if he arranges, manages or assists in arranging or managing a meeting which he knows is—

    (a) to support a proscribed organisation,

    (b) to further the activities of a proscribed organisation, or

    (c) to be addressed by a person who belongs or professes to belong to a proscribed organisation.

(3) A person commits an offence if he addresses a meeting and the purpose of his address is to encourage support for a proscribed organisation or to further its activities.

(4) Where a person is charged with an offence under subsection (2)(c) in respect of a private meeting it is a defence for him to prove that he had no reasonable cause to believe that the address mentioned in subsection (2)(c) would support a proscribed organisation or further its activities.

(5) In subsections (2) to (4)—

    (a) 'meeting' means a meeting of three or more persons, whether or not the public are admitted, and

    (b) a meeting is private if the public are not admitted.

(6) A person guilty of an offence under this section shall be liable—

    (a) on conviction on indictment, to imprisonment for a term not exceeding ten years, to a fine or to both, or

    (b) on summary conviction, to imprisonment for a term not exceeding six months, to a fine not exceeding the statutory maximum or to both.

13 Uniform

(1) A person in a public place commits an offence if he—

    (a) wears an item of clothing, or

    (b) wears, carries or displays an article, in such a way or in such circumstances as to arouse reasonable suspicion that he is a member or supporter of a proscribed organisation.

(2) A constable in Scotland may arrest a person without a warrant if he has reasonable grounds to suspect that the person is guilty of an offence under this section.

(3) A person guilty of an offence under this section shall be liable on summary conviction to—

    (a) imprisonment for a term not exceeding six months,

    (b) a fine not exceeding level 5 on the standard scale, or

    (c) both.

14 *****

Offences

15 Fund-raising

(1) A person commits an offence if he—

    (a) invites another to provide money or other property, and

    (b) intends that it should be used, or has reasonable cause to suspect that it may be used, for the purposes of terrorism.

(2) A person commits an offence if he—

    (a) receives money or other property, and

    (b) intends that it should be used, or has reasonable cause to suspect that it may be used, for the purposes of terrorism.

(3) A person commits an offence if he—

    (a) provides money or other property, and

    (b) knows or has reasonable cause to suspect that it will or may be used for the purposes of terrorism.

(4) In this section a reference to the provision of money or other property is a reference to its being given, lent or otherwise made available, whether or not for consideration.

16–18 *****

19 Disclosure of information: duty

(1) This section applies where a person—

    (a) believes or suspects that another person has committed an offence under any of sections 15 to 18, and

    (b) bases his belief or suspicion on information which [comes to his attention—

        (i) in the course of a trade, profession or business, or

        (ii) in the course of his employment (whether or not in the course of a trade, profession or business)].

[(1A) But this section does not apply if the information came to the person in the course of a business in the regulated sector.]

(2) The person commits an offence if he does not disclose to a constable as soon as is reasonably practicable—

    (a) his belief or suspicion, and

    (b) the information on which it is based.

(3) It is a defence for a person charged with an offence under subsection (2) to prove that he had a reasonable excuse for not making the disclosure.

(4) Where—

    (a) a person is in employment,

    (b) his employer has established a procedure for the making of disclosures of the matters specified in subsection (2), and

    (c) he is charged with an offence under that subsection,

it is a defence for him to prove that he disclosed the matters specified in that subsection in accordance with the procedure.

(5) Subsection (2) does not require disclosure by a professional legal adviser of—

    (a) information which he obtains in privileged circumstances, or

    (b) a belief or suspicion based on information which he obtains in privileged circumstances.

(6) For the purpose of subsection (5) information is obtained by an adviser in privileged circumstances if it comes to him, otherwise than with a view to furthering a criminal purpose—

    (a) from a client or a client's representative, in connection with the provision of legal advice by the adviser to the client,

    (b) from a person seeking legal advice from the adviser, or from the person's representative, or

    (c) from any person, for the purpose of actual or contemplated legal proceedings.

(7)–(8) *****

20–39 *****

PART V COUNTER-TERRORIST POWERS

Suspected terrorists

40 Terrorist: interpretation

(1) In this Part 'terrorist' means a person who—

    (a) has committed an offence under any of sections 11, 12, 15 to 18, 54 and 56 to 63, or

    (b) is or has been concerned in the commission, preparation or instigation of acts of terrorism.

(2) The reference in subsection (1)(b) to a person who has been concerned in the commission, preparation or instigation of acts of terrorism includes a reference to a person who has been, whether before or after the passing of this Act, concerned in the commission, preparation or instigation of acts of terrorism within the meaning given by section 1.

41 Arrest without warrant

(1) A constable may arrest without a warrant a person whom he reasonably suspects to be a terrorist.

(2) Where a person is arrested under this section the provisions of Schedule 8 (detention: treatment, review and extension) shall apply.

(3) Subject to subsections (4) to (7), a person detained under this section shall (unless detained under any other power) be released not later than the end of the period of 48 hours beginning—

(a) with the time of his arrest under this section, or

(b) if he was being detained under Schedule 7 when he was arrested under this section, with the time when his examination under that Schedule began.

(4) If on a review of a person's detention under Part II of Schedule 8 the review officer does not authorise continued detention, the person shall (unless detained in accordance with subsection (5) or (6) or under any other power) be released.

(5) Where a police officer intends to make an application for a warrant under paragraph 29 of Schedule 8 extending a person's detention, the person may be detained pending the making of the application.

(6) Where an application has been made under paragraph 29 or 36 of Schedule 8 in respect of a person's detention, he may be detained pending the conclusion of proceedings on the application.

(7) Where an application under paragraph 29 or 36 of Schedule 8 is granted in respect of a person's detention, he may be detained, subject to paragraph 37 of that Schedule, during the period specified in the warrant.

(8) The refusal of an application in respect of a person's detention under paragraph 29 or 36 of Schedule 8 shall not prevent his continued detention in accordance with this section.

(9) A person who has the powers of a constable in one Part of the United Kingdom may exercise the power under subsection (1) in any Part of the United Kingdom.

42 Search of premises

(1) A justice of the peace may on the application of a constable issue a warrant in relation to specified premises if he is satisfied that there are reasonable grounds for suspecting that a person whom the constable reasonably suspects to be a person falling within section 40(1)(b) is to be found there.

(2) A warrant under this section shall authorise any constable to enter and search the specified premises for the purpose of arresting the person referred to in subsection (1) under section 41.

(3) In the application of subsection (1) to Scotland—

(a) 'justice of the peace' includes the sheriff, and

(b) the justice of the peace or sheriff can be satisfied as mentioned in that subsection only by having heard evidence on oath.

43 Search of persons

(1) A constable may stop and search a person whom he reasonably suspects to be a terrorist to discover whether he has in his possession anything which may constitute evidence that he is a terrorist.

(2) A constable may search a person arrested under section 41 to discover whether he has in his possession anything which may constitute evidence that he is a terrorist.

(3) A search of a person under this section must be carried out by someone of the same sex.

(4) A constable may seize and retain anything which he discovers in the course of a search of a person under subsection (1) or (2) and which he reasonably suspects may constitute evidence that the person is a terrorist.

(5) A person who has the powers of a constable in one Part of the United Kingdom may exercise a power under this section in any Part of the United Kingdom.

44–58A *****

Inciting terrorism overseas

59 England and Wales

(1) A person commits an offence if—

(a) he incites another person to commit an act of terrorism wholly or partly outside the United Kingdom, and

(b) the act would, if committed in England and Wales, constitute one of the offences listed in subsection (2).

(2) Those offences are—

(a) murder,

(b) an offence under section 18 of the Offences against the Person Act 1861 (wounding with intent),

(c) an offence under section 23 or 24 of that Act (poison),

(d) an offence under section 28 or 29 of that Act (explosions), and

(e) an offence under section 1(2) of the Criminal Damage Act 1971 (endangering life by damaging property).

(3) A person guilty of an offence under this section shall be liable to any penalty to which he would be liable on conviction of the offence listed in subsection (2) which corresponds to the act which he incites.

(4) For the purposes of subsection (1) it is immaterial whether or not the person incited is in the United Kingdom at the time of the incitement.

(5) Nothing in this section imposes criminal liability on any person acting on behalf of, or holding office under, the Crown.

[Note: There is equivalent provision for Northern Ireland in s. 60 and for Scotland in s. 61.]

60, 61   *****

Terrorist bombing and finance offences

62   Terrorist bombing: jurisdiction

(1) If—

(a) a person does anything outside the United Kingdom as an act of terrorism or for the purposes of terrorism, and

(b) his action would have constituted the commission of one of the offences listed in subsection (2) if it had been done in the United Kingdom,

he shall be guilty of the offence.

(2) The offences referred to in subsection (1)(b) are—

(a) an offence under section 2, 3 or 5 of the Explosive Substances Act 1883 (causing explosions, &c.),

(b) an offence under section 1 of the Biological Weapons Act 1974 (biological weapons), and

(c) an offence under section 2 of the Chemical Weapons Act 1996 (chemical weapons).

63   *****

[63A   Other terrorist offences under this Act: jurisdiction]

[(1) If—

(a) a United Kingdom national or a United Kingdom resident does anything outside the United Kingdom, and

(b) his action, if done in any part of the United Kingdom, would have constituted an offence under . . . any of sections 56 to 61,

he shall be guilty in that part of the United Kingdom of the offence.

(2) For the purposes of this section and sections 63B and 63C a 'United Kingdom national' means an individual who is—

(a) a British citizen, a British overseas territories citizen, a British National (Overseas) or a British Overseas citizen.

(b) a person who under the British Nationality Act 1981 is a British subject, or

(c) a British protected person within the meaning of that Act.

(3) For the purposes of this section and sections 63B and 63C a 'United Kingdom resident' means an individual who is resident in the United Kingdom.]

[63B   Terrorist attacks abroad by UK nationals or residents: jurisdiction]

[(1) If—

    (a) a United Kingdom national or a United Kingdom resident does anything outside the United Kingdom as an act of terrorism or for the purposes of terrorism, and

    (b) his action, if done in any part of the United Kingdom, would have constituted an offence listed in subsection (2).

he shall be guilty in that part of the United Kingdom of the offence.

(2) These are the offences—

    (a) murder, manslaughter, culpable homicide, rape, assault causing injury, assault to injury, kidnapping, abduction or false imprisonment,

    (b) an offence under section 4, 16, 18, 20, 21, 22, 23, 24, 28, 29, 30 or 64 of the Offences against the Person Act 1861,

    (c) an offence under any of sections 1 to 5 of the Forgery and Counterfeiting Act 1981,

    (d) the uttering of a forged document or an offence under section 46A of the Criminal Law (Consolidation) (Scotland) Act 1995,

    (e) an offence under section 1 or 2 of the Criminal Damage Act 1971,

    (f) an offence under Article 3 or 4 of the Criminal Damage (Northern Ireland) Order 1977,

    (g) malicious mischief,

    (h) wilful fire-raising.]

[63C   Terrorist attacks abroad on UK nationals, residents and diplomatic staff etc: jurisdiction]

[(1) If—

    (a) a person does anything outside the United Kingdom as an act of terrorism or for the purposes of terrorism,

    (b) his action is done to, or in relation to, a United Kingdom national, a United Kingdom resident or a protected person, and

    (c) his action, if done in any part of the United Kingdom, would have constituted an offence listed in subsection (2),

he shall be guilty in that part of the United Kingdom of the offence.

(2) These are the offences—

    (a) murder, manslaughter, culpable homicide, rape, assault causing injury, assault to injury, kidnapping, abduction or false imprisonment,

    (b) an offence under section 4, 16, 18, 20, 21, 22, 23, 24, 28, 29, 30 or 64 of the Offences against the Person Act 1861,

    (c) an offence under section 1, 2, 3, 4 or 5(1) or (3) of the Forgery and Counterfeiting Act 1981,

    (d) the uttering of a forged document or an offence under section 46A(1) of the Criminal Law (Consolidation) (Scotland) Act 1995.]

(3)–(5) *****

63D–113   *****

PART VIII GENERAL

114   Police powers

(1) A power conferred by virtue of this Act on a constable—

    (a) is additional to powers which he has at common law or by virtue of any other enactment, and

    (b) shall not be taken to affect those powers.

(2) A constable may if necessary use reasonable force for the purpose of exercising a power conferred on him by virtue of this Act (apart from paragraphs 2 and 3 of Schedule 7).

(3) Where anything is seized by a constable under a power conferred by virtue of this Act, it may (unless the contrary intention appears) be retained for so long as is necessary in all the circumstances.
*****

SCHEDULE 2   PROSCRIBED ORGANISATIONS

The Irish Republican Army
Cumann na mBan
Fianna na hEireann
The Red Hand Commando
Saor Eire
The Ulster Freedom Fighters
The Ulster Volunteer Force
The Irish National Liberation Army
The Irish People's Liberation Organisation
The Ulster Defence Association
The Loyalist Volunteer Force
The Continuity Army Council
The Orange Volunteers
The Red Hand Defenders
[Al-Qa'ida
Egyptian Islamic Jihad
Al-Gama'at al-Islamiya
Armed Islamic Group (Groupe Islamique Armée) (GIA)
Salafist Group for Call and Combat (Groupe Salafiste pour la Prédication et le Combat) (GSPC)
Babbar Khalsa
International Sikh Youth Federation
Harakat Mujahideen
Jaish e Mohammed
Lashkar e Tayyaba
Liberation Tigers of Tamil Eelam (LTTE)
[The military wing of Hizballah, including the Jihad Council and all units reporting to it (including the Hizballah External Security Organisation).]
Hamas-Izz al-Din al-Qassem Brigades
Palestinian Islamic Jihad—Shaqaqi
Abu Nidal Organisation
Islamic Army of Aden
. . .
Kurdistan Workers' Party (Partiya Karkeren Kurdistan) (PKK)
Revolutionary Peoples' Liberation Party—Front (Devrimci Halk Kurtulus Partisi-Cephesi) (DHKP-C)
Basque Homeland and Liberty (Euskadi ta Askatasuna) (ETA)
17 November Revolutionary Organisation (N17)]
[Abu Sayyaf Group
Asbat Al-Ansar
Islamic Movement of Uzbekistan
Jemaah Islamiyah]
[Al Ittihad Al Islamia
Ansar Al Islam
Ansar Al Sunna
Groupe Islamique Combattant Marocain

Harakat-ul-Jihad-ul Islami
Harakat-ul-Jihad-ul Islami (Bangladesh)
Harakat-ul-Mujahideen/Alami
Hezb-e-Islami Gulbuddin
Islamic Jihad Union
Jamaat ul-Furquan
Jundallah
Khuddam ul-Islam
Lashkar-e Jhangvi
Libyan Islamic Fighting Group
Sipah-e Sahaba Pakistan]
[Al-Ghurabaa
The Saved Sect
Baluchistan Liberation Army
Teyrebaz Azadiye Kurdistan]
[Jammat-ul Mujahideen Bangladesh
Tehrik Nefaz-e Shari'at Muhammadi]
[Al-Shabaab]
[Tehrik-e Taliban Pakistan]

[**Note:** The entry for The Orange Volunteers refers to the organisation which uses that name and in the name of which a statement described as a press release was published on 14 October 1998.

The entry for Jemaah Islamiyah refers to the organisation using that name that is based in south-east Asia, members of which were arrested by the Singapore authorities in December 2001 in connection with a plot to attack US and other Western targets in Singapore.]

SCHEDULES 3–5 *****

SCHEDULE 6 FINANCIAL INFORMATION

Orders

1.—(1) Where an order has been made under this paragraph in relation to a terrorist investigation, a constable named in the order may require a financial institution [to which the order applies] to provide customer information for the purposes of the investigation.

(1A) *****

(2) The information shall be provided—

(a) in such manner and within such time as the constable may specify, and

(b) notwithstanding any restriction on the disclosure of information imposed by statute or otherwise.

(3) An institution which fails to comply with a requirement under this paragraph shall be guilty of an offence.

(4) It is a defence for an institution charged with an offence under sub-paragraph (3) to prove—

(a) that the information required was not in the institution's possession, or

(b) that it was not reasonably practicable for the institution to comply with the requirement.

(5) An institution guilty of an offence under sub-paragraph (3) shall be liable on summary conviction to a fine not exceeding level 5 on the standard scale.

2.–4. *****

Criteria for making order

5. An order under paragraph 1 may be made only if the person making it is satisfied that—

(a) the order is sought for the purposes of a terrorist investigation,

(b) the tracing of terrorist property is desirable for the purposes of the investigation, and

(c) the order will enhance the effectiveness of the investigation.

*****

[**Note:** Schedule 8 (not reproduced) contains provisions for the detention and treatment of persons arrested under this Act, equivalent to provisions for persons arrested under s. 24 Police and Criminal Evidence Act 1984 contained in that Act. The Terrorism Act 2006 amends Sch. 8, and allows for a maximum period of detention following arrest of 28 days (para. 36).]

Anti-terrorism, Crime and Security Act 2001

(2001, c. 24)

An Act to amend the Terrorism Act 2000; to make further provision about terrorism and security; to provide for the freezing of assets; to make provision about immigration and asylum; to amend or extend the criminal law and powers for preventing crime and enforcing that law: to make provision about the control of pathogens and toxins; to provide for the retention of communications data; to provide for implementation of Title VI of the Treaty on European Union; and for connected purposes. [14th December 2001]

Territorial extent: United Kingdom (provisions reproduced here)

1–3 *****

PART 2 FREEZING ORDERS

Orders

4 Power to make order

(1) The Treasury may make a freezing order if the following two conditions are satisfied.

(2) The first condition is that the Treasury reasonably believe that—

(a) action to the detriment of the United Kingdom's economy (or part of it) has been or is likely to be taken by a person or persons, or

(b) action constituting a threat to the life or property of one or more nationals of the United Kingdom or residents of the United Kingdom has been or is likely to be taken by a person or persons.

(3) If one person is believed to have taken or to be likely to take the action the second condition is that the person is—

(a) the government of a country or territory outside the United Kingdom, or

(b) a resident of a country or territory outside the United Kingdom.

(4) If two or more persons are believed to have taken or to be likely to take the action the second condition is that each of them falls within paragraph (a) or (b) of subsection (3); and different persons may fall within different paragraphs.

5 Contents of order

(1) A freezing order is an order which prohibits persons from making funds available to or for the benefit of a person or persons specified in the order.

(2) The order must provide that these are the persons who are prohibited—

(a) all persons in the United Kingdom, and

(b) all persons elsewhere who are nationals of the United Kingdom or are bodies incorporated under the law of any part of the United Kingdom or are Scottish partnerships.

(3) The order may specify the following (and only the following) as the person or persons to whom or for whose benefit funds are not to be made available—

(a) the person or persons reasonably believed by the Treasury to have taken or to be likely to take the action referred to in section 4;

(b) any person the Treasury reasonably believe has provided or is likely to provide assistance (directly or indirectly) to that person or any of those persons.

(4) A person may be specified under subsection (3) by—

(a) being named in the order, or

(b) falling within a description of persons set out in the order.

(5) The description must be such that a reasonable person would know whether he fell within it.

(6) Funds are financial assets and economic benefits of any kind.

6   *****

7   Review of order

The Treasury must keep a freezing order under review.

8   Duration of order

A freezing order ceases to have effect at the end of the period of 2 years starting with the day on which it is made.

9   *****

Orders: procedure etc.

10   Procedure for making freezing orders

(1) A power to make a freezing order is exercisable by statutory instrument.

(2) A freezing order—

(a) must be laid before Parliament after being made;

(b) ceases to have effect at the end of the relevant period unless before the end of that period the order is approved by a resolution of each House of Parliament (but without that affecting anything done under the order or the power to make a new order).

(3) The relevant period is a period of 28 days starting with the day on which the order is made.

(4), (5)   *****

11–14   *****

15   The Crown

(1) A freezing order binds the Crown, subject to the following provisions of this section.

(2) No contravention by the Crown of a provision of a freezing order makes the Crown criminally liable; but the High Court or in Scotland the Court of Session may, on the application of a person appearing to the Court to have an interest, declare unlawful any act or omission of the Crown which constitutes such a contravention.

(3) Nothing in this section affects Her Majesty in her private capacity; and this is to be construed as if section 38(3) of the Crown Proceedings Act 1947 (meaning of Her Majesty in her private capacity) were contained in this Act.

16–20   *****

21–33   . . .

34–46   *****

PART 6   WEAPONS OF MASS DESTRUCTION

Nuclear weapons

47   Use etc. of nuclear weapons

(1) A person who—

(a) knowingly causes a nuclear weapon explosion;

(b) develops or produces, or participates in the development or production of, a nuclear weapon;

(c) has a nuclear weapon in his possession;

(d) participates in the transfer of a nuclear weapon; or

(e) engages in military preparations, or in preparations of a military nature, intending to use, or threaten to use, a nuclear weapon,

is guilty of an offence.

(2) Subsection (1) has effect subject to the exceptions and defences in sections 48 and 49.

(3)–(9) *****

48   Exceptions

(1) Nothing in section 47 applies—

    (a) to an act which is authorised under subsection (2); or

    (b) to an act done in the course of an armed conflict.

(2) The Secretary of State may—

    (a) authorise any act which would otherwise contravene section 47 in such manner and on such terms as he thinks fit; and

    (b) withdraw or vary any authorisation given under this subsection.

(3) Any question arising in proceedings for an offence under section 47 as to whether anything was done in the course of an armed conflict shall be determined by the Secretary of State.

(4) *****

49   Defences

(1) In proceedings for an offence under section 47(1)(c) or (d) relating to an object it is a defence for the accused to show that he did not know and had no reason to believe that the object was a nuclear weapon.

(2) But he shall be taken to have shown that fact if—

    (a) sufficient evidence is adduced to raise an issue with respect to it; and

    (b) the contrary is not proved by the prosecution beyond reasonable doubt.

(3) In proceedings for such an offence it is also a defence for the accused to show that he knew or believed that the object was a nuclear weapon but, as soon as reasonably practicable after he first knew or believed that fact, he took all reasonable steps to inform the Secretary of State or a constable of his knowledge or belief.

*****

SCHEDULES

*****

SCHEDULE 3   FREEZING ORDERS

*****

Compensation

10.—(1) A freezing order may include provision for the award of compensation to or on behalf of a person on the grounds that he has suffered loss as a result of—

    (a) the order;

    (b) the fact that a licence has not been granted under the order;

    (c) the fact that a licence under the order has been granted on particular terms rather than others;

    (d) the fact that a licence under the order has been varied or revoked.

(2) In particular, the order may include—

    (a) provision about the person who may make a claim for an award;

    (b) provision about the person to whom a claim for an award is to be made (which may be provision that it is to be made to the High Court or, in Scotland, the Court of Session);

    (c) provision about the procedure for making and deciding a claim;

    (d) provision that no compensation is to be awarded unless the claimant has behaved reasonably (which may include provision requiring him to mitigate his loss, for instance by applying for a licence);

    (e) provision that compensation must be awarded in specified circumstances or may be awarded in specified circumstances (which may include provision that the circumstances involve negligence or other fault);

    (f) provision about the amount that may be awarded;

    (g) provision about who is to pay any compensation awarded (which may include provision that it is to be paid or reimbursed by the Treasury);

    (h) provision about how compensation is to be paid (which may include provision for payment to a person other than the claimant).

Treasury's duty to give reasons

11. A freezing order must include provision that if—

    (a) a person is specified in the order as a person to whom or for whose benefit funds are not to be made available, and

    (b) he makes a written request to the Treasury to give him the reason why he is so specified, as soon as is practicable the Treasury must give the person the reason in writing.

*****

Criminal Justice and Police Act 2001

(2001, c. 16)

An Act to make provision for combating crime and disorder; to make provision about the disclosure of information relating to criminal matters and about powers of search and seizure; to amend the Police and Criminal Evidence Act 1984, the Police and Criminal Evidence (Northern Ireland) Order 1989 and the Terrorism Act 2000; to make provision about the police, the National Criminal Intelligence Service, and the National Crime Squad; to make provision about the powers of the Courts in relation to criminal matters; and for connected purposes. [11th May 2001]

Territorial extent: England and Wales, but Parts 2, 5 (National Criminal Intelligence Service) extend to the United Kingdom

1–38 *****

39 Intimidation of witnesses

    (1) A person commits an offence if—

        (a) he does an act which intimidates, and is intended to intimidate, another person ('the victim');

        (b) he does the act—

            (i) knowing or believing that the victim is or may be a witness in any relevant proceedings; and

            (ii) intending, by his act, to cause the course of justice to be obstructed, perverted or interfered with;

        and

        (c) the act is done after the commencement of those proceedings.

    (2) For the purposes of subsection (1) it is immaterial—

        (a) whether or not the act that is done is done in the presence of the victim;

        (b) whether that act is done to the victim himself or to another person; and

        (c) whether or not the intention to cause the course of justice to be obstructed, perverted or interfered with is the predominating intention of the person doing the act in question.

    (3) If, in proceedings against a person for an offence under this section, it is proved—

(a) that he did any act that intimidated, and was intended to intimidate, another person, and

(b) that he did that act knowing or believing that that other person was or might be a witness in any relevant proceedings that had already commenced,

he shall be presumed, unless the contrary is shown, to have done the act with the intention of causing the course of justice to be obstructed, perverted or interfered with.

(4) A person guilty of an offence under this section shall be liable—

(a) on conviction on indictment, to imprisonment for a term not exceeding five years or to a fine, or to both;

(b) on summary conviction, to imprisonment for a term not exceeding six months or to a fine not exceeding the statutory maximum, or to both.

(5)–(7) *****

40 Harming witnesses etc.

(1) A person commits an offence if, in circumstances falling within subsection (2)—

(a) he does an act which harms, and is intended to harm, another person; or

(b) intending to cause another person to fear harm, he threatens to do an act which would harm that other person.

(2) The circumstances fall within this subsection if—

(a) the person doing or threatening to do the act does so knowing or believing that some person (whether or not the person harmed or threatened or the person against whom harm is threatened) has been a witness in relevant proceedings; and

(b) he does or threatens to do that act because of that knowledge or belief.

(3) If, in proceedings against a person for an offence under this section, it is proved that, within the relevant period—

(a) he did an act which harmed, and was intended to harm, another person, or

(b) intending to cause another person to fear harm, he threatened to do an act which would harm that other person,

and that he did the act, or (as the case may be) threatened to do the act, with the knowledge or belief required by paragraph (a) of subsection (2), he shall be presumed, unless the contrary is shown, to have done the act, or (as the case may be) threatened to do the act, because of that knowledge or belief.

(4) For the purposes of this section it is immaterial—

(a) whether or not the act that is done or threatened, or the threat that is made, is or would be done or is made in the presence of the person who is or would be harmed or of the person who is threatened;

(b) whether or not the motive mentioned in subsection (2)(b) is the predominating motive for the act or threat; and

(c) whether the harm that is done or threatened is physical or financial or is harm to a person or to his property.

(5) A person guilty of an offence under this section shall be liable—

(a) on conviction on indictment, to imprisonment for a term not exceeding five years or to a fine, or to both;

(b) on summary conviction, to imprisonment for a term not exceeding six months or to a fine not exceeding the statutory maximum, or to both.

(6) In this section 'the relevant period', in relation to an act done, or threat made, with the knowledge or belief that a person has been a witness in any relevant proceedings, means the period that begins with the commencement of those proceedings and ends one year after they are finally concluded.

(7), (8) *****

41 Relevant proceedings

(1) A reference in section 39 or 40 to relevant proceedings is a reference to any proceedings in or before the Court of Appeal, the High Court, the Crown Court or any county court or magistrates' court which—

(a) are not proceedings for an offence; and

(b) were commenced after the coming into force of that section.

(2)–(5) *****

42 Police directions stopping the harassment etc. of a person in his home

(1) Subject to the following provisions of this section, a constable who is at the scene may give a direction under this section to any person if—

(a) that person is present outside or in the vicinity of any premises that are used by any individual ('the resident') as his dwelling;

(b) that constable believes, on reasonable grounds, that that person is present there for the purpose (by his presence or otherwise) of representing to the resident or another individual (whether or not one who uses the premises as his dwelling), or of persuading the resident or such another individual—

(i) that he should not do something that he is entitled or required to do; or

(ii) that he should do something that he is not under any obligation to do; and

(c) that constable also believes, on reasonable grounds, that the presence of that person (either alone or together with that of any other persons who are also present)—

(i) amounts to, or is likely to result in, the harassment of the resident; or

(ii) is likely to cause alarm or distress to the resident.

(2) A direction under this section is a direction requiring the person to whom it is given to do all such things as the constable giving it may specify as the things he considers necessary to prevent one or both of the following—

(a) the harassment of the resident; or

(b) the causing of any alarm or distress to the resident.

(3) A direction under this section may be given orally; and where a constable is entitled to give a direction under this section to each of several persons outside, or in the vicinity of, any premises, he may give that direction to those persons by notifying them of his requirements either individually or all together.

[(4) The requirements that may be imposed by a direction under this section include—

(a) a requirement to leave the vicinity of the premises in question, and

(b) a requirement to leave that vicinity, and not to return to it within such period as the constable may specify, not being longer than 3 months;

and (in either case) the requirement to leave the vicinity may be to do so immediately or after a specified period of time.]

(5) A direction under this section may make exceptions to any requirement imposed by the direction, and may make any such exception subject to such conditions as the constable giving the direction thinks fit; and those conditions may include—

(a) conditions as to the distance from the premises in question at which, or otherwise as to the location where, persons who do not leave their vicinity must remain; and

(b) conditions as to the number or identity of the persons who are authorised by the exception to remain in the vicinity of those premises.

(6) The power of a constable to give a direction under this section shall not include—

(a) any power to give a direction at any time when there is a more senior-ranking police officer at the scene; or

(b) any power to direct a person to refrain from conduct that is lawful under section 220 of the Trade Union and Labour Relations (Consolidation) Act 1992 (c. 52) (right peacefully to picket a work place);

but it shall include power to vary or withdraw a direction previously given under this section.

(7) Any person who knowingly [fails to comply with a requirement in a direction given to him under this section (other than a requirement under subsection (4)(b))] shall be guilty of an offence and liable, on summary conviction, to imprisonment for a term not exceeding three months or to a fine not exceeding level 4 on the standard scale, or to both.

[(7A) Any person to whom a constable has given a direction including a requirement under subsection (4)(b) commits an offence if he—

> (a) returns to the vicinity of the premises in question within the period specified in the direction beginning with the date on which the direction is given; and
>
> (b) does so for the purpose described in subsection (1)(b).

(7B) A person guilty of an offence under subsection (7A) shall be liable, on summary conviction, to imprisonment for a term not exceeding six months or to a fine not exceeding level 4 on the standard scale, or to both.]

(7C) *****

(8) . . .

(9) In this section 'dwelling' has the same meaning as in Part 1 of the Public Order Act 1986 (c. 64).

42A–47 *****

48, 49 . . .

PART 2 POWERS OF SEIZURE

Additional powers of seizure

50 Additional powers of seizure from premises

(1) Where—

> (a) a person who is lawfully on any premises finds anything on those premises that he has reasonable grounds for believing may be or may contain something for which he is authorised to search on those premises,
>
> (b) a power of seizure to which this section applies or the power conferred by subsection (2) would entitle him, if he found it, to seize whatever it is that he has grounds for believing that thing to be or to contain, and
>
> (c) in all the circumstances, it is not reasonably practicable for it to be determined, on those premises—
>
> > (i) whether what he has found is something that he is entitled to seize, or
> >
> > (ii) the extent to which what he has found contains something that he is entitled to seize,

that person's powers of seizure shall include power under this section to seize so much of what he has found as it is necessary to remove from the premises to enable that to be determined.

(2) Where—

> (a) a person who is lawfully on any premises finds anything on those premises ('the seizable property') which he would be entitled to seize but for its being comprised in something else that he has (apart from this subsection) no power to seize,
>
> (b) the power under which that person would have power to seize the seizable property is a power to which this section applies, and
>
> (c) in all the circumstances it is not reasonably practicable for the seizable property to be separated, on those premises, from that in which it is comprised,

that person's powers of seizure shall include power under this section to seize both the seizable property and that from which it is not reasonably practicable to separate it.

(3)–(6) *****

51 Additional powers of seizure from the person

(1) Where—

> (a) a person carrying out a lawful search of any person finds something that he has reasonable grounds for believing may be or may contain something for which he is authorised to search,

    (b) a power of seizure to which this section applies or the power conferred by subsection (2) would entitle him, if he found it, to seize whatever it is that he has grounds for believing that thing to be or to contain, and

    (c) in all the circumstances it is not reasonably practicable for it to be determined, at the time and place of the search—

        (i)   whether what he has found is something that he is entitled to seize, or

        (ii) the extent to which what he has found contains something that he is entitled to seize,

that person's powers of seizure shall include power under this section to seize so much of what he has found as it is necessary to remove from that place to enable that to be determined.

    (2)–(5) *****

52–58 *****

Remedies and safeguards

59   Application to the appropriate judicial authority

    (1) This section applies where anything has been seized in exercise, or purported exercise, of a relevant power of seizure.

    (2) Any person with a relevant interest in the seized property may apply to the appropriate judicial authority, on one or more of the grounds mentioned in subsection (3), for the return of the whole or a part of the seized property.

    (3) Those grounds are—

    (a) that there was no power to make the seizure;

    (b) that the seized property is or contains an item subject to legal privilege that is not comprised in property falling within section 54(2);

    (c) that the seized property is or contains any excluded material or special procedure material which—

        (i)   has been seized under a power to which section 55 applies;

        (ii) is not comprised in property falling within section 55(2) or (3); and

        (iii) is not property the retention of which is authorised by section 56;

    (d) that the seized property is or contains something seized under section 50 or 51 which does not fall within section 53(3);

and subsections (5) and (6) of section 55 shall apply for the purposes of paragraph (c) as they apply for the purposes of that section.

    (4) Subject to subsection (6), the appropriate judicial authority, on an application under subsection (2), shall—

    (a) if satisfied as to any of the matters mentioned in subsection (3), order the return of so much of the seized property as is property in relation to which the authority is so satisfied; and

    (b) to the extent that that authority is not so satisfied, dismiss the application.

    (5)–(12) *****

*****

International Criminal Court Act 2001

(2001, c. 17)

An Act to give effect to the Statute of the International Criminal Court; to provide for offences under the law of England and Wales and Northern Ireland corresponding to offences within the jurisdiction of that Court; and for connected purposes.   [11th May 2001]

Territorial extent: The United Kingdom (but ss. 28 and 51 and Sch. 3 apply only to England and Wales)

PART 1 THE INTERNATIONAL CRIMINAL COURT

1 The ICC and the ICC Statute

(1) In this Act—

'the ICC' means the International Criminal Court established by the Statute of the International Criminal Court, done at Rome on 17th July 1998;

'the ICC Statute' means that Statute; and

'ICC crime' means a crime (other than the crime of aggression) over which the ICC has jurisdiction in accordance with the ICC Statute.

(2) References in this Act to articles are, unless otherwise indicated, to articles of the ICC Statute.

(3) Schedule 1 to this Act contains supplementary provisions relating to the ICC.

PART 2 ARREST AND DELIVERY OF PERSONS

Proceedings on request

2 Request for arrest and surrender

(1) Where the Secretary of State receives a request from the ICC for the arrest and surrender of a person alleged to have committed an ICC crime, or to have been convicted by the ICC, he shall transmit the request and the documents accompanying it to an appropriate judicial officer.

(2) If it appears to the Secretary of State that the request should be considered by an appropriate judicial officer in Scotland, he shall transmit the request and the documents accompanying it to the Scottish Ministers who shall transmit them to an appropriate judicial officer.

(3) If the request is accompanied by a warrant of arrest and the appropriate judicial officer is satisfied that the warrant appears to have been issued by the ICC, he shall endorse the warrant for execution in the United Kingdom.

(4) If in the case of a person convicted by the ICC the request is not accompanied by a warrant of arrest, but is accompanied by—

  (a) a copy of the judgment of conviction,

  (b) information to demonstrate that the person sought is the one referred to in the judgment of conviction, and

  (c) where the person sought has been sentenced, a copy of the sentence imposed and a statement of any time already served and the time remaining to be served,

the officer shall issue a warrant for the arrest of the person to whom the request relates.

(5) In this Part a warrant endorsed or issued under this section is referred to as a 'section 2 warrant'.

3 Request for provisional arrest

(1) This section applies where the Secretary of State receives from the ICC a request for the provisional arrest of a person alleged to have committed an ICC crime or to have been convicted by the ICC.

(2) If it appears to the Secretary of State that application for a warrant should be made in England and Wales—

  (a) he shall transmit the request to a constable and direct the constable to apply for a warrant for the arrest of that person, and

  (b) on an application by a constable stating on oath that he has reason to believe—

    (i) that a request has been made on grounds of urgency by the ICC for the arrest of a person, and

    (ii) that the person is in, or on his way to, the United Kingdom, an appropriate judicial officer shall issue a warrant for the arrest of that person.

(3), (4) *****

(5) In this Part a warrant issued under this section is referred to as a 'provisional warrant'.

4   Dealing with person arrested under provisional warrant

(1) A person arrested under a provisional warrant shall be brought before a competent court as soon as is practicable.

(2) If there is produced to the court a section 2 warrant in respect of that person, the court shall proceed as if he had been arrested under that warrant.

(3) If no such warrant is produced, the court shall remand him pending the production of such a warrant.

(4)–(7) ****

5   Proceedings for delivery order

(1) A person arrested under a section 2 warrant shall be brought before a competent court as soon as is practicable.

(2) If the competent court is satisfied—

    (a) that the warrant—

        (i)   is a warrant of the ICC and has been duly endorsed under section 2(3), or

        (ii) has been duly issued under section 2(4), and

    (b) that the person brought before the court is the person named or described in the warrant,

it shall make a delivery order.

(3) A 'delivery order' is an order that the person be delivered up—

    (a) into the custody of the ICC, or

    (b) if the ICC so directs in the case of a person convicted by the ICC, into the custody of the state of enforcement,

in accordance with arrangements made by the Secretary of State.

(4) In the case of a person alleged to have committed an ICC crime, the competent court may adjourn the proceedings pending the outcome of any challenge before the ICC to the admissibility of the case or to the jurisdiction of the ICC.

(5) In deciding whether to make a delivery order the court is not concerned to enquire—

    (a) whether any warrant issued by the ICC was duly issued, or

    (b) in the case of a person alleged to have committed an ICC crime, whether there is evidence to justify his trial for the offence he is alleged to have committed.

(6)–(9) *****

6–22   *****

Supplementary provisions

23   Provisions as to state or diplomatic immunity

(1) Any state or diplomatic immunity attaching to a person by reason of a connection with a state party to the ICC Statute does not prevent proceedings under this Part in relation to that person.

(2) Where—

    (a) state or diplomatic immunity attaches to a person by reason of a connection with a state other than a state party to the ICC Statute, and

    (b) waiver of that immunity is obtained by the ICC in relation to a request for that person's surrender,

the waiver shall be treated as extending to proceedings under this Part in connection with that request.

(3)–(6) *****

24–27   *****

28   Questioning

(1) This section applies where the Secretary of State receives a request from the ICC for assistance in questioning a person being investigated or prosecuted.

(2) The person concerned shall not be questioned in pursuance of the request unless—

(a) he has been informed of his rights under article 55, and

(b) he consents to be interviewed.

(3) The provisions of article 55 are set out in Schedule 3 to this Act.

(4) Consent for the purposes of subsection (2)(b) may be given—

(a) by the person himself, or

(b) in circumstances in which it is inappropriate for the person to act for himself, by reason of his physical or mental condition or his youth, by an appropriate person acting on his behalf.

(5) Such consent may be given orally or in writing, but if given orally it shall be recorded in writing as soon as is reasonably practicable.

29–50   *****

51   Genocide, crimes against humanity and war crimes

(1) It is an offence against the law of England and Wales for a person to commit genocide, a crime against humanity or a war crime.

(2) This section applies to acts committed—

(a) in England or Wales, or

(b) outside the United Kingdom by a United Kingdom national, a United Kingdom resident or a person subject to UK service jurisdiction.

*****

SCHEDULE 3   RIGHTS OF PERSONS DURING INVESTIGATION: ARTICLE 55

Article 55   Rights of persons during an investigation

1. In respect of an investigation under this Statute, a person:

(a) Shall not be compelled to incriminate himself or herself or to confess guilt;

(b) Shall not be subjected to any form of coercion, duress or threat, to torture or to any other form of cruel, inhuman or degrading treatment or punishment;

(c) Shall, if questioned in a language other than a language the person fully understands and speaks, have, free of any cost, the assistance of a competent interpreter and such translations as are necessary to meet the requirements of fairness; and

(d) Shall not be subjected to arbitrary arrest or detention, and shall not be deprived of his or her liberty except on such grounds and in accordance with such procedures as are established in this Statute.

2. Where there are grounds to believe that a person has committed a crime within the jurisdiction of the Court and that person is about to be questioned either by the Prosecutor, or by national authorities pursuant to a request made under Part 9, that person shall also have the following rights of which he or she shall be informed prior to being questioned:

(a) To be informed, prior to being questioned, that there are grounds to believe that he or she has committed a crime within the jurisdiction of the Court;

(b) To remain silent, without such silence being a consideration in the determination of guilt or innocence;

(c) To have legal assistance of the person's choosing, or, if the person does not have legal assistance, to have legal assistance assigned to him or her, in any case where the interests of justice so require, and without payment by the person in any such case if the person does not have sufficient means to pay for it; and

(d) To be questioned in the presence of counsel unless the person has voluntarily waived his or her right to counsel.

*****

European Parliamentary Elections Act 2002

(2002, c. 24)

An Act to consolidate the European Parliamentary Elections Acts 1978, 1993 and 1999 [24th July 2002]

Territorial extent: United Kingdom, and Gibraltar (by virtue of the European Parliament (Representation) Act 2003, s. 19)

Introductory

[1   Number of MEPs and electoral regions

(1) There shall be [73] members of the European Parliament ('MEPs') elected for the United Kingdom.

(2) For the purposes of electing those MEPs—

   (a) [the area of England and Gibraltar] is divided into the nine electoral regions specified in Schedule 1; and

   (b) Scotland, Wales and Northern Ireland are each single electoral regions.

[(3) The number of MEPs to be elected for each electoral region is as follows—

East Midlands	5
Eastern	7
London	8
North East	3
North West	8
South East	10
South West	6
[West Midlands	7]
Yorkshire and the Humber	6
Scotland	6
Wales	4
Northern Ireland	3.]]

(Table of constituencies omitted.)

1A   *****

General elections

2   Voting system in Great Britain [and Gibraltar]

(1) The system of election of MEPs in an electoral region [other than Northern Ireland] is to be a regional list system.

(2) The Secretary of State must by regulations—

   (a) make provision for the nomination of registered parties in relation to an election in such a region, and

   (b) require a nomination under paragraph (a) to be accompanied by a list of candidates numbering no more than the MEPs to be elected for the region.

(3) The system of election must comply with the following conditions.

(4) A vote may be cast for a registered party or an individual candidate named on the ballot paper.

(5) The first seat is to be allocated to the party or individual candidate with the greatest number of votes.

(6) The second and subsequent seats are to be allocated in the same way, except that the number of votes given to a party to which one or more seats have already been allocated are to be divided by the number of seats allocated plus one.

(7) In allocating the second or any subsequent seat there are to be disregarded any votes given to—

(a) a party to which there has already been allocated a number of seats equal to the number of names on the party's list of candidates, and

(b) an individual candidate to whom a seat has already been allocated.

(8) Seats allocated to a party are to be filled by the persons named on the party's list of candidates in the order in which they appear on that list.

(9) For the purposes of subsection (6) fractions are to be taken into account.

(10) In this section 'registered party' means a party registered under Part 2 of the Political Parties, Elections and Referendums Act 2000.

3　Voting system in Northern Ireland

The system of election of MEPs in Northern Ireland is to be a single transferable vote system under which—

(a) a vote is capable of being given so as to indicate the voter's order of preference for the candidates, and

(b) a vote is capable of being transferred to the next choice—

(i) when the vote is not required to give a prior choice the necessary quota of votes, or

(ii) when, owing to the deficiency in the number of votes given for a prior choice, that choice is eliminated from the list of candidates.

4–7 *****

Entitlement to vote

8　Persons entitled to vote

(1) A person is entitled to vote as an elector at an election to the European Parliament in an electoral region if he is within any of subsections (2) to (5).

(2) A person is within this subsection if on the day of the poll he would be entitled to vote as an elector at a parliamentary election in a parliamentary constituency wholly or partly comprised in the electoral region, and—

(a) the address in respect of which he is registered in the relevant register of parliamentary electors is within the electoral region, or

(b) his registration in the relevant register of parliamentary electors results from an overseas elector's declaration which specifies an address within the electoral region.

(3) A person is within this subsection if—

(a) he is a peer who on the day of the poll would be entitled to vote at a local government election in an electoral area wholly or partly comprised in the electoral region, and

(b) the address in respect of which he is registered in the relevant register of local government electors is within the electoral region.

(4) A person is within this subsection if he is entitled to vote in the electoral region by virtue of section 3 of the Representation of the People Act 1985 (peers resident outside the United Kingdom).

(5) A person is within this subsection if he is entitled to vote in the electoral region by virtue of the European Parliamentary Elections (Franchise of Relevant Citizens of the Union) Regulations 2001 (citizens of the European Union other than Commonwealth and Republic of Ireland citizens).

(6)–(8) *****

9 *****

Entitlement to be MEP

10　Disqualification

(1) A person is disqualified for the office of MEP if—

(a) he is disqualified for membership of the House of Commons, . . .

(b) . . .

(2) But a person is not disqualified for the office of MEP under subsection (1)(a) merely because—

(a) he is a peer,

      (b) he is a Lord Spiritual,

      (c) he holds an office mentioned in section 4 of the House of Commons Disqualification Act 1975 (stewardship of Chiltern Hundreds etc), or

      (d) he holds any of the offices described in Part 2 or 3 of Schedule 1 to that Act which are designated by order by the Secretary of State for the purposes of this section.

    (3) A citizen of the European Union who is resident in the United Kingdom [or Gibraltar] is not disqualified for the office of MEP under subsection (1)(a) merely because he is disqualified for membership of the House of Commons under section 3 of the Act of Settlement (disqualification of persons, other than [qualifying Commonwealth citizens] and Republic of Ireland citizens, who are born outside Great Britain and Ireland and the dominions).

    (3A)–(8) *****

*****

Police Reform Act 2002

(2002, c. 30)

An Act to make new provision about the supervision, administration, functions and conduct of police forces, police officers, and other persons serving with, or carrying out functions in relation to, the police; to amend police powers and provide for the exercise of police powers by persons who are not police officers; to amend the law relating to anti-social behaviour orders; to amend the law relating to sex offender orders; and for connected purposes.　　　　　　　　　　　　　　　　　　　　　　　　　[24th July 2002]

Territorial extent: England and Wales (material reproduced here)

1–7 *****

8 . . .

The Independent Police Complaints Commission

9　The Independent Police Complaints Commission

    (1) There shall be a body corporate to be known as the Independent Police Complaints Commission (in this Part referred to as 'the Commission').

    (2) The Commission shall consist of—

      (a) a chairman appointed by Her Majesty; and

      (b) not less than ten other members appointed by the Secretary of State.

    (3) A person shall not be appointed as the chairman of the Commission, or as another member of the Commission, if—

      (a) he holds or has held office as a constable in any part of the United Kingdom;

      (b) he is or has been under the direction and control of a chief officer or of any person holding an equivalent office in Scotland or Northern Ireland;

      (c)–(f) *****

    (4)–(7) *****

10　General functions of the Commission

    (1) The functions of the Commission shall be—

      (a) to secure the maintenance by the Commission itself, and by [local policing bodies] and chief officers, of suitable arrangements with respect to the matters mentioned in subsection (2);

      (b) to keep under review all arrangements maintained with respect to those matters;

      (c) to secure that arrangements maintained with respect to those matters comply with the requirements of the following provisions of this Part, are efficient and effective and contain and manifest an appropriate degree of independence;

(d) to secure that public confidence is established and maintained in the existence of suitable arrangements with respect to those matters and with the operation of the arrangements that are in fact maintained with respect to those matters;

(e) to make such recommendations, and to give such advice, for the modification of the arrangements maintained with respect to those matters, and also of police practice in relation to other matters, as appear, from the carrying out by the Commission of its other functions, to be necessary or desirable; ...

(f) to such extent as it may be required to do so by regulations made by the Secretary of State, to carry out functions in relation to ... bodies of constables maintained otherwise than by [local policing bodies] which broadly correspond to those conferred on the Commission in relation to police forces by the preceding paragraphs of this subsection[; ...

(g) to carry out functions in relation to the Serious Organised Crime Agency which correspond to those conferred on the Commission in relation to police forces by paragraph (e) of this subsection][; and

(h) to carry out functions in relation to the National Policing Improvement Agency which correspond to those conferred on the Commission in relation to police forces by paragraph (e) of this subsection]

(2) Those matters are—

    (a)   the handling of complaints made about the conduct of persons serving with the police;

    (b)   the recording of matters from which it appears that there may have been conduct by such persons which constitutes or involves the commission of a criminal offence or behaviour justifying disciplinary proceedings;

    [(ba) the recording of matters from which it appears that a person has died or suffered serious injury during, or following, contact with a person serving with the police;]

    (c)   the manner in which any such complaints or any such matters as are mentioned in paragraph (b) [or (ba)] are investigated or otherwise handled and dealt with.

(3)–(7) *****

(8) Nothing in this Part shall confer any function on the Commission in relation to so much of any complaint or conduct matter as relates to the direction and control of a police force by—

    (a) the chief officer of police of that force; or

    (b) a person for the time being carrying out the functions of the chief officer of police of that force.

(9) *****

11 Reports to the Secretary of State

(1) As soon as practicable after the end of each of its financial years, the Commission shall make a report to the Secretary of State on the carrying out of its functions during that year.

(2) The Commission shall also make such reports to the Secretary of State about matters relating generally to the carrying out of its functions as he may, from time to time, require.

(3) The Commission may, from time to time, make such other reports to the Secretary of State as it considers appropriate for drawing his attention to matters which—

    (a) have come to the Commission's notice; and

    (b) are matters that it considers should be drawn to his attention by reason of their gravity or of other exceptional circumstances.

(4)–(11) *****

Application of Part 2

12 Complaints, matters and persons to which Part 2 applies

(1) In this Part references to a complaint are references (subject to the following provisions of this section) to any complaint about the conduct of a person serving with the police which is made (whether in writing or otherwise) by—

(a) a member of the public who claims to be the person in relation to whom the conduct took place;

(b) a member of the public not falling within paragraph (a) who claims to have been adversely affected by the conduct;

(c) a member of the public who claims to have witnessed the conduct;

(d) a person acting on behalf of a person falling within any of paragraphs (a) to (c).

(2) In this Part 'conduct matter' means (subject to the following provisions of this section, paragraph 2(4) of Schedule 3 and any regulations made by virtue of section 23(2)(d)) any matter which is not and has not been the subject of a complaint but in the case of which there is an indication (whether from the circumstances or otherwise) that a person serving with the police may have—

(a) committed a criminal offence; or

(b) behaved in a manner which would justify the bringing of disciplinary proceedings.

[(2A) In this Part 'death or serious injury matter' (or 'DSI matter' for short) means any circumstances (other than those which are or have been the subject of a complaint or which amount to a conduct matter)—

(a) in or in consequence of which a person has died or has sustained serious injury; and

(b) in relation to which the requirements of either subsection (2B) or subsection (2C) are satisfied.

(2B) The requirements of this subsection are that at the time of the death or serious injury the person—

(a) had been arrested by a person serving with the police and had not been released from that arrest; or

(b) was otherwise detained in the custody of a person serving with the police.

(2C) The requirements of this subsection are that—

(a) at or before the time of the death or serious injury the person had contact (of whatever kind, and whether direct or indirect) with a person serving with the police who was acting in the execution of his duties; and

(b) there is an indication that the contact may have caused (whether directly or indirectly) or contributed to the death or serious injury.

(2D) In subsection (2A) the reference to a person includes a person serving with the police, but in relation to such a person 'contact' in subsection (2C) does not include contact that he has whilst acting in the execution of his duties.]

(3)–(7) *****

13–14 *****

Co-operation, assistance and information

15 General duties of [local policing bodies], chief officers and inspectors

(1)–(3) *****

(4) It shall be the duty of—

(a) every [local policing body] maintaining a police force,

(b) the chief officer of police of every police force, [and

(c) the Serious Organised Crime Agency,]

to provide the Commission and every member of the Commission's staff with all such assistance as the Commission or that member of staff may reasonably require for the purposes of, or in connection with, the carrying out of any investigation by the Commission under this Part.

(5) It shall be the duty of—

(a) every [local policing body] maintaining a police force,

(b) the chief officer of every police force, [and

(c) the Serious Organised Crime Agency,]

to ensure that a person appointed under paragraph 16, 17 or 18 of Schedule 3 to carry out an investigation is given all such assistance and co-operation in the carrying out of that investigation as that person may reasonably require.

(6)–(10) *****

16, 16A *****

17 Provision of information to the Commission

(1) It shall be the duty of—

    (a) every [local policing body], and

    (b) every chief officer,

at such times, in such circumstances and in accordance with such other requirements as may be set out in regulations made by the Secretary of State, to provide the Commission with all such information and documents as may be specified or described in regulations so made.

(2) It shall also be the duty of every [local policing body] and of every chief officer—

    (a) to provide the Commission with all such other information and documents specified or described in a notification given by the Commission to that [body] or chief officer, and

    (b) to produce or deliver up to the Commission all such evidence and other things so specified or described,

as appear to the Commission to be required by it for the purposes of the carrying out of any of its functions.

(3)–(6) *****

18 Inspections of police premises on behalf of the Commission

(1) Where—

    (a) the Commission requires—

        (i)   a [local policing body] maintaining any police force, or

        (ii) the chief officer of police of any such force,

        to allow a person nominated for the purpose by the Commission to have access to any premises occupied for the purposes of that force and to documents and other things on those premises, and

    (b) the requirement is imposed for any of the purposes mentioned in subsection (2),

it shall be the duty of the [body] or, as the case may be, of the chief officer to secure that the required access is allowed to the nominated person.

(2) Those purposes are—

    (a) the purposes of any examination by the Commission of the efficiency and effectiveness of the arrangements made by the force in question for handling complaints or dealing with recordable conduct matters [or DSI matters];

    (b) the purposes of any investigation by the Commission under this Part or of any investigation carried out under its supervision or management.

(3) A requirement imposed under this section for the purposes mentioned in subsection (2)(a) must be notified to the [body] or chief officer at least 48 hours before the time at which access is required.

(4) Where—

    (a) a requirement imposed under this section for the purposes mentioned in subsection (2)(a) requires access to any premises, document or thing to be allowed to any person, but

    (b) there are reasonable grounds for not allowing that person to have the required access at the time at which he seeks to have it,

the obligation to secure that the required access is allowed shall have effect as an obligation to secure that the access is allowed to that person at the earliest practicable time after there cease to be any such grounds as that person may specify.

(5) *****

19 Use of investigatory powers by or on behalf of the Commission

(1) The Secretary of State may by order make such provision as he thinks appropriate for the purpose of authorising—

(a) the use of directed and intrusive surveillance, and

(b) the conduct and use of covert human intelligence sources,

for the purposes of, or for purposes connected with, the carrying out of the Commission's functions.

(2)–(4) *****

20, 21 *****

Guidance and regulations

22 Power of the Commission to issue guidance

(1) The Commission may issue guidance—

(a) to [local policing bodies],

(b) to chief officers, and

(c) to persons who are serving with the police otherwise than as chief officers,

concerning the exercise or performance, by the persons to whom the guidance is issued, of any of the powers or duties specified in subsection (2).

(2) Those powers and duties are—

(a) those that are conferred or imposed by or under this Part; and

(b) those that are otherwise conferred or imposed but relate to—

(i)   the handling of complaints;

(ii)   the means by which recordable conduct matters [or DSI matters] are dealt with; or

(iii) the detection or deterrence of misconduct by persons serving with the police.

(3) Before issuing any guidance under this section, the Commission shall consult with—

[(a) such persons as appear to the Commission to represent the views of police and crime commissioners;

(aa) the Mayor's office for Policing and Crime;

(ab) the Common Council;]

(b)   the Association of Chief Police Officers; and]

(c)   such other persons as it thinks fit.

(4) The approval of the Secretary of State shall be required for the issue by the Commission of any guidance under this section.

(5) *****

(6) Nothing in this section shall authorise the issuing of any guidance about a particular case.

(7) It shall be the duty of every person to whom any guidance under this section is issued to have regard to that guidance in exercising or performing the powers and duties to which the guidance relates.

(8) A failure by a person to whom guidance under this section is issued to have regard to the guidance shall be admissible in evidence in any disciplinary proceedings or on any appeal from a decision taken in any such proceedings.

23–49 *****

Power to require name and address

50 Persons acting in an anti-social manner

(1) If a constable in uniform has reason to believe that a person has been acting, or is acting, in an anti-social manner (within the meaning of section 1 of the Crime and Disorder Act 1998 (anti-social behaviour orders)), he may require that person to give his name and address to the constable.

(2) Any person who—

(a) fails to give his name and address when required to do so under subsection (1), or

(b) gives a false or inaccurate name or address in response to a requirement under that subsection,

is guilty of an offence and shall be liable, on summary conviction, to a fine not exceeding level 3 on the standard scale.

*****

Proceeds of Crime Act 2002

(2002, c. 29)

An Act to establish the Assets Recovery Agency and make provision about the appointment of its Director and his functions (including Revenue functions), to provide for confiscation orders in relation to persons who benefit from criminal conduct and for restraint orders to prohibit dealing with property, to allow the recovery of property which is or represents property obtained through unlawful conduct or which is intended to be used in unlawful conduct, to make provision about money laundering, to make provision about investigations relating to benefit from criminal conduct or to property which is or represents property obtained through unlawful conduct or to money laundering, to make provision to give effect to overseas requests and orders made where property is found or believed to be obtained through criminal conduct, and for connected purposes.   [24th July 2002]

Territorial extent: England and Wales. Part 3 of the Act makes equivalent provisions for Scotland and Part 4 for Northern Ireland; these are not reproduced for reasons of space

1–5 ****

PART 2   CONFISCATION: ENGLAND AND WALES

Confiscation orders

6   Making of order

(1) The Crown Court must proceed under this section if the following two conditions are satisfied.

(2) The first condition is that a defendant falls within any of the following paragraphs—

    (a) he is convicted of an offence or offences in proceedings before the Crown Court;

    (b) he is committed to the Crown Court for sentence in respect of an offence or offences under [section 3, 3A, 3B, 3C, 4, 4A or 6] of the Sentencing Act;

    (c) he is committed to the Crown Court in respect of an offence or offences under section 70 below (committal with a view to a confiscation order being considered).

(3) The second condition is that—

    (a) the prosecutor . . . asks the court to proceed under this section, or

    (b) the court believes it is appropriate for it to do so.

(4) The court must proceed as follows—

    (a) it must decide whether the defendant has a criminal lifestyle;

    (b) if it decides that he has a criminal lifestyle it must decide whether he has benefited from his general criminal conduct;

    (c) if it decides that he does not have a criminal lifestyle it must decide whether he has benefited from his particular criminal conduct.

(5) If the court decides under subsection (4)(b) or (c) that the defendant has benefited from the conduct referred to it must—

    (a) decide the recoverable amount, and

    (b) make an order (a confiscation order) requiring him to pay that amount.

(6)–(9) *****

7   Recoverable amount

(1) The recoverable amount for the purposes of section 6 is an amount equal to the defendant's benefit from the conduct concerned.

(2) But if the defendant shows that the available amount is less than that benefit the recoverable amount is—

    (a) the available amount, or

    (b) a nominal amount, if the available amount is nil.

(3)–(5) *****

8   *****

9   Available amount

(1) For the purposes of deciding the recoverable amount, the available amount is the aggregate of—

    (a) the total of the values (at the time the confiscation order is made) of all the free property then held by the defendant minus the total amount payable in pursuance of obligations which then have priority, and

    (b) the total of the values (at that time) of all tainted gifts.

(2) An obligation has priority if it is an obligation of the defendant—

    (a) to pay an amount due in respect of a fine or other order of a court which was imposed or made on conviction of an offence and at any time before the time the confiscation order is made, or

    (b) to pay a sum which would be included among the preferential debts if the defendant's bankruptcy had commenced on the date of the confiscation order or his winding up had been ordered on that date.

(3) 'Preferential debts' has the meaning given by section 386 of the Insolvency Act 1986.

10   Assumptions to be made in case of criminal lifestyle

(1) If the court decides under section 6 that the defendant has a criminal lifestyle it must make the following four assumptions for the purpose of—

    (a) deciding whether he has benefited from his general criminal conduct, and

    (b) deciding his benefit from the conduct.

(2) The first assumption is that any property transferred to the defendant at any time after the relevant day was obtained by him—

    (a) as a result of his general criminal conduct, and

    (b) at the earliest time he appears to have held it.

(3) The second assumption is that any property held by the defendant at any time after the date of conviction was obtained by him—

    (a) as a result of his general criminal conduct, and

    (b) at the earliest time he appears to have held it.

(4) The third assumption is that any expenditure incurred by the defendant at any time after the relevant day was met from property obtained by him as a result of his general criminal conduct.

(5) The fourth assumption is that, for the purpose of valuing any property obtained (or assumed to have been obtained) by the defendant, he obtained it free of any other interests in it.

(6) But the court must not make a required assumption in relation to particular property or expenditure if—

    (a) the assumption is shown to be incorrect, or

    (b) there would be a serious risk of injustice if the assumption were made.

(7) If the court does not make one or more of the required assumptions it must state its reasons.

(8) The relevant day is the first day of the period of six years ending with—

    (a) the day when proceedings for the offence concerned were started against the defendant, or

    (b) if there are two or more offences and proceedings for them were started on different days, the earliest of those days.

(9), (10)   *****

11–74   *****

Interpretation

75   Criminal lifestyle

(1) A defendant has a criminal lifestyle if (and only if) the following condition is satisfied.

(2) The condition is that the offence (or any of the offences) concerned satisfies any of these tests—

(a) it is specified in Schedule 2;

(b) it constitutes conduct forming part of a course of criminal activity;

(c) it is an offence committed over a period of at least six months and the defendant has benefited from the conduct which constitutes the offence.

(3) Conduct forms part of a course of criminal activity if the defendant has benefited from the conduct and—

(a) in the proceedings in which he was convicted he was convicted of three or more other offences, each of three or more of them constituting conduct from which he has benefited, or

(b) in the period of six years ending with the day when those proceedings were started (or, if there is more than one such day, the earliest day) he was convicted on at least two separate occasions of an offence constituting conduct from which he has benefited.

(4) But an offence does not satisfy the test in subsection (2)(b) or (c) unless the defendant obtains relevant benefit of not less than £5000.

(5) Relevant benefit for the purposes of subsection (2)(b) is—

(a) benefit from conduct which constitutes the offence;

(b) benefit from any other conduct which forms part of the course of criminal activity and which constitutes an offence of which the defendant has been convicted;

(c) benefit from conduct which constitutes an offence which has been or will be taken into consideration by the court in sentencing the defendant for an offence mentioned in paragraph (a) or (b).

(6) Relevant benefit for the purposes of subsection (2)(c) is—

(a) benefit from conduct which constitutes the offence;

(b) benefit from conduct which constitutes an offence which has been or will be taken into consideration by the court in sentencing the defendant for the offence mentioned in paragraph (a).

(7) The Secretary of State may by order amend Schedule 2.

(8) The Secretary of State may by order vary the amount for the time being specified in subsection (4).

76 Conduct and benefit

(1) Criminal conduct is conduct which—

(a) constitutes an offence in England and Wales, or

(b) would constitute such an offence if it occurred in England and Wales.

(2) General criminal conduct of the defendant is all his criminal conduct, and it is immaterial—

(a) whether conduct occurred before or after the passing of this Act;

(b) whether property constituting a benefit from conduct was obtained before or after the passing of this Act.

(3) Particular criminal conduct of the defendant is all his criminal conduct which falls within the following paragraphs—

(a) conduct which constitutes the offence or offences concerned;

(b) conduct which constitutes offences of which he was convicted in the same proceedings as those in which he was convicted of the offence or offences concerned;

(c) conduct which constitutes offences which the court will be taking into consideration in deciding his sentence for the offence or offences concerned.

(4)–(7) *****

77–83 *****

84 Property: general provisions

(1) Property is all property wherever situated and includes—

(a) money;

   (b) all forms of real or personal property;
   (c) things in action and other intangible or incorporeal property.
 (2) The following rules apply in relation to property—
   (a) property is held by a person if he holds an interest in it;
   (b) property is obtained by a person if he obtains an interest in it;
   (c) property is transferred by one person to another if the first one transfers or grants an interest in it to the second;
   (d) references to property held by a person include references to property vested in his trustee in bankruptcy, permanent or interim trustee (within the meaning of the Bankruptcy (Scotland) Act 1985) or liquidator;
   (e) references to an interest held by a person beneficially in property include references to an interest which would be held by him beneficially if the property were not so vested;
   (f) references to an interest, in relation to land in England and Wales or Northern Ireland, are to any legal estate or equitable interest or power;
   (g) references to an interest, in relation to land in Scotland, are to any estate, interest, servitude or other heritable right in or over land, including a heritable security;
   (h) references to an interest, in relation to property other than land, include references to a right (including a right to possession).

85–462 *****

<h1 style="text-align:center">SCHEDULE 1 ...</h1>

Section 75   <h1 style="text-align:center">SCHEDULE 2</h1>

LIFESTYLE OFFENCES: ENGLAND AND WALES

Drug trafficking

   1.—(1) An offence under any of the following provisions of the Misuse of Drugs Act 1971 (c. 38)—
   (a) section 4(2) or (3) (unlawful production or supply of controlled drugs);
   (b) section 5(3) (possession of controlled drug with intent to supply);
   (c) section 8 (permitting certain activities relating to controlled drugs);
   (d) section 20 (assisting in or inducing the commission outside the UK of an offence punishable under a corresponding law).

   (2) An offence under any of the following provisions of the Customs and Excise Management Act 1979 (c. 2) if it is committed in connection with a prohibition or restriction on importation or exportation which has effect by virtue of section 3 of the Misuse of Drugs Act 1971—
   (a) section 50(2) or (3) (improper importation of goods);
   (b) section 68(2) (exploration of prohibited or restricted goods);
   (c) section 170 (fraudulent evasion).

   (3) An offence under either of the following provisions of the Criminal Justice (International Co-operation) Act 1990 (c. 5)—
   (a) section 12 (manufacture or supply of a substance for the time being specified in Schedule 2 to that Act);
   (b) section 19 (using a ship for illicit traffic in controlled drugs).

Money laundering

   2. An offence under either of the following provisions of this Act—

(a) section 327 (concealing etc criminal property);

(b) section 328 (assisting another to retain criminal property).

Directing terrorism

3.   An offence under section 56 of the Terrorism Act 2000 (c. 11) (directing the activities of a terrorist organisation).

People trafficking

[4.—(1) An offence under section 25, 25A or 25B of the Immigration Act 1971 (c. 77) (assisting unlawful immigration etc).]

[(2) An offence under any of sections 57 to 59 of the Sexual Offences Act 2003 (trafficking for sexual exploitation).]

[(3) An offence under section 4 of the Asylum and Immigration (Treatment of Claimants, etc) Act 2004 (exploitation).]

Arms trafficking

5.—(1) An offence under either of the following provisions of the Customs and Excise Management Act 1979 if it is committed in connection with a firearm or ammunition—

(a) section 68(2) (exportation of prohibited goods);

(b) section 170 (fraudulent evasion).

(2) An offence under section 3(1) of the Firearms Act 1968 (c. 27) (dealing in firearms or ammunition by way of trade or business).

(3) In this paragraph 'firearm' and 'ammunition' have the same meanings as in section 57 of the Firearms Act 1968 (c. 27).

Counterfeiting

6.   An offence under any of the following provisions of the Forgery and Counterfeiting Act 1981 (c. 45)—

(a) section 14 (making counterfeit notes or coins);

(b) section 15 (passing etc counterfeit notes or coins);

(c) section 16 (having counterfeit notes or coins);

(d) section 17 (making or possessing materials or equipment for counterfeiting).

Intellectual property

7.—(1) An offence under any of the following provisions of the Copyright, Designs and Patents Act 1988 (c. 48)—

(a) section 107(1) (making or dealing in an article which infringes copyright);

(b) section 107(2) (making or possessing an article designed or adapted for making a copy of a copyright work);

(c) section 198(1) (making or dealing in an illicit recording);

(d) section 297A (making or dealing in unauthorised decoders).

(2) An offence under section 92(1), (2) or (3) of the Trade Marks Act 1994 (c. 26) (unauthorised use etc of trade mark).

[Prostitution and child sex

8.—(1) An offence under section 33 or 34 of the Sexual Offences Act 1956 (keeping or letting premises for use as a brothel).

(2) An offence under any of the following provisions of the Sexual Offences Act 2003—

(a) section 14 (arranging or facilitating commission of a child sex offence);

(b) section 48 (causing or inciting child prostitution or pornography);

(c) section 49 (controlling a child prostitute or a child involved in pornography);

(d) section 50 (arranging or facilitating child prostitution or pornography);

(e) section 52 (causing or inciting prostitution for gain);

(f) section 53 (controlling prostitution for gain).]

Blackmail

9. An offence under section 21 of the Theft Act 1968 (c. 60) (blackmail).

[9A. An offence under section 12(1) or (2) of the Gangmasters (Licensing) Act 2004 (acting as a gangmaster other than under the authority of a licence, possession of false documents etc).]

Inchoate offences

10.—(1) An offence of attempting, conspiring or inciting the commission of an offence specified in this Schedule.

[(1A) An offence under section 44 of the Serious Crime Act 2007 of doing an act capable of encouraging or assisting the commission of an offence specified in this Schedule.]

(2) An offence of aiding, abetting, counselling or procuring the commission of such an offence.
*****

Criminal Justice Act 2003

(2003, c. 44)

An Act to make provision about criminal justice (including the powers and duties of the police) and about dealing with offenders; to amend the law relating to jury service; to amend Chapter 1 of Part 1 of the Crime and Disorder Act 1998 and Part 5 of the Police Act 1997; to make provision about civil proceedings brought by offenders; and for connected purposes   [20th November 2003]

Territorial extent: England and Wales (and Northern Ireland, subject to certain modifications)
*****

PART 10   RETRIAL FOR SERIOUS OFFENCES

Cases that may be retried

75   Cases that may be retried

(1) This Part applies where a person has been acquitted of a qualifying offence in proceedings—

    (a) on indictment in England and Wales,

    (b) on appeal against a conviction, verdict or finding in proceedings on indictment in England and Wales, or

    (c) on appeal from a decision on such an appeal.

(2) A person acquitted of an offence in proceedings mentioned in subsection (1) is treated for the purposes of that subsection as also acquitted of any qualifying offence of which he could have been convicted in the proceedings because of the first-mentioned offence being charged in the indictment, except an offence—

    (a) of which he has been convicted,

    (b) of which he has been found not guilty by reason of insanity, or

    (c) in respect of which, in proceedings where he has been found to be under a disability (as defined by section 4 of the Criminal Procedure (Insanity) Act 1964 (c. 84)), a finding has been made that he did the act or made the omission charged against him.

(3) References in subsections (1) and (2) to a qualifying offence do not include references to an offence which, at the time of the acquittal, was the subject of an order under section 77(1) or (3).

(4) This Part also applies where a person has been acquitted, in proceedings elsewhere than in the United Kingdom, of an offence under the law of the place where the proceedings were held, if the commission of the offence as alleged would have amounted to or included the commission (in the United Kingdom or elsewhere) of a qualifying offence.

(5) Conduct punishable under the law in force elsewhere than in the United Kingdom is an offence under that law for the purposes of subsection (4), however it is described in that law.

(6) This Part applies whether the acquittal was before or after the passing of this Act.

(7) References in this Part to acquittal are to acquittal in circumstances within subsection (1) or (4).

(8) In this Part 'qualifying offence' means an offence listed in Part 1 of Schedule 5.

Application for retrial

76 Application to Court of Appeal

(1) A prosecutor may apply to the Court of Appeal for an order—

    (a) quashing a person's acquittal in proceedings within section 75(1), and

    (b) ordering him to be retried for the qualifying offence.

(2) A prosecutor may apply to the Court of Appeal, in the case of a person acquitted elsewhere than in the United Kingdom, for—

    (a) a determination whether the acquittal is a bar to the person being tried in England and Wales for the qualifying offence, and

    (b) if it is, an order that the acquittal is not to be a bar.

(3)–(5) *****

77 Determination by Court of Appeal

(1) On an application under section 76(1), the Court of Appeal—

    (a) if satisfied that the requirements of sections 78 and 79 are met, must make the order applied for;

    (b) otherwise, must dismiss the application.

(2) Subsections (3) and (4) apply to an application under section 76(2).

(3) Where the Court of Appeal determines that the acquittal is a bar to the person being tried for the qualifying offence, the court—

    (a) if satisfied that the requirements of sections 78 and 79 are met, must make the order applied for;

    (b) otherwise, must make a declaration to the effect that the acquittal is a bar to the person being tried for the offence.

(4) Where the Court of Appeal determines that the acquittal is not a bar to the person being tried for the qualifying offence, it must make a declaration to that effect.

78 New and compelling evidence

(1) The requirements of this section are met if there is new and compelling evidence against the acquitted person in relation to the qualifying offence.

(2) Evidence is new if it was not adduced in the proceedings in which the person was acquitted (nor, if those were appeal proceedings, in earlier proceedings to which the appeal related).

(3) Evidence is compelling if—

    (a) it is reliable,

    (b) it is substantial, and

    (c) in the context of the outstanding issues, it appears highly probative of the case against the acquitted person.

(4) The outstanding issues are the issues in dispute in the proceedings in which the person was acquitted and, if those were appeal proceedings, any other issues remaining in dispute from earlier proceedings to which the appeal related.

(5) For the purposes of this section, it is irrelevant whether any evidence would have been admissible in earlier proceedings against the acquitted person.

79 Interests of justice

(1) The requirements of this section are met if in all the circumstances it is in the interests of justice for the court to make the order under section 77.

(2) That question is to be determined having regard in particular to—

    (a) whether existing circumstances make a fair trial unlikely;

    (b) for the purposes of that question and otherwise, the length of time since the qualifying offence was allegedly committed;

(c) whether it is likely that the new evidence would have been adduced in the earlier proceedings against the acquitted person but for a failure by an officer or by a prosecutor to act with due diligence or expedition;

(d) whether, since those proceedings or, if later, since the commencement of this Part, any officer or prosecutor has failed to act with due diligence or expedition.

(3), (4) *****

80, 81 *****

82 Restrictions on publication in the interests of justice

(1) Where it appears to the Court of Appeal that the inclusion of any matter in a publication would give rise to a substantial risk of prejudice to the administration of justice in a retrial, the court may order that the matter is not to be included in any publication while the order has effect.

(2) In subsection (1) 'retrial' means the trial of an acquitted person for a qualifying offence pursuant to any order made or that may be made under section 77.

(3) The court may make an order under this section only if it appears to it necessary in the interests of justice to do so.

(4) An order under this section may apply to a matter which has been included in a publication published before the order takes effect, but such an order—

(a) applies only to the later inclusion of the matter in a publication (whether directly or by inclusion of the earlier publication), and

(b) does not otherwise affect the earlier publication.

(5)–(11) *****

*****

Extradition Act 2003

(2003, c. 41)

An Act to make provision about extradition.   [20th November 2003]

Territorial extent: United Kingdom

PART 1 EXTRADITION TO CATEGORY 1 TERRITORIES

Introduction

1 Extradition to category 1 territories

(1) This Part deals with extradition from the United Kingdom to the territories designated for the purposes of this Part by order made by the Secretary of State.

(2) In this Act references to category 1 territories are to the territories designated for the purposes of this Part.

(3) A territory may not be designated for the purposes of this Part if a person found guilty in the territory of a criminal offence may be sentenced to death for the offence under the general criminal law of the territory.

2 Part 1 warrant and certificate

(1) This section applies if the designated authority receives a Part 1 warrant in respect of a person.

(2) A Part 1 warrant is an arrest warrant which is issued by a judicial authority of a category 1 territory and which contains—

(a) the statement referred to in subsection (3) and the information referred to in subsection (4), or

    (b) the statement referred to in subsection (5) and the information referred to in subsection (6).

(3) The statement is one that—

    (a) the person in respect of whom the Part 1 warrant is issued is accused in the category 1 territory of the commission of an offence specified in the warrant, and

    (b) the Part 1 warrant is issued with a view to his arrest and extradition to the category 1 territory for the purpose of being prosecuted for the offence.

(4) The information is—

    (a) particulars of the person's identity;

    (b) particulars of any other warrant issued in the category 1 territory for the person's arrest in respect of the offence;

    (c) particulars of the circumstances in which the person is alleged to have committed the offence, including the conduct alleged to constitute the offence, the time and place at which he is alleged to have committed the offence and any provision of the law of the category 1 territory under which the conduct is alleged to constitute an offence;

    (d) particulars of the sentence which may be imposed under the law of the category 1 territory in respect of the offence if the person is convicted of it.

(5) The statement is one that—

    (a) the person in respect of whom the Part 1 warrant is issued is [has been convicted] of an offence specified in the warrant by a court in the category 1 territory, and

    (b) the Part 1 warrant is issued with a view to his arrest and extradition to the category 1 territory for the purpose of being sentenced for the offence or of serving a sentence of imprisonment or another form of detention imposed in respect of the offence.

(6) The information is—

    (a) particulars of the person's identity;

    (b) particulars of the conviction;

    (c) particulars of any other warrant issued in the category 1 territory for the person's arrest in respect of the offence;

    (d) particulars of the sentence which may be imposed under the law of the category 1 territory in respect of the offence, if the person has not been sentenced for the offence;

    (e) particulars of the sentence which has been imposed under the law of the category 1 territory in respect of the offence, if the person has been sentenced for the offence.

(7)–(10) *****

Arrest

3   Arrest under certified Part 1 warrant

(1) This section applies if a certificate is issued under section 2 in respect of a Part 1 warrant issued in respect of a person.

(2) The warrant may be executed by a constable or a customs officer in any part of the United Kingdom.

(3)–(5) *****

(6) ...

4   Person arrested under Part 1 warrant

(1) This section applies if a person is arrested under a Part 1 warrant.

(2) A copy of the warrant must be given to the person as soon as practicable after his arrest.

(3) The person must be brought as soon as practicable before the appropriate judge.

(4) If subsection (2) is not complied with and the person applies to the judge to be discharged, the judge may order his discharge.

(5) If subsection (3) is not complied with and the person applies to the judge to be discharged, the judge must order his discharge.

(6) A person arrested under the warrant must be treated as continuing in legal custody until he is brought before the appropriate judge under subsection (3) or he is discharged under subsection (4) or (5).

5   Provisional arrest

(1) A constable, a customs officer or a service policeman may arrest a person without a warrant if he has reasonable grounds for believing—

(a) that a Part 1 warrant has been or will be issued in respect of the person by an authority of a category 1 territory, and

(b) that the authority has the function of issuing arrest warrants in the category 1 territory.

(2) A constable or a customs officer may arrest a person under subsection (1) in any part of the United Kingdom.

(3)–(4) *****

(5) …

6–9   *****

10   Initial stage of extradition hearing

(1) This section applies if a person in respect of whom a Part 1 warrant is issued appears or is brought before the appropriate judge for the extradition hearing.

(2) The judge must decide whether the offence specified in the Part 1 warrant is an extradition offence.

(3) If the judge decides the question in subsection (2) in the negative he must order the person's discharge.

(4) If the judge decides that question in the affirmative he must proceed under section 11.

11   Bars to extradition

(1) If the judge is required to proceed under this section he must decide whether the person's extradition to the category 1 territory is barred by reason of—

(a) the rule against double jeopardy;

(b) extraneous considerations;

(c) the passage of time;

(d) the person's age;

(e) hostage-taking considerations;

(f) speciality;

(g) the person's earlier extradition to the United Kingdom from another category 1 territory;

(h) the person's earlier extradition to the United Kingdom from a non-category 1 territory;

[(i) the person's earlier transfer to the United Kingdom by the International Criminal Court;]

[(j) forum].

(2) [Sections 12 to 19B apply] for the interpretation of subsection (1).

(3) If the judge decides any of the questions in subsection (1) in the affirmative he must order the person's discharge.

(4) If the judge decides those questions in the negative and the person is alleged to be unlawfully at large after conviction of the extradition offence, the judge must proceed under section 20.

(5) If the judge decides those questions in the negative and the person is accused of the commission of the extradition offence but is not alleged to be unlawfully at large after conviction of it, the judge must proceed under section 21.

12   Rule against double jeopardy

A person's extradition to a category 1 territory is barred by reason of the rule against double jeopardy if (and only if) it appears that he would be entitled to be discharged under any rule of law relating to previous acquittal or conviction on the assumption—

(a) that the conduct constituting the extradition offence constituted an offence in the part of the United Kingdom where the judge exercises jurisdiction;

(b) that the person were charged with the extradition offence in that part of the United Kingdom.

13   Extraneous considerations

A person's extradition to a category 1 territory is barred by reason of extraneous considerations if (and only if) it appears that—

(a) the Part 1 warrant issued in respect of him (though purporting to be issued on account of the extradition offence) is in fact issued for the purpose of prosecuting or punishing him on account of his race, religion, nationality, gender, sexual orientation or political opinions, or

(b) if extradited he might be prejudiced at his trial or punished, detained or restricted in his personal liberty by reason of his race, religion, nationality, gender, sexual orientation or political opinions.

14   Passage of time

A person's extradition to a category 1 territory is barred by reason of the passage of time if (and only if) it appears that it would be unjust or oppressive to extradite him by reason of the passage of time [since he is alleged to have—

(a) committed the extradition offence (where he is accused of its commission), or

(b) become unlawfully at large (where he is alleged to have been convicted of it)].

15   Age

A person's extradition to a category 1 territory is barred by reason of his age if (and only if) it would be conclusively presumed because of his age that he could not be guilty of the extradition offence on the assumption—

(a) that the conduct constituting the extradition offence constituted an offence in the part of the United Kingdom where the judge exercises jurisdiction;

(b) that the person carried out the conduct when the extradition offence was committed (or alleged to be committed);

(c) that the person carried out the conduct in the part of the United Kingdom where the judge exercises jurisdiction.

16   *****

17   Speciality

(1) A person's extradition to a category 1 territory is barred by reason of speciality if (and only if) there are no speciality arrangements with the category 1 territory.

(2) There are speciality arrangements with a category 1 territory if, under the law of that territory or arrangements made between it and the United Kingdom, a person who is extradited to the territory from the United Kingdom may be dealt with in the territory for an offence committed before his extradition only if—

(a) the offence is one falling within subsection (3), or

(b) the condition in subsection (4) is satisfied.

(3) The offences are—

(a) the offence in respect of which the person is extradited;

(b) an extradition offence disclosed by the same facts as that offence;

(c) an extradition offence in respect of which the appropriate judge gives his consent under section 55 to the person being dealt with;

(d) an offence which is not punishable with imprisonment or another form of detention;

(e) an offence in respect of which the person will not be detained in connection with his trial, sentence or appeal;

(f) an offence in respect of which the person waives the right that he would have (but for this paragraph) not to be dealt with for the offence.

(4) The condition is that the person is given an opportunity to leave the category 1 territory and—

(a) he does not do so before the end of the permitted period, or

(b) if he does so before the end of the permitted period, he returns there.

(5) The permitted period is 45 days starting with the day on which the person arrives in the category 1 territory.

(6), (7) *****

18, 19 *****

[19A   Earlier transfer to United Kingdom by International Criminal Court]

[(1) A person's extradition to a category 1 territory is barred by reason of his earlier transfer by the International Criminal Court if (and only if)—

    (a) the person was transferred to the United Kingdom to serve a sentence imposed by the Court;

    (b) under arrangements between the United Kingdom and the Court, the consent of the Presidency of the Court is required to the person's extradition from the United Kingdom to the category 1 territory in respect of the extradition offence under consideration;

    (c) that consent has not been given.

(2) Subsection (1) does not apply if the person has served the sentence imposed by the Court and has subsequently—

    (a) remained voluntarily in the United Kingdom for more than 30 days, or

    (b) left the United Kingdom and returned to it.]

[19B   Forum]

[(1) A person's extradition to a category 1 territory ('the requesting territory') is barred by reason of forum if (and only if) it appears that—

    (a) a significant part of the conduct alleged to constitute the extradition offence is conduct in the United Kingdom, and

    (b) in view of that and all the other circumstances, it would not be in the interests of justice for the person to be tried for the offence in the requesting territory.

(2) For the purposes of subsection (1)(b) the judge must take into account whether the relevant prosecution authorities in the United Kingdom have decided not to take proceedings against the person in respect of the conduct in question.

(3) This section does not apply if the person is alleged to be unlawfully at large after conviction of the extradition offence.]

[**Note:** Section 19B is not yet (April 2012) in force.]

20   Case where person has been convicted

(1) If the judge is required to proceed under this section (by virtue of section 11) he must decide whether the person was convicted in his presence.

(2) If the judge decides the question in subsection (1) in the affirmative he must proceed under section 21.

(3) If the judge decides that question in the negative he must decide whether the person deliberately absented himself from his trial.

(4) If the judge decides the question in subsection (3) in the affirmative he must proceed under section 21.

(5) If the judge decides that question in the negative he must decide whether the person would be entitled to a retrial or (on appeal) to a review amounting to a retrial.

(6) If the judge decides the question in subsection (5) in the affirmative he must proceed under section 21.

(7) If the judge decides that question in the negative he must order the person's discharge.

(8) The judge must not decide the question in subsection (5) in the affirmative unless, in any proceedings that it is alleged would constitute a retrial or a review amounting to a retrial, the person would have these rights—

    (a) the right to defend himself in person or through legal assistance of his own choosing or, if he had not sufficient means to pay for legal assistance, to be given it free when the interests of justice so required;

(b) the right to examine or have examined witnesses against him and to obtain the attendance and examination of witnesses on his behalf under the same conditions as witnesses against him.

21 Human rights

(1) If the judge is required to proceed under this section (by virtue of section 11 or 20) he must decide whether the person's extradition would be compatible with the Convention rights within the meaning of the Human Rights Act 1998 (c. 42).

(2) If the judge decides the question in subsection (1) in the negative he must order the person's discharge.

(3) If the judge decides that question in the affirmative he must order the person to be extradited to the category 1 territory in which the warrant was issued.

(4) If the judge makes an order under subsection (3) he must remand the person in custody or on bail to wait for his extradition to the category 1 territory.

(5) If the person is remanded in custody, the appropriate judge] may later grant bail.

22–68A *****

PART 2 EXTRADITION TO CATEGORY 2 TERRITORIES

Introduction

69 Extradition to category 2 territories

(1) This Part deals with extradition from the United Kingdom to the territories designated for the purposes of this Part by order made by the Secretary of State.

(2) In this Act references to category 2 territories are to the territories designated for the purposes of this Part.

70–79 *****

80 Rule against double jeopardy

A person's extradition to a category 2 territory is barred by reason of the rule against double jeopardy if (and only if) it appears that he would be entitled to be discharged under any rule of law relating to previous acquittal or conviction if he were charged with the extradition offence in the part of the United Kingdom where the judge exercises his jurisdiction.

81 Extraneous considerations

A person's extradition to a category 2 territory is barred by reason of extraneous considerations if (and only if) it appears that—

(a) the request for his extradition (though purporting to be made on account of the extradition offence) is in fact made for the purpose of prosecuting or punishing him on account of his race, religion, nationality, gender, sexual orientation or political opinions, or

(b) if extradited he might be prejudiced at his trial or punished, detained or restricted in his personal liberty by reason of his race, religion, nationality, gender, sexual orientation or political opinions.

82 Passage of time

A person's extradition to a category 2 territory is barred by reason of the passage of time if (and only if) it appears that it would be unjust or oppressive to extradite him by reason of the passage of time [since he is alleged to have—

(a) committed the extradition offence (where he is accused of its commission), or

(b) become unlawfully at large (where he is alleged to have been convicted of it)].

83–86 ******

87 Human rights

(1) If the judge is required to proceed under this section (by virtue of section 84, 85 or 86) he must decide whether the person's extradition would be compatible with the Convention rights within the meaning of the Human Rights Act 1998 (c. 42).

(2) If the judge decides the question in subsection (1) in the negative he must order the person's discharge.

(3) If the judge decides that question in the affirmative he must send the case to the Secretary of State for his decision whether the person is to be extradited.

88–93 ******

94 Death penalty

(1) The Secretary of State must not order a person's extradition to a category 2 territory if he could be, will be or has been sentenced to death for the offence concerned in the category 2 territory.

(2) Subsection (1) does not apply if the Secretary of State receives a written assurance which he considers adequate that a sentence of death—

    (a) will not be imposed, or

    (b) will not be carried out (if imposed).

*****

Asylum and Immigration (Treatment of Claimants etc.) Act 2004

(2004, c. 19)

An Act to make provision about asylum and immigration.   [22nd July 2004]

Territorial extent: United Kingdom; may be extended by Order to any of the Channel Islands and the Isle of Man

Offences

1 ******

2 Entering United Kingdom without passport, &c.

(1) A person commits an offence if at a leave or asylum interview he does not have with him an immigration document which—

    (a) is in force, and

    (b) satisfactorily establishes his identity and nationality or citizenship.

(2) A person commits an offence if at a leave or asylum interview he does not have with him, in respect of any dependent child with whom he claims to be travelling or living, an immigration document which—

    (a) is in force, and

    (b) satisfactorily establishes the child's identity and nationality or citizenship.

(3) But a person does not commit an offence under subsection (1) or (2) if—

    (a) the interview referred to in that subsection takes place after the person has entered the United Kingdom, and

    (b) within the period of three days beginning with the date of the interview the person provides to an immigration officer or to the Secretary of State a document of the kind referred to in that subsection.

(4) It is a defence for a person charged with an offence under subsection (1)—

    (a) to prove that he is an EEA national,

(b) to prove that he is a member of the family of an EEA national and that he is exercising a right under the Community Treaties in respect of entry to or residence in the United Kingdom,

(c) to prove that he has a reasonable excuse for not being in possession of a document of the kind specified in subsection (1),

(d) to produce a false immigration document and to prove that he used that document as an immigration document for all purposes in connection with his journey to the United Kingdom, or

(e) to prove that he travelled to the United Kingdom without, at any stage since he set out on the journey, having possession of an immigration document.

(5), (6) *****

(7) For the purposes of subsections (4) to (6)—

(a) the fact that a document was deliberately destroyed or disposed of is not a reasonable excuse for not being in possession of it or for not providing it in accordance with subsection (3), unless it is shown that the destruction or disposal was—

(i) for a reasonable cause, or

(ii) beyond the control of the person charged with the offence, and

(b) in paragraph (a)(i) 'reasonable cause' does not include the purpose of—

(i) delaying the handling or resolution of a claim or application or the taking of a decision,

(ii) increasing the chances of success of a claim or application, or

(iii) complying with instructions or advice given by a person who offers advice about, or facilitates, immigration into the United Kingdom, unless in the circumstances of the case it is unreasonable to expect non-compliance with the instructions or advice.

(8) A person shall be presumed for the purposes of this section not to have a document with him if he fails to produce it to an immigration officer or official of the Secretary of State on request.

(9) A person guilty of an offence under this section shall be liable—

(a) on conviction on indictment, to imprisonment for a term not exceeding two years, to a fine or to both, or

(b) on summary conviction, to imprisonment for a term not exceeding twelve months, to a fine not exceeding the statutory maximum or to both.

(10)–(17) *****

3 ...

4 Trafficking people for exploitation

(1) A person commits an offence if he arranges or facilitates the arrival in[, or entry into,] the United Kingdom of an individual (the 'passenger') and—

(a) he intends to exploit the passenger in the United Kingdom or elsewhere, or

(b) he believes that another person is likely to exploit the passenger in the United Kingdom or elsewhere.

(2) A person commits an offence if he arranges or facilitates travel within the United Kingdom by an individual (the 'passenger') in respect of whom he believes that an offence under subsection (1) may have been committed and—

(a) he intends to exploit the passenger in the United Kingdom or elsewhere, or

(b) he believes that another person is likely to exploit the passenger in the United Kingdom or elsewhere.

(3) A person commits an offence if he arranges or facilitates the departure from the United Kingdom of an individual (the 'passenger') and—

(a) he intends to exploit the passenger outside the United Kingdom, or

(b) he believes that another person is likely to exploit the passenger outside the United Kingdom.

[(3A)] ***** (not yet in force)

(4) For the purposes of this section a person is exploited if (and only if)—

    (a)   he is the victim of behaviour that contravenes Article 4 of the Human Rights Convention (slavery and forced labour),

    (b)   he is encouraged, required or expected to do anything as a result of which he or another person would commit an offence under [Part 1 of the Human Tissues (Scotland) Act 2006 (asp 4)] or [under section 32 or 33 of the Human Tissue Act 2004],

    [(ba)]   ***** (not yet in force)

    (c)   he is subjected to force, threats or deception designed to induce him—

        (i)   to provide services of any kind,

        (ii)   to provide another person with benefits of any kind, or

        (iii)   to enable another person to acquire benefits of any kind, or

    [(d)   a person uses or attempts to use him for any purpose within sub-paragraph (i), (ii) or (iii) of paragraph (c), having chosen him for that purpose on the grounds that—

        (i)   he is mentally or physically ill or disabled, he is young or he has a family relationship with a person, and

        (ii)   a person without the illness, disability, youth or family relationship would be likely to refuse to be used for that purpose].

(5) A person guilty of an offence under this section shall be liable—

    (a) on conviction on indictment, to imprisonment for a term not exceeding 14 years, to a fine or to both, or

    (b) on summary conviction, to imprisonment for a term not exceeding twelve months, to a fine not exceeding the statutory maximum or to both.

5–7 *****

Treatment of claimants

8 Claimant's credibility

(1) In determining whether to believe a statement made by or on behalf of a person who makes an asylum claim or a human rights claim, a deciding authority shall take account, as damaging the claimant's credibility, of any behaviour to which this section applies.

(2) This section applies to any behaviour by the claimant that the deciding authority thinks—

    (a) is designed or likely to conceal information,

    (b) is designed or likely to mislead, or

    (c) is designed or likely to obstruct or delay the handling or resolution of the claim or the taking of a decision in relation to the claimant.

(3) *****

(4) This section also applies to failure by the claimant to take advantage of a reasonable opportunity to make an asylum claim or human rights claim while in a safe country.

(5) This section also applies to failure by the claimant to make an asylum claim or human rights claim before being notified of an immigration decision, unless the claim relies wholly on matters arising after the notification.

(6) This section also applies to failure by the claimant to make an asylum claim or human rights claim before being arrested under an immigration provision, unless—

    (a) he had no reasonable opportunity to make the claim before the arrest, or

    (b) the claim relies wholly on matters arising after the arrest.

(7)–(11) *****

(12) This section shall not prevent a deciding authority from determining not to believe a statement on the grounds of behaviour to which this section does not apply.

(13) . . .

9–32   *****

Removal and detention

33   Removing asylum seeker to safe country

(1) Schedule 3 (which concerns the removal of persons claiming asylum to countries known to protect refugees and to respect human rights) shall have effect.

(2), (3) *****

34   *****

35   Deportation or removal: cooperation

(1) The Secretary of State may require a person to take specified action if the Secretary of State thinks that—

 (a) the action will or may enable a travel document to be obtained by or for the person, and

 (b) possession of the travel document will facilitate the person's deportation or removal from the United Kingdom.

(2) In particular, the Secretary of State may require a person to—

 (a) provide information or documents to the Secretary of State or to any other person;

 (b) obtain information or documents;

 (c) provide fingerprints, submit to the taking of a photograph or provide information, or submit to a process for the recording of information, about external physical characteristics (including, in particular, features of the iris or any other part of the eye);

 (d) make, or consent to or cooperate with the making of, an application to a person acting for the government of a State other than the United Kingdom;

 (e) cooperate with a process designed to enable determination of an application;

 (f) complete a form accurately and completely;

 (g) attend an interview and answer questions accurately and completely;

 (h) make an appointment.

(3) A person commits an offence if he fails without reasonable excuse to comply with a requirement of the Secretary of State under subsection (1).

(4)–(11) *****

36   Electronic monitoring

(1) In this section—

 (a) 'residence restriction' means a restriction as to residence imposed under—

  (i)   paragraph 21 of Schedule 2 to the Immigration Act 1971 (c. 77) (control on entry) (including that paragraph as applied by another provision of the Immigration Acts), or

  (ii) Schedule 3 to that Act (deportation),

 (b) 'reporting restriction' means a requirement to report to a specified person imposed under any of those provisions,

 (c), (d) *****

(2) Where a residence restriction is imposed on an adult—

 (a) he may be required to cooperate with electronic monitoring, and

 (b) failure to comply with a requirement under paragraph (a) shall be treated for all purposes of the Immigration Acts as failure to observe the residence restriction.

(3) Where a reporting restriction could be imposed on an adult—

 (a) he may instead be required to cooperate with electronic monitoring, and

 (b) the requirement shall be treated for all purposes of the Immigration Acts as a reporting restriction.

(4) Immigration bail may be granted to an adult subject to a requirement that he cooperate with electronic monitoring; and the requirement may (but need not) be imposed as a condition of a recognizance or bail bond.

(5) In this section a reference to requiring an adult to cooperate with electronic monitoring is a reference to requiring him to cooperate with such arrangements as the person imposing the requirement may specify for detecting and recording by electronic means the location of the adult, or his presence in or absence from a location—

(a) at specified times,

(b) during specified periods of time, or

(c) throughout the currency of the arrangements.

(6)–(11) *****

(12) ...

*****

SCHEDULE 3   REMOVAL OF ASYLUM SEEKER TO SAFE COUNTRY

PART 1 INTRODUCTORY

1.—(1) In this Schedule—

'asylum claim' means a claim by a person that to remove him from or require him to leave the United Kingdom would breach the United Kingdom's obligations under the Refugee Convention,

'Convention rights' means the rights identified as Convention rights by section 1 of the Human Rights Act 1998 (c. 42) (whether or not in relation to a State that is a party to the Convention),

'human rights claim' means a claim by a person that to remove him from or require him to leave the United Kingdom would be unlawful under section 6 of the Human Rights Act 1998 (public authority not to act contrary to Convention) as being incompatible with his Convention rights,

'immigration appeal' means an appeal under section 82(1) of the Nationality, Immigration and Asylum Act 2002 (c. 41) (appeal against immigration decision), and

'the Refugee Convention' means the Convention relating to the Status of Refugees done at Geneva on 28th July 1951 and its Protocol.

(2) In this Schedule a reference to anything being done in accordance with the Refugee Convention is a reference to the thing being done in accordance with the principles of the Convention, whether or not by a signatory to it.

PART 2 FIRST LIST OF SAFE COUNTRIES (REFUGEE CONVENTION AND HUMAN RIGHTS (1))

2. This Part applies to—

(a) Austria,

(b) Belgium,

[(ba) Bulgaria,]

(c) Republic of Cyprus,

(d) Czech Republic,

(e) Denmark,

(f) Estonia,

(g) Finland,

(h) France,

(i) Germany,

(j) Greece,

(k) Hungary,

(l) Iceland,

(m) Ireland,

(n) Italy,

    (o) Latvia,
    (p) Lithuania,
    (q) Luxembourg,
    (r) Malta,
    (s) Netherlands,
    (t) Norway,
    (u) Poland,
    (v) Portugal,
   [(va) Romania,]
    (w) Slovak Republic,
    (x) Slovenia,
    (y) Spain, ...
    (z) Sweden,
  [(z1)] Switzerland].

3.—(1) This paragraph applies for the purposes of the determination by any person, tribunal or court whether a person who has made an asylum claim or a human rights claim may be removed—

    (a) from the United Kingdom, and
    (b) to a State of which he is not a national or citizen.

(2) A State to which this Part applies shall be treated, in so far as relevant to the question mentioned in sub-paragraph (1), as a place—

    (a) where a person's life and liberty are not threatened by reason of his race, religion, nationality, membership of a particular social group or political opinion,
    (b) from which a person will not be sent to another State in contravention of his Convention rights, and
    (c) from which a person will not be sent to another State otherwise than in accordance with the Refugee Convention.

4. Section 77 of the Nationality, Immigration and Asylum Act 2002 (c. 41) (no removal while claim for asylum pending) shall not prevent a person who has made a claim for asylum from being removed—

    (a) from the United Kingdom, and
    (b) to a State to which this Part applies,

provided that the Secretary of State certifies that in his opinion the person is not a national or citizen of the State.

5.—(1) This paragraph applies where the Secretary of State certifies that—

    (a) it is proposed to remove a person to a State to which this Part applies, and
    (b) in the Secretary of State's opinion the person is not a national or citizen of the State.

(2) The person may not bring an immigration appeal by virtue of section 92(2) or (3) of that Act (appeal from within United Kingdom: general).

(3) The person may not bring an immigration appeal by virtue of section 92(4)(a) of that Act (appeal from within United Kingdom: asylum or human rights) in reliance on—

    (a) an asylum claim which asserts that to remove the person to a specified State to which this Part applies would breach the United Kingdom's obligations under the Refugee Convention, or
    (b) a human rights claim in so far as it asserts that to remove the person to a specified State to which this Part applies would be unlawful under section 6 of the Human Rights Act 1998 because of the possibility of removal from that State to another State.

(4) The person may not bring an immigration appeal by virtue of section 92(4)(a) of that Act in reliance on a human rights claim to which this sub-paragraph applies if the Secretary of State certifies that the claim is clearly unfounded; and the Secretary of State shall certify a human rights claim to which this sub-paragraph applies unless satisfied that the claim is not clearly unfounded.

(5) Sub-paragraph (4) applies to a human rights claim if, or in so far as, it asserts a matter other than that specified in sub-paragraph (3)(b).

6. A person who is outside the United Kingdom may not bring an immigration appeal on any ground that is inconsistent with treating a State to which this Part applies as a place—

(a) where a person's life and liberty are not threatened by reason of his race, religion, nationality, membership of a particular social group or political opinion,

(b) from which a person will not be sent to another State in contravention of his Convention rights, and

(c) from which a person will not be sent to another State otherwise than in accordance with the Refugee Convention.

PART 3 SECOND LIST OF SAFE COUNTRIES (REFUGEE CONVENTION AND HUMAN RIGHTS (2))

7.—(1) This Part applies to such States as the Secretary of State may by order specify.

(2) An order under this paragraph—

(a) shall be made by statutory instrument, and

(b) shall not be made unless a draft has been laid before and approved by resolution of each House of Parliament.

8.—(1) This paragraph applies for the purposes of the determination by any person, tribunal or court whether a person who has made an asylum claim may be removed—

(a) from the United Kingdom, and

(b) to a State of which he is not a national or citizen

(2) A State to which this Part applies shall be treated, in so far as relevant to the question mentioned in sub-paragraph (1), as a place—

(a) where a person's life and liberty are not threatened by reason of his race, religion, nationality, membership of a particular social group or political opinion, and

(b) from which a person will not be sent to another State otherwise than in accordance with the Refugee Convention.

9.–16. *****

PART 5 COUNTRIES CERTIFIED AS SAFE FOR INDIVIDUALS

17. This Part applies to a person who has made an asylum claim if the Secretary of State certifies that—

(a) it is proposed to remove the person to a specified State,

(b) in the Secretary of State's opinion the person is not a national or citizen of the specified State, and

(c) in the Secretary of State's opinion the specified State is a place—

(i)   where the person's life and liberty will not be threatened by reason of his race, religion, nationality, membership of a particular social group or political opinion, and

(ii) from which the person will not be sent to another State otherwise than in accordance with the Refugee Convention.

18. Where this Part applies to a person section 77 of the Nationality, Immigration and Asylum Act 2002 (c. 41) (no removal while claim for asylum pending) shall not prevent his removal to the State specified under paragraph 17.

19. Where this Part applies to a person—

(a) he may not bring an immigration appeal by virtue of section 92(2) or (3) of that Act (appeal from within United Kingdom: general),

(b) he may not bring an immigration appeal by virtue of section 92(4)(a) of that Act (appeal from within United Kingdom: asylum or human rights) in reliance on an asylum claim which asserts that to remove the person to the State specified under paragraph 17 would breach the United Kingdom's obligations under the Refugee Convention,

      (c) he may not bring an immigration appeal by virtue of section 92(4)(a) of that Act in reliance on a human rights claim if the Secretary of State certifies that the claim is clearly unfounded, and

      (d) he may not while outside the United Kingdom bring an immigration appeal on any ground that is inconsistent with the opinion certified under paragraph 17(c).

    20., 21. *****

*****

Civil Contingencies Act 2004

(2004, c. 36)

An Act to make provision about civil contingencies   [18th November 2004]

Territorial extent: United Kingdom

1–18 *****

PART 2 EMERGENCY POWERS

19 Meaning of 'emergency'

    (1) In this Part 'emergency' means—

      (a) an event or situation which threatens serious damage to human welfare in the United Kingdom or in a Part or region,

      (b) an event or situation which threatens serious damage to the environment of the United Kingdom or of a Part or region, or

      (c) war, or terrorism, which threatens serious damage to the security of the United Kingdom.

    (2) For the purposes of subsection (1)(a) an event or situation threatens damage to human welfare only if it involves, causes or may cause—

      (a) loss of human life,

      (b) human illness or injury,

      (c) homelessness,

      (d) damage to property,

      (e) disruption of a supply of money, food, water, energy or fuel,

      (f) disruption of a system of communication,

      (g) disruption of facilities for transport, or

      (h) disruption of services relating to health.

    (3) For the purposes of subsection (1)(b) an event or situation threatens damage to the environment only if it involves, causes or may cause—

      (a) contamination of land, water or air with biological, chemical or radio-active matter, or

      (b) disruption or destruction of plant life or animal life.

    (4)–(6) *****

20 Power to make emergency regulations

    (1) Her Majesty may by Order in Council make emergency regulations if satisfied that the conditions in section 21 are satisfied.

    (2) A senior Minister of the Crown may make emergency regulations if satisfied—

      (a) that the conditions in section 21 are satisfied, and

      (b) that it would not be possible, without serious delay, to arrange for an Order in Council under subsection (1).

    (3) In this Part 'senior Minister of the Crown' means—

      (a) the First Lord of the Treasury (the Prime Minister),

      (b) any of Her Majesty's Principal Secretaries of State, and

(c) the Commissioners of Her Majesty's Treasury.

(4) In this Part 'serious delay' means a delay that might—

(a) cause serious damage, or

(b) seriously obstruct the prevention, control or mitigation of serious damage.

(5) *****

21   Conditions for making emergency regulations

(1) This section specifies the conditions mentioned in section 20.

(2) The first condition is that an emergency has occurred, is occurring or is about to occur.

(3) The second condition is that it is necessary to make provision for the purpose of preventing, controlling or mitigating an aspect or effect of the emergency.

(4) The third condition is that the need for provision referred to in subsection (3) is urgent.

(5), (6) *****

22   Scope of emergency regulations

(1) Emergency regulations may make any provision which the person making the regulations is satisfied is appropriate for the purpose of preventing, controlling or mitigating an aspect or effect of the emergency in respect of which the regulations are made.

(2) In particular, emergency regulations may make any provision which the person making the regulations is satisfied is appropriate for the purpose of—

(a) protecting human life, health or safety,

(b) treating human illness or injury,

(c) protecting or restoring property,

(d) protecting or restoring a supply of money, food, water, energy or fuel,

(e) protecting or restoring a system of communication,

(f) protecting or restoring facilities for transport,

(g) protecting or restoring the provision of services relating to health,

(h) protecting or restoring the activities of banks or other financial institutions,

(i) preventing, containing or reducing the contamination of land, water or air,

(j) preventing, reducing or mitigating the effects of disruption or destruction of plant life or animal life,

(k) protecting or restoring activities of Parliament, of the Scottish Parliament, of the Northern Ireland Assembly or of the National Assembly for Wales, or

(l) protecting or restoring the performance of public functions.

(3) Emergency regulations may make provision of any kind that could be made by Act of Parliament or by the exercise of the Royal Prerogative; in particular, regulations may—

(a) confer a function on a Minister of the Crown, on the Scottish Ministers, on the National Assembly for Wales, on a Northern Ireland department, on a coordinator appointed under section 24 or on any other specified person (and a function conferred may, in particular, be—

(i)   a power, or duty, to exercise a discretion;

(ii) a power to give directions or orders, whether written or oral);

(b) provide for or enable the requisition or confiscation of property (with or without compensation);

(c) provide for or enable the destruction of property, animal life or plant life (with or without compensation);

(d) prohibit, or enable the prohibition of, movement to or from a specified place;

(e) require, or enable the requirement of, movement to or from a specified place;

(f) prohibit, or enable the prohibition of, assemblies of specified kinds, at specified places or at specified times;

(g) prohibit, or enable the prohibition of, travel at specified times;

(h) prohibit, or enable the prohibition of, other specified activities;

(i) create an offence of—

        (i)   failing to comply with a provision of the regulations;

        (ii) failing to comply with a direction or order given or made under the regulations;

        (iii) obstructing a person in the performance of a function under or by virtue of the regulations;

    (j) disapply or modify an enactment or a provision made under or by virtue of an enactment;

    (k) require a person or body to act in performance of a function (whether the function is conferred by the regulations or otherwise and whether or not the regulations also make provision for remuneration or compensation);

    (l) enable the Defence Council to authorise the deployment of Her Majesty's armed forces;

    (m) make provision (which may include conferring powers in relation to property) for facilitating any deployment of Her Majesty's armed forces;

    (n) confer jurisdiction on a court or tribunal (which may include a tribunal established by the regulations);

    (o) make provision which has effect in relation to, or to anything done in—

        (i)   an area of the territorial sea,

        (ii) an area within British fishery limits, or

        (iii) an area of the continental shelf;

    (p) make provision which applies generally or only in specified circumstances or for a specified purpose;

    (q) make different provision for different circumstances or purposes.

(4) In subsection (3) 'specified' means specified by, or to be specified in accordance with, the regulations.

(5) A person making emergency regulations must have regard to the importance of ensuring that Parliament, the High Court and the Court of Session are able to conduct proceedings in connection with—

    (a) the regulations, or

    (b) action taken under the regulations.

23 Limitations of emergency regulations

(1) Emergency regulations may make provision only if and in so far as the person making the regulations is satisfied—

    (a) that the provision is appropriate for the purpose of preventing, controlling or mitigating an aspect or effect of the emergency in respect of which the regulations are made, and

    (b) that the effect of the provision is in due proportion to that aspect or effect of the emergency.

(2) Emergency regulations must specify the Parts of the United Kingdom or regions in relation to which the regulations have effect.

(3) Emergency regulations may not—

    (a) require a person, or enable a person to be required, to provide military service, or

    (b) prohibit or enable the prohibition of participation in, or any activity in connection with, a strike or other industrial action.

(4) Emergency regulations may not—

    (a) create an offence other than one of the kind described in section 22(3)(i),

    (b) create an offence other than one which is triable only before a magistrates' court or, in Scotland, before a sheriff under summary procedure,

    (c) create an offence which is punishable—

        (i)   with imprisonment for a period exceeding three months, or

        (ii) with a fine exceeding level 5 on the standard scale, or

    (d) alter procedure in relation to criminal proceedings.

(5) Emergency regulations may not amend—

    (a) this Part of this Act, or

    (b) the Human Rights Act 1998 (c. 42).

24, 25   *****

26 Duration

(1) Emergency regulations shall lapse—

    (a) at the end of the period of 30 days beginning with the date on which they are made, or

    (b) at such earlier time as may be specified in the regulations.

(2) Subsection (1)—

    (a) shall not prevent the making of new regulations, and

    (b) shall not affect anything done by virtue of the regulations before they lapse.

27 Parliamentary scrutiny

(1) Where emergency regulations are made—

    (a) a senior Minister of the Crown shall as soon as is reasonably practicable lay the regulations before Parliament, and

    (b) the regulations shall lapse at the end of the period of seven days beginning with the date of laying unless during that period each House of Parliament passes a resolution approving them.

(2) If each House of Parliament passes a resolution that emergency regulations shall cease to have effect, the regulations shall cease to have effect—

    (a) at such time, after the passing of the resolutions, as may be specified in them, or

    (b) if no time is specified in the resolutions, at the beginning of the day after that on which the resolutions are passed (or, if they are passed on different days, at the beginning of the day after that on which the second resolution is passed).

(3) If each House of Parliament passes a resolution that emergency regulations shall have effect with a specified amendment, the regulations shall have effect as amended, with effect from—

    (a) such time, after the passing of the resolutions, as may be specified in them, or

    (b) if no time is specified in the resolutions, the beginning of the day after that on which the resolutions are passed (or, if they are passed on different days, the beginning of the day after that on which the second resolution is passed).

(4) Nothing in this section—

    (a) shall prevent the making of new regulations, or

    (b) shall affect anything done by virtue of regulations before they lapse, cease to have effect or are amended under this section.

*****

Civil Partnership Act 2004

(2004, c. 33)

An Act to make provision for and in connection with civil partnership   [18th November 2004]

Territorial extent: United Kingdom (s. 1); England and Wales (remaining sections printed; equivalent provisions for Scotland and Northern Ireland respectively are in Parts 3 and 4 of the Act)

PART 1 INTRODUCTION

1 Civil partnership

(1) A civil partnership is a relationship between two people of the same sex ('civil partners')—

    (a) which is formed when they register as civil partners of each other—

        (i)   in England or Wales (under Part 2),

        (ii) in Scotland (under Part 3),

        (iii) in Northern Ireland (under Part 4), or

(iv) outside the United Kingdom under an Order in Council made under Chapter 1 of Part 5 (registration at British consulates etc. or by armed forces personnel), or

(b) which they are treated under Chapter 2 of Part 5 as having formed (at the time determined under that Chapter) by virtue of having registered an overseas relationship.

(2) Subsection (1) is subject to the provisions of this Act under or by virtue of which a civil partnership is void.

(3) A civil partnership ends only on death, dissolution or annulment.

(4) The references in subsection (3) to dissolution and annulment are to dissolution and annulment having effect under or recognised in accordance with this Act.

(5) References in this Act to an overseas relationship are to be read in accordance with Chapter 2 of Part 5.

PART 2 CIVIL PARTNERSHIP: ENGLAND AND WALES

Chapter 1   Registration

Formation, eligibility and parental etc. consent

2 Formation of civil partnership by registration

(1) For the purposes of section 1, two people are to be regarded as having registered as civil partners of each other once each of them has signed the civil partnership document—

(a) at the invitation of, and in the presence of, a civil partnership registrar, and

(b) in the presence of each other and two witnesses.

(2) Subsection (1) applies regardless of whether subsections (3) and (4) are complied with.

(3) After the civil partnership document has been signed under subsection (1), it must also be signed, in the presence of the civil partners and each other, by—

(a) each of the two witnesses, and

(b) the civil partnership registrar.

(4) After the witnesses and the civil partnership registrar have signed the civil partnership document, the relevant registration authority must ensure that—

(a) the fact that the two people have registered as civil partners of each other, and

(b) Any other information prescribed by regulations,

is recorded in the register as soon as is practicable.

(5) No religious service is to be used while the civil partnership registrar is officiating at the signing of a civil partnership document.

(6) 'The civil partnership document' has the meaning given by section 7(1).

(7) 'The relevant registration authority' means the registration authority in whose area the registration takes place.

3 Eligibility

(1) Two people are not eligible to register as civil partners of each other if—

(a) they are not of the same sex,

(b) either of them is already a civil partner or lawfully married,

(c) either of them is under 16, or

(d) they are within prohibited degrees of relationship.

(2) Part 1 of Schedule 1 contains provisions for determining when two people are within prohibited degrees of relationship.

4, 5 *****

Registration procedure: general

6 Place of registration

(1) The place at which two people may register as civil partners of each other—

(a) must be in England or Wales,

(b) ...
(c) must be specified in the notices, or notice, of proposed civil partnership required by this Chapter.
(2) ...
[(3) Subsections (3A) and (3B) apply in the case of registration under the standard procedure (including that procedure modified as mentioned in section 5).
(3A) The place must be—
(a) on approved premises, or
(b) in a register office.
(3B) If it is in a register office, the place must be open to any person wishing to attend the registration.
(3C) In this chapter 'register office' means a register office provided under section 10 of the Registration Service Act 1953.]
(4), (5) ...
*****

Gender Recognition Act 2004

(2004, c. 7)

An Act to make provision for and in connection with change of gender [1st July 2004]

Territorial extent: United Kingdom (provisions reproduced)

Applications for gender recognition certificate

1 Applications
(1) A person of either gender who is aged at least 18 may make an application for a gender recognition certificate on the basis of—
(a) living in the other gender, or
(b) having changed gender under the law of a country or territory outside the United Kingdom.
(2) In this Act 'the acquired gender', in relation to a person by whom an application under subsection (1) is or has been made, means—
(a) in the case of an application under paragraph (a) of that subsection, the gender in which the person is living, or
(b) in the case of an application under paragraph (b) of that subsection, the gender to which the person has changed under the law of the country or territory concerned.
(3) An application under subsection (1) is to be determined by a Gender Recognition Panel.
(4) Schedule 1 (Gender Recognition Panels) has effect.

2 Determination of applications
(1) In the case of an application under section 1(1)(a), the Panel must grant the application if satisfied that the applicant—
(a) has or has had gender dysphoria,
(b) has lived in the acquired gender throughout the period of two years ending with the date on which the application is made,
(c) intends to continue to live in the acquired gender until death, and
(d) complies with the requirements imposed by and under section 3.
(2) In the case of an application under section 1(1)(b), the Panel must grant the application if satisfied—
(a) that the country or territory under the law of which the applicant has changed gender is an approved country or territory, and
(b) that the applicant complies with the requirements imposed by and under section 3.

(3) The Panel must reject an application under section 1(1) if not required by subsection (1) or (2) to grant it.

(4) In this Act 'approved country or territory' means a country or territory prescribed by order made by the Secretary of State after consulting the Scottish Ministers and the Department of Finance and Personnel in Northern Ireland.

3 Evidence

(1) An application under section 1(1)(a) must include either—
(a) a report made by a registered medical practitioner practising in the field of gender dysphoria and a report made by another registered medical practitioner (who may, but need not, practise in that field), or
(b) a report made by a [registered psychologist] practising in that field and a report made by a registered medical practitioner (who may, but need not, practise in that field).

(2) But subsection (1) is not complied with unless a report required by that subsection and made by—
(a) a registered medical practitioner, or
(b) a [registered psychologist],
practising in the field of gender dysphoria includes details of the diagnosis of the applicant's gender dysphoria.

(3) And subsection (1) is not complied with in a case where—
(a) the applicant has undergone or is undergoing treatment for the purpose of modifying sexual characteristics, or
(b) treatment for that purpose has been prescribed or planned for the applicant,
unless at least one of the reports required by that subsection includes details of it.

(4) An application under section 1(1)(a) must also include a statutory declaration by the applicant that the applicant meets the conditions in section 2(1)(b) and (c).

(5) An application under section 1(1)(b) must include evidence that the applicant has changed gender under the law of an approved country or territory.

(6)–(8) *****

4 Successful applications

(1) If a Gender Recognition Panel grants an application under section 1(1) it must issue a gender recognition certificate to the applicant.

(2) Unless the applicant is married [or a civil partner], the certificate is to be a full gender recognition certificate.

(3) If the applicant is married [or a civil partner], the certificate is to be an interim gender recognition certificate.

(4), (5) *****

5 [Issue of full certificates where applicant has been married]

(1) A court which—
(a) makes absolute a decree of nullity granted on the ground that an interim gender recognition certificate has been issued to a party to the marriage, or
(b) (in Scotland) grants a decree of divorce on that ground,
must, on doing so, issue a full gender recognition certificate to that party and send a copy to the Secretary of State.

(2) If an interim gender recognition certificate has been issued to a person and either—
(a) the person's marriage is dissolved or annulled (otherwise than on the ground mentioned in subsection (1)) in proceedings instituted during the period of six months beginning with the day on which it was issued, or
(b) the person's spouse dies within that period,
the person may make an application for a full gender recognition certificate at any time within the period specified in subsection (3) (unless the person is again married [or is a civil partner]).

(3) That period is the period of six months beginning with the day on which the marriage is dissolved or annulled or the death occurs.

(4)–(7) *****

*****

Hunting Act 2004

(2004, c. 37)

An Act to make provision about hunting wild mammals with dogs; to prohibit hare coursing; and for connected purposes   [18th November 2004]

Territorial extent: England and Wales

BE IT ENACTED by The Queen's most Excellent Majesty, by and with the advice and consent of the Commons in this present Parliament assembled, in accordance with the provisions of the Parliament Acts 1911 and 1949, and by the authority of the same, as follows:—

PART 1   OFFENCES

1   Hunting wild mammals with dogs

A person commits an offence if he hunts a wild mammal with a dog, unless his hunting is exempt.

2   Exempt hunting

(1) Hunting is exempt if it is within a class specified in Schedule 1.

(2) The Secretary of State may by order amend Schedule 1 so as to vary a class of exempt hunting.

3   Hunting: assistance

(1) A person commits an offence if he knowingly permits land which belongs to him to be entered or used in the course of the commission of an offence under section 1.

(2) A person commits an offence if he knowingly permits a dog which belongs to him to be used in the course of the commission of an offence under section 1.

4   Hunting: defence

It is a defence for a person charged with an offence under section 1 in respect of hunting to show that he reasonably believed that the hunting was exempt.

5   *****

PART 2   ENFORCEMENT

6   Penalty

A person guilty of an offence under this Act shall be liable on summary conviction to a fine not exceeding level 5 on the standard scale.

7   . . .

*****

Constitutional Reform Act 2005

(2005, c. 4)

An Act to make provision for modifying the office of Lord Chancellor, and to make provision relating to the functions of that office; to establish a Supreme Court of the United Kingdom, and to abolish the appellate jurisdiction of the [Supreme Court]; to make provision about the jurisdiction of the Judicial Committee of the Privy Council and the judicial functions of the President of the Council; to make other provision about the judiciary, their appointment and discipline; and for connected purposes.   [24th March 2005]

Territorial extent: The United Kingdom

PART 1 THE RULE OF LAW

1 The rule of law

This Act does not adversely affect—

 (a) the existing constitutional principle of the rule of law, or

 (b) the Lord Chancellor's existing constitutional role in relation to that principle.

PART 2 ARRANGEMENTS TO MODIFY THE OFFICE OF LORD CHANCELLOR

Qualifications for office of Lord Chancellor

2 Lord Chancellor to be qualified by experience

 (1) A person may not be recommended for appointment as Lord Chancellor unless he appears to the Prime Minister to be qualified by experience.

 (2) The Prime Minister may take into account any of these—

 (a) experience as a Minister of the Crown;

 (b) experience as a member of either House of Parliament;

 (c) experience as a qualifying practitioner;

 (d) experience as a teacher of law in a university;

 (e) other experience that the Prime Minister considers relevant.

 (3) In this section 'qualifying practitioner' means any of these—

 (a) a person who has a Senior Courts qualification, within the meaning of section 71 of the Courts and Legal Services Act 1990 (c. 41);

 (b) an advocate in Scotland or a solicitor entitled to appear in the Court of Session and the High Court of Justiciary;

 (c) a member of the Bar of Northern Ireland or a solicitor of the Court of Judicature of Northern Ireland.

Continued judicial independence

3 Guarantee of continued judicial independence

 (1) The Lord Chancellor, other Ministers of the Crown and all with responsibility for matters relating to the judiciary or otherwise to the administration of justice must uphold the continued independence of the judiciary.

 (2) Subsection (1) does not impose any duty which it would be within the legislative competence of the Scottish Parliament to impose.

 (3) A person is not subject to the duty imposed by subsection (1) if he is subject to the duty imposed by section 1(1) of the Justice (Northern Ireland) Act 2002 (c. 26).

 (4) The following particular duties are imposed for the purpose of upholding that independence.

 (5) The Lord Chancellor and other Ministers of the Crown must not seek to influence particular judicial decisions through any special access to the judiciary.

 (6) The Lord Chancellor must have regard to—

 (a) the need to defend that independence;

 (b) the need for the judiciary to have the support necessary to enable them to exercise their functions;

(c) the need for the public interest in regard to matters relating to the judiciary or otherwise to the administration of justice to be properly represented in decisions affecting those matters.

(7) In this section 'the judiciary' includes the judiciary of any of the following—

(a) the Supreme Court;

(b) any other court established under the law of any part of the United Kingdom;

(c) any international court.

[(7A) In this section 'the judiciary' also includes every person who—

(a) holds an office listed in Schedule 14 or holds an office listed in subsection (7B), and

(b) but for this subsection would not be a member of the judiciary for the purposes of this section.

(7B) The offices are those of—

(a) Senior President of Tribunals;

(b) President of Employment Tribunals (Scotland);

(c) Vice President of Employment Tribunals (Scotland);

(d) member of a panel of chairmen of Employment Tribunals (Scotland);

(e) member of a panel of members of employment tribunals that is not a panel of chairmen;

(f) ...]

(8) *****

4 *****

Representations by senior judges

5 Representations to Parliament

(1) The chief justice of any part of the United Kingdom may lay before Parliament written representations on matters that appear to him to be matters of importance relating to the judiciary, or otherwise to the administration of justice, in that part of the United Kingdom.

(2)–(4) *****

(5) In this section 'chief justice' means—

(a) in relation to England and Wales or Northern Ireland, the Lord Chief Justice of that part of the United Kingdom;

(b) in relation to Scotland, the Lord President of the Court of Session.

6–18 *****

Functions subject to transfer, modification or abolition

19 Transfer, modification or abolition of functions by order

(1) The Lord Chancellor may by order make provision for any of these purposes—

(a) to transfer an existing function of the Lord Chancellor to another person;

(b) to direct that an existing function of the Lord Chancellor is to be exercisable concurrently with another person;

(c) to direct that an existing function of the Lord Chancellor exercisable concurrently with another person is to cease to be exercisable by the Lord Chancellor;

(d) to modify an existing function of the Lord Chancellor;

(e) to abolish an existing function of the Lord Chancellor.

(2)–(8) *****

20–22 *****

PART 3 THE SUPREME COURT

The Supreme Court

23 The Supreme Court

(1) There is to be a Supreme Court of the United Kingdom.

(2) The Court consists of 12 judges appointed by Her Majesty by letters patent.

(3) Her Majesty may from time to time by Order in Council amend subsection (2) so as to increase or further increase the number of judges of the Court.

(4) No recommendation may be made to Her Majesty in Council to make an Order under subsection (3) unless a draft of the Order has been laid before and approved by resolution of each House of Parliament.

(5) Her Majesty may by letters patent appoint one of the judges to be President and one to be Deputy President of the Court.

(6) The judges other than the President and Deputy President are to be styled 'Justices of the Supreme Court'.

(7) The Court is to be taken to be duly constituted despite any vacancy among the judges of the Court or in the office of President or Deputy President.

24   First members of the Court

On the commencement of section 23—

     (a) the persons who immediately before that commencement are Lords of Appeal in Ordinary become judges of the Supreme Court,

     (b) the person who immediately before that commencement is the senior Lord of Appeal in Ordinary becomes the President of the Court, and

     (c) the person who immediately before that commencement is the second senior Lord of Appeal in Ordinary becomes the Deputy President of the Court.

Appointment of judges

25   Qualification for appointment

(1) A person is not qualified to be appointed a judge of the Supreme Court unless he has (at any time)—

     (a)   held high judicial office for a period of at least 2 years,

     [(b) satisfied the judicial-appointment eligibility condition on a 15 year basis, or

     (c)   been a qualifying practitioner for a period of at least 15 years].

(2) A person is a qualifying practitioner for the purposes of this section at any time when—

     (a) ...

     (b) he is an advocate in Scotland or a solicitor entitled to appear in the Court of Session and the High Court of Justiciary, or

     (c) he is a member of the Bar of Northern Ireland or a solicitor of the Court of Judicature of Northern Ireland.

26   Selection of members of the Court

(1) This section applies to a recommendation for an appointment to one of the following offices—

     (a) judge of the Supreme Court;

     (b) President of the Court;

     (c) Deputy President of the Court.

(2) A recommendation may be made only by the Prime Minister.

(3) The Prime Minister—

     (a) must recommend any person whose name is notified to him under section 29;

     (b) may not recommend any other person.

(4) A person who is not a judge of the Court must be recommended for appointment as a judge if his name is notified to the Prime Minister for an appointment as President or Deputy President.

(5) If there is a vacancy in one of the offices mentioned in subsection (1), or it appears to him that there will soon be such a vacancy, the Lord Chancellor must convene a selection commission for the selection of a person to be recommended.

     (6)–(8) *****

27   Selection process

(1) The commission must—

    (a) determine the selection process to be applied,

    (b) apply the selection process, and

    (c) make a selection accordingly.

(2) As part of the selection process the commission must consult each of the following—

    (a) such of the senior judges as are not members of the commission and are not willing to be considered for selection;

    (b) the Lord Chancellor;

    (c) the First Minister in Scotland;

    (d) [the First Minister for Wales];

    (e) the Secretary of State for Northern Ireland.

(3) If for any part of the United Kingdom no judge of the courts of that part is to be consulted under subsection (2)(a), the commission must consult as part of the selection process the most senior judge of the courts of that part who is not a member of the commission and is not willing to be considered for selection.

(4) Subsections (5) to (10) apply to any selection under this section or section 31.

(5) Selection must be on merit.

(6) A person may be selected only if he meets the requirements of section 25.

(7) A person may not be selected if he is a member of the commission.

(8) In making selections for the appointment of judges of the Court the commission must ensure that between them the judges will have knowledge of, and experience of practice in, the law of each part of the United Kingdom.

(9) The commission must have regard to any guidance given by the Lord Chancellor as to matters to be taken into account (subject to any other provision of this Act) in making a selection.

(10) Any selection must be of one person only.

28   Report

(1) After complying with section 27 the commission must submit a report to the Lord Chancellor.

(2) The report must—

    (a) state who has been selected;

    (b) state the senior judges consulted under section 27(2)(a) and any judge consulted under section 27(3);

    (c) contain any other information required by the Lord Chancellor.

(3) The report must be in a form approved by the Lord Chancellor.

(4) After submitting the report the commission must provide any further information the Lord Chancellor may require.

(5) When he receives the report the Lord Chancellor must consult each of the following—

    (a) the senior judges consulted under section 27(2)(a);

    (b) any judge consulted under section 27(3);

    (c) the First Minister in Scotland;

    (d) [the First Minister for Wales];

    (e) the Secretary of State for Northern Ireland.

29   The Lord Chancellor's options

(1) This section refers to the following stages—

Stage 1: where a person has been selected under section 27

Stage 2: where a person has been selected following a rejection or reconsideration at stage 1

Stage 3: where a person has been selected following a rejection or reconsideration at stage 2.

(2) At stage 1 the Lord Chancellor must do one of the following—

    (a) notify the selection;

    (b) reject the selection;

(c) require the commission to reconsider the selection.

(3) At stage 2 the Lord Chancellor must do one of the following—

(a) notify the selection;

(b) reject the selection, but only if it was made following a reconsideration at stage 1;

(c) require the commission to reconsider the selection, but only if it was made following a rejection at stage 1.

(4) At stage 3 the Lord Chancellor must notify the selection, unless subsection (5) applies and he makes a notification under it.

(5) If a person whose selection the Lord Chancellor required to be reconsidered at stage 1 or 2 was not selected again at the next stage, the Lord Chancellor may at stage 3 notify that person's name to the Prime Minister.

(6) In this Part references to the Lord Chancellor notifying a selection are references to his notifying to the Prime Minister the name of the person selected.

30 Exercise of powers to reject or require reconsideration

(1) The power of the Lord Chancellor under section 29 to reject a selection at stage 1 or 2 is exercisable only on the grounds that, in the Lord Chancellor's opinion, the person selected is not suitable for the office concerned.

(2) The power of the Lord Chancellor under section 29 to require the commission to reconsider a selection at stage 1 or 2 is exercisable only on the grounds that, in the Lord Chancellor's opinion—

(a) there is not enough evidence that the person is suitable for the office concerned,

(b) there is evidence that the person is not the best candidate on merit, or

(c) there is not enough evidence that if the person were appointed the judges of the Court would between them have knowledge of, and experience of practice in, the law of each part of the United Kingdom.

(3) The Lord Chancellor must give the commission reasons in writing for rejecting or requiring reconsideration of a selection.

31 Selection following rejection or requirement to reconsider

(1) If under section 29 the Lord Chancellor rejects or requires reconsideration of a selection at stage 1 or 2, the commission must select a person in accordance with this section.

(2) If the Lord Chancellor rejects a selection, the commission—

(a) may not select the person rejected, and

(b) where the rejection is following reconsideration of a selection, may not select the person (if different) whose selection it reconsidered.

(3) If the Lord Chancellor requires a selection to be reconsidered, the commission—

(a) may select the same person or a different person, but

(b) where the requirement is following a rejection, may not select the person rejected.

(4) The commission must inform the Lord Chancellor of the person selected following a rejection or requirement to reconsider.

32 *****

33 Tenure

A judge of the Supreme Court holds that office during good behaviour, but may be removed from it on the address of both Houses of Parliament.

34–39 *****

Jurisdiction, relation to other courts etc.

40 Jurisdiction

(1) The Supreme Court is a superior court of record.

(2) An appeal lies to the Court from any order or judgment of the Court of Appeal in England and Wales in civil proceedings.

(3) An appeal lies to the Court from any order or judgment of a court in Scotland if an appeal lay from that court to the [Supreme Court] at or immediately before the commencement of this section.

(4), (5) *****

(6) An appeal under subsection (2) lies only with the permission of the Court of Appeal or the Supreme Court; but this is subject to provision under any other enactment restricting such an appeal.

41   Relation to other courts etc

(1) Nothing in this Part is to affect the distinctions between the separate legal systems of the parts of the United Kingdom.

(2) A decision of the Supreme Court on appeal from a court of any part of the United Kingdom, other than a decision on a devolution matter, is to be regarded as the decision of a court of that part of the United Kingdom.

(3) A decision of the Supreme Court on a devolution matter—

(a) is not binding on that Court when making such a decision;

(b) otherwise, is binding in all legal proceedings.

(4) In this section 'devolution matter' means—

(a) a question referred to the Supreme Court under [section . . . 99 or 112 of the Government of Wales Act 2006,] section 33 of the Scotland Act 1998 (c. 46) or section 11 of the Northern Ireland Act 1998 (c. 47);

(b) a devolution issue as defined in [Schedule 9 to the Government of Wales Act 2006], Schedule 6 to the Scotland Act 1998 or Schedule 10 to the Northern Ireland Act 1998.

Composition for proceedings

42   Composition

(1) The Supreme Court is duly constituted in any proceedings only if all of the following conditions are met—

(a) the Court consists of an uneven number of judges;

(b) the Court consists of at least three judges;

(c) more than half of those judges are permanent judges.

(2) Paragraphs (a) and (b) of subsection (1) are subject to any directions that in specified proceedings the Court is to consist of a specified number of judges that is both uneven and greater than three.

(3) Paragraph (b) of subsection (1) is subject to any directions that in specified descriptions of proceedings the Court is to consist of a specified minimum number of judges that is greater than three.

(4) This section is subject to section 43.

(5), (6) *****

43   Changes in composition

(1) This section applies if in any proceedings the Court ceases to be duly constituted in accordance with section 42, or in accordance with a direction under this section, because one or more members of the Court are unable to continue.

(2) The presiding judge may direct that the Court is still duly constituted in the proceedings.

(3) The presiding judge may give a direction under this section only if—

(a) the parties agree;

(b) the Court still consists of at least three judges (whether the number of judges is even or uneven);

(c) at least half of those judges are permanent judges.

(4) Subsections (2) and (3) are subject to directions given by the President of the Court.

(5), (6) *****

Practice and procedure

44 Specially qualified advisers

(1) If the Supreme Court thinks it expedient in any proceedings, it may hear and dispose of the proceedings wholly or partly with the assistance of one or more specially qualified advisers appointed by it.

(2) Any remuneration payable to such an adviser is to be determined by the Court unless agreed between the adviser and the parties to the proceedings.

(3) Any remuneration forms part of the costs of the proceedings.

45–60 *****

PART 4 JUDICIAL APPOINTMENTS AND DISCIPLINE

Chapter 1 Commission and Ombudsman

61 The Judicial Appointments Commission

(1) There is to be a body corporate called the Judicial Appointments Commission.

(2) Schedule 12 is about the Commission.

62 Judicial Appointments and Conduct Ombudsman

(1) There is to be a Judicial Appointments and Conduct Ombudsman.

(2) Schedule 13 is about the Ombudsman.

[**Note:** Schedules 12 and 13 are not reproduced.]

Chapter 2   Appointments

General provisions

63 Merit and good character

(1) Subsections (2) and (3) apply to any selection under this Part by the Commission or a selection panel ('the selecting body').

(2) Selection must be solely on merit.

(3) A person must not be selected unless the selecting body is satisfied that he is of good character.

64 Encouragement of diversity

(1) The Commission, in performing its functions under this Part, must have regard to the need to encourage diversity in the range of persons available for selection for appointments.

(2) This section is subject to section 63.

65 Guidance about procedures

(1) The Lord Chancellor may issue guidance about procedures for the performance by the Commission or a selection panel of its functions of—

(a) identifying persons willing to be considered for selection under this Part, and

(b) assessing such persons for the purposes of selection.

(2) The guidance may, among other things, relate to consultation or other steps in determining such procedures.

(3) The purposes for which guidance may be issued under this section include the encouragement of diversity in the range of persons available for selection.

(4) The Commission and any selection panel must have regard to the guidance in matters to which it relates.

66–98 *****

Complaints and references

99 Complaints: interpretation

(1) This section applies for the purposes of this Part.

(2) A Commission complaint is a complaint by a qualifying complainant of maladministration by the Commission or a committee of the Commission.

(3) A departmental complaint is a complaint by a qualifying complainant of maladministration by the Lord Chancellor or his department in connection with any of the following—

(a) selection under this Part;

(b) recommendation for or appointment to an office listed in Schedule 14.

(4) A qualifying complainant is a complainant who claims to have been adversely affected, as an applicant for selection or as a person selected under this Part, by the maladministration complained of.

100 Complaints to the Commission or the Lord Chancellor

(1) The Commission must make arrangements for investigating any Commission complaint made to it.

(2) The Lord Chancellor must make arrangements for investigating any departmental complaint made to him.

(3) Arrangements under this section need not apply to a complaint made more than 28 days after the matter complained of.

101 Complaints to the Ombudsman

(1) Subsections (2) and (3) apply to a complaint which the complainant—

(a) has made to the Commission or the Lord Chancellor in accordance with arrangements under section 100, and

(b) makes to the Ombudsman not more than 28 days after being notified of the Commission's or Lord Chancellor's decision on the complaint.

(2) If the Ombudsman considers that investigation of the complaint is not necessary, he must inform the complainant.

(3) Otherwise he must investigate the complaint.

(4) The Ombudsman may investigate a complaint which the complainant—

(a) has made to the Commission or the Lord Chancellor in accordance with arrangements under section 100, and

(b) makes to the Ombudsman at any time.

(5) The Ombudsman may investigate a transferred complaint made to him, and no such complaint may be made under the Judicial Appointments Order after the commencement of this section.

(6) The Judicial Appointments Order is the Judicial Appointments Order in Council 2001, which sets out the functions of Her Majesty's Commissioners for Judicial Appointments.

(7) A transferred complaint is a complaint that lay to those Commissioners (whether or not it was made to them) in respect of the application of appointment procedures before the commencement of this section, but not a complaint that those Commissioners had declined to investigate or on which they had concluded their investigation.

(8) Any complaint to the Ombudsman under this section must be in a form approved by him.

102 Report and recommendations

(1) The Ombudsman must prepare a report on any complaint he has investigated under section 101.

(2) The report must state—

(a) what findings the Ombudsman has made;

(b) whether he considers the complaint should be upheld in whole or part;

(c) if he does, what if any action he recommends should be taken by the Commission or the Lord Chancellor as a result of the complaint.

(3) The recommendations that may be made under subsection (2)(c) include recommendations for the payment of compensation.

(4) Such a recommendation must relate to loss which appears to the Ombudsman to have been suffered by the complainant as a result of maladministration and not as a result of any failure to be appointed to an office to which the complaint related.

103 *****

104 References by the Lord Chancellor

(1) If the Lord Chancellor refers to the Ombudsman any matter relating to the procedures of the Commission or a committee of the Commission, the Ombudsman must investigate it.

(2) The matter may relate to such procedures generally or in a particular case.

(3) The Ombudsman must report to the Lord Chancellor on any investigation under this section.

(4) The report must state—

(a) what findings the Ombudsman has made;

(b) what if any action he recommends should be taken by any person in relation to the matter.

(5) The report must be signed by the Ombudsman.

105 Information

The Commission and the Lord Chancellor must provide the Ombudsman with such information as he may reasonably require relating to the subject matter of any investigation by him under section 101 or 104.

106, 107 *****

Chapter 3   Discipline

Disciplinary powers

108 Disciplinary powers

(1) Any power of the Lord Chancellor to remove a person from an office listed in Schedule 14 is exercisable only after the Lord Chancellor has complied with prescribed procedures (as well as any other requirements to which the power is subject).

(2) The Lord Chief Justice may exercise any of the following powers but only with the agreement of the Lord Chancellor and only after complying with prescribed procedures.

(3) The Lord Chief Justice may give a judicial office holder formal advice, or a formal warning or reprimand, for disciplinary purposes (but this section does not restrict what he may do informally or for other purposes or where any advice or warning is not addressed to a particular office holder).

(4) He may suspend a person from a judicial office for any period during which any of the following applies—

(a) the person is subject to criminal proceedings;

(b) the person is serving a sentence imposed in criminal proceedings;

(c) the person has been convicted of an offence and is subject to prescribed procedures in relation to the conduct constituting the offence.

(5) He may suspend a person from a judicial office for any period if—

(a) the person has been convicted of a criminal offence,

(b) it has been determined under prescribed procedures that the person should not be removed from office, and

(c) it appears to the Lord Chief Justice with the agreement of the Lord Chancellor that the suspension is necessary for maintaining confidence in the judiciary.

(6) He may suspend a person from office as a senior judge for any period during which the person is subject to proceedings for an Address.

(7) He may suspend the holder of an office listed in Schedule 14 for any period during which the person—

(a) is under investigation for an offence, or

(b) is subject to prescribed procedures.

(8) While a person is suspended under this section from any office he may not perform any of the functions of the office (but his other rights as holder of the office are not affected).

[**Note:** Schedule 14 is not reproduced.]

109 *****

Applications for review and references

110   Applications to the Ombudsman

(1) This section applies if an interested party makes an application to the Ombudsman for the review of the exercise by any person of a regulated disciplinary function, on the grounds that there has been—

(a) a failure to comply with prescribed procedures, or

(b) some other maladministration.

(2) The Ombudsman must carry out a review if the following three conditions are met.

(3) The first condition is that the Ombudsman considers that a review is necessary.

(4) The second condition is that—

(a) the application is made within the permitted period,

(b) the application is made within such longer period as the Ombudsman considers appropriate in the circumstances, or

(c) the application is made on grounds alleging undue delay and the Ombudsman considers that the application has been made within a reasonable time.

(5) The third condition is that the application is made in a form approved by the Ombudsman.

(6) But the Ombudsman may not review the merits of a decision made by any person.

(7) If any of the conditions in subsections (3) to (5) is not met, or if the grounds of the application relate only to the merits of a decision, the Ombudsman—

(a) may not carry out a review, and

(b) must inform the applicant accordingly.

(8)–(10) *****

111–114 *****

General

115   Regulations about procedures

The Lord Chief Justice may, with the agreement of the Lord Chancellor, make regulations providing for the procedures that are to be followed in—

(a) the investigation and determination of allegations by any person of misconduct by judicial office holders;

(b) reviews and investigations (including the making of applications or references) under sections 110 to 112.

116–136 *****

*****

Serious Organised Crime and Police Act 2005

(2005, c. 15)

An Act to provide for the establishment and functions of the Serious Organised Crime Agency; to make provision about investigations, prosecutions, offenders and witnesses in criminal proceedings and the protection of persons involved in investigations or proceedings; to provide for the implementation of certain international obligations relating to criminal matters; to amend the proceeds of Crime Act 2002; to make further provision for combating crime and disorder, including new provision about powers of arrest and search warrants and about parental compensation orders; to make further provision about the police and policing and persons supporting the police; to make provision for protecting certain organisations from interference with their activities; to make provision about criminal records; to provide for the Private Security Industry Act 2001 to extend to Scotland; and for connected purposes.   [7th April 2005]

Territorial extent: See s. 179 (reproduced below)

PART 1 THE SERIOUS ORGANISED CRIME AGENCY

Chapter 1 SOCA: establishment and activities

Establishment of SOCA

1   Establishment of Serious Organised Crime Agency

(1) There shall be a body corporate to be known as the Serious Organised Crime Agency ('SOCA').

(2) *******

(3) Each of the following bodies shall cease to exist on such date as the Secretary of State appoints by order—

(a) the National Criminal Intelligence Service and its Service Authority, and

(b) the National Crime Squad and its Service Authority.

Functions

2   Functions of SOCA as to serious organised crime

(1) SOCA has the functions of—

(a) preventing and detecting serious organised crime, and

(b) contributing to the reduction of such crime in other ways and to the mitigation of its consequences.

(2) SOCA's functions under subsection (1) are exercisable subject to subsections (3) to (5) (but subsection (3) does not apply to Scotland).

(3) If, in exercising its function under subsection (1)(a), SOCA becomes aware of conduct appearing to SOCA to involve serious or complex fraud, SOCA may thereafter exercise that function in relation to the fraud in question only—

(a) with the agreement of the Director, or an authorised officer, of the Serious Fraud Office, or

(b) if the Serious Fraud Office declines to act in relation to it.

(4) If, in exercising its function under subsection (1)(a), SOCA becomes aware of conduct appearing to SOCA to involve revenue fraud, SOCA may thereafter exercise that function in relation to the fraud in question only with the agreement of the Commissioners.

(5) Before exercising its function under subsection (1)(b) in any way in relation to revenue fraud, SOCA must consult the Commissioners.

(6) The issue of whether SOCA's function under subsection (1)(a) continued to be exercisable in any circumstances within subsection (3) or (4) may not be raised in any criminal proceedings.

(7) In this section 'revenue fraud' includes fraud relating to taxes, duties and national insurance contributions.

(8) In this Chapter 'the Commissioners' means the Commissioners for Her Majesty's Revenue and Customs.

[2A   Functions of SOCA as to the recovery of assets]

[SOCA has the functions conferred on it (whether directly or through its staff) by the Proceeds of Crime Act 2002 (c. 29) (functions relating to the recovery of assets).]

3 Functions of SOCA as to information relating to crime

(1) SOCA has the function of gathering, storing, analysing and disseminating information relevant to—

(a) the prevention, detection, investigation or prosecution of offences, . . .

(b) the reduction of crime in other ways or the mitigation of its consequences [; or

(c) exploitation proceeds investigations (within the meaning of section 341(5) of the Proceeds of Crime Act 2002) or exploitation proceeds orders within the meaning of Part 7 of the Coroners and Justice Act 2009 (or applications for such orders)].

(2) SOCA may disseminate such information to—

(a) police forces within subsection (3),

(b) special police forces,

(c) law enforcement agencies, or

(d) such other persons as it considers appropriate in connection with any of the matters mentioned in subsection [(1)(a), (b) or (c)].

(3)–(5) *****

4 *****

General powers

5 SOCA's general powers

(1) SOCA has the general powers conferred by this section.

(2) SOCA may—

(a) institute criminal proceedings in England and Wales or Northern Ireland;

(b) at the request of the chief officer of a police force within section 3(3) or of a special police force, act in support of any activities of that force;

(c) at the request of any law enforcement agency, act in support of any activities of that agency;

(d) enter into other arrangements for co-operating with bodies or persons (in the United Kingdom or elsewhere) which it considers appropriate in connection with the exercise of any of SOCA's functions under section 2 or 3 [or mentioned in section 2A] or any activities within subsection (3).

(3) Despite the references to serious organised crime in section 2(1), SOCA may carry on activities in relation to other crime if they are carried on for the purposes of any of the functions conferred on SOCA by section 2 or 3 [or mentioned in section 2A].

(4)–(7) *****

6–59 *****

PART 2 INVESTIGATIONS, PROSECUTIONS, PROCEEDINGS AND PROCEEDS OF CRIME

Chapter 1 Investigatory powers of DPP, etc.

Introductory

60 Investigatory powers of DPP etc.

(1) This Chapter confers powers on—

(a) the Director of Public Prosecutions,

(b) the Director of Revenue and Customs Prosecutions,

(c) the Lord Advocate, [and

(d) the Director of Public Prosecutions for Northern Ireland,]

in relation to the giving of disclosure notices in connection with the investigation of offences to which this Chapter applies [or in connection with a terrorist investigation].

(2)–(6) *****

[(7) In this Chapter 'terrorist investigation' means an investigation of—

    (a) the commission, preparation or instigation of acts of terrorism,

    (b) any act or omission which appears to have been for the purposes of terrorism and which consists in or involves the commission, preparation or instigation of an offence, or

    (c) the commission, preparation or instigation of an offence under the Terrorism Act 2000 (c 11) or under Part 1 of the Terrorism Act 2006 other than an offence under section 1 or 2 of that Act.]

61 Offences to which this Chapter applies

(1) This Chapter applies to the following offences—

    (a)   any offence listed in Schedule 2 to the Proceeds of Crime Act 2002 (c 29) (lifestyle offences: England and Wales);

    (b)   any offence listed in Schedule 4 to that Act (lifestyle offences: Scotland);

    [(ba)   any offence listed in Schedule 5 to that Act (lifestyle offences: Northern Ireland);]

    (c)   any offence under sections 15 to 18 of the Terrorism Act 2000 (c 11) (offences relating to fund-raising, money laundering etc.);

    (d)   any offence under section 170 of the Customs and Excise Management Act 1979 (c 2) (fraudulent evasion of duty) or section 72 of the Value Added Tax Act 1994 (c 23) (offences relating to VAT) which is a qualifying offence;

    (e)   any offence under section 17 of the Theft Act 1968 (c 60) [or section 17 of the Theft Act (Northern Ireland) 1969] (false accounting), or any offence at common law of cheating in relation to the public revenue, which is a qualifying offence;

    (f)   any offence under section 1 of the Criminal Attempts Act 1981 (c 47) [or Article 3 of the Criminal Attempts and Conspiracy (Northern Ireland) Order 1983], or in Scotland at common law, of attempting to commit any offence in paragraph (c) or any offence in paragraph (d) or (e) which is a qualifying offence;

    (g)   any offence under section 1 of the Criminal Law Act 1977 (c 45) [or Article 9 of the Criminal Attempts and Conspiracy (Northern Ireland) Order 1983], or in Scotland at common law, of conspiracy to commit any offence in paragraph (c) or any offence in paragraph (d) or (e) which is a qualifying offence;

    [(h)   any offence under the Bribery Act 2010].

(2) For the purposes of subsection (1) an offence in paragraph (d) or (e) of that subsection is a qualifying offence if the Investigating Authority certifies that in his opinion—

    (a) in the case of an offence in paragraph (d) or an offence of cheating the public revenue, the offence involved or would have involved a loss, or potential loss, to the public revenue of an amount not less than £5,000;

    (b) in the case of an offence under section 17 of the Theft Act 1968 (c 60) [or section 17 of the Theft Act (Northern Ireland) 1969], the offence involved or would have involved a loss or gain, or potential loss or gain, of an amount not less than £5,000.

(3)–(5) *****

Disclosure notices

62 Disclosure notices

(1) If it appears to the Investigating Authority—

    (a) that there are reasonable grounds for suspecting that an offence to which this Chapter applies has been committed,

    (b) that any person has information (whether or not contained in a document) which relates to a matter relevant to the investigation of that offence, and

    (c) that there are reasonable grounds for believing that information which may be provided by that person in compliance with a disclosure notice is likely to be of substantial value (whether or not by itself) to that investigation, he may give, or authorise an appropriate person to give, a disclosure notice to that person.

    (1A) *****

    (2) In this Chapter 'appropriate person' means—

        (a) a constable,

        (b) a member of the staff of SOCA who is for the time being designated under section 43, or

        (c) an officer of Revenue and Customs.

[But in the application of this Chapter to Northern Ireland, this subsection has effect as if paragraph (b) were omitted.]

    (3) In this Chapter 'disclosure notice' means a notice in writing requiring the person to whom it is given to do all or any of the following things in accordance with the specified requirements, namely—

        (a) answer questions with respect to any matter relevant to the investigation;

        (b) provide information with respect to any such matter as is specified in the notice;

        (c) produce such documents, or documents of such descriptions, relevant to the investigation as are specified in the notice.

    (4)–(6) *****

63   Production of documents

    (1) This section applies where a disclosure notice has been given under section 62.

    (2) An authorised person may—

        (a) take copies of or extracts from any documents produced in compliance with the notice, and

        (b) require the person producing them to provide an explanation of any of them.

    (3) Documents so produced may be retained for so long as the Investigating Authority considers that it is necessary to retain them (rather than copies of them) in connection with the investigation for the purposes of which the disclosure notice was given.

    (4)–(7) *****

64   Restrictions on requiring information etc.

    (1) A person may not be required under section 62 or 63—

        (a) to answer any privileged question,

        (b) to provide any privileged information, or

        (c) to produce any privileged document,

except that a lawyer may be required to provide the name and address of a client of his.

    (2) A 'privileged question' is a question which the person would be entitled to refuse to answer on grounds of legal professional privilege in proceedings in the High Court.

    (3) 'Privileged information' is information which the person would be entitled to refuse to provide on grounds of legal professional privilege in such proceedings.

    (4) A 'privileged document' is a document which the person would be entitled to refuse to produce on grounds of legal professional privilege in such proceedings.

    (5) A person may not be required under section 62 to produce any excluded material (as defined by section 11 of the Police and Criminal Evidence Act 1984 (c 60) [or, in relation to Northern Ireland, Article 13 of the Police and Criminal Evidence (Northern Ireland) Order 1989]).

    (6), (7) *****

    (8) A person may not be required under section 62 or 63 to disclose any information or produce any document in respect of which he owes an obligation of confidence by virtue of carrying on any banking business, unless—

        (a) the person to whom the obligation of confidence is owed consents to the disclosure or production, or

        (b) the requirement is made by, or in accordance with a specific authorisation given by, the Investigating Authority.

    (9) Subject to the preceding provisions, any requirement under section 62 or 63 has effect despite any restriction on disclosure (however imposed).

65 *****

Enforcement

66   Power to enter and seize documents

(1) A justice of the peace may issue a warrant under this section if, on an information on oath laid by the Investigating Authority, he is satisfied—

- (a) that any of the conditions mentioned in subsection (2) is met in relation to any documents of a description specified in the information, and
- (b) that the documents are on premises so specified.

(2) The conditions are—

- (a) that a person has been required by a disclosure notice to produce the documents but has not done so;
- (b) that it is not practicable to give a disclosure notice requiring their production;
- (c) that giving such a notice might seriously prejudice the investigation of an offence to which this Chapter applies.

(3) A warrant under this section is a warrant authorising an appropriate person named in it—

- (a) to enter and search the premises, using such force as is reasonably necessary;
- (b) to take possession of any documents appearing to be documents of a description specified in the information, or to take any other steps which appear to be necessary for preserving, or preventing interference with, any such documents;
- (c) in the case of any such documents consisting of information recorded otherwise than in legible form, to take possession of any computer disk or other electronic storage device which appears to contain the information in question, or to take any other steps which appear to be necessary for preserving, or preventing interference with, that information;
- (d) to take copies of or extracts from any documents or information falling within paragraph (b) or (c);
- (e) to require any person on the premises to provide an explanation of any such documents or information or to state where any such documents or information may be found;
- (f) to require any such person to give the appropriate person such assistance as he may reasonably require for the taking of copies or extracts as mentioned in paragraph (d).

(4) A person executing a warrant under this section may take other persons with him, if it appears to him to be necessary to do so.

(5) A warrant under this section must, if so required, be produced for inspection by the owner or occupier of the premises or anyone acting on his behalf.

(6) If the premises are unoccupied or the occupier is temporarily absent, a person entering the premises under the authority of a warrant under this section must leave the premises as effectively secured against trespassers as he found them.

(7)–(11) *****

67–70   *****

Chapter 2 Offenders assisting investigations and prosecutions

71   Assistance by offender: immunity from prosecution

(1) If a specified prosecutor thinks that for the purposes of the investigation or prosecution of [an indictable offence or an offence triable either way] it is appropriate to offer any person immunity from prosecution [for any offence] he may give the person a written notice under this subsection (an "immunity notice").

(2) If a person is given an immunity notice, no proceedings for an offence of a description specified in the notice may be brought against that person in England and Wales or Northern Ireland except in circumstances specified in the notice.

(3) An immunity notice ceases to have effect in relation to the person to whom it is given if the person fails to comply with any conditions specified in the notice.

(4) Each of the following is a specified prosecutor—

    (a) the Director of Public Prosecutions;

    (b) the Director of Revenue and Customs Prosecutions;

    (c) the Director of the Serious Fraud Office;

    (d) the Director of Public Prosecutions for Northern Ireland;

   [(da) the Financial Services Authority;

   (db) the Secretary of State for Business, Innovation and Skills, acting personally;]

    (e) a prosecutor designated for the purposes of this section by a prosecutor mentioned in paragraphs (a) to [(db)].

(5)–(7) *****

72 Assistance by offender: undertakings as to use of evidence

(1) If a specified prosecutor thinks that for the purposes of the investigation or prosecution of [an indictable offence or an offence triable either way] it is appropriate to offer any person an undertaking that information of any description will not be used against the person in any proceedings to which this section applies he may give the person a written notice under this subsection (a 'restricted use undertaking').

(2) This section applies to—

    (a) [any] criminal proceedings;

    (b) proceedings under Part 5 of the Proceeds of Crime Act 2002 (c. 29).

(3) If a person is given a restricted use undertaking the information described in the undertaking must not be used against that person in any proceedings to which this section applies brought in England and Wales or Northern Ireland except in the circumstances specified in the undertaking.

(4) A restricted use undertaking ceases to have effect in relation to the person to whom it is given if the person fails to comply with any conditions specified in the undertaking.

(5)–(7) *****

73 Assistance by defendant: reduction in sentence

(1) This section applies if a defendant—

    (a) following a plea of guilty is either convicted of an offence in proceedings in the Crown Court or is committed to the Crown Court for sentence, and

    (b) has, pursuant to a written agreement made with a specified prosecutor, assisted or offered to assist the investigator or prosecutor in relation to that or any other offence.

(2) In determining what sentence to pass on the defendant the court may take into account the extent and nature of the assistance given or offered.

(3) If the court passes a sentence which is less than it would have passed but for the assistance given or offered, it must state in open court—

    (a) that it has passed a lesser sentence than it would otherwise have passed, and

    (b) what the greater sentence would have been.

(4) Subsection (3) does not apply if the court thinks that it would not be in the public interest to disclose that the sentence has been discounted; but in such a case the court must give written notice of the matters specified in paragraphs (a) and (b) of subsection (3) to both the prosecutor and the defendant.

(5)–(10) *****

74 Assistance by defendant: review of sentence

(1) This section applies if—

    (a) the Crown Court has passed a sentence on a person in respect of an offence, and

    (b) the person falls within subsection (2).

(2) A person falls within this subsection if—

(a) he receives a discounted sentence in consequence of his having offered in pursuance of a written agreement to give assistance to the prosecutor or investigator of an offence but he knowingly fails to any extent to give assistance in accordance with the agreement;

(b) he receives a discounted sentence in consequence of his having offered in pursuance of a written agreement to give assistance to the prosecutor or investigator of an offence and, having given the assistance in accordance with the agreement, in pursuance of another written agreement gives or offers to give further assistance;

(c) he receives a sentence which is not discounted but in pursuance of a written agreement he subsequently gives or offers to give assistance to the prosecutor or investigator of an offence.

(3) A specified prosecutor may at any time refer the case back to the court by which the sentence was passed if—

(a) the person is still serving his sentence, and

(b) the specified prosecutor thinks it is in the interests of justice to do so.

(4) A case so referred must, if possible, be heard by the judge who passed the sentence to which the referral relates.

(5) If the court is satisfied that a person who falls within subsection (2)(a) knowingly failed to give the assistance it may substitute for the sentence to which the referral relates such greater sentence (not exceeding that which it would have passed but for the agreement to give assistance) as it thinks appropriate.

(6) In a case of a person who falls within subsection (2)(b) or (c) the court may—

(a) take into account the extent and nature of the assistance given or offered;

(b) substitute for the sentence to which the referral relates such lesser sentence as it thinks appropriate.

(7) Any part of the sentence to which the referral relates which the person has already served must be taken into account in determining when a greater or lesser sentence imposed by subsection (5) or (6) has been served.

(8) A person in respect of whom a reference is made under this section and the specified prosecutor may with the leave of the Court of Appeal appeal to the Court of Appeal against the decision of the Crown Court.

(9)–(15) *****

75–127   *****

Trespass on designated site

128   Offence of trespassing on designated site

(1) A person commits an offence if he enters, or is on, any [protected] site in England and Wales or Northern Ireland as a trespasser.

[(1A) In this section 'protected site' means—

(a) a nuclear site; or

(b) a designated site.]

(1B), (1C) *****

(2) A 'designated site' means a site—

(a) specified or described (in any way) in an order made by the Secretary of State, and

(b) designated for the purposes of this section by the order.

(3) The Secretary of State may only designate a site for the purposes of this section if—

(a) it is comprised in Crown land; or

(b) it is comprised in land belonging to Her Majesty in Her private capacity or to the immediate heir to the Throne in his private capacity; or

(c) it appears to the Secretary of State that it is appropriate to designate the site in the interests of national security.

(4) It is a defence for a person charged with an offence under this section to prove that he did not know, and had no reasonable cause to suspect, that the site in relation to which the offence is alleged to have been committed was a [protected] site.

(5) A person guilty of an offence under this section is liable on summary conviction—

(a) to imprisonment for a term not exceeding 51 weeks, or

(b) to a fine not exceeding level 5 on the standard scale, or to both.

(6)–(10) *****

129 Corresponding Scottish offence

(1) A person commits an offence if he enters, or is on, any [protected] Scottish site without lawful authority.

[(1A) In this section 'protected Scottish site' means—

(a) a nuclear site in Scotland; or

(b) a designated Scottish site.]

(1B), (1C) *****

(2) A 'designated Scottish site' means a site in Scotland—

(a) specified or described (in any way) in an order made by the Secretary of State, and

(b) designated for the purposes of this section by the order.

(3) The Secretary of State may only designate a site for the purposes of this section if it appears to him that it is appropriate to designate the site in the interests of national security.

(4)–(7) *****

130–144   *****

PART 5 MISCELLANEOUS

Protection of activities of certain organisations

145 Interference with contractual relationships so as to harm animal research organisation

(1) A person (A) commits an offence if, with the intention of harming an animal research organisation, he—

(a) does a relevant act, or

(b) threatens that he or somebody else will do a relevant act,

in circumstances in which that act or threat is intended or likely to cause a second person (B) to take any of the steps in subsection (2).

(2) The steps are—

(a) not to perform any contractual obligation owed by B to a third person (C) (whether or not such non-performance amounts to a breach of contract);

(b) to terminate any contract B has with C;

(c) not to enter into a contract with C.

(3) For the purposes of this section, a 'relevant act' is—

(a) an act amounting to a criminal offence, or

(b) a tortious act causing B to suffer loss or damage of any description;

but paragraph (b) does not include an act which is actionable on the ground only that it induces another person to break a contract with B.

(4) For the purposes of this section, 'contract' includes any other arrangement (and 'contractual' is to be read accordingly).

(5) For the purposes of this section, to 'harm' an animal research organisation means—

(a) to cause the organisation to suffer loss or damage of any description, or

(b) to prevent or hinder the carrying out by the organisation of any of its activities.

(6) This section does not apply to any act done wholly or mainly in contemplation or furtherance of a trade dispute.

(7) *****

146   Intimidation of persons connected with animal research organisation

(1) A person (A) commits an offence if, with the intention of causing a second person (B) to abstain from doing something which B is entitled to do (or to do something which B is entitled to abstain from doing)—

    (a) A threatens B that A or somebody else will do a relevant act, and

    (b) A does so wholly or mainly because B is a person falling within subsection (2).

(2) A person falls within this subsection if he is—

    (a) an employee or officer of an animal research organisation;

    (b) a student at an educational establishment that is an animal research organisation;

    (c) a lessor or licensor of any premises occupied by an animal research organisation;

    (d) a person with a financial interest in, or who provides financial assistance to, an animal research organisation;

    (e) a customer or supplier of an animal research organisation;

    (f) a person who is contemplating becoming someone within paragraph (c), (d) or (e);

    (g) a person who is, or is contemplating becoming, a customer or supplier of someone within paragraph (c), (d), (e) or (f);

    (h) an employee or officer of someone within paragraph (c), (d), (e), (f) or (g);

    (i) a person with a financial interest in, or who provides financial assistance to, someone within paragraph (c), (d), (e), (f) or (g);

    (j) a spouse, civil partner, friend or relative of, or a person who is known personally to, someone within any of paragraphs (a) to (i);

    (k) a person who is, or is contemplating becoming, a customer or supplier of someone (l) within paragraph (a), (b), (h), (i) or (j); or

    (l) an employer of someone within paragraph (j).

(3), (4) *****

(5) For the purposes of this section, a 'relevant act' is—

    (a) an act amounting to a criminal offence, or

    (b) a tortious act causing B or another person to suffer loss or damage of any description.

(6) *****

(7) This section does not apply to any act done wholly or mainly in contemplation or furtherance of a trade dispute.

(8) *****

147   Penalty for offences under sections 145 and 146

(1) A person guilty of an offence under section 145 or 146 is liable—

    (a) on summary conviction, to imprisonment for a term not exceeding 12 months or to a fine not exceeding the statutory maximum, or to both;

    (b) on conviction on indictment, to imprisonment for a term not exceeding five years or to a fine, or to both.

(2) No proceedings for an offence under either of those sections may be instituted except by or with the consent of the Director of Public Prosecutions.

148   *****

149   Extension of sections 145 to 147

(1) The Secretary of State may by order provide for sections 145, 146 and 147 to apply in relation to persons or organisations of a description specified in the order as they apply in relation to animal research organisations.

(2) The Secretary of State may, however, only make an order under this section if satisfied that a series of acts has taken place and—

(a) that those acts were directed at persons or organisations of the description specified in the order or at persons having a connection with them, and

(b) that, if those persons or organisations had been animal research organisations, those acts would have constituted offences under section 145 or 146.

(3) In this section 'organisation' and 'animal research organisation' have the meanings given by section 148.

150–178 *****

179   Short title and extent

(1) This Act may be cited as the Serious Organised Crime and Police Act 2005.

(2) Subject to the following provisions, this Act extends to England and Wales only.

(3) The following extend also to Scotland—

(a) sections 1 to 54, [and 56 to] 58,

(b) sections 60 to 68, 70, 79 to 96, 98 to 106, 107(1) and (4) and 108,

(c) section 123,

(d) section 131,

(e) sections 150 to 153, 156(6), 158, 163(1) and (2), 164, 165(1) and (2), 166(2), 167 and 171(1),

(f) sections 172, 173, 176 to 178 and this section,

(g) Schedules 1, 3, 5 and 15.

(4) The following extend to Scotland only—

(a) section 77 and 107(3),

(b) sections 129 and 130(3),

(c) sections 156(1) to (5), 166(1) and 171(2).

(5) The following extend also to Northern Ireland—

(a) sections 1 to 54 [and 56 to] 58,

(b) sections [60] to 75, 79 to 106, 107(1), (2) and (4) and 108,

(c) Section 123(1),

(d) sections 128, 131 and 144,

(e)–(g) *****

(6)–(10) *****

*****

European Union (Accessions) Act 2006

(2006, c. 2)

An Act to make provision consequential on the Treaty concerning the accession of the Republic of Bulgaria and Romania to the European Union, signed at Luxembourg on 25th April 2005; and to make provision in relation to the entitlement of nationals of those states to enter or reside in the United Kingdom as workers.   [16th February 2006]

Territorial extent: The United Kingdom

1 *****

2   Freedom of movement for workers

(1) The Secretary of State may by regulations make provision concerning—

(a) the entitlement of a national of an acceding State to enter or reside in the United Kingdom as a worker;

(b) any matter ancillary to that entitlement.

(2) The provision that may be made by regulations under this section includes provision which applies (with or without modification) a specified enactment relating to—

     (a) the entitlement of a national of an EEA State to enter or reside in the United Kingdom as a worker, or

     (b) any matter ancillary to that entitlement,

to a national of an acceding State as it applies in relation to a national of an EEA State.

  (3) Regulations under this section may (in particular) include provision the effect of which is—

     (a) to make it a requirement that a national of an acceding State working in the United Kingdom be registered in accordance with the regulations;

     (b) to make it a requirement that a fee is payable in respect of applications or registration under the regulations;

     (c) to make it an offence for an employer to employ a national of an acceding State unless his employment of that person is authorised by the regulations.

  (4)–(6) *****

  (7) No regulations may be made containing (with or without other provision) any provision the power to make which is conferred by this section unless—

     (a) a draft of the regulations has been laid before Parliament and approved by a resolution of each House; or

     (b) the regulations contain a declaration by the Secretary of State that the urgency of the matter makes it necessary for the regulations to be made without that approval.

  (8) Regulations under this section that contain such a declaration—

     (a) must be laid before Parliament after being made; and

     (b) if not approved by a resolution of each House before the end of 40 days beginning with the day on which they were made, shall cease to have effect at the end of that period;

but, where regulations cease to have effect in accordance with this subsection, that does not affect anything previously done under them, or prevent the making of new regulations to the same or similar effect.

  (9), (10) *****

*****

Equality Act 2006

(2006, c. 3)

An Act to make provision for the establishment of the Commission for Equality and Human Rights; to dissolve the Equal Opportunities Commission, the Commission for Racial Equality and the Disability Rights Commission; to make provision about discrimination on grounds of religion or belief; to enable provision to be made about discrimination on grounds of sexual orientation; to impose duties relating to sex discrimination on persons performing public functions; to amend the Disability Discrimination Act 1995; and for connected purposes.   [16th February 2006]

Territorial Extent: England and Wales, Scotland

PART 1 THE COMMISSION FOR EQUALITY AND HUMAN RIGHTS

The Commission

1 Establishment

There shall be a body corporate known as the Commission for Equality and Human Rights.

2 *****

3 General duty

The Commission shall exercise its functions under this Part with a view to encouraging and supporting the development of a society in which—

(a) people's ability to achieve their potential is not limited by prejudice or discrimination,

(b) there is respect for and protection of each individual's human rights,

(c) there is respect for the dignity and worth of each individual,

(d) each individual has an equal opportunity to participate in society, and

(e) there is mutual respect between groups based on understanding and valuing of diversity and on shared respect for equality and human rights.

4–7   *****

8   Equality and diversity

(1) The Commission shall, by exercising the powers conferred by this Part—

(a) promote understanding of the importance of equality and diversity,

(b) encourage good practice in relation to equality and diversity,

(c) promote equality of opportunity,

(d) promote awareness and understanding of rights under the [Equality Act 2010],

(e) enforce [that Act],

(f) work towards the elimination of unlawful discrimination, and

(g) work towards the elimination of unlawful harassment.

(2) In subsection (1)—

'diversity' means the fact that individuals are different,

'equality' means equality between individuals, and

'unlawful' is to be construed in accordance with section 34.

(3) In promoting equality of opportunity between disabled persons and others, the Commission may, in particular, promote the favourable treatment of disabled persons.

(4) In this Part 'disabled person' means a person who—

(a) is a disabled person within the meaning of the [Equality Act 2010], or

(b) has been a disabled person within that meaning (whether or not at a time when that Act had effect).

9   Human rights

(1) The Commission shall, by exercising the powers conferred by this Part—

(a) promote understanding of the importance of human rights,

(b) encourage good practice in relation to human rights,

(c) promote awareness, understanding and protection of human rights, and

(d) encourage public authorities to comply with section 6 of the Human Rights Act 1998 (c 42) (compliance with Convention rights).

(2) In this Part 'human rights' means—

(a) the Convention rights within the meaning given by section 1 of the Human Rights Act 1998, and

(b) other human rights.

(3) In determining what action to take in pursuance of this section the Commission shall have particular regard to the importance of exercising the powers conferred by this Part in relation to the Convention rights.

(4) In fulfilling a duty under section 8 or 10 the Commission shall take account of any relevant human rights.

(5) A reference in this Part (including this section) to human rights does not exclude any matter by reason only of its being a matter to which section 8 or 10 relates.

10   Groups

(1) The Commission shall, by exercising the powers conferred by this Part—

(a) promote understanding of the importance of good relations—

(i) between members of different groups, and

(ii) between members of groups and others,

    (b) encourage good practice in relation to relations—
        (i)   between members of different groups, and
        (ii) between members of groups and others,
    (c) work towards the elimination of prejudice against, hatred of and hostility towards members of groups, and
    (d) work towards enabling members of groups to participate in society.

(2) In this Part 'group' means a group or class of persons who share a common attribute in respect of any of the following matters—
    (a)   age,
    (b)   disability,
    (c)   gender,
    [(d) gender reassignment (within the meaning of section 7 of the Equality Act 2010)].
    (e)   race,
    (f)   religion or belief, and
    (g)   sexual orientation.
(3)–(7) *****

11 Monitoring the law

(1) The Commission shall monitor the effectiveness of the equality and human rights enactments.

(2) The Commission may—
    (a) advise central government about the effectiveness of any of the equality and human rights enactments;
    (b) recommend to central government the amendment, repeal, consolidation (with or without amendments) or replication (with or without amendments) of any of the equality and human rights enactments;
    (c) advise central or devolved government about the effect of an enactment (including an enactment in or under an Act of the Scottish Parliament);
    (d) advise central or devolved government about the likely effect of a proposed change of law.

(3) *****

12 Monitoring progress

(1) The Commission shall from time to time identify—
    (a) changes in society that have occurred or are expected to occur and are relevant to the aim specified in section 3,
    (b) results at which to aim for the purpose of encouraging and supporting the development of the society described in section 3 ('outcomes'), and
    (c) factors by reference to which progress towards those results may be measured ('indicators').

(2)–(5) *****

13 ****

14 Codes of practice

(1) The Commission may issue a code of practice in connection with a matter addressed by [the Equality Act 2010].

(2) A code of practice under subsection (1) shall contain provision designed—
    (a) to ensure or facilitate compliance with [the Equality Act 2010 or an enactment made under that Act], or
    (b) to promote equality of opportunity.

(3), (4) *****

(5) The Commission shall comply with a direction of the [Secretary of State] to issue a code under this section in connection with a specified matter if—

(a) the matter is not [a matter addressed by the Equality Act 2010], but

(b) the [Secretary of State] expects to add it by order under section 15(6).

(6) Before issuing a code under this section the Commission shall—

(a) publish proposals, and

(b) consult such persons as it thinks appropriate.

(7) Before issuing a code under this section the Commission shall submit a draft to the [Secretary of State], who shall—

(a) if he approves the draft—

    (i) notify the Commission, and

    (ii) lay a copy before Parliament, or

(b) otherwise, give the Commission written reasons why he does not approve the draft.

(8) Where a draft is laid before Parliament under subsection (7)(a)(ii), if neither House passes a resolution disapproving the draft within 40 days—

(a) the Commission may issue the code in the form of the draft, and

(b) it shall come into force in accordance with provision made by the [Secretary of State] by order.

(9), (10) *****

15   *****

16   Inquiries

(1) The Commission may conduct an inquiry into a matter relating to any of the Commission's duties under sections 8, 9 and 10.

(2) If in the course of an inquiry the Commission begins to suspect that a person may have committed an unlawful act—

(a) in continuing the inquiry the Commission shall, so far as possible, avoid further consideration of whether or not the person has committed an unlawful act,

(b) the Commission may commence an investigation into that question under section 20,

(c) the Commission may use information or evidence acquired in the course of the inquiry for the purpose of the investigation, and

(d) the Commission shall so far as possible ensure (whether by aborting or suspending the inquiry or otherwise) that any aspects of the inquiry which concern the person investigated, or may require his involvement, are not pursued while the investigation is in progress.

(3) The report of an inquiry—

(a) may not state (whether expressly or by necessary implication) that a specified or identifiable person has committed an unlawful act, and

(b) shall not otherwise refer to the activities of a specified or identifiable person unless the Commission thinks that the reference—

    (i) will not harm the person, or

    (ii) is necessary in order for the report adequately to reflect the results of the inquiry.

(4) Subsections (2) and (3) shall not prevent an inquiry from considering or reporting a matter relating to human rights (whether or not a necessary implication arises in relation to the [Equality Act 2010]).

(5) Before settling a report of an inquiry which records findings which in the Commission's opinion are of an adverse nature and relate (whether expressly or by necessary implication) to a specified or identifiable person the Commission shall—

(a) send a draft of the report to the person,

(b) specify a period of at least 28 days during which he may make written representations about the draft, and

(c) consider any representations made.

(6) *****

17–19   *****

20   Investigations

(1) The Commission may investigate whether or not a person—

    (a) has committed an unlawful act,

    (b) has complied with a requirement imposed by an unlawful act notice under section 21, or

    (c) has complied with an undertaking given under section 23.

(2) The Commission may conduct an investigation under subsection (1)(a) only if it suspects that the person concerned may have committed an unlawful act.

(3) A suspicion for the purposes of subsection (2) may (but need not) be based on the results of, or a matter arising during the course of, an inquiry under section 16.

(4), (5) *****

21   Unlawful act notice

(1) The Commission may give a person a notice under this section (an 'unlawful act notice') if—

    (a) he is or has been the subject of an investigation under section 20(1)(a), and

    (b) the Commission is satisfied that he has committed an unlawful act.

(2) A notice must specify—

    (a) the unlawful act, and

    (b) the provision of the [Equality Act 2010] by virtue of which the act is unlawful.

(3) A notice must inform the recipient of the effect of—

    (a) subsections (5) to (7),

    (b) section 20(1)(b), and

    (c) section 24(1).

(4) A notice may—

    (a) require the person to whom the notice is given to prepare an action plan for the purpose of avoiding repetition or continuation of the unlawful act;

    (b) recommend action to be taken by the person for that purpose.

(5) A person who is given a notice may, within the period of six weeks beginning with the day on which the notice is given, appeal to the appropriate court or tribunal on the grounds—

    (a) that he has not committed the unlawful act specified in the notice, or

    (b) that a requirement for the preparation of an action plan imposed under subsection (4)(a) is unreasonable.

(6) An appeal under subsection (5) the court or tribunal may—

    (a) affirm a notice;

    (b) annul a notice;

    (c) vary a notice;

    (d) affirm a requirement;

    (e) annul a requirement;

    (f) vary a requirement;

    (g) make an order for costs or expenses.

(7) In subsection (5) 'the appropriate court or tribunal' means—

    (a) an employment tribunal, if a claim in respect of the alleged unlawful act could be made to it, or

    (b) a county court (in England and Wales) or the sheriff (in Scotland), if a claim in respect of the alleged unlawful act could be made to it or to him.

22   Action plans

(1) This section applies where a person has been given a notice under section 21 which requires him (under section 21(4)(a)) to prepare an action plan.

(2) The notice must specify a time by which the person must give the Commission a first draft plan.

(3) After receiving a first draft plan from a person the Commission shall—

    (a) approve it, or

(b) give the person a notice which—
    (i)   states that the draft is not adequate,
    (ii) requires the person to give the Commission a revised draft by a specified time, and
    (iii) may make recommendations about the content of the revised draft.
(4)–(9) *****

23 Agreements

(1) The Commission may enter into an agreement with a person under which—
    (a) the person undertakes—
        (i)   not to commit an unlawful act of a specified kind, and
        (ii) to take, or refrain from taking, other specified action (which may include the preparation of a plan for the purpose of avoiding an unlawful act), and
    (b) the Commission undertakes not to proceed against the person under section 20 or 21 in respect of any unlawful act of the kind specified under paragraph (a)(i).

(2) The Commission may enter into an agreement with a person under this section only if it thinks that the person has committed an unlawful act.

(3) But a person shall not be taken to admit to the commission of an unlawful act by reason only of entering into an agreement under this section.

(4), (5) *****

24 Applications to court

(1) If the Commission thinks that a person is likely to commit an unlawful act, it may apply—
    (a) in England and Wales, to a county court for an injunction restraining the person from committing the act, or
    (b) in Scotland, to the sheriff for an interdict prohibiting the person from committing the act.

(2) Subsection (3) applies if the Commission thinks that a party to an agreement under section 23 has failed to comply, or is likely not to comply, with an undertaking under the agreement.

(3) The Commission may apply to a county court (in England and Wales) or to the sheriff (in Scotland) for an order requiring the person—
    (a) to comply with his undertaking, and
    (b) to take such other action as the court or the sheriff may specify.

24A–27 *****

28 Legal assistance

(1) The Commission may assist an individual who is or may become party to legal proceedings if—
    (a) the proceedings relate or may relate (wholly or partly) to a provision of the [Equality Act 2010], and
    (b) the individual alleges that he has been the victim of behaviour contrary to a provision of [that Act].

(2)–(13) *****

29 *****

30 Judicial review and other legal proceedings

(1) The Commission shall have capacity to institute or intervene in legal proceedings, whether for judicial review or otherwise, if it appears to the Commission that the proceedings are relevant to a matter in connection with which the Commission has a function.

(2) The Commission shall be taken to have title and interest in relation to the subject matter of any legal proceedings in Scotland which it has capacity to institute, or in which it has capacity to intervene, by virtue of subsection (1).

(3)–(4) *****

31–42 *****

43–81 ...

82 *****

83–90 ...

91–95 *****

SCHEDULE 1   *****

SCHEDULE 2 INQUIRIES, INVESTIGATIONS AND ASSESSMENTS

Introduction

1. This Schedule applies to—
   (a) inquiries under section 16,
   (b) investigations under section 20, and
   (c) assessments under section 31.

Terms of reference

2. Before conducting an inquiry the Commission shall—
   (a) publish the terms of reference of the inquiry in a manner that the Commission thinks is likely to bring the inquiry to the attention of persons whom it concerns or who are likely to be interested in it, and
   (b) in particular, give notice of the terms of reference to any persons specified in them.
3. Before conducting an investigation the Commission shall—
   (a) prepare terms of reference specifying the person to be investigated and the nature of the unlawful act which the Commission suspects,
   (b) give the person to be investigated notice of the proposed terms of reference,
   (c) give the person to be investigated an opportunity to make representations about the proposed terms of reference,
   (d) consider any representations made, and
   (e) publish the terms of reference once settled.
4. Before conducting an assessment of a person's compliance with a duty the Commission shall—
   (a) prepare terms of reference,
   (b) give the person notice of the proposed terms of reference,
   (c) give the person an opportunity to make representations about the proposed terms of reference,
   (d) consider any representations made, and
   (e) publish the terms of reference once settled.
5. Paragraphs 2 to 4 shall apply in relation to revised terms of reference as they apply in relation to original terms of reference.

Representations

6.—(1) The Commission shall make arrangements for giving persons an opportunity to make representations in relation to inquiries, investigations and assessments.

(2) In particular, in the course of an investigation, inquiry or assessment the Commission must give any person specified in the terms of reference an opportunity to make representations.

7. Arrangements under paragraph 6 may (but need not) include arrangements for oral representations.

8.—(1) The Commission shall consider representations made in relation to an inquiry, investigation or assessment.

(2) But the Commission may, where they think it appropriate, refuse to consider representations—

    (a) made neither by nor on behalf of a person specified in the terms of reference, or

    (b) made on behalf of a person specified in the terms of reference by a person who is not a [relevant lawyer].

[(2A) 'Relevant lawyer' means—

    (a) an advocate or solicitor in Scotland, or

    (b) a person who, for the purposes of the Legal Services Act 2007, is an authorised person in relation to an activity which constitutes the exercise of a right of audience or the conduct of litigation (within the meaning of that Act).]

(3) If the Commission refuse to consider representations in reliance on sub-paragraph (2) they shall give the person who makes them written notice of the Commission's decision and the reasons for it.

Evidence

9. In the course of an inquiry, investigation or assessment the Commission may give a notice under this paragraph to any person.

10.—(1) A notice given to a person under paragraph 9 may require him—

    (a) to provide information in his possession,

    (b) to produce documents in his possession, or

    (c) to give oral evidence.

2. A notice under paragraph 9 may include provision about—

    (a) the form of information, documents or evidence;

    (b) timing.

3. A notice under paragraph 9—

    (a) may not require a person to provide information that he is prohibited from disclosing by virtue of an enactment,

    (b) may not require a person to do anything that he could not be compelled to do in proceedings before the High Court or the Court of Session, and

    (c) may not require a person to attend at a place unless the Commission undertakes to pay the expenses of his journey.

11. The recipient of a notice under paragraph 9 may apply to a county court (in England and Wales) or to the sheriff (in Scotland) to have the notice cancelled on the grounds that the requirement imposed by the notice is—

    (a) unnecessary having regard to the purpose of the inquiry, investigation or assessment to which the notice relates, or

    (b) otherwise unreasonable.

12.–20. *****

*****

Government of Wales Act 2006

(2006, c. 32)

An Act to make provision about the government of Wales.   [25th July 2006]

PART 1 NATIONAL ASSEMBLY FOR WALES

The Assembly

1   The Assembly

(1) There is to be an Assembly for Wales to be known as the National Assembly for Wales or Cynulliad Cenedlaethol Cymru (referred to in this Act as "the Assembly").

(2) The Assembly is to consist of—

(a) one member for each Assembly constituency (referred to in this Act as 'Assembly constituency members'), and

(b) members for each Assembly electoral region (referred to in this Act as "Assembly regional members").

(3) Members of the Assembly (referred to in this Act as "Assembly members") are to be returned in accordance with the provision made by and under this Act for—

(a) the holding of general elections of Assembly members (for the return of the entire Assembly), and

(b) the filling of vacancies in Assembly seats.

(4) The validity of any Assembly proceedings is not affected by any vacancy in its membership.

(5) In this Act 'Assembly proceedings' means any proceedings of—

(a) the Assembly,

(b) committees of the Assembly, or

(c) sub-committees of such committees.

2 Assembly constituencies and electoral regions

(1) The Assembly constituencies are the parliamentary constituencies in Wales(as specified in the Parliamentary Constituencies and Assembly Electoral Regions (Wales) Order 2006 (SI 2006/1041)).

(2) There are five Assembly electoral regions.

(3) The Assembly electoral regions are as specified in the Parliamentary Constituencies and Assembly Electoral Regions (Wales) Order 2006.

(4) There are four seats for each Assembly electoral region.

(5), (6) . . .

3 Ordinary general elections

(1) The poll at an ordinary general election is to be held on the first Thursday in May in the fourth calendar year following that in which the previous ordinary general election was held, unless provision is made for the day of the poll by an order under section 4.

(2) If the poll is to be held on the first Thursday in May, the Assembly—

(a) is dissolved by virtue of this section at the beginning of the minimum period which ends with that day, and

(b) must meet within the period of seven days beginning immediately after the day of the poll.

(3) In subsection (2) 'the minimum period' means the period determined in accordance with an order under section 13.

(4) *****

4 Power to vary date of ordinary general election

(1) The Secretary of State may by order provide for the poll at an ordinary general election to be held on a day which is neither—

(a) more than one month earlier, nor

(b) more than one month later,

than the first Thursday in May.

(2) An order under this section must make provision for the Assembly—

(a) to be dissolved on a day specified in the order, and

(b) to meet within the period of seven days beginning immediately after the day of the poll.

(3) *****

(4) An order under this section may make provision for—

(a) any provision of, or made under, the Representation of the People Acts, or

(b) any other enactment relating to the election of Assembly members,

to have effect with such modifications or exceptions as the Secretary of State considers appropriate in connection with the alteration of the day of the poll.

(5) No order is to be made under this section unless the Secretary of State has consulted the Welsh Ministers about it.

(6) A statutory instrument containing an order under this section is subject to annulment in pursuance of a resolution of either House of Parliament.

5–24 *****

25 Presiding Officer etc.

(1) The Assembly must, at its first meeting following a general election, elect from among the Assembly members—

    (a) a presiding officer (referred to in this Act as 'the Presiding Officer'), and

    (b) a deputy presiding officer (referred to in this Act as 'the Deputy Presiding Officer').

(2) The person elected under paragraph (a) of subsection (1) is to be known as the Presiding Officer or by such other title as the standing orders may provide; and the person elected under paragraph (b) of that subsection is to be known as the Deputy Presiding Officer or by such other title as the standing orders may provide.

(3) The Presiding Officer holds office until the conclusion of the next election of a Presiding Officer under subsection (1).

(4) The Deputy Presiding Officer holds office until the Assembly is dissolved.

(5) But the Presiding Officer or Deputy Presiding Officer—

    (a) may at any time resign,

    (b) ceases to hold office on ceasing to be an Assembly member otherwise than by reason of a dissolution, and

    (c) may be removed from office by the Assembly.

(6) If the Presiding Officer or the Deputy Presiding Officer ceases to hold office under subsection (5) (or dies), the Assembly must elect a replacement from among the Assembly members.

(7) Subject to subsection (9), the Presiding Officer and the Deputy Presiding Officer must not belong to—

    (a) the same political group, or

    (b) different political groups both of which are political groups with an executive role.

(8) For the purposes of this Act a political group is a political group with an executive role if the First Minister or one or more of the Welsh Ministers appointed under section 48 belong to it.

(9) The Assembly may resolve that subsection(7) is not to apply for so long as the resolution so provides; but if the motion for the resolution is passed on a vote it is of no effect unless at least two-thirds of the Assembly members voting support it.

(10) The Presiding Officer's functions may be exercised by the Deputy Presiding Officer if—

    (a) the office of Presiding Officer is vacant, or

    (b) the Presiding Officer is for any reason unable to act.

(11) The Presiding Officer may (subject to the standing orders) authorise the Deputy Presiding Officer to exercise functions of the Presiding Officer.

(12) The standing orders may include provision for the Presiding Officer's functions to be exercisable by any person specified in, or determined in accordance with, the standing orders if—

    (a) the office of Presiding Officer is vacant or the Presiding Officer is for any reason unable to act, and

    (b) the office of Deputy Presiding Officer is vacant or the Deputy Presiding Officer is for any reason unable to act.

(13) The standing orders may include provision as to the participation (including voting) in Assembly proceedings of the Presiding Officer and Deputy Presiding Officer and any person acting by virtue of subsection (12).

(14) The validity of any act of a person as Presiding Officer or Deputy Presiding Officer, or of any person acting by virtue of subsection (12), is not affected by any defect in the person's appointment by the Assembly.

(15) *****

26 *****

27 Assembly Commission

(1) There is to be a body corporate to be known as the National Assembly for Wales Commission or Comisiwn Cynulliad Cenedlaethol Cymru (referred to in this Act as 'the Assembly Commission').

(2) The members of the Assembly Commission are to be—

> (a) the Presiding Officer, and

> (b) four other Assembly members.

(3) The standing orders must make provision for the appointment of the four other Assembly members as members of the Assembly Commission.

(4) The provision included in the standing orders in compliance with subsection (3) must (so far as it is reasonably practicable to do so) secure that not more than one of the members of the Assembly Commission (other than the Presiding Officer) belongs to any one political group.

(5) The Assembly Commission must—

> (a) provide to the Assembly, or

> (b) ensure that the Assembly is provided with,

the property, staff and services required for the Assembly's purposes.

(6) The Assembly may give special or general directions to the Assembly Commission for the purpose of, or in connection with, the exercise of the Assembly Commission's functions.

(7), (8) *****

28–30 *****

Proceedings etc.

31 Standing orders

(1) Assembly proceedings are to be regulated by standing orders (referred to in this Act as 'the standing orders').

(2) The standing orders must include provision for preserving order in Assembly proceedings, including provision for—

> (a) preventing conduct which would constitute a criminal offence or contempt of court, and

> (b) a sub judice rule.

(3) The standing orders may include provision for excluding an Assembly member from Assembly proceedings.

(4) The standing orders may include provision for withdrawing from an Assembly member any or all of the rights and privileges of membership of the Assembly.

(5) The standing orders—

> (a) must include provision requiring the proceedings of the Assembly to be held in public, and for proceedings of a committee of the Assembly or a sub-committee of such a committee to be held in public except in circumstances provided for in the standing orders, and

> (b) may include provision as to the conditions to be complied with by members of the public attending the proceedings (including provision for excluding any member of the public who does not comply with the conditions).

(6) The standing orders must include provision—

> (a) for reporting the proceedings of the Assembly, and for reporting proceedings of committees of the Assembly and sub-committees of such committees which are held in public, and

> (b) for publishing the reports of proceedings as soon as reasonably practicable after the proceedings take place.

(7) The Assembly may by resolution remake or revise the standing orders; but if the motion for a resolution to remake or revise the standing orders is passed on a vote, it has no effect unless at least two-thirds of the Assembly members voting support it.

(8) The Clerk must from time to time publish the standing orders.

32   *****

33   Consultation about UK Government's legislative programme

(1) As soon as is reasonably practicable after the beginning of each session of Parliament, the Secretary of State for Wales must undertake with the Assembly such consultation about the UK Government's legislative programme for the session as appears to the Secretary of State to be appropriate.

(2) The consultation in relation to the UK Government's legislative programme for a session must include participating in proceedings of the Assembly relating to it on at least one occasion.

(3) For this purpose the UK Government's legislative programme for a session of Parliament consists of the bills which, at the beginning of the session, are intended to be introduced into either House of Parliament during the session by a Minister of the Crown.

(4) If, at any time after the beginning of a session of Parliament, it is decided that a bill should be introduced into either House of Parliament during the session by a Minister of the Crown and no consultation about the bill has been undertaken under subsection (1), the Secretary of State for Wales must undertake with the Assembly such consultation about the bill as appears to the Secretary of State to be appropriate.

(5) This section does not require the undertaking of consultation with the Assembly about a bill if it appears to the Secretary of State for Wales that there are considerations relating to the bill that make such consultation inappropriate.

34–44   *****

PART 2 WELSH ASSEMBLY GOVERNMENT

Government

45   Welsh Assembly Government

(1) There is to be a Welsh Assembly Government, or Llywodraeth Cynulliad Cymru, whose members are—

    (a) the First Minister or Prif Weinidog (see sections 46 and 47),

    (b) the Welsh Ministers, or Gweinidogion Cymru, appointed under section 48,

    (c) the Counsel General to the Welsh Assembly Government or Cwnsler Cyffredinol i Lywodraeth Cynulliad Cymru (see section 49) (referred to in this Act as "the Counsel General"), and

    (d) the Deputy Welsh Ministers or Dirprwy Weinidogion Cymru (see section 50).

(2) In this Act and in any other enactment or instrument the First Minister and the Welsh Ministers appointed under section 48 are referred to collectively as the Welsh Ministers.

46   The First Minister

(1) The First Minister is to be appointed by Her Majesty after nomination in accordance with section 47.

(2) The First Minister holds office at Her Majesty's pleasure.

(3) The First Minister may at any time tender resignation to Her Majesty and ceases to hold office as First Minister when it is accepted.

(4) A person ceases to hold office as the First Minister if another person is appointed to that office.

(5) The functions of the First Minister are exercisable by a person designated by the Presiding Officer if—

    (a) the office of the First Minister is vacant,

    (b) the First Minister is for any reason unable to act, or

    (c) the First Minister has ceased to be an Assembly member.

(6) A person may not be designated to exercise the functions of the First Minister unless the person is—

    (a) an Assembly member, or

    (b) if the Assembly has been dissolved, a person who ceased to be an Assembly member by reason of the dissolution.

(7) A person may be designated to exercise the functions of the First Minister only on the recommendation of the Welsh Ministers (unless there is no-one holding office as a Welsh Minister appointed under section 48).

(8) If a person is designated to exercise the functions of the First Minister, the designation continues to have effect even if the Assembly is dissolved.

47 Choice of First Minister

(1) If one of the following events occurs, the Assembly must, before the end of the relevant period, nominate an Assembly member for appointment as First Minister.

(2) The events are—

    (a) the holding of a poll at a general election,

    (b) the Assembly resolving that the Welsh Ministers no longer enjoy the confidence of the Assembly,

    (c) the First Minister tendering resignation to Her Majesty,

    (d) the First Minister dying or becoming permanently unable to act and to tender resignation, and

    (e) the First Minister ceasing to be an Assembly member otherwise than by reason of a dissolution.

(3) The relevant period is the period of 28 days beginning with the day on which the event occurs; but—

    (a) if another of those events occurs within that period, the relevant period is (subject to paragraph (b)) extended to end with the period of 28 days beginning with the day on which that other event occurs, and

    (b) the relevant period ends if the Assembly passes a resolution under section 5(2)(a) or when Her Majesty appoints a person as the First Minister.

(4) The Presiding Officer must recommend to Her Majesty the appointment of the person nominated by the Assembly under subsection (1).

48 Welsh Ministers

(1) The First Minister may, with the approval of Her Majesty, appoint Welsh Ministers from among the Assembly members.

(2) A Welsh Minister appointed under this section holds office at Her Majesty's pleasure.

(3) A Welsh Minister appointed under this section may be removed from office by the First Minister.

(4) A Welsh Minister appointed under this section may at any time resign.

(5) A Welsh Minister appointed under this section must resign if the Assembly resolves that the Welsh Ministers no longer enjoy the confidence of the Assembly.

(6) A Welsh Minister appointed under this section who resigns ceases to hold office immediately.

(7) A Welsh Minister appointed under this section ceases to hold office on ceasing to be an Assembly member otherwise than by reason of a dissolution.

49–55 *****

56 Introduction

(1) The persons to whom this section applies have the functions conferred or imposed on them by or by virtue of this Act or any other enactment or prerogative instrument.

(2) This section applies to the Welsh Ministers, the First Minister and the Counsel General.

57   Exercise of functions

(1) Functions may be conferred or imposed on the Welsh Ministers by that name.

(2) Functions of the Welsh Ministers, the First Minister and the Counsel General are exercisable on behalf of Her Majesty.

(3) Functions of the Welsh Ministers are exercisable by the First Minister or any of the Welsh Ministers appointed under section 48.

(4) Any act or omission of, or in relation to, the First Minister or any of the Welsh Ministers appointed under section 48 is to be treated as an act or omission of, or in relation to, each of them.

(5) But subsection (4) does not apply in relation to the exercise of functions conferred or imposed on the First Minister alone.

(6) Where a function conferred or imposed on the Counsel General is (either generally or in particular circumstances) exercisable concurrently by the Welsh Ministers or the First Minister, subsection (4) applies in relation to the exercise of the function (or to its exercise in those circumstances) as if the Counsel General were included among the Welsh Ministers.

58   Transfer of Ministerial functions

(1) Her Majesty may by Order in Council—

    (a) provide for the transfer to the Welsh Ministers, the First Minister or the Counsel General of any function so far as exercisable by a Minister of the Crown in relation to Wales [or the Welsh zone],

    (b) direct that any function so far as so exercisable is to be exercisable by the Welsh Ministers, the First Minister or the Counsel General concurrently with the Minister of the Crown, or

    (c) direct that any function so far as exercisable by a Minister of the Crown in relation to Wales [or the Welsh zone] is to be exercisable by the Minister of the Crown only with the agreement of, or after consultation with, the Welsh Ministers, the First Minister or the Counsel General.

(1A), (1B) *****

(2) An Order in Council under this section may, in particular, provide for any function exercisable by the Welsh Ministers, the First Minister or the Counsel General by virtue of an Order in Council under subsection (1)(a) or (b) to be exercisable either generally or in such circumstances as may be specified in the Order in Council, concurrently with any other of the Welsh Ministers, the First Minister or the Counsel General.

(3) An Order in Council under this section may make such modifications of—

    (a) any enactment (including any enactment comprised in or made under this Act) or prerogative instrument, or

    (b) any other instrument or document,

as Her Majesty considers appropriate in connection with the provision made by the Order in Council.

(4) No recommendation is to be made to Her Majesty in Council to make an Order in Council under this section unless a draft of the statutory instrument containing the Order in Council—

    (a) has been laid before, and approved by a resolution of, each House of Parliament, and

    (b) has been approved by the Welsh Ministers.

(5) *****

59   *****

60   Promotion etc. of well-being

(1) The Welsh Ministers may do anything which they consider appropriate to achieve any one or more of the following objects—

    (a) the promotion or improvement of the economic well-being of Wales,

    (b) the promotion or improvement of the social well-being of Wales, and

    (c) the promotion or improvement of the environmental well-being of Wales.

(2) The power under subsection (1) may be exercised in relation to or for the benefit of—

    (a) the whole or any part of Wales, or

(b) all or any persons resident or present in Wales.

(3) The power under subsection (1) includes power to do anything in relation to or for the benefit of any area outside Wales, or all or any persons resident or present anywhere outside Wales, if the Welsh Ministers consider that it is likely to achieve one or more of the objects in that subsection.

(4) The power under subsection (1) includes power—

(a) to enter into arrangements or agreements with any person,

(b) to co-operate with, or facilitate or co-ordinate the activities of, any person,

(c) to exercise on behalf of any person any functions of that person, and

(d) to provide staff, goods, services or accommodation to any person.

61   Support of culture etc.

The Welsh Ministers may do anything which they consider appropriate to support—

(a) archaeological remains in Wales,

(b) ancient monuments in Wales,

(c) buildings and places of historical or architectural interest in Wales,

(d) historic wrecks in Wales,

(e) arts and crafts relating to Wales,

(f) museums and galleries in Wales,

(g) libraries in Wales,

(h) archives and historical records relating to Wales,

(i) cultural activities and projects relating to Wales,

(j) sport and recreational activities relating to Wales, and

(k) the Welsh language.

62–86 *****

Property, rights and liabilities

87   Property, rights and liabilities of Welsh Ministers etc.

(1) Property, rights and liabilities may belong to—

(a) the Welsh Ministers by that name,

(b) the First Minister by that name, or

(c) the Counsel General by that name.

(2) Property and rights acquired by or transferred to the Welsh Ministers belong to, and liabilities incurred by the Welsh Ministers are liabilities of, the Welsh Ministers for the time being.

(3) Property and rights acquired by or transferred to any of the Welsh Ministers appointed under section 48 belong to, and liabilities incurred by any of those Welsh Ministers are liabilities of, the Welsh Ministers for the time being.

(4) Property and rights acquired by or transferred to the First Minister belong to, and liabilities incurred by the First Minister are liabilities of, the First Minister for the time being.

(5) Property and rights acquired by or transferred to the Counsel General belong to, and liabilities incurred by the Counsel General are liabilities of, the Counsel General for the time being.

(6) In relation to property and rights acquired by or transferred to (or belonging to), or to liabilities incurred by—

(a) the Welsh Ministers or any of the Welsh Ministers appointed under section 48,

(b) the First Minister, or

(c) the Counsel General,

references to the Welsh Ministers, the First Minister or the Counsel General in any register or other document are to be read in accordance with this section.

88–92 *****

PART 3 ASSEMBLY MEASURES

Power

93 Assembly Measures

(1) The Assembly may make laws, to be known as Measures of the National Assembly for Wales or Mesurau Cynulliad Cenedlaethol Cymru (referred to in this Act as 'Assembly Measures').

(2) A proposed Assembly Measure is enacted by being passed by the Assembly and approved by Her Majesty in Council.

(3) The validity of an Assembly Measure is not affected by any invalidity in the Assembly proceedings leading to its enactment.

(4) Every Assembly Measure is to be judicially noticed.

(5) This Part does not affect the power of the Parliament of the United Kingdom to make laws for Wales.

94 Legislative competence

(1) Subject to the provisions of this Part, an Assembly Measure may make any provision that could be made by an Act of Parliament.

(2) An Assembly Measure is not law so far as any provision of the Assembly Measure is outside the Assembly's legislative competence.

(3) A provision of an Assembly Measure is within the Assembly's legislative competence only if it falls within subsection (4) or (5).

(4) A provision of an Assembly Measure falls within this subsection if—

  (a) it relates to one or more of the matters specified in Part 1 of Schedule 5 [and does not fall within any of the exceptions specified in paragraph A1 of Part 2 of that Schedule (whether or not the exception is under a heading corresponding to the field which includes the matter)], and

  (b) it neither applies otherwise than in relation to Wales nor confers, imposes, modifies or removes (or gives power to confer, impose, modify or remove) functions exercisable otherwise than in relation to Wales.

(5) A provision of an Assembly Measure falls within this subsection if—

  (a) it provides for the enforcement of a provision (of that or any other Assembly Measure) which falls within subsection (4) or it is otherwise appropriate for making such a provision effective, or

  (b) it is otherwise incidental to, or consequential on, such a provision.

(6) But a provision which falls within subsection (4) or (5) is outside the Assembly's legislative competence if—

  (a) it breaches any of the restrictions in [paragraphs 1 to 6 of] Part 2 of Schedule 5, having regard to any exception in Part 3 of that Schedule from those restrictions,

  (b) it extends otherwise than only to England and Wales, or

  (c) it is incompatible with the Convention rights or with [EU] law.

(7) For the purposes of this section the question whether a provision of an Assembly Measure relates to one or more of the matters specified in Part 1 of Schedule 5 [(or falls within any of the exceptions specified in paragraph A1 of Part 2 of that Schedule)] is to be determined by reference to the purpose of the provision, having regard (among other things) to its effect in all the circumstances.

95 Legislative competence: supplementary

(1) Her Majesty may by Order in Council—

  (a) amend Part 1 of Schedule 5 to add a matter which relates to one or more of the fields listed in that Part, or to vary or remove any matter,

  (b) amend that Part to add a new field or to vary or remove any field, or

  (c) amend Part 2 or 3 of that Schedule.

(2) An Order in Council under this section does not have effect to amend Part 1 of Schedule 5 by adding a field if, at the time when the amendment comes into force, no functions in the field are exercisable by the Welsh Ministers, the First Minister or the Counsel General.

(3) An Order in Council under this section may make such modifications of—

(a) any enactment (including any enactment comprised in or made under this Act) or prerogative instrument, or

(b) any other instrument or document,

as Her Majesty considers appropriate in connection with the provision made by the Order in Council.

(4) An Order in Council under this section may make provision having retrospective effect.

(5) No recommendation is to be made to Her Majesty in Council to make an Order in Council under this section unless a draft of the statutory instrument containing the Order in Council—

(a) has been laid before, and approved by a resolution of, the Assembly, and

(b) having been so approved, has been laid before, and approved by a resolution of, each House of Parliament.

(6) As soon as is reasonably practicable after the draft of an Order in Council under this section has been approved by a resolution of the Assembly, the First Minister must ensure that—

(a) notice in writing of the resolution, and

(b) a copy of the draft,

is sent to the Secretary of State.

(7) The Secretary of State must, before the end of the period of 60 days beginning immediately after the day on which notice of the Assembly's resolution is received, either—

(a) lay the draft before each House of Parliament, or

(b) give notice in writing to the First Minister of the Secretary of State's refusal to do so and the reasons for that refusal.

(8) As soon as is reasonably practicable after the First Minister receives notice of the Secretary of State's refusal to lay the draft before each House of Parliament and the reasons for that refusal—

(a) the First Minister must lay a copy of the notice before the Assembly, and

(b) the Assembly must ensure that it is published.

(9) In reckoning the period of 60 days mentioned in subsection (7) no account is to be taken of any period during which Parliament is dissolved or prorogued or both Houses are adjourned for more than four days.

(10) The amendment of Schedule 5 by an Order in Council under this section does not affect—

(a) the validity of an Assembly Measure passed before the amendment comes into force, or

(b) the previous or continuing operation of such an Assembly Measure.

96 Scrutiny of proposed Orders in Council

The Counsel General or the Attorney General may refer to the [Supreme Court] for decision the question whether a matter which a proposed Order in Council under section 95 proposes to add to Part 1 of Schedule 5 relates to a field listed in that Part.

Procedure

97 Introduction of proposed Assembly Measures

(1) A proposed Assembly Measure may, subject to the standing orders, be introduced in the Assembly—

(a) by the First Minister, any Welsh Minister appointed under section 48, any Deputy Welsh Minister or the Counsel General, or

(b) by any other Assembly member.

(2) The person in charge of a proposed Assembly Measure must, on or before the introduction of the proposed Assembly Measure, state that, in that person's view, its provisions would be within the Assembly's legislative competence.

(3) The Presiding Officer must, on or before the introduction of a proposed Assembly Measure in the Assembly—

    (a) decide whether or not, in the view of the Presiding Officer, the provisions of the proposed Assembly Measure would be within the Assembly's legislative competence, and

    (b) state that decision.

(4) A statement under this section must be made in both English and Welsh; but, subject to that, the form of the statement and the manner in which it is to be made are to be determined under the standing orders.

(5) *****

98–102 *****

PART 4 ACTS OF THE ASSEMBLY

Referendum

103 Referendum about commencement of Assembly Act provisions

(1) Her Majesty may by Order in Council cause a referendum to be held throughout Wales about whether the Assembly Act provisions should come into force.

(2)–(8) *****

104 Proposal for referendum by Assembly

(1) This section applies if—

    (a) the Assembly passes a resolution moved by the First Minister or a Welsh Minister appointed under section 48 that, in its opinion, a recommendation should be made to Her Majesty in Council to make an Order in Council under section 103(1), and

    (b) the resolution of the Assembly is passed on a vote in which the number of Assembly members voting in favour of it is not less than two-thirds of the total number of Assembly seats.

(2) The First Minister must, as soon as is reasonably practicable after the resolution is passed, ensure that notice in writing of the resolution is given to the Secretary of State.

(3) The Secretary of State must, within the period of 120 days beginning immediately after the day on which it is received—

    (a) lay a draft of a statutory instrument containing an Order in Council under section 103(1) before each House of Parliament, or

    (b) give notice in writing to the First Minister of the Secretary of State's refusal to do so and the reasons for that refusal.

(4) *****

105, 106 *****

Power

107 Acts of the Assembly

(1) The Assembly may make laws, to be known as Acts of the National Assembly for Wales or Deddfau Cynulliad Cenedlaethol Cymru (referred to in this Act as "Acts of the Assembly").

(2) Proposed Acts of the Assembly are to be known as Bills; and a Bill becomes an Act of the Assembly when it has been passed by the Assembly and has received Royal Assent.

(3) The validity of an Act of the Assembly is not affected by any invalidity in the Assembly proceedings leading to its enactment.

(4) Every Act of the Assembly is to be judicially noticed.

(5) This Part does not affect the power of the Parliament of the United Kingdom to make laws for Wales.

108 Legislative competence

(1) Subject to the provisions of this Part, an Act of the Assembly may make any provision that could be made by an Act of Parliament.

(2) An Act of the Assembly is not law so far as any provision of the Act is outside the Assembly's legislative competence.

(3) A provision of an Act of the Assembly is within the Assembly's legislative competence only if it falls within subsection (4) or (5).

(4) A provision of an Act of the Assembly falls within this subsection if—

    (a) it relates to one or more of the subjects listed under any of the headings in Part 1 of Schedule 7 and does not fall within any of the exceptions specified in that Part of that Schedule (whether or not under that heading or any of those headings), and

    (b) it neither applies otherwise than in relation to Wales nor confers, imposes, modifies or removes (or gives power to confer, impose, modify or remove) functions exercisable otherwise than in relation to Wales.

(5) A provision of an Act of the Assembly falls within this subsection if—

    (a) it provides for the enforcement of a provision (of that or any other Act of the Assembly) which falls within subsection (4) or a provision of an Assembly Measure or it is otherwise appropriate for making such a provision effective, or

    (b) it is otherwise incidental to, or consequential on, such a provision.

(6) But a provision which falls within subsection (4) or (5) is outside the Assembly's legislative competence if—

    (a) it breaches any of the restrictions in Part 2 of Schedule 7, having regard to any exception in Part 3 of that Schedule from those restrictions,

    (b) it extends otherwise than only to England and Wales, or

    (c) it is incompatible with the Convention rights or with [EU] law.

(7) For the purposes of this section the question whether a provision of an Act of the Assembly relates to one or more of the subjects listed in Part 1 of Schedule 7 (or falls within any of the exceptions specified in that Part of that Schedule) is to be determined by reference to the purpose of the provision, having regard (among other things) to its effect in all the circumstances.

109 Legislative competence: supplementary

(1) Her Majesty may by Order in Council amend Schedule 7.

(2) An Order in Council under this section may make such modifications of—

    (a) any enactment (including any enactment comprised in or made under this Act) or prerogative instrument, or

    (b) any other instrument or document, as Her Majesty considers appropriate in connection with the provision made by the Order in Council.

(3) An Order in Council under this section may make provision having retrospective effect.

(4), (5) *****

110–166 *****

*****

SCHEDULES 1–4 *****

SCHEDULE 5 ASSEMBLY MEASURES

PART 1 MATTERS

Field 1: agriculture, fisheries, forestry and rural development
Field 2: ancient monuments and historic buildings
Field 3: culture
Field 4: economic development

Field 5: education and training
Field 6: environment
Field 7: fire and rescue services and promotion of fire safety
Field 8: food
Field 9: health and health services
Field 10: highways and transport
Field 11: housing
Field 12: local government
Field 13: National Assembly for Wales
Field 14: public administration
Field 15: social welfare
Field 16: sport and recreation
Field 17: tourism
Field 18: town and country planning
Field 19: water and flood defence
Field 20: Welsh language

[**Note:** The above list includes the main headings for the fields and not the precise matters, which have not been included.]

*****

PART 2 [EXCEPTIONS TO MATTERS AND GENERAL RESTRICTIONS]

Functions of Ministers of the Crown

1.—(1) A provision of an Assembly Measure cannot remove or modify, or confer power by subordinate legislation to remove or modify, any function of a Minister of the Crown.

(2) A provision of an Assembly Measure cannot confer or impose, or confer power by subordinate legislation to confer or impose, any function on a Minister of the Crown.

Criminal offences

2.—(1) A provision of an Assembly Measure cannot create, or confer power by subordinate legislation to create, any criminal offence punishable—

(a) on summary conviction, with imprisonment for a period exceeding the prescribed term or with a fine exceeding the amount specified as level 5 on the standard scale, or

(b) on conviction on indictment, with a period of imprisonment exceeding two years.

(2) In sub-paragraph (1) 'the prescribed term' means—

(a) where the offence is a summary offence, 51 weeks, and

(b) where the offence is triable either way, twelve months.

[2A. A provision of an Assembly Measure cannot make any alteration in police areas.]

Enactments other than this Act

3. A provision of an Assembly Measure cannot make modifications of, or confer power by subordinate legislation to make modifications of, any of the provisions listed in the Table below—

[Table omitted]

4. A provision of an Assembly Measure cannot make modifications of, or confer power by subordinate legislation to make modifications of, any provision of an Act of Parliament other than this Act which requires sums required for the repayment of, or the payment of interest on, amounts borrowed by the Welsh Ministers to be charged on the Welsh Consolidated Fund.

5. A provision of an Assembly Measure cannot make modifications of, or confer power by subordinate legislation to make modifications of, any functions of the Comptroller and Auditor General [or the National Audit Office].

This Act

6.—(1) A provision of an Assembly Measure cannot make modifications of, or confer power by subordinate legislation to make modifications of, provisions contained in this Act.

[(2) Sub-paragraph (1) does not apply to—
(a) sections 20, 22, 24, 35(1), 36(1) to (5) and (7) to (11), 53, 54, 78 and 156(2) to (5); or
(b) paragraph 8(3) of Schedule 2.]

(3) Sub-paragraph (1) does not apply to any provision—
(a) making modifications of so much of any enactment as is modified by this Act, or
(b) repealing so much of any provision of this Act as amends any enactment, if the provision ceases to have effect in consequence of any provision of, or made under, an Assembly Measure.

PART 3 [EXCEPTIONS FROM GENERAL RESTRICTIONS IN PART 2]

[Interpretation

6Z.   In this Part "general restrictions in Part 2" means paragraphs 1 to 6 of Part 2.]

Functions of Ministers of the Crown

7.   [(1)] [The general restrictions in Part 2 do not] prevent a provision of an Assembly Measure removing or modifying, or conferring power by subordinate legislation to remove or modify, any function of a Minister of the Crown if the Secretary of State consents to the provision.

[(2) Part 2 does not prevent a provision of an Assembly Measure relating to matter 20.1 or 20.2 of Part 1, conferring or imposing, or conferring power by subordinate legislation to confer or impose, any function on a Minister of the Crown if the Secretary of State consents to the provision, but functions so conferred or imposed may not be made enforceable against Ministers of the Crown by means of criminal offences.]

[Police areas

7A.   [The general restrictions in Part 2 do not] prevent a provision of an Assembly Measure making an alteration to the boundary of a police area in Wales if the Secretary of State consents to the provision.]

Comptroller and Auditor General [and National Audit Office]

8.   [The general restrictions in Part 2 do not] prevent a provision of an Assembly Measure modifying, or conferring power by subordinate legislation to modify, any enactment relating to the Comptroller and Auditor General [or the National Audit Office] if the Secretary of State consents to the provision.

Restatement

9.   [The general restrictions in Part 2 do not] prevent a provision of an Assembly Measure—
(a) restating the law (or restating it with such modifications as are not prevented by that Part), or
(b) repealing or revoking any spent enactment,
or conferring power by subordinate legislation to do so.

Subordinate legislation

10.   [The general restrictions in Part 2 do not] prevent an Assembly Measure making modifications of, or conferring power by subordinate legislation to make modifications of, an enactment for or in connection with any of the following purposes—

(a) making different provision about the document by which a power to make, confirm or approve subordinate legislation is to be exercised,

(b) making provision (or no provision) for the procedure, in relation to the Assembly, to which legislation made in the exercise of such a power (or the instrument or other document in which it is contained) is to be subject, and

(c) applying any enactment comprised in or made under an Assembly Measure relating to the documents by which such powers may be exercised.

[Data Protection Act 1998

11.   [The general restrictions in Part 2 do not] prevent an Assembly Measure making modifications of, or conferring power by subordinate legislation to make modifications of, section 31(6) of the Data Protection Act 1998 so that it applies to complaints under any Assembly Measure relating to matter 9.1 in Part 1.]

SCHEDULE 6   ****

SCHEDULE 7   ACTS OF THE ASSEMBLY

[**Note:** The first part of the schedule lists the subjects to which a provision in an Act of the Assembly must relate. These follow the headings in Sch. 5 but contain exceptions limiting the legislative competence of the Assembly. Space does not allow their inclusion here. The more general restrictions in Parts 2 and 3 of the Schedule largely mirror Parts 2 and 3 of Sch. 5.]

SCHEDULE 8   ****

SCHEDULE 9 DEVOLUTION ISSUES

PART 1 PRELIMINARY

1.—(1) In this Schedule 'devolution issue' means—

(a) a question whether an Assembly Measure or Act of the Assembly, or any provision of an Assembly Measure or Act of the Assembly, is within the Assembly's legislative competence,

(b) a question whether any function (being a function which any person has purported, or is proposing, to exercise) is exercisable by the Welsh Ministers, the First Minister or the Counsel General,

(c) a question whether the purported or proposed exercise of a function by the Welsh Ministers, the First Minister or the Counsel General is, or would be, within the powers of the Welsh Ministers, the First Minister or the Counsel General (including a question whether a purported or proposed exercise of a function is, or would be, outside those powers by virtue of section 80(8) or 81(1)),

(d) a question whether there has been any failure to comply with a duty imposed on the Welsh Ministers, the First Minister or the Counsel General (including any obligation imposed by virtue of section 80(1) or (7)), or

(e) a question of whether a failure to act by the Welsh Ministers, the First Minister or the Counsel General is incompatible with any of the Convention rights.

(2) *****

2. A devolution issue is not to be taken to arise in any proceedings merely because of any contention of a party to the proceedings which appears to the court or tribunal before which the proceedings take place to be frivolous or vexatious.

PART 2 PROCEEDINGS IN ENGLAND AND WALES

Application of Part 2

3. This Part applies in relation to devolution issues in proceedings in England and Wales.

Institution of proceedings

4.—(1) Proceedings for the determination of a devolution issue may be instituted by the Attorney General or the Counsel General.

(2) The Counsel General may defend any such proceedings instituted by the Attorney General.

(3) This paragraph does not limit any power to institute or defend proceedings exercisable apart from this paragraph by any person.

Notice of devolution issue

5.—(1) A court or tribunal must order notice of any devolution issue which arises in any proceedings before it to be given to the Attorney General and the Counsel General (unless a party to the proceedings).

(2) A person to whom notice is given in pursuance of sub-paragraph (1) may take part as a party in the proceedings, so far as they relate to a devolution issue.

Reference of devolution issue to High Court or Court of Appeal

6. A magistrates' court may refer any devolution issue which arises in civil proceedings before it to the High Court.

7.—(1) A court may refer any devolution issue which arises in civil proceedings before it to the Court of Appeal.

(2) Sub-paragraph (1) does not apply—

(a) to a magistrates' court, the Court of Appeal or the [Supreme Court], or

(b) to the High Court if the devolution issue arises in proceedings on a reference under paragraph 6.

8. A tribunal from which there is no appeal must refer any devolution issue which arises in proceedings before it to the Court of Appeal; and any other tribunal may make such a reference.

9. A court, other than the Court of Appeal or the [Supreme Court], may refer any devolution issue which arises in criminal proceedings before it to—

(a) the High Court if the proceedings are summary proceedings, or

(b) the Court of Appeal if the proceedings are proceedings on indictment.

References from Court of Appeal to [Supreme Court]

10. The Court of Appeal may refer any devolution issue which arises in proceedings before it (otherwise than on a reference under paragraph 7, 8 or 9) to the [Supreme Court].

Appeals from superior courts to [Supreme Court]

11. An appeal against a determination of a devolution issue by the High Court or the Court of Appeal on a reference under paragraph 6, 7, 8 or 9 lies to the [Supreme Court] but only—

(a) with [permission] of the court from which the appeal lies, or

(b) failing such [permission], with [permission] of the [Supreme Court].

*****

Immigration, Asylum and Nationality Act 2006

(2006, c. 13)

An Act to make provision about immigration, asylum and nationality; and for connected purposes.

[30th March 2006]

Territorial extent: The United Kingdom

1–14 *****

Employment

15 Penalty

(1) It is contrary to this section to employ an adult subject to immigration control if—

    (a) he has not been granted leave to enter or remain in the United Kingdom, or

    (b) his leave to enter or remain in the United Kingdom—

        (i) is invalid,

        (ii) has ceased to have effect (whether by reason of curtailment, revocation, cancellation, passage of time or otherwise), or

        (iii) is subject to a condition preventing him from accepting the employment.

(2) The Secretary of State may give an employer who acts contrary to this section a notice requiring him to pay a penalty of a specified amount not exceeding the prescribed maximum.

(3) An employer is excused from paying a penalty if he shows that he complied with any prescribed requirements in relation to the employment.

(4) But the excuse in subsection (3) shall not apply to an employer who knew, at any time during the period of the employment, that it was contrary to this section.

(5) The Secretary of State may give a penalty notice without having established whether subsection (3) applies.

(6) A penalty notice must—

    (a) state why the Secretary of State thinks the employer is liable to the penalty,

    (b) state the amount of the penalty,

    (c) specify a date, at least 28 days after the date specified in the notice as the date on which it is given, before which the penalty must be paid,

    (d) specify how the penalty must be paid,

    (e) explain how the employer may object to the penalty, and

    (f) explain how the Secretary of State may enforce the penalty.

(7) An order prescribing requirements for the purposes of subsection (3) may, in particular—

    (a) require the production to an employer of a document of a specified description;

    (b) require the production to an employer of one document of each of a number of specified descriptions;

    (c) require an employer to take specified steps to verify, retain, copy or record the content of a document produced to him in accordance with the order;

    (d) require action to be taken before employment begins;

    (e) require action to be taken at specified intervals or on specified occasions during the course of employment.

16 Objection

(1) This section applies where an employer to whom a penalty notice is given objects on the ground that—

    (a) he is not liable to the imposition of a penalty,

    (b) he is excused payment by virtue of section 15(3), or

    (c) the amount of the penalty is too high.

(2) The employer may give a notice of objection to the Secretary of State.

(3) A notice of objection must—

    (a) be in writing,

    (b) give the objector's reasons,

    (c) be given in the prescribed manner, and

    (d) be given before the end of the prescribed period.

(4) Where the Secretary of State receives a notice of objection to a penalty he shall consider it and—

    (a) cancel the penalty,

    (b) reduce the penalty,

    (c) increase the penalty, or

    (d) determine to take no action.

(5) Where the Secretary of State considers a notice of objection he shall—

    (a) have regard to the code of practice under section 19 (in so far as the objection relates to the amount of the penalty),

    (b) inform the objector of his decision before the end of the prescribed period or such longer period as he may agree with the objector,

    (c) if he increases the penalty, issue a new penalty notice under section 15, and

    (d) if he reduces the penalty, notify the objector of the reduced amount.

17 Appeal

(1) An employer to whom a penalty notice is given may appeal to the court on the ground that—

    (a) he is not liable to the imposition of a penalty,

    (b) he is excused payment by virtue of section 15(3), or

    (c) the amount of the penalty is too high.

(2) The court may—

    (a) allow the appeal and cancel the penalty,

    (b) allow the appeal and reduce the penalty, or

    (c) dismiss the appeal.

(3) An appeal shall be a re-hearing of the Secretary of State's decision to impose a penalty and shall be determined having regard to—

    (a) the code of practice under section 19 that has effect at the time of the appeal (in so far as the appeal relates to the amount of the penalty), and

    (b) any other matters which the court thinks relevant (which may include matters of which the Secretary of State was unaware);

and this subsection has effect despite any provision of rules of court.

(4)–(6) *****

18 *****

19 Code of practice

(1) The Secretary of State shall issue a code of practice specifying factors to be considered by him in determining the amount of a penalty imposed under section 15.

(2) The code—

    (a) shall not be issued unless a draft has been laid before Parliament, and

    (b) shall come into force in accordance with provision made by order of the Secretary of State.

(3) The Secretary of State shall from time to time review the code and may revise and re-issue it following a review; and a reference in this section to the code includes a reference to the code as revised.

20 *****

21 Offence

(1) A person commits an offence if he employs another ('the employee') knowing that the employee is an adult subject to immigration control and that—

    (a) he has not been granted leave to enter or remain in the United Kingdom, or

    (b) his leave to enter or remain in the United Kingdom—

        (i)   is invalid,

        (ii) has ceased to have effect (whether by reason of curtailment, revocation, cancellation, passage of time or otherwise), or

        (iii) is subject to a condition preventing him from accepting the employment.

(2)–(4) *****

22   Offence: bodies corporate, etc.

(1) For the purposes of section 21(1) a body (whether corporate or not) shall be treated as knowing a fact about an employee if a person who has responsibility within the body for an aspect of the employment knows the fact.

(2) If an offence under section 21(1) is committed by a body corporate with the consent or connivance of an officer of the body, the officer, as well as the body, shall be treated as having committed the offence.

(3), (4) *****

23   Discrimination: code of practice

(1) The Secretary of State shall issue a code of practice specifying what an employer should or should not do in order to ensure that, while avoiding liability to a penalty under section 15 and while avoiding the commission of an offence under section 21, he also avoids contravening—

    (a) [the Equality Act 2010, so far as relating to race], or

    (b) the Race Relations (Northern Ireland) Order 1997 (S.I. 869 (N.I. 6)).

(2), (3) *****

(4) A breach of the code—

    (a) shall not make a person liable to civil or criminal proceedings, but

    (b) may be taken into account by a court or tribunal.

(5) The Secretary of State shall from time to time review the code and may revise and re-issue it following a review; and a reference in this section to the code includes a reference to the code as revised.

(6) *****

24–31   *****

32   Passenger and crew information: police powers

(1) This section applies to ships and aircraft which are—

    [(a) arriving, or expected to arrive, at any place in the United Kingdom (whether from a place in the United Kingdom or from outside the United Kingdom), or

    (b) leaving, or expected to leave, from any place in the United Kingdom (whether for a place in the United Kingdom or for outside the United Kingdom)].

(2) The owner or agent of a ship or aircraft shall comply with any requirement imposed by a constable of the rank of superintendent or above to provide passenger or service information.

(3) A passenger or member of crew shall provide to the owner or agent of a ship or aircraft any information that he requires for the purpose of complying with a requirement imposed by virtue of subsection (2).

(4) A constable may impose a requirement under subsection (2) only if he thinks it necessary—

    (a) in the case of a constable in England, Wales or Northern Ireland, for police purposes, or

    (b) in the case of a constable in Scotland, for police purposes which are or relate to reserved matters.

(5), (6) *****

(7) The Secretary of State may make an order specifying a kind of information under subsection (5)(a) only if satisfied that the nature of the information is such that there are likely to be circumstances in which it can be required under subsection (2) without breaching Convention rights (within the meaning of the Human Rights Act 1998 (c. 42)).

(8) *****

33–35   *****

36   Duty to share information

(1) This section applies to—

    [(a) designated customs officials,

    (aa) immigration officers,

(ab) the Secretary of State in so far as the Secretary of State has general customs functions,

(ac) the Secretary of State in so far as the Secretary of State has functions relating to immigration, asylum or nationality,

(ad) the Director of Border Revenue and any person exercising functions of the Director,]

(b) a chief officer of police, and

(c) Her Majesty's Revenue and Customs.

(2) The persons specified in subsection (1) shall share information to which subsection (4) applies and which is obtained or held by them in the course of their functions to the extent that the information is likely to be of use for—

(a) immigration purposes,

(b) police purposes, or

(c) Revenue and Customs purposes.

(3) But a chief officer of police in Scotland shall share information under subsection (2) only to the extent that it is likely to be of use for—

(a) immigration purposes,

(b) police purposes, in so far as they are or relate to reserved matters within the meaning of the Scotland Act 1998, or

(c) Revenue and Customs purposes other than the prosecution of crime.

(4) This subsection applies to information which—

(a) is obtained or held in the exercise of a power specified by the Secretary of State and the Treasury jointly by order and relates to—

(i)   passengers on a ship or aircraft,

(ii)   crew of a ship or aircraft,

(iii) freight on a ship or aircraft, or

(iv) flights or voyages, or

(b) relates to such other matters in respect of travel or freight as the Secretary of State and the Treasury may jointly specify by order.

(5) The Secretary of State and the Treasury may make an order under subsection (4) which has the effect of requiring information to be shared only if satisfied that—

(a) the sharing is likely to be of use for—

(i)   immigration purposes,

(ii)   police purposes, or

(iii) Revenue and Customs purposes, and

(b) the nature of the information is such that there are likely to be circumstances in which it can be shared under subsection (2) without breaching Convention rights (within the meaning of the Human Rights Act 1998 (c. 42)).

(6) Information shared in accordance with subsection (2)—

(a) shall be made available to each of the persons [or descriptions of persons] specified in subsection (1), and

(b) may be used for immigration purposes, police purposes or Revenue and Customs purposes (regardless of its source).

(7)–(10) *****

37   Information sharing: code of practice

(1) The Secretary of State and the Treasury shall jointly issue one or more codes of practice about—

(a) the use of information shared in accordance with section 36(2), and

(b) the extent to which, or form or manner in which, shared information is to be made available in accordance with section 36(6).

(2) A code—

(a) shall not be issued unless a draft has been laid before Parliament, and

(b) shall come into force in accordance with provision made by order of the Secretary of State and the Treasury jointly.

(3), (4) *****

38 ...

*****

Legislative and Regulatory Reform Act 2006

(2006, c. 51)

An Act to enable provision to be made for the purpose of removing or reducing burdens resulting from legislation and promoting regulatory principles; to make provision about the exercise of regulatory functions; to make provision about the interpretation of legislation relating to the European Communities and the European Economic Area; to make provision relating to section 2(2) of the European Communities Act 1972; and for connected purposes.   [8th November 2006]

Territorial extent: United Kingdom

PART 1   ORDER-MAKING POWERS

Powers

1   Power to remove or reduce burdens

(1) A Minister of the Crown may by order under this section make any provision which he considers would serve the purpose in subsection (2).

(2) That purpose is removing or reducing any burden, or the overall burdens, resulting directly or indirectly for any person from any legislation.

(3) In this section 'burden' means any of the following—

   (a) a financial cost;

   (b) an administrative inconvenience;

   (c) an obstacle to efficiency, productivity or profitability; or

   (d) a sanction, criminal or otherwise, which affects the carrying on of any lawful activity.

(4) Provision may not be made under subsection (1) in relation to any burden which affects only a Minister of the Crown or government department, unless it affects the Minister or department in the exercise of a regulatory function.

(5) For the purposes of subsection (2), a financial cost or administrative inconvenience may result from the form of any legislation (for example, where the legislation is hard to understand).

(6) In this section 'legislation' means any of the following or a provision of any of the following—

   (a)   a public general Act or local Act (whether passed before or after the commencement of this section), ...

   [(aa) a Measure or Act of the Assembly, or]

   (b)   any Order in Council, order, rules, regulations, scheme, warrant, byelaw or other subordinate instrument made at any time [under—

       (a) an Act referred to in paragraph (a), or

       (b) a Measure or Act of the Assembly],

but does not include any instrument which is, or is made under, Northern Ireland legislation.

(7) Subject to this Part, the provision that may be made under subsection (1) includes—

   (a) provision abolishing, conferring or transferring, or providing for the delegation of, functions of any description,

   (b) provision creating or abolishing a body or office,

and provision made by amending or repealing any enactment.

(8) An order under this section may contain such consequential, supplementary, incidental or transitional provision (including provision made by amending or repealing any enactment or other provision) as the Minister making it considers appropriate.

(9) An order under this section may bind the Crown.

(10) An order under this section must be made in accordance with this Part.

2 Power to promote regulatory principles

(1) A Minister of the Crown may by order under this section make any provision which he considers would serve the purpose in subsection (2).

(2) That purpose is securing that regulatory functions are exercised so as to comply with the principles in subsection (3).

(3) Those principles are that—

    (a) regulatory activities should be carried out in a way which is transparent, accountable, proportionate and consistent;

    (b) regulatory activities should be targeted only at cases in which action is needed.

(4) Subject to this Part, the provision that may be made under subsection (1) for the purpose in subsection (2) includes—

    (a) provision modifying the way in which a regulatory function is exercised by any person,

    (b) provision amending the constitution of a body exercising regulatory functions which is established by or under an enactment,

    (c) provision transferring, or providing for the delegation of, the regulatory functions conferred on any person,

and provision made by amending or repealing any enactment.

(5) The provision referred to in subsection (4)(c) includes provision—

    (a) to create a new body to which, or a new office to the holder of which, regulatory functions are transferred;

    (b) to abolish a body from which, or office from the holder of which, regulatory functions are transferred.

(6) The provision that may be made under subsection (1) does not include provision conferring any new regulatory function or abolishing any regulatory function.

(7) An order under this section may contain such consequential, supplementary, incidental or transitional provision (including provision made by amending or repealing any enactment or other provision) as the Minister making it considers appropriate.

(8) An order under this section may bind the Crown.

(9) An order under this section must be made in accordance with this Part.

3 Preconditions

(1) A Minister may not make provision under section 1(1) or 2(1), other than provision which merely restates an enactment, unless he considers that the conditions in subsection (2), where relevant, are satisfied in relation to that provision.

(2) Those conditions are that—

    (a) the policy objective intended to be secured by the provision could not be satisfactorily secured by non-legislative means;

    (b) the effect of the provision is proportionate to the policy objective;

    (c) the provision, taken as a whole, strikes a fair balance between the public interest and the interests of any person adversely affected by it;

    (d) the provision does not remove any necessary protection;

    (e) the provision does not prevent any person from continuing to exercise any right or freedom which that person might reasonably expect to continue to exercise;

    (f) the provision is not of constitutional significance.

(3) A Minister may not make provision under section 1(1) or 2(1) which merely restates an enactment unless he considers that the condition in subsection (4) is satisfied in relation to that provision.

(4) That condition is that the provision made would make the law more accessible or more easily understood.

(5) In this section and sections 4 to 7, to 'restate' an enactment means to replace it with alterations only of form or arrangement (and for these purposes to remove an ambiguity is to make an alteration other than one of form or arrangement).

4 Subordinate legislation

(1) An order under this Part may only confer or transfer a function of legislating on or to—

  (a) a Minister of the Crown;

  (b) any person on or to whom functions are conferred or have been transferred by an enactment; or

  (c) a body which, or the holder of an office which, is created by the order.

(2) An order under this Part may not make provision for the delegation of any function of legislating.

(3) An order under this Part may not make provision to confer a function of legislating on a Minister of the Crown (alone or otherwise) unless the conditions in subsections (4) and (5) are satisfied.

[(3A) An order under this Part may not make provision to confer a function of legislating on the Welsh Ministers, the First Minister for Wales or the Counsel General to the Welsh Assembly Government (alone or otherwise) unless the conditions in subsections (4) and (5A) are satisfied.]

(4) The condition in this subsection is that the function is exercisable by statutory instrument.

(5) The condition in this subsection is that such a statutory instrument—

  (a) is an instrument to which section 5(1) of the Statutory Instruments Act 1946 (c 36) applies (instruments subject to annulment by resolution of either House of Parliament); or

  (b) is not to be made unless a draft of the statutory instrument has been laid before and approved by a resolution of each House of Parliament.

[(5A) The condition in this subsection is that such a statutory instrument—

  (a) is an instrument to which section 5(1) of the Statutory Instruments Act 1946 applies (instruments subject to annulment); or

  (b) is not to be made unless a draft of the statutory instrument has been laid before and approved by a resolution of the Assembly.]

(6) Subsections (1) to [(3A)] do not apply to provision which merely restates an enactment.

(7) For the purposes of this section a 'function of legislating' is a function of legislating by order, rules, regulations or other subordinate instrument.

5 Taxation

(1) An order under this Part may not make provision to impose, abolish or vary any tax.

(2)–(7) *****

6 Criminal penalties

(1) An order under this Part may not make provision to create a new offence that is punishable, or increase the penalty for an existing offence so that it is punishable—

  (a) on indictment, with imprisonment for a term exceeding two years; or

  (b) on summary conviction, with—

    (i) imprisonment for a term exceeding the normal maximum term; or

    (ii) a fine exceeding level 5 on the standard scale.

(2) In subsection (1)(b)(i), 'the normal maximum term' means—

  (a) in relation to England and Wales—

    (i) in the case of a summary offence, 51 weeks; and

    (ii) in the case of an offence triable either way, twelve months; and

  (b) in relation to Scotland or Northern Ireland, six months.

(3)–(6) *****

7 Forcible entry etc.

(1) An order under this Part may not make provision to—

    (a) authorise any forcible entry, search or seizure; or

    (b) compel the giving of evidence.

(2) Subsection (1) does not prevent an order under this Part from extending any power for purposes similar to those to which the power applied before the order was made.

(3) Subsection (1) does not apply to provision which merely restates an enactment.

8 Excepted enactments

An order under this Part may not make provision amending or repealing any provision of—

    (a) this Part; or

    (b) the Human Rights Act 1998 (c. 42).

9 Scotland

An order under this Part may not, except by virtue of section 1(8) or 2(7), make provision which would be within the legislative competence of the Scottish Parliament if it were contained in an Act of that Parliament.

10 Northern Ireland

An order under this Part may not, except by virtue of section 1(8) or 2(7), make provision to amend or repeal any Northern Ireland legislation.

[11 Wales]

[(1) Except with the agreement of the Assembly, an order under this Part may not make provision which would be within the legislative competence of the Assembly if the provision were contained in—

    (a) an Assembly Measure (until the Assembly Act provisions of the Government of Wales Act 2006 come into force), or

    (b) an Act of the Assembly (after those provisions come into force).

(2) An order under this Part may not make any provision—

    (a) conferring a function on the Welsh Ministers, the First Minister for Wales or the Counsel General to the Welsh Assembly Government,

    (b) modifying or removing a function of the Welsh Ministers, the First Minister for Wales or the Counsel General to the Welsh Assembly Government,

    (c) restating any provision which confers a function on the Welsh Ministers, the First Minister for Wales or the Counsel General to the Welsh Assembly Government, or

    (d) that could be made by the Welsh Ministers, the First Minister for Wales or the Counsel General to the Welsh Assembly Government in the exercise of any of their functions,

except with the agreement of the Welsh Ministers.

(3) Subsections (1) and (2)(d) do not apply to any provision of an order under this Part falling within sections 1(8) or 2(7).]

Procedure

12 Procedure: introductory

(1) An order under this Part must be made by statutory instrument.

(2) A Minister may not make an order under this Part unless—

    (a) he has consulted in accordance with section 13;

    (b) following that consultation, he has laid a draft order and explanatory document before Parliament in accordance with section 14; and

    (c) the order is made, as determined under section 15, in accordance with—

        (i) the negative resolution procedure (see section 16);

        (ii) the affirmative resolution procedure (see section 17); or

        (iii) the super-affirmative resolution procedure (see section 18).

13 Consultation

(1) If a Minister proposes to make an order under this Part he must—

    (a) consult such organisations as appear to him to be representative of interests substantially affected by the proposals;

    (b) where the proposals relate to the functions of one or more statutory bodies, consult those bodies, or persons appearing to him to be representative of those bodies;

    [(c) consult the Welsh Ministers where the proposals, so far as applying in or as regards Wales, relate to any matter in relation to which the Welsh Ministers, the First Minister for Wales or the Counsel General to the Welsh Assembly Government exercise functions (and where the agreement of the Welsh Ministers is not required under section 11);]

    (d) in such cases as he considers appropriate, consult the Law Commission, the Scottish Law Commission or the Northern Ireland Law Commission; and

    (e) consult such other persons as he considers appropriate.

(2) If, as a result of any consultation required by subsection (1), it appears to the Minister that it is appropriate to change the whole or any part of his proposals, he must undertake such further consultation with respect to the changes as he considers appropriate.

(3)–(5) *****

14 Draft order and explanatory document laid before Parliament

(1) If, after the conclusion of the consultation required by section 13, the Minister considers it appropriate to proceed with the making of an order under this Part, he must lay before Parliament—

    (a) a draft of the order, together with

    (b) an explanatory document.

(2) The explanatory document must—

    (a) explain under which power or powers in this Part the provision contained in the order is made;

    (b) introduce and give reasons for the provision;

    (c) explain why the Minister considers that—

        (i)   the conditions in section 3(2) are satisfied (where relevant); or

        (ii) the condition in section 3(4) is satisfied;

    (d) in the case of an order under section 1, include, so far as appropriate, an assessment of the extent to which the provision made by the order would remove or reduce any burden or burdens (within the meaning of subsection (2) of that section);

    (e) identify and give reasons for—

        (i)   any functions of legislating conferred by the order; and

        (ii) the procedural requirements attaching to the exercise of those functions; and

    (f) give details of—

        (i)   any consultation undertaken under section 13;

        (ii) any representations received as a result of the consultation;

        (iii) the changes (if any) made as a result of those representations.

(3)–(6) *****

15 Determination of Parliamentary procedure

(1) The explanatory document laid with a draft order under section 14 must contain a recommendation by the Minister as to which of the following should apply in relation to the making of an order pursuant to the draft order—

    (a) the negative resolution procedure (see section 16);

    (b) the affirmative resolution procedure (see section 17); or

    (c) the super-affirmative resolution procedure (see section 18).

(2) The explanatory document must give reasons for the Minister's recommendation.

(3) Where the Minister's recommendation is that the negative resolution procedure should apply, that procedure shall apply unless, within the 30-day period—

(a) either House of Parliament requires that the super-affirmative resolution procedure shall apply, in which case that procedure shall apply; or

(b) in a case not falling within paragraph (a), either House of Parliament requires that the affirmative resolution procedure shall apply, in which case that procedure shall apply.

(4) Where the Minister's recommendation is that the affirmative resolution procedure should apply, that procedure shall apply unless, within the 30-day period, either House of Parliament requires that the super-affirmative resolution procedure shall apply, in which case the super-affirmative resolution procedure shall apply.

(5) Where the Minister's recommendation is that the super-affirmative resolution procedure should apply, that procedure shall apply.

(6) For the purposes of this section a House of Parliament shall be taken to have required a procedure within the 30-day period if—

(a) that House resolves within that period that that procedure shall apply; or

(b) in a case not falling within paragraph (a), a committee of that House charged with reporting on the draft order has recommended within that period that that procedure should apply and the House has not by resolution rejected that recommendation within that period.

(7) In this section the '30-day period' means the period of 30 days beginning with the day on which the draft order was laid before Parliament under section 14.

16 Negative resolution procedure

(1) For the purposes of this Part, the 'negative resolution procedure' in relation to the making of an order pursuant to a draft order laid under section 14 is as follows.

(2) The Minister may make an order in the terms of the draft order subject to the following provisions of this section.

(3) The Minister may not make an order in the terms of the draft order if either House of Parliament so resolves within the 40-day period.

(4) A committee of either House charged with reporting on the draft order may, at any time after the expiry of the 30-day period and before the expiry of the 40-day period, recommend under this subsection that the Minister not make an order in the terms of the draft order.

(5) Where a recommendation is made by a committee of either House under subsection (4) in relation to a draft order, the Minister may not make an order in the terms of the draft order unless the recommendation is, in the same Session, rejected by resolution of that House.

(6) For the purposes of this section an order is made in the terms of a draft order if it contains no material changes to the provisions of the draft order.

(7) In this section—

(a) the '30-day period' has the meaning given by section 15(7); and

(b) the '40-day period' means the period of 40 days beginning with the day on which the draft order was laid before Parliament under section 14.

(8) For the purpose of calculating the 40-day period in a case where a recommendation is made under subsection (4) by a committee of either House but the recommendation is rejected by that House under subsection (5), no account shall be taken of any day between the day on which the recommendation was made and the day on which the recommendation was rejected.

17 Affirmative resolution procedure

(1) For the purposes of this Part the 'affirmative resolution procedure' in relation to the making of an order pursuant to a draft order laid under section 14 is as follows.

(2) If after the expiry of the 40-day period the draft order is approved by a resolution of each House of Parliament, the Minister may make an order in the terms of the draft.

(3) However, a committee of either House charged with reporting on the draft order may, at any time after the expiry of the 30-day period and before the expiry of the 40-day period, recommend under this subsection that no further proceedings be taken in relation to the draft order.

(4) Where a recommendation is made by a committee of either House under subsection (3) in relation to a draft order, no proceedings may be taken in relation to the draft order in that House under subsection (2) unless the recommendation is, in the same Session, rejected by resolution of that House.

(5) For the purposes of subsection (2) an order is made in the terms of a draft order if it contains no material changes to the provisions of the draft order.

(6)–(7) *****

18   Super-affirmative resolution procedure

(1) For the purposes of this Part the 'super-affirmative resolution procedure' in relation to the making of an order pursuant to a draft order laid under section 14 is as follows.

(2) The Minister must have regard to—

    (a) any representations,

    (b) any resolution of either House of Parliament, and

    (c) any recommendations of a committee of either House of Parliament charged with reporting on the draft order,

made during the 60-day period with regard to the draft order.

(3) If, after the expiry of the 60-day period, the Minister wishes to make an order in the terms of the draft, he must lay before Parliament a statement—

    (a) stating whether any representations were made under subsection (2)(a); and

    (b) if any representations were so made, giving details of them.

(4) The Minister may after the laying of such a statement make an order in the terms of the draft if it is approved by a resolution of each House of Parliament.

(5) However, a committee of either House charged with reporting on the draft order may, at any time after the laying of a statement under subsection (3) and before the draft order is approved by that House under subsection (4), recommend under this subsection that no further proceedings be taken in relation to the draft order.

(6) Where a recommendation is made by a committee of either House under subsection (5) in relation to a draft order, no proceedings may be taken in relation to the draft order in that House under subsection (4) unless the recommendation is, in the same Session, rejected by resolution of that House.

(7)–(13) *****

19   Calculation of time periods

In calculating any period of days for the purposes of sections 15 to 18, no account shall be taken of any time during which Parliament is dissolved or prorogued or during which either House is adjourned for more than four days.

20   Combination with powers under European Communities Act 1972

(1) The power to make an order under this Part may be exercised together with, and by the same instrument as, the power to make an order under section 2(2) of the European Communities Act 1972 (c 68).

(2) Where the powers referred to in subsection (1) are so exercised—

    (a) sections 12(2) to 18 above apply to the order under section 2(2) of the European Communities Act 1972 as to the order under this Part; and

    (b) paragraph 2(2) of Schedule 2 to the European Communities Act 1972 does not apply.

PART 2 REGULATORS

Exercise of regulatory functions

21   Principles

(1) Any person exercising a regulatory function to which this section applies must have regard to the principles in subsection (2) in the exercise of the function.

(2) Those principles are that—
    (a) regulatory activities should be carried out in a way which is transparent, accountable, proportionate and consistent;
    (b) regulatory activities should be targeted only at cases in which action is needed.

(3) The duty in subsection (1) is subject to any other requirement affecting the exercise of the regulatory function.

*****

Terrorism Act 2006

(2006, c. 11)

An Act to make provision for and about offences relating to conduct carried out, or capable of being carried out, for purposes connected with terrorism; to amend enactments relating to terrorism; to amend the Intelligence Services Act 1994 and the Regulation of Investigatory Powers Act 2000; and for connected purposes.   [30th March 2006]

Territorial extent: The United Kingdom; for the application of the Act outside the United Kingdom, see s. 17

PART 1   OFFENCES

Encouragement etc. of terrorism

1 Encouragement of terrorism

(1) This section applies to a statement that is likely to be understood by some or all of the members of the public to whom it is published as a direct or indirect encouragement or other inducement to them to the commission, preparation or instigation of acts of terrorism or Convention offences.

(2) A person commits an offence if—
    (a) he publishes a statement to which this section applies or causes another to publish such a statement; and
    (b) at the time he publishes it or causes it to be published, he—
        (i) intends members of the public to be directly or indirectly encouraged or otherwise induced by the statement to commit, prepare or instigate acts of terrorism or Convention offences; or
        (ii) is reckless as to whether members of the public will be directly or indirectly encouraged or otherwise induced by the statement to commit, prepare or instigate such acts or offences.

(3) For the purposes of this section, the statements that are likely to be understood by members of the public as indirectly encouraging the commission or preparation of acts of terrorism or Convention offences include every statement which—
    (a) glorifies the commission or preparation (whether in the past, in the future or generally) of such acts or offences; and
    (b) is a statement from which those members of the public could reasonably be expected to infer that what is being glorified is being glorified as conduct that should be emulated by them in existing circumstances.

(4) For the purposes of this section the questions how a statement is likely to be understood and what members of the public could reasonably be expected to infer from it must be determined having regard both—
    (a) to the contents of the statement as a whole; and

(b) to the circumstances and manner of its publication.

(5) It is irrelevant for the purposes of subsections (1) to (3)—

(a) whether anything mentioned in those subsections relates to the commission, preparation or instigation of one or more particular acts of terrorism or Convention offences, of acts of terrorism or Convention offences of a particular description or of acts of terrorism or Convention offences generally; and,

(b) whether any person is in fact encouraged or induced by the statement to commit, prepare or instigate any such act or offence.

(6) In proceedings for an offence under this section against a person in whose case it is not proved that he intended the statement directly or indirectly to encourage or otherwise induce the commission, preparation or instigation of acts of terrorism or Convention offences, it is a defence for him to show—

(a) that the statement neither expressed his views nor had his endorsement (whether by virtue of section 3 or otherwise); and

(b) that it was clear, in all the circumstances of the statement's publication, that it did not express his views and (apart from the possibility of his having been given and failed to comply with a notice under subsection(3)of that section) did not have his endorsement.

(7) A person guilty of an offence under this section shall be liable—

(a) on conviction on indictment, to imprisonment for a term not exceeding 7 years or to a fine, or to both;

(b) on summary conviction in England and Wales, to imprisonment for a term not exceeding 12 months or to a fine not exceeding the statutory maximum, or to both;

(c) on summary conviction in Scotland or Northern Ireland, to imprisonment for a term not exceeding 6 months or to a fine not exceeding the statutory maximum, or to both.

(8) In relation to an offence committed before the commencement of section 154(1) of the Criminal Justice Act 2003 (c. 44), the reference in subsection (7)(b) to 12 months is to be read as a reference to 6 months.

2   Dissemination of terrorist publications

(1) A person commits an offence if he engages in conduct falling within subsection (2) and, at the time he does so—

(a) he intends an effect of his conduct to be a direct or indirect encouragement or other inducement to the commission, preparation or instigation of acts of terrorism;

(b) he intends an effect of his conduct to be the provision of assistance in the commission or preparation of such acts; or

(c) he is reckless as to whether his conduct has an effect mentioned in paragraph (a) or (b).

(2) For the purposes of this section a person engages in conduct falling within this subsection if he—

(a) distributes or circulates a terrorist publication;

(b) gives, sells or lends such a publication;

(c) offers such a publication for sale or loan;

(d) provides a service to others that enables them to obtain, read, listen to or look at such a publication, or to acquire it by means of a gift, sale or loan;

(e) transmits the contents of such a publication electronically; or

(f) has such a publication in his possession with a view to its becoming the subject of conduct falling within any of paragraphs (a) to (e).

(3) For the purposes of this section a publication is a terrorist publication, in relation to conduct falling within subsection (2), if matter contained in it is likely—

(a) to be understood, by some or all of the persons to whom it is or may become available as a consequence of that conduct, as a direct or indirect encouragement or other inducement to them to the commission, preparation or instigation of acts of terrorism; or

(b) to be useful in the commission or preparation of such acts and to be understood, by some or all of those persons, as contained in the publication, or made available to them, wholly or mainly for the purpose of being so useful to them.

(4) For the purposes of this section matter that is likely to be understood by a person as indirectly encouraging the commission or preparation of acts of terrorism includes any matter which—

(a) glorifies the commission or preparation (whether in the past, in the future or generally) of such acts; and

(b) is matter from which that person could reasonably be expected to infer that what is being glorified is being glorified as conduct that should be emulated by him in existing circumstances.

(5) For the purposes of this section the question whether a publication is a terrorist publication in relation to particular conduct must be determined—

(a) as at the time of that conduct; and

(b) having regard both to the contents of the publication as a whole and to the circumstances in which that conduct occurs.

(6) In subsection (1) references to the effect of a person's conduct in relation to a terrorist publication include references to an effect of the publication on one or more persons to whom it is or may become available as a consequence of that conduct.

(7) It is irrelevant for the purposes of this section whether anything mentioned in subsections (1) to (4) is in relation to the commission, preparation or instigation of one or more particular acts of terrorism, of acts of terrorism of a particular description or of acts of terrorism generally.

(8) For the purposes of this section it is also irrelevant, in relation to matter contained in any article whether any person—

(a) is in fact encouraged or induced by that matter to commit, prepare or instigate acts of terrorism; or

(b) in fact makes use of it in the commission or preparation of such acts.

(9) In proceedings for an offence under this section against a person in respect of conduct to which subsection (10) applies, it is a defence for him to show—

(a) that the matter by reference to which the publication in question was a terrorist publication neither expressed his views nor had his endorsement (whether by virtue of section 3 or otherwise); and

(b) that it was clear, in all the circumstances of the conduct, that that matter did not express his views and (apart from the possibility of his having been given and failed to comply with a notice under subsection (3) of that section) did not have his endorsement.

(10) This subsection applies to the conduct of a person to the extent that—

(a) the publication to which his conduct related contained matter by reference to which it was a terrorist publication by virtue of subsection (3)(a); and

(b) that person is not proved to have engaged in that conduct with the intention specified in subsection (1)(a).

(11) A person guilty of an offence under this section shall be liable—

(a) on conviction on indictment, to imprisonment for a term not exceeding 7 years or to a fine, or to both;

(b) on summary conviction in England and Wales, to imprisonment for a term not exceeding 12 months or to a fine not exceeding the statutory maximum, or to both;

(c) on summary conviction in Scotland or Northern Ireland, to imprisonment for a term not exceeding 6 months or to a fine not exceeding the statutory maximum, or to both.

(12) In relation to an offence committed before the commencement of section 154(1) of the Criminal Justice Act 2003 (c. 44), the reference in subsection (11)(b) to 12 months is to be read as a reference to 6 months.

(13) In this section—

'lend' includes let on hire, and 'loan' is to be construed accordingly;

'publication' means an article or record of any description that contains any of the following, or any combination of them—

(a) matter to be read;

(b) matter to be listened to;

(c) matter to be looked at or watched.

3 Application of ss. 1 and 2 to internet activity etc.

(1) This section applies for the purposes of sections 1 and 2 in relation to cases where—

    (a) a statement is published or caused to be published in the course of, or in connection with, the provision or use of a service provided electronically; or

    (b) conduct falling within section 2(2) was in the course of, or in connection with, the provision or use of such a service.

(2) The cases in which the statement, or the article or record to which the conduct relates, is to be regarded as having the endorsement of a person (the relevant person') at any time include a case in which—

    (a) a constable has given him a notice under subsection (3);

    (b) that time falls more than 2 working days after the day on which the notice was given; and

    (c) the relevant person has failed, without reasonable excuse, to comply with the notice.

(3) A notice under this subsection is a notice which—

    (a) declares that, in the opinion of the constable giving it, the statement or the article or record is unlawfully terrorism-related;

    (b) requires the relevant person to secure that the statement or the article or record, so far as it is so related, is not available to the public or is modified so as no longer to be so related;

    (c) warns the relevant person that a failure to comply with the notice within 2 working days will result in the statement, or the article or record, being regarded as having his endorsement; and

    (d) explains how, under subsection (4), he may become liable by virtue of the notice if the statement, or the article or record, becomes available to the public after he has complied with the notice.

(4) Where—

    (a) a notice under subsection (3) has been given to the relevant person in respect of a statement, or an article or record, and he has complied with it, but

    (b) he subsequently publishes or causes to be published a statement which is, or is for all practical purposes, the same or to the same effect as the statement to which the notice related, or to matter contained in the article or record to which it related, (a 'repeat statement');

the requirements of subsection (2)(a) to (c) shall be regarded as satisfied in the case of the repeat statement in relation to the times of its subsequent publication by the relevant person.

(5)–(6) *****

(7) For the purposes of this section a statement or an article or record is unlawfully terrorism-related if it constitutes, or if matter contained in the article or record constitutes—

    (a) something that is likely to be understood, by any one or more of the persons to whom it has or may become available, as a direct or indirect encouragement or other inducement to the commission, preparation or instigation of acts of terrorism or Convention offences; or

    (b) information which—

        (i) is likely to be useful to any one or more of those persons in the commission or preparation of such acts; and

        (ii) is in a form or context in which it is likely to be understood by any one or more of those persons as being wholly or mainly for the purpose of being so useful.

(8) The reference in subjection (7) to something that is likely to be understood as an indirect encouragement to the commission or preparation of acts of terrorism or Convention offences includes anything which is likely to be understood as—

    (a) the glorification of the commission or preparation (whether in the past, in the future or generally) of such acts or such offences; and

(b) a suggestion that what is being glorified as conduct that should be emulated in existing circumstances.

(9) *****

4 *****

Preparation of terrorist acts and terrorist training

5 Preparation of terrorist acts

(1) A person commits an offence if, with the intention of—

(a) committing acts of terrorism, or

(b) assisting another to commit such acts,

he engages in any conduct in preparation for giving effect to his intention.

(2) It is irrelevant for the purposes of subsection (1) whether the intention and preparations relate to one or more particular acts of terrorism, acts of terrorism of a particular description or acts of terrorism generally.

(3) A person guilty of an offence under this section shall be liable, on conviction on indictment, to imprisonment for life.

6 Training for terrorism

(1) A person commits an offence if—

(a) he provides instruction or training in any of the skills mentioned in subsection (3); and

(b) at the time he provides the instruction or training, he knows that a person receiving it intends to use the skills in which he is being instructed or trained—

(i) for or in connection with the commission or preparation of acts of terrorism or Convention offences; or

(ii) for assisting the commission or preparation by others of such acts or offences.

(2) A person commits an offence if—

(a) he receives instruction or training in any of the skills mentioned in subsection (3); and

(b) at the time of the instruction or training, he intends to use the skills in which he is being instructed or trained—

(i) for or in connection with the commission or preparation of acts of terrorism or Convention offences; or

(ii) for assisting the commission or preparation by others of such acts or offences.

(3) The skills are—

(a) the making, handling or use of a noxious substance, or of substances of a description of such substances;

(b) the use of any method or technique for doing anything else that is capable of being done for the purposes of terrorism, in connection with the commission or preparation of an act of terrorism or Convention offence or in connection with assisting the commission or preparation by another of such an act or offence; and

(c) the design or adaptation for the purposes of terrorism, or in connection with the commission or preparation of an act of terrorism or Convention offence, of any method or technique for doing anything.

(4) It is irrelevant for the purposes of subsections (1) and (2)—

(a) whether any instruction or training that is provided is provided to one or more particular persons or generally;

(b) whether the acts or offences in relation to which a person intends to use skills in which he is instructed or trained consist of one or more particular acts of terrorism or Convention offences, acts of terrorism or Convention offences of a particular description or acts of terrorism or Convention offences generally; and

(c) whether assistance that a person intends to provide to others is intended to be provided to one or more particular persons or to one or more persons whose identities are not yet known.

(5) A person guilty of an offence under this section shall be liable—

    (a) on conviction on indictment, to imprisonment for a term not exceeding 10 years or to a fine, or to both;

    (b) on summary conviction in England and Wales, to imprisonment for a term not exceeding 12 months or to a fine not exceeding the statutory maximum, or to both;

    (c) on summary conviction in Scotland or Northern Ireland, to imprisonment for a term not exceeding 6 months or to a fine not exceeding the statutory maximum, or to both.

(6) In relation to an offence committed before the commencement of section 154(1) of the Criminal Justice Act 2003 (c. 44), the reference in subsection (5)(b) to 12 months is to be read as a reference to 6 months.

(7) In this section—

'noxious substance' means—

    (a) a dangerous substance within the meaning of Part 7 of the Anti-terrorism, Crime and Security Act 2001 (c. 24); or

    (b) any other substance which is hazardous or noxious or which may be or become hazardous or noxious only in certain circumstances;

'substance' includes any natural or artificial substance (whatever its origin or method of production and whether in solid or liquid form or in the form of a gas or vapour) and any mixture of substances.

7 Powers of forfeiture in respect of offences under s. 6

(1) A court before which a person is convicted of an offence under section 6 may order the forfeiture of anything the court considers to have been in the person's possession for purposes connected with the offence.

(2)–(7) *****

8 Attendance at a place used for terrorist training

(1) A person commits an offence if—

    (a) he attends at any place, whether in the United Kingdom or elsewhere;

    (b) while he is at that place, instruction or training of the type mentioned in section 6(1) of this Act or section 54(1) of the Terrorism Act 2000 (c. 11) (weapons training) is provided there;

    (c) that instruction or training is provided there wholly or partly for purposes connected with the commission or preparation of acts of terrorism or Convention offences; and

    (d) the requirements of subsection (2) are satisfied in relation to that person.

(2) The requirements of this subsection are satisfied in relation to a person if—

    (a) he knows or believes that instruction or training is being provided there wholly or partly for purposes connected with the commission or preparation of acts of terrorism or Convention offences; or

    (b) a person attending at that place throughout the period of that person's attendance could not reasonably have failed to understand that instruction or training was being provided there wholly or partly for such purposes.

(3) It is immaterial for the purposes of this section—

    (a) whether the person concerned receives the instruction or training himself; and

    (b) whether the instruction or training is provided for purposes connected with one or more particular acts of terrorism or Convention offences, acts of terrorism or Convention offences of a particular description or acts of terrorism or Convention offences generally.

(4) A person guilty of an offence under this section shall be liable—

    (a) on conviction on indictment, to imprisonment for a term not exceeding 10 years or to a fine, or to both;

    (b) on summary conviction in England and Wales, to imprisonment for a term not exceeding 12 months or to a fine not exceeding the statutory maximum, or to both;

(c) on summary conviction in Scotland or Northern Ireland, to imprisonment for a term not exceeding 6 months or to a fine not exceeding the statutory maximum, or to both.

(5) In relation to an offence committed before the commencement of section 154(1) of the Criminal Justice Act 2003 (c. 44), the reference in subsection (4)(b) to 12 months is to be read as a reference to 6 months.

(6) References in this section to instruction or training being provided include references to its being made available.

Offences involving radioactive devices and materials and nuclear facilities and sites

9 Making and possession of devices or materials

(1) A person commits an offence if—

(a) he makes or has in his possession a radioactive device, or

(b) he has in his possession radioactive material,

with the intention of using the device or material in the course of or in connection with the commission or preparation of an act of terrorism or for the purposes of terrorism, or of making it available to be so used.

(2) It is irrelevant for the purposes of subsection (1) whether the act of terrorism to which an intention relates is a particular act of terrorism, an act of terrorism of a particular description or an act of terrorism generally.

(3) A person guilty of an offence under this section shall be liable, on conviction on indictment, to imprisonment for life.

(4), (5) *****

10 Misuse of devices or material and misuse and damage of facilities

(1) A person commits an offence if he uses—

(a) a radioactive device, or

(b) radioactive material,

in the course of or in connection with the commission of an act of terrorism or for the purposes of terrorism.

(2) A person commits an offence if, in the course of or in connection with the commission of an act of terrorism or for the purposes of terrorism, he uses or damages a nuclear facility in a manner which—

(a) causes a release of radioactive material; or

(b) creates or increases a risk that such material will be released.

(3) A person guilty of an offence under this section shall be liable, on conviction on indictment, to imprisonment for life.

(4), (5) *****

11 Terrorist threats relating to devices, materials or facilities

(1) A person commits an offence if, in the course of or in connection with the commission of an act of terrorism or for the purposes of terrorism—

(a) he makes a demand—

(i) for the supply to himself or to another of a radioactive device or of radioactive material;

(ii) for a nuclear facility to be made available to himself or to another; or

(iii) for access to such a facility to be given to himself or to another;

(b) he supports the demand with a threat that he or another will take action if the demand is not met; and

(c) the circumstances and manner of the threat are such that it is reasonable for the person to whom it is made to assume that there is real risk that the threat will be carried out if the demand is not met.

(2) A person also commits an offence if—

(a) he makes a threat falling within subsection (3) in the course of or in connection with the commission of an act of terrorism or for the purposes of terrorism; and

(b) the circumstances and manner of the threat are such that it is reasonable for the person to whom it is made to assume that there is real risk that the threat will be carried out, or would be carried out if demands made in association with the threat are not met.

(3) A threat falls within this subsection if it is—

(a) a threat to use radioactive material;

(b) a threat to use a radioactive device; or

(c) a threat to use or damage a nuclear facility in a manner that releases radioactive material or creates or increases a risk that such material will be released.

(4) A person guilty of an offence under this section shall be liable, on conviction on indictment, to imprisonment for life.

(5) *****

[11A   Forfeiture of devices, materials or facilities]

[(1) A court by or before which a person is convicted of an offence under section 9 or 10 may order the forfeiture of any radioactive device or radioactive material, or any nuclear facility, made or used in committing the offence.

(2) A court by or before which a person is convicted of an offence under section 11 may order the forfeiture of any radioactive device or radioactive material, or any nuclear facility, which is the subject of—

(a) a demand under subsection (1) of that section, or

(b) a threat falling within subsection (3) of that section.

(3) Before making an order under this section, a court must give an opportunity to be heard to any person, other than the convicted person, who claims to be the owner or otherwise interested in anything which can be forfeited under this section.

(4) An order under this section does not come into force until there is no further possibility of it being varied, or set aside, on appeal (disregarding any power of a court to grant leave to appeal out of time).

(5)–(7) *****

12–16   *****

17   Commission of offences abroad

(1) If—

(a) a person does anything outside the United Kingdom, and

(b) his action, if done in a part of the United Kingdom, would constitute an offence falling within subsection (2),

he shall be guilty in that part of the United Kingdom of the offence.

(2) The offences falling within this subsection are—

(a) an offence under section 1 or 6 of this Act so far as it is committed in relation to any statement, instruction or training in relation to which that section has effect by reason of its relevance to the commission, preparation or instigation of one or more Convention offences;

(b) an offence under any of sections 8 to 11 of this Act;

(c) an offence under section 11(1) of the Terrorism Act 2000 (c. 11) (membership of proscribed organisations);

(d) an offence under section 54 of that Act (weapons training);

(e) conspiracy to commit an offence falling within this subsection;

(f) inciting a person to commit such an offence;

(g) attempting to commit such an offence;

(h) aiding, abetting, counselling or procuring the commission of such an offence.

(3) Subsection (1) applies irrespective of whether the person is a British citizen or, in the case of a company, a company incorporated in a part of the United Kingdom.

(4) In the case of an offence falling within subsection (2) which is committed wholly or partly outside the United Kingdom—

    (a) proceedings for the offence may be taken at any place in the United Kingdom; and

    (b) the offence may for all incidental purposes be treated as having been committed at any such place.

(5), (6) *****

18 *****

19 Consents to prosecutions

(1) Proceedings for an offence under this Part—

    (a) may be instituted in England and Wales only with the consent of the Director of Public Prosecutions; and

    (b) may be instituted in Northern Ireland only with the consent of the Director of Public Prosecutions for Northern Ireland.

(2) But if it appears to the Director of Public Prosecutions or the Director of Public Prosecutions for Northern Ireland that an offence under this Part has been committed [outside the United Kingdom or] for a purpose wholly or partly connected with the affairs of a country other than the United Kingdom, his consent for the purposes of this section may be given only with the permission—

    (a) in the case of the Director of Public Prosecutions, of the Attorney General; and

    (b) in the case of the Director of Public Prosecutions for Northern Ireland, of the Advocate General for Northern Ireland.

(3) In relation to any time before the coming into force of section 27(1) of the Justice (Northern Ireland) Act 2002 (c. 26), the reference in subsection (2)(b) to the Advocate General for Northern Ireland is to be read as a reference to the Attorney General for Northern Ireland.

Interpretation of Part 1

20 Interpretation of Part 1

(1) Expressions used in this Part and in the Terrorism Act 2000 (c. 11) have the same meanings in this Part as in that Act.

(2) In this Part—

'act of terrorism' includes anything constituting an action taken for the purposes of terrorism, within the meaning of the Terrorism Act 2000 (see section 1(5) of that Act);

'article' includes anything for storing data;

'Convention offence' means an offence listed in Schedule 1 or an equivalent offence under the law of a country or territory outside the United Kingdom;

'glorification' includes any form of praise or celebration, and cognate expressions are to be construed accordingly;

'public' is to be construed in accordance with subsection (3);

'publish' and cognate expressions are to be construed in accordance with subsection (4);

'record' means a record so far as not comprised in an article, including a temporary record created electronically and existing solely in the course of, and for the purposes of, the transmission of the whole or a part of its contents;

'statement' is to be construed in accordance with subsection (6).

(3) In this Part references to the public—

    (a) are references to the public of any part of the United Kingdom or of a country or territory outside the United Kingdom, or any section of the public; and

    (b) except in section 9(4), also include references to a meeting or other group of persons which is open to the public (whether unconditionally or on the making of a payment or the satisfaction of other conditions).

(4) In this Part references to a person's publishing a statement are references to—

    (a) his publishing it in any manner to the public;

    (b) his providing electronically any service by means of which the public have access to the statement; or

    (c) his using a service provided to him electronically by another so as to enable or to facilitate access by the public to the statement;

but this subsection does not apply to the references to a publication in section 2.

    (5)–(11) *****

21–35 *****

PART 3 SUPPLEMENTAL PROVISIONS

36 Review of terrorism legislation

(1) The Secretary of State must appoint a person to review the operation of the provisions of the Terrorism Act 2000 and of Part 1 of this Act.

(2) That person may, from time to time, carry out a review of those provisions and, where he does so, must send a report on the outcome of his review to the Secretary of State as soon as reasonably practicable after completing the review.

[(2A)] ***** (not yet in force)

(3) That person must carry out and report on his first review under this section before the end of the period of 12 months after the laying before Parliament of the last report to be so laid under section 126 of the Terrorism Act 2000 before the commencement of this section.

(4) That person must carry out and report on a review under this section at least once in every twelve month period ending with an anniversary of the end of the twelve month period mentioned in subsection (3).

(5) In receiving a report under this section, the Secretary of State must lay a copy of it before Parliament.

(6) The Secretary of State may, out of money provided by Parliament, pay a person appointed to carry out a review under this section, both his expenses and also such allowances as the Secretary of State determines.

37–39 ****

Section 20

SCHEDULE 1

CONVENTION OFFENCES

Explosives offences

1.—(1) Subject to sub-paragraph (3), an offence under any of sections 28 to 30 of the Offences against the Person Act 1861 (c. 100) (causing injury by explosions, causing explosions and handling or placing explosives).

(2) Subject to sub-paragraph (3), an offence under any of the following provisions of the Explosive Substances Act 1883 (c. 3)—

    (a) section 2 (causing an explosion likely to endanger life);

    (b) section 3 (preparation of explosions);

    (c) section 5 (ancillary offences).

(3) An offence in or as regards Scotland is a Convention offence by virtue of this paragraph only if it consists in—

    (a) the doing of an act as an act of terrorism; or

    (b) an action for the purposes of terrorism.

Biological weapons

2. An offence under section 1 of the Biological Weapons Act 1974 (c. 6) (development etc. of biological weapons).

Offences against internationally protected persons

3.—(1) Subject to sub-paragraph (4), an offence mentioned in section 1(1)(a) of the Internationally Protected Persons Act 1978 (c. 17) (attacks against protected persons committed outside the United Kingdom) which is committed (whether in the United Kingdom or elsewhere) in relation to a protected person.

(2) Subject to sub-paragraph (4), an offence mentioned in section 1(1)(b) of that Act (attacks on relevant premises etc.) which is committed (whether in the United Kingdom or elsewhere) in connection with an attack—

(a) on relevant premises or on a vehicle ordinarily used by a protected person, and

(b) at a time when a protected person is in or on the premises or vehicle.

(3) Subject to sub-paragraph (4), an offence under section 1(3) of that Act (threats etc. in relation to protected persons).

(4) An offence in or as regards Scotland is a Convention offence by virtue of this paragraph only if it consists in—

(a) the doing of an act as an act of terrorism; or

(b) an action for the purposes of terrorism.

(5) Expressions used in this paragraph and section 1 of that Act have the same meanings in this paragraph as in that section.

Hostage-taking

4. An offence under section 1 of the Taking of Hostages Act 1982 (c. 28) (hostage-taking).

Hijacking and other offences against aircraft

5. Offences under any of the following provisions of the Aviation Security Act 1982 (c. 36)—

(a) section 1 (hijacking);

(b) section 2 (destroying, damaging or endangering safety of aircraft);

(c) section 3 (other acts endangering or likely to endanger safety of aircraft);

(d) section 6(2) (ancillary offences).

Offences involving nuclear material [or nuclear facilities]

6.—(1) An offence mentioned in section 1(1) [(a) to (d)] of the Nuclear Material (Offences) Act 1983 (c. 18) (offences in relation to nuclear material committed outside the United Kingdom) which is committed (whether in the United Kingdom or elsewhere) in relation to or by means of nuclear material.

[(2) An offence mentioned in section 1(1)(a) or (b) of that Act where the act making the person guilty of the offence (whether done in the United Kingdom or elsewhere)—

(a) is directed at a nuclear facility or interferes with the operation of such a facility, and

(b) causes death, injury or damage resulting from the emission of ionising radiation or the release of radioactive material.

(3) An offence under any of the following provisions of that Act—

(a) section 1B (offences relating to damage to environment);

(b) section 1C (offences of importing or exporting etc nuclear material: extended jurisdiction);

(c) section 2 (offences involving preparatory acts and threats).

(4) Expressions used in this paragraph and that Act have the same meanings in this paragraph as in that Act.]

[6A—(1) Any of the following offences under the Customs and Excise Management Act 1979—

    (a) an offence under section 50(2) or (3) (improper importation of goods) in connection with a prohibition or restriction relating to the importation of nuclear material;

    (b) an offence under section 68(2) (exportation of prohibited or restricted goods) in connection with a prohibition or restriction relating to the exportation or shipment as stores of nuclear material;

    (c) an offence under section 170(1) or (2) (fraudulent evasion of duty etc) in connection with a prohibition or restriction relating to the importation, exportation or shipment as stores of nuclear material.

(2) In this paragraph "nuclear material" has the same meaning as in the Nuclear Material (Offences) Act 1983 (see section 6 of that Act).]

Offences under the Aviation and Maritime Security Act 1990 (c. 31)

7. Offences under any of the following provisions of the Aviation and Maritime Security Act 1990—

    (a) section 1 (endangering safety at aerodromes);

    (b) section 9 (hijacking of ships);

    (c) section 10 (seizing or exercising control of fixed platforms);

    (d) section 11 (destroying ships or fixed platforms or endangering their safety);

    (e) section 12 (other acts endangering or likely to endanger safe navigation);

    (f) section 13 (offences involving threats relating to ships or fixed platforms);

    (g) section 14 (ancillary offences).

Offences involving chemical weapons

8. An offence under section 2 of the Chemical Weapons Act 1996 (c. 6) (use, development etc. of chemical weapons).

Terrorist funds

9. An offence under any of the following provisions of the Terrorism Act 2000 (c. 11)—

    (a) section 15 (terrorist fund-raising);

    (b) section 16 (use or possession of terrorist funds);

    (c) section 17 (funding arrangements for terrorism);

    (d) section 18 (money laundering of terrorist funds).

Directing terrorist organisations

10. An offence under section 56 of the Terrorism Act 2000 (directing a terrorist organisation).

Offences involving nuclear weapons

11. An offence under section 47 of the Anti-terrorism, Crime and Security Act 2001 (c. 24) (use, development etc. of nuclear weapons).

Conspiracy etc.

12. Any of the following offences—

    (a) conspiracy to commit a Convention offence;

    (b) inciting the commission of a Convention offence;

    (c) attempting to commit a Convention offence;

    (d) aiding, abetting, counselling or procuring the commission of a Convention offence.

*****

Legal Services Act 2007

(2007, c. 29)

An Act to make provision for the establishment of the Legal Services Board and in respect of its functions; to make provision for, and in connection with, the regulation of persons who carry on certain legal activities; to make provision for the establishment of the Office for Legal Complaints and for a scheme to consider

and determine legal complaints; to make provision about claims management services and about immigra-
tion advice and immigration services; to make provision in respect of legal representation provided free of
charge; to make provision about the application of the Legal Profession and Legal Aid (Scotland) Act 2007;
to make provision about the Scottish legal services ombudsman; and for connected purposes.

[30th October 2007]

Territorial extent: England and Wales

PART 1   THE REGULATORY OBJECTIVES

1   The regulatory objectives

(1) In this Act a reference to 'the regulatory objectives' is a reference to the objectives of—

    (a) protecting and promoting the public interest;

    (b) supporting the constitutional principle of the rule of law;

    (c) improving access to justice;

    (d) protecting and promoting the interests of consumers;

    (e) promoting competition in the provision of services within subsection (2);

    (f) encouraging an independent, strong, diverse and effective legal profession;

    (g) increasing public understanding of the citizen's legal rights and duties;

    (h) promoting and maintaining adherence to the professional principles.

(2) The services within this subsection are services such as are provided by authorised persons (including services which do not involve the carrying on of activities which are reserved legal activities).

(3) The 'professional principles' are—

    (a) that authorised persons should act with independence and integrity,

    (b) that authorised persons should maintain proper standards of work,

    (c) that authorised persons should act in the best interests of their clients,

    (d) that persons who exercise before any court a right of audience, or conduct litigation in relation to proceedings in any court, by virtue of being authorised persons should comply with their duty to the court to act with independence in the interests of justice, and

    (e) that the affairs of clients should be kept confidential.

(4) In this section 'authorised persons' means authorised persons in relation to activities which are reserved legal activities.

PART 2   THE LEGAL SERVICES BOARD

Constitution

2   The Legal Services Board

(1) There is to be a body corporate called the Legal Services Board ("the Board").

(2) Schedule 1 is about the Board.

General functions

3   The Board's duty to promote the regulatory objectives etc

(1) In discharging its functions the Board must comply with the requirements of this section.

(2) The Board must, so far as is reasonably practicable, act in a way—

    (a) which is compatible with the regulatory objectives, and

    (b) which the Board considers most appropriate for the purpose of meeting those objectives.

(3) The Board must have regard to—

    (a) the principles under which regulatory activities should be transparent, accountable, proportionate, consistent and targeted only at cases in which action is needed, and

(b) any other principle appearing to it to represent the best regulatory practice.

4 Standards of regulation, education and training

The Board must assist in the maintenance and development of standards in relation to—

(a) the regulation by approved regulators of persons authorised by them to carry on activities which are reserved legal activities, and

(b) the education and training of persons so authorised.

5 Corporate governance

In managing its affairs, the Board must have regard to such generally accepted principles of good corporate governance as it is reasonable to regard as applicable to it.

*****

Serious Crime Act 2007

(2007, c. 27)

An Act to make provision about serious crime prevention orders; to create offences in respect of the encouragement or assistance of crime; to enable information to be shared or processed to prevent fraud or for purposes relating to proceeds of crime; to enable data matching to be conducted both in relation to fraud and for other purposes; to transfer functions of the Director of the Assets Recovery Agency to the Serious Organised Crime Agency and other persons and to make further provision in connection with the abolition of the Agency and the office of Director; to amend the Proceeds of Crime Act 2002 in relation to certain investigations and in relation to accredited financial investigators, management receivers and enforcement receivers, cash recovery proceedings and search warrants; to extend stop and search powers in connection with incidents involving serious violence; to make amendments relating to Her Majesty's Revenue and Customs in connection with the regulation of investigatory powers; and for connected purposes.   [30th October 2007]

Territorial extent: England and Wales, Northern Ireland

PART 1   SERIOUS CRIME PREVENTION ORDERS

General

1 Serious crime prevention orders

(1) The High Court in England and Wales may make an order if—

(a) it is satisfied that a person has been involved in serious crime (whether in England and Wales or elsewhere); and

(b) it has reasonable grounds to believe that the order would protect the public by preventing, restricting or disrupting involvement by the person in serious crime in England and Wales.

(2) *****

(3) An order under this section may contain—

(a) such prohibitions, restrictions or requirements; and

(b) such other terms;

as the court considers appropriate for the purpose of protecting the public by preventing, restricting or disrupting involvement by the person concerned in serious crime in England and Wales or (as the case may be) Northern Ireland.

(4) The powers of the court in respect of an order under this section are subject to sections 6 to 15 (safeguards).

(5) In this Part 'serious crime prevention order' means—

(a) an order under this section; or

(b) an order under section 19 (corresponding order of the Crown Court on conviction).

(6) For the purposes of this Part references to the person who is the subject of a serious crime prevention order are references to the person against whom the public are to be protected.

2 Involvement in serious crime: England and Wales orders

(1) For the purposes of this Part, a person has been involved in serious crime in England and Wales if he—

(a) has committed a serious offence in England and Wales;

(b) has facilitated the commission by another person of a serious offence in England and Wales; or

(c) has conducted himself in a way that was likely to facilitate the commission by himself or another person of a serious offence in England and Wales (whether or not such an offence was committed).

(2) In this Part 'a serious offence in England and Wales' means an offence under the law of England and Wales which, at the time when the court is considering the application or matter in question—

(a) is specified, or falls within a description specified, in Part 1 of Schedule 1; or

(b) is one which, in the particular circumstances of the case, the court considers to be sufficiently serious to be treated for the purposes of the application or matter as if it were so specified.

(3) For the purposes of this Part, involvement in serious crime in England and Wales is any one or more of the following—

(a) the commission of a serious offence in England and Wales;

(b) conduct which facilitates the commission by another person of a serious offence in England and Wales;

(c) conduct which is likely to facilitate the commission, by the person whose conduct it is or another person, of a serious offence in England and Wales (whether or not such an offence is committed).

(4) For the purposes of section 1(1)(a), a person has been involved in serious crime elsewhere than in England and Wales if he—

(a) has committed a serious offence in a country outside England and Wales;

(b) has facilitated the commission by another person of a serious offence in a country outside England and Wales; or

(c) has conducted himself in a way that was likely to facilitate the commission by himself or another person of a serious offence in a country outside England and Wales (whether or not such an offence was committed).

(5)–(7) *****

3 *****

4 Involvement in serious crime: supplementary

(1) In considering for the purposes of this Part whether a person has committed a serious offence—

(a) the court must decide that the person has committed the offence if—

(i) he has been convicted of the offence; and

(ii) the conviction has not been quashed on appeal nor has the person been pardoned of the offence; but

(b) the court must not otherwise decide that the person has committed the offence.

(2) In deciding for the purposes of this Part whether a person ('the respondent') facilitates the commission by another person of a serious offence, the court must ignore—

(a) any act that the respondent can show to be reasonable in the circumstances; and

(b) subject to this, his intentions, or any other aspect of his mental state, at the time.

(3) In deciding for the purposes of this Part whether a person ('the respondent') conducts himself in a way that is likely to facilitate the commission by himself or another person of a serious offence (whether or not such an offence is committed), the court must ignore—

(a) any act that the respondent can show to be reasonable in the circumstances; and

(b) subject to this, his intentions, or any other aspect of his mental state, at the time.

(4) *****

5   Type of provision that may be made by orders

(1) This section contains examples of the type of provision that may be made by a serious crime prevention order but it does not limit the type of provision that may be made by such an order.

(2) Examples of prohibitions, restrictions or requirements that may be imposed by serious crime prevention orders in England and Wales or Northern Ireland include prohibitions, restrictions or requirements in relation to places other than England and Wales or (as the case may be) Northern Ireland.

(3) Examples of prohibitions, restrictions or requirements that may be imposed on individuals (including partners in a partnership) by serious crime prevention orders include prohibitions or restrictions on, or requirements in relation to—

(a) an individual's financial, property or business dealings or holdings;

(b) an individual's working arrangements;

(c) the means by which an individual communicates or associates with others, or the persons with whom he communicates or associates;

(d) the premises to which an individual has access;

(e) the use of any premises or item by an individual;

(f) an individual's travel (whether within the United Kingdom, between the United Kingdom and other places or otherwise).

(4) Examples of prohibitions, restrictions or requirements that may be imposed on bodies corporate, partnerships and unincorporated associations by serious crime prevention orders include prohibitions or restrictions on, or requirements in relation to—

(a) financial, property or business dealings or holdings of such persons;

(b) the types of agreements to which such persons may be a party;

(c) the provision of goods or services by such persons;

(d) the premises to which such persons have access;

(e) the use of any premises or item by such persons;

(f) the employment of staff by such persons.

(5) Examples of requirements that may be imposed on any persons by serious crime prevention orders include—

(a) a requirement on a person to answer questions, or provide information, specified or described in an order—

(i) at a time, within a period or at a frequency;

(ii) at a place;

(iii) in a form and manner; and

(iv) to a law enforcement officer or description of law enforcement officer;

notified to the person by a law enforcement officer specified or described in the order;

(b) a requirement on a person to produce documents specified or described in an order—

(i) at a time, within a period or at a frequency;

(ii) at a place;

(iii) in a manner; and

(iv) to a law enforcement officer or description of law enforcement officer;

notified to the person by a law enforcement officer specified or described in the order.

(6) The prohibitions, restrictions or requirements that may be imposed on individuals by serious crime prevention orders include prohibitions, restrictions or requirements in relation to an individual's private dwelling (including, for example, prohibitions or restrictions on, or requirements in relation to, where an individual may reside).

(7), (8) *****

*****

Tribunals, Courts and Enforcement Act 2007

(2007, c. 15)

An Act to make provision about tribunals and inquiries; to establish an Administrative Justice and Tribunals Council; to amend the law relating to judicial appointments and appointments to the Law Commission; to amend the law relating to the enforcement of judgments and debts; to make further provision about the management and relief of debt; to make provision protecting cultural objects from seizure or forfeiture in certain circumstances; to amend the law relating to the taking of possession of land affected by compulsory purchase; to alter the powers of the High Court in judicial review applications; and for connected purposes.   [19th July 2007]

Territorial extent: United Kingdom (provisions reproduced here)

PART 1 TRIBUNALS AND INQUIRIES

Chapter 1 Tribunal judiciary: independence and Senior President

[Section 1 amends the Constitutional Reform Act 2005 (q.v.) by inserting s. 3(7A) and (7B).]

2   Senior President of Tribunals

(1) Her Majesty may, on the recommendation of the Lord Chancellor, appoint a person to the office of Senior President of Tribunals.

(2) Schedule 1 makes further provision about the Senior President of Tribunals and about recommendations for appointment under subsection (1).

(3) A holder of the office of Senior President of Tribunals must, in carrying out the functions of that office, have regard to—

(a) the need for tribunals to be accessible,

(b) the need for proceedings before tribunals—

(i) to be fair, and

(ii) to be handled quickly and efficiently,

(c) the need for members of tribunals to be experts in the subject-matter of, or the law to be applied in, cases in which they decide matters, and

(d) the need to develop innovative methods of resolving disputes that are of a type that may be brought before tribunals.

(4) In subsection (3) 'tribunals' means—

(a) the First-tier Tribunal,

(b) the Upper Tribunal,

(c) employment tribunals, [and]

(d) the Employment Appeal Tribunal, . . .

(e) . . .

Chapter 2 First-tier Tribunal and Upper Tribunal

Establishment

3   The First-tier Tribunal and the Upper Tribunal

(1) There is to be a tribunal, known as the First-tier Tribunal, for the purpose of exercising the functions conferred on it under or by virtue of this Act or any other Act.

(2) There is to be a tribunal, known as the Upper Tribunal, for the purpose of exercising the functions conferred on it under or by virtue of this Act or any other Act.

(3) Each of the First-tier Tribunal, and the Upper Tribunal, is to consist of its judges and other members.

(4) The Senior President of Tribunals is to preside over both of the First-tier Tribunal and the Upper Tribunal.

(5) The Upper Tribunal is to be a superior court of record.

Members and composition of tribunals

4 Judges and other members of the First-tier Tribunal

(1) A person is a judge of the First-tier Tribunal if the person—

(a) is a judge of the First-tier Tribunal by virtue of appointment under paragraph 1(1) of Schedule 2,

(b) is a transferred-in judge of the First-tier Tribunal (see section 31(2)),

(c) is a judge of the Upper Tribunal,

(d) . . . or

(e) is a member of a panel of chairmen of employment tribunals.

(2) A person is also a judge of the First-tier Tribunal, but only as regards functions of the tribunal in relation to appeals such as are mentioned in subsection (1) of section 5 of the Criminal Injuries Compensation Act 1995 (c. 53), if the person is an adjudicator appointed under that section by the Scottish Ministers.

(3) A person is one of the other members of the First-tier Tribunal if the person—

(a) is a member of the First-tier Tribunal by virtue of appointment under paragraph 2(1) of Schedule 2,

(b) is a transferred-in other member of the First-tier Tribunal (see section 31(2)),

(c) is one of the other members of the Upper Tribunal, or

(d) is a member of a panel of members of employment tribunals that is not a panel of chairmen of employment tribunals.

(4) Schedule 2—

contains provision for the appointment of persons to be judges or other members of the First-tier Tribunal, and makes further provision in connection with judges and other members of the First-tier Tribunal.

5, 6 *****

7 Chambers: jurisdiction and Presidents

(1) The Lord Chancellor may, with the concurrence of the Senior President of Tribunals, by order make provision for the organisation of each of the First-tier Tribunal and the Upper Tribunal into a number of chambers.

(2) There is—

(a) for each chamber of the First-tier Tribunal, and

(b) for each chamber of the Upper Tribunal,

to be a person, or two persons, to preside over that chamber.

(3) A person may not at any particular time preside over more than one chamber of the First-tier Tribunal and may not at any particular time preside over more than one chamber of the Upper Tribunal (but may at the same time preside over one chamber of the First-tier Tribunal and over one chamber of the Upper Tribunal).

(4) A person appointed under this section to preside over a chamber is to be known as a Chamber President.

(5)–(9) *****

8–10 *****

Review of decisions and appeals

11 Right to appeal to Upper Tribunal

(1) For the purposes of subsection (2), the reference to a right of appeal is to a right to appeal to the Upper Tribunal on any point of law arising from a decision made by the First-tier Tribunal other than an excluded decision.

(2) Any party to a case has a right of appeal, subject to subsection (8).

(3) That right may be exercised only with permission (or, in Northern Ireland, leave).

(4) Permission (or leave) may be given by—

    (a) the First-tier Tribunal, or

    (b) the Upper Tribunal,

on an application by the party.

(5)–(8) *****

12 Proceedings on appeal to Upper Tribunal

(1) Subsection (2) applies if the Upper Tribunal, in deciding an appeal under section 11, finds that the making of the decision concerned involved the making of an error on a point of law.

(2) The Upper Tribunal—

    (a) may (but need not) set aside the decision of the First-tier Tribunal, and

    (b) if it does, must either—

        (i)   remit the case to the First-tier Tribunal with directions for its reconsideration, or

        (ii) re-make the decision.

(3) In acting under subsection (2)(b)(i), the Upper Tribunal may also—

    (a) direct that the members of the First-tier Tribunal who are chosen to reconsider the case are not to be the same as those who made the decision that has been set aside;

    (b) give procedural directions in connection with the reconsideration of the case by the First-tier Tribunal.

(4) In acting under subsection (2)(b)(ii), the Upper Tribunal—

    (a) may make any decision which the First-tier Tribunal could make if the First-tier Tribunal were re-making the decision, and

    (b) may make such findings of fact as it considers appropriate.

13 Right to appeal to Court of Appeal etc.

(1) For the purposes of subsection (2), the reference to a right of appeal is to a right to appeal to the relevant appellate court on any point of law arising from a decision made by the Upper Tribunal other than an excluded decision.

(2) Any party to a case has a right of appeal, subject to subsection (14).

(3) That right may be exercised only with permission (or, in Northern Ireland, leave).

(4) Permission (or leave) may be given by—

    (a) the Upper Tribunal, or

    (b) the relevant appellate court,

on an application by the party.

(5) An application may be made under subsection (4) to the relevant appellate court only if permission (or leave) has been refused by the Upper Tribunal.

(6) The Lord Chancellor may, as respects an application under subsection (4) that falls within subsection (7) and for which the relevant appellate court is the Court of Appeal in England and Wales or the Court of Appeal in Northern Ireland, by order make provision for permission (or leave) not to be granted on the application unless the Upper Tribunal or (as the case may be) the relevant appellate court considers—

    (a) that the proposed appeal would raise some important point of principle or practice, or

    (b) that there is some other compelling reason for the relevant appellate court to hear the appeal.

(7)–(15) *****

14 *****

'Judicial review'

15 Upper Tribunal's 'judicial review' jurisdiction

(1) The Upper Tribunal has power, in cases arising under the law of England and Wales or under the law of Northern Ireland, to grant the following kinds of relief—

    (a) a mandatory order;

    (b) a prohibiting order;

    (c) a quashing order;

    (d) a declaration;

    (e) an injunction.

(2) The power under subsection (1) may be exercised by the Upper Tribunal if—

    (a) certain conditions are met (see section 18), or

    (b) the tribunal is authorised to proceed even though not all of those conditions are met (see section 19(3) and (4)).

(3) Relief under subsection (1) granted by the Upper Tribunal—

    (a) has the same effect as the corresponding relief granted by the High Court on an application for judicial review, and

    (b) is enforceable as if it were relief granted by the High Court on an application for judicial review.

(4) In deciding whether to grant relief under subsection (1)(a), (b) or (c), the Upper Tribunal must apply the principles that the High Court would apply in deciding whether to grant that relief on an application for judicial review.

(5) In deciding whether to grant relief under subsection (1)(d) or (e), the Upper Tribunal must—

    (a) in cases arising under the law of England and Wales apply the principles that the High Court would apply in deciding whether to grant that relief under section 31(2) of the Supreme Court Act 1981 (c. 54) on an application for judicial review, and

    (b) in cases arising under the law of Northern Ireland apply the principles that the High Court would apply in deciding whether to grant that relief on an application for judicial review.

(6) *****

16 Application for relief under section 15(1)

(1) This section applies in relation to an application to the Upper Tribunal for relief under section 15(1).

(2) The application may be made only if permission (or, in a case arising under the law of Northern Ireland, leave) to make it has been obtained from the tribunal.

(3) The tribunal may not grant permission (or leave) to make the application unless it considers that the applicant has a sufficient interest in the matter to which the application relates.

(4) Subsection (5) applies where the tribunal considers—

    (a) that there has been undue delay in making the application, and

    (b) that granting the relief sought on the application would be likely to cause substantial hardship to, or substantially prejudice the rights of, any person or would be detrimental to good administration.

(5) The tribunal may—

    (a) refuse to grant permission (or leave) for the making of the application;

    (b) refuse to grant any relief sought on the application.

(6) The tribunal may award to the applicant damages, restitution or the recovery of a sum due if—

    (a) the application includes a claim for such an award arising from any matter to which the application relates, and

    (b) the tribunal is satisfied that such an award would have been made by the High Court if the claim had been made in an action begun in the High Court by the applicant at the time of making the application.

(7)–(9) *****

17–43 *****

Chapter 5   Oversight of administrative justice system, tribunals and inquiries

44   The Administrative Justice and Tribunals Council

(1) There is to be a council to be known as the Administrative Justice and Tribunals Council.

(2) In Schedule 7—

Part 1 makes provision about membership and committees of the Council,

Part 2 makes provision about functions of the Council,

Part 3 requires the Council to be consulted before procedural rules for certain tribunals are made, confirmed etc., and

Part 4 contains interpretative provisions.

45   Abolition of the Council on Tribunals

(1) The following are abolished—

(a) the Council on Tribunals, and

(b) the Scottish Committee of the Council on Tribunals.

(2), (3) *****

46–149 *****

SCHEDULE 1 *****

SCHEDULE 2   JUDGES AND OTHER MEMBERS OF THE FIRST-TIER TRIBUNAL

Power to appoint judges of First-tier Tribunal

1.—(1) The Lord Chancellor may appoint a person to be one of the judges of the First-tier Tribunal.

(2) A person is eligible for appointment under sub-paragraph (1) only if the person—

(a) satisfies the judicial-appointment eligibility condition on a 5-year basis,

(b) is an advocate or solicitor in Scotland of at least five years' standing,

(c) is a barrister or solicitor in Northern Ireland of at least five years' standing, or

(d) in the Lord Chancellor's opinion, has gained experience in law which makes the person as suitable for appointment as if the person satisfied any of paragraphs (a) to (c).

(3) Section 52(2) to (5) (meaning of "gain experience in law") apply for the purposes of sub-paragraph (2)(d), but as if section 52(4)(i) referred to the Lord Chancellor instead of to the relevant decision-maker.

Power to appoint other members of First-tier Tribunal

2.—(1) The Lord Chancellor may appoint a person to be one of the members of the First-tier Tribunal who are not judges of the tribunal.

(2) A person is eligible for appointment under sub-paragraph (1) only if the person has qualifications prescribed in an order made by the Lord Chancellor with the concurrence of the Senior President of Tribunals.

Appointed and transferred-in judges and other members: removal from office

3.—(1) This paragraph applies to any power by which—

(a) a person appointed under paragraph 1(1) or 2(1),

(b) a transferred-in judge of the First-tier Tribunal, or

(c) a transferred-in other member of the First-tier Tribunal,

may be removed from office.

(2) If the person exercises functions wholly or mainly in Scotland, the power may be exercised only with the concurrence of the Lord President of the Court of Session.

(3) If the person exercises functions wholly or mainly in Northern Ireland, the power may be exercised only with the concurrence of the Lord Chief Justice of Northern Ireland.

(4) If neither of sub-paragraphs (2) and (3) applies, the power may be exercised only with the concurrence of the Lord Chief Justice of England and Wales.

Terms of appointment

4.—(1) This paragraph applies—
  (a) to a person appointed under paragraph 1(1) or 2(1),
  (b) to a transferred-in judge of the First-tier Tribunal, and
  (c) to a transferred-in other member of the First-tier Tribunal.

(2) If the terms of the person's appointment provide that he is appointed on a salaried (as opposed to fee-paid) basis, the person may be removed from office—
  (a) only by the Lord Chancellor (and in accordance with paragraph 3), and
  (b) only on the ground of inability or misbehaviour.

(3) Subject to sub-paragraph (2) (and to the Judicial Pensions and Retirement Act 1993 (c. 8)), the person is to hold and vacate office in accordance with the terms of his appointment.

5.–9. *****

SCHEDULES 3–6   *****

SCHEDULE 7   ADMINISTRATIVE JUSTICE AND TRIBUNALS COUNCIL

PART 1   MEMBERS AND COMMITTEES

Membership

1.—(1) The Council is to consist of—
  (a) the Parliamentary Commissioner for Administration, and
  (b) not more than fifteen nor fewer than ten appointed members.

(2) Of the appointed members—
  (a) either two or three are to be appointed by the Scottish Ministers with the concurrence of the Lord Chancellor and the Welsh Ministers,
  (b) either one or two are to be appointed by the Welsh Ministers with the concurrence of the Lord Chancellor and the Scottish Ministers, and
  (c) the others are to be appointed by the Lord Chancellor with the concurrence of the Scottish Ministers and the Welsh Ministers.

2.–11. *****

PART 2   FUNCTIONS

Introductory

12. The Council has the functions conferred on it by this Schedule or any other statutory provision.

Functions with respect to the administrative justice system

13.—(1) The Council is to—
  (a) keep the administrative justice system under review,
  (b) consider ways to make the system accessible, fair and efficient,
  (c) advise the persons mentioned in sub-paragraph (2) on the development of the system,
  (d) refer proposals for changes in the system to those persons, and

(e) make proposals for research into the system.

(2) Those persons are—

(a) the Lord Chancellor,

(b) the Scottish Ministers,

(c) the Welsh Ministers, and

(d) the Senior President of Tribunals.

(3) The Council may make such reports as it considers appropriate on any of the matters mentioned in sub-paragraph (1).

(4) In this paragraph 'the administrative justice system' means the overall system by which decisions of an administrative or executive nature are made in relation to particular persons, including—

(a) the procedures for making such decisions,

(b) the law under which such decisions are made, and

(c) the systems for resolving disputes and airing grievances in relation to such decisions.

General functions with respect to tribunals

14.—(1) The Council is to—

(a) keep under review, and report on, the constitution and working—

(i)   of listed tribunals in general, and

(ii) of each listed tribunal,

(b) consider, and report on, any other matter—

(i)   that relates to listed tribunals in general or to a particular listed tribunal, and

(ii) that the Council determines to be of special importance, and

(c) consider, and report on, any particular matter referred to the Council—

(i)   that relates to tribunals in general or to any particular tribunal, and

(ii) whose referral to the Council falls within paragraph 16.

(2) The Council may scrutinise and comment on legislation, existing or proposed, relating to tribunals or to any particular tribunal.

(3) The Council must—

(a) consult the Scottish Committee before exercising the power conferred by sub-paragraph (2) with respect to legislation, existing or proposed, that relates to at least one tribunal with jurisdiction in cases arising in Scotland;

(b) consult the Welsh Committee before exercising that power with respect to legislation, existing or proposed, that relates to at least one tribunal with jurisdiction in cases arising in Wales.

(4) In sub-paragraphs (1)(c), (2) and (3)—

'legislation' includes procedural rules;

'tribunal' includes a proposed tribunal.

General functions with respect to statutory inquiries

15. The Council is to—

(a) keep under review, and report on, the constitution and working of statutory inquiries, both in general and by reference to statutory provisions under which statutory inquiries of different descriptions may be held,

(b) consider, and report on, any other matter—

(i)   that relates to statutory inquiries in general, to statutory inquiries of a particular description or to any particular statutory inquiry, and

(ii) that the Council determines to be of special importance, and

(c) consider, and report on, any particular matter referred to the Council—

(i)   that relates to statutory inquiries in general, to statutory inquiries of a particular description or to any particular statutory inquiry, and

(ii) whose referral to the Council falls within paragraph 16.

16.–21. *****

Right to attend proceedings

22.—(1) A member of any of—

    (a) the Council,

    (b) the Scottish Committee, and

    (c) the Welsh Committee,

may attend (as observer) proceedings of a listed tribunal or of a statutory inquiry.

    (2) The right under sub-paragraph (1) applies even in respect of proceedings—

    (a) taking the form of a hearing held in private, or

    (b) not taking the form of a hearing.

    (3) The right under sub-paragraph (1) is subject to any statutory provision by which members of the Council, members of the Scottish Committee or members of the Welsh Committee are expressly excluded from proceedings.

    23.–28. *****

*****

UK Borders Act 2007

(2007, c. 30)

An Act to make provision about immigration and asylum; and for connected purposes.

[30th October 2007]

Territorial extent: England, Scotland Wales, Northern Ireland (ss. 1–3); United Kingdom (other provisions reproduced here)

Detention at ports

1 Designated immigration officers

    (1) The Secretary of State may designate immigration officers for the purposes of section 2.

    (2) The Secretary of State may designate only officers who the Secretary of State thinks are—

    (a) fit and proper for the purpose, and

    (b) suitably trained.

    (3) A designation—

    (a) may be permanent or for a specified period, and

    (b) may (in either case) be revoked.

2 Detention

    (1) A designated immigration officer at a port in England, Wales or Northern Ireland may detain an individual if the immigration officer thinks that the individual—

    (a) may be liable to arrest by a constable under section 24(1), (2) or (3) of the Police and Criminal Evidence Act 1984 (c. 60) or Article 26(1), (2) or (3) of the Police and Criminal Evidence (Northern Ireland) Order 1989 (S.I. 1989/1341 (N.I. 12)), or

    (b) is subject to a warrant for arrest.

[(1A) A designated immigration officer at a port in Scotland may detain an individual if the immigration officer thinks that the individual is subject to a warrant for arrest.]

    (2) A designated immigration officer who detains an individual—

    (a) must arrange for a constable to attend as soon as is reasonably practicable,

    (b) may search the individual for, and retain, anything that might be used to assist escape or to cause physical injury to the individual or another person,

    (c) must retain anything found on a search which the immigration officer thinks may be evidence of the commission of an offence, and

    (d) must, when the constable arrives, deliver to the constable the individual and anything retained on a search.

    (3) An individual may not be detained under this section for longer than three hours.

(4) A designated immigration officer may use reasonable force for the purpose of exercising a power under this section.

(5) Where an individual whom a designated immigration officer has detained or attempted to detain under this section leaves the port, a designated immigration officer may—

   (a) pursue the individual, and
   (b) return the individual to the port.

(6) Detention under this section shall be treated as detention under the Immigration Act 1971 (c. 77) for the purposes of Part 8 of the Immigration and Asylum Act 1999 (c. 33) (detained persons).

3   Enforcement

(1) An offence is committed by a person who—

   (a) absconds from detention under section 2,
   (b) assaults an immigration officer exercising a power under section 2, or
   (c) obstructs an immigration officer in the exercise of a power under section 2.

(2) A person guilty of an offence under subsection (1)(a) or (b) shall be liable on summary conviction to—

   (a) imprisonment for a term not exceeding [51 weeks],
   (b) a fine not exceeding level 5 on the standard scale, or
   (c) both.

(3) A person guilty of an offence under subsection (1)(c) shall be liable on summary conviction to—

   (a) imprisonment for a term not exceeding [51 weeks],
   (b) a fine not exceeding level 3 on the standard scale, or
   (c) both.

(4), (4A), (5) *****

4–31 *****

Deportation of criminals

32   Automatic deportation

(1) In this section 'foreign criminal' means a person—

   (a) who is not a British citizen,
   (b) who is convicted in the United Kingdom of an offence, and
   (c) to whom Condition 1 or 2 applies.

(2) Condition 1 is that the person is sentenced to a period of imprisonment of at least 12 months.

(3) Condition 2 is that—

   (a) the offence is specified by order of the Secretary of State under section 72(4)(a) of the Nationality, Immigration and Asylum Act 2002 (c. 41) (serious criminal), and
   (b) the person is sentenced to a period of imprisonment.

(4) For the purpose of section 3(5)(a) of the Immigration Act 1971 (c. 77), the deportation of a foreign criminal is conducive to the public good.

(5) The Secretary of State must make a deportation order in respect of a foreign criminal (subject to section 33).

(6) The Secretary of State may not revoke a deportation order made in accordance with subsection (5) unless—

   (a) he thinks that an exception under section 33 applies,
   (b) the application for revocation is made while the foreign criminal is outside the United Kingdom, or
   (c) section 34(4) applies.

(7) Subsection (5) does not create a private right of action in respect of consequences of non-compliance by the Secretary of State.

33 Exceptions

(1) Section 32(4) and (5)—

   (a) do not apply where an exception in this section applies (subject to subsection (7) below), and

   (b) are subject to sections 7 and 8 of the Immigration Act 1971 (Commonwealth citizens, Irish citizens, crew and other exemptions).

(2) Exception 1 is where removal of the foreign criminal in pursuance of the deportation order would breach—

   (a) a person's Convention rights, or

   (b) the United Kingdom's obligations under the Refugee Convention.

(3) Exception 2 is where the Secretary of State thinks that the foreign criminal was under the age of 18 on the date of conviction.

(4) Exception 3 is where the removal of the foreign criminal from the United Kingdom in pursuance of a deportation order would breach rights of the foreign criminal under the [EU] treaties.

(5) Exception 4 is where the foreign criminal—

   (a) is the subject of a certificate under section 2 or 70 of the Extradition Act 2003 (c. 41),

   (b) is in custody pursuant to arrest under section 5 of that Act,

   (c) is the subject of a provisional warrant under section 73 of that Act,

   (d) is the subject of an authority to proceed under section 7 of the Extradition Act 1989 (c. 33) or an order under paragraph 4(2) of Schedule 1 to that Act, or

   (e) is the subject of a provisional warrant under section 8 of that Act or of a warrant under paragraph 5(1)(b) of Schedule 1 to that Act.

(6), (6A), (7) *****

34 Timing

(1) Section 32(5) requires a deportation order to be made at a time chosen by the Secretary of State.

(2) A deportation order may not be made under section 32(5) while an appeal or further appeal against the conviction or sentence by reference to which the order is to be made—

   (a) has been instituted and neither withdrawn nor determined, or

   (b) could be brought.

(3) For the purpose of subsection (2)(b)—

   (a) the possibility of an appeal out of time with permission shall be disregarded, and

   (b) a person who has informed the Secretary of State in writing that the person does not intend to appeal shall be treated as being no longer able to appeal.

(4) *****

35   *****

36 Detention

(1) A person who has served a period of imprisonment may be detained under the authority of the Secretary of State—

   (a) while the Secretary of State considers whether section 32(5) applies, and

   (b) where the Secretary of State thinks that section 32(5) applies, pending the making of the deportation order.

(2) Where a deportation order is made in accordance with section 32(5) the Secretary of State shall exercise the power of detention under paragraph 2(3) of Schedule 3 to the Immigration Act 1971 (c. 77) (detention pending removal) unless in the circumstances the Secretary of State thinks it inappropriate.

(3) A court determining an appeal against conviction or sentence may direct release from detention under subsection (1) or (2).

(4), (5) *****

37 Family

(1) Where a deportation order against a foreign criminal states that it is made in accordance with section 32(5) ('the automatic deportation order') this section shall have effect in place of the words from 'A deportation order' to 'after the making of the deportation order against him' in section 5(3) of the Immigration Act 1971 (period during which family members may also be deported).

(2) A deportation order may not be made against a person as belonging to the family of the foreign criminal after the end of the relevant period of 8 weeks.

(3) In the case of a foreign criminal who has not appealed in respect of the automatic deportation order, the relevant period begins when an appeal can no longer be brought (ignoring any possibility of an appeal out of time with permission).

(4) In the case of a foreign criminal who has appealed in respect of the automatic deportation order, the relevant period begins when the appeal is no longer pending (within the meaning of section 104 of the Nationality, Immigration and Asylum Act 2002 (c. 41)).

38 Interpretation

(1) In section 32(2) the reference to a person who is sentenced to a period of imprisonment of at least 12 months—

    (a) does not include a reference to a person who receives a suspended sentence (unless a court subsequently orders that the sentence or any part of it (of whatever length) is to take effect),

    (b) does not include a reference to a person who is sentenced to a period of imprisonment of at least 12 months only by virtue of being sentenced to consecutive sentences amounting in aggregate to more than 12 months,

    (c) includes a reference to a person who is sentenced to detention, or ordered or directed to be detained, in an institution other than a prison (including, in particular, a hospital or an institution for young offenders) for at least 12 months, and

    (d) includes a reference to a person who is sentenced to imprisonment or detention, or ordered or directed to be detained, for an indeterminate period (provided that it may last for 12 months).

(2)–(4) *****

*****

Counter-Terrorism Act 2008

(2008, c. 28)

An Act to confer further powers to gather and share information for counter-terrorism and other purposes; to make further provision about the detention and questioning of terrorist suspects and the prosecution and punishment of terrorist offences; to impose notification requirements on persons convicted of such offences; to confer further powers to act against terrorist financing, money laundering and certain other activities; to provide for review of certain Treasury decisions and about evidence in, and other matters connected with, review proceedings; to amend the law relating to inquiries; to amend the definition of "terrorism"; to amend the enactments relating to terrorist offences, control orders and the forfeiture of terrorist cash; to provide for recovering the costs of policing at certain gas facilities; to amend provisions about the appointment of special advocates in Northern Ireland; and for connected purposes.

[26th November 2008]

Territorial extent: United Kingdom

[**Note:** The early sections of this Act have been omitted as they are not yet in force (April 2012).]

Disclosure of information and the intelligence services

19 Disclosure and the intelligence services

(1) A person may disclose information to any of the intelligence services for the purposes of the exercise by that service of any of its functions.

(2) Information obtained by any of the intelligence services in connection with the exercise of any of its functions may be used by that service in connection with the exercise of any of its other functions.

(3) Information obtained by the Security Service for the purposes of any of its functions may be disclosed by it—

  (a) for the purpose of the proper discharge of its functions,

  (b) for the purpose of the prevention or detection of serious crime, or

  (c) for the purpose of any criminal proceedings.

(4) Information obtained by the Secret Intelligence Service for the purposes of any of its functions may be disclosed by it—

  (a) for the purpose of the proper discharge of its functions,

  (b) in the interests of national security,

  (c) for the purpose of the prevention or detection of serious crime, or

  (d) for the purpose of any criminal proceedings.

(5) Information obtained by GCHQ for the purposes of any of its functions may be disclosed by it—

  (a) for the purpose of the proper discharge of its functions, or

  (b) for the purpose of any criminal proceedings.

(6) A disclosure under this section does not breach—

  (a) any obligation of confidence owed by the person making the disclosure, or

  (b) any other restriction on the disclosure of information (however imposed).

(7) The provisions of this section are subject to section 20 (savings and other supplementary provisions).

20   Disclosure and the intelligence services: supplementary provisions

(1) The provisions of section 19 (disclosure and use of information) do not affect the duties with respect to the obtaining or disclosure of information imposed—

  (a) on the Director-General of the Security Service, by section 2(2) of the Security Service Act 1989;

  (b) on the Chief of the Intelligence Service, by section 2(2) of the Intelligence Services Act 1994;

  (c) on the Director of GCHQ, by section 4(2) of that Act.

(2) Nothing in that section authorises a disclosure that—

  (a) contravenes the Data Protection Act 1998 (c. 29), or

  (b) is prohibited by Part 1 of the Regulation of Investigatory Powers Act 2000 (c. 23).

(3) The provisions of that section are without prejudice to any rule of law authorising the obtaining, use or disclosure of information by any of the intelligence services.

(4) *****

21   Disclosure and the intelligence services: interpretation

(1) In sections 19 and 20 "the intelligence services" means the Security Service, the Secret Intelligence Service and GCHQ.

(2)–(4) *****

22   Post-charge questioning: England and Wales

(1) The following provisions apply in England and Wales.

(2) A judge of the Crown Court may authorise the questioning of a person about an offence—

  (a) after the person has been charged with the offence or been officially informed that they may be prosecuted for it, or

  (b) after the person has been sent for trial for the offence,

if the offence is a terrorism offence or it appears to the judge that the offence has a terrorist connection.

(3) The judge—

    (a) must specify the period during which questioning is authorised, and

    (b) may impose such conditions as appear to be necessary in the interests of justice, which may include conditions as to the place where the questioning is to be carried out.

(4) The period during which questioning is authorised—

    (a) begins when questioning pursuant to the authorisation begins and runs continuously from that time (whether or not questioning continues), and

    (b) must not exceed 48 hours.

This is without prejudice to any application for a further authorisation under this section.

(5) Where the person is in prison or otherwise lawfully detained, the judge may authorise the person's removal to another place and detention there for the purpose of being questioned.

(6) A judge must not authorise the questioning of a person under this section unless satisfied—

    (a) that further questioning of the person is necessary in the interests of justice,

    (b) that the investigation for the purposes of which the further questioning is proposed is being conducted diligently and expeditiously, and

    (c) that what is authorised will not interfere unduly with the preparation of the person's defence to the charge in question or any other criminal charge.

(7) Codes of practice under section 66 of the Police and Criminal Evidence Act 1984 (c. 60) must make provision about the questioning of a person by a constable in accordance with this section.

(8) Nothing in this section prevents codes of practice under that section making other provision for the questioning of a person by a constable about an offence—

    (a) after the person has been charged with the offence or been officially informed that they may be prosecuted for it, or

    (b) after the person has been sent for trial for the offence.

(9), (10) *****

[**Note**: Sections 23 and 24 repeat these powers for the Sheriff (Scotland) and District Judge (Northern Ireland).]

25 Recording of interviews

(1) This section applies to any interview of a person by a constable under section 22, 23 or 24 (post-charge questioning).

(2) Any such interview must be video recorded, and the video recording must be with sound.

(3) The Secretary of State must issue a code of practice about the video recording of interviews to which this section applies.

(4) The interview and video recording must be conducted in accordance with that code of practice.

(5) A code of practice under this section—

    (a) may make provision in relation to a particular part of the United Kingdom, and

    (b) may make different provision for different parts of the United Kingdom.

26 Issue and revision of code of practice

(1) This section applies to the code of practice under section 25 (recording of interviews).

(2) The Secretary of State must—

    (a) publish a draft of the proposed code, and

    (b) consider any representations made about the draft,

and may modify the draft in the light of the representations made.

(3) The Secretary of State must lay a draft of the code before Parliament.

(4) After laying the draft code before Parliament the Secretary of State may bring it into operation by order.

(5) The order is subject to affirmative resolution procedure.

(6) The Secretary of State may revise a code and issue the revised code, and subsections (2) to (5) apply to a revised code as they apply to an original code.

(7) Failure to observe a provision of a code does not of itself render a constable liable to criminal or civil proceedings.

(8) A code—

(a) is admissible in evidence in criminal and civil proceedings, and

(b) shall be taken into account by a court or tribunal in any case in which it appears to the court or tribunal to be relevant.

27   Meaning of "terrorism offence"

(1) For the purposes of sections 22 to 24 (post-charge questioning) the following are terrorism offences—

(a) an offence under any of the following provisions of the Terrorism Act 2000 (c. 11)—
    sections 11 to 13 (offences relating to proscribed organisations), sections 15 to 19, 21A and 21D (offences relating to terrorist property), sections 38B and 39 (disclosure of and failure to disclose information about terrorism), section 54 (weapons training), sections 56 to 58A (directing terrorism, possessing things and collecting information for the purposes of terrorism), sections 59 to 61 (inciting terrorism outside the United Kingdom), paragraph 14 of Schedule 5 (order for explanation of material: false or misleading statements), paragraph 1 of Schedule 6 (failure to provide customer information in connection with a terrorist investigation), paragraph 18 of Schedule 7 (offences in connection with port and border controls);

(b) an offence in respect of which there is jurisdiction by virtue of any of sections 62 to 63D of that Act (extra-territorial jurisdiction in respect of certain offences committed outside the United Kingdom for the purposes of terrorism etc);

(c) an offence under section 113 of the Anti-Terrorism, Crime and Security Act 2001 (c. 24) (use of noxious substances or things);

(d) an offence under any of the following provisions of Part 1 of the Terrorism Act 2006 (c. 11)—
    sections 1 and 2 (encouragement of terrorism), sections 5, 6 and 8 (preparation and training for terrorism), sections 9, 10 and 11 (offences relating to radioactive devices and material and nuclear facilities);

(e) an offence in respect of which there is jurisdiction by virtue of section 17 of that Act (extra-territorial jurisdiction in respect of certain offences committed outside the United Kingdom for the purposes of terrorism etc);

(f) an offence under paragraph 8 or 9 of Schedule 3 to the Justice and Security (Northern Ireland) Act 2007 (c. 6) (offences in connection with searches for munitions and transmitters in Northern Ireland).

(2) Any ancillary offence in relation to an offence listed in subsection (1) is a terrorism offence for the purposes of sections 22 to 24.

(3) The Secretary of State may by order amend subsection (1).

(4) Any such order is subject to affirmative resolution procedure.

PART 3 PROSECUTION AND PUNISHMENT OF TERRORIST OFFENCES

28   Jurisdiction to try offences committed in the UK

(1) Where an offence to which this section applies is committed in the United Kingdom—

(a) proceedings for the offence may be taken at any place in the United Kingdom, and

(b) the offence may for all incidental purposes be treated as having been committed at any such place.

(2) The section applies to—

(a) an offence under any of the following provisions of the Terrorism Act 2000 (c. 11)—
    sections 11 to 13 (offences relating to proscribed organisations), sections 15 to 19, 21A and 21D (offences relating to terrorist property), sections 38B and 39 (disclosure of

and failure to disclose information about terrorism), section 47 (offences relating to stop and search powers), section 51 (parking a vehicle in contravention of an authorisation or restriction), section 54 (weapons training), sections 56 to 58A (directing terrorism and possessing things or collecting information for the purposes of terrorism), section 116 (failure to stop a vehicle when required to do so), paragraph 1 of Schedule 6 (failure to provide customer information in connection with a terrorist investigation), paragraph 18 of Schedule 7 (offences in connection with port and border controls);

(b) an offence under section 113 of the Anti-terrorism, Crime and Security Act 2001 (c. 24) (use of noxious substances or things to cause harm and intimidate);

(c) an offence under any of the following provisions of the Terrorism Act 2006 (c. 11)—
sections 1 and 2 (encouragement of terrorism), sections 5, 6 and 8 (preparation and training for terrorism), sections 9, 10 and 11 (offences relating to radioactive devices etc).

[(d) an offence under any provision of Part 1 of the Terrorist Asset-Freezing etc Act 2010].

(3) The Secretary of State may by order amend subsection (2).

(4) Any such order is subject to affirmative resolution procedure.

(5) The power conferred by subsection (3) may be exercised so as to add offences to subsection (2) only if it appears to the Secretary of State necessary to do so for the purpose of dealing with terrorism.

(6) *****

29–39 *****

PART 4 NOTIFICATION REQUIREMENTS

40   Scheme of this Part

(1) This Part imposes notification requirements on persons dealt with in respect of certain offences—
(a) sections 41 to 43 specify the offences to which this Part applies;
(b) sections 44 to 46 make provision as to the sentences or orders triggering the notification requirements;
(c) sections 47 to 52 contain the notification requirements; and
(d) section 53 makes provision as to the period for which the requirements apply.

(2) This Part also provides for—
(a) orders applying the notification requirements to persons dealt with outside the United Kingdom for corresponding foreign offences (see section 57 and Schedule 4); and
(b) orders imposing restrictions on travel outside the United Kingdom on persons subject to the notification requirements (see section 58 and Schedule 5).

(3) Schedule 6 provides for the application of this Part to service offences and related matters.

41   Offences to which this Part applies: terrorism offences

(1) This Part applies to—
(a) an offence under any of the following provisions of the Terrorism Act 2000 (c. 11)—
section 11 or 12 (offences relating to proscribed organisations), sections 15 to 18 (offences relating to terrorist property), section 38B (failure to disclose information about acts of terrorism), section 54 (weapons training), sections 56 to 61 (directing terrorism, possessing things and collecting information for the purposes of terrorism and inciting terrorism outside the United Kingdom);
(b) an offence in respect of which there is jurisdiction by virtue of any of sections 62 to 63D of that Act (extra-territorial jurisdiction in respect of certain offences committed outside the United Kingdom for the purposes of terrorism etc);
(c) an offence under section 113 of the Anti-terrorism, Crime and Security Act 2001 (c. 24) (use of noxious substances or things);
(d) an offence under any of the following provisions of Part 1 of the Terrorism Act 2006 (c. 11)—

sections 1 and 2 (encouragement of terrorism), sections 5, 6 and 8 (preparation and training for terrorism), sections 9, 10 and 11 (offences relating to radioactive devices and material and nuclear facilities);

(e) an offence in respect of which there is jurisdiction by virtue of section 17 of that Act (extra-territorial jurisdiction in respect of certain offences committed outside the United Kingdom for the purposes of terrorism etc).

(2) This Part also applies to any ancillary offence in relation to an offence listed in subsection (1).

(3) The Secretary of State may by order amend subsection (1).

(4) Any such order is subject to affirmative resolution procedure.

(5) An order adding an offence applies only in relation to offences dealt with after the order comes into force.

(6) An order removing an offence has effect in relation to offences whenever dealt with, whether before or after the order comes into force.

(7) Where an offence is removed from the list, a person subject to the notification requirements by reason of that offence being listed (and who is not otherwise subject to those requirements) ceases to be subject to them when the order comes into force.

42   Offences to which this Part applies: offences having a terrorist connection

(1) This Part applies to—

(a) an offence as to which a court has determined under section 30 (sentences for offences with a terrorist connection: England and Wales) that the offence has a terrorist connection, and

(b) an offence in relation to which section 31 applies (sentences for offences with terrorist connection: Scotland).

(2) A person to whom the notification requirements apply by virtue of such a determination as is mentioned in subsection (1)(a) may appeal against it to the same court, and subject to the same conditions, as an appeal against sentence.

(3) If the determination is set aside on appeal, the notification requirements are treated as never having applied to that person in respect of the offence.

(4) Where an order is made under section 33 removing an offence from the list in Schedule 2, a person subject to the notification requirements by reason of that offence being so listed (and who is not otherwise subject to those requirements) ceases to be subject to them when the order comes into force.

43   Offences dealt with before commencement

(1) This Part applies to a person dealt with for an offence before the commencement of this Part only if—

(a) the offence is on the commencement of this Part within section 41(1) or (2) (offences to which this Part applies: terrorism offences), and

(b) immediately before the commencement of this Part the person—

(i) is imprisoned or detained in pursuance of the sentence passed or order made in respect of the offence,

(ii) would be so imprisoned or detained but for being unlawfully at large, absent without leave, on temporary leave or leave of absence, or on bail pending an appeal, or

(iii) is on licence, having served the custodial part of a sentence of imprisonment in respect of the offence.

(2) In relation to a person dealt with for an offence before the commencement of this Part—

(a) any reference in this Part to a sentence or order under a specified statutory provision includes a sentence or order under any corresponding earlier statutory provision;

(b) any reference in this Part to a person being or having been found to be under a disability and to have done the act charged against them in respect of an offence includes a reference to their being or having been found—

(i) unfit to be tried for the offence,

(ii) insane so that their trial for the offence cannot or could not proceed, or

      (iii) unfit to be tried and to have done the act charged against them in respect of the offence.

44 Persons to whom the notification requirements apply

The notification requirements apply to a person who—

    (a) is aged 16 or over at the time of being dealt with for an offence to which this Part applies, and

    (b) is made subject in respect of the offence to a sentence or order within section 45 (sentences or orders triggering notification requirements).

45 Sentences or orders triggering notification requirements

  (1) The notification requirements apply to a person who in England and Wales—

    (a) has been convicted of an offence to which this Part applies and sentenced in respect of the offence to—

      (i) imprisonment or custody for life,

      (ii) imprisonment or detention in a young offender institution for a term of 12 months or more,

      (iii) imprisonment or detention in a young offender institution for public protection under section 225 of the Criminal Justice Act 2003 (c. 44),

      (iv) detention for life or for a period of 12 months or more under section 91 of the Powers of Criminal Courts (Sentencing) Act 2000 (c. 6) (offenders under 18 convicted of certain serious offences),

      (v) a detention and training order for a term of 12 months or more under section 100 of that Act (offenders under age of 18),

      (vi) detention for public protection under section 226 of the Criminal Justice Act 2003 (serious offences committed by persons under 18), or

      (vii) detention during Her Majesty's pleasure; or

    (b) has been—

      (i) convicted of an offence to which this Part applies carrying a maximum term of imprisonment of 12 months or more,

      (ii) found not guilty by reason of insanity of such an offence, or

      (iii) found to be under a disability and to have done the act charged against them in respect of such an offence,

    and made subject in respect of the offence to a hospital order.

  (2)–(5) *****

46 Power to amend specified terms or periods of imprisonment or detention

  (1) The Secretary of State may by order amend the provisions of section 45 referring to a specified term or period of imprisonment or detention.

  (2)–(4) *****

47 Initial notification

  (1) A person to whom the notification requirements apply must notify the following information to the police within the period of three days beginning with the day on which the person is dealt with in respect of the offence in question.

  (2) The information required is—

    (a) date of birth;

    (b) national insurance number;

    (c) name on the date on which the person was dealt with in respect of the offence (where the person used one or more other names on that date, each of those names);

    (d) home address on that date;

    (e) name on the date on which notification is made (where the person uses one or more other names on that date, each of those names);

    (f) home address on the date on which notification is made;

    (g) address of any other premises in the United Kingdom at which, at the time the notification is made, the person regularly resides or stays;

    (h) any prescribed information.

(3) In subsection (2) "prescribed" means prescribed by regulations made by the Secretary of State.

Such regulations are subject to affirmative resolution procedure.

(4) In determining the period within which notification is to be made under this section, there shall be disregarded any time when the person is—

    (a) remanded in or committed to custody by an order of a court,

    (b) serving a sentence of imprisonment or detention,

    (c) detained in a hospital, or

    (d) detained under the Immigration Acts.

(5) This section does not apply to a person who—

    (a) is subject to the notification requirements in respect of another offence (and does not cease to be so subject before the end of the period within which notification is to be made), and

    (b) has complied with this section in respect of that offence.

(6) In the application of this section to a person dealt with for an offence before the commencement of this Part who, immediately before commencement—

    (a) would be imprisoned or detained in respect of the offence but for being unlawfully at large, absent without leave, on temporary leave or leave of absence, or on bail pending an appeal, or

    (b) is on licence, having served the custodial part of a sentence of imprisonment in respect of the offence,

the reference in subsection (1) to the day on which the person is dealt with in respect of the offence shall be read as a reference to the commencement of this Part.

48   Notification of changes

(1) A person to whom the notification requirements apply who uses a name that has not previously been notified to the police must notify the police of that name.

(2) If there is a change of the home address of a person to whom the notification requirements apply, the person must notify the police of the new home address.

(3) A person to whom the notification requirements apply who resides or stays at premises in the United Kingdom the address of which has previously not been notified to the police—

    (a) for a period of 7 days, or

    (b) for two or more periods, in any period of 12 months, that taken together amount to 7 days,

must notify the police of the address of those premises.

(4) A person to whom the notification requirements apply who is released—

    (a) from custody pursuant to an order of a court,

    (b) from imprisonment or detention pursuant to a sentence of a court,

    (c) from detention in a hospital, or

    (d) from detention under the Immigration Acts,

must notify the police of that fact.

This does not apply if the person is at the same time required to notify the police under section 47 (initial notification).

(5) A person who is required to notify information within section 47(2)(h) (prescribed information) must notify the police of the prescribed details of any prescribed changes in that information.

(6) In subsection (5) "prescribed" means prescribed by regulations made by the Secretary of State.

Such regulations are subject to affirmative resolution procedure.

(7) Notification under this section must be made before the end of the period of three days beginning with the day on which the event in question occurs. Where subsection (3) applies that is the day with which the period referred to in paragraph (a) or (b) (as the case may be) ends.

(8) In determining the period within which notification is to be made under this section, there shall be disregarded any time when the person is—

    (a) remanded in or committed to custody by an order of a court,

    (b) serving a sentence of imprisonment or detention,

    (c) detained in a hospital, or

    (d) detained under the Immigration Acts.

(9) References in this section to previous notification are to previous notification by the person under section 47 (initial notification), this section, section 49 (periodic re-notification) or section 56 (notification on return after absence from UK).

(10) Notification under this section must be accompanied by re-notification of the other information mentioned in section 47(2).

49 Periodic re-notification

(1) A person to whom the notification requirements apply must, within the period of one year after last notifying the police in accordance with—

    (a) section 47 (initial notification),

    (b) section 48 (notification of change),

    (c) this section, or

    (d) section 56 (notification on return after absence from UK),

re-notify to the police the information mentioned in section 47(2).

(2) Subsection (1) does not apply if the period referred to in that subsection ends at a time when the person is—

    (a) remanded in or committed to custody by an order of a court,

    (b) serving a sentence of imprisonment or detention,

    (c) detained in a hospital, or

    (d) detained under the Immigration Acts.

(3) In that case section 48(4) and (10) (duty to notify of release and to re-notify other information) apply when the person is released.

50 Method of notification and related matters

(1) This section applies to notification under—

    (a) section 47 (initial notification),

    (b) section 48 (notification of change),

    (c) section 49 (periodic re-notification), or

    (d) section 56 (notification on return after absence from UK).

(2) Notification must be made by the person—

    (a) attending at a police station in the person's local police area, and

    (b) making an oral notification to a police officer or to a person authorised for the purpose by the officer in charge of the station.

(3) A person making a notification under section 48 (notification of change) in relation to premises referred to in subsection (3) of that section may make the notification at a police station that would fall within subsection (2)(a) above if the address of those premises were the person's home address.

(4) The notification must be acknowledged.

(5) The acknowledgement must be in writing, and in such form as the Secretary of State may direct.

(6) The person making the notification must, if requested to do so by the police officer or person to whom the notification is made, allow the officer or person to—

    (a) take the person's fingerprints,

    (b) photograph any part of the person, or

    (c) do both these things,

for the purpose of verifying the person's identity.

(7) *****

51   Meaning of "local police area"

(1) For the purposes of section 50(2) (method of notification) a person's "local police area" means—

(a) the police area in which the person's home address is situated;

(b) in the absence of a home address, the police area in which the home address last notified is situated;

(c) in the absence of a home address and of any such notification, the police area in which the court of trial was situated.

(2) In subsection (1)(c) "the court of trial" means—

(a) the court by or before which the conviction or finding was made by virtue of which the notification requirements apply to the person, or

(b) if that conviction or finding was one substituted on an appeal or reference, the court by or before which the proceedings were taken from which the appeal or reference was brought.

(3) This section and section 50(2) apply in relation to Northern Ireland as if Northern Ireland were a police area.

52   Travel outside the United Kingdom

(1) The Secretary of State may by regulations make provision requiring a person to whom the notification requirements apply who leaves the United Kingdom—

(a) to notify the police of their departure before they leave, and

(b) to notify the police of their return if they subsequently return to the United Kingdom.

(2) Notification of departure must disclose—

(a) the date on which the person intends to leave the United Kingdom;

(b) the country (or, if there is more than one, the first country) to which the person will travel;

(c) the person's point of arrival (determined in accordance with the regulations) in that country;

(d) any other information required by the regulations.

(3) Notification of return must disclose such information as is required by the regulations about the person's return to the United Kingdom.

(4), (5) *****

53   Period for which notification requirements apply

(1) The period for which the notification requirements apply is—

(a) 30 years in the case of a person who—

(i)   is aged 18 or over at the time of conviction for the offence, and

(ii) receives in respect of the offence a sentence within subsection (2);

(b) 15 years in the case of a person who—

(i)   is aged 18 or over at the time of conviction for the offence, and

(ii) receives in respect of the offence a sentence within subsection (3);

(c) 10 years in any other case.

(2) The sentences in respect of which a 30 year period applies are—

(a) in England and Wales—

(i)   imprisonment or custody for life,

(ii) imprisonment or detention in a young offender institution for a term of 10 years or more,

(iii) imprisonment or detention in a young offender institution for public protection under section 225 of the Criminal Justice Act 2003 (c. 44),

(iv) detention during Her Majesty's pleasure;

(b) in Scotland—

(i)   imprisonment or detention in a young offenders institution for life,

(ii) imprisonment or detention in a young offenders institution for a term of 10 years or more,

(iii) an order for lifelong restriction under section 210F of the Criminal Procedure (Scotland) Act 1995 (c. 46);

(c) in Northern Ireland—
   (i) imprisonment for life,
   (ii) imprisonment for a term of 10 years or more,
   (iii) an indeterminate custodial sentence under Article 13 of the Criminal Justice (Northern Ireland) Order 2008 (S.I. 2008/1216 (N.I. 1)),
   (iv) an extended custodial sentence for a term of 10 years or more under Article 14(5) of that Order (offenders under 21 convicted of certain offences),
   (v) detention during the pleasure of the Secretary of State under Article 45(1) of the Criminal Justice (Children) (Northern Ireland) Order 1998 (S.I. 1998/1504 (N.I. 9)).

(3) The sentences in respect of which a 15 year period applies are—
   (a) in England and Wales, imprisonment or detention in a young offender institution for a term of 5 years or more but less than 10 years;
   (b) in Scotland, imprisonment or detention in a young offenders institution for a term of 5 years or more but less than 10 years;
   (c) in Northern Ireland—
      (i) imprisonment for a term of 5 years or more but less than 10 years,
      (ii) an extended custodial sentence for a term of 5 years or more but less than 10 years under Article 14(5) of the Criminal Justice (Northern Ireland) Order 2008 (S.I. 2008/1216 (N.I. 1)) (offenders under 21 convicted of certain offences).

(4) The period begins with the day on which the person is dealt with for the offence.

(5) If a person who is the subject of a finding within section 45(1)(b)(iii), (2)(b)(iii) or (3)(b)(iii) (finding of disability, etc.) is subsequently tried for the offence, the period resulting from that finding ends—
   (a) if the person is acquitted, at the conclusion of the trial;
   (b) if the person is convicted, when the person is again dealt with in respect of the offence.

(6) For the purposes of determining the length of the period—
   (a) a person who has been sentenced in respect of two or more offences to which this Part applies to consecutive terms of imprisonment is treated as if sentenced, in respect of each of the offences, to a term of imprisonment equal to the aggregate of the terms; and
   (b) a person who has been sentenced in respect of two or more such offences to concurrent terms of imprisonment (X and Y) that overlap for a period (Z) is treated as if sentenced, in respect of each of the offences, to a term of imprisonment equal to X plus Y minus Z.

(7) In determining whether the period has expired, there shall be disregarded any period when the person was—
   (a) remanded in or committed to custody by an order of a court,
   (b) serving a sentence of imprisonment or detention,
   (c) detained in a hospital, or
   (d) detained under the Immigration Acts.

54 Offences relating to notification

(1) A person commits an offence who—
   (a) fails without reasonable excuse to comply with—
      section 47 (initial notification), section 48 (notification of changes), section 49 (periodic re-notification), section 50(6) (taking of fingerprints or photographs), any regulations made under section 52(1) (travel outside United Kingdom), or section 56 (notification on return after absence from UK); or
   (b) notifies to the police in purported compliance with—
      section 47 (initial notification), section 48 (notification of changes), section 49 (periodic re-notification), any regulations made under section 52(1) (travel outside United Kingdom), or section 56 (notification on return after absence from UK),
      any information that the person knows to be false.

(2), (3) *****

(4) A person—

    (a) commits an offence under subsection (1)(a) above on the day on which the person first fails without reasonable excuse to comply with—

        section 47 (initial notification), section 48 (notification of changes), section 49 (periodic re-notification), any regulations made under section 52(1) (travel outside United Kingdom), or section 56 (notification on return after absence from UK), and

    (b) continues to commit it throughout any period during which the failure continues.

But a person must not be prosecuted under subsection (1) more than once in respect of the same failure.

(5) Proceedings for an offence under this section may be commenced in any court having jurisdiction in any place where the person charged with the offence resides or is found.

55 Effect of absence abroad

(1) If a person to whom the notification requirements apply is absent from the United Kingdom for any period the following provisions apply.

(2) During the period of absence the period for which the notification requirements apply continues to run.

(3) The period of absence does not affect the obligation under section 47 (initial notification). This is subject to subsection (4).

(4) Section 47 does not apply if—

    (a) the period of absence begins before the end of the period within which notification must be made under that section, and

    (b) the person's absence results from the person's removal from the United Kingdom.

(5) Section 48 (notification of changes)—

    (a) applies in relation to an event that occurs before the period of absence, but

    (b) does not apply in relation to an event that occurs during the period of absence.

Paragraph (a) is subject to subsection (6).

(6) Section 48 does not apply in relation to an event that occurs before the period of absence if—

    (a) the period of absence begins before the end of the period within which notification must be made under that section, and

    (b) the person's absence results from the person's removal from the United Kingdom.

(7) Section 49 (periodic re-notification) does not apply if the period referred to in subsection (1) of that section ends during the period of absence.

(8) Section 53(7) (disregard of period of custody etc.) applies in relation to the period of absence as if it referred to any period when the person was—

    (a) remanded in or committed to custody by an order of a court outside the United Kingdom,

    (b) serving a sentence of imprisonment or detention imposed by such a court,

    (c) detained in a hospital pursuant to an order of such a court that is equivalent to a hospital order, or

    (d) subject to a form of detention outside the United Kingdom that is equivalent to detention under the Immigration Acts.

(9) References in this section and section 56 to a person's removal from the United Kingdom include—

    (a) the person's removal from the United Kingdom in accordance with the Immigration Acts,

    (b) the person's extradition from the United Kingdom, or

    (c) the person's transfer from the United Kingdom to another country pursuant to a warrant under section 1 of the Repatriation of Prisoners Act 1984 (c. 47).

56 Notification on return after absence from UK

(1) This section applies if, before the end of the period for which the notification requirements apply, a person to whom the requirements apply returns to the United Kingdom after a period of absence and—

(a) the person was not required to make a notification under section 47 (initial notification),

(b) there has been a change to any of the information last notified to the police in accordance with—

    (i)   section 47,

    (ii) section 48 (notification of changes),

    (iii) section 49 (periodic re-notification), or

    (iv) this section, or

(c) the period referred to in section 49(1) (period after which re-notification required) ended during the period of absence.

(2) The person must notify or (as the case may be) re-notify to the police the information mentioned in section 47(2) within the period of three days beginning with the day of return.

(3) In determining the period within which notification is to be made under this section, there shall be disregarded any time when the person is—

(a) remanded in or committed to custody by an order of a court,

(b) serving a sentence of imprisonment or detention,

(c) detained in a hospital, or

(d) detained under the Immigration Acts.

(4) This section does not apply if—

(a) the person subsequently leaves the United Kingdom,

(b) the period of absence begins before the end of the period within which notification must be made under this section, and

(c) the person's absence results from the person's removal from the United Kingdom.

(5) The obligation under this section does not affect any obligation to notify information under section 52(3) (regulations requiring notification of return etc.).

57 Notification orders

Schedule 4 makes provision for notification orders applying the notification requirements of this Part to persons who have been dealt with outside the United Kingdom in respect of a corresponding foreign offence.

58 Foreign travel restriction orders

Schedule 5 makes provision for foreign travel restriction orders prohibiting persons to whom the notification requirements apply from—

(a) travelling to a country outside the United Kingdom named or described in the order,

(b) travelling to any country outside the United Kingdom other than a country named or described in the order, or

(c) travelling to any country outside the United Kingdom.

59 Application of Part to service offences and related matters

Schedule 6 makes provision for the application of this Part to service offences and related matters.

[**Note:** For reasons of space schedules 4–6 are not reproduced here.]

*****

Criminal Justice and Immigration Act 2008

(2008, c. 4)

An Act to make further provision about criminal justice (including provision about the police) and dealing with offenders and defaulters; to make further provision about the management of offenders; to amend the criminal law; to make further provision for combating crime and disorder; to make provision about the mutual recognition of financial penalties; to amend the Repatriation of Prisoners Act 1984; to make provision for a new immigration status in certain cases involving criminality; to make provision about the automatic deportation of criminals under the UK Borders Act 2007; to amend section 127 of the Criminal

Justice and Public Order Act 1994 and to confer power to suspend the operation of that section; and for connected purposes.   [8th May 2008]

Territorial extent: England, Wales and Northern Ireland (in the case of Part 5 below)
*****

PART 5 CRIMINAL LAW

Pornography etc.

63 Possession of extreme pornographic images

(1) It is an offence for a person to be in possession of an extreme pornographic image.

(2) An "extreme pornographic image" is an image which is both—

(a) pornographic, and

(b) an extreme image.

(3) An image is "pornographic" if it is of such a nature that it must reasonably be assumed to have been produced solely or principally for the purpose of sexual arousal.

(4) Where (as found in the person's possession) an image forms part of a series of images, the question whether the image is of such a nature as is mentioned in subsection (3) is to be determined by reference to—

(a) the image itself, and

(b) (if the series of images is such as to be capable of providing a context for the image) the context in which it occurs in the series of images.

(5) So, for example, where—

(a) an image forms an integral part of a narrative constituted by a series of images, and

(b) having regard to those images as a whole, they are not of such a nature that they must reasonably be assumed to have been produced solely or principally for the purpose of sexual arousal,

the image may, by virtue of being part of that narrative, be found not to be pornographic, even though it might have been found to be pornographic if taken by itself.

(6) An "extreme image" is an image which—

(a) falls within subsection (7), and

(b) is grossly offensive, disgusting or otherwise of an obscene character.

(7) An image falls within this subsection if it portrays, in an explicit and realistic way, any of the following—

(a) an act which threatens a person's life,

(b) an act which results, or is likely to result, in serious injury to a person's anus, breasts or genitals,

(c) an act which involves sexual interference with a human corpse, or

(d) a person performing an act of intercourse or oral sex with an animal (whether dead or alive),

and a reasonable person looking at the image would think that any such person or animal was real.

(8) In this section "image" means—

(a) a moving or still image (produced by any means); or

(b) data (stored by any means) which is capable of conversion into an image within paragraph (a).

(9) In this section references to a part of the body include references to a part surgically constructed (in particular through gender reassignment surgery).

(10) Proceedings for an offence under this section may not be instituted—

(a) in England and Wales, except by or with the consent of the Director of Public Prosecutions; or

(b) in Northern Ireland, except by or with the consent of the Director of Public Prosecutions for Northern Ireland.

64   Exclusion of classified films etc.

(1) Section 63 does not apply to excluded images.

(2) An "excluded image" is an image which forms part of a series of images contained in a recording of the whole or part of a classified work.

(3) But such an image is not an "excluded image" if—

  (a) it is contained in a recording of an extract from a classified work, and

  (b) it is of such a nature that it must reasonably be assumed to have been extracted (whether with or without other images) solely or principally for the purpose of sexual arousal.

(4) Where an extracted image is one of a series of images contained in the recording, the question whether the image is of such a nature as is mentioned in subsection (3)(b) is to be determined by reference to—

  (a) the image itself, and

  (b) (if the series of images is such as to be capable of providing a context for the image) the context in which it occurs in the series of images;

and section 63(5) applies in connection with determining that question as it applies in connection with determining whether an image is pornographic.

(5) In determining for the purposes of this section whether a recording is a recording of the whole or part of a classified work, any alteration attributable to—

  (a) a defect caused for technical reasons or by inadvertence on the part of any person, or

  (b) the inclusion in the recording of any extraneous material (such as advertisements),

is to be disregarded.

(6) Nothing in this section is to be taken as affecting any duty of a designated authority to have regard to section 63 (along with other enactments creating criminal offences) in determining whether a video work is suitable for a classification certificate to be issued in respect of it.

(7) In this section—

  "classified work" means (subject to subsection (8)) a video work in respect of which a classification certificate has been issued by a designated authority (whether before or after the commencement of this section);

  "classification certificate" and "video work" have the same meanings as in the Video Recordings Act 1984 (c. 39);

  "designated authority" means an authority which has been designated by the Secretary of State under section 4 of that Act;

  "extract" includes an extract consisting of a single image;

  "image" and "pornographic" have the same meanings as in section 63;

  "recording" means any disc, tape or other device capable of storing data electronically and from which images may be produced (by any means).

(8) *****

65   Defences: general

(1) Where a person is charged with an offence under section 63, it is a defence for the person to prove any of the matters mentioned in subsection (2).

(2) The matters are—

  (a) that the person had a legitimate reason for being in possession of the image concerned;

  (b) that the person had not seen the image concerned and did not know, nor had any cause to suspect, it to be an extreme pornographic image;

  (c) that the person—

    (i)   was sent the image concerned without any prior request having been made by or on behalf of the person, and

    (ii) did not keep it for an unreasonable time.

(3) *****

66   Defence: participation in consensual acts

(1) This section applies where—

    (a) a person ("D") is charged with an offence under section 63, and

    (b) the offence relates to an image that portrays an act or acts within paragraphs (a) to (c) (but none within paragraph (d)) of subsection (7) of that section.

(2) It is a defence for D to prove—

    (a) that D directly participated in the act or any of the acts portrayed, and

    (b) that the act or acts did not involve the infliction of any non-consensual harm on any person, and

    (c) if the image portrays an act within section 63(7)(c), that what is portrayed as a human corpse was not in fact a corpse.

(3) For the purposes of this section harm inflicted on a person is "non-consensual" harm if—

    (a) the harm is of such a nature that the person cannot, in law, consent to it being inflicted on himself or herself; or

    (b) where the person can, in law, consent to it being so inflicted, the person does not in fact consent to it being so inflicted.

67   Penalties etc. for possession of extreme pornographic images

(1) This section has effect where a person is guilty of an offence under section 63.

(2) Except where subsection (3) applies to the offence, the offender is liable—

    (a) on summary conviction, to imprisonment for a term not exceeding the relevant period or a fine not exceeding the statutory maximum or both;

    (b) on conviction on indictment, to imprisonment for a term not exceeding 3 years or a fine or both.

(3) If the offence relates to an image that does not portray any act within section 63(7)(a) or (b), the offender is liable—

    (a) on summary conviction, to imprisonment for a term not exceeding the relevant period or a fine not exceeding the statutory maximum or both;

    (b) on conviction on indictment, to imprisonment for a term not exceeding 2 years or a fine or both.

(4) In subsection (2)(a) or (3)(a) "the relevant period" means—

    (a) in relation to England and Wales, 12 months;

    (b) in relation to Northern Ireland, 6 months.

*****

Borders, Citizenship and Immigration Act 2009

(2009, c. 11)

An Act to provide for customs functions to be exercisable by the Secretary of State, the Director of Border Revenue and officials designated by them; to make provision about the use and disclosure of customs information; to make provision for and in connection with the exercise of customs functions and functions relating to immigration, asylum or nationality; to make provision about citizenship and other nationality matters; to make further provision about immigration and asylum; and for connected purposes.   [21st July 2009]

Territorial extent: England, Wales and Northern Ireland (ss. 22 and 23) and also Scotland in relation to s. 55.

*****

Investigations and detention

22   Application of the PACE orders

(1) Subject as follows, the PACE orders—

(a) apply to criminal investigations conducted by designated customs officials and relating to a general customs matter or customs revenue matter as they apply to relevant investigations conducted by officers of Revenue and Customs, and

(b) apply to persons detained by designated customs officials as they apply to persons detained by officers of Revenue and Customs.

(2) Each of the following is a PACE order for the purposes of this section—

  (a) the Police and Criminal Evidence Act 1984 (Application to Revenue and Customs) Order 2007 (SI 2007/3175);

  (b) the Police and Criminal Evidence (Application to Revenue and Customs) Order (Northern Ireland) 2007 (SR 2007/464).

(3) In the application of the PACE orders by virtue of this section—

  (a) subject to the following provisions of this subsection, references in those orders to an officer of Revenue and Customs are to be read as references to a designated customs official;

  (b) references in those orders to the Commissioners are to be read as references to—

    (i) the Secretary of State in relation to general customs matters, or

    (ii) the Director of Border Revenue in relation to customs revenue matters;

  (c) references in those orders to Her Majesty's Revenue and Customs or to Revenue and Customs are to be read as references to—

    (i)   the Secretary of State in so far as the Secretary of State has general customs functions,

    (ii) the Director of Border Revenue, and

    (iii) designated customs officials;

  (d) references in those orders to an office of Revenue and Customs are to be read as references to an office of the UK Border Agency;

  (e) references in those orders to a designated office of Revenue and Customs are to be read as references to a designated office of the UK Border Agency;

  (f) references in those orders to a relevant indictable offence are to be read as references to an indictable offence that relates to a general customs matter or a customs revenue matter;

  (g) references in those orders to a relevant investigation are to be read as references to a criminal investigation conducted by a designated customs official that relates to a general customs matter or a customs revenue matter;

  (h) references in those orders to a person being in Revenue and Customs detention are to be read as references to a person being in UK Border Agency detention;

  (i) references in those orders to an officer of Revenue and Customs of at least the grade of officer are to be read as references to a designated customs official of at least the grade of immigration officer or executive officer;

  (j) references in those orders to an officer of Revenue and Customs of at least the grade of higher officer are to be read as references to a designated customs official of at least the grade of chief immigration officer or higher executive officer;

  (k) references in those orders to an officer of Revenue and Customs of at least the grade of senior officer are to be read as references to a designated customs official of at least the grade of immigration inspector or senior executive officer;

  (l) any other references in those orders to an officer of Revenue and Customs occupying a specified post or grade are to be read as references to the Secretary of State.

(4) For the purposes of this section—

  (a) a person is in UK Border Agency detention if—

    (i) the person has been taken to an office of the UK Border Agency after being arrested for an offence, or

    (ii) the person is arrested at an office of the UK Border Agency after attending voluntarily at the office or accompanying a designated customs official to it, and is detained there or is detained elsewhere in the charge of a designated customs official, and

(b) "office of the UK Border Agency" means premises wholly or partly occupied by designated customs officials.

(5) This section does not apply to the following provisions of the PACE orders—

(a) in article 2(1) of the Police and Criminal Evidence Act 1984 (Application to Revenue and Customs) Order 2007 (SI 2007/3175), the definitions of "the Commissioners", "office of Revenue and Customs", "relevant indictable offence" and "relevant investigation";

(b) article 2(2) of that order (Revenue and Customs detention);

(c) article 7 of that order (restriction on other powers to apply for production of documents);

(d) article 19 of that order (authorisation);

(e) in article 2(1) of the Police and Criminal Evidence (Application to Revenue and Customs) Order (Northern Ireland) 2007 (SR 2007/464), the definitions of "the Commissioners", "office of Revenue and Customs", "relevant indictable offence" and "relevant investigation";

(f) article 2(2) of that order (Revenue and Customs detention);

(g) article 7 of that order (restriction on other powers to apply for production of documents);

(h) article 15 of that order (authorisation).

(6) A person may be transferred—

(a) between UK Border Agency detention and Revenue and Customs detention;

(b) between Revenue and Customs detention and UK Border Agency detention;

(c) between UK Border Agency detention and police detention;

(d) between police detention and UK Border Agency detention.

(7) The references to police detention in subsection (6)—

(a) in relation to England and Wales, are to be construed in accordance with the Police and Criminal Evidence Act 1984 (c 60);

(b) in relation to Northern Ireland, are to be construed in accordance with the Police and Criminal Evidence (Northern Ireland) Order 1989 (SI 1989/1341 (NI 12)).

(8) Expressions used in this section that are defined in a PACE order have the same meaning as in that PACE order.

(9) This section does not affect the generality of sections 1(4), 3(5), 7(5) and 11(4) (construction of statutory etc references to the Commissioners for Her Majesty's Revenue and Customs, officers of Revenue and Customs and Her Majesty's Revenue and Customs).

23   Investigations and detention: England and Wales and Northern Ireland

(1) The Secretary of State may by order provide for any provision of an enactment listed in subsection (2) that relates to investigations of offences conducted by police officers or to persons detained by the police to apply, subject to such modifications as the order may specify, in relation to—

(a) investigations conducted by designated customs officials,

(b) persons detained by designated customs officials,

(c) investigations conducted by immigration officers, or

(d) persons detained by immigration officers.

(2) Those enactments are—

(a) the Police and Criminal Evidence Act 1984 (c 60), and

(b) the Police and Criminal Evidence (Northern Ireland) Order 1989 (SI 1989/1341 (NI 12)).

(3) An order under this section may make, in relation to designated customs officials, immigration officers, the Secretary of State or the Director of Border Revenue, provision similar to that which may be made in relation to officers of Revenue and Customs or the Commissioners for Her Majesty's Revenue and Customs under—

(a) section 114 of the Police and Criminal Evidence Act 1984, or

(b) article 85 of the Police and Criminal Evidence (Northern Ireland) Order 1989.

(4) If an order under this section provides that a function may be exercised only by a person acting with the authority of the Secretary of State or the Director of Border Revenue, a certificate of the Secretary of State or (as the case may be) the Director that the person had authority to exercise the function is conclusive evidence of that fact.

(5) An order under this section may amend or repeal section 22 (application of the PACE orders).

23–54 *****

Children

55 Duty regarding the welfare of children

(1) The Secretary of State must make arrangements for ensuring that—

    (a) the functions mentioned in subsection (2) are discharged having regard to the need to safeguard and promote the welfare of children who are in the United Kingdom, and

    (b) any services provided by another person pursuant to arrangements which are made by the Secretary of State and relate to the discharge of a function mentioned in subsection (2) are provided having regard to that need.

(2) The functions referred to in subsection (1) are—

    (a) any function of the Secretary of State in relation to immigration, asylum or nationality;

    (b) any function conferred by or by virtue of the Immigration Acts on an immigration officer;

    (c) any general customs function of the Secretary of State;

    (d) any customs function conferred on a designated customs official.

(3) A person exercising any of those functions must, in exercising the function, have regard to any guidance given to the person by the Secretary of State for the purpose of subsection (1).

(4) The Director of Border Revenue must make arrangements for ensuring that—

    (a) the Director's functions are discharged having regard to the need to safeguard and promote the welfare of children who are in the United Kingdom, and

    (b) any services provided by another person pursuant to arrangements made by the Director in the discharge of such a function are provided having regard to that need.

(5) A person exercising a function of the Director of Border Revenue must, in exercising the function, have regard to any guidance given to the person by the Secretary of State for the purpose of subsection (4).

(6) In this section—

"children" means persons who are under the age of 18;

"customs function", "designated customs official" and "general customs function" have the meanings given by Part 1.

(7) A reference in an enactment (other than this Act) to the Immigration Acts includes a reference to this section.

(8) Section 21 of the UK Borders Act 2007 (c 30) (children) ceases to have effect.
*****

Parliamentary Standards Act 2009

(2009, c. 13)

An Act to make provision establishing a body corporate known as the Independent Parliamentary Standards Authority and an officer known as the Commissioner for Parliamentary Investigations; to make provision relating to salaries and allowances for members of the House of Commons and to their financial interests and conduct; and for connected purposes. [21st July 2009]

Territorial extent: United Kingdom

Introductory

1   Bill of Rights

Nothing in this Act shall be construed by any court in the United Kingdom as affecting Article IX of the Bill of Rights 1689.

2   House of Lords

(1) Nothing in this Act shall affect the House of Lords.

(2) *****

Independent Parliamentary Standards Authority etc.

3   Independent Parliamentary Standards Authority etc.

(1) There is to be a body corporate known as the Independent Parliamentary Standards Authority ("IPSA").

(2) *****

(3) There is to be an officer known as the Commissioner for Parliamentary Investigations ("the Commissioner").

(4)–(6) *****

[3A   General duties of the IPSA]

[(1) In carrying out its functions the IPSA must have regard to the principle that it should act in a way which is efficient, cost-effective and transparent.

(2) In carrying out its functions the IPSA must have regard to the principle that members of the House of Commons should be supported in efficiently, cost-effectively and transparently carrying out their Parliamentary functions.]

Salaries and allowances for MPs

4   [MPs' salaries]

[(1) Members of the House of Commons are to receive a salary for the relevant period.

(2) The salaries are to be paid by the IPSA.

(3) Salaries are to be paid on a monthly basis in arrears.

(4) The amounts of the salaries are to be determined by the IPSA (see section 4A).

(5) "Relevant period", in relation to a person who is a member of the House of Commons, means the period beginning with the day after the day of the poll for the parliamentary election at which the member was elected and ending with—

> (a) if the person is a member immediately before Parliament is dissolved, the day of the poll for the parliamentary general election which follows the dissolution;
>
> (b) otherwise, the day on which the person ceases to be a member.

(6) No payment of salary is to be made to a member before the member has made and subscribed the oath required by the Parliamentary Oaths Act 1866 (or the corresponding affirmation).

(7) The duty of the IPSA to pay a salary to a member is subject to anything done in relation to the member in the exercise of the disciplinary powers of the House of Commons.]

[4A   Determination of MPs' salaries]

[(1) This section is about determinations under section 4(4).

(2) A determination may provide for higher salaries to be payable to members while holding an office or position specified for the purposes of this subsection in a resolution of the House of Commons.

(3) A determination by virtue of subsection (2) may make different provision for different offices or positions or different classes of member (and may include exceptions).

(4) A determination may include a formula or other mechanism for adjusting salaries from time to time.

(5) A determination (other than the first determination) may have retrospective effect.

(6) The IPSA must review the current determination (and make a new determination as appropriate)—

    (a) in the first year of each Parliament;

    (b) at any other time it considers appropriate.

(7) In reviewing a determination (and before making the first determination) the IPSA must consult—

    (a) the Review Body on Senior Salaries,

    (b) persons appearing to the IPSA to represent persons likely to be affected by the determination or the review,

    (c) the Minister for the Civil Service,

    (d) the Treasury, and

    (e) any other person the IPSA considers appropriate.

(8) After making a determination, the IPSA must publish in a way it considers appropriate—

    (a) the determination, and

    (b) a statement of how it arrived at the determination.

(9) If the IPSA reviews the current determination but decides not to make a new determination, it must publish in a way it considers appropriate a statement of how it arrived at that decision.

(10) The IPSA may delegate to the Review Body on Senior Salaries its function of reviewing a determination (but not its function of deciding whether or not to make a new determination).]

5 MPs' allowances scheme

(1) The IPSA is to pay allowances to members of the House of Commons in accordance with the MPs' allowances scheme.

(2) In this Act "the MPs' allowances scheme" means the scheme prepared under this section as it is in effect for the time being.

(3) The IPSA must—

    (a) prepare the scheme;

    (b) review the scheme regularly and revise it as appropriate.

(4) In preparing or revising the scheme, the IPSA must consult—

    (a) the Speaker of the House of Commons,

    (b) the Committee on Standards in Public Life,

    (c) the Leader of the House of Commons,

    (d) any committee of the House of Commons nominated by the Speaker,

    (e) members of the House of Commons,

    (f) the Review Body on Senior Salaries,

    (g) Her Majesty's Revenue and Customs,

    (h) the Treasury, and

    (i) any other person the IPSA considers appropriate.

(5) The Speaker must lay the scheme (or revision) before the House of Commons.

[(5A) When the scheme (or revision) is laid, the IPSA must publish in a way it considers appropriate—

    (a) the scheme (or revision), and

    (b) a statement of its reasons for adopting that scheme (or making that revision).]

(6) The scheme (or revision) comes into effect on the date specified in the scheme (or revision).

(7) The scheme may, for example—

    (a) provide for allowances to be payable in respect of specified kinds of expenditure or in specified circumstances;

    (b) provide for allowances to be payable only on specified conditions (such as a condition that claims for allowances must be supported by documentary evidence);

    (c) impose limits on the amounts that may be paid.

(8) The scheme may provide for allowances to be payable in connection with a person's ceasing to be a member of the House of Commons; [and in relation to any such allowances, references in this Act to a member of the House of Commons include a former member of that House].

[(8A) Any duty of the IPSA to pay an allowance to a member is subject to anything done in relation to the member in the exercise of the disciplinary powers of the House of Commons.]

(9), (10) *****

6 Dealing with claims under the scheme

(1) No allowance is to be paid to a member of the House of Commons under the MPs' allowances scheme unless a claim for the allowance has been made to the IPSA.

(2) The claim must be made by the member (except where the scheme provides otherwise).

(3) On receipt of a claim, the IPSA must—

(a) determine whether to allow or refuse the claim, and

(b) if it is allowed, determine how much of the amount claimed is to be allowed and pay it accordingly.

(4) ...

(5) ...

(6) The MPs' allowances scheme may include—

(a) further provision about how claims are to be dealt with;

[(b) provision for deducting amounts within subsection (6A) from allowances payable under the scheme or salaries payable under section 4;

(c) provision about how such deductions, and deductions under paragraph 5 or 12 of Schedule 4, are to be made].

(6A)–(10) *****

[6A] *****

7 Information and guidance ...

[(A1) The IPSA must—

(a) prepare guidance for members of the House of Commons about making claims under the MPs' allowances scheme;

(b) review the guidance regularly and revise it as appropriate;

(c) publish the guidance in a way the IPSA considers appropriate;

(d) provide to any member on request such further advice about making claims as the IPSA considers appropriate.]

(1) The IPSA must provide to members of the House of Commons—

(a) details of any general information or guidance about taxation issues published by HMRC that it considers they should be aware of, and

(b) any other general information or guidance about taxation issues that it considers appropriate (consulting HMRC for this purpose as it considers appropriate).

(2), (3) *****

8 ...

Investigation and enforcement

[9 Investigations]

[(1) The Compliance Officer may conduct an investigation if the Compliance Officer has reason to believe that a member of the House of Commons may have been paid an amount under the MPs' allowances scheme that should not have been allowed.

(2) An investigation may be conducted—

(a) on the Compliance Officer's own initiative,

(b) at the request of the IPSA,

(c) at the request of the member, or

(d) in response to a complaint by an individual.

(3) For the purposes of the investigation the member and the IPSA—

(a) must provide the Compliance Officer with any information (including documents) the Compliance Officer reasonably requires, and

(b) must do so within such period as the Compliance Officer reasonably requires.

(4) The Compliance Officer must, after giving the member and the IPSA an opportunity to make representations to the Compliance Officer, prepare a statement of the Compliance Officer's provisional findings.

(5) The Compliance Officer must, after giving the member and the IPSA an opportunity to make representations to the Compliance Officer about the provisional findings, prepare a statement of the Compliance Officer's findings (subject to subsection (7)).

(6) Provisional findings under subsection (4) and findings under subsection (5) may include—

    (a) a finding that the member failed to comply with subsection (3),

    (b) findings about the role of the IPSA in the matters under investigation, including findings that the member's being paid an amount under the MPs' allowances scheme that should not have been allowed was wholly or partly the IPSA's fault.

(7) If subsection (8) applies, the Compliance Officer need not make a finding under subsection (5) as to whether the member was paid an amount under the MPs' allowances scheme that should not have been allowed.

(8) This subsection applies if—

    (a) the member accepts a provisional finding that the member was paid an amount under the MPs' allowances scheme that should not have been allowed,

    (b) such other conditions as may be specified by the IPSA are, in the Compliance Officer's view, met in relation to the case, and

    (c) the member agrees to repay to the IPSA, in such manner and within such period as the Compliance Officer considers reasonable, such amount as the Compliance Officer considers reasonable (and makes the repayment accordingly).

(9) Before specifying conditions under subsection (8)(b) the IPSA must consult the persons listed in section 9A(6).

(10) References in this section (and section 9A) to a member of the House of Commons include a former member of that House.]

9A, 9B   *****

10   Offence of providing false or misleading information for allowances claims

(1) A member of the House of Commons commits an offence if the member—

    (a) makes a claim under the MPs' allowances scheme, and

    (b) provides information for the purposes of the claim that the member knows to be false or misleading in a material respect.

(2) A person guilty of an offence under subsection (1) is liable—

    (a) on summary conviction, to imprisonment for a term not exceeding 12 months or to a fine not exceeding the statutory maximum or to both;

    (b) on conviction on indictment, to imprisonment for a term not exceeding 12 months or to a fine or to both.

(3) *****

10A   *****

11 ...
*****

Bribery Act 2010

(2010, c. 23)

An Act to make provision about offences relating to bribery; and for connected purposes.

[8th April 2010]

Territorial extent: United Kingdom

General bribery offences

1 Offences of bribing another person

(1) A person ("P") is guilty of an offence if either of the following cases applies.

(2) Case 1 is where—

    (a) P offers, promises or gives a financial or other advantage to another person, and

    (b) P intends the advantage—

        (i)   to induce a person to perform improperly a relevant function or activity, or

        (ii)   to reward a person for the improper performance of such a function or activity.

(3) Case 2 is where—

    (a) P offers, promises or gives a financial or other advantage to another person, and

    (b) P knows or believes that the acceptance of the advantage would itself constitute the improper performance of a relevant function or activity.

(4) In case 1 it does not matter whether the person to whom the advantage is offered, promised or given is the same person as the person who is to perform, or has performed, the function or activity concerned.

(5) In cases 1 and 2 it does not matter whether the advantage is offered, promised or given by P directly or through a third party.

2 Offences relating to being bribed

(1) A person ("R") is guilty of an offence if any of the following cases applies.

(2) Case 3 is where R requests, agrees to receive or accepts a financial or other advantage intending that, in consequence, a relevant function or activity should be performed improperly (whether by R or another person).

(3) Case 4 is where—

    (a) R requests, agrees to receive or accepts a financial or other advantage, and

    (b) the request, agreement or acceptance itself constitutes the improper performance by R of a relevant function or activity.

(4) Case 5 is where R requests, agrees to receive or accepts a financial or other advantage as a reward for the improper performance (whether by R or another person) of a relevant function or activity.

(5) Case 6 is where, in anticipation of or in consequence of R requesting, agreeing to receive or accepting a financial or other advantage, a relevant function or activity is performed improperly—

    (a) by R, or

    (b) by another person at R's request or with R's assent or acquiescence.

(6) In cases 3 to 6 it does not matter—

    (a) whether R requests, agrees to receive or accepts (or is to request, agree to receive or accept) the advantage directly or through a third party,

    (b) whether the advantage is (or is to be) for the benefit of R or another person.

(7) In cases 4 to 6 it does not matter whether R knows or believes that the performance of the function or activity is improper.

(8) In case 6, where a person other than R is performing the function or activity, it also does not matter whether that person knows or believes that the performance of the function or activity is improper.

3 Function or activity to which bribe relates

(1) For the purposes of this Act a function or activity is a relevant function or activity if—

    (a) it falls within subsection (2), and

    (b) meets one or more of conditions A to C.

(2) The following functions and activities fall within this subsection—

    (a) any function of a public nature,

    (b) any activity connected with a business,

    (c) any activity performed in the course of a person's employment,

(d) any activity performed by or on behalf of a body of persons (whether corporate or unincorporate).

(3) Condition A is that a person performing the function or activity is expected to perform it in good faith.

(4) Condition B is that a person performing the function or activity is expected to perform it impartially.

(5) Condition C is that a person performing the function or activity is in a position of trust by virtue of performing it.

(6) A function or activity is a relevant function or activity even if it—

    (a) has no connection with the United Kingdom, and

    (b) is performed in a country or territory outside the United Kingdom.

(7) In this section "business" includes trade or profession.

4 Improper performance to which bribe relates

(1) For the purposes of this Act a relevant function or activity—

    (a) is performed improperly if it is performed in breach of a relevant expectation, and

    (b) is to be treated as being performed improperly if there is a failure to perform the function or activity and that failure is itself a breach of a relevant expectation.

(2) In subsection (1) "relevant expectation"—

    (a) in relation to a function or activity which meets condition A or B, means the expectation mentioned in the condition concerned, and

    (b) in relation to a function or activity which meets condition C, means any expectation as to the manner in which, or the reasons for which, the function or activity will be performed that arises from the position of trust mentioned in that condition.

(3) Anything that a person does (or omits to do) arising from or in connection with that person's past performance of a relevant function or activity is to be treated for the purposes of this Act as being done (or omitted) by that person in the performance of that function or activity.

5 Expectation test

(1) For the purposes of sections 3 and 4, the test of what is expected is a test of what a reasonable person in the United Kingdom would expect in relation to the performance of the type of function or activity concerned.

(2) In deciding what such a person would expect in relation to the performance of a function or activity where the performance is not subject to the law of any part of the United Kingdom, any local custom or practice is to be disregarded unless it is permitted or required by the written law applicable to the country or territory concerned.

(3) In subsection (2) "written law" means law contained in—

    (a) any written constitution, or provision made by or under legislation, applicable to the country or territory concerned, or

    (b) any judicial decision which is so applicable and is evidenced in published written sources.

Bribery of foreign public officials

6 Bribery of foreign public officials

(1) A person ("P") who bribes a foreign public official ("F") is guilty of an offence if P's intention is to influence F in F's capacity as a foreign public official.

(2) P must also intend to obtain or retain—

    (a) business, or

    (b) an advantage in the conduct of business.

(3) P bribes F if, and only if—

    (a) directly or through a third party, P offers, promises or gives any financial or other advantage—

(i)   to F, or

(ii)   to another person at F's request or with F's assent or acquiescence, and

(b)   F is neither permitted nor required by the written law applicable to F to be influenced in F's capacity as a foreign public official by the offer, promise or gift.

(4)   References in this section to influencing F in F's capacity as a foreign public official mean influencing F in the performance of F's functions as such an official, which includes—

(a)   any omission to exercise those functions, and

(b)   any use of F's position as such an official, even if not within F's authority.

(5)   "Foreign public official" means an individual who—

(a)   holds a legislative, administrative or judicial position of any kind, whether appointed or elected, of a country or territory outside the United Kingdom (or any subdivision of such a country or territory),

(b)   exercises a public function—

(i)   for or on behalf of a country or territory outside the United Kingdom (or any subdivision of such a country or territory), or

(ii)   for any public agency or public enterprise of that country or territory (or subdivision), or

(c)   is an official or agent of a public international organisation.

(6)   "Public international organisation" means an organisation whose members are any of the following—

(a)   countries or territories,

(b)   governments of countries or territories,

(c)   other public international organisations,

(d)   a mixture of any of the above.

(7)   For the purposes of subsection (3)(b), the written law applicable to F is—

(a)   where the performance of the functions of F which P intends to influence would be subject to the law of any part of the United Kingdom, the law of that part of the United Kingdom,

(b)   where paragraph (a) does not apply and F is an official or agent of a public international organisation, the applicable written rules of that organisation,

(c)   where paragraphs (a) and (b) do not apply, the law of the country or territory in relation to which F is a foreign public official so far as that law is contained in—

(i)   any written constitution, or provision made by or under legislation, applicable to the country or territory concerned, or

(ii)   any judicial decision which is so applicable and is evidenced in published written sources.

(8)   For the purposes of this section, a trade or profession is a business.

Failure of commercial organisations to prevent bribery

7   Failure of commercial organisations to prevent bribery

(1)   A relevant commercial organisation ("C") is guilty of an offence under this section if a person ("A") associated with C bribes another person intending—

(a)   to obtain or retain business for C, or

(b)   to obtain or retain an advantage in the conduct of business for C.

(2)   But it is a defence for C to prove that C had in place adequate procedures designed to prevent persons associated with C from undertaking such conduct.

(3)   For the purposes of this section, A bribes another person if, and only if, A—

(a)   is, or would be, guilty of an offence under section 1 or 6 (whether or not A has been prosecuted for such an offence), or

(b)   would be guilty of such an offence if section 12(2)(c) and (4) were omitted.

(4)   See section 8 for the meaning of a person associated with C and see section 9 for a duty on the Secretary of State to publish guidance.

(5) In this section—

"partnership" means—

    (a) a partnership within the Partnership Act 1890, or

    (b) a limited partnership registered under the Limited Partnerships Act 1907,

or a firm or entity of a similar character formed under the law of a country or territory outside the United Kingdom,

"relevant commercial organisation" means—

    (a) a body which is incorporated under the law of any part of the United Kingdom and which carries on a business (whether there or elsewhere),

    (b) any other body corporate (wherever incorporated) which carries on a business, or part of a business, in any part of the United Kingdom,

    (c) a partnership which is formed under the law of any part of the United Kingdom and which carries on a business (whether there or elsewhere), or

    (d) any other partnership (wherever formed) which carries on a business, or part of a business, in any part of the United Kingdom,

and, for the purposes of this section, a trade or profession is a business.

8–11   *****

Other provisions about offences

12   Offences under this Act: territorial application

(1) An offence is committed under section 1, 2 or 6 in England and Wales, Scotland or Northern Ireland if any act or omission which forms part of the offence takes place in that part of the United Kingdom.

(2) Subsection (3) applies if—

    (a) no act or omission which forms part of an offence under section 1, 2 or 6 takes place in the United Kingdom,

    (b) a person's acts or omissions done or made outside the United Kingdom would form part of such an offence if done or made in the United Kingdom, and

    (c) that person has a close connection with the United Kingdom.

(3) In such a case—

    (a) the acts or omissions form part of the offence referred to in subsection (2)(a), and

    (b) proceedings for the offence may be taken at any place in the United Kingdom.

(4) For the purposes of subsection (2)(c) a person has a close connection with the United Kingdom if, and only if, the person was one of the following at the time the acts or omissions concerned were done or made—

    (a) a British citizen,

    (b) a British overseas territories citizen,

    (c) a British National (Overseas),

    (d) a British Overseas citizen,

    (e) a person who under the British Nationality Act 1981 was a British subject,

    (f) a British protected person within the meaning of that Act,

    (g) an individual ordinarily resident in the United Kingdom,

    (h) a body incorporated under the law of any part of the United Kingdom,

    (i) a Scottish partnership.

(5) An offence is committed under section 7 irrespective of whether the acts or omissions which form part of the offence take place in the United Kingdom or elsewhere.

(6) Where no act or omission which forms part of an offence under section 7 takes place in the United Kingdom, proceedings for the offence may be taken at any place in the United Kingdom.

(7)–(9)   *****

13   Defence for certain bribery offences etc.

(1) It is a defence for a person charged with a relevant bribery offence to prove that the person's conduct was necessary for—

(a) the proper exercise of any function of an intelligence service, or

(b) the proper exercise of any function of the armed forces when engaged on active service.

(2) The head of each intelligence service must ensure that the service has in place arrangements designed to ensure that any conduct of a member of the service which would otherwise be a relevant bribery offence is necessary for a purpose falling within subsection (1)(a).

(3) The Defence Council must ensure that the armed forces have in place arrangements designed to ensure that any conduct of—

(a) a member of the armed forces who is engaged on active service, or

(b) a civilian subject to service discipline when working in support of any person falling within paragraph (a),

which would otherwise be a relevant bribery offence is necessary for a purpose falling within subsection (1)(b).

(4)–(6) *****

14, 15 *****

Supplementary and final provisions

16   Application to Crown

This Act applies to individuals in the public service of the Crown as it applies to other individuals.
*****

Constitutional Reform and Governance Act 2010

(2010, c. 25)

An Act to make provision relating to the civil service of the State; to make provision in relation to section 3 of the Act of Settlement; to make provision relating to the ratification of treaties; to make provision relating to the counting of votes in parliamentary elections; to amend the Parliamentary Standards Act 2009 and the European Parliament (Pay and Pensions) Act 1979 and to make provision relating to pensions for members of the House of Commons, Ministers and other office holders; to make provision for treating members of the House of Commons and members of the House of Lords as resident, ordinarily resident and domiciled in the United Kingdom for taxation purposes; to amend the Government Resources and Accounts Act 2000 and to make corresponding provision in relation to Wales; to amend the Public Records Act 1958 and the Freedom of Information Act 2000.   [8th April 2010]

Territorial extent: United Kingdom

PART 1 THE CIVIL SERVICE

Chapter 1 Statutory Basis for Management of the Civil Service

Application

1   Application of Chapter

(1) Subject to subsections (2) and (3), this Chapter applies to the civil service of the State.

(2) This Chapter does not apply to the following parts of the civil service of the State—

(a) the Secret Intelligence Service;

(b) the Security Service;

    (c) the Government Communications Headquarters;

    (d) the Northern Ireland Civil Service;

    (e) the Northern Ireland Court Service.

(3) Further, this Chapter—

    (a) does not apply in relation to the making, outside the United Kingdom, of selections of persons who are not members of the civil service of the State for appointment to that service for the purpose only of duties to be carried out wholly outside the United Kingdom;

    (b) does not apply in relation to the appointment of a person to the civil service of the State who was selected for the appointment as mentioned in paragraph (a);

    (c) does not apply to the civil service of the State so far as it consists of persons—

      (i) who were appointed to the civil service of the State as mentioned in paragraph (b), and

      (ii) all of whose duties are carried out wholly outside the United Kingdom.

(4) In this Chapter references to the civil service—

    (a) are to the civil service of the State excluding the parts mentioned in subsections (2) and (3)(c);

    (b) are to be read subject to subsection (3)(a) and (b);

and references to civil servants are to be read accordingly.

Civil Service Commission

2 Establishment of the Civil Service Commission

(1) There is to be a body corporate called the Civil Service Commission ("the Commission").

(2) Schedule 1 (which is about the Commission) has effect.

(3) The Commission has the role in relation to selections for appointments to the civil service set out in sections 11 to 14.

(4) See also—

    (a) section 9 (which sets out the Commission's role in dealing with conduct that conflicts with civil service codes of conduct);

    (b) section 17 (under which the Commission may be given additional functions).

Power to manage the civil service

3 Management of the civil service

(1) The Minister for the Civil Service has the power to manage the civil service (excluding the diplomatic service).

(2) The Secretary of State has the power to manage the diplomatic service.

(3) The powers in subsections (1) and (2) include (among other things) power to make appointments.

(4) But they do not cover national security vetting (and, accordingly, subsections (1) and (2) do not affect any power relating to national security vetting).

(5) The agreement of the Minister for the Civil Service is required for any exercise of the power in subsection (2) in relation to—

    (a) remuneration of civil servants (including compensation payable on leaving the civil service), or

    (b) the conditions on which a civil servant may retire.

(6) In exercising his power to manage the civil service, the Minister for the Civil Service shall have regard to the need to ensure that civil servants who advise Ministers are aware of the constitutional significance of Parliament and of the conventions governing the relationship between Parliament and Her Majesty's Government.

4 *****

Codes of conduct

5   Civil service code

(1) The Minister for the Civil Service must publish a code of conduct for the civil service (excluding the diplomatic service).

(2) For this purpose, the Minister may publish separate codes of conduct covering civil servants who serve the Scottish Executive or the Welsh Assembly Government.

(3) Before publishing a code (or any revision of a code) under subsection (2), the Minister must consult the First Minister for Scotland or the First Minister for Wales (as the case may be).

(4) In this Chapter "civil service code" means a code of conduct published under this section as it is in force for the time being.

(5) The Minister for the Civil Service must lay any civil service code before Parliament.

(6) The First Minister for Scotland must lay before the Scottish Parliament any civil service code under subsection (2) that covers civil servants who serve the Scottish Executive.

(7) The First Minister for Wales must lay before the National Assembly for Wales any civil service code under subsection (2) that covers civil servants who serve the Welsh Assembly Government.

(8) A civil service code forms part of the terms and conditions of service of any civil servant covered by the code.

6–19   *****

PART 2 RATIFICATION OF TREATIES

20   Treaties to be laid before Parliament before ratification

(1) Subject to what follows, a treaty is not to be ratified unless—
  (a) a Minister of the Crown has laid before Parliament a copy of the treaty,
  (b) the treaty has been published in a way that a Minister of the Crown thinks appropriate, and
  (c) period A has expired without either House having resolved, within period A, that the treaty should not be ratified.

(2) Period A is the period of 21 sitting days beginning with the first sitting day after the date on which the requirement in subsection (1)(a) is met.

(3) Subsections (4) to (6) apply if the House of Commons resolved as mentioned in subsection (1)(c) (whether or not the House of Lords also did so).

(4) The treaty may be ratified if—
  (a) a Minister of the Crown has laid before Parliament a statement indicating that the Minister is of the opinion that the treaty should nevertheless be ratified and explaining why, and
  (b) period B has expired without the House of Commons having resolved, within period B, that the treaty should not be ratified.

(5) Period B is the period of 21 sitting days beginning with the first sitting day after the date on which the requirement in subsection (4)(a) is met.

(6) A statement may be laid under subsection (4)(a) in relation to the treaty on more than one occasion.

(7) Subsection (8) applies if—
  (a) the House of Lords resolved as mentioned in subsection (1)(c), but
  (b) the House of Commons did not.

(8) The treaty may be ratified if a Minister of the Crown has laid before Parliament a statement indicating that the Minister is of the opinion that the treaty should nevertheless be ratified and explaining why.

(9) "Sitting day" means a day on which both Houses of Parliament sit.

21   Extension of 21 sitting day period

(1) A Minister of the Crown may, in relation to a treaty, extend the period mentioned in section 20(1)(c) by 21 sitting days or less.

(2) The Minister does that by laying before Parliament a statement—

    (a) indicating that the period is to be extended, and

    (b) setting out the length of the extension.

(3) The statement must be laid before the period would have expired without the extension.

(4) The Minister must publish the statement in a way the Minister thinks appropriate.

(5) The period may be extended more than once.

22   Section 20 not to apply in exceptional cases

(1) Section 20 does not apply to a treaty if a Minister of the Crown is of the opinion that, exceptionally, the treaty should be ratified without the requirements of that section having been met.

(2) But a treaty may not be ratified by virtue of subsection (1) after either House has resolved, as mentioned in section 20(1)(c), that the treaty should not be ratified.

(3) If a Minister determines that a treaty is to be ratified by virtue of subsection (1), the Minister must, either before or as soon as practicable after the treaty is ratified—

    (a) lay before Parliament a copy of the treaty,

    (b) arrange for the treaty to be published in a way that the Minister thinks appropriate, and

    (c) lay before Parliament a statement indicating that the Minister is of the opinion mentioned in subsection (1) and explaining why.

23   Section 20 not to apply to certain descriptions of treaties

(1) Section 20 does not apply to—

    (a) a treaty covered by section 12 of the European Parliamentary Elections Act 2002 (treaty providing for increase in European Parliament's powers not to be ratified unless approved by Act of Parliament);

    (b) a treaty covered by section 5 of the European Union (Amendment) Act 2008 (treaty amending founding Treaties not to be ratified unless approved by Act of Parliament).

(2) Section 20 does not apply to a treaty in relation to which an Order in Council may be made under one or more of the following—

    (a) section 158 of the Inheritance Tax Act 1984 (double taxation conventions);

    (b) section 2 of the Taxation (International and Other Provisions) Act 2010 (double taxation arrangements);

    (c) section 173 of the Finance Act 2006 (international tax enforcement arrangements).

(3) Section 20 does not apply to a treaty concluded (under authority given by the government of the United Kingdom) by the government of a British overseas territory, of any of the Channel Islands or of the Isle of Man.

(4) Section 20 does not apply to a treaty a copy of which is presented to Parliament by command of Her Majesty before that section comes into force.

24   Explanatory memoranda

In laying a treaty before Parliament under this Part, a Minister shall accompany the treaty with an explanatory memorandum explaining the provisions of the treaty, the reasons for Her Majesty's Government seeking ratification of the treaty, and such other matters as the Minister considers appropriate.

25–40   *****

PART 4 TAX STATUS OF MPS AND MEMBERS OF THE HOUSE OF LORDS

41   Tax status of MPs and members of the House of Lords

(1) Subsection (2) applies if a person is for any part of a tax year—

(a) a member of the House of Commons, or

(b) a member of the House of Lords.

(2) The person is to be treated for the purposes of the taxes listed in subsection (3) as resident, ordinarily resident and domiciled in the United Kingdom for the whole of that tax year.

(3) The taxes are—

(a) income tax,

(b) capital gains tax, and

(c) inheritance tax.

(4) For the purposes of this section a person—

(a) becomes a member of the House of Commons when (having been elected to that House) the person makes and subscribes the oath required by the Parliamentary Oaths Act 1866 (or the corresponding affirmation), and

(b) ceases to be a member of that House when—

(i)   the Parliament to which the person was elected is dissolved, or

(ii) the person's seat is otherwise vacated.

(5) For the purposes of this section and section 42 a person is a member of the House of Lords if the person is entitled to receive writs of summons to attend that House.

(6) In relation to a member of the House of Lords, in subsection (1) the reference to any part of a tax year excludes any part of the year during which—

(a) section 137(3) of the Constitutional Reform Act 2005 applies to the member, or

(b) the member is entitled to receive writs of summons to attend the House of Lords by virtue of being an archbishop or bishop.

(7)–(10) *****

*****

Crime and Security Act 2010

(2010, c. 17)

An Act to make provision about police powers of stop and search; about the taking, retention, destruction and use of evidential material; for the protection of victims of domestic violence; about injunctions in respect of gang-related violence; about anti-social behaviour orders; about the private security industry; about possession and use of electronic communications devices in prison; about air weapons; for the compensation of victims of overseas terrorism; about licensing the sale and supply of alcohol; about searches in relation to persons subject to control orders; and for connected purposes.

[8th April 2010]

Territorial extent: ss. 23, 47–49 (UK) ss. 24–26 (England and Wales)
*****

23   National DNA Database Strategy Board

(1) The Secretary of State must make arrangements for a National DNA Database Strategy Board to oversee the operation of the National DNA Database.

(2) The National DNA Database Strategy Board must issue guidance about the immediate destruction of DNA samples and DNA profiles which are, or may be, retained under—

(a) the Police and Criminal Evidence Act 1984, or

(b) the Police and Criminal Evidence (Northern Ireland) Order 1989.

(3) The following must act in accordance with any guidance issued under this section—

(a) any chief officer of a police force in England and Wales;

(b) the Chief Constable of the Police Service of Northern Ireland.

(4) The Secretary of State must publish the governance rules of the National DNA Database Strategy Board and lay a copy of the rules before Parliament.

(5) The National DNA Database Strategy Board must make an annual report to the Secretary of State about the exercise of its functions.

(6) The Secretary of State must publish the report and must lay a copy of the published report before Parliament.

(7) The Secretary of State may exclude from publication any part of the report if in the opinion of the Secretary of State the publication of that part would be against the interests of national security.

Domestic violence

24   Power to issue a domestic violence protection notice

(1) A member of a police force not below the rank of superintendent ("the authorising officer") may issue a domestic violence protection notice ("a DVPN") under this section.

(2) A DVPN may be issued to a person ("P") aged 18 years or over if the authorising officer has reasonable grounds for believing that—

(a) P has been violent towards, or has threatened violence towards, an associated person, and

(b) the issue of the DVPN is necessary to protect that person from violence or a threat of violence by P.

(3) Before issuing a DVPN, the authorising officer must, in particular, consider—

(a) the welfare of any person under the age of 18 whose interests the officer considers relevant to the issuing of the DVPN (whether or not that person is an associated person),

(b) the opinion of the person for whose protection the DVPN would be issued as to the issuing of the DVPN,

(c) any representations made by P as to the issuing of the DVPN, and

(d) in the case of provision included by virtue of subsection (8), the opinion of any other associated person who lives in the premises to which the provision would relate.

(4) The authorising officer must take reasonable steps to discover the opinions mentioned in subsection (3).

(5) But the authorising officer may issue a DVPN in circumstances where the person for whose protection it is issued does not consent to the issuing of the DVPN.

(6) A DVPN must contain provision to prohibit P from molesting the person for whose protection it is issued.

(7) Provision required to be included by virtue of subsection (6) may be expressed so as to refer to molestation in general, to particular acts of molestation, or to both.

(8) If P lives in premises which are also lived in by a person for whose protection the DVPN is issued, the DVPN may also contain provision—

(a) to prohibit P from evicting or excluding from the premises the person for whose protection the DVPN is issued,

(b) to prohibit P from entering the premises,

(c) to require P to leave the premises, or

(d) to prohibit P from coming within such distance of the premises as may be specified in the DVPN.

(9) An "associated person" means a person who is associated with P within the meaning of section 62 of the Family Law Act 1996.

(10) Subsection (11) applies where a DVPN includes provision in relation to premises by virtue of subsection (8)(b) or (8)(c) and the authorising officer believes that—

(a) P is a person subject to service law in accordance with sections 367 to 369 of the Armed Forces Act 2006, and

(b) the premises fall within paragraph (a) of the definition of "service living accommodation" in section 96(1) of that Act.

(11) The authorising officer must make reasonable efforts to inform P's commanding officer (within the meaning of section 360 of the Armed Forces Act 2006) of the issuing of the notice.

25   Contents and service of a domestic violence protection notice

(1) A DVPN must state—

(a) the grounds on which it has been issued,

(b) that a constable may arrest P without warrant if the constable has reasonable grounds for believing that P is in breach of the DVPN,

(c) that an application for a domestic violence protection order under section 27 will be heard within 48 hours of the time of service of the DVPN and a notice of the hearing will be given to P,

(d) that the DVPN continues in effect until that application has been determined, and

(e) the provision that a magistrates' court may include in a domestic violence protection order.

(2) A DVPN must be in writing and must be served on P personally by a constable.

(3) On serving P with a DVPN, the constable must ask P for an address for the purposes of being given the notice of the hearing of the application for the domestic violence protection order.

26   Breach of a domestic violence protection notice

(1) A person arrested by virtue of section 25(1)(b) for a breach of a DVPN must be held in custody and brought before the magistrates' court which will hear the application for the DVPO under section 27—

(a) before the end of the period of 24 hours beginning with the time of the arrest, or

(b) if earlier, at the hearing of that application.

(2) If the person is brought before the court by virtue of subsection (1)(a), the court may remand the person.

(3) If the court adjourns the hearing of the application by virtue of section 27(8), the court may remand the person.

(4) In calculating when the period of 24 hours mentioned in subsection (1)(a) ends, Christmas Day, Good Friday, any Sunday and any day which is a bank holiday in England and Wales under the Banking and Financial Dealings Act 1971 are to be disregarded.

27–46   *****

Compensation of victims of overseas terrorism

47   Introductory

(1) The Secretary of State may make arrangements for making payments to, or in respect of, persons who are injured as a result of an act designated under subsection (2).

(2) The Secretary of State may designate an act under this subsection if—

(a) it took place outside the United Kingdom,

(b) it took place on or after 18 January 2010,

(c) in the view of the Secretary of State the act constitutes terrorism within the meaning of the Terrorism Act 2000 (see section 1 of that Act), and

(d) having regard to all the circumstances, the Secretary of State considers that it would be appropriate to designate it.

(3) Nothing in this section affects any power of the Secretary of State to make payments to, or in respect of, persons who are injured as a result of terrorism outside the United Kingdom.

(4) In sections 47 to 54, "injury" includes fatal injury (and "injured" is to be construed accordingly).

48 Compensation scheme

(1) Arrangements under section 47 may include the making of a scheme providing, in particular, for—

    (a) the circumstances in which payments may be made, and

    (b) the categories of person to whom payments may be made.

(2) The scheme is to be known as the Victims of Overseas Terrorism Compensation Scheme ("the Scheme").

(3) Sums required for payments to be made in accordance with the Scheme are to be provided by the Secretary of State.

(4) Schedule 2 (which makes consequential amendments relating to the Scheme) is part of this section.

49 Eligibility and applications

(1) The Scheme may make provision about a person's eligibility for a payment under it by reference to any or all of the following factors—

    (a) the nationality of the person (or the injured person);

    (b) the place of residence of the person (or the injured person);

    (c) the length of time the person (or the injured person) has resided there;

    (d) any other factors that the Secretary of State considers appropriate.

(2) The Scheme may provide that applications for payments under it may only be made—

    (a) by eligible persons;

    (b) within a period specified in the Scheme (and the Scheme may specify different periods for different descriptions of act);

    (c) in a manner or form specified in the Scheme.

*****

Equality Act 2010

(2010, c. 15)

An Act to make provision to require Ministers of the Crown and others when making strategic decisions about the exercise of their functions to have regard to the desirability of reducing socio-economic inequalities; to reform and harmonise equality law and restate the greater part of the enactments relating to discrimination and harassment related to certain personal characteristics; to enable certain employers to be required to publish information about the differences in pay between male and female employees; to prohibit victimisation in certain circumstances; to require the exercise of certain functions to be with regard to the need to eliminate discrimination and other prohibited conduct; to enable duties to be imposed in relation to the exercise of public procurement functions; to increase equality of opportunity; to amend the law relating to rights and responsibilities in family relationships; and for connected purposes.

[8th April 2010]

Territorial extent: England and Wales

PART 1 SOCIO-ECONOMIC INEQUALITIES

1 Public sector duty regarding socio-economic inequalities

(1) An authority to which this section applies must, when making decisions of a strategic nature about how to exercise its functions, have due regard to the desirability of exercising them in a way that is designed to reduce the inequalities of outcome which result from socio-economic disadvantage.

(2) In deciding how to fulfil a duty to which it is subject under subsection (1), an authority must take into account any guidance issued by a Minister of the Crown.

(3) The authorities to which this section applies are—

    (a) a Minister of the Crown;

    (b) a government department other than the Security Service, the Secret Intelligence Service or the Government Communications Headquarters;

    (c) a county council or district council in England;

    (d) the Greater London Authority;

    (e) a London borough council;

    (f) the Common Council of the City of London in its capacity as a local authority;

    (g) the Council of the Isles of Scilly;

    (h) . . .;

    (i) . . .;

    (j) . . .;

    (k) [police and crime commissioner] established for an area in England.

(4) This section also applies to an authority that—

    (a) is a partner authority in relation to a responsible local authority, and

    (b) does not fall within subsection (3),

but only in relation to its participation in the preparation or modification of a sustainable community strategy.

(5) In subsection (4)—

"partner authority" has the meaning given by section 104 of the Local Government and Public Involvement in Health Act 2007;

"responsible local authority" has the meaning given by section 103 of that Act;

"sustainable community strategy" means a strategy prepared under section 4 of the Local Government Act 2000.

(6) The reference to inequalities in subsection (1) does not include any inequalities experienced by a person as a result of being a person subject to immigration control within the meaning given by section 115(9) of the Immigration and Asylum Act 1999.

2   *****

3 Enforcement

A failure in respect of a performance of a duty under section 1 does not confer a cause of action at private law.

PART 2 EQUALITY: KEY CONCEPTS

Chapter 1 Protected Characteristics

4 The protected characteristics

The following characteristics are protected characteristics—

    age;

    disability;

    gender reassignment;

    marriage and civil partnership;

    pregnancy and maternity;

    race;

    religion or belief;

    sex;

    sexual orientation.

5 Age

(1) In relation to the protected characteristic of age—

    (a) a reference to a person who has a particular protected characteristic is a reference to a person of a particular age group;

(b) a reference to persons who share a protected characteristic is a reference to persons of the same age group.

(2) A reference to an age group is a reference to a group of persons defined by reference to age, whether by reference to a particular age or to a range of ages.

6 Disability

(1) A person (P) has a disability if—

    (a) P has a physical or mental impairment, and

    (b) the impairment has a substantial and long-term adverse effect on P's ability to carry out normal day-to-day activities.

(2) A reference to a disabled person is a reference to a person who has a disability.

(3) In relation to the protected characteristic of disability—

    (a) a reference to a person who has a particular protected characteristic is a reference to a person who has a particular disability;

    (b) a reference to persons who share a protected characteristic is a reference to persons who have the same disability.

(4) This Act (except Part 12 and section 190) applies in relation to a person who has had a disability as it applies in relation to a person who has the disability; accordingly (except in that Part and that section)—

    (a) a reference (however expressed) to a person who has a disability includes a reference to a person who has had the disability, and

    (b) a reference (however expressed) to a person who does not have a disability includes a reference to a person who has not had the disability.

(5), (6) *****

7 Gender reassignment

(1) A person has the protected characteristic of gender reassignment if the person is proposing to undergo, is undergoing or has undergone a process (or part of a process) for the purpose of reassigning the person's sex by changing physiological or other attributes of sex.

(2) A reference to a transsexual person is a reference to a person who has the protected characteristic of gender reassignment.

(3) In relation to the protected characteristic of gender reassignment—

    (a) a reference to a person who has a particular protected characteristic is a reference to a transsexual person;

    (b) a reference to persons who share a protected characteristic is a reference to transsexual persons.

8 Marriage and civil partnership

(1) A person has the protected characteristic of marriage and civil partnership if the person is married or is a civil partner.

(2) In relation to the protected characteristic of marriage and civil partnership—

    (a) a reference to a person who has a particular protected characteristic is a reference to a person who is married or is a civil partner;

    (b) a reference to persons who share a protected characteristic is a reference to persons who are married or are civil partners.

9 Race

(1) Race includes—

    (a) colour;

    (b) nationality;

    (c) ethnic or national origins.

(2) In relation to the protected characteristic of race—

    (a) a reference to a person who has a particular protected characteristic is a reference to a person of a particular racial group;

(b) a reference to persons who share a protected characteristic is a reference to persons of the same racial group.

(3) A racial group is a group of persons defined by reference to race; and a reference to a person's racial group is a reference to a racial group into which the person falls.

(4) The fact that a racial group comprises two or more distinct racial groups does not prevent it from constituting a particular racial group.

(5), (6) *****

10 Religion or belief

(1) Religion means any religion and a reference to religion includes a reference to a lack of religion.

(2) Belief means any religious or philosophical belief and a reference to belief includes a reference to a lack of belief.

(3) In relation to the protected characteristic of religion or belief—

(a) a reference to a person who has a particular protected characteristic is a reference to a person of a particular religion or belief;

(b) a reference to persons who share a protected characteristic is a reference to persons who are of the same religion or belief.

11 Sex

In relation to the protected characteristic of sex—

(a) a reference to a person who has a particular protected characteristic is a reference to a man or to a woman;

(b) a reference to persons who share a protected characteristic is a reference to persons of the same sex.

12 Sexual orientation

(1) Sexual orientation means a person's sexual orientation towards—

(a) persons of the same sex,

(b) persons of the opposite sex, or

(c) persons of either sex.

(2) In relation to the protected characteristic of sexual orientation—

(a) a reference to a person who has a particular protected characteristic is a reference to a person who is of a particular sexual orientation;

(b) a reference to persons who share a protected characteristic is a reference to persons who are of the same sexual orientation.

Chapter 2 Prohibited Conduct

Discrimination

13 Direct discrimination

(1) A person (A) discriminates against another (B) if, because of a protected characteristic, A treats B less favourably than A treats or would treat others.

(2) If the protected characteristic is age, A does not discriminate against B if A can show A's treatment of B to be a proportionate means of achieving a legitimate aim.

(3) If the protected characteristic is disability, and B is not a disabled person, A does not discriminate against B only because A treats or would treat disabled persons more favourably than A treats B.

(4) If the protected characteristic is marriage and civil partnership, this section applies to a contravention of Part 5 (work) only if the treatment is because it is B who is married or a civil partner.

(5) If the protected characteristic is race, less favourable treatment includes segregating B from others.

(6) If the protected characteristic is sex—

(a) less favourable treatment of a woman includes less favourable treatment of her because she is breast-feeding;

     (b) in a case where B is a man, no account is to be taken of special treatment afforded to a woman in connection with pregnancy or childbirth.

(7) Subsection (6)(a) does not apply for the purposes of Part 5 (work).

(8) *****

14 Combined discrimination: dual characteristics

(1) A person (A) discriminates against another (B) if, because of a combination of two relevant protected characteristics, A treats B less favourably than A treats or would treat a person who does not share either of those characteristics.

(2) The relevant protected characteristics are—

     (a) age;

     (b) disability;

     (c) gender reassignment;

     (d) race

     (e) religion or belief;

     (f) sex;

     (g) sexual orientation.

(3) For the purposes of establishing a contravention of this Act by virtue of subsection (1), B need not show that A's treatment of B is direct discrimination because of each of the characteristics in the combination (taken separately).

(4) But B cannot establish a contravention of this Act by virtue of subsection (1) if, in reliance on another provision of this Act or any other enactment, A shows that A's treatment of B is not direct discrimination because of either or both of the characteristics in the combination.

(5) Subsection (1) does not apply to a combination of characteristics that includes disability in circumstances where, if a claim of direct discrimination because of disability were to be brought, it would come within section 116 (special educational needs).

(6), (7) *****

15–18 *****

19 Indirect discrimination

(1) A person (A) discriminates against another (B) if A applies to B a provision, criterion or practice which is discriminatory in relation to a relevant protected characteristic of B's.

(2) For the purposes of subsection (1), a provision, criterion or practice is discriminatory in relation to a relevant protected characteristic of B's if—

     (a) A applies, or would apply, it to persons with whom B does not share the characteristic,

     (b) it puts, or would put, persons with whom B shares the characteristic at a particular disadvantage when compared with persons with whom B does not share it,

     (c) it puts, or would put, B at that disadvantage, and

     (d) A cannot show it to be a proportionate means of achieving a legitimate aim.

(3) The relevant protected characteristics are—

     age;

     disability;

     gender reassignment;

     marriage and civil partnership;

     race;

     religion or belief;

     sex;

     sexual orientation.

*****

Identity Documents Act 2010

(2010, c. 40)

An Act to make provision for and in connection with the repeal of the Identity Cards Act 2006.   [21st December 2010]

Territorial extent: United Kingdom

1 *****

2 Cancellation of ID cards etc

(1) No ID cards are to be issued by the Secretary of State at any time on or after the day on which this Act is passed.

(2) All ID cards that are valid immediately before that day are to be treated as cancelled by the Secretary of State at the end of the period of one month beginning with that day.

(3) As soon as reasonably practicable after that day, the Secretary of State must send a letter to every cardholder—

    (a) informing the cardholder that the cardholder's ID card is to be treated as cancelled as mentioned in subsection (2), and

    (b) providing the cardholder with such information about the consequences of its cancellation as the Secretary of State considers appropriate.

(4), (5) *****

(6) In this section "ID card" has the same meaning as in the Identity Cards Act 2006.

3 Destruction of information recorded in National Identity Register

The Secretary of State must ensure that all the information recorded in the National Identity Register is destroyed before the end of the period of two months beginning with the day on which this Act is passed.

False identity documents etc

4 Possession of false identity documents etc with improper intention

(1) It is an offence for a person ("P") with an improper intention to have in P's possession or under P's control—

    (a) an identity document that is false and that P knows or believes to be false,

    (b) an identity document that was improperly obtained and that P knows or believes to have been improperly obtained, or

    (c) an identity document that relates to someone else.

(2) Each of the following is an improper intention—

    (a) the intention of using the document for establishing personal information about P;

    (b) the intention of allowing or inducing another to use it for establishing, ascertaining or verifying personal information about P or anyone else.

(3) In subsection (2)(b) the reference to P or anyone else does not include, in the case of a document within subsection (1)(c), the individual to whom it relates.

(4) A person guilty of an offence under this section is liable, on conviction on indictment, to imprisonment for a term not exceeding 10 years or a fine (or both).

5 Apparatus designed or adapted for the making of false identity documents etc

(1) It is an offence for a person ("P") with the prohibited intention to make or to have in P's possession or under P's control—

    (a) any apparatus which, to P's knowledge, is or has been specially designed or adapted for the making of false identity documents, or

    (b) any article or material which, to P's knowledge, is or has been specially designed or adapted to be used in the making of such documents.

(2) The prohibited intention is the intention—

    (a) that P or another will make a false identity document, and

    (b) that the document will be used by somebody for establishing, ascertaining or verifying personal information about a person.

(3) A person guilty of an offence under this section is liable, on conviction on indictment, to imprisonment for a term not exceeding 10 years or a fine (or both).

6 Possession of false identity documents etc without reasonable excuse

(1) It is an offence for a person ("P"), without reasonable excuse, to have in P's possession or under P's control—

    (a) an identity document that is false,

    (b) an identity document that was improperly obtained,

    (c) an identity document that relates to someone else,

    (d) any apparatus which, to P's knowledge, is or has been specially designed or adapted for the making of false identity documents, or

    (e) any article or material which, to P's knowledge, is or has been specially designed or adapted to be used in the making of such documents.

(2) A person guilty of an offence under this section is liable—

    (a) on conviction on indictment, to imprisonment for a term not exceeding 2 years or a fine (or both), or

    (b) on summary conviction, to imprisonment for a term not exceeding the maximum period or a fine not exceeding the statutory maximum (or both).

(3), (4) *****

7 Meaning of "identity document"

(1) For the purposes of sections 4 to 6 "identity document" means any document that is or purports to be—

    (a) an immigration document,

    (b) a United Kingdom passport (within the meaning of the Immigration Act 1971),

    (c) a passport issued by or on behalf of the authorities of a country or territory outside the United Kingdom or by or on behalf of an international organisation,

    (d) a document that can be used (in some or all circumstances) instead of a passport,

    (e) a licence to drive a motor vehicle granted under Part 3 of the Road Traffic 1988 or under Part 2 of the Road Traffic (Northern Ireland) Order 1981, or

    (f) a driving licence issued by or on behalf of the authorities of a country or territory outside the United Kingdom.

(2) In subsection (1)(a) "immigration document" means—

    (a) a document used for confirming the right of a person under the EU Treaties in respect of entry or residence in the United Kingdom,

    (b) a document that is given in exercise of immigration functions and records information about leave granted to a person to enter or to remain in the United Kingdom, or

    (c) a registration card (within the meaning of section 26A of the Immigration Act 1971).

(3)–(6) *****

8 Meaning of "personal information"

(1) For the purposes of sections 4 and 5 "personal information", in relation to an individual ("A"), means—

    (a) A's full name,

    (b) other names by which A is or has previously been known,

    (c) A's gender,

    (d) A's date and place of birth,

    (e) external characteristics of A that are capable of being used for identifying A,

    (f) the address of A's principal place of residence in the United Kingdom,

(g) the address of every other place in the United Kingdom or elsewhere where A has a place of residence,

(h) where in the United Kingdom and elsewhere A has previously been resident,

(i) the times at which A was resident at different places in the United Kingdom or elsewhere,

(j) A's current residential status,

(k) residential statuses previously held by A, and

(l) information about numbers allocated to A for identification purposes and about the documents (including stamps or labels) to which they relate.

(2) In subsection (1) "residential status" means—

(a) A's nationality,

(b) A's entitlement to remain in the United Kingdom, and

(c) if that entitlement derives from a grant of leave to enter or remain in the United Kingdom, the terms and conditions of that leave.

9   Other definitions

(1) "Apparatus" includes any equipment, machinery or device and any wire or cable, together with any software used with it.

(2) *****

(3) An identity document was "improperly obtained" if—

(a) false information was provided in, or in connection with, the application for its issue to the person who issued it, or

(b) false information was provided in, or in connection with, an application for its modification to a person entitled to modify it.

(4)–(6) *****

*****

Terrorist Asset-Freezing etc Act 2010

(2010, c. 38)

An Act to make provision for imposing financial restrictions on, and in relation to, certain persons believed or suspected to be, or to have been, involved in terrorist activities; to amend Schedule 7 to the Counter-Terrorism Act 2008; and for connected purposes.   [16th December 2010]

Territorial extent: United Kingdom

PART 1   TERRORIST ASSET-FREEZING

Chapter 1   Designated Persons

Introductory

1   Meaning of "designated person"

In this Part "designated person" means—

(a) a person designated by the Treasury for the purposes of this Part, or

(b) a natural or legal person, group or entity included in the list provided for by Article 2(3) of Council Regulation (EC) No 2580/2001 of 27 December 2001 on specific restrictive measures directed against certain persons and entities with a view to combating terrorism.

Final designations

2   Treasury's power to make final designation

(1) The Treasury may make a final designation of a person for the purposes of this Part if—

(a) they reasonably believe—

      (i)   that the person is or has been involved in terrorist activity,

      (ii) that the person is owned or controlled directly or indirectly by a person within sub-paragraph (i), or

      (iii) that the person is acting on behalf of or at the direction of a person within sub-paragraph (i), and

  (b) they consider that it is necessary for purposes connected with protecting members of the public from terrorism that financial restrictions should be applied in relation to the person.

(2) For this purpose involvement in terrorist activity is any one or more of the following—

  (a) the commission, preparation or instigation of acts of terrorism;

  (b) conduct that facilitates the commission, preparation or instigation of such acts, or that is intended to do so;

  (c) conduct that gives support or assistance to persons who are known or believed by the person concerned to be involved in conduct falling within paragraph (a) or (b) of this subsection.

(3) It is immaterial whether the acts of terrorism in question are specific acts of terrorism or acts of terrorism generally.

(4) In this section—

"terrorism" has the same meaning as in the Terrorism Act 2000 (see section 1(1) to (4) of that Act);

and the reference in subsection (1)(b) above to financial restrictions includes a reference to restrictions relating to economic resources.

3 Notification of final designation

(1) Where the Treasury make a final designation of a person, they must—

  (a) give written notice of the designation to the designated person, and

  (b) take steps to publicise the designation.

(2) Unless one or more of the following conditions is met, the Treasury must take steps to publicise the designation generally.

(3) The conditions are that—

  (a) the Treasury believe that the designated person is an individual under the age of 18, or

  (b) the Treasury consider that disclosure of the designation should be restricted—

      (i)   in the interests of national security,

      (ii) for reasons connected with the prevention or detection of serious crime, or

      (iii) in the interests of justice.

(4) If one or more of those conditions is met, the Treasury must inform only such persons as they consider appropriate.

(5) If that ceases to be the case, the Treasury must—

  (a) give written notice of that fact to the designated person, and

  (b) take steps to publicise the designation generally.

4 Duration of final designation

(1) A final designation expires at the end of the period of one year beginning with the date on which it was made, unless it is renewed.

(2) The Treasury may renew a final designation at any time before it expires, if the requirements in section 2(1)(a) and (b) continue to be met.

(3) A renewed final designation expires at the end of the period of one year beginning with the date on which it was renewed (or last renewed), unless it is renewed again.

(4) The provisions of section 3 (notification of final designation) apply where a final designation is renewed (or further renewed) as in relation to the original making of a final designation.

(5) Where a final designation expires the Treasury must—

  (a) give written notice of that fact to the designated person, and

  (b) take reasonable steps to bring that fact to the attention of the persons informed of the designation.

5   Variation or revocation of final designation

(1) The Treasury may vary or revoke a final designation at any time.

(2) Where a final designation is varied or revoked the Treasury must—

    (a) give written notice of the variation or revocation to the designated person, and

    (b) take reasonable steps to bring the variation or revocation to the attention of the persons informed of the designation.

Interim designations

6   Treasury's power to make interim designation

(1) The Treasury may make an interim designation of a person for the purposes of this Part if—

    (a) they reasonably suspect—

        (i)   that the person is or has been involved in terrorist activity,

        (ii)   that the person is owned or controlled directly or indirectly by a person within sub-paragraph (i), or

        (iii) that the person is acting on behalf of or at the direction of a person within sub-paragraph (i), and

    (b) they consider that it is necessary for purposes connected with protecting members of the public from terrorism that financial restrictions should be applied in relation to the person.

(2) Subsections (2) to (4) of section 2 (Treasury's power to make final designation: definitions) apply for the purposes of this section as they apply for the purposes of that section.

(3) The Treasury may not make more than one interim designation of the same person in relation to the same, or substantially the same, evidence.

7–9   *****

Confidential information

10   Confidential information

(1) Where the Treasury in accordance with section 3(4) or 7(4) inform only certain persons of a designation, they may specify that information contained in it is to be treated as confidential.

(2) A person ("P") who—

    (a) is provided with information that is to be treated as confidential in accordance with sub-section (1), or

    (b) obtains such information,

must not, subject to subsection (3), disclose it if P knows, or has reasonable cause to suspect, that the information is to be treated as confidential.

(3) The prohibition in subsection (2) does not apply to any disclosure made by P with lawful authority.

(4)–(7)   *****

Chapter 2   Prohibitions in Relation to Designated Persons

Prohibitions

11   Freezing of funds and economic resources

(1) A person ("P") must not deal with funds or economic resources owned, held or controlled by a designated person if P knows, or has reasonable cause to suspect, that P is dealing with such funds or economic resources.

(2) In subsection (1) "deal with" means—

    (a) in relation to funds—

        (i)   use, alter, move, allow access to or transfer,

        (ii)   deal with the funds in any other way that would result in any change in volume, amount, location, ownership, possession, character or destination, or

        (iii) make any other change that would enable use, including portfolio management;

    (b) in relation to economic resources, exchange or use in exchange for funds, goods or services.

(3) Subsection (1) is subject to sections 16 and 17 (exceptions and licences).

(4) A person who contravenes the prohibition in subsection (1) commits an offence.

12 Making funds or financial services available to designated person

(1) A person ("P") must not make funds or financial services available (directly or indirectly) to a designated person if P knows, or has reasonable cause to suspect, that P is making the funds or financial services so available.

(2) Subsection (1) is subject to sections 16 and 17 (exceptions and licences).

(3) A person who contravenes the prohibition in subsection (1) commits an offence.

13 Making funds or financial services available for benefit of designated person

(1) A person ("P") must not make funds or financial services available to any person for the benefit of a designated person if P knows, or has reasonable cause to suspect, that P is making the funds or financial services so available.

(2) For the purposes of this section—

    (a) funds are made available for the benefit of a designated person only if that person thereby obtains, or is able to obtain, a significant financial benefit, and

    (b) "financial benefit" includes the discharge of a financial obligation for which the designated person is wholly or partly responsible.

(3) Subsection (1) is subject to sections 16 and 17 (exceptions and licences).

(4) A person who contravenes the prohibition in subsection (1) commits an offence.

14 Making economic resources available to designated person

(1) A person ("P") must not make economic resources available (directly or indirectly) to a designated person if P knows, or has reasonable cause to suspect—

    (a) that P is making the economic resources so available, and

    (b) that the designated person would be likely to exchange the economic resources, or use them in exchange, for funds, goods or services.

(2) Subsection (1) is subject to section 17 (licences).

(3) A person who contravenes the prohibition in subsection (1) commits an offence.

15 Making economic resources available for benefit of designated person

(1) A person ("P") must not make economic resources available to any person for the benefit of a designated person if P knows, or has reasonable cause to suspect, that P is making the economic resources so available.

(2) For the purposes of this section—

    (a) economic resources are made available for the benefit of a designated person only if that person thereby obtains, or is able to obtain, a significant financial benefit, and

    (b) "financial benefit" includes the discharge of a financial obligation for which the designated person is wholly or partly responsible.

(3) Subsection (1) is subject to section 17 (licences).

(4) A person who contravenes the prohibition in subsection (1) commits an offence.

Exceptions and licences

16 Exceptions

(1) The prohibitions in sections 11 to 13 are not contravened by a relevant institution crediting a frozen account with—

    (a) interest or other earnings due on the account, or

    (b) payments due under contracts, agreements or obligations that were concluded or arose before the account became a frozen account.

(2) The prohibitions in sections 12 and 13 on making funds available do not prevent a relevant institution from crediting a frozen account where it receives funds transferred to the account.

(3) The prohibition in section 13 is not contravened by the making of a payment which—

(a) is a benefit under or by virtue of an enactment relating to social security (irrespective of the name or nature of the benefit), and

(b) is made to a person who is not a designated person,

whether or not the payment is made in respect of a designated person.

(4) A relevant institution must inform the Treasury without delay if it credits a frozen account in accordance with subsection (1)(b) or (2).

(5) In this section "frozen account" means an account with a relevant institution which is held or controlled (directly or indirectly) by a designated person.

17   Licences

(1) The prohibitions in sections 11 to 15 do not apply to anything done under the authority of a licence granted by the Treasury.

(2) Where relevant such a licence also constitutes authorisation under Article 6 of Council Regulation (EC) No 2580/2001 of 27 December 2001 on specific restrictive measures directed against certain persons and entities with a view to combating terrorism.

(3) A licence must specify the acts authorised by it and may be—

(a) general or granted to a category of persons or to a particular person;

(b) subject to conditions;

(c) of indefinite duration or subject to an expiry date.

(4) The Treasury may vary or revoke a licence at any time.

(5) On the grant, variation or revocation of a licence, the Treasury must—

(a) in the case of a licence granted to a particular person, give written notice of the grant, variation or revocation to that person;

(b) in the case of a general licence or a licence granted to a category of persons, take such steps as the Treasury consider appropriate to publicise the grant, variation or revocation of the licence.

(6) A person commits an offence who, for the purpose of obtaining a licence, knowingly or recklessly—

(a) provides information that is false in a material respect, or

(b) provides or produces a document that is not what it purports to be.

(7) A person who purports to act under the authority of a licence but who fails to comply with any conditions included in the licence commits an offence.

Circumventing prohibitions etc

18   Circumventing prohibitions etc

A person commits an offence who intentionally participates in activities knowing that the object or effect of them is (whether directly or indirectly)—

(a) to circumvent any of the prohibitions in sections 11 to 15, or

(b) to enable or facilitate the contravention of any such prohibition.

*****

European Union Act 2011

(2011, c. 12)

An Act to make provision about treaties relating to the European Union and decisions made under them, including provision implementing the Protocol signed at Brussels on 23 June 2010 amending the Protocol (No. 36) on transitional provisions annexed to the Treaty on European Union, to the Treaty on the Functioning of the European Union and to the Treaty establishing the European Atomic Energy Community; and to make provision about the means by which directly applicable or directly effective European Union law has effect in the United Kingdom.   [19th July 2011]

Territorial extent: United Kingdom

PART 1

RESTRICTIONS ON TREATIES AND DECISIONS RELATING TO EU

Introductory

1 Interpretation of Part 1

(1) This section has effect for the interpretation of this Part.

(2) "TEU" means the Treaty on European Union.

(3) "TFEU" means the Treaty on the Functioning of the European Union.

(4) A reference to a treaty which amends TEU or TFEU includes a reference to—

(a) a treaty resulting from the application of Article 48(2) to (5) of TEU (ordinary revision procedure);

(b) an agreement under Article 49 of TEU (admission of new members).

(5) An "Article 48(6) decision" means a decision under Article 48(6) of TEU (simplified revision procedure).

(6) Except in a reference to "the European Council", "the Council" means the Council of the European Union.

(7) A reference to a Minister of the Crown voting in favour of or otherwise supporting a decision is a reference to a Minister of the Crown—

(a) voting in favour of the decision in the European Council or the Council, or

(b) allowing the decision to be adopted by consensus or unanimity by the European Council or the Council.

Restrictions relating to amendments of TEU or TFEU

2 Treaties amending or replacing TEU or TFEU

(1) A treaty which amends or replaces TEU or TFEU is not to be ratified unless—

(a) a statement relating to the treaty was laid before Parliament in accordance with section 5,

(b) the treaty is approved by Act of Parliament, and

(c) the referendum condition or the exemption condition is met.

(2) The referendum condition is that—

(a) the Act providing for the approval of the treaty provides that the provision approving the treaty is not to come into force until a referendum about whether the treaty should be ratified has been held throughout the United Kingdom or, where the treaty also affects Gibraltar, throughout the United Kingdom and Gibraltar,

(b) the referendum has been held, and

(c) the majority of those voting in the referendum are in favour of the ratification of the treaty.

(3) The exemption condition is that the Act providing for the approval of the treaty states that the treaty does not fall within section 4.

3 Amendment of TFEU under simplified revision procedure

(1) Where the European Council has adopted an Article 48(6) decision subject to its approval by the member States, a Minister of the Crown may not confirm the approval of the decision by the United Kingdom unless—

(a) a statement relating to the decision was laid before Parliament in accordance with section 5,

(b) the decision is approved by Act of Parliament, and

(c) the referendum condition, the exemption condition or the significance condition is met.

(2) The referendum condition is that—

(a) the Act providing for the approval of the decision provides that the provision approving the decision is not to come into force until a referendum about whether the decision should be approved has been held throughout the United Kingdom or, where the decision also affects Gibraltar, throughout the United Kingdom and Gibraltar,

(b) the referendum has been held,

(c) the majority of those voting in the referendum are in favour of the approval of the decision.

(3) The exemption condition is that the Act providing for the approval of the decision states that the decision does not fall within section 4.

(4) The significance condition is that the Act providing for the approval of the decision states that—

(a) the decision falls within section 4 only because of provision of the kind mentioned in subsection (1)(i) or (j) of that section, and

(b) the effect of that provision in relation to the United Kingdom is not significant.

4 Cases where treaty or Article 48(6) decision attracts a referendum

(1) Subject to subsection (4), a treaty or an Article 48(6) decision falls within this section if it involves one or more of the following—

(a) the extension of the objectives of the EU as set out in Article 3 of TEU;

(b) the conferring on the EU of a new exclusive competence;

(c) the extension of an exclusive competence of the EU;

(d) the conferring on the EU of a new competence shared with the member States;

(e) the extension of any competence of the EU that is shared with the member States;

(f) the extension of the competence of the EU in relation to—

(i) the co-ordination of economic and employment policies, or

(ii) common foreign and security policy;

(g) the conferring on the EU of a new competence to carry out actions to support, co-ordinate or supplement the actions of member States;

(h) the extension of a supporting, co-ordinating or supplementing competence of the EU;

(i) the conferring on an EU institution or body of power to impose a requirement or obligation on the United Kingdom, or the removal of any limitation on any such power of an EU institution or body;

(j) the conferring on an EU institution or body of new or extended power to impose sanctions on the United Kingdom;

(k) any amendment of a provision listed in Schedule 1 that removes a requirement that anything should be done unanimously, by consensus or by common accord;

(l) any amendment of Article 31(2) of TEU (decisions relating to common foreign and security policy to which qualified majority voting applies) that removes or amends the provision enabling a member of the Council to oppose the adoption of a decision to be taken by qualified majority voting;

(m) any amendment of any of the provisions specified in subsection (3) that removes or amends the provision enabling a member of the Council, in relation to a draft legislative act, to ensure the suspension of the ordinary legislative procedure.

(2) Any reference in subsection (1) to the extension of a competence includes a reference to the removal of a limitation on a competence.

(3) The provisions referred to in subsection (1)(m) are—

(a) Article 48 of TFEU (social security),

(b) Article 82(3) of TFEU (judicial co-operation in criminal matters), and

(c) Article 83(3) of TFEU (particularly serious crime with a cross-border dimension).

(4) A treaty or Article 48(6) decision does not fall within this section merely because it involves one or more of the following—

> (a) the codification of practice under TEU or TFEU in relation to the previous exercise of an existing competence;
>
> (b) the making of any provision that applies only to member States other than the United Kingdom;
>
> (c) in the case of a treaty, the accession of a new member State.

5 Statement to be laid before Parliament

(1) If a treaty amending TEU or TFEU is agreed in an inter-governmental conference, a Minister of the Crown must lay the required statement before Parliament before the end of the 2 months beginning with the date on which the treaty is agreed.

(2) If an Article 48(6) decision is adopted by the European Council subject to its approval by the member States, a Minister of the Crown must lay the required statement before Parliament before the end of the 2 months beginning with the date on which the decision is adopted.

(3) The required statement is a statement as to whether, in the Minister's opinion, the treaty or Article 48(6) decision falls within section 4.

(4) If the Minister is of the opinion that an Article 48(6) decision falls within section 4 only because of provision of the kind mentioned in subsection (1)(i) or (j) of that section, the statement must indicate whether in the Minister's opinion the effect of that provision in relation to the United Kingdom is significant.

(5) The statement must give reasons for the Minister's opinion under subsection (3) and, if relevant, subsection (4).

(6) *****

Restrictions relating to other decisions under TEU or TFEU

6 Decisions requiring approval by Act and by referendum

(1) A Minister of the Crown may not vote in favour of or otherwise support a decision to which this subsection applies unless—

> (a) the draft decision is approved by Act of Parliament, and
>
> (b) the referendum condition is met.

(2) Where the European Council has recommended to the member States the adoption of a decision under Article 42(2) of TEU in relation to a common EU defence, a Minister of the Crown may not notify the European Council that the decision is adopted by the United Kingdom unless—

> (a) the decision is approved by Act of Parliament, and
>
> (b) the referendum condition is met.

(3) A Minister of the Crown may not give a notification under Article 4 of Protocol (No. 21) on the position of the United Kingdom and Ireland in respect of the area of freedom, security and justice annexed to TEU and TFEU which relates to participation by the United Kingdom in a European Public Prosecutor's Office or an extension of the powers of that Office unless—

> (a) the notification has been approved by Act of Parliament, and
>
> (b) the referendum condition is met.

(4) The referendum condition is that set out in section 3(2), with references to a decision being read for the purposes of subsection (1) as references to a draft decision and for the purposes of subsection (3) as references to a notification.

(5), (6) *****

7 Decisions requiring approval by Act

(1) A Minister of the Crown may not confirm the approval by the United Kingdom of a decision to which this subsection applies unless the decision is approved by Act of Parliament.

(2) The decisions to which subsection (1) applies are—

(a) a decision under the provision of Article 25 of TFEU that permits the adoption of provisions to strengthen or add to the rights listed in Article 20(2) of that Treaty (rights of citizens of the European Union);

(b) a decision under the provision of Article 223(1) of TFEU that permits the laying down of the provisions necessary for the election of the members of the European Parliament in accordance with that Article;

(c) a decision under the provision of Article 262 of TFEU that permits the conferring of jurisdiction on the Court of Justice of the European Union in disputes relating to the application of acts adopted on the basis of the EU Treaties which create European intellectual property rights;

(d) a decision under the third paragraph of Article 311 of TFEU to adopt a decision laying down provisions relating to the system of own resources of the European Union.

(3) A Minister of the Crown may not vote in favour of or otherwise support a decision to which this subsection applies unless the draft decision is approved by Act of Parliament.

(4) The decisions to which subsection (3) applies are—

(a) a decision under the provision of Article 17(5) of TEU that permits the alteration of the number of members of the European Commission;

(b) a decision under Article 48(7) of TEU which in relation to any provision not listed in Schedule 1—

(i) adopts qualified majority voting, or

(ii) applies the ordinary legislative procedure in place of a special legislative procedure requiring the Council to act unanimously;

(c) a decision under the provision of Article 64(3) of TFEU that permits the adoption of measures which constitute a step backwards in European Union law as regards the liberalisation of the movement of capital to or from third countries;

(d) a decision under the provision of Article 126(14) of TFEU that permits the adoption of provisions to replace the Protocol (No. 12) on the excessive deficit procedure annexed to TEU and TFEU;

(e) a decision under the provision of Article 333(1) of TFEU (enhanced cooperation) that permits the adoption of qualified majority voting, where the decision relates to a provision not listed in Schedule 1 and the United Kingdom is a participant in the enhanced co-operation to which the decision relates;

(f) a decision under the provision of Article 333(2) of TFEU (enhanced cooperation) that permits the adoption of the ordinary legislative procedure in place of a special legislative procedure, where—

(i) the decision relates to a provision not listed in Schedule 1,

(ii) the special legislative procedure requires the Council to act unanimously, and

(iii) the United Kingdom is a participant in the enhanced cooperation to which the decision relates.

8   Decisions under Article 352 of TFEU

(1) A Minister of the Crown may not vote in favour of or otherwise support an Article 352 decision unless one of subsections (3) to (5) is complied with in relation to the draft decision.

(2) An Article 352 decision is a decision under the provision of Article 352 of TFEU that permits the adoption of measures to attain one of the objectives set out in the EU Treaties (but for which those Treaties have not provided the necessary powers).

(3)–(7) *****

9   Approval required in connection with Title V of Part 3 of TFEU

(1) A Minister of the Crown may not give a notification to which this subsection applies unless Parliamentary approval has been given in accordance with subsection (3).

(2) Subsection (1) applies in relation to a notification under Article 3 of Protocol (No. 21) on the position of the United Kingdom and Ireland in respect of the area of freedom, security and justice

annexed to TEU and TFEU (the "AFSJ Protocol") that the United Kingdom wishes to take part in the adoption and application of a measure proposed under any of the following—

    (a) the provision of Article 81(3) of TFEU (family law) that permits the application of the ordinary legislative procedure in place of a special legislative procedure;

    (b) the provision of Article 82(2)(d) of TFEU (criminal procedure) that permits the identification of further specific aspects of criminal procedure to which directives adopted under the ordinary legislative procedure may relate;

    (c) the provision of Article 83(1) of TFEU (particularly serious crime with a cross-border dimension) that permits the identification of further areas of crime to which directives adopted under the ordinary legislative procedure may relate.

  (3) Parliamentary approval is given if—

    (a) in each House of Parliament a Minister of the Crown moves a motion that the House approves Her Majesty's Government's intention to give a notification in respect of a specified measure, and

    (b) each House agrees to the motion without amendment.

  (4)–(6) *****

10 Parliamentary control of certain decisions not requiring approval by Act

  (1) A Minister of the Crown may not vote in favour of or otherwise support a decision under any of the following unless Parliamentary approval has been given in accordance with this section—

    (a) the provision of Article 56 of TFEU that permits the extension of the provisions of Chapter 3 of Title IV of Part 3 of that Treaty (free movement of services) to nationals of a third country;

    (b) Article 129(3) of TFEU (amendment of provisions of the Statute of the European System of Central Banks or of the European Central Bank);

    (c) the provision of Article 252 of TFEU that permits an increase in the number of Advocates-General;

    (d) the provision of Article 257 of TFEU that permits the establishment of specialised courts attached to the General Court;

    (e) the provision of Article 281 of TFEU that permits the amendment of the Statute of the Court of Justice of the European Union;

    (f) the provision of Article 308 of TFEU that permits the amendment of the Statute of the European Investment Bank.

  (2) A Minister of the Crown may not vote in favour of or otherwise support a decision to which this subsection applies unless Parliamentary approval has been given in accordance with this section.

  (3) Subsection (2) applies to a decision under Article 48(7) of TEU which in relation to a provision of TFEU applies the ordinary legislative procedure in place of a special legislative procedure not requiring the Council to act unanimously.

  (4) A Minister of the Crown may not confirm the approval by the United Kingdom of a decision under Article 218(8) of TFEU for the accession of the European Union to the European Convention for the Protection of Human Rights and Fundamental Freedoms in accordance with Article 6(2) of TEU unless Parliamentary approval has been given in accordance with this section.

  (5) Parliamentary approval is given if—

    (a) in each House of Parliament a Minister of the Crown moves a motion that the House approves Her Majesty's Government's intention to support the adoption of a specified draft decision, and

    (b) each House agrees to the motion without amendment.

11–17 *****

PART 3

GENERAL

Status of EU law

18   Status of EU law dependent on continuing statutory basis

Directly applicable or directly effective EU law (that is, the rights, powers, liabilities, obligations, restrictions, remedies and procedures referred to in section 2(1) of the European Communities Act 1972) falls to be recognised and available in law in the United Kingdom only by virtue of that Act or where it is required to be recognised and available in law by virtue of any other Act.
*****

Fixed-term Parliaments Act 2011

(2011, c. 14)

An Act to make provision about the dissolution of Parliament and the determination of polling days for parliamentary general elections; and for connected purposes.   [15th September 2011]

Territorial extent: United Kingdom

1   Polling days for parliamentary general elections

(1) This section applies for the purposes of the Timetable in rule 1 in Schedule 1 to the Representation of the People Act 1983 and is subject to section 2.

(2) The polling day for the next parliamentary general election after the passing of this Act is to be 7 May 2015.

(3) The polling day for each subsequent parliamentary general election is to be the first Thursday in May in the fifth calendar year following that in which the polling day for the previous parliamentary general election fell.

(4) But, if the polling day for the previous parliamentary general election—

(a) was appointed under section 2(7), and

(b) in the calendar year in which it fell, fell before the first Thursday in May,

subsection (3) has effect as if for "fifth" there were substituted "fourth".

(5) The Prime Minister may by order made by statutory instrument provide that the polling day for a parliamentary general election in a specified calendar year is to be later than the day determined under subsection (2) or (3), but not more than two months later.

(6) A statutory instrument containing an order under subsection (5) may not be made unless a draft has been laid before and approved by a resolution of each House of Parliament.

(7) The draft laid before Parliament must be accompanied by a statement setting out the Prime Minister's reasons for proposing the change in the polling day.

2   Early parliamentary general elections

(1) An early parliamentary general election is to take place if—

(a) the House of Commons passes a motion in the form set out in subsection (2), and

(b) if the motion is passed on a division, the number of members who vote in favour of the motion is a number equal to or greater than two thirds of the number of seats in the House (including vacant seats).

(2) The form of motion for the purposes of subsection (1)(a) is—

"That there shall be an early parliamentary general election."

(3) An early parliamentary general election is also to take place if—

(a) the House of Commons passes a motion in the form set out in subsection (4), and

(b) the period of 14 days after the day on which that motion is passed ends without the House passing a motion in the form set out in subsection (5).

(4) The form of motion for the purposes of subsection (3)(a) is—

"That this House has no confidence in Her Majesty's Government."

(5) The form of motion for the purposes of subsection (3)(b) is—

"That this House has confidence in Her Majesty's Government."

(6) Subsection (7) applies for the purposes of the Timetable in rule 1 in Schedule 1 to the Representation of the People Act 1983.

(7) If a parliamentary general election is to take place as provided for by subsection (1) or (3), the polling day for the election is to be the day appointed by Her Majesty by proclamation on the recommendation of the Prime Minister (and, accordingly, the appointed day replaces the day which would otherwise have been the polling day for the next election determined under section 1).

3 Dissolution of Parliament

(1) The Parliament then in existence dissolves at the beginning of the 17th working day before the polling day for the next parliamentary general election as determined under section 1 or appointed under section 2(7).

(2) Parliament cannot otherwise be dissolved.

(3) Once Parliament dissolves, the Lord Chancellor and, in relation to Northern Ireland, the Secretary of State have the authority to have the writs for the election sealed and issued (see rule 3 in Schedule 1 to the Representation of the People Act 1983).

(4) Once Parliament dissolves, Her Majesty may issue the proclamation summoning the new Parliament which may—

(a) appoint the day for the first meeting of the new Parliament; Fixed-term Parliaments Act 2011 (c. 14)

(b) deal with any other matter which was normally dealt with before the passing of this Act by proclamations summoning new Parliaments (except a matter dealt with by subsection (1) or (3)).

(5), (6) *****

4, 5   *****

6 Supplementary provisions

(1) This Act does not affect Her Majesty's power to prorogue Parliament.

(2)–(3) *****

*****

Localism Act 2011

(2011, c. 20)

An Act to make provision about the functions and procedures of local and certain other authorities; to make provision about the functions of the Commission for Local Administration in England; to enable the recovery of financial sanctions imposed by the Court of Justice of the European Union on the United Kingdom from local and public authorities; to make provision about local government finance; to make provision about town and country planning, the Community Infrastructure Levy and the authorisation of nationally signifi-cant infrastructure projects; to make provision about social and other housing; to make provision about regeneration in London; and for connected purposes.   [15th November 2011]

Territorial extent: For the sections reproduced here, England and Wales only except for section 48 which applies also to Scotland and Northern Ireland

PART 1

LOCAL GOVERNMENT

General Powers of Authorities

1 Local authority's general power of competence

(1) A local authority has power to do anything that individuals generally may do.

(2) Subsection (1) applies to things that an individual may do even though they are in nature, extent or otherwise—

(a) unlike anything the authority may do apart from subsection (1), or

(b) unlike anything that other public bodies may do.

(3) In this section "individual" means an individual with full capacity.

(4) Where subsection (1) confers power on the authority to do something, it confers power (subject to sections 2 to 4) to do it in any way whatever, including—

(a) power to do it anywhere in the United Kingdom or elsewhere,

(b) power to do it for a commercial purpose or otherwise for a charge, or without charge, and

(c) power to do it for, or otherwise than for, the benefit of the authority, its area or persons resident or present in its area.

(5) The generality of the power conferred by subsection (1) ("the general power") is not limited by the existence of any other power of the authority which (to any extent) overlaps the general power.

(6) Any such other power is not limited by the existence of the general power (but see section 5(2)).

(7) Schedule 1 (consequential amendments) has effect.

2 Boundaries of the general power

(1) If exercise of a pre-commencement power of a local authority is subject to restrictions, those restrictions apply also to exercise of the general power so far as it is overlapped by the pre-commencement power.

(2) The general power does not enable a local authority to do—

(a) anything which the authority is unable to do by virtue of a precommencement limitation, or

(b) anything which the authority is unable to do by virtue of a postcommencement limitation which is expressed to apply—

(i) to the general power,

(ii) to all of the authority's powers, or

(iii) to all of the authority's powers but with exceptions that do not include the general power.

(3) The general power does not confer power to—

(a) make or alter arrangements of a kind which may be made under Part 6 of the Local Government Act 1972 (arrangements for discharge of authority's functions by committees, joint committees, officers etc);

(b) make or alter arrangements of a kind which are made, or may be made, by or under Part 1A of the Local Government Act 2000 (arrangements for local authority governance in England);

(c) make or alter any contracting-out arrangements, or other arrangements within neither of paragraphs (a) and (b), that authorise a person to exercise a function of a local authority.

(4) In this section—

"post-commencement limitation" means a prohibition, restriction or other limitation expressly imposed by a statutory provision that—

    (a) is contained in an Act passed after the end of the Session in which this Act is passed, or

    (b) is contained in an instrument made under an Act and comes into force on or after the commencement of section 1;

"pre-commencement limitation" means a prohibition, restriction or other limitation expressly imposed by a statutory provision that—

    (a) is contained in this Act, or in any other Act passed no later than the end of the Session in which this Act is passed, or

    (b) is contained in an instrument made under an Act and comes into force before the commencement of section 1;

"pre-commencement power" means power conferred by a statutory provision that—

    (a) is contained in this Act, or in any other Act passed no later than the end of the Session in which this Act is passed, or

    (b) is contained in an instrument made under an Act and comes into force before the commencement of section 1.

3   Limits on charging in exercise of general power

(1) Subsection (2) applies where—

    (a) a local authority provides a service to a person otherwise than for a commercial purpose, and

    (b) its providing the service to the person is done, or could be done, in exercise of the general power.

(2) The general power confers power to charge the person for providing the service to the person only if—

    (a) the service is not one that a statutory provision requires the authority to provide to the person,

    (b) the person has agreed to its being provided, and

    (c) ignoring this section and section 93 of the Local Government Act 2003, the authority does not have power to charge for providing the service.

(3) The general power is subject to a duty to secure that, taking one financial year with another, the income from charges allowed by subsection (2) does not exceed the costs of provision.

(4) The duty under subsection (3) applies separately in relation to each kind of service.

4   Limits on doing things for commercial purpose in exercise of general power

(1) The general power confers power on a local authority to do things for a commercial purpose only if they are things which the authority may, in exercise of the general power, do otherwise than for a commercial purpose.

(2) Where, in exercise of the general power, a local authority does things for a commercial purpose, the authority must do them through a company.

(3) A local authority may not, in exercise of the general power, do things for a commercial purpose in relation to a person if a statutory provision requires the authority to do those things in relation to the person.

(4) *****

5–14   *****

Transfer and Delegation of Functions to Certain Authorities

15   Power to transfer local public functions to permitted authorities

(1) The Secretary of State may by order make provision—

    (a) transferring a local public function from the public authority whose function it is to a per-
        mitted authority;

    (b) about the discharge of local public functions that are transferred to permitted authorities
        under this section (including provision enabling the discharge of those functions to be
        delegated).

(2) An order under this section may modify any enactment (whenever passed or made) for the purpose of making the provision mentioned in subsection (1).

(3) The power to modify an enactment in subsection (2) is a power—

    (a) to apply that enactment with or without modifications,

    (b) to extend, disapply or amend that enactment, or

    (c) to repeal or revoke that enactment with or without savings.

(4) An order under this section may disapply, or modify the application of, Chapter 4 of Part 1A of the Local Government Act 2000 (changing local authority governance arrangements) in relation to a county council or district council to which the order transfers a local public function.

(5) The Secretary of State may not make an order under this section unless the Secretary of State considers that it is likely that making the order would—

    (a) promote economic development or wealth creation, or

    (b) increase local accountability in relation to each local public function transferred by the
        order.

(6) For the purposes of subsection (5)(b), in relation to a local public function, local accountability is increased if the exercise of the function becomes more accountable to persons living or working in the area of the permitted authority to which it is transferred.

(7) The Secretary of State may not make an order under this section unless the Secretary of State considers that the local public function transferred by the order can appropriately be exercised by the permitted authority to which it is transferred.

(8) The Secretary of State may not make an order under this section transferring a local public function to a permitted authority unless the authority has consented to the transfer.

(9) Before making an order under this section, the Secretary of State must consult such persons as the Secretary of State considers appropriate.

16   Delegation of functions by Ministers to permitted authorities

(1) A Minister of the Crown may, to such extent and subject to such conditions as that Minister thinks fit, delegate to a permitted authority any of the Minister's eligible functions.

(2) A function is eligible for the purposes of subsection (1) if—

    (a) it does not consist of a power to make regulations or other instruments of a legislative
        character or a power to fix fees or charges, and

    (b) the Minister of the Crown considers that it can appropriately be exercised by the permitted
        authority.

(3) No delegation under subsection (1), and no variation of a delegation under that subsection, may be made without the agreement of the permitted authority.

(4) Before delegating a function under subsection (1), the Minister of the Crown must consult such persons as the Minister considers appropriate.

(5) A delegation under subsection (1) may be revoked at any time by any Minister of the Crown.

17   Transfer schemes

(1) The Secretary of State may make a scheme for the transfer of property, rights or liabilities from the person who, or body which, would have a local public function but for an order under section 15 to the permitted authority to which the function is transferred.

(2) A Minister of the Crown may make a scheme for the transfer from the Crown to a permitted authority of such property, rights or liabilities as the Minister of the Crown considers appropriate in consequence of a delegation, or the variation of a delegation, under section 16 of a function of any Minister of the Crown to the permitted authority.

(3) A Minister of the Crown may make a scheme for the transfer from a permitted authority to the Crown of such property, rights or liabilities as the Minister of the Crown considers appropriate in consequence of a variation or revocation of a delegation under section 16 of a function of any Minister of the Crown to the permitted authority.

(4) The things that may be transferred under a transfer scheme include—

(a) property, rights or liabilities that could not otherwise be transferred;

(b) property acquired, or rights or liabilities arising, after the making of the order.

(5)–(8) *****

18 Duty to consider proposals for exercise of powers under sections 15 and 17

(1) If the Secretary of State receives a relevant proposal from a permitted authority, the Secretary of State must—

(a) consider the proposal, and

(b) notify the permitted authority of what action, if any, the Secretary of State will take in relation to the proposal.

(2) The Secretary of State may by regulations specify criteria to which the Secretary of State must have regard in considering a relevant proposal.

(3) For the purposes of this section, a "relevant proposal" is a proposal—

(a) for the exercise of the Secretary of State's powers in sections 15 and 17 in relation to the permitted authority, and

(b) that is accompanied by such information and evidence as the Secretary of State may specify by regulations.

(4) Before making regulations under this section, the Secretary of State must consult such persons as the Secretary of State considers appropriate.

19–24 *****

Predetermination

25 Prior indications of view of a matter not to amount to predetermination etc

(1) Subsection (2) applies if—

(a) as a result of an allegation of bias or predetermination, or otherwise, there is an issue about the validity of a decision of a relevant authority, and

(b) it is relevant to that issue whether the decision-maker, or any of the decision-makers, had or appeared to have had a closed mind (to any extent) when making the decision.

(2) A decision-maker is not to be taken to have had, or to have appeared to have had, a closed mind when making the decision just because—

(a) the decision-maker had previously done anything that directly or indirectly indicated what view the decision-maker took, or would or might take, in relation to a matter, and

(b) the matter was relevant to the decision.

(3)–(5) *****

26 *****

27 Duty to promote and maintain high standards of conduct

(1) A relevant authority must promote and maintain high standards of conduct by members and co-opted members of the authority.

(2) In discharging its duty under subsection (1), a relevant authority must, in particular, adopt a code dealing with the conduct that is expected of members and co-opted members of the authority when they are acting in that capacity.

(3) A relevant authority that is a parish council—

(a) may comply with subsection (2) by adopting the code adopted under that subsection by its principal authority, where relevant on the basis that references in that code to its principal authority's register are to its register, and

(b) may for that purpose assume that its principal authority has complied with section 28(1) and (2).

(4) In this Chapter "co-opted member", in relation to a relevant authority, means a person who is not a member of the authority but who—

(a) is a member of any committee or sub-committee of the authority, or

(b) is a member of, and represents the authority on, any joint committee or joint sub-committee of the authority,

and who is entitled to vote on any question that falls to be decided at any meeting of that committee or sub-committee.

(5) A reference in this Chapter to a joint committee or joint sub-committee of a relevant authority is a reference to a joint committee on which the authority is represented or a sub-committee of such a committee.

(6)–(10) *****

28 Codes of conduct

(1) A relevant authority must secure that a code adopted by it under section 27(2) (a "code of conduct") is, when viewed as a whole, consistent with the following principles—

(a) selflessness;

(b) integrity;

(c) objectivity;

(d) accountability;

(e) openness;

(f) honesty;

(g) leadership.

(2) A relevant authority must secure that its code of conduct includes the provision the authority considers appropriate in respect of the registration in its register, and disclosure, of—

(a) pecuniary interests, and

(b) interests other than pecuniary interests.

(3) Sections 29 to 34 do not limit what may be included in a relevant authority's code of conduct, but nothing in a relevant authority's code of conduct prejudices the operation of those sections.

(4) A failure to comply with a relevant authority's code of conduct is not be dealt with otherwise than in accordance with arrangements made under subsection (6); in particular, a decision is not invalidated just because something that occurred in the process of making the decision involved a failure to comply with the code.

(5) A relevant authority may—

(a) revise its existing code of conduct, or

(b) adopt a code of conduct to replace its existing code of conduct.

(6) A relevant authority other than a parish council must have in place—

(a) arrangements under which allegations can be investigated, and

(b) arrangements under which decisions on allegations can be made.

(7) Arrangements put in place under subsection (6)(b) by a relevant authority must include provision for the appointment by the authority of at least one independent person—

(a) whose views are to be sought, and taken into account, by the authority before it makes its decision on an allegation that it has decided to investigate, and

(b) whose views may be sought—

(i) by the authority in relation to an allegation in circumstances not within paragraph (a),

(ii) by a member, or co-opted member, of the authority if that person's behaviour is the subject of an allegation, and

(iii) by a member, or co-opted member, of a parish council if that person's behaviour is the subject of an allegation and the authority is the parish council's principal authority.

(8)–(13) *****

29 Register of interests

(1) The monitoring officer of a relevant authority must establish and maintain a register of interests of members and co-opted members of the authority.

(2) Subject to the provisions of this Chapter, it is for a relevant authority to determine what is to be entered in the authority's register.

(3) Nothing in this Chapter requires an entry to be retained in a relevant authority's register once the person concerned—

    (a) no longer has the interest, or

    (b) is (otherwise than transitorily on re-election or re-appointment) neither a member nor a co-opted member of the authority.

(4) In the case of a relevant authority that is a parish council, references in this Chapter to the authority's monitoring officer are to the monitoring officer of the parish council's principal authority.

(5) The monitoring officer of a relevant authority other than a parish council must secure—

    (a) that a copy of the authority's register is available for inspection at a place in the authority's area at all reasonable hours, and

    (b) that the register is published on the authority's website.

(6) The monitoring officer of a relevant authority that is a parish council must—

    (a) secure that a copy of the parish council's register is available for inspection at a place in the principal authority's area at all reasonable hours,

    (b) secure that the register is published on the principal authority's website, and

    (c) provide the parish council with any data it needs to comply with subsection (7).

(7) A parish council must, if it has a website, secure that its register is published on its website.

(8)–(10) *****

30 Disclosure of pecuniary interests on taking office

(1) A member or co-opted member of a relevant authority must, before the end of 28 days beginning with the day on which the person becomes a member or coopted member of the authority, notify the authority's monitoring officer of any disclosable pecuniary interests which the person has at the time when the notification is given.

(2) Where a person becomes a member or co-opted member of a relevant authority as a result of re-election or re-appointment, subsection (1) applies only as regards disclosable pecuniary interests not entered in the authority's register when the notification is given.

(3) For the purposes of this Chapter, a pecuniary interest is a "disclosable pecuniary interest" in relation to a person ("M") if it is of a description specified in regulations made by the Secretary of State and either—

    (a) it is an interest of M's, or

    (b) it is an interest of—

        (i) M's spouse or civil partner,

        (ii) a person with whom M is living as husband and wife, or

        (iii) a person with whom M is living as if they were civil partners,

        and M is aware that that other person has the interest.

(4) Where a member or co-opted member of a relevant authority gives a notification for the purposes of subsection (1), the authority's monitoring officer is to cause the interests notified to be entered in the authority's register (whether or not they are disclosable pecuniary interests).

31 Pecuniary interests in matters considered at meetings or by a single member

(1) Subsections (2) to (4) apply if a member or co-opted member of a relevant authority—

    (a) is present at a meeting of the authority or of any committee, subcommittee, joint committee or joint sub-committee of the authority,

    (b) has a disclosable pecuniary interest in any matter to be considered, or being considered, at the meeting, and

    (c) is aware that the condition in paragraph (b) is met.

(2) If the interest is not entered in the authority's register, the member or co-opted member must disclose the interest to the meeting, but this is subject to section 32(3).

(3) If the interest is not entered in the authority's register and is not the subject of a pending notification, the member or co-opted member must notify the authority's monitoring officer of the interest before the end of 28 days beginning with the date of the disclosure.

(4) The member or co-opted member may not—

    (a) participate, or participate further, in any discussion of the matter at the meeting, or

    (b) participate in any vote, or further vote, taken on the matter at the meeting,

but this is subject to section 33.

(5)–(11) *****

32   Sensitive interests

(1) Subsections (2) and (3) apply where—

    (a) a member or co-opted member of a relevant authority has an interest (whether or not a disclosable pecuniary interest), and

    (b) the nature of the interest is such that the member or co-opted member, and the authority's monitoring officer, consider that disclosure of the details of the interest could lead to the member or co-opted member, or a person connected with the member or co-opted member, being subject to violence or intimidation.

(2) If the interest is entered in the authority's register, copies of the register that are made available for inspection, and any published version of the register, must not include details of the interest (but may state that the member or co-opted member has an interest the details of which are withheld under this subsection).

(3) If section 31(2) applies in relation to the interest, that provision is to be read as requiring the member or co-opted member to disclose not the interest but merely the fact that the member or co-opted member has a disclosable pecuniary interest in the matter concerned.

33   Dispensations from section 31(4)

(1) A relevant authority may, on a written request made to the proper officer of the authority by a member or co-opted member of the authority, grant a dispensation relieving the member or co-opted member from either or both of the restrictions in section 31(4) in cases described in the dispensation.

(2) A relevant authority may grant a dispensation under this section only if, after having had regard to all relevant circumstances, the authority—

    (a) considers that without the dispensation the number of persons prohibited by section 31(4) from participating in any particular business would be so great a proportion of the body transacting the business as to impede the transaction of the business,

    (b) considers that without the dispensation the representation of different political groups on the body transacting any particular business would be so upset as to alter the likely outcome of any vote relating to the business,

    (c) considers that granting the dispensation is in the interests of persons living in the authority's area,

    (d) if it is an authority to which Part 1A of the Local Government Act 2000 applies and is operating executive arrangements, considers that without the dispensation each member of the authority's executive would be prohibited by section 31(4) from participating in any particular business to be transacted by the authority's executive, or

    (e) considers that it is otherwise appropriate to grant a dispensation.

(3) A dispensation under this section must specify the period for which it has effect, and the period specified may not exceed four years.

(4) Section 31(4) does not apply in relation to anything done for the purpose of deciding whether to grant a dispensation under this section.

34   Offences

(1) A person commits an offence if, without reasonable excuse, the person—

(a) fails to comply with an obligation imposed on the person by section 30(1) or 31(2), (3) or (7),

(b) participates in any discussion or vote in contravention of section 31(4), or

(c) takes any steps in contravention of section 31(8).

(2) A person commits an offence if under section 30(1) or 31(2), (3) or (7) the person provides information that is false or misleading and the person—

(a) knows that the information is false or misleading, or

(b) is reckless as to whether the information is true and not misleading.

(3) A person who is guilty of an offence under this section is liable on summary conviction to a fine not exceeding level 5 on the standard scale.

(4) A court dealing with a person for an offence under this section may (in addition to any other power exercisable in the person's case) by order disqualify the person, for a period not exceeding five years, for being or becoming (by election or otherwise) a member or co-opted member of the relevant authority in question or any other relevant authority.

(5) A prosecution for an offence under this section is not to be instituted except by or on behalf of the Director of Public Prosecutions.

(6)–(14) *****

35–47 *****

EU FINANCIAL SANCTIONS

48   Power to require public authorities to make payments in respect of certain EU financial sanctions

(1) A Minister of the Crown may, in accordance with the provisions of this Part, require public authorities to make payments of amounts determined by a Minister of the Crown in respect of an EU financial sanction to which this Part applies.

(2) A requirement to make a payment under this Part—

(a) may only be imposed on a public authority if—

(i)   the authority has been designated under section 52; and

(ii) the EU financial sanction concerned is one to which the designation applies; and

(b) must be imposed by a notice given to the authority under section 56 (referred to in this Part as a final notice).

(3) If a final notice is registered in accordance with rules of court or any practice direction, it is enforceable in the same manner as an order of the High Court.

(4) Any sums paid by a public authority under this Part are to be paid into the Consolidated Fund.

(5) In this Part—

(a) "EU financial sanction" means a sanction consisting of a lump sum or penalty payment (or both) imposed by the Court of Justice in Article 260(2) proceedings for an infraction of EU law;

(b) "infraction of EU law", in relation to an EU financial sanction, means the failure to comply with a judgment of the Court of Justice given in proceedings under Article 258 or 259 of the Treaty on the Functioning of the European Union; and

(c) "Article 260(2) proceedings" means proceedings under Article 260(2) of that Treaty.

49–80 *****

Community Right to Challenge

81   Duty to consider expression of interest

(1) A relevant authority must consider an expression of interest in accordance with this Chapter if—

    (a) it is submitted to the authority by a relevant body, and

    (b) it is made in writing and complies with such other requirements for expressions of interest as the Secretary of State may specify by regulations.

This is subject to section 82 (timing of expressions of interest). [**Note:** not reproduced here.]

(2) In this Chapter "relevant authority" means—

    (a) a county council in England,

    (b) a district council,

    (c) a London borough council, or

    (d) such other person or body carrying on functions of a public nature as the Secretary of State may specify by regulations.

(3) The persons or bodies who may be specified by regulations under subsection (2)(d) include a Minister of the Crown or a government department.

(4)–(10) *****

*****

Police Reform and Social Responsibility Act 2011

(2011, c. 13)

An Act to make provision about the administration and governance of police forces; about the licensing of, and for the imposition of a late night levy in relation to, the sale and supply of alcohol, and for the repeal of provisions about alcohol disorder zones; for the repeal of sections 132 to 138 of the Serious Organised Crime and Police Act 2005 and for the prohibition of certain activities in Parliament Square; to enable provision in local authority byelaws to include powers of seizure and forfeiture; about the control of dangerous or otherwise harmful drugs; to restrict the issue of arrest warrants for certain extra-territorial offences; and for connected purposes. [15th September 2011]

Territorial extent: England and Wales

PART 1

POLICE REFORM

Chapter 1   Police areas outside London

1   Police and crime commissioners

(1) There is to be a police and crime commissioner for each police area listed in Schedule 1 to the Police Act 1996 (police areas outside London).

(2) A police and crime commissioner is a corporation sole.

(3) The name of the police and crime commissioner for a police area is "the Police and Crime Commissioner for" with the addition of the name of the police area.

(4) The police and crime commissioner for a police area is to be elected, and hold office, in accordance with Chapter 6.

(5) A police and crime commissioner has—

    (a) the functions conferred by this section,

    (b) the functions relating to community safety and crime prevention conferred by Chapter 3, and

(c) the other functions conferred by this Act and other enactments.

(6) The police and crime commissioner for a police area must—

(a) secure the maintenance of the police force for that area, and

(b) secure that the police force is efficient and effective.

(7) The police and crime commissioner for a police area must hold the relevant chief constable to account for the exercise of—

(a) the functions of the chief constable, and

(b) the functions of persons under the direction and control of the chief constable.

(8)–(10) *****

2   Chief constables

(1) Each police force is to have a chief constable.

(2) The chief constable of a police force is to be appointed, and hold office, in accordance with—

(a) section 38, and

(b) the terms and conditions of the appointment.

(3) A police force, and the civilian staff of a police force, are under the direction and control of the chief constable of the force.

(4) A chief constable has the other functions conferred by this Act and by other enactments.

(5) A chief constable must exercise the power of direction and control conferred by subsection (3) in such a way as is reasonable to assist the relevant police and crime commissioner to exercise the commissioner's functions.

(6)–(8) *****

Chapter 2   Metropolitan police district

3   Mayor's Office for Policing and Crime

(1) There is to be a body with the name "The Mayor's Office for Policing and Crime" for the metropolitan police district.

(2) The Mayor's Office for Policing and Crime is a corporation sole.

(3) The person who is Mayor of London for the time being is to be the occupant for the time being of the Mayor's Office for Policing and Crime.

(4) Accordingly, where a person is the occupant of the Mayor's Office for Policing and Crime by virtue of a particular term of office as Mayor of London (the "relevant mayoral term"), the person's term as the occupant of the Mayor's Office for Policing and Crime—

(a) begins at the same time as the relevant mayoral term, and

(b) ends at the same time as the relevant mayoral term.

(5) The Mayor's Office for Policing and Crime has—

(a) the functions conferred by this section,

(b) the functions relating to community safety and crime prevention conferred by Chapter 3, and

(c) the other functions conferred by this Act and other enactments.

(6) The Mayor's Office for Policing and Crime must—

(a) secure the maintenance of the metropolitan police force, and

(b) secure that the metropolitan police force is efficient and effective.

(7) The Mayor's Office for Policing and Crime must hold the Commissioner of Police of the Metropolis to account for the exercise of—

(a) the functions of the Commissioner, and

(b) the functions of persons under the direction and control of the Commissioner.

(8) The Mayor's Office for Policing and Crime must, in particular, hold the Commissioner to account for—

(a) the exercise of the duty imposed by section 8(4) (duty to have regard to police and crime plan);

(b) the exercise of the duty under section 37A(2) of the Police Act 1996 (duty to have regard to strategic policing requirement);

(c) the exercise of the duty imposed by section 39A(7) of the Police Act 1996 (duty to have regard to codes of practice issued by Secretary of State);

(d) the effectiveness and efficiency of the Commissioner's arrangements for co-operating with other persons in the exercise of the Commissioner's functions (whether under section 22A of the Police Act 1996 or otherwise);

(e) the effectiveness and efficiency of the Commissioner's arrangements under section 34 (engagement with local people);

(f) the extent to which the Commissioner has complied with section 35 (value for money);

(g) the exercise of duties relating to equality and diversity imposed on the Commissioner by any enactment;

(h) the exercise of duties in relation to the safeguarding of children and the promotion of child welfare that are imposed on the Commissioner by sections 10 and 11 of the Children Act 2004.

(9)–(11) *****

(12) The Metropolitan Police Authority is abolished.

(13) *****

4   Commissioner of Police of the Metropolis

(1) There is to be a corporation sole with the name "the Commissioner of Police of the Metropolis".

(2) The Commissioner of Police of the Metropolis is to be appointed, and hold office, in accordance with—

(a) sections 42 and 48, and

(b) the terms and conditions of the appointment.

(3) The metropolitan police force, and the civilian staff of the metropolitan police force, are under the direction and control of the Commissioner of Police of the Metropolis.

(4) The Commissioner of Police of the Metropolis has the other functions conferred by this Act and by other enactments.

(5) The Commissioner of Police of the Metropolis must exercise the power of direction and control conferred by subsection (3) in such a way as is reasonable to assist the Mayor's Office for Policing and Crime to exercise that Office's functions.

(6)–(7) *****

Chapter 3   Functions of elected local policing bodies etc

Community safety and crime prevention

5   Police and crime commissioners to issue police and crime plans

(1) The police and crime commissioner for a police area must issue a police and crime plan within the financial year in which each ordinary election is held.

(2) A police and crime commissioner must comply with the duty under subsection (1) as soon as practicable after the commissioner takes office.

(3) A police and crime commissioner may, at any time, issue a police and crime plan.

(4) A police and crime commissioner may vary a police and crime plan.

(5)–(13) *****

6   Mayor's Office for Policing and Crime to issue police and crime plans

(1) The Mayor's Office for Policing and Crime must issue a police and crime plan within the financial year in which each ordinary election is held.

(2) The Mayor's Office for Policing and Crime must comply with the duty under subsection (1) as soon as practicable after the person elected in the ordinary election takes office.

(3) The Mayor's Office for Policing and Crime may, at any time, issue a police and crime plan.

(4) The Mayor's Office for Policing and Crime may vary a police and crime plan.

(5) In issuing or varying a police and crime plan, the Mayor's Office for Policing and Crime must have regard to the strategic policing requirement issued by the Secretary of State under section 37A of the Police Act 1996.

(6)–(13) *****

7   Police and crime plans

(1) A police and crime plan is a plan which sets out, in relation to the planning period, the following matters—

(a) the elected local policing body's police and crime objectives;

(b) the policing of the police area which the chief officer of police is to provide;

(c) the financial and other resources which the elected local policing body is to provide to the chief officer of police for the chief officer to exercise the functions of chief officer;

(d) the means by which the chief officer of police will report to the elected local policing body on the chief officer's provision of policing;

(e) the means by which the chief officer of police's performance in providing policing will be measured;

(f) the crime and disorder reduction grants which the elected local policing body is to make, and the conditions (if any) to which such grants are to be made.

(2) The elected local policing body's police and crime objectives are the body's objectives for—

(a) the policing of the body's area,

(b) crime and disorder reduction in that area, and

(c) the discharge by the relevant police force of its national or international functions.

(3) A police and crime plan has effect from the start of the planning period until—

(a) the end of that planning period, or

(b) if another police and crime plan is issued in relation to the elected local policing body's area before the end of that planning period, the day when that other plan first has effect.

(4) The Secretary of State may give guidance to elected local policing bodies about the matters to be dealt with in police and crime plans.

(5) An elected local policing body must have regard to such guidance.

(6), (7) *****

8   Duty to have regard to police and crime plan

(1) A police and crime commissioner must, in exercising the functions of commissioner, have regard to the police and crime plan issued by the commissioner.

(2)–(7) *****

9–27 *****

Chapter 4   Accountability of elected local policing bodies

Scrutiny of police and crime commissioners

28   Police and crime panels outside London

(1) Each police area, other than the metropolitan police district, is to have a police and crime panel established and maintained in accordance with Schedule 6 (police and crime panels).

(2) The functions of the police and crime panel for a police area must be exercised with a view to supporting the effective exercise of the functions of the police and crime commissioner for that police area.

(3) A police and crime panel must—

    (a) review the draft police and crime plan, or draft variation, given to the panel by the relevant police and crime commissioner in accordance with section 5(6)(c), and

    (b) make a report or recommendations on the draft plan or variation to the commissioner.

(4), (5) *****

(6) A police and crime panel must—

    (a) review or scrutinise decisions made, or other action taken, by the relevant police and crime commissioner in connection with the discharge of the commissioner's functions; and

    (b) make reports or recommendations to the relevant police and crime commissioner with respect to the discharge of the commissioner's functions,

insofar as the panel is not otherwise required to do so by subsection (3) or (4) or by Schedule 1, 5 or 8.

(7) A police and crime panel must publish any reports or recommendations made to the relevant police and crime commissioner.

(8)–(11) *****

29   Power to require attendance and information

(1) A police and crime panel may require the relevant police and crime commissioner, and members of that commissioner's staff, to attend before the panel (at reasonable notice) to answer any question which appears to the panel to be necessary in order for it to carry out its functions.

(2) Nothing in subsection (1) requires a member of the police and crime commissioner's staff to give any evidence, or produce any document, which discloses advice given to the commissioner by that person.

(3) A police and crime panel may require the relevant police and crime commissioner to respond in writing (within a reasonable period determined by the panel) to any report or recommendation made by the panel to the commissioner.

(4) The police and crime commissioner must comply with any requirement imposed by the panel under subsection (1) or (3).

(5) Members of the staff of the police and crime commissioner must comply with any requirement imposed on them under subsection (1).

(6) If a police and crime panel requires the relevant police and crime commissioner to attend before the panel, the panel may (at reasonable notice) request the relevant chief constable to attend before the panel on the same occasion to answer any question which appears to the panel to be necessary in order for it to carry out its functions.

30   Suspension of police and crime commissioner

(1) A police and crime panel may suspend the relevant police and crime commissioner if it appears to the panel that—

    (a) the commissioner has been charged in the United Kingdom, the Channel Islands or the Isle of Man with an offence, and

    (b) the offence is one which carries a maximum term of imprisonment exceeding two years.

(2) The suspension of the police and crime commissioner ceases to have effect upon the occurrence of the earliest of these events—

    (a) the charge being dropped;

    (b) the police and crime commissioner being acquitted of the offence;

    (c) the police and crime commissioner being convicted of the offence but not being disqualified under section 66 by virtue of the conviction;

    (d) the termination of the suspension by the police and crime panel.

(3) For the purposes of salary, pensions and allowances in respect of times during a period of suspension, the police and crime commissioner is to be treated as not holding that office during that suspension.

(4) *****

31–33 *****

Chapter 5   Police forces in areas with elected local policing bodies

Chief officers of police

34   Engagement with local people

(1) A chief officer of police must make arrangements for obtaining the views ofpersons within each neighbourhood in the relevant police area about crime and disorder in that neighbourhood.

(2) A chief officer of police must make arrangements for providing persons within each neighbourhood in the relevant police area with information about policing in that neighbourhood (including information about how policing in that neighbourhood is aimed at dealing with crime and disorder there).

(3)–(4) *****

35   Value for money

(1) In exercising functions, a chief officer of police must secure that good value for money is obtained.

(2) That includes securing that the persons under the direction and control of the chief officer of police obtain good value for money in exercising their functions.

36, 37 *****

Police forces outside London

38   Appointment, suspension and removal of chief constables

(1) The police and crime commissioner for a police area is to appoint the chief constable of the police force for that area.

(2) The police and crime commissioner for a police area may suspend from duty the chief constable of the police force for that area.

(3) The police and crime commissioner for a police area may call upon the chief constable of the police force for that area to resign or retire.

(4) The chief constable must retire or resign if called upon to do so by the relevant police and crime commissioner in accordance with subsection (3).

(5)–(7) *****
*****

Public Bodies Act 2011

(2011, c. 24)

An Act to confer powers on Ministers of the Crown in relation to certain public bodies and offices; to confer powers on Welsh Ministers in relation to environmental and other public bodies; to make provision about delegation and shared services in relation to persons exercising environmental functions; to abolish regional development agencies; to make provision about the funding of Sianel Pedwar Cymru; to make provision about the powers of bodies established under the National Heritage Act 1983 to form companies; to repeal provisions of the Coroners and Justice Act 2009 relating to appeals to the Chief Coroner;

to make provision about amendment of Schedule 1 to the Superannuation Act 1972; and for connected purposes.   [14th December 2011]

Territorial extent: United Kingdom

Powers of Ministers

1   Power to abolish

(1) A Minister may by order abolish a body or office specified in Schedule 1.

(2) An order under subsection (1) may include provision transferring functions from the body or office being abolished to an eligible person.

(3) In this Act, "eligible person" means—

(a) a Minister, the Scottish Ministers, a Northern Ireland department or the Welsh Ministers,

(b) any other person exercising public functions,

(c) a company limited by guarantee,

(d) a community interest company,

(e) a co-operative society,

(f) a community benefit society,

(g) a charitable incorporated organisation, or

(h) a body of trustees or other unincorporated body of persons.

2   Power to merge

(1) A Minister may by order merge any group of bodies or offices specified in Schedule 2.

(2) In this section, to "merge" a group means—

(a) to abolish all the bodies or offices in the group, create a new body corporate or office and transfer some or all of the functions of the abolished bodies or offices to the new one, or

(b) to abolish all but one of the bodies or offices in the group and to transfer some or all of the functions of the abolished bodies or offices to the remaining one.

(3) An order under subsection (1) may include provision to transfer a function from a body or office being abolished to an eligible person not included in the group.

3   Power to modify constitutional arrangements

(1) A Minister may by order modify the constitutional arrangements of a body or office specified in Schedule 3.

(2) In this Act, references to the constitutional arrangements of a body include matters relating to—

(a) the name of the body;

(b) the chair of the body (including qualifications and procedures for appointment and functions);

(c) members of the body (including the number of members, qualifications and procedures for appointment and functions);

(d) employees of the body exercising functions on its behalf (including qualifications and procedures for appointment and functions);

(e) the body's powers to employ staff;

(f) governing procedures and arrangements (including the role and membership of committees and sub-committees);

(g) reports and accounts;

(h) the extent to which the body is accountable to Ministers;

(i) the extent to which the body exercises functions on behalf of the Crown.

(3) In this Act, references to the constitutional arrangements of an office include matters relating to—

(a) the name of the office;

(b) appointment of the office-holder (including qualifications and procedures for appointment);

(c) the office-holder's powers to employ staff;

(d) reports and accounts;

(e) the extent to which the office-holder is accountable to Ministers;

(f) the extent to which the office-holder exercises functions on behalf of the Crown.

4 Power to modify funding arrangements

(1) A Minister may by order modify the funding arrangements of a body or office specified in Schedule 4.

(2) The consent of the Treasury is required to make an order under this section.

(3) In this Act, references to modifying the funding arrangements of a body or office include—

(a) modifying the extent to which it is funded by a Minister;

(b) conferring power on the body, or the office-holder, to charge fees for the exercise of a function (and to determine their amount).

5 Power to modify or transfer functions

(1) A Minister may by order—

(a) modify the functions of a body, or the holder of an office, specified in Schedule 5, or

(b) transfer a function of such a person to an eligible person.

(2) In this Act, references to modifying the functions of a person include—

(a) conferring a function on the person;

(b) abolishing a function of the person;

(c) changing the purpose or objective for which the person exercises a function;

(d) changing the conditions under which the person exercises a function.

6 *****

Powers of Ministers: supplementary

7 Restrictions on Ministerial powers

(1) The modification or transfer of a function by an order under sections 1 to 5 must not prevent it (to the extent that it continues to be exercisable) from being exercised independently of Ministers in any of the following cases.

(2) Those cases are—

(a) where the function is a judicial function (whether or not exercised by a court or a tribunal);

(b) where the function's exercise involves enforcement activities in relation to obligations imposed on a Minister;

(c) where the function's exercise otherwise constitutes the exercise of oversight or scrutiny of the actions of a Minister.

(3) Provision made by an order under sections 1 to 5 must be proportionate to the reasons for the order.

(4) In this section "enforcement activities" means—

(a) the bringing of legal proceedings or the provision of assistance with the bringing of legal proceedings,

(b) the carrying out of an investigation with a view to bringing legal proceedings or to providing such assistance, or

(c) the taking of steps preparatory to any of those things.

8 Purpose and conditions

(1) A Minister may make an order under sections 1 to 5 only if the Minister considers that the order serves the purpose of improving the exercise of public functions, having regard to—

(a) efficiency,

(b) effectiveness,

(c) economy, and

(d) securing appropriate accountability to Ministers.

(2) A Minister may make an order under those sections only if the Minister considers that—

  (a) the order does not remove any necessary protection, and
  (b) the order does not prevent any person from continuing to exercise any right or freedom which that person might reasonably expect to continue to exercise.

9 Devolution

  (1) An order under sections 1 to 5 requires the consent of the Scottish Parliament to make provision—
  (a) which would be within the legislative competence of the Scottish Parliament if it were contained in an Act of that Parliament, or
  (b) which modifies the functions of the Scottish Ministers.
  (2) Consent is not required under subsection (1)(b) in relation to provision abolishing a function of the Scottish Ministers which relates to a body abolished under section 1 or 2.
  (3) An order under sections 1 to 5 requires the consent of the Northern Ireland Assembly to make provision—
  (a) which would be within the legislative competence of the Northern Ireland Assembly if it were contained in an Act of the Assembly, or
  (b) which modifies the functions of a person within subsection (4).
  (4) The persons referred to in subsection (3)(b) are—
  (a) the First Minister and deputy First Minister of Northern Ireland;
  (b) a Northern Ireland Minister;
  (c) the Attorney General for Northern Ireland;
  (d) a Northern Ireland department;
  (e) a person exercising public functions in relation to a transferred matter (within the meaning of the Northern Ireland Act 1998).
  (5) Consent is not required under subsection (3)(a) in relation to any provision if—
  (a) a Bill for an Act of the Northern Ireland Assembly containing the provision would require the consent of the Secretary of State under section 8 of the Northern Ireland Act 1998, and
  (b) the provision does not affect, other than incidentally, a transferred matter (within the meaning of that Act).
  (6) An order under sections 1 to 5 requires the consent of the National Assembly for Wales to make provision which would be within the legislative competence of the Assembly if it were contained in an Act of the Assembly.
  (7)–(8) *****

10 Consultation

  (1) A Minister proposing to make an order under sections 1 to 5 must consult—
  (a) the body or the holder of the office to which the proposal relates,
  (b) such other persons as appear to the Minister to be representative of interests substantially affected by the proposal,
  (c) the Scottish Ministers, if the proposal relates to any matter, so far as applying in or as regards Scotland, in relation to which the Scottish Ministers exercise functions (and where the consent of the Scottish Parliament is not required under section 9),
  (d) a Northern Ireland department, if the proposal relates to any matter, so far as applying in or as regards Northern Ireland, in relation to which the department exercises functions (and where the consent of the Northern Ireland Assembly is not required under section 9),
  (e) the Welsh Ministers, if the proposal relates to any matter, so far as applying in or as regards Wales, in relation to which the Welsh Ministers exercise functions (and where the consent of the National Assembly for Wales or the Welsh Ministers is not required under section 9),
  (f) where the functions affected by the proposal relate to the administration of justice, the Lord Chief Justice, and

(g) such other persons as the Minister considers appropriate.

(2)–(4) *****

11 Procedure

(1) If after consultation under section 10 the Minister considers it appropriate to proceed with the making of an order under sections 1 to 5, the Minister may lay before Parliament—

(a) a draft order, and

(b) an explanatory document.

(2) The explanatory document must—

(a) introduce and give reasons for the order,

(b) explain why the Minister considers that—

(i)   the order serves the purpose in section 8(1), and

(ii) the conditions in section 8(2)(a) and (b) are satisfied,

(c) if the order contains provision made by virtue of more than one entry in Schedules 1 to 5, explain why the Minister considers it appropriate for it to do so, and

(d) contain a summary of representations received in the consultation.

(3)–(12)*****

12–39   *****

SCHEDULES

SCHEDULE 1   POWER TO ABOLISH: BODIES AND OFFICES

Administrative Justice and Tribunals Council.

Advisory Committee on Hazardous Substances (established under section 140(5) of the Environmental Protection Act 1990).

Advisory Committee on Pesticides and Advisory Committee on Pesticides for Northern Ireland (bodies established under section 16(7) of the Food and Environment Protection Act 1985).

Agricultural dwelling-house advisory committees for areas in England.

Agricultural Wages Board for England and Wales.

Agricultural wages committees for areas in England.

Aircraft and Shipbuilding Industries Arbitration Tribunal.

British Shipbuilders and any subsidiary of British Shipbuilders (within the meaning of section 1159 of the Companies Act 2006).

BRB (Residuary) Limited.

Child Maintenance and Enforcement Commission.

Commission for Rural Communities.

Committee on Agricultural Valuation (the body established under section 92 of the Agricultural Holdings Act 1986).

Competition Service.

Courts boards.

Crown Court Rule Committee.

Disability Living Allowance Advisory Board.

Disabled Persons Transport Advisory Committee.

Environment Protection Advisory Committees established under section 12 of the Environment Act 1995 other than the one established pursuant to subsection (6) of that section (Wales).

Food from Britain.

Home Grown Timber Advisory Committee.

Inland Waterways Advisory Council.

Her Majesty's Inspectorate of Court Administration.
Library Advisory Council for England.
Magistrates' Courts Rule Committee (established under section 144 of the
Magistrates' Courts Act 1980).
National Consumer Council ("Consumer Focus").
National Endowment for Science, Technology and the Arts.
Plant Varieties and Seeds Tribunal.
Public Guardian Board.
Railway Heritage Committee.
Regional and local fisheries advisory committees established under section
13 of the Environment Act 1995 other than the one established pursuant to
subsection (5) of that section (Wales).
Registrar of Public Lending Right.
Sports Grounds Safety Authority.
Valuation Tribunal Service.
Victims' Advisory Panel.

*****

SCHEDULE 2   POWER TO MERGE: BODIES AND OFFICES

Group 1

Central Arbitration Committee.
Certification Officer.

Group 2

Gambling Commission.
National Lottery Commission.

Group 3

Pensions Ombudsman.
Ombudsman for the Board of the Pension Protection Fund.

Group 4

Director of Public Prosecutions.
Director of Revenue and Customs Prosecutions.

Group 5

Competition Commission.
Office of Fair Trading ("OFT").

SCHEDULE 3   POWER TO MODIFY CONSTITUTIONAL ARRANGEMENTS: BODIES AND OFFICES

Administrative Justice and Tribunals Council.
British Hallmarking Council.
Broads Authority.
Commission for Equality and Human Rights.
English Tourist Board.
Internal drainage boards for areas wholly or mainly in England.
Joint Nature Conservation Committee.
National Park authorities in England.

Passengers' Council ("Passenger Focus").

Sianel Pedwar Cymru ("S4C").

Theatres Trust.

SCHEDULE 4   POWER TO MODIFY FUNDING ARRANGEMENTS: BODIES AND OFFICES

Administrative Justice and Tribunals Council.

Commission for Equality and Human Rights.

Inspectors appointed by the Secretary of State under section 86 of the Water Industry Act 1991.

Marine Management Organisation.

Natural England.

Office of Communications ("Ofcom").

SCHEDULE 5   POWER TO MODIFY OR TRANSFER FUNCTIONS: BODIES AND OFFICES

Administrative Justice and Tribunals Council.

Advisory Council on Public Records.

British Hallmarking Council.

British Waterways Board.

Commission for Equality and Human Rights.

Dover Harbour Board.

Environment Agency.

Her Majesty's Stationery Office.

Horserace Betting Levy Board.

Human Fertilisation and Embryology Authority.

Human Tissue Authority.

Internal drainage boards for areas wholly or mainly in England.

Keeper of Public Records.

Office of Communications ("Ofcom").

Office of Fair Trading ("OFT").

Public Record Office.

*****

Terrorism Prevention and Investigation Measures Act 2011

(2011, c. 23)

An Act to abolish control orders and make provision for the imposition of terrorism prevention and investigation measures.   [14th December 2011]

Territorial extent: United Kingdom

New regime to protect the public from terrorism

1   *****

2   Imposition of terrorism prevention and investigation measures

(1) The Secretary of State may by notice (a "TPIM notice") impose specified terrorism prevention and investigation measures on an individual if conditions A to E in section 3 are met.

(2) In this Act "terrorism prevention and investigation measures" means requirements, restrictions and other provision which may be made in relation to an individual by virtue of Schedule 1 (terrorism prevention and investigation measures).

(3) In this section and Part 1 of Schedule 1 "specified" means specified in the TPIM notice.

3   Conditions A to E

(1) Condition A is that the Secretary of State reasonably believes that the individual is, or has been, involved in terrorism-related activity (the "relevant activity").

(2) Condition B is that some or all of the relevant activity is new terrorism-related activity.

(3) Condition C is that the Secretary of State reasonably considers that it is necessary, for purposes connected with protecting members of the public from a risk of terrorism, for terrorism prevention and Investigation measures to be imposed on the individual.

(4) Condition D is that the Secretary of State reasonably considers that it is necessary, for purposes connected with preventing or restricting the individual's involvement in terrorism-related activity, for the specified terrorism prevention and investigation measures to be imposed on the individual.

(5) Condition E is that—

  (a) the court gives the Secretary of State permission under section 6, or
  (b) the Secretary of State reasonably considers that the urgency of the case requires terrorism prevention and investigation measures to be imposed without obtaining such permission.

(6) In this section "new terrorism-related activity" means—

  (a) if no TPIM notice relating to the individual has ever been in force, terrorism-related activity occurring at any time (whether before or after the coming into force of this Act);
  (b) if only one TPIM notice relating to the individual has ever been in force, terrorism-related activity occurring after that notice came into force; or
  (c) if two or more TPIM notices relating to the individual have been in force, terrorism-related activity occurring after such a notice came into force most recently.

4   Involvement in terrorism-related activity

(1) For the purposes of this Act, involvement in terrorism-related activity is any one or more of the following—

  (a) the commission, preparation or instigation of acts of terrorism;
  (b) conduct which facilitates the commission, preparation or instigation of such acts, or which is intended to do so;
  (c) conduct which gives encouragement to the commission, preparation or instigation of such acts, or which is intended to do so;
  (d) conduct which gives support or assistance to individuals who are known or believed by the individual concerned to be involved in conduct falling within paragraphs (a) to (c);

and for the purposes of this Act it is immaterial whether the acts of terrorism in question are specific acts of terrorism or acts of terrorism in general.

(2) For the purposes of this Act, it is immaterial whether an individual's involvement in terrorism-related activity occurs before or after the coming into force of this Act.

Two year limit on imposition of measures without new terrorism-related activity

5   Two year limit for TPIM notices

(1) A TPIM notice—

  (a) comes into force when the notice is served on the individual or, if later, at the time specified for this purpose in the notice; and
  (b) is in force for the period of one year.

(2) The Secretary of State may by notice extend a TPIM notice for a period of one year beginning when the TPIM notice would otherwise expire.

(3) A TPIM notice—

(a) may be extended under subsection (2) only if conditions A, C and D are met; and

(b) may be so extended on only one occasion.

(4) *****

Court scrutiny of imposition of measures

6 Prior permission of the court

(1) This section applies if the Secretary of State—

(a) makes the relevant decisions in relation to an individual, and

(b) makes an application to the court for permission to impose measures on the individual.

(2) The application must set out a draft of the proposed TPIM notice.

(3) The function of the court on the application is—

(a) to determine whether the relevant decisions of the Secretary of State are obviously flawed, and

(b) to determine whether to give permission to impose measures on the individual and (where applicable) whether to exercise the power of direction under subsection (9).

(4) The court may consider the application—

(a) in the absence of the individual;

(b) without the individual having been notified of the application; and

(c) without the individual having been given an opportunity (if the individual was aware of the application) of making any representations to the court.

(5) But that does not limit the matters about which rules of court may be made.

(6) In determining the application, the court must apply the principles applicable on an application for judicial review.

(7) In a case where the court determines that a decision of the Secretary of State that condition A, condition B, or condition C is met is obviously flawed, the court may not give permission under this section.

(8) In any other case, the court may give permission under this section.

(9) If the court determines that the Secretary of State's decision that condition D is met is obviously flawed, the court may (in addition to giving permission under subsection (8)) give directions to the Secretary of State in relation to the measures to be imposed on the individual.

(10) In this section "relevant decisions" means the decisions that the following conditions are met—

(a) condition A;

(b) condition B;

(c) condition C; and

(d) condition D.

7, 8 *****

9 Review hearing

(1) On a review hearing held in compliance with directions under section 8(4), the function of the court is to review the decisions of the Secretary of State that the relevant conditions were met and continue to be met.

(2) In doing so, the court must apply the principles applicable on an application for judicial review.

(3) The court—

(a) must discontinue the review hearing if the individual requests the court to do so; and

(b) may discontinue the review hearing in any other circumstances.

(4) The court may not discontinue the review hearing in accordance with subsection (3)(b) without giving the Secretary of State and the individual the opportunity to make representations.

(5) The court has the following powers (and only those powers) on a review hearing—

(a) power to quash the TPIM notice;

(b) power to quash measures specified in the TPIM notice;

(c) power to give directions to the Secretary of State for, or in relation to,—

    (i) the revocation of the TPIM notice, or

    (ii) the variation of measures specified in the TPIM notice.

(6) If the court does not exercise any of its powers under subsection (5), the court must decide that the TPIM notice is to continue in force.

(7) If the court exercises a power under subsection (5)(b) or (c)(ii), the court must decide that the TPIM notice is to continue in force subject to that exercise of that power.

(8) In this section "relevant conditions" means—

(a) condition A;

(b) condition B;

(c) condition C; and

(d) condition D.

10 *****

Review of ongoing necessity

11 Review of ongoing necessity

During the period that a TPIM notice is in force, the Secretary of State must keep under review whether conditions C and D are met.

12–16 *****

17 Jurisdiction in relation to decisions under this Act

(1) TPIM decisions are not to be questioned in any legal proceedings other than—

(a) proceedings in the court; or

(b) proceedings on appeal from such proceedings.

(2) The court is the appropriate tribunal for the purposes of section 7 of the Human Rights Act 1998 in relation to proceedings all or any part of which call a TPIM decision into question.

(3) *****

*****

Part II

Other constitutional materials

The Constitution of the United States (1787)

We the People of the United States, in order to form a more perfect Union, establish Justice, ensure Domestic Tranquillity, provide for the common Defence, promote the general Welfare, and secure the Blessings of Liberty to ourselves and our Posterity, do ordain and establish this CONSTITUTION for the United States of America.

Articles I–VII
*****

Amendments to the Constitution

Article I
Congress shall make no law respecting an establishment of religion, or prohibiting the free exercise thereof; or abridging the freedom of speech or of the press; or the right of the people peaceably to assemble, and to petition the government for a redress of grievances.

Article II
A well-regulated militia being necessary to the security of a free state, the right of the people to keep and bear arms shall not be infringed.

Article III
No soldier shall, in time of peace, be quartered in any house without the consent of the owner, nor in time of war but in a manner to be prescribed by law.

Article IV
The right of the people to be secure in their persons, houses, papers, and effects, against unreasonable searches and seizures, shall not be violated, and no warrants shall issue but upon probable cause, supported by oath or affirmation, and particularly describing the place to be searched, and the persons or things to be seized.

Article V
No person shall be held to answer for a capital or other infamous crime unless on a presentment or indictment of a grand jury, except in cases arising in the land or naval forces, or in the militia, when in actual service, in time of war or public danger; nor shall any person be subject for the same offence to be twice put in jeopardy of life or limb; nor shall be compelled in any criminal case to be a witness against himself, nor be deprived of life, liberty, or property, without due process of law; nor shall private property be taken for public use without just compensation.

Article VI
In all criminal prosecutions, the accused shall enjoy the right to a speedy and public trial, by an impartial jury of the state and district wherein the crime shall have been committed, which district shall

have been previously ascertained by law, and to be informed of the nature and cause of the accusation; to be confronted with the witnesses against him; to have compulsory process for obtaining witnesses in his favor, and to have the assistance of counsel for his defence.

Article VII

In suits at common law, where the value in controversy shall exceed twenty dollars, the right of trial by jury shall be preserved, and no fact tried by a jury shall be otherwise re-examined in any court of the United States than according to the rules of the common law.

Article VIII

Excessive bail shall not be required, nor excessive fines imposed, nor cruel and unusual punishments inflicted.

Article IX

The enumeration in the constitution of certain rights shall not be construed to deny or disparage others retained by the people.

Article X

The powers not delegated to the United States by the constitution, nor prohibited by it to the states, are reserved to the states respectively, or to the people.

[*The foregoing ten amendments were adopted at the first session of Congress, and were declared to be in force, 15th December 1791.*]

Articles XI–XIII

*****

Article XIV

1. All persons born or naturalized in the United States, and subject to the jurisdiction thereof, are citizens of the United States and of the state wherein they reside. No state shall make or enforce any law which shall abridge the privileges or immunities of citizens of the United States; nor shall any state deprive any person of life, liberty, or property without due process of law; nor deny to any person within its jurisdiction the equal protection of the law.

2.–4. *****

5. The Congress shall have power to enforce, by appropriate legislation, the provisions of this article.

[*Declared in force, 28th July 1868.*]

*****

United Nations Universal Declaration of Human Rights (December 1948)*

Preamble

Whereas recognition of the inherent dignity and of the equal and inalienable rights of all members of the human family is the foundation of freedom, justice and peace in the world,

Whereas disregard and contempt for human rights have resulted in barbarous acts which have outraged the conscience of mankind, and the advent of a world in which human beings shall enjoy freedom of speech and belief and freedom from fear and want has been proclaimed as the highest aspiration of the common people,

Whereas it is essential, if man is not to be compelled to have recourse, as a last resort, to rebellion against tyranny and oppression, that human rights should be protected by the rule of law,

Whereas it is essential to promote the development of friendly relations between nations,

---

* Reproduced with permission from the United Nations.

Whereas the peoples of the United Nations have in the Charter reaffirmed their faith in fundamental human rights, in the dignity and worth of the human person and in the equal rights of men and women and have determined to promote social progress and better standards of life in larger freedom,

Whereas Member States have pledged themselves to achieve, in co-operation with the United Nations, the promotion of universal respect for and observance of human rights and fundamental freedoms,

Whereas a common understanding of these rights and freedoms is of the greatest importance for the full realization of this pledge,

Now, Therefore THE GENERAL ASSEMBLY proclaims THIS UNIVERSAL DECLARATION OF HUMAN RIGHTS as a common standard of achievement for all peoples and all nations, to the end that every individual and every organ of society, keeping this Declaration constantly in mind, shall strive by teaching and education to promote respect for these rights and freedoms and by progressive measures, national and international, to secure their universal and effective recognition and observance, both among the peoples of Member States themselves and among the peoples of territories under their jurisdiction.

Article 1

All human beings are born free and equal in dignity and rights. They are endowed with reason and conscience and should act towards one another in a spirit of brotherhood.

Article 2

Everyone is entitled to all the rights and freedoms set forth in this Declaration, without distinction of any kind, such as race, colour, sex, language, religion, political or other opinion, national or social origin, property, birth or other status. Furthermore, no distinction shall be made on the basis of the political, jurisdictional or international status of the country or territory to which a person belongs, whether it be independent, trust, non-self-governing or under any other limitation of sovereignty.

Article 3

Everyone has the right to life, liberty and security of person.

Article 4

No one shall be held in slavery or servitude; slavery and the slave trade shall be prohibited in all their forms.

Article 5

No one shall be subjected to torture or to cruel, inhuman or degrading treatment or punishment.

Article 6

Everyone has the right to recognition everywhere as a person before the law.

Article 7

All are equal before the law and are entitled without any discrimination to equal protection of the law. All are entitled to equal protection against any discrimination in violation of this Declaration and against any incitement to such discrimination.

Article 8

Everyone has the right to an effective remedy by the competent national tribunals for acts violating the fundamental rights granted him by the constitution or by law.

Article 9

No one shall be subjected to arbitrary arrest, detention or exile.

Article 10

Everyone is entitled in full equality to a fair and public hearing by an independent and impartial tribunal, in the determination of his rights and obligations and of any criminal charge against him.

Article 11

(1) Everyone charged with a penal offence has the right to be presumed innocent until proved guilty according to law in a public trial at which he has had all the guarantees necessary for his defence.

(2) No one shall be held guilty of any penal offence on account of any act or omission which did not constitute a penal offence, under national or international law, at the time when it was committed. Nor shall a heavier penalty be imposed than the one that was applicable at the time the penal offence was committed.

Article 12

No one shall be subjected to arbitrary interference with his privacy, family, home or correspondence, nor to attacks upon his honour and reputation. Everyone has the right to the protection of the law against such interference or attacks.

Article 13

(1) Everyone has the right to freedom of movement and residence within the borders of each state.

(2) Everyone has the right to leave any country, including his own, and to return to his country.

Article 14

(1) Everyone has the right to seek and to enjoy in other countries asylum from persecution.

(2) This right may not be invoked in the case of prosecutions genuinely arising from non-political crimes or from acts contrary to the purposes and principles of the United Nations.

Article 15

(1) Everyone has the right to a nationality.

(2) No one shall be arbitrarily deprived of his nationality nor denied the right to change his nationality.

Article 16

(1) Men and women of full age, without any limitation due to race, nationality or religion, have the right to marry and to found a family. They are entitled to equal rights as to marriage, during marriage and at its dissolution.

(2) Marriage shall be entered into only with the free and full consent of the intending spouses.

(3) The family is the natural and fundamental group unit of society and is entitled to protection by society and the State.

Article 17

(1) Everyone has the right to own property alone as well as in association with others.

(2) No one shall be arbitrarily deprived of his property.

Article 18

Everyone has the right to freedom of thought, conscience and religion; this right includes freedom to change his religion or belief, and freedom, either alone or in community with others and in public or private, to manifest his religion or belief in teaching, practice, worship and observance.

Article 19

Everyone has the right to freedom of opinion and expression; this right includes freedom to hold opinions without interference and to seek, receive and impart information and ideas through any media and regardless of frontiers.

Article 20

(1) Everyone has the right to freedom of peaceful assembly and association.

(2) No one may be compelled to belong to an association.

Article 21

(1) Everyone has the right to take part in the government of his country, directly or through freely chosen representatives.

(2) Everyone has the right of equal access to public service in his country.

(3) The will of the people shall be the basis of the authority of government; this will shall be expressed in periodic and genuine elections which shall be by universal and equal suffrage and shall be held by secret vote or by equivalent free voting procedures.

Article 22

Everyone, as a member of society, has the right to social security and is entitled to realization, through national effort and international co-operation and in accordance with the organization and resources of each State, of the economic, social and cultural rights indispensable for his dignity and the free development of his personality.

Article 23

(1) Everyone has the right to work, to free choice of employment, to just and favourable conditions of work and to protection against unemployment.

(2) Everyone, without any discrimination, has the right to equal pay for equal work.

(3) Everyone who works has the right to just and favourable remuneration ensuring for himself and his family an existence worthy of human dignity, and supplemented, if necessary, by other means of social protection.

(4) Everyone has the right to form and to join trade unions for the protection of his interests.

Article 24

Everyone has the right to rest and leisure, including reasonable limitation of working hours and periodic holidays with pay.

Article 25

(1) Everyone has the right to a standard of living adequate for the health and well-being of himself and of his family, including food, clothing, housing and medical care and necessary social services, and the right to security in the event of unemployment, sickness, disability, widowhood, old age or other lack of livelihood in circumstances beyond his control.

(2) Motherhood and childhood are entitled to special care and assistance. All children, whether born in or out of wedlock, shall enjoy the same social protection.

Article 26

(1) Everyone has the right to education. Education shall be free, at least in the elementary and fundamental stages. Elementary education shall be compulsory. Technical and professional education shall be made generally available and higher education shall be equally accessible to all on the basis of merit.

(2) Education shall be directed to the full development of the human personality and to the strengthening of respect for human rights and fundamental freedoms. It shall promote understanding, tolerance and friendship among all nations, racial or religious groups, and shall further the activities of the United Nations for the maintenance of peace.

(3) Parents have a prior right to choose the kind of education that shall be given to their children.

Article 27

(1) Everyone has the right freely to participate in the cultural life of the community, to enjoy the arts and to share in scientific advancement and its benefits.

(2) Everyone has the right to the protection of the moral and material interests resulting from any scientific, literary or artistic production of which he is the author.

Article 28

Everyone is entitled to a social and international order in which the rights and freedoms set forth in this Declaration can be fully realized.

Article 29

(1) Everyone has duties to the community in which alone the free and full development of his personality is possible.

(2) In the exercise of his rights and freedoms, everyone shall be subject only to such limitations as are determined by law solely for the purpose of securing due recognition and respect for the rights and freedoms of others and of meeting the just requirements of morality, public order and the general welfare in a democratic society.

(3) These rights and freedoms may in no case be exercised contrary to the purposes and principles of the United Nations.

Article 30

Nothing in this Declaration may be interpreted as implying for any State, group or person any right to engage in any activity or to perform any act aimed at the destruction of any of the rights and freedoms set forth herein.

European Convention for the Protection of Human Rights and Fundamental Freedoms (1950)*

[*The European Convention on Human Rights*]

The Governments signatory hereto, being Members of the Council of Europe,

Considering the Universal Declaration of Human Rights proclaimed by the General Assembly of the United Nations on 10 December 1948;

Considering that this Declaration aims at securing the universal and effective recognition and observance of the Rights therein declared;

Considering that the aim of the Council of Europe is the achievement of greater unity between its Members and that one of the methods by which the aim is to be pursued is the maintenance and further realization of Human Rights and Fundamental Freedoms;

Reaffirming their profound belief in those Fundamental Freedoms which are the foundation of justice and peace in the world and are best maintained on the one hand by an effective political democracy and on the other by a common understanding and observance of the Human Rights upon which they depend;

Being resolved, as the Governments of European countries which are like-minded and have a common heritage of political traditions, ideals, freedom and the rule of law to take the first steps for the collective enforcement of certain of the Rights stated in the Universal Declaration;

Have agreed as follows:

Article 1   Obligation to respect human rights

The High Contracting Parties shall secure to everyone within their jurisdiction the rights and freedoms defined in Section I of this Convention.

Section I Rights and Freedoms

Article 2   Right to life

1. Everyone's right to life shall be protected by law. No one shall be deprived of his life intentionally save in the execution of a sentence of a court following his conviction of a crime for which this penalty is provided by law.

2. Deprivation of life shall not regarded as inflicted in contravention of this article when it results from the use of force which is no more than absolutely necessary:

    (a) in defence of any person from unlawful violence;

    (b) in order to effect a lawful arrest or to prevent the escape of a person lawfully detained;

    (c) in action lawfully taken for the purpose of quelling a riot or insurrection.

Article 3   Prohibition of torture

No one shall be subjected to torture or to inhuman or degrading treatment or punishment.

Article 4   Prohibition of slavery and forced labour

1. No one shall be held in slavery or servitude.
2. No one shall be required to perform forced or compulsory labour.
3. For the purpose of this article the term 'forced or compulsory labour' shall not include:
   (a) any work required to be done in the ordinary course of detention imposed according to the provisions of Article 5 of this Convention or during conditional release from such detention;
   (b) any service of a military character or, in case of conscientious objectors in countries where they are recognized, service exacted instead of compulsory military service;
   (c) any service exacted in case of an emergency or calamity threatening the life or well- being of the community;
   (d) any work or service which forms part of normal civic obligations.

Article 5   Right to liberty and security

1. Everyone has the right to liberty and security of person.

No one shall be deprived of his liberty save in the following cases and in accordance with a procedure prescribed by law:
   (a) the lawful detention of a person after conviction by a competent court;
   (b) the lawful arrest or detention of a person for non-compliance with the lawful order of a court or in order to secure the fulfilment of any obligation prescribed by law;
   (c) the lawful arrest or detention of a person effected for the purpose of bringing him before the competent legal authority on reasonable suspicion of having committed an offence or when it is reasonably considered necessary to prevent his committing an offence or fleeing after having done so;
   (d) the detention of a minor by lawful order for the purpose of educational supervision or his lawful detention for the purpose of bringing him before the competent legal authority;
   (e) the lawful detention of persons for the prevention of the spreading of infectious diseases, of persons of unsound mind, alcoholics or drug addicts, or vagrants;
   (f) the lawful arrest or detention of a person to prevent his effecting an unauthorized entry into the country or of a person against whom action is being taken with a view to deportation or extradition.

2. Everyone who is arrested shall be informed promptly, in a language which he understands, of the reasons for his arrest and of any charge against him.

3. Everyone arrested or detained in accordance with the provisions of paragraph 1(c) of this article shall be brought promptly before a judge or other officer authorized by law to exercise judicial power and shall be entitled to trial within a reasonable time or to release pending trial. Release may be conditioned by guarantees to appear for trial.

4. Everyone who is deprived of his liberty by arrest or detention shall be entitled to take proceedings by which the lawfulness of his detention shall be decided speedily by a court and his release ordered if the detention is not lawful.

5. Everyone who has been the victim of arrest or detention in contravention of the provisions of this article shall have an enforceable right to compensation.

Article 6   Right to a fair trial

1. In the determination of his civil rights and obligations or of any criminal charge against him, everyone is entitled to a fair and public hearing within a reasonable time by an independent and impartial tribunal established by law. Judgment shall be pronounced publicly but the press and public may be excluded from all or part of the trial in the interest of morals, public order or national security in a democratic society, where the interests of juveniles or the protection of the private life of the parties so require, or to the extent strictly necessary in the opinion of the court in special circumstances where publicity would prejudice the interests of justice.

Everyone charged with a criminal offence shall be presumed innocent until proved guilty ꞁing to law.

ɔ. Everyone charged with a criminal offence has the following minimum rights:

(a) to be informed promptly, in a language which he understands and in detail, of the nature and cause of the accusation against him;

(b) to have adequate time and facilities for the preparation of his defence;

(c) to defend himself in person or through legal assistance of his own choosing or, if he has not sufficient means to pay for legal assistance, to be given it free when the interests of justice so require;

(d) to examine or have examined witnesses against him and to obtain the attendance and examination of witnesses on his behalf under the same conditions as witnesses against him;

(e) to have the free assistance of an interpreter if he cannot understand or speak the language used in court.

Article 7   No punishment without law

1. No one shall be held guilty of any criminal offence on account of any act or omission which did not constitute a criminal offence under national or international law at the time when it was committed. Nor shall a heavier penalty be imposed than the one that was applicable at the time the criminal offence was committed.

2. This article shall not prejudice the trial and punishment of any person for any act or omission which, at the time when it was committed, was criminal according to the general principles of law recognized by civilized nations.

Article 8   Right to respect for private and family life

1. Everyone has the right to respect for his private and family life, his home and his correspondence.

2. There shall be no interference by a public authority with the exercise of this right except such as is in accordance with the law and is necessary in a democratic society in the interests of national security, public safety or the economic well-being of the country, for the prevention of disorder or crime, for the protection of health or morals, or for the protection of the rights and freedoms of others.

Article 9   Freedom of thought, conscience and religion

1. Everyone has the right to freedom of thought, conscience and religion; this right includes freedom to change his religion or belief, and freedom, either alone or in community with others and in public or private, to manifest his religion or belief, in worship, teaching, practice and observance.

2. Freedom to manifest one's religion or beliefs shall be subject only to such limitations as are prescribed by law and are necessary in a democratic society in the interests of public safety, for the protection of public order, health or morals, or for the protection of the rights and freedoms of others.

Article 10   Freedom of expression

1. Everyone has the right to freedom of expression. This right shall include freedom to hold opinions and to receive and impart information and ideas without interference by public authority and regardless of frontiers. This article shall not prevent States from requiring the licensing of broadcasting, television or cinema enterprises.

2. The exercise of these freedoms, since it carries with it duties and responsibilities, may be subject to such formalities, conditions, restrictions or penalties as are prescribed by law and are necessary in a democratic society, in the interests of national security, territorial integrity or public safety, for the prevention of disorder or crime, for the protection of health or morals, for the protection of the reputation or rights of others, for preventing the disclosure of information received in confidence, or for maintaining the authority and impartiality of the judiciary.

Article 11   Freedom of assembly and association

1. Everyone has the right to freedom of peaceful assembly and to freedom of association with others, including the right to form and to join trade unions for the protection of his interests.

2. No restrictions shall be placed on the exercise of these rights other than such as are prescribed by law and are necessary in a democratic society in the interests of national security or public safety, for the prevention of disorder or crime, of the protection of health or morals or for the protection of the rights and freedoms of others. This article shall not prevent the imposition of lawful restrictions on the exercise of these rights by members of the armed forces, of the police or of the administration of the State.

Article 12   Right to marry
Men and women of marriageable age have the right to marry and to found a family, according to the national laws governing the exercise of this right.

Article 13   Right to an effective remedy
Everyone whose rights and freedoms as set forth in this Convention are violated shall have an effective remedy before a national authority notwithstanding that the violation has been committed by persons acting in an official capacity.

Article 14   Prohibition of discrimination
The enjoyment of the rights and freedoms set forth in this Convention shall be secured without discrimination on any ground such as sex, race, colour, language, religion, political or other opinion, national or social origin, association with a national minority, property, birth or other status.

Article 15   Derogation in time of emergency
1. In time of war or other public emergency threatening the life of the nation any High Contracting Party may take measures derogating from its obligations under this Convention to the extent strictly required by the exigencies of the situation, provided that such measures are not inconsistent with its other obligations under international law.

2. No derogation from Article 2, except in respect of deaths resulting from lawful acts of war, or from Articles 3, 4 (paragraph 1) and 7 shall be made under this provision.

3. Any High Contracting Party availing itself of this right of derogation shall keep the Secretary-General of the Council of Europe fully informed of the measures which it has taken and the reasons therefor. It shall also inform the Secretary-General of the Council of Europe when such measures have ceased to operate and the provisions of the Convention are again being fully executed.

Article 16   Restrictions on political activity of aliens
Nothing in Articles 10, 11, and 14 shall be regarded as preventing the High Contracting Parties from imposing restrictions on the political activity of aliens.

Article 17   Prohibition of abuse of rights
Nothing in this Convention may be interpreted as implying for any State, group or person any right to engage in any activity or perform any act aimed at the destruction of any of the rights and freedoms set forth herein or at their limitation to a greater extent than is provided for in the Convention.

Article 18   Limitation on use of restrictions on rights
The restrictions permitted under this Convention to the said rights and freedoms shall not be applied for any purpose other than those for which they have been prescribed.

Section II European Court of Human Rights

Article 19   Establishment of the Court
To ensure the observance of the engagements undertaken by the High Contracting Parties in the Convention and the protocols thereto, there shall be set up a European Court of Human Rights, hereinafter referred to as 'the Court'. It shall function on a permanent basis.

Article 20   Number of judges
The Court shall consist of a number of judges equal to that of the High Contracting Parties.

Article 21   Criteria for office

1. The judges shall be of high moral character and must either possess the qualifications required for appointment to high judicial office or be jurisconsults of recognised competence.

2. The judges shall sit on the Court in their individual capacity.

3. During their term of office the judges shall not engage in any activity which is incompatible with their independence, impartiality or with the demands of a full-time office; all questions arising from the application of this paragraph shall be decided by the Court.

Article 22   Election of judges

The judges shall be elected by the Parliamentary Assembly with respect to each High Contracting Party by a majority of votes cast from a list of three candidates nominated by the High Contracting Party.

Article 23   Terms of office and dismissal

1. The judges shall be elected for a period of nine years. They may not be re-elected.

2. The terms of office of judges shall expire when they reach the age of 70.

3. The judges shall hold office until replaced. They shall, however, continue to deal with such cases as they already have under consideration.

4. No judge may be dismissed from office unless the other judges decide by a majority of two-thirds that that judge has ceased to fulfil the required conditions.

Article 24   Registry and rapporteurs

1. The Court shall have a registry, the functions and organisation of which shall be laid down in the rules of the Court.

2. When sitting in a single-judge formation, the Court shall be assisted by rapporteurs who shall function under the authority of the President of the Court. They shall form part of the Court's registry.

Article 25   Plenary Court

The plenary Court shall

(a) elect its President and one or two Vice-Presidents for a period of three years; they may be re-elected;

(b) set up Chambers, constituted for a fixed period of time;

(c) elect the Presidents of the Chambers of the Court; they may be re-elected;

(d) adopt the rules of the Court;

(e) elect the Registrar and one or more Deputy Registrars;

(f) make any request under Article 26, paragraph 2.

Article 26   Single-judge formation, committees, Chambers and Grand Chamber

1. To consider cases brought before it, the Court shall sit in a single-judge formation, in committees of three judges, in Chambers of seven judges and in a Grand Chamber of seventeen judges. The Court's Chambers shall set up committees for a fixed period of time.

2. At the request of the plenary Court, the Committee of Ministers may, by a unanimous decision and for a fixed period, reduce to five the number of judges of the Chambers.

3. When sitting as a single judge, a judge shall not examine any application against the High Contracting Party in respect of which that judge has been elected.

4. There shall sit as an *ex officio member* of the Chamber and the Grand Chamber the judge elected in respect of the High Contracting Party concerned. If there is none or if that judge is unable to sit, a person chosen by the President of the Court from a list submitted in advance by that Party shall sit in the capacity of judge.

5. The Grand Chamber shall also include the President of the Court, the Vice-Presidents, the Presidents of the Chambers and other judges chosen in accordance with the rules of the Court. When a case is referred to the Grand Chamber under Article 43, no judge from the Chamber which rendered

the judgment shall sit in the Grand Chamber, with the exception of the President of the Chamber and the judge who sat in respect of the High Contracting Party concerned.

Article 27   Competence of single judges

1. A single judge may declare inadmissible or strike out of the Court's list of cases an application submitted under Article 34, where such a decision can be taken without further examination.

2. The decision shall be final.

3. If the single judge does not declare an application inadmissible or strike it out, that judge shall forward it to a committee or to a Chamber for further examination.

Article 28   Competence of committees

1. In respect of an application submitted under Article 34, a committee may, by a unanimous vote,

    (a) declare it inadmissible or strike it out of its list of cases, where such decision can be taken without further examination; or

    (b) declare it admissible and render at the same time a judgment on the merits, if the underlying question in the case, concerning the interpretation or the application of the Convention or the Protocols thereto, is already the subject of well-established case-law of the Court.

2. Decisions and judgments under paragraph 1 shall be final.

3. If the judge elected in respect of the High Contracting Party concerned is not a member of the committee, the committee may at any stage of the proceedings invite that judge to take the place of one of the members of the committee, having regard to all relevant factors, including whether that Party has contested the application of the procedure under paragraph 1.b.

Article 29   Decisions by Chambers on admissibility and merits

1. If no decision is taken under Article 27 or 28, or no judgment rendered under Article 28, a Chamber shall decide on the admissibility and merits of individual applications submitted under Article 34. The decision on admissibility may be taken separately.

2. A Chamber shall decide on the admissibility and merits of inter-State applications submitted under Article 33. The decision on admissibility shall be taken separately unless the Court, in exceptional cases, decides otherwise.

Article 30   Relinquishment of jurisdiction to the Grand Chamber

Where a case pending before a Chamber raises a serious question affecting the interpretation of the Convention or the protocols thereto, or where the resolution of a question before the Chamber might have a result inconsistent with a judgment previously delivered by the Court, the Chamber may, at any time before it has rendered its judgment, relinquish jurisdiction in favour of the Grand Chamber, unless one of the parties to the case objects.

Article 31   Powers of the Grand Chamber

The Grand Chamber shall:

    (a) determine applications submitted either under Article 33 or Article 34 when a Chamber has relinquished jurisdiction under Article 30 or when the case has been referred to it under Article 43;

    (b) decide on issues referred to the Court by the Committee of Ministers in accordance with Article 46, paragraph 4; and

    (c) consider requests for advisory opinions submitted in Article 47.

Article 32   Jurisdiction of the Court

1. The jurisdiction of the Court shall extend to all matters concerning the interpretation and application of the Convention and the protocols thereto which are referred to it as provided in Articles 33, 34 and 47.

2. In the event of dispute as to whether the Court has jurisdiction, the Court shall decide.

Article 33   Inter-State cases

Any High Contracting Party may refer to the Court any alleged breach of the provisions of the Convention and the protocols thereto by another High Contracting Party.

Article 34   Individual applications

The Court may receive applications from any person, non-governmental organisation or group of individuals claiming to be the victim of a violation by one of the High Contracting Parties of the rights set forth in the Convention or the protocols thereto. The High Contracting Parties undertake not to hinder in any way the effective exercise of this right.

Article 35   Admissibility criteria

1. The Court may only deal with the matter after all domestic remedies have been exhausted, according to the generally recognised rules of international law, and within a period of six months from the date on which the final decision was taken.

2. The Court shall not deal with any individual application submitted under Article 34 that:

    (a) is anonymous; or

    (b) is substantially the same as a matter that has already been examined by the Court or has already been submitted to another procedure of international investigation or settlement and contains no relevant new information.

3. The Court shall declare inadmissible any individual application submitted under Article 34 if it considers that:

    (a) the application is incompatible with the provisions of the Convention or the Protocols thereto, manifestly ill-founded, or an abuse of the right of individual application; or

    (b) the applicant has not suffered a significant disadvantage, unless respect for human rights as defined in the Convention and the Protocols thereto requires an examination of the application on the merits and provided that no case may be rejected on this ground which has not been duly considered by a domestic tribunal.

4. The Court shall reject any application which it considers inadmissible under this Article. It may do so at any stage of the proceedings.

Article 36   Third party intervention

1. In all cases before a Chamber or the Grand Chamber, a High Contracting Party one of whose nationals is an applicant shall have the right to submit written comments and to take part in hearings.

2. The President of the Court may, in the interest of the proper administration of justice, invite any High Contracting Party which is not a party to the proceedings or any person concerned who is not the applicant to submit written comments or take part in hearings.

3. In all cases before a Chamber of the Grand Chamber, the Council of Europe Commissioner for Human Rights may submit written comments and take part in hearings.

Article 37   Striking out applications

1. The Court may at any stage of the proceedings decide to strike an application out of its list of cases where the circumstances lead to the conclusion that:

    (a) the applicant does not intend to pursue his application; or

    (b) the matter has been resolved; or

    (c) for any other reason established by the Court, it is no longer justified to continue the examination of the application.

However, the Court shall continue the examination of the application if respect for human rights as defined in the Convention and the protocols thereto so requires.

2. The Court may decide to restore an application to its list of cases if it considers that the circumstances justify such a course.

Article 38   Examination of the case

The Court shall examine the case together with the representatives of the parties and, if need be, undertake an investigation, for the effective conduct of which the High Contracting Parties concerned shall furnish all necessary facilities.

Article 39   Friendly settlements

1. At any stage of the proceedings, the Court may place itself at the disposal of the parties concerned with a view to securing a friendly settlement of the matter on the basis of respect for human rights as defined in the Convention and the Protocols thereto.

2. Proceedings conducted under paragraph 1 shall be confidential.

3. If a friendly settlement is effected, the Court shall strike the case out of its list by means of a decision which shall be confined to a brief statement of the facts and of the solution reached.

4. This decision shall be transmitted to the Committee of Ministers, which shall supervise the execution of the terms of the friendly settlement as set out in the decision.

Article 40   Public hearings and access to documents

1. Hearings shall be public unless the Court in exceptional circumstances decides otherwise.

2. Documents deposited with the Registrar shall be accessible to the public unless the President of the Court decides otherwise.

Article 41   Just satisfaction

If the Court finds that there has been a violation of the Convention or the protocols thereto, and if the internal law of the High Contracting Party concerned allows only partial reparation to be made, the Court shall, if necessary, afford just satisfaction to the injured party.

Article 42   Judgments of Chambers

Judgments of Chambers shall become final in accordance with the provisions of Article 44, paragraph 2.

Article 43   Referral to the Grand Chamber

1. Within a period of three months from the date of the judgment of the Chamber, any party to the case may, in exceptional cases, request that the case be referred to the Grand Chamber.

2. A panel of five judges of the Grand Chamber shall accept the request if the case raises a serious question affecting the interpretation or application of the Convention or the protocols thereto, or a serious issue of general importance.

3. If the panel accepts the request, the Grand Chamber shall decide the case by means of a judgment.

Article 44   Final judgments

1. The judgment of the Grand Chamber shall be final.

2. The judgment of a Chamber shall become final:
    (a) when the parties declare that they will not request that the case be referred to the Grand Chamber; or
    (b) three months after the date of the judgment, if reference of the case to the Grand Chamber has not been requested; or
    (c) when the panel of the Grand Chamber rejects the request to refer under Article 43.

3. The final judgment shall be published.

Article 45   Reasons for judgments and decisions

1. Reasons shall be given for judgments as well as for decisions declaring applications admissible or inadmissible.

2. If a judgment does not represent, in whole or in part, the unanimous opinion of the judges, any judge shall be entitled to deliver a separate opinion.

Article 46   Binding force and execution of judgments

1. The High Contracting Parties undertake to abide by the final judgment of the Court in any case to which they are parties.

2. The final judgment of the Court shall be transmitted to the Committee of Ministers, which shall supervise its execution.

3. If the Committee of Ministers considers that the supervision of the execution of a final judgment is hindered by a problem of interpretation of the judgment, it may refer the matter to the Court for a ruling on the question of interpretation. A referral decision shall require a majority vote of two thirds of the representatives entitled to sit on the Committee.

4. If the Committee of Ministers considers that a High Contracting Party refuses to abide by a final judgment in a case to which it is a party, it may, after serving formal notice on that Party and by decision adopted by a majority vote of two thirds of the representatives entitled to sit on the Committee, refer to the Court the question whether that Party has failed to fulfil its obligation under paragraph 1.

5. If the Court finds a violation of paragraph 1, it shall refer the case to the Committee of Ministers for consideration of the measures to be taken. If the Court finds no violation of paragraph 1, it shall refer the case to the Committee of Ministers, which shall close its examination of the case.

Article 47 Advisory opinions

1. The Court may, at the request of the Committee of Ministers, give advisory opinions on legal questions concerning the interpretation of the Convention and the protocols thereto.

2. Such opinions shall not deal with any question relating to the content or scope of the rights or freedoms defined in Section I of the Convention and the protocols thereto, or with any other question which the Court or the Committee of Ministers might have to consider in consequence of any such proceedings as could be instituted in accordance with the Convention.

3. Decisions of the Committee of Ministers to request an advisory opinion of the Court shall require a majority vote of the representatives entitled to sit on the Committee.

Article 48 Advisory jurisdiction of the Court

The Court shall decide whether a request for an advisory opinion submitted by the Committee of Ministers is within its competence as defined in Article 47.

Article 49 Reasons for advisory opinions

1. Reasons shall be given for advisory opinions of the Court.

2. If the advisory opinion does not represent, in whole or in part, the unanimous opinion of the judges, any judge shall be entitled to deliver a separate opinion.

3. Advisory opinions of the Court shall be communicated to the Committee of Ministers.

Article 50 Expenditure on the Court

The expenditure on the Court shall be borne by the Council of Europe.

Article 51 Privileges and immunities of judges

The judges shall be entitled, during the exercise of their functions, to the privileges and immunities provided for in Article 40 of the Statute of the Council of Europe and in the agreements made thereunder.

Section III Miscellaneous Provisions

Article 52 *****

Article 53 Safeguard for existing human rights

Nothing in this Convention shall be construed as limiting or derogating from any of the human rights and fundamental freedoms which may be ensured under the laws of any High Contracting Party or under any other agreement to which it is a Party.

Articles 54–56 *****

Article 57 Reservations

1. Any State may, when signing this Convention or when depositing its instrument of ratification, make a reservation in respect of any particular provision of the Convention to the extent that any law then in force in its territory is not in conformity with the provision. Reservations of a general character shall not be permitted under this article.

2. Any reservation made under this article shall contain a brief statement of the law concerned.
*****

Protocols

Enforcement of certain Rights and Freedoms not included in Section I of the Convention

The Governments signatory hereto, being Members of the Council of Europe,

Being resolved to take steps to ensure the collective enforcement of certain rights and freedoms other than those already included in Section I of the Convention for the Protection of Human Rights and Fundamental Freedoms signed at Rome on 4th November 1950 (herein-after referred to as 'the Convention'),

Have agreed as follows:

Article 1   Protection of property

Every natural or legal person is entitled to the peaceful enjoyment of his possessions. No one shall be deprived of his possessions except in the public interest and subject to the conditions provided for by law and by the general principles of international law.

The preceding provisions shall not, however, in any way impair the right of a State to enforce such laws as it deems necessary to control the use of property in accordance with the general interest or to secure the payment of taxes or other contributions or penalties.

Article 2   Right to education

No person shall be denied the right to education. In the exercise of any functions which it assumes in relation to education and to teaching, the State shall respect the right of parents to ensure such education and teaching in conformity with their own religious and philosophical convictions.

Article 3   Right to free elections

The High Contracting Parties undertake to hold free elections at reasonable intervals by secret ballot, under conditions which will ensure the free expression of the opinion of the people in the choice of the legislature.

*****

4.   Protecting certain additional rights

The Governments signatory hereto, being Members of the Council of Europe.

Being resolved to take steps to ensure the collective enforcement of certain rights and freedoms other than those already included in Section I of the Convention for the Protection of Human Rights and Fundamental Freedoms signed at Rome on 4 November 1950 (hereinafter referred to as 'the Convention') and in Articles 1 to 3 of the First Protocol to the Convention, signed at Paris on 20 March 1952,

Have agreed as follows:

Article 1   Prohibition of imprisonment for debt

No one shall be deprived of his liberty merely on the ground of inability to fulfil a contractual obligation.

Article 2   Freedom of movement

1. Everyone lawfully within the territory of a State shall, within that territory, have the right to liberty of movement and freedom to choose his residence.

2. Everyone shall be free to leave any country, including his own.

3. No restrictions shall be placed on the exercise of these rights other than such as are in accordance with law and are necessary in a democratic society in the interests of national security or public safety, for the maintenance of 'order public', for the prevention of crime, for the protection of the rights and freedoms of others.

4. The rights set forth in paragraph 1 may also be subject, in particular areas, to restrictions imposed in accordance with law and justified by the public interest in a democratic society.

Article 3   Prohibition of expulsion of nationals

1. No one shall be expelled, by means either of an individual or of a collective measure, from the territory of the State of which he is a national.

2. No one shall be deprived of the right to enter the territory of the State of which he is a national.

Article 4   Prohibition of collective expulsion of aliens
Collective expulsion of aliens is prohibited.
*****
[**Note:** This Protocol has not yet been ratified by the United Kingdom.]

13.   The Death Penalty

Article 1   Abolition of the death penalty
The death penalty shall be abolished. No one shall be condemned to such penalty or executed.
*****

International Covenant on Civil and Political Rights (December 1966)*

Preamble

The States Parties to the present Covenant,

Considering that, in accordance with the principles proclaimed in the Charter of the United Nations, recognition of the inherent dignity and of the equal and inalienable rights of all members of the human family is the foundation of freedom, justice and peace in the world,

Recognizing that these rights derive from the inherent dignity of the human person,

Recognizing that, in accordance with the Universal Declaration of Human Rights, the ideal of free human beings enjoying civil and political freedom and freedom from fear and want can only be achieved if conditions are created whereby everyone may enjoy his civil and political rights, as well as his economic, social and cultural rights,

Considering the obligation of States under the Charter of the United Nations to promote universal respect for, and observance of, human rights and freedoms,

Realizing that the individual, having duties to other individuals and to the community to which he belongs, is under a responsibility to strive for the promotion and observance of the rights recognized in the present Covenant,

Agree upon the following articles:

Part I

Article 1
1. All peoples have the right of self-determination. By virtue of that right they freely determine their political status and freely pursue their economic, social and cultural development.

2. All peoples may, for their own ends, freely dispose of their natural wealth and resources without prejudice to any obligations arising out of international economic co-operation, based upon the principle of mutual benefit, and international law. In no case may a people be deprived of its own means of subsistence.

3. The States Parties to the present Covenant, including those having responsibility for the administration of Non-Self-Governing and Trust Territories, shall promote the realization of the right of self-determination, and shall respect that right, in conformity with the provisions of the Charter of the United Nations.

---

* This document has been reproduced from the website for the Office of the High Commission of Human Rights (OHCHR): http://www.ohchr.org/

Part II

Article 2

1. Each State Party to the present Covenant undertakes to respect and to ensure to all individuals within its territory and subject to its jurisdiction the rights recognized in the present Covenant, without distinction of any kind, such as race, colour, sex, language, religion, political or other opinion, national or social origin, property, birth or other status.

2. Where not already provided for by existing legislative or other measures, each State Party to the present Covenant undertakes to take the necessary steps, in accordance with its constitutional processes and with the provisions of the present Covenant, to adopt such laws or other measures as may be necessary to give effect to the rights recognized in the present Covenant.

3. Each State Party to the present Covenant undertakes:

   (a) To ensure that any person whose rights or freedoms as herein recognized are violated shall have an effective remedy, notwithstanding that the violation has been committed by persons acting in an official capacity;

   (b) To ensure that any person claiming such a remedy shall have his right thereto determined by competent judicial, administrative or legislative authorities, or by any other competent authority provided for by the legal system of the State, and to develop the possibilities of judicial remedy;

   (c) To ensure that the competent authorities shall enforce such remedies when granted.

Article 3

The States Parties to the present Covenant undertake to ensure the equal right of men and women to the enjoyment of all civil and political rights set forth in the present Covenant.

Article 4

1. In time of public emergency which threatens the life of the nation and the existence of which is officially proclaimed, the States Parties to the present Covenant may take measures derogating from their obligations under the present Covenant to the extent strictly required by the exigencies of the situation, provided that such measures are not inconsistent with their other obligations under international law and do not involve discrimination solely on the ground of race, colour, sex, language, religion or social origin.

2. No derogation from articles 6, 7, 8 (paragraphs 1 and 2), 11, 15, 16 and 18 may be made under this provision.

3. Any State Party to the present Covenant availing itself of the right of derogation shall immediately inform the other States Parties to the present Covenant, through the intermediary of the Secretary-General of the United Nations, of the provisions from which it has derogated and of the reasons by which it was actuated. A further communication shall be made, through the same intermediary, on the date on which it terminates such derogation.

Article 5

1. Nothing in the present Covenant may be interpreted as implying for any State, group or person any right to engage in any activity or perform any act aimed at the destruction of any of the rights and freedoms recognized herein or at their limitation to a greater extent than is provided for in the present Covenant.

2. There shall be no restriction upon or derogation from any of the fundamental human rights recognized or existing in any State Party to the present Covenant pursuant to law, conventions, regulations or custom on the pretext that the present Covenant does not recognize such rights or that it recognizes them to a lesser extent.

Part III

Article 6

1. Every human being has the inherent right to life. This right shall be protected by law. No one shall be arbitrarily deprived of his life.

2. In countries which have not abolished the death penalty, sentence of death may be imposed only for the most serious crimes in accordance with the law in force at the time of the commission of the crime and not contrary to the provisions of the present Covenant and to the Convention on the Prevention and Punishment of the Crime of Genocide. This penalty can only be carried out pursuant to a final judgement rendered by a competent court.

3. When deprivation of life constitutes the crime of genocide, it is understood that nothing in this article shall authorize any State Party to the present Covenant to derogate in any way from any obligation assumed under the provisions of the Convention on the Prevention and Punishment of the Crime of Genocide.

4. Anyone sentenced to death shall have the right to seek pardon or commutation of the sentence. Amnesty, pardon or commutation of the sentence of death may be granted in all cases.

5. Sentence of death shall not be imposed for crimes committed by persons below eighteen years of age and shall not be carried out on pregnant women.

6. Nothing in this article shall be invoked to delay or to prevent the abolition of capital punishment by any State Party to the present Covenant.

Article 7

No one shall be subjected to torture or to cruel, inhuman or degrading treatment or punishment. In particular, no one shall be subjected without his free consent to medical or scientific experimentation.

Article 8

1. No one shall be held in slavery; slavery and the slave-trade in all their forms shall be prohibited.

2. No one shall be held in servitude.

3. (a) No one shall be required to perform forced or compulsory labour;

    (b) Paragraph 3 (a) shall not be held to preclude, in countries where imprisonment with hard labour may be imposed as a punishment for a crime, the performance of hard labour in pursuance of a sentence to such punishment by a competent court;

    (c) For the purpose of this paragraph the term 'forced or compulsory labour' shall not include:

        (i) Any work or service, not referred to in subparagraph (b), normally required of a person who is under detention in consequence of a lawful order of a court, or of a person during conditional release from such detention;

        (ii) Any service of a military character and, in countries where conscientious objection is recognized, any national service required by law of conscientious objectors;

        (iii) Any service exacted in cases of emergency or calamity threatening the life or well-being of the community;

        (iv) Any work or service which forms part of normal civil obligations.

Article 9

1. Everyone has the right to liberty and security of person. No one shall be subjected to arbitrary arrest or detention. No one shall be deprived of his liberty except on such grounds and in accordance with such procedure as are established by law.

2. Anyone who is arrested shall be informed, at the time of arrest, of the reasons for his arrest and shall be promptly informed of any charges against him.

3. Anyone arrested or detained on a criminal charge shall be brought promptly before a judge or other officer authorized by law to exercise judicial power and shall be entitled to trial within a reasonable time or to release. It shall not be the general rule that persons awaiting trial shall be detained in custody, but release may be subject to guarantees to appear for trial, at any other stage of the judicial proceedings, and, should occasion arise, for execution of the judgement.

4. Anyone who is deprived of his liberty by arrest or detention shall be entitled to take proceedings before a court, in order that court may decide without delay on the lawfulness of his detention and order his release if the detention is not lawful.

5. Anyone who has been the victim of unlawful arrest or detention shall have an enforceable right to compensation.

Article 10

1. All persons deprived of their liberty shall be treated with humanity and with respect for the inherent dignity of the human person.

2. (a) Accused persons shall, save in exceptional circumstances, be segregated from convicted persons and shall be subject to separate treatment appropriate to their status as unconvicted persons;

(b) Accused juvenile persons shall be separated from adults and brought as speedily as possible for adjudication.

3. The penitentiary system shall comprise treatment of prisoners the essential aim of which shall be their reformation and social rehabilitation. Juvenile offenders shall be segregated from adults and be accorded treatment appropriate to their age and legal status.

Article 11

No one shall be imprisoned merely on the ground of inability to fulfil a contractual obligation.

Article 12

1. Everyone lawfully within the territory of a State shall, within that territory, have the right to liberty of movement and freedom to choose his residence.

2. Everyone shall be free to leave any country, including his own.

3. The above-mentioned rights shall not be subject to any restrictions except those which are provided by law, are necessary to protect national security, public order (ordre public), public health or morals or the rights and freedoms of others, and are consistent with the other rights recognized in the present Covenant.

4. No one shall be arbitrarily deprived of the right to enter his own country.

Article 13

An alien lawfully in the territory of a State Party to the present Covenant may be expelled therefrom only in pursuance of a decision reached in accordance with law and shall, except where compelling reasons of national security otherwise require, be allowed to submit the reasons against his expulsion and to have his case reviewed by, and be represented for the purpose before, the competent authority or a person or persons especially designated by the competent authority.

Article 14

1. All persons shall be equal before the courts and tribunals. In the determination of any criminal charge against him, or of his rights and obligations in a suit at law, everyone shall be entitled to a fair and public hearing by a competent, independent and impartial tribunal established by law. The press and the public may be excluded from all or part of a trial for reasons of morals, public order (ordre public) or national security in a democratic society, or when the interest of the private lives of the parties so requires, or to the extent strictly necessary in the opinion of the court in special circumstances where publicity would prejudice the interests of justice; but any judgement rendered in a criminal case or in a suit at law shall be made public except where the interest of juvenile persons otherwise requires or the proceedings concern matrimonial disputes or the guardianship of children.

2. Everyone charged with a criminal offence shall have the right to be presumed innocent until proved guilty according to law.

3. In the determination of any criminal charge against him, everyone shall be entitled to the following minimum guarantees, in full equality:

(a) To be informed promptly and in detail in a language which he understands of the nature and cause of the charge against him;

(b) To have adequate time and facilities for the preparation of his defence and to communicate with counsel of his own choosing;

(c) To be tried without undue delay;

   (d) To be tried in his presence, and to defend himself in person or through legal assistance of his own choosing; to be informed, if he does not have legal assistance, of this right; and to have legal assistance assigned to him, in any case where the interests of justice so require, and without payment by him in any such case if he does not have sufficient means to pay for it;

   (e) To examine, or have examined, the witnesses against him and to obtain the attendance and examination of witnesses on his behalf under the same conditions as witnesses against him;

   (f) To have the free assistance of an interpreter if he cannot understand or speak the language used in court;

   (g) Not to be compelled to testify against himself or to confess guilt.

   4. In the case of juvenile persons, the procedure shall be such as will take account of their age and the desirability of promoting their rehabilitation.

   5. Everyone convicted of a crime shall have the right to his conviction and sentence being reviewed by a higher tribunal according to law.

   6. When a person has by a final decision been convicted of a criminal offence and when subsequently his conviction has been reversed or he has been pardoned on the ground that a new or newly discovered fact shows conclusively that there has been a miscarriage of justice, the person who has suffered punishment as a result of such conviction shall be compensated according to law, unless it is proved that the non-disclosure of the unknown fact in time is wholly or partly attributable to him.

   7. No one shall be liable to be tried or punished again for an offence for which he has already been finally convicted or acquitted in accordance with the law and penal procedure of each country.

Article 15

   1. No one shall be held guilty of any criminal offence on account of any act or omission which did not constitute a criminal offence, under national or international law, at the time when it was committed. Nor shall a heavier penalty be imposed than the one that was applicable at the time when the criminal offence was committed. If, subsequent to the commission of the offence, provision is made by law for the imposition of the lighter penalty, the offender shall benefit thereby.

   2. Nothing in this article shall prejudice the trial and punishment of any person for any act or omission which, at the time when it was committed, was criminal according to the general principles of law recognized by the community of nations.

Article 16

Everyone shall have the right to recognition everywhere as a person before the law.

Article 17

   1. No one shall be subjected to arbitrary or unlawful interference with his privacy, family, home or correspondence, nor to unlawful attacks on his honour and reputation.

   2. Everyone has the right to the protection of the law against such interference or attacks.

Article 18

   1. Everyone shall have the right to freedom of thought, conscience and religion. This right shall include freedom to have or to adopt a religion or belief of his choice, and freedom, either individually or in community with others and in public or private, to manifest his religion or belief in worship, observance, practice and teaching.

   2. No one shall be subject to coercion which would impair his freedom to have or to adopt a religion or belief of his choice.

   3. Freedom to manifest one's religion or beliefs may be subject only to such limitations as are prescribed by law and are necessary to protect public safety, order, health, or morals or the fundamental rights and freedoms of others.

   4. The States Parties to the present Covenant undertake to have respect for the liberty of parents and, when applicable, legal guardians to ensure the religious and moral education of their children in conformity with their own convictions.

Article 19

1. Everyone shall have the right to hold opinions without interference.

2. Everyone shall have the right to freedom of expression; this right shall include freedom to seek, receive and impart information and ideas of all kinds, regardless of frontiers, either orally, in writing or in print, in the form of art, or through any other media of his choice.

3. The exercise of the rights provided for in paragraph 2 of this article carries with it special duties and responsibilities. It may therefore be subject to certain restrictions, but these shall only be such as are provided by law and are necessary:

    (a) For respect of the rights or reputations of others;

    (b) For the protection of national security or of public order (ordre public), or of public health or morals.

Article 20

1. Any propaganda for war shall be prohibited by law.

2. Any advocacy of national, racial or religious hatred that constitutes incitement to discrimination, hostility or violence shall be prohibited by law.

Article 21

The right of peaceful assembly shall be recognized. No restrictions may be placed on the exercise of this right other than those imposed in conformity with the law and which are necessary in a democratic society in the interests of national security or public safety, public order (ordre public), the protection of public health or morals or the protection of the rights and freedoms of others.

Article 22

1. Everyone shall have the right to freedom of association with others, including the right to form and join trade unions for the protection of his interests.

2. No restrictions may be placed on the exercise of this right other than those which are prescribed by law and which are necessary in a democratic society in the interests of national security or public safety, public order (ordre public), the protection of public health or morals or the protection of the rights and freedoms of others. This article shall not prevent the imposition of lawful restrictions on members of the armed forces and of the police in their exercise of this right.

3. Nothing in this article shall authorize States Parties to the International Labour Organisation Convention of 1948 concerning Freedom of Association and Protection of the Right to Organize to take legislative measures which would prejudice, or to apply the law in such a manner as to prejudice, the guarantees provided for in that Convention.

Article 23

1. The family is the natural and fundamental group unit of society and is entitled to protection by society and the State.

2. The right of men and women of marriageable age to marry and to found a family shall be recognized.

3. No marriage shall be entered into without the free and full consent of the intending spouses.

4. States Parties to the present Covenant shall take appropriate steps to ensure equality of rights and responsibilities of spouses as to marriage, during marriage and at its dissolution. In the case of dissolution, provision shall be made for the necessary protection of any children.

Article 24

1. Every child shall have, without any discrimination as to race, colour, sex, language, religion, national or social origin, property or birth, the right to such measures of protection as are required by his status as a minor, on the part of his family, society and the State.

2. Every child shall be registered immediately after birth and shall have a name.

3. Every child has the right to acquire a nationality.

Article 25

Every citizen shall have the right and the opportunity, without any of the distinctions mentioned in article 2 and without unreasonable restrictions:

    (a) To take part in the conduct of public affairs, directly or through freely chosen representatives;

    (b) To vote and to be elected at genuine periodic elections which shall be by universal and equal suffrage and shall be held by secret ballot, guaranteeing the free expression of the will of the electors;

    (c) To have access, on general terms of equality, to public service in his country.

Article 26

All persons are equal before the law and are entitled without any discrimination the equal protection of the law. In this respect, the law shall prohibit any discrimination and guarantee to all persons equal and effective protection against discrimination on any ground such as race, colour, sex, language, religion, political or other opinion, national or social origin, property, birth or other status.

Article 27

In those States in which ethnic, religious or linguistic minorities exist, persons belonging to such minorities shall not be denied the right, in community with the other members of their group, to enjoy their own culture, to profess and practise their own religion, or to use their own language.

Articles 28–53   *****

Consolidated versions of the Treaty on European Union and the Treaty on the Functioning of the European Union

[**Note**: This is the consolidated version of both the Treaty on European Union and the Treaty on the Functioning of the European Union as amended by the Treaty of Lisbon, signed on 13 December 2007 in Lisbon.]

CONSOLIDATED VERSION OF THE TREATY ON EUROPEAN UNION

Title I Common Provisions

Article 1

By this Treaty, the HIGH CONTRACTING PARTIES establish among themselves a EUROPEAN UNION, hereinafter called 'the Union' on which the Member States confer competences to attain objectives they have in common.

This Treaty marks a new stage in the process of creating an ever closer union among the peoples of Europe, in which decisions are taken as openly as possible and as closely as possible to the citizen.

The Union shall be founded on the present Treaty and on the Treaty on the Functioning of the European Union (hereinafter referred to as 'the Treaties'). Those two Treaties shall have the same legal value. The Union shall replace and succeed the European Community.

Article 2

The Union is founded on the values of respect for human dignity, freedom, democracy, equality, the rule of law and respect for human rights, including the rights of persons belonging to minorities. These values are common to the Member States in a society in which pluralism, non-discrimination, tolerance, justice, solidarity and equality between women and men prevail.

Article 3

    1. The Union's aim is to promote peace, its values and the well-being of its peoples.

2. The Union shall offer its citizens an area of freedom, security and justice without internal frontiers, in which the free movement of persons is ensured in conjunction with appropriate measures with respect to external border controls, asylum, immigration and the prevention and combating of crime.

3. The Union shall establish an internal market. It shall work for the sustainable development of Europe based on balanced economic growth and price stability, a highly competitive social market economy, aiming at full employment and social progress, and a high level of protection and improvement of the quality of the environment. It shall promote scientific and technological advance.

It shall combat social exclusion and discrimination, and shall promote social justice and protection, equality between women and men, solidarity between generations and protection of the rights of the child.

It shall promote economic, social and territorial cohesion, and solidarity among Member States.

It shall respect its rich cultural and linguistic diversity, and shall ensure that Europe's cultural heritage is safeguarded and enhanced.

4. The Union shall establish an economic and monetary union whose currency is the euro.

5. In its relations with the wider world, the Union shall uphold and promote its values and interests and contribute to the protection of its citizens. It shall contribute to peace, security, the sustainable development of the Earth, solidarity and mutual respect among peoples, free and fair trade, eradication of poverty and the protection of human rights, in particular the rights of the child, as well as to the strict observance and the development of international law, including respect for the principles of the United Nations Charter.

6. The Union shall pursue its objectives by appropriate means commensurate with the competences which are conferred upon it in the Treaties.

Article 4 *****

Article 5

1. The limits of Union competences are governed by the principle of conferral. The use of Union competences is governed by the principles of subsidiarity and proportionality.

2. Under the principle of conferral, the Union shall act only within the limits of the competences conferred upon it by the Member States in the Treaties to attain the objectives set out therein.

Competences not conferred upon the Union in the Treaties remain with the Member States.

3. Under the principle of subsidiarity, in areas which do not fall within its exclusive competence, the Union shall act only if and in so far as the objectives of the proposed action cannot be sufficiently achieved by the Member States, either at central level or at regional and local level, but can rather, by reason of the scale or effects of the proposed action, be better achieved at Union level.

The institutions of the Union shall apply the principle of subsidiarity as laid down in the Protocol on the application of the principles of subsidiarity and proportionality. National Parliaments ensure compliance with the principle of subsidiarity in accordance with the procedure set out in that Protocol.

4. Under the principle of proportionality, the content and form of Union action shall not exceed what is necessary to achieve the objectives of the Treaties.

The institutions of the Union shall apply the principle of proportionality as laid down in the Protocol on the application of the principles of subsidiarity and proportionality.

Article 6

1. The Union recognises the rights, freedoms and principles set out in the Charter of Fundamental Rights of the European Union of 7 December 2000, as adapted at Strasbourg, on 12 December 2007, which shall have the same legal value as the Treaties.

The provisions of the Charter shall not extend in any way the competences of the Union as defined in the Treaties.

The rights, freedoms and principles in the Charter shall be interpreted in accordance with the general provisions in Title VII of the Charter governing its interpretation and application and with due regard to the explanations referred to in the Charter, that set out the sources of those provisions.

2. The Union shall accede to the European Convention for the Protection of Human Rights and Fundamental Freedoms. Such accession shall not affect the Union's competences as defined in the Treaties.

3. Fundamental rights, as guaranteed by the European Convention for the Protection of Human Rights and Fundamental Freedoms and as they result from the constitutional traditions common to the Member States, shall constitute general principles of the Union's law.

Articles 7–10 *****

Article 11

1. The institutions shall, by appropriate means, give citizens and representative associations the opportunity to make known and publicly exchange their views in all areas of Union action.

2. The institutions shall maintain an open, transparent and regular dialogue with representative associations and civil society.

3. The European Commission shall carry out broad consultations with parties concerned in order to ensure that the Union's actions are coherent and transparent.

4. Not less than one million citizens who are nationals of a significant number of Member States may take the initiative of inviting the European Commission, within the framework of its powers, to submit any appropriate proposal on matters where citizens consider that a legal act of the Union is required for the purpose of implementing the Treaties.

The procedures and conditions required for such a citizens' initiative shall be determined in accordance with the first paragraph of Article 24 of the Treaty on the Functioning of the European Union.

Article 12 *****

Title III Provisions on the Institutions

Article 13

1. The Union shall have an institutional framework which shall aim to promote its values, advance its objectives, serve its interests, those of its citizens and those of the Member States, and ensure the consistency, effectiveness and continuity of its policies and actions.

The Union's institutions shall be:
- the European Parliament,
- the European Council,
- the Council,
- the European Commission (hereinafter referred to as 'the Commission'),
- the Court of Justice of the European Union,
- the European Central Bank,
- the Court of Auditors.

2. Each institution shall act within the limits of the powers conferred on it in the Treaties, and in conformity with the procedures, conditions and objectives set out in them. The institutions shall practice mutual sincere cooperation.

3. The provisions relating to the European Central Bank and the Court of Auditors and detailed provisions on the other institutions are set out in the Treaty on the Functioning of the European Union.

4. The European Parliament, the Council and the Commission shall be assisted by an Economic and Social Committee and a Committee of the Regions acting in an advisory capacity.

Article 14

1. The European Parliament shall, jointly with the Council, exercise legislative and budgetary functions. It shall exercise functions of political control and consultation as laid down in the Treaties. It shall elect the President of the Commission.

2. The European Parliament shall be composed of representatives of the Union's citizens. They shall not exceed seven hundred and fifty in number, plus the President. Representation of citizens

shall be degressively proportional, with a minimum threshold of six members per Member State. No Member State shall be allocated more than ninety-six seats.

The European Council shall adopt by unanimity, on the initiative of the European Parliament and with its consent, a decision establishing the composition of the European Parliament, respecting the principles referred to in the first subparagraph.

3. The members of the European Parliament shall be elected for a term of five years by direct universal suffrage in a free and secret ballot.

4. The European Parliament shall elect its President and its officers from among its members.

Article 15

1. The European Council shall provide the Union with the necessary impetus for its development and shall define the general political directions and priorities thereof. It shall not exercise legislative functions.

2. The European Council shall consist of the Heads of State or Government of the Member States, together with its President and the President of the Commission. The High Representative of the Union for Foreign Affairs and Security Policy shall take part in its work.

3. The European Council shall meet twice every six months, convened by its President. When the agenda so requires, the members of the European Council may decide each to be assisted by a minister and, in the case of the President of the Commission, by a member of the Commission. When the situation so requires, the President shall convene a special meeting of the European Council.

4. Except where the Treaties provide otherwise, decisions of the European Council shall be taken by consensus.

5. The European Council shall elect its President, by a qualified majority, for a term of two and a half years, renewable once. In the event of an impediment or serious misconduct, the European Council can end the President's term of office in accordance with the same procedure.

6. The President of the European Council:
   (a) shall chair it and drive forward its work;
   (b) shall ensure the preparation and continuity of the work of the European Council in cooperation with the President of the Commission, and on the basis of the work of the General Affairs Council;
   (c) shall endeavour to facilitate cohesion and consensus within the European Council;
   (d) shall present a report to the European Parliament after each of the meetings of the European Council.

The President of the European Council shall, at his level and in that capacity, ensure the external representation of the Union on issues concerning its common foreign and security policy, without prejudice to the powers of the High Representative of the Union for Foreign Affairs and Security Policy.

The President of the European Council shall not hold a national office.

Article 16

1. The Council shall, jointly with the European Parliament, exercise legislative and budgetary functions. It shall carry out policy-making and coordinating functions as laid down in the Treaties.

2. The Council shall consist of a representative of each Member State at ministerial level, who may commit the government of the Member State in question and cast its vote.

3. The Council shall act by a qualified majority except where the Treaties provide otherwise.

4. As from 1 November 2014, a qualified majority shall be defined as at least 55 % of the members of the Council, comprising at least fifteen of them and representing Member States comprising at least 65% of the population of the Union.

A blocking minority must include at least four Council members, failing which the qualified majority shall be deemed attained.

The other arrangements governing the qualified majority are laid down in Article 238(2) of the Treaty on the Functioning of the European Union.

5. The transitional provisions relating to the definition of the qualified majority which shall be applicable until 31 October 2014 and those which shall be applicable from 1 November 2014 to 31 March 2017 are laid down in the Protocol on transitional provisions.

6. The Council shall meet in different configurations, the list of which shall be adopted in accordance with Article 236 of the Treaty on the Functioning of the European Union.

The General Affairs Council shall ensure consistency in the work of the different Council configurations. It shall prepare and ensure the follow-up to meetings of the European Council, in liaison with the President of the European Council and the Commission.

The Foreign Affairs Council shall elaborate the Union's external action on the basis of strategic guidelines laid down by the European Council and ensure that the Union's action is consistent.

7. A Committee of Permanent Representatives of the Governments of the Member States shall be responsible for preparing the work of the Council.

8. The Council shall meet in public when it deliberates and votes on a draft legislative act. To this end, each Council meeting shall be divided into two parts, dealing respectively with deliberations on Union legislative acts and non-legislative activities.

9. The Presidency of Council configurations, other than that of Foreign Affairs, shall be held by Member State representatives in the Council on the basis of equal rotation, in accordance with the conditions established in accordance with Article 236 of the Treaty on the Functioning of the European Union.

Article 17

1. The Commission shall promote the general interest of the Union and take appropriate initiatives to that end. It shall ensure the application of the Treaties, and of measures adopted by the institutions pursuant to them. It shall oversee the application of Union law under the control of the Court of Justice of the European Union. It shall execute the budget and manage programmes. It shall exercise coordinating, executive and management functions, as laid down in the Treaties. With the exception of the common foreign and security policy, and other cases provided for in the Treaties, it shall ensure the Union's external representation. It shall initiate the Union's annual and multiannual programming with a view to achieving interinstitutional agreements.

2. Union legislative acts may only be adopted on the basis of a Commission proposal, except where the Treaties provide otherwise. Other acts shall be adopted on the basis of a Commission proposal where the Treaties so provide.

3. The Commission's term of office shall be five years.

The members of the Commission shall be chosen on the ground of their general competence and European commitment from persons whose independence is beyond doubt.

In carrying out its responsibilities, the Commission shall be completely independent. Without prejudice to Article 18(2), the members of the Commission shall neither seek nor take instructions from any Government or other institution, body, office or entity. They shall refrain from any action incompatible with their duties or the performance of their tasks.

4. The Commission appointed between the date of entry into force of the Treaty of Lisbon and 31 October 2014, shall consist of one national of each Member State, including its President and the High Representative of the Union for Foreign Affairs and Security Policy who shall be one of its Vice-Presidents.

5. As from 1 November 2014, the Commission shall consist of a number of members, including its President and the High Representative of the Union for Foreign Affairs and Security Policy, corresponding to two thirds of the number of Member States, unless the European Council, acting unanimously, decides to alter this number.

The members of the Commission shall be chosen from among the nationals of the Member States on the basis of a system of strictly equal rotation between the Member States, reflecting the demographic and geographical range of all the Member States. This system shall be established unanimously by the European Council in accordance with Article 244 of the Treaty on the Functioning of the European Union.

6. The President of the Commission shall:

    (a) lay down guidelines within which the Commission is to work;

    (b) decide on the internal organisation of the Commission, ensuring that it acts consistently, efficiently and as a collegiate body;

    (c) appoint Vice-Presidents, other than the High Representative of the Union for Foreign Affairs and Security Policy, from among the members of the Commission.

A member of the Commission shall resign if the President so requests. The High Representative of the Union for Foreign Affairs and Security Policy shall resign, in accordance with the procedure set out in Article 18(1), if the President so requests.

7. Taking into account the elections to the European Parliament and after having held the appropriate consultations, the European Council, acting by a qualified majority, shall propose to the European Parliament a candidate for President of the Commission. This candidate shall be elected by the European Parliament by a majority of its component members. If he does not obtain the required majority, the European Council, acting by a qualified majority, shall within one month propose a new candidate who shall be elected by the European Parliament following the same procedure.

The Council, by common accord with the President-elect, shall adopt the list of the other persons whom it proposes for appointment as members of the Commission. They shall be selected, on the basis of the suggestions made by Member States, in accordance with the criteria set out in paragraph 3, second subparagraph, and paragraph 5, second subparagraph.

The President, the High Representative of the Union for Foreign Affairs and Security Policy and the other members of the Commission shall be subject as a body to a vote of consent by the European Parliament. On the basis of this consent the Commission shall be appointed by the European Council, acting by a qualified majority.

8. The Commission, as a body, shall be responsible to the European Parliament. In accordance with Article 234 of the Treaty on the Functioning of the European Union, the European Parliament may vote on a motion of censure of the Commission. If such a motion is carried, the members of the Commission shall resign as a body and the High Representative of the Union for Foreign Affairs and Security Policy shall resign from the duties that he carries out in the Commission.

Article 18

1. The European Council, acting by a qualified majority, with the agreement of the President of the Commission, shall appoint the High Representative of the Union for Foreign Affairs and Security Policy. The European Council may end his term of office by the same procedure.

2. The High Representative shall conduct the Union's common foreign and security policy. He shall contribute by his proposals to the development of that policy, which he shall carry out as mandated by the Council. The same shall apply to the common security and defence policy.

3. The High Representative shall preside over the Foreign Affairs Council.

4. The High Representative shall be one of the Vice-Presidents of the Commission. He shall ensure the consistency of the Union's external action. He shall be responsible within the Commission for responsibilities incumbent on it in external relations and for coordinating other aspects of the Union's external action. In exercising these responsibilities within the Commission, and only for these responsibilities, the High Representative shall be bound by Commission procedures to the extent that this is consistent with paragraphs 2 and 3.

Article 19

1. The Court of Justice of the European Union shall include the Court of Justice, the General Court and specialised courts. It shall ensure that in the interpretation and application of the Treaties the law is observed.

Member States shall provide remedies sufficient to ensure effective legal protection in the fields covered by Union law.

2. The Court of Justice shall consist of one judge from each Member State. It shall be assisted by Advocates-General.

The General Court shall include at least one judge per Member State.

The Judges and the Advocates-General of the Court of Justice and the Judges of the General Court shall be chosen from persons whose independence is beyond doubt and who satisfy the conditions set out in Articles 253 and 254 of the Treaty on the Functioning of the European Union. They shall be appointed by common accord of the governments of the Member States for six years. Retiring Judges and Advocates-General may be reappointed.

3. The Court of Justice of the European Union shall, in accordance with the Treaties:

    (a) rule on actions brought by a Member State, an institution or a natural or legal person;

    (b) give preliminary rulings, at the request of courts or tribunals of the Member States, on the interpretation of Union law or the validity of acts adopted by the institutions;

    (c) rule in other cases provided for in the Treaties.

*****

Article 27

1. The High Representative of the Union for Foreign Affairs and Security Policy, who shall chair the Foreign Affairs Council, shall contribute through his proposals towards the preparation of the common foreign and security policy and shall ensure implementation of the decisions adopted by the European Council and the Council.

2. The High Representative shall represent the Union for matters relating to the common foreign and security policy. He shall conduct political dialogue with third parties on the Union's behalf and shall express the Union's position in international organisations and at international conferences.

3. In fulfilling his mandate, the High Representative shall be assisted by a European External Action Service. This service shall work in cooperation with the diplomatic services of the Member States and shall comprise officials from relevant departments of the General Secretariat of the Council and of the Commission as well as staff seconded from national diplomatic services of the Member States. The organisation and functioning of the European External Action Service shall be established by a decision of the Council. The Council shall act on a proposal from the High Representative after consulting the European Parliament and after obtaining the consent of the Commission.

*****

CONSOLIDATED VERSION OF THE TREATY ON THE FUNCTIONING OF THE EUROPEAN UNION

PART ONE (PRINCIPLES)

Article 1

1. This Treaty organises the functioning of the Union and determines the areas of, delimitation of, and arrangements for exercising its competences.

2. This Treaty and the Treaty on European Union constitute the Treaties on which the Union is founded. These two Treaties, which have the same legal value, shall be referred to as 'the Treaties'.

Title I Categories and Areas of Union Competence

Article 2

1. When the Treaties confer on the Union exclusive competence in a specific area, only the Union may legislate and adopt legally binding acts, the Member States being able to do so themselves only if so empowered by the Union or for the implementation of Union acts.

2. When the Treaties confer on the Union a competence shared with the Member States in a specific area, the Union and the Member States may legislate and adopt legally binding acts in that area.

The Member States shall exercise their competence to the extent that the Union has not exercised its competence. The Member States shall again exercise their competence to the extent that the Union has decided to cease exercising its competence.

3. The Member States shall coordinate their economic and employment policies within arrangements as determined by this Treaty, which the Union shall have competence to provide.

4. The Union shall have competence, in accordance with the provisions of the Treaty on European Union, to define and implement a common foreign and security policy, including the progressive framing of a common defence policy.

5. In certain areas and under the conditions laid down in the Treaties, the Union shall have competence to carry out actions to support, coordinate or supplement the actions of the Member States, without thereby superseding their competence in these areas.

Legally binding acts of the Union adopted on the basis of the provisions of the Treaties relating to these areas shall not entail harmonisation of Member States' laws or regulations.

6. The scope of and arrangements for exercising the Union's competences shall be determined by the provisions of the Treaties relating to each area.

Articles 3–6 *****

Title II Provisions Having General Application

Article 7
The Union shall ensure consistency between its policies and activities, taking all of its objectives into account and in accordance with the principle of conferral of powers.

Article 8
In all its activities, the Union shall aim to eliminate inequalities, and to promote equality, between men and women.

Article 9
In defining and implementing its policies and activities, the Union shall take into account requirements linked to the promotion of a high level of employment, the guarantee of adequate social protection, the fight against social exclusion, and a high level of education, training and protection of human health.

Article 10
In defining and implementing its policies and activities, the Union shall aim to combat discrimination based on sex, racial or ethnic origin, religion or belief, disability, age or sexual orientation.

Article 11
Environmental protection requirements must be integrated into the definition and implementation of the Union policies and activities, in particular with a view to promoting sustainable development.

Article 12
Consumer protection requirements shall be taken into account in defining and implementing other Union policies and activities.

Articles 13–16 *****

Article 17
1. The Union respects and does not prejudice the status under national law of churches and religious associations or communities in the Member States.

2. The Union equally respects the status under national law of philosophical and non-confessional organisations.

3. Recognising their identity and their specific contribution, the Union shall maintain an open, transparent and regular dialogue with these churches and organisations.

PART TWO (NON-DISCRIMINATION AND CITIZENSHIP OF THE UNION)

Article 18

Within the scope of application of the Treaties, and without prejudice to any special provisions contained therein, any discrimination on grounds of nationality shall be prohibited.

The European Parliament and the Council, acting in accordance with the ordinary legislative procedure, may adopt rules designed to prohibit such discrimination.

Article 19

1. Without prejudice to the other provisions of the Treaties and within the limits of the powers conferred by them upon the Union, the Council, acting unanimously in accordance with a special legislative procedure and after obtaining the consent of the European Parliament, may take appropriate action to combat discrimination based on sex, racial or ethnic origin, religion or belief, disability, age or sexual orientation.

2. By way of derogation from paragraph 1, the European Parliament and the Council, acting in accordance with the ordinary legislative procedure, may adopt the basic principles of Union incentive measures, excluding any harmonisation of the laws and regulations of the Member States, to support action taken by the Member States in order to contribute to the achievement of the objectives referred to in paragraph 1.

Article 20

1. Citizenship of the Union is hereby established. Every person holding the nationality of a Member State shall be a citizen of the Union. Citizenship of the Union shall be additional to and not replace national citizenship.

2. Citizens of the Union shall enjoy the rights and be subject to the duties provided for in the Treaties. They shall have, *inter alia*:

    (a) the right to move and reside freely within the territory of the Member States;

    (b) the right to vote and to stand as candidates in elections to the European Parliament and in municipal elections in their Member State of residence, under the same conditions as nationals of that State;

    (c) the right to enjoy, in the territory of a third country in which the Member State of which they are nationals is not represented, the protection of the diplomatic and consular authorities of any Member State on the same conditions as the nationals of that State;

    (d) the right to petition the European Parliament, to apply to the European Ombudsman, and to address the institutions and advisory bodies of the Union in any of the Treaty languages and to obtain a reply in the same language.

These rights shall be exercised in accordance with the conditions and limits defined by the Treaties and by the measures adopted thereunder.

Articles 21–25   *****

PART THREE (UNION POLICIES AND INTERNAL ACTIONS)

Title I The Internal Market

Article 26

1. The Union shall adopt measures with the aim of establishing or ensuring the functioning of the internal market, in accordance with the relevant provisions of the Treaties.

2. The internal market shall comprise an area without internal frontiers in which the free movement of goods, persons, services and capital is ensured in accordance with the provisions of the Treaties.

3. The Council, on a proposal from the Commission, shall determine the guidelines and conditions necessary to ensure balanced progress in all the sectors concerned.

Article 27 *****

Title II Free Movement of Goods

Article 28

1. The Union shall comprise a customs union which shall cover all trade in goods and which shall involve the prohibition between Member States of customs duties on imports and exports and of all charges having equivalent effect, and the adoption of a common customs tariff in their relations with third countries.

2. The provisions of Article 30 and of Chapter 2 of this Title shall apply to products originating in Member States and to products coming from third countries which are in free circulation in Member States.

Articles 29–33 *****

Chapter 3 (Prohibition of Quantitative Restrictions between Member States)

Article 34

Quantitative restrictions on imports and all measures having equivalent effect shall be prohibited between Member States.

Article 35 *****

Article 36

The provisions of Articles 34 and 35 shall not preclude prohibitions or restrictions on imports, exports or goods in transit justified on grounds of public morality, public policy or public security; the protection of health and life of humans, animals or plants; the protection of national treasures possessing artistic, historic or archaeological value; or the protection of industrial and commercial property. Such prohibitions or restrictions shall not, however, constitute a means of arbitrary discrimination or a disguised restriction on trade between Member States.

Articles 37–44 *****

Title IV Free Movement of Persons, Services and Capital

Chapter 1 (Workers)

Article 45

1. Freedom of movement for workers shall be secured within the Union.

2. Such freedom of movement shall entail the abolition of any discrimination based on nationality between workers of the Member States as regards employment, remuneration and other conditions of work and employment.

3. It shall entail the right, subject to limitations justified on grounds of public policy, public security or public health:

   (a) to accept offers of employment actually made;

   (b) to move freely within the territory of Member States for this purpose;

(c) to stay in a Member State for the purpose of employment in accordance with the provisions governing the employment of nationals of that State laid down by law, regulation or administrative action;

(d) to remain in the territory of a Member State after having been employed in that State, subject to conditions which shall be embodied in regulations to be drawn up by the Commission.

4. The provisions of this Article shall not apply to employment in the public service.

Articles 46   *****

Article 47
The Union shall have legal personality.

Article 48
1. The Treaties may be amended in accordance with an ordinary revision procedure. They may also be amended in accordance with simplified revision procedures.

Ordinary revision procedure

2. The Government of any Member State, the European Parliament or the Commission may submit to the Council proposals for the amendment of the Treaties. These proposals may, inter alia, serve either to increase or to reduce the competences conferred on the Union in the Treaties. These proposals shall be submitted to the European Council by the Council and the national Parliaments shall be notified.

3. If the European Council, after consulting the European Parliament and the Commission, adopts by a simple majority a decision in favour of examining the proposed amendments, the President of the European Council shall convene a Convention composed of representatives of the national Parliaments, of the Heads of State or Government of the Member States, of the European Parliament and of the Commission. The European Central Bank shall also be consulted in the case of institutional changes in the monetary area. The Convention shall examine the proposals for amendments and shall adopt by consensus a recommendation to a conference of representatives of the governments of the Member States as provided for in paragraph 4.

The European Council may decide by a simple majority, after obtaining the consent of the European Parliament, not to convene a Convention should this not be justified by the extent of the proposed amendments. In the latter case, the European Council shall define the terms of reference for a conference of representatives of the governments of the Member States.

4. A conference of representatives of the governments of the Member States shall be convened by the President of the Council for the purpose of determining by common accord the amendments to be made to the Treaties.

The amendments shall enter into force after being ratified by all the Member States in accordance with their respective constitutional requirements.

5. If, two years after the signature of a treaty amending the Treaties, four fifths of the Member States have ratified it and one or more Member States have encountered difficulties in proceeding with ratification, the matter shall be referred to the European Council.

Simplified revision procedures

6. The Government of any Member State, the European Parliament or the Commission may submit to the European Council proposals for revising all or part of the provisions of Part Three of the Treaty on the Functioning of the European Union relating to the internal policies and action of the Union.

The European Council may adopt a decision amending all or part of the provisions of Part Three of the Treaty on the Functioning of the European Union. The European Council shall act by unanimity after consulting the European Parliament and the Commission, and the European Central Bank in the case of institutional changes in the monetary area. That decision shall not enter into force until it is approved by the Member States in accordance with their respective constitutional requirements.

The decision referred to in the second subparagraph shall not increase the competences conferred on the Union in the Treaties.

7. Where the Treaty on the Functioning of the European Union or Title V of this Treaty provides for the Council to act by unanimity in a given area or case, the European Council may adopt a decision authorising the Council to act by a qualified majority in that area or in that case. This subparagraph shall not apply to decisions with military implications or those in the area of defence.

Where the Treaty on the Functioning of the European Union provides for legislative acts to be adopted by the Council in accordance with a special legislative procedure, the European Council may adopt a decision allowing for the adoption of such acts in accordance with the ordinary legislative procedure.

Any initiative taken by the European Council on the basis of the first or the second subparagraph shall be notified to the national Parliaments. If a national Parliament makes known its opposition within six months of the date of such notification, the decision referred to in the first or the second subparagraph shall not be adopted. In the absence of opposition, the European Council may adopt the decision.

For the adoption of the decisions referred to in the first and second subparagraphs, the European Council shall act by unanimity after obtaining the consent of the European Parliament, which shall be given by a majority of its component members.

Chapter 2 (Right of Establishment)

Article 49
Within the framework of the provisions set out below, restrictions on the freedom of establishment of nationals of a Member State in the territory of another Member State shall be prohibited. Such prohibition shall also apply to restrictions on the setting-up of agencies, branches or subsidiaries by nationals of any Member State established in the territory of any Member State.

Freedom of establishment shall include the right to take up and pursue activities as self-employed persons and to set up and manage undertakings, in particular companies or firms within the meaning of the second paragraph of Article 54, under the conditions laid down for its own nationals by the law of the country where such establishment is effected, subject to the provisions of the Chapter relating to capital.

Articles 50–53 *****

Article 54
Companies or firms formed in accordance with the law of a Member State and having their registered office, central administration or principal place of business within the Union shall, for the purposes of this Chapter, be treated in the same way as natural persons who are nationals of Member States.

'Companies or firms' means companies or firms constituted under civil or commercial law, including cooperative societies, and other legal persons governed by public or private law, save for those which are non-profit-making.

Article 55 *****

Chapter 3 (Services)

Article 56
Within the framework of the provisions set out below, restrictions on freedom to provide services within the Union shall be prohibited in respect of nationals of Member States who are established in a Member State other than that of the person for whom the services are intended.

The European Parliament and the Council, acting in accordance with the ordinary legislative procedure, may extend the provisions of the Chapter to nationals of a third country who provide services and who are established within the Union.

Article 57

Services shall be considered to be 'services' within the meaning of the Treaties where they are normally provided for remuneration, in so far as they are not governed by the provisions relating to freedom of movement for goods, capital and persons.

'Services' shall in particular include:

    (a) activities of an industrial character;

    (b) activities of a commercial character;

    (c) activities of craftsmen;

    (d) activities of the professions.

Without prejudice to the provisions of the Chapter relating to the right of establishment, the person providing a service may, in order to do so, temporarily pursue his activity in the Member State where the service is provided, under the same conditions as are imposed by that State on its own nationals.

    *****

Chapter 4 (Judicial Cooperation in Criminal Matters)

Article 82

1. Judicial cooperation in criminal matters in the Union shall be based on the principle of mutual recognition of judgments and judicial decisions and shall include the approximation of the laws and regulations of the Member States in the areas referred to in paragraph 2 and in Article 83.

The European Parliament and the Council, acting in accordance with the ordinary legislative procedure, shall adopt measures to:

    (a) lay down rules and procedures for ensuring recognition throughout the Union of all forms of judgments and judicial decisions;

    (b) prevent and settle conflicts of jurisdiction between Member States;

    (c) support the training of the judiciary and judicial staff;

    (d) facilitate cooperation between judicial or equivalent authorities of the Member States in relation to proceedings in criminal matters and the enforcement of decisions.

2. To the extent necessary to facilitate mutual recognition of judgments and judicial decisions and police and judicial cooperation in criminal matters having a cross-border dimension, the European Parliament and the Council may, by means of directives adopted in accordance with the ordinary legislative procedure, establish minimum rules. Such rules shall take into account the differences between the legal traditions and systems of the Member States.

They shall concern:

    (a) mutual admissibility of evidence between Member States;

    (b) the rights of individuals in criminal procedure;

    (c) the rights of victims of crime;

    (d) any other specific aspects of criminal procedure which the Council has identified in advance by a decision; for the adoption of such a decision, the Council shall act unanimously after obtaining the consent of the European Parliament.

Adoption of the minimum rules referred to in this paragraph shall not prevent Member States from maintaining or introducing a higher level of protection for individuals.

    3. *****

Article 83

1. The European Parliament and the Council may, by means of directives adopted in accordance with the ordinary legislative procedure, establish minimum rules concerning the definition of criminal offences and sanctions in the areas of particularly serious crime with a cross-border dimension resulting from the nature or impact of such offences or from a special need to combat them on a common basis.

These areas of crime are the following: terrorism, trafficking in human beings and sexual exploitation of women and children, illicit drug trafficking, illicit arms trafficking, money laundering, corruption, counterfeiting of means of payment, computer crime and organised crime.

On the basis of developments in crime, the Council may adopt a decision identifying other areas of crime that meet the criteria specified in this paragraph. It shall act unanimously after obtaining the consent of the European Parliament.

   2, 3 *****

Articles 84–86   *****

Chapter 5   (Police Cooperation)

Article 87

1. The Union shall establish police cooperation involving all the Member States' competent authorities, including police, customs and other specialised law enforcement services in relation to the prevention, detection and investigation of criminal offences.

2. For the purposes of paragraph 1, the European Parliament and the Council, acting in accordance with the ordinary legislative procedure, may establish measures concerning:

  (a) the collection, storage, processing, analysis and exchange of relevant information;

  (b) support for the training of staff, and cooperation on the exchange of staff, on equipment and on research into crime-detection;

  (c) common investigative techniques in relation to the detection of serious forms of organised crime.

3. The Council, acting in accordance with a special legislative procedure, may establish measures concerning operational cooperation between the authorities referred to in this Article. The Council shall act unanimously after consulting the European Parliament.

In case of the absence of unanimity in the Council, a group of at least nine Member States may request that the draft measures be referred to the European Council. In that case, the procedure in the Council shall be suspended. After discussion, and in case of a consensus, the European Council shall, within four months of this suspension, refer the draft back to the Council for adoption.

Within the same timeframe, in case of disagreement, and if at least nine Member States wish to establish enhanced cooperation on the basis of the draft measures concerned, they shall notify the European Parliament, the Council and the Commission accordingly. In such a case, the authorisation to proceed with enhanced cooperation referred to in Article 20(2) of the Treaty on European Union and Article 329(1) of this Treaty shall be deemed to be granted and the provisions on enhanced cooperation shall apply.

The specific procedure provided for in the second and third subparagraphs shall not apply to acts which constitute a development of the Schengen *acquis*.

   *****

Title VII   Common Rules on Competition, Taxation and Approximation of Laws

Chapter 1   (Rules on Competition)

Section 1   Rules applying to undertakings

Article 101

1. The following shall be prohibited as incompatible with the internal market: all agreements between undertakings, decisions by associations of undertakings and concerted practices which may affect trade between Member States and which have as their object or effect the prevention, restriction or distortion of competition within the internal market, and in particular those which:

  (a) directly or indirectly fix purchase or selling prices or any other trading conditions;

  (b) limit or control production, markets, technical development, or investment;

  (c) share markets or sources of supply;

(d) apply dissimilar conditions to equivalent transactions with other trading parties, thereby placing them at a competitive disadvantage;

(e) make the conclusion of contracts subject to acceptance by the other parties of supplementary obligations which, by their nature or according to commercial usage, have no connection with the subject of such contracts.

2. Any agreements or decisions prohibited pursuant to this Article shall be automatically void.

3. The provisions of paragraph 1 may, however, be declared inapplicable in the case of:

— any agreement or category of agreements between undertakings,

— any decision or category of decisions by associations of undertakings,

— any concerted practice or category of concerted practices,

which contributes to improving the production or distribution of goods or to promoting technical or economic progress, while allowing consumers a fair share of the resulting benefit, and which does not:

(a) impose on the undertakings concerned restrictions which are not indispensable to the attainment of these objectives;

(b) afford such undertakings the possibility of eliminating competition in respect of a substantial part of the products in question.

Articles 102–106   *****

Section 2 Aids granted by States

Article 107

1. Save as otherwise provided in the Treaties, any aid granted by a Member State or through State resources in any form whatsoever which distorts or threatens to distort competition by favouring certain undertakings or the production of certain goods shall, in so far as it affects trade between Member States, be incompatible with the internal market.

2. The following shall be compatible with the internal market:

(a) aid having a social character, granted to individual consumers, provided that such aid is granted without discrimination related to the origin of the products concerned;

(b) aid to make good the damage caused by natural disasters or exceptional occurrences;

(c) aid granted to the economy of certain areas of the Federal Republic of Germany affected by the division of Germany, in so far as such aid is required in order to compensate for the economic disadvantages caused by that division. Five years after the entry into force of the Treaty of Lisbon, the Council, acting on a proposal from the Commission, may adopt a decision repealing this point.

3. The following may be considered to be compatible with the internal market:

(a) aid to promote the economic development of areas where the standard of living is abnormally low or where there is serious underemployment, and of the regions referred to in Article 349, in view of their structural, economic and social situation;

(b) aid to promote the execution of an important project of common European interest or to remedy a serious disturbance in the economy of a Member State;

(c) aid to facilitate the development of certain economic activities or of certain economic areas, where such aid does not adversely affect trading conditions to an extent contrary to the common interest;

(d) aid to promote culture and heritage conservation where such aid does not affect trading conditions and competition in the Union to an extent that is contrary to the common interest;

(e) such other categories of aid as may be specified by decision of the Council on a proposal from the Commission.

Articles 108–113   *****

Chapter 3 (Approximation of Laws)

Article 114

1. Save where otherwise provided in the Treaties, the following provisions shall apply for the achievement of the objectives set out in Article 26. The European Parliament and the Council shall, acting in accordance with the ordinary legislative procedure and after consulting the Economic and Social Committee, adopt the measures for the approximation of the provisions laid down by law, regulation or administrative action in Member States which have as their object the establishment and functioning of the internal market.

2. Paragraph 1 shall not apply to fiscal provisions, to those relating to the free movement of persons nor to those relating to the rights and interests of employed persons.

3. The Commission, in its proposals envisaged in paragraph 1 concerning health, safety, environmental protection and consumer protection, will take as a base a high level of protection, taking account in particular of any new development based on scientific facts. Within their respective powers, the European Parliament and the Council will also seek to achieve this objective.

4. If, after the adoption of a harmonisation measure by the European Parliament and the Council, by the Council or by the Commission, a Member State deems it necessary to maintain national provisions on grounds of major needs referred to in Article 36, or relating to the protection of the environment or the working environment, it shall notify the Commission of these provisions as well as the grounds for maintaining them.

5–10 *****

Articles 115–118   *****

Title VIII Economic and Monetary Policy

Article 119

1. For the purposes set out in Article 3 of the Treaty on European Union, the activities of the Member States and the Union shall include, as provided in the Treaties, the adoption of an economic policy which is based on the close coordination of Member States' economic policies, on the internal market and on the definition of common objectives, and conducted in accordance with the principle of an open market economy with free competition.

2. Concurrently with the foregoing, and as provided in the Treaties and in accordance with the procedures set out therein, these activities shall include a single currency, the euro, and the definition and conduct of a single monetary policy and exchange-rate policy the primary objective of both of which shall be to maintain price stability and, without prejudice to this objective, to support the general economic policies in the Union, in accordance with the principle of an open market economy with free competition.

3. These activities of the Member States and the Union shall entail compliance with the following guiding principles: stable prices, sound public finances and monetary conditions and a sustainable balance of payments.

*****

Title X Social Policy

Article 151

The Union and the Member States, having in mind fundamental social rights such as those set out in the European Social Charter signed at Turin on 18 October 1961 and in the 1989 Community Charter of the Fundamental Social Rights of Workers, shall have as their objectives the promotion of employment, improved living and working conditions, so as to make possible their harmonisation while the improvement is being maintained, proper social protection, dialogue between management and labour, the development of human resources with a view to lasting high employment and the combating of exclusion.

To this end the Union and the Member States shall implement measures which take account of the diverse forms of national practices, in particular in the field of contractual relations, and the need to maintain the competitiveness of the Union economy.

They believe that such a development will ensue not only from the functioning of the internal market, which will favour the harmonisation of social systems, but also from the procedures provided for in the Treaties and from the approximation of provisions laid down by law, regulation or administrative action.

Article 152   *****

Article 153

1. With a view to achieving the objectives of Article 151, the Union shall support and complement the activities of the Member States in the following fields:
   (a) improvement in particular of the working environment to protect workers' health and safety;
   (b) working conditions;
   (c) social security and social protection of workers;
   (d) protection of workers where their employment contract is terminated;
   (e) the information and consultation of workers;
   (f) representation and collective defence of the interests of workers and employers, including co-determination, subject to paragraph 5;
   (g) conditions of employment for third-country nationals legally residing in Union territory;
   (h) the integration of persons excluded from the labour market, without prejudice to Article 166;
   (i) equality between men and women with regard to labour market opportunities and treatment at work;
   (j) the combating of social exclusion;
   (k) the modernisation of social protection systems without prejudice to point (c).

2. To this end, the European Parliament and the Council:
   (a) may adopt measures designed to encourage cooperation between Member States through initiatives aimed at improving knowledge, developing exchanges of information and best practices, promoting innovative approaches and evaluating experiences, excluding any harmonisation of the laws and regulations of the Member States;
   (b) may adopt, in the fields referred to in paragraph 1(a) to (i), by means of directives, minimum requirements for gradual implementation, having regard to the conditions and technical rules obtaining in each of the Member States. Such directives shall avoid imposing administrative, financial and legal constraints in a way which would hold back the creation and development of small and medium-sized undertakings.

The European Parliament and the Council shall act in accordance with the ordinary legislative procedure after consulting the Economic and Social Committee and the Committee of the Regions.

In the fields referred to in paragraph 1(c), (d), (f) and (g), the Council shall act unanimously, in accordance with a special legislative procedure, after consulting the European Parliament and the said Committees.

The Council, acting unanimously on a proposal from the Commission, after consulting the European Parliament, may decide to render the ordinary legislative procedure applicable to paragraph 1(d), (f) and (g).

3. A Member State may entrust management and labour, at their joint request, with the implementation of directives adopted pursuant to paragraph 2, or, where appropriate, with the implementation of a Council decision adopted in accordance with Article 155.

In this case, it shall ensure that, no later than the date on which a directive or a decision must be transposed or implemented, management and labour have introduced the necessary measures by agreement, the Member State concerned being required to take any necessary measure enabling it at any time to be in a position to guarantee the results imposed by that directive or that decision.

4. The provisions adopted pursuant to this Article:

— shall not affect the right of Member States to define the fundamental principles of their social security systems and must not significantly affect the financial equilibrium thereof,

— shall not prevent any Member State from maintaining or introducing more stringent protective measures compatible with the Treaties.

5. The provisions of this Article shall not apply to pay, the right of association, the right to strike or the right to impose lock-outs.

Article 154

1. The Commission shall have the task of promoting the consultation of management and labour at Union level and shall take any relevant measure to facilitate their dialogue by ensuring balanced support for the parties.

2. To this end, before submitting proposals in the social policy field, the Commission shall consult management and labour on the possible direction of Union action.

3. If, after such consultation, the Commission considers Union action advisable, it shall consult management and labour on the content of the envisaged proposal. Management and labour shall forward to the Commission an opinion or, where appropriate, a recommendation.

4. On the occasion of the consultation referred to in paragraphs 2 and 3, management and labour may inform the Commission of their wish to initiate the process provided for in Article 155. The duration of this process shall not exceed nine months, unless the management and labour concerned and the Commission decide jointly to extend it.

Article 155

1. Should management and labour so desire, the dialogue between them at Union level may lead to contractual relations, including agreements.

2. Agreements concluded at Union level shall be implemented either in accordance with the procedures and practices specific to management and labour and the Member States or, in matters covered by Article 153, at the joint request of the signatory parties, by a Council decision on a proposal from the Commission. The European Parliament shall be informed.

The Council shall act unanimously where the agreement in question contains one or more provisions relating to one of the areas for which unanimity is required pursuant to Article 153(2).

Article 156

With a view to achieving the objectives of Article 151 and without prejudice to the other provisions of the Treaties, the Commission shall encourage cooperation between the Member States and facilitate the coordination of their action in all social policy fields under this Chapter, particularly in matters relating to:

— employment,

— labour law and working conditions,

— basic and advanced vocational training,

— social security,

— prevention of occupational accidents and diseases,

— occupational hygiene,

— the right of association and collective bargaining between employers and workers.

To this end, the Commission shall act in close contact with Member States by making studies, delivering opinions and arranging consultations both on problems arising at national level and on those of concern to international organisations, in particular initiatives aiming at the establishment of guidelines and indicators, the organisation of exchange of best practice, and the preparation of the necessary elements for periodic monitoring and evaluation. The European Parliament shall be kept fully informed.

Before delivering the opinions provided for in this Article, the Commission shall consult the Economic and Social Committee.

Article 157

1. Each Member State shall ensure that the principle of equal pay for male and female workers for equal work or work of equal value is applied.

2. For the purpose of this Article, 'pay' means the ordinary basic or minimum wage or salary and any other consideration, whether in cash or in kind, which the worker receives directly or indirectly, in respect of his employment, from his employer.

Equal pay without discrimination based on sex means:

(a) that pay for the same work at piece rates shall be calculated on the basis of the same unit of measurement;

(b) that pay for work at time rates shall be the same for the same job.

3. The European Parliament and the Council, acting in accordance with the ordinary legislative procedure, and after consulting the Economic and Social Committee, shall adopt measures to ensure the application of the principle of equal opportunities and equal treatment of men and women in matters of employment and occupation, including the principle of equal pay for equal work or work of equal value.

4. With a view to ensuring full equality in practice between men and women in working life, the principle of equal treatment shall not prevent any Member State from maintaining or adopting measures providing for specific advantages in order to make it easier for the underrepresented sex to pursue a vocational activity or to prevent or compensate for disadvantages in professional careers.

******

Title V International Agreements

Article 216

1. The Union may conclude an agreement with one or more third countries or international organisations where the Treaties so provide or where the conclusion of an agreement is necessary in order to achieve, within the framework of the Union's policies, one of the objectives referred to in the Treaties, or is provided for in a legally binding Union act or is likely to affect common rules or alter their scope.

2. Agreements concluded by the Union are binding upon the institutions of the Union and on its Member States.

Article 217

The Union may conclude with one or more third countries or international organisations agreements establishing an association involving reciprocal rights and obligations, common action and special procedure.

Articles 218–222   *****

PART SIX (INSTITUTIONAL AND FINANCIAL PROVISIONS)

Title I Institutional Provisions

Chapter 1 (The Institutions)

Section 1 The European Parliament

Article 223

1. The European Parliament shall draw up a proposal to lay down the provisions necessary for the election of its Members by direct universal suffrage in accordance with a uniform procedure in all Member States or in accordance with principles common to all Member States.

The Council, acting unanimously in accordance with a special legislative procedure and after obtaining the consent of the European Parliament, which shall act by a majority of its component Members, shall lay down the necessary provisions. These provisions shall enter into force following their approval by the Member States in accordance with their respective constitutional requirements.

2. The European Parliament, acting by means of regulations on its own initiative in accordance with a special legislative procedure after seeking an opinion from the Commission and with the approval of the Council, shall lay down the regulations and general conditions governing the performance of the duties of its Members. All rules or conditions relating to the taxation of Members or former Members shall require unanimity within the Council.

Article 224

The European Parliament and the Council, acting in accordance with the ordinary legislative procedure, by means of regulations, shall lay down the regulations governing political parties at European level referred to in Article 10(4) of the Treaty on European Union and in particular the rules regarding their funding.

Article 225

The European Parliament may, acting by a majority of its component Members, request the Commission to submit any appropriate proposal on matters on which it considers that a Union act is required for the purpose of implementing the Treaties. If the Commission does not submit a proposal, it shall inform the European Parliament of the reasons.

Article 226

In the course of its duties, the European Parliament may, at the request of a quarter of its component Members, set up a temporary Committee of Inquiry to investigate, without prejudice to the powers conferred by the Treaties on other institutions or bodies, alleged contraventions or maladministration in the implementation of Union law, except where the alleged facts are being examined before a court and while the case is still subject to legal proceedings.

The temporary Committee of Inquiry shall cease to exist on the submission of its report.

The detailed provisions governing the exercise of the right of inquiry shall be determined by the European Parliament, acting by means of regulations on its own initiative in accordance with a special legislative procedure, after obtaining the consent of the Council and the Commission.

Article 227

Any citizen of the Union, and any natural or legal person residing or having its registered office in a Member State, shall have the right to address, individually or in association with other citizens or persons, a petition to the European Parliament on a matter which comes within the Union's fields of activity and which affects him, her or it directly.

Article 228

1. A European Ombudsman, elected by the European Parliament, shall be empowered to receive complaints from any citizen of the Union or any natural or legal person residing or having its registered office in a Member State concerning instances of maladministration in the activities of the Union institutions, bodies, offices or agencies, with the exception of the Court of Justice of the European Union acting in its judicial role. He or she shall examine such complaints and report on them.

In accordance with his duties, the Ombudsman shall conduct inquiries for which he finds grounds, either on his own initiative or on the basis of complaints submitted to him direct or through a Member of the European Parliament, except where the alleged facts are or have been the subject of legal proceedings. Where the Ombudsman establishes an instance of maladministration, he shall refer the matter to the institution, body, office or agency concerned, which shall have a period of three months in which to inform him of its views. The Ombudsman shall then forward a report to the European Parliament and the institution, body, office or agency concerned. The person lodging the complaint shall be informed of the outcome of such inquiries.

The Ombudsman shall submit an annual report to the European Parliament on the outcome of his inquiries.

2. The Ombudsman shall be elected after each election of the European Parliament for the duration of its term of office. The Ombudsman shall be eligible for reappointment.

The Ombudsman may be dismissed by the Court of Justice at the request of the European Parliament if he no longer fulfils the conditions required for the performance of his duties or if he is guilty of serious misconduct.

3. The Ombudsman shall be completely independent in the performance of his duties. In the performance of those duties he shall neither seek nor take instructions from any Government, institution, body, office or entity. The Ombudsman may not, during his term of office, engage in any other occupation, whether gainful or not.

4. The European Parliament acting by means of regulations on its own initiative in accordance with a special legislative procedure shall, after seeking an opinion from the Commission and with the approval of the Council, lay down the regulations and general conditions governing the performance of the Ombudsman's duties.

Article 229

The European Parliament shall hold an annual session. It shall meet, without requiring to be convened, on the second Tuesday in March.

The European Parliament may meet in extraordinary part-session at the request of a majority of its component Members or at the request of the Council or of the Commission.

Article 230

The Commission may attend all the meetings and shall, at its request, be heard.

The Commission shall reply orally or in writing to questions put to it by the European Parliament or by its Members.

The European Council and the Council shall be heard by the European Parliament in accordance with the conditions laid down in the Rules of Procedure of the European Council and those of the Council.

Article 231

Save as otherwise provided in the Treaties, the European Parliament shall act by a majority of the votes cast.

The Rules of Procedure shall determine the quorum.

Article 232

The European Parliament shall adopt its Rules of Procedure, acting by a majority of its Members.

The proceedings of the European Parliament shall be published in the manner laid down in the Treaties and in its Rules of Procedure.

Article 233

The European Parliament shall discuss in open session the annual general report submitted to it by the Commission.

Article 234

If a motion of censure on the activities of the Commission is tabled before it, the European Parliament shall not vote thereon until at least three days after the motion has been tabled and only by open vote.

If the motion of censure is carried by a two-thirds majority of the votes cast, representing a majority of the component Members of the European Parliament, the members of the Commission shall resign as a body and the High Representative of the Union for Foreign Affairs and Security Policy shall resign from duties that he or she carries out in the Commission. They shall remain in office and continue to deal with current business until they are replaced in accordance with Article 17 of the Treaty on European Union. In this case, the term of office of the members of the Commission appointed to replace them shall expire on the date on which the term of office of the members of the Commission obliged to resign as a body would have expired.

Section 2   The European Council

Article 235

1. Where a vote is taken, any member of the European Council may also act on behalf of not more than one other member.

Article 16(4) of the Treaty on European Union and Article 238(2) of this Treaty shall apply to the European Council when it is acting by a qualified majority. Where the European Council decides by vote, its President and the President of the Commission shall not take part in the vote.

Abstentions by members present in person or represented shall not prevent the adoption by the European Council of acts which require unanimity.

2. The President of the European Parliament may be invited to be heard by the European Council.

3. The European Council shall act by a simple majority for procedural questions and for the adoption of its Rules of Procedure.

4. The European Council shall be assisted by the General Secretariat of the Council.

Article 236

The European Council shall adopt by a qualified majority:

(a) a decision establishing the list of Council configurations, other than those of the General Affairs Council and of the Foreign Affairs Council, in accordance with Article 16(6) of the Treaty on European Union;

(b) a decision on the Presidency of Council configurations, other than that of Foreign Affairs, in accordance with Article 16(9) of the Treaty on European Union.

Section 3 The Council

Article 237

The Council shall meet when convened by its President on his own initiative or at the request of one of its Members or of the Commission.

Article 238

1. Where it is required to act by a simple majority, the Council shall act by a majority of its component members.

2. By way of derogation from Article 16(4) of the Treaty on European Union, as from 1 November 2014 and subject to the provisions laid down in the Protocol on transitional provisions, where the Council does not act on a proposal from the Commission or from the High Representative of the Union for Foreign Affairs and Security Policy, the qualified majority shall be defined as at least 72 % of the members of the Council, representing Member States comprising at least 65 % of the population of the Union.

3. As from 1 November 2014 and subject to the provisions laid down in the Protocol on transitional provisions, in cases where, under the Treaties, not all the members of the Council participate in voting, a qualified majority shall be defined as follows:

(a) A qualified majority shall be defined as at least 55 % of the members of the Council representing the participating Member States, comprising at least 65 % of the population of these States.

A blocking minority must include at least the minimum number of Council members representing more than 35 % of the population of the participating Member States, plus one member, failing which the qualified majority shall be deemed attained;

(b) By way of derogation from point (a), where the Council does not act on a proposal from the Commission or from the High Representative of the Union for Foreign Affairs and Security Policy, the qualified majority shall be defined as at least 72 % of the members of the Council representing the participating Member States, comprising at least 65 % of the population of these States.

4. Abstentions by Members present in person or represented shall not prevent the adoption by the Council of acts which require unanimity.

Articles 239–243   *****

Section 4 The Commission

Article 244

In accordance with Article 17(5) of the Treaty on European Union, the Members of the Commission shall be chosen on the basis of a system of rotation established unanimously by the European Council and on the basis of the following principles:

    (a) Member States shall be treated on a strictly equal footing as regards determination of the sequence of, and the time spent by, their nationals as members of the Commission; consequently, the difference between the total number of terms of office held by nationals of any given pair of Member States may never be more than one;

    (b) subject to point (a), each successive Commission shall be so composed as to reflect satisfactorily the demographic and geographical range of all the Member States.

Articles 245–250 *****

Section 5 The Court of Justice of the European Union

Article 251

The Court of Justice shall sit in chambers or in a Grand Chamber, in accordance with the rules laid down for that purpose in the Statute of the Court of Justice of the European Union.

When provided for in the Statute, the Court of Justice may also sit as a full Court.

Article 252

The Court of Justice shall be assisted by eight Advocates-General. Should the Court of Justice so request, the Council, acting unanimously, may increase the number of Advocates-General.

It shall be the duty of the Advocate-General, acting with complete impartiality and independence, to make, in open court, reasoned submissions on cases which, in accordance with the Statute of the Court of Justice of the European Union, require his involvement.

Article 253

The Judges and Advocates-General of the Court of Justice shall be chosen from persons whose independence is beyond doubt and who possess the qualifications required for appointment to the highest judicial offices in their respective countries or who are jurisconsults of recognised competence; they shall be appointed by common accord of the governments of the Member States for a term of six years, after consultation of the panel provided for in Article 255.

Every three years there shall be a partial replacement of the Judges and Advocates-General, in accordance with the conditions laid down in the Statute of the Court of Justice of the European Union.

The Judges shall elect the President of the Court of Justice from among their number for a term of three years. He may be re-elected.

Retiring Judges and Advocates-General may be reappointed.

The Court of Justice shall appoint its Registrar and lay down the rules governing his service.

The Court of Justice shall establish its Rules of Procedure. Those Rules shall require the approval of the Council.

Article 254

The number of Judges of the General Court shall be determined by the Statute of the Court of Justice of the European Union. The Statute may provide for the General Court to be assisted by Advocates-General.

The members of the General Court shall be chosen from persons whose independence is beyond doubt and who possess the ability required for appointment to high judicial office. They shall be appointed by common accord of the governments of the Member States for a term of six years, after consultation of the panel provided for in Article 255. The membership shall be partially renewed every three years.

Retiring members shall be eligible for reappointment.

The Judges shall elect the President of the General Court from among their number for a term of three years. He may be re-elected.

The General Court shall appoint its Registrar and lay down the rules governing his service.

The General Court shall establish its Rules of Procedure in agreement with the Court of Justice. Those Rules shall require the approval of the Council.

Unless the Statute of the Court of Justice of the European Union provides otherwise, the provisions of the Treaties relating to the Court of Justice shall apply to the General Court.

Article 255

A panel shall be set up in order to give an opinion on candidates' suitability to perform the duties of Judge and Advocate-General of the Court of Justice and the General Court before the governments of the Member States make the appointments referred to in Articles 253 and 254.

The panel shall comprise seven persons chosen from among former members of the Court of Justice and the General Court, members of national supreme courts and lawyers of recognised competence, one of whom shall be proposed by the European Parliament. The Council shall adopt a decision establishing the panel's operating rules and a decision appointing its members. It shall act on the initiative of the President of the Court of Justice.

Article 256

1. The General Court shall have jurisdiction to hear and determine at first instance actions or proceedings referred to in Articles 263, 265, 268, 270 and 272, with the exception of those assigned to a specialised court set up under Article 257 and those reserved in the Statute for the Court of Justice. The Statute may provide for the General Court to have jurisdiction for other classes of action or proceeding.

Decisions given by the General Court under this paragraph may be subject to a right of appeal to the Court of Justice on points of law only, under the conditions and within the limits laid down by the Statute.

2. The General Court shall have jurisdiction to hear and determine actions or proceedings brought against decisions of the specialised courts.

Decisions given by the General Court under this paragraph may exceptionally be subject to review by the Court of Justice, under the conditions and within the limits laid down by the Statute, where there is a serious risk of the unity or consistency of Union law being affected.

3. The General Court shall have jurisdiction to hear and determine questions referred for a preliminary ruling under Article 267, in specific areas laid down by the Statute.

Where the General Court considers that the case requires a decision of principle likely to affect the unity or consistency of Union law, it may refer the case to the Court of Justice for a ruling.

Decisions given by the General Court on questions referred for a preliminary ruling may exceptionally be subject to review by the Court of Justice, under the conditions and within the limits laid down by the Statute, where there is a serious risk of the unity or consistency of Union law being affected.

Article 257

The European Parliament and the Council, acting in accordance with the ordinary legislative procedure, may establish specialised courts attached to the General Court to hear and determine at first instance certain classes of action or proceeding brought in specific areas. The European Parliament and the Council shall act by means of regulations either on a proposal from the Commission after consultation of the Court of Justice or at the request of the Court of Justice after consultation of the Commission.

The regulation establishing a specialised court shall lay down the rules on the organisation of the court and the extent of the jurisdiction conferred upon it.

Decisions given by specialised courts may be subject to a right of appeal on points of law only or, when provided for in the regulation establishing the specialised court, a right of appeal also on matters of fact, before the General Court.

The members of the specialised courts shall be chosen from persons whose independence is beyond doubt and who possess the ability required for appointment to judicial office. They shall be appointed by the Council, acting unanimously.

The specialised courts shall establish their Rules of Procedure in agreement with the Court of Justice. Those Rules shall require the approval of the Council.

Unless the regulation establishing the specialised court provides otherwise, the provisions of the Treaties relating to the Court of Justice of the European Union and the provisions of the Statute of the Court of Justice of the European Union shall apply to the specialised courts. Title I of the Statute and Article 64 thereof shall in any case apply to the specialised courts.

Article 258

If the Commission considers that a Member State has failed to fulfil an obligation under the Treaties, it shall deliver a reasoned opinion on the matter after giving the State concerned the opportunity to submit its observations.

If the State concerned does not comply with the opinion within the period laid down by the Commission, the latter may bring the matter before the Court of Justice of the European Union.

Article 259

A Member State which considers that another Member State has failed to fulfil an obligation under the Treaties may bring the matter before the Court of Justice of the European Union.

Before a Member State brings an action against another Member State for an alleged infringement of an obligation under the Treaties, it shall bring the matter before the Commission.

The Commission shall deliver a reasoned opinion after each of the States concerned has been given the opportunity to submit its own case and its observations on the other party's case both orally and in writing.

If the Commission has not delivered an opinion within three months of the date on which the matter was brought before it, the absence of such opinion shall not prevent the matter from being brought before the Court.

Article 260

1. If the Court of Justice of the European Union finds that a Member State has failed to fulfil an obligation under the Treaties, the State shall be required to take the necessary measures to comply with the judgment of the Court.

2. If the Commission considers that the Member State concerned has not taken the necessary measures to comply with the judgment of the Court, it may bring the case before the Court after giving that State the opportunity to submit its observations. It shall specify the amount of the lump sum or penalty payment to be paid by the Member State concerned which it considers appropriate in the circumstances.

If the Court finds that the Member State concerned has not complied with its judgment it may impose a lump sum or penalty payment on it.

This procedure shall be without prejudice to Article 259.

3. When the Commission brings a case before the Court pursuant to Article 258 on the grounds that the Member State concerned has failed to fulfil its obligation to notify measures transposing a directive adopted under a legislative procedure, it may, when it deems appropriate, specify the amount of the lump sum or penalty payment to be paid by the Member State concerned which it considers appropriate in the circumstances.

If the Court finds that there is an infringement it may impose a lump sum or penalty payment on the Member State concerned not exceeding the amount specified by the Commission. The payment obligation shall take effect on the date set by the Court in its judgment.

Article 261

Regulations adopted jointly by the European Parliament and the Council, and by the Council, pursuant to the provisions of the Treaties, may give the Court of Justice of the European Union unlimited jurisdiction with regard to the penalties provided for in such regulations.

Article 262 *****

Article 263

The Court of Justice of the European Union shall review the legality of legislative acts, of acts of the Council, of the Commission and of the European Central Bank, other than recommendations and opinions, and of acts of the European Parliament and of the European Council intended to produce legal effects *vis-à-vis* third parties. It shall also review the legality of acts of bodies, offices or agencies of the Union intended to produce legal effects *vis-à-vis* third parties.

It shall for this purpose have jurisdiction in actions brought by a Member State, the European Parliament, the Council or the Commission on grounds of lack of competence, infringement of an essential procedural requirement, infringement of the Treaties or of any rule of law relating to their application, or misuse of powers.

The Court shall have jurisdiction under the same conditions in actions brought by the Court of Auditors, by the European Central Bank and by the Committee of the Regions for the purpose of protecting their prerogatives.

Any natural or legal person may, under the conditions laid down in the first and second paragraphs, institute proceedings against an act addressed to that person or which is of direct and individual concern to them, and against a regulatory act which is of direct concern to them and does not entail implementing measures.

Acts setting up bodies, offices and agencies of the Union may lay down specific conditions and arrangements concerning actions brought by natural or legal persons against acts of these bodies, offices or agencies intended to produce legal effects in relation to them.

The proceedings provided for in this Article shall be instituted within two months of the publication of the measure, or of its notification to the plaintiff, or, in the absence thereof, of the day on which it came to the knowledge of the latter, as the case may be.

Article 264

If the action is well founded, the Court of Justice of the European Union shall declare the act concerned to be void.

However, the Court shall, if it considers this necessary, state which of the effects of the act which it has declared void shall be considered as definitive.

Articles 265, 266 *****

Article 267

The Court of Justice of the European Union shall have jurisdiction to give preliminary rulings concerning:

    (a) the interpretation of the Treaties;
    (b) the validity and interpretation of acts of the institutions, bodies, offices or agencies of the Union;

Where such a question is raised before any court or tribunal of a Member State, that court or tribunal may, if it considers that a decision on the question is necessary to enable it to give judgment, request the Court to give a ruling thereon.

Where any such question is raised in a case pending before a court or tribunal of a Member State against whose decisions there is no judicial remedy under national law, that court or tribunal shall bring the matter before the Court.

If such a question is raised in a case pending before a court or tribunal of a Member State with regard to a person in custody, the Court of Justice of the European Union shall act with the minimum of delay.

Articles 268–274 *****

Article 275

The Court of Justice of the European Union shall not have jurisdiction with respect to the provisions relating to the common foreign and security policy nor with respect to acts adopted on the basis of those provisions.

However, the Court shall have jurisdiction to monitor compliance with Article 40 of the Treaty on European Union and to rule on proceedings, brought in accordance with the conditions laid down in the fourth paragraph of Article 263 of this Treaty, reviewing the legality of decisions providing for restrictive measures against natural or legal persons adopted by the Council on the basis of Chapter 2 of Title V of the Treaty on European Union.

*****

Chapter 2 (Legal Acts of the Union, Adoption Procedures and Other Provisions)

Section 1 The legal acts of the Union

Article 288

To exercise the Union's competences, the institutions shall adopt regulations, directives, decisions, recommendations and opinions.

A regulation shall have general application. It shall be binding in its entirety and directly applicable in all Member States.

A directive shall be binding, as to the result to be achieved, upon each Member State to which it is addressed, but shall leave to the national authorities the choice of form and methods.

A decision shall be binding in its entirety. A decision which specifies those to whom it is addressed shall be binding only on them.

Recommendations and opinions shall have no binding force.

Articles 289–293 *****

Article 294

1. Where reference is made in the Treaties to the ordinary legislative procedure for the adoption of an act, the following procedure shall apply.

2. The Commission shall submit a proposal to the European Parliament and the Council.

First reading

3. The European Parliament shall adopt its position at first reading and communicate it to the Council.

4. If the Council approves the European Parliament's position, the act concerned shall be adopted in the wording which corresponds to the position of the European Parliament.

5. If the Council does not approve the European Parliament's position, it shall adopt its position at first reading and communicate it to the European Parliament.

6. The Council shall inform the European Parliament fully of the reasons which led it to adopt its position at first reading. The Commission shall inform the European Parliament fully of its position.

Second reading

7. If, within three months of such communication, the European Parliament:
    (a) approves the Council's position at first reading or has not taken a decision, the act concerned shall be deemed to have been adopted in the wording which corresponds to the position of the Council;
    (b) rejects, by a majority of its component members, the Council's position at first reading, the proposed act shall be deemed not to have been adopted;
    (c) proposes, by a majority of its component members, amendments to the Council's position at first reading, the text thus amended shall be forwarded to the Council and to the Commission, which shall deliver an opinion on those amendments.

8. If, within three months of receiving the European Parliament's amendments, the Council, acting by a qualified majority:

    (a) approves all those amendments, the act in question shall be deemed to have been adopted;

    (b) does not approve all the amendments, the President of the Council, in agreement with the President of the European Parliament, shall within six weeks convene a meeting of the Conciliation Committee.

9. The Council shall act unanimously on the amendments on which the Commission has delivered a negative opinion.

Conciliation

10. The Conciliation Committee, which shall be composed of the members of the Council or their representatives and an equal number of members representing the European Parliament, shall have the task of reaching agreement on a joint text, by a qualified majority of the members of the Council or their representatives and by a majority of the members representing the European Parliament within six weeks of its being convened, on the basis of the positions of the European Parliament and the Council at second reading.

11. The Commission shall take part in the Conciliation Committee's proceedings and shall take all necessary initiatives with a view to reconciling the positions of the European Parliament and the Council.

12. If, within six weeks of its being convened, the Conciliation Committee does not approve the joint text, the proposed act shall be deemed not to have been adopted.

Third reading

13. If, within that period, the Conciliation Committee approves a joint text, the European Parliament, acting by a majority of the votes cast, and the Council, acting by a qualified majority, shall each have a period of six weeks from that approval in which to adopt the act in question in accordance with the joint text. If they fail to do so, the proposed act shall be deemed not to have been adopted.

14. The periods of three months and six weeks referred to in this Article shall be extended by a maximum of one month and two weeks respectively at the initiative of the European Parliament or the Council.

Special provisions

15. Where, in the cases provided for in the Treaties, a legislative act is submitted to the ordinary legislative procedure on the initiative of a group of Member States, on a recommendation by the European Central Bank, or at the request of the Court of Justice, paragraph 2, the second sentence of paragraph 6, and paragraph 9 shall not apply.

In such cases, the European Parliament and the Council shall communicate the proposed act to the Commission with their positions at first and second readings. The European Parliament or the Council may request the opinion of the Commission throughout the procedure, which the Commission may also deliver on its own initiative. It may also, if it deems it necessary, take part in the Conciliation Committee in accordance with paragraph 11.

*****

PART SEVEN (GENERAL AND FINAL PROVISIONS)

*****

Article 352

1. If action by the Union should prove necessary, within the framework of the policies defined in the Treaties, to attain one of the objectives set out in the Treaties, and the Treaties have not provided the necessary powers, the Council, acting unanimously on a proposal from the Commission and after obtaining the consent of the European Parliament, shall adopt the appropriate measures. Where the

measures in question are adopted by the Council in accordance with a special legislative procedure, it shall also act unanimously on a proposal from the Commission and after obtaining the consent of the European Parliament.

2. Using the procedure for monitoring the subsidiarity principle referred to in Article 5(3) of the Treaty on European Union, the Commission shall draw national Parliaments' attention to proposals based on this Article.

3. Measures based on this Article shall not entail harmonisation of Member States' laws or regulations in cases where the Treaties exclude such harmonisation.

4. This Article cannot serve as a basis for attaining objectives pertaining to the common foreign and security policy and any acts adopted pursuant to this Article shall respect the limits set out in Article 40, second paragraph, of the Treaty on European Union.

Article 353–355 *****

Article 356
This Treaty is concluded for an unlimited period.
*****

PROTOCOLS

PROTOCOL (NO 1) ON THE ROLE OF NATIONAL PARLIAMENTS IN THE EUROPEAN UNION

Article 1
Commission consultation documents (green and white papers and communications) shall be forwarded directly by the Commission to national Parliaments upon publication. The Commission shall also forward the annual legislative programme as well as any other instrument of legislative planning or policy to national Parliaments, at the same time as to the European Parliament and the Council.

Article 2
Draft legislative acts sent to the European Parliament and to the Council shall be forwarded to national Parliaments.

For the purposes of this Protocol, 'draft legislative acts' shall mean proposals from the Commission, initiatives from a group of Member States, initiatives from the European Parliament, requests from the Court of Justice, recommendations from the European Central Bank and requests from the European Investment Bank for the adoption of a legislative act.

Draft legislative acts originating from the Commission shall be forwarded to national Parliaments directly by the Commission, at the same time as to the European Parliament and the Council.

Draft legislative acts originating from the European Parliament shall be forwarded to national Parliaments directly by the European Parliament.

Draft legislative acts originating from a group of Member States, the Court of Justice, the European Central Bank or the European Investment Bank shall be forwarded to national Parliaments by the Council.

Article 3
National Parliaments may send to the Presidents of the European Parliament, the Council and the Commission a reasoned opinion on whether a draft legislative act complies with the principle of subsidiarity, in accordance with the procedure laid down in the Protocol on the application of the principles of subsidiarity and proportionality.

If the draft legislative act originates from a group of Member States, the President of the Council shall forward the reasoned opinion or opinions to the governments of those Member States.

If the draft legislative act originates from the Court of Justice, the European Central Bank or the European Investment Bank, the President of the Council shall forward the reasoned opinion or opinions to the institution or body concerned.

Article 4

An eight-week period shall elapse between a draft legislative act being made available to national Parliaments in the official languages of the Union and the date when it is placed on a provisional agenda for the Council for its adoption or for adoption of a position under a legislative procedure. Exceptions shall be possible in cases of urgency, the reasons for which shall be stated in the act or position of the Council. Save in urgent cases for which due reasons have been given, no agreement may be reached on a draft legislative act during those eight weeks. Save in urgent cases for which due reasons have been given, a ten-day period shall elapse between the placing of a draft legislative act on the provisional agenda for the Council and the adoption of a position.

Article 5

The agendas for and the outcome of meetings of the Council, including the minutes of meetings where the Council is deliberating on draft legislative acts, shall be forwarded directly to national Parliaments, at the same time as to Member States' governments.

Article 6

When the European Council intends to make use of the first or second subparagraphs of Article 48(7) of the Treaty on European Union, national Parliaments shall be informed of the initiative of the European Council at least six months before any decision is adopted.

Article 7

The Court of Auditors shall forward its annual report to national Parliaments, for information, at the same time as to the European Parliament and to the Council.

Article 8

Where the national Parliamentary system is not unicameral, Articles 1 to 7 shall apply to the component chambers.

9, 10 *****
*****

European Union Charter of Fundamental Rights (2000)*

Preamble

The peoples of Europe, in creating an ever closer union among them, are resolved to share a peaceful future based on common values.

Conscious of its spiritual and moral heritage, the Union is founded on the indivisible, universal values of human dignity, freedom, equality and solidarity; it is based on the principles of democracy and the rule of law. It places the individual at the heart of its activities, by establishing the citizenship of the Union and by creating an area of freedom, security and justice.

The Union contributes to the preservation and to the development of these common values while respecting the diversity of the cultures and traditions of the peoples of Europe as well as the national identities of the Member States and the organisation of their public authorities at national, regional and local levels; it seeks to promote balanced and sustainable development and ensures free movement of persons, goods, services and capital, and the freedom of establishment.

To this end, it is necessary to strengthen the protection of fundamental rights in the light of changes in society, social progress and scientific and technological developments by making those rights more visible in a Charter.

This Charter reaffirms, with due regard for the powers and tasks of the Community and the Union and the principle of subsidiarity, the rights as they result, in particular, from the constitutional traditions and international obligations common to the Member States, the European Convention for the Protection of Human Rights and Fundamental Freedoms, the Social Charters adopted by the Union and by the Council of Europe and the case law of the Court of Justice of the European Union and of the European Court of Human Rights. In this context the Charter will be interpreted by the courts of the Union and the Member States with due regard to the explanations prepared under the authority of the Praesidium of the Convention which drafted the Charter and updated under the responsibility of the Praesidium of the European Convention.

Enjoyment of these rights entails responsibilities and duties with regard to other persons, to the human community and to future generations.

The Union therefore recognises the rights, freedoms and principles set out hereafter.

Chapter I Dignity

Article 1 Human dignity
Human dignity is inviolable. It must be respected and protected.

Article 2 Right to life
1. Everyone has the right to life.
2. No one shall be condemned to the death penalty, or executed.

Article 3 Right to the integrity of the person
1. Everyone has the right to respect for his or her physical and mental integrity.
2. In the fields of medicine and biology, the following must be respected in particular:

  • the free and informed consent of the person concerned, according to the procedures laid down by law,

  • the prohibition of eugenic practices, in particular those aiming at the selection of persons,

  • the prohibition on making the human body and its parts as such a source of financial gain,

  • the prohibition of the reproductive cloning of human beings.

Article 4 Prohibition of torture and inhuman or degrading treatment or punishment
No one shall be subjected to torture or to inhuman or degrading treatment or punishment.

Article 5 Prohibition of slavery and forced labour
1. No one shall be held in slavery or servitude.
2. No one shall be required to perform forced or compulsory labour.
3. Trafficking in human beings is prohibited.

Chapter II Freedoms

Article 6 Right to liberty and security
Everyone has the right to liberty and security of person.

Article 7 Respect for private and family life
Everyone has the right to respect for his or her private and family life, home and communications.

Article 8 Protection of personal data
1. Everyone has the right to the protection of personal data concerning him or her.

2. Such data must be processed fairly for specified purposes and on the basis of the consent of the person concerned or some other legitimate basis laid down by law. Everyone has the right of access to data which has been collected concerning him or her, and the right to have it rectified.

3. Compliance with these rules shall be subject to control by an independent authority.

Article 9   Right to marry and right to found a family

The right to marry and the right to found a family shall be guaranteed in accordance with the national laws governing the exercise of these rights.

Article 10   Freedom of thought, conscience and religion

1. Everyone has the right to freedom of thought, conscience and religion. This right includes freedom to change religion or belief and freedom, either alone or in community with others and in public or in private, to manifest religion or belief, in worship, teaching, practice and observance.

2. The right to conscientious objection is recognised, in accordance with the national laws governing the exercise of this right.

Article 11   Freedom of expression and information

1. Everyone has the right to freedom of expression. This right shall include freedom to hold opinions and to receive and impart information and ideas without interference by public authority and regardless of frontiers.

2. The freedom and pluralism of the media shall be respected.

Article 12   Freedom of assembly and of association

1. Everyone has the right to freedom of peaceful assembly and to freedom of association at all levels, in particular in political, trade union and civic matters, which implies the right of everyone to form and to join trade unions for the protection of his or her interests.

2. Political parties at Union level contribute to expressing the political will of the citizens of the Union.

Article 13   Freedom of the arts and sciences

The arts and scientific research shall be free of constraint. Academic freedom shall be respected.

Article 14   Right to education

1. Everyone has the right to education and to have access to vocational and continuing training.

2. This right includes the possibility to receive free compulsory education.

3. The freedom to found educational establishments with due respect for democratic principles and the right of parents to ensure the education and teaching of their children in conformity with their religious, philosophical and pedagogical convictions shall be respected, in accordance with the national laws governing the exercise of such freedom and right.

Article 15   Freedom to choose an occupation and right to engage in work

1. Everyone has the right to engage in work and to pursue a freely chosen or accepted occupation.

2. Every citizen of the Union has the freedom to seek employment, to work, to exercise the right of establishment and to provide services in any Member State.

3. Nationals of third countries who are authorised to work in the territories of the Member States are entitled to working conditions equivalent to those of citizens of the Union.

Article 16   Freedom to conduct a business

The freedom to conduct a business in accordance with Community law and national laws and practices is recognised.

Article 17   Right to property

1. Everyone has the right to own, use, dispose of and bequeath his or her lawfully acquired possessions. No one may be deprived of his or her possessions, except in the public interest and in the cases and under the conditions provided for by law, subject to fair compensation being paid in good

time for their loss. The use of property may be regulated by law insofar as is necessary for the general interest.

2. Intellectual property shall be protected.

Article 18   Right to asylum

The right to asylum shall be guaranteed with due respect for the rules of the Geneva Convention of 28 July 1951 and the Protocol of 31 January 1967 relating to the status of refugees and in accordance with the Treaty on European Union and the Treaty on the Functioning of the European Union (hereinafter referred to as 'the Treaties').

Article 19   Protection in the event of removal, expulsion or extradition

1. Collective expulsions are prohibited.

2. No one may be removed, expelled or extradited to a State where there is a serious risk that he or she would be subjected to the death penalty, torture or other inhuman or degrading treatment or punishment.

Chapter III Equality

Article 20   Equality before the law

Everyone is equal before the law.

Article 21   Non-discrimination

1. Any discrimination based on any ground such as sex, race, colour, ethnic or social origin, genetic features, language, religion or belief, political or any other opinion, membership of a national minority, property, birth, disability, age or sexual orientation shall be prohibited.

2. Within the scope of application of the Treaty establishing the European Community and of the Treaty on European Union, and without prejudice to the special provisions of those Treaties, any discrimination on grounds of nationality shall be prohibited.

Article 22   Cultural, religious and linguistic diversity

The Union shall respect cultural, religious and linguistic diversity.

Article 23   Equality between men and women

Equality between men and women must be ensured in all areas, including employment, work and pay.

The principle of equality shall not prevent the maintenance or adoption of measures providing for specific advantages in favour of the under-represented sex.

Article 24   The rights of the child

1. Children shall have the right to such protection and care as is necessary for their well-being. They may express their views freely. Such views shall be taken into consideration on matters which concern them in accordance with their age and maturity.

2. In all actions relating to children, whether taken by public authorities or private institutions, the child's best interests must be a primary consideration.

3. Every child shall have the right to maintain on a regular basis a personal relationship and direct contact with both his or her parents, unless that is contrary to his or her interests.

Article 25   The rights of the elderly

The Union recognises and respects the rights of the elderly to lead a life of dignity and independence and to participate in social and cultural life.

Article 26   Integration of persons with disabilities

The Union recognises and respects the right of persons with disabilities to benefit from measures designed to ensure their independence, social and occupational integration and participation in the life of the community.

Chapter IV Solidarity

Article 27   Workers' right to information and consultation within the undertaking

Workers or their representatives must, at the appropriate levels, be guaranteed information and consultation in good time in the cases and under the conditions provided for by Community law and national laws and practices.

Article 28   Right of collective bargaining and action

Workers and employers, or their respective organisations, have, in accordance with Community law and national laws and practices, the right to negotiate and conclude collective agreements at the appropriate levels and, in cases of conflicts of interest, to take collective action to defend their interests, including strike action.

Article 29   Right of access to placement services

Everyone has the right of access to a free placement service.

Article 30   Protection in the event of unjustified dismissal

Every worker has the right to protection against unjustified dismissal, in accordance with Community law and national laws and practices.

Article 31   Fair and just working conditions

1. Every worker has the right to working conditions which respect his or her health, safety and dignity.

2. Every worker has the right to limitation of maximum working hours, to daily and weekly rest periods and to an annual period of paid leave.

Article 32   Prohibition of child labour and protection of young people at work

The employment of children is prohibited. The minimum age of admission to employment may not be lower than the minimum school-leaving age, without prejudice to such rules as may be more favourable to young people and except for limited derogations.

Young people admitted to work must have working conditions appropriate to their age and be protected against economic exploitation and any work likely to harm their safety, health or physical, mental, moral or social development or to interfere with their education.

Article 33   Family and professional life

1. The family shall enjoy legal, economic and social protection.

2. To reconcile family and professional life, everyone shall have the right to protection from dismissal for a reason connected with maternity and the right to paid maternity leave and to parental leave following the birth or adoption of a child.

Article 34   Social security and social assistance

1. The Union recognises and respects the entitlement to social security benefits and social services providing protection in cases such as maternity, illness, industrial accidents, dependency or old age, and in the case of loss of employment, in accordance with the procedures laid down by Community law and national laws and practices.

2. Everyone residing and moving legally within the European Union is entitled to social security benefits and social advantages in accordance with Community law and national laws and practices.

3. In order to combat social exclusion and poverty, the Union recognises and respects the right to social and housing assistance so as to ensure a decent existence for all those who lack sufficient resources, in accordance with the procedures laid down by Community law and national laws and practices.

Article 35   Health care

Everyone has the right of access to preventive health care and the right to benefit from medical treatment under the conditions established by national laws and practices. A high level of human health protection shall be ensured in the definition and implementation of all Union policies and activities.

Article 36   Access to services of general economic interest

The Union recognises and respects access to services of general economic interest as provided for in national laws and practices, in accordance with the Treaties, in order to promote the social and territorial cohesion of the Union.

Article 37   Environmental protection

A high level of environmental protection and the improvement of the quality of the environment must be integrated into the polices of the Union and ensured in accordance with the principle of sustainable development.

Article 38   Consumer protection

Union policies shall ensure a high level of consumer protection.

Chapter V Citizen's Rights

Article 39   Right to vote and to stand as a candidate at elections to the European Parliament

1. Every citizen of the Union has the right to vote and to stand as a candidate at elections to the European Parliament in the Member State in which he or she resides, under the same conditions as nationals of that State.

2. Members of the European Parliament shall be elected by direct universal suffrage in a free and secret ballot.

Article 40   Right to vote and to stand as a candidate at municipal elections

Every citizen of the Union has the right to vote and to stand as a candidate at municipal elections in the Member State in which he or she resides under the same conditions as nationals of that State.

Article 41   Right to good administration

1. Every person has the right to have his or her affairs handled impartially, fairly and within a reasonable time by the institutions and bodies of the Union.

2. This right includes:

- the right of every person to be heard, before any individual measure which would affect him or her adversely is taken;
- the right of every person to have access to his or her file, while respecting the legitimate interests of confidentiality and of professional and business secrecy;
- the obligation of the administration to give reasons for its decisions.

3. Every person has the right to have the Union make good any damage caused by its institutions or by its servants in the performance of their duties, in accordance with the general principles common to the laws of the Member States.

4. Every person may write to the institutions of the Union in one of the languages of the Treaties and must have an answer in the same language.

Article 42   Right of access to documents

Any citizen of the Union, and any natural or legal person residing or having its registered office in a Member State, has a right of access to documents of the institutions, bodies, offices and agencies of the Union, whatever their medium.

Article 43   European Ombudsman

Any citizen of the Union and any natural or legal person residing or having its registered office in a Member State has the right to refer to the European Ombudsman cases of maladministration in the activities of the institutions, bodies, offices or agencies of the Union, with the exception of the Court of Justice of the European Union acting in its judicial role.

Article 44   Right to petition

Any citizen of the Union and any natural or legal person residing or having its registered office in a Member State has the right to petition the European Parliament.

Article 45   Freedom of movement and of residence

1. Every citizen of the Union has the right to move and reside freely within the territory of the Member States.

2. Freedom of movement and residence may be granted, in accordance with the Treaties, to nationals of third countries legally resident in the territory of a Member State.

Article 46   Diplomatic and consular protection

Every citizen of the Union shall, in the territory of a third country in which the Member State of which he or she is a national is not represented, be entitled to protection by the diplomatic or consular authorities of any Member State, on the same conditions as the nationals of that Member State.

Chapter VI Justice

Article 47   Right to an effective remedy and to a fair trial

Everyone whose rights and freedoms guaranteed by the law of the Union are violated has the right to an effective remedy before a tribunal in compliance with the conditions laid down in this Article. Everyone is entitled to a fair and public hearing within a reasonable time by an independent and impartial tribunal previously established by law. Everyone shall have the possibility of being advised, defended and represented.

Legal aid shall be made available to those who lack sufficient resources insofar as such aid is necessary to ensure effective access to justice.

Article 48   Presumption of innocence and right of defence

1. Everyone who has been charged shall be presumed innocent until proved guilty according to law.

2. Respect for the rights of the defence of anyone who has been charged shall be guaranteed.

Article 49   Principles of legality and proportionality of criminal offences and penalties

1. No one shall be held guilty of any criminal offence on account of any act or omission which did not constitute a criminal offence under national law or international law at the time when it was committed. Nor shall a heavier penalty be imposed than that which was applicable at the time the criminal offence was committed. If, subsequent to the commission of a criminal offence, the law provides for a lighter penalty, that penalty shall be applicable.

2. This Article shall not prejudice the trial and punishment of any person for any act or omission which, at the time when it was committed, was criminal according to the general principles recognised by the community of nations.

3. The severity of penalties must not be disproportionate to the criminal offence.

Article 50   Right not to be tried or punished twice in criminal proceedings for the same criminal offence

No one shall be liable to be tried or punished again in criminal proceedings for an offence for which he or she has already been finally acquitted or convicted within the Union in accordance with the Law.

Chapter VII General Provisions Governing the Interpretation and Application of the Charter

Article 51   Field of Application

1. The provisions of this Charter are addressed to the institutions, bodies, offices and agencies of the Union with due regard for the principle of subsidiarity and to the Member States only when

they are implementing Union law. They shall therefore respect the rights, observe the principles and promote the application thereof in accordance with their respective powers and respecting the limits of the powers of the Union as conferred on it in the Treaties.

2. The Charter does not extend the field of application of Union law beyond the powers of the Union or establish any new power or task for the Union, or modify powers and tasks as defined in the Treaties.

Article 52   Scope and interpretation of rights and principles

1. Any limitation on the exercise of the rights and freedoms recognised by this Charter must be provided for by law and respect the essence of those rights and freedoms. Subject to the principle of proportionality, limitations may be made only if they are necessary and genuinely meet objectives of general interest recognized by the Union or the need to protect the rights and freedoms of others.

2. Rights recognised by this Charter for which provision is made in the Treaties shall be exercised under the conditions and within the limits defined by those Treaties.

3. Insofar as this Charter contains rights which correspond to rights guaranteed by the Convention for the Protection of Human Rights and Fundamental Freedoms, the meaning and scope of those rights shall be the same as those laid down by the said Convention. This provision shall not prevent Union law providing more extensive protection.

4. In so far as this Charter recognises fundamental rights as they result from the constitutional traditions common to the Member States, those rights shall be interpreted in harmony with those traditions.

5. The provisions of this Charter which contain principles may be implemented by legislative and executive acts taken by institutions, bodies, offices and agencies of the Union, and by acts of Member States when they are implementing Union law, in the exercise of their respective powers. They shall be judicially cognisable only in the interpretation of such acts and in the ruling on their legality.

6. Full account shall be taken of national laws and practices as specified in the Charter.

7. The explanations drawn up as a way of providing guidance in the interpretation of this Charter shall be given due regard by the courts of the Union and of the Member States.

Article 53   Level of protection

Nothing in this Charter shall be interpreted as restricting or adversely affecting human rights and fundamental freedoms as recognised, in their respective fields of application, by Union law and international law and by international agreements to which the Union, or all the Member States are party, including the European Convention for the Protection of Human Rights and Fundamental Freedoms, and by the Member States' constitutions.

Article 54   Prohibition of abuse of rights

Nothing in this Charter shall be interpreted as implying any right to engage in any activity or to perform any act aimed at the destruction of any of the rights and freedoms recognised in this Charter or at their limitation to a greater extent than is provided for herein.

Part III

PACE Codes

Note: For the legal status of the Codes and other issues relating to them, see ss. 66 and 67 of the Police and Criminal Evidence Act 1984 *(supra)*. The Codes have been revised regularly in accordance with s. 67(7) of the Act. The most recent revised versions of the Codes reproduced here took effect on 1st January 2006 (Code B), 25th July 2006 (Code C) and 31st July 2006 (Code A) respectively; they were further revised with effect from 31st January 2008, and these revisions are incorporated in the text. Code H is a new Code, which came into effect in August 2006. Codes D (on methods used by the police to identify people in connection with the investigation of offences), E (on tape recording of interviews with suspects in the police station) and F (on the visual recording of interviews with suspects) are not reproduced here. The Codes apply only to England and Wales. A Welsh language edition of the Codes is available.

Code A Code of Practice for the Exercise by Police Officers of Statutory Powers of Stop and Search

General
This code of practice must be readily available at all police stations for consultation by police officers, police staff, detained persons and members of the public. The notes for guidance included are not provisions of this code, but are guidance to police officers and others about its application and interpretation. Provisions in the annexes to the code are provisions of this code.
*****

1 Principles governing stop and search
1.1 Powers to stop and search must be used fairly, responsibly, with respect for people being searched and without unlawful discrimination. The Equality Act 2010 makes it unlawful for police officers to discriminate against, harass or victimise any person on the grounds of the 'protected characteristics' of age, disability, gender reassignment, race, religion or belief, sex and sexual orientation, marriage and civil partnership, pregnancy and maternity when using their powers. When police forces are carrying out their functions they also have a duty to have regard to the need to eliminate unlawful discrimination, harassment and victimisation and to take steps to foster good relations.

1.2 The intrusion on the liberty of the person stopped or searched must be brief and detention for the purposes of a search must take place at or near the location of the stop.

1.3 If these fundamental principles are not observed the use of powers to stop and search may be drawn into question. Failure to use the powers in the proper manner reduces their effectiveness. Stop and search can play an important role in the detection and prevention of crime, and using the powers fairly makes them more effective.

1.4 The primary purpose of stop and search powers is to enable officers to allay or confirm suspicions about individuals without exercising their power of arrest. Officers may be required to justify the use or authorisation of such powers, in relation both to individual searches and the overall pattern of their activity in this regard, to their supervisory officers or in court. Any misuse of the powers is likely to be harmful to policing and lead to mistrust of the police. Officers must also be able to explain their actions to the member of the public searched. The misuse of these powers can lead to disciplinary action.

1.5 An officer must not search a person, even with his or her consent, where no power to search is applicable. Even where a person is prepared to submit to a search voluntarily, the person must not be searched unless the necessary legal power exists, and the search must be in accordance with the relevant power and the provisions of this Code. The only exception, where an officer does not require a specific power, applies to searches of persons entering sports grounds or other premises carried out with their consent given as a condition of entry.

2   Explanation of powers to stop and search

2.1 This code applies to powers of stop and search as follows:

(a) powers which require reasonable grounds for suspicion, before they may be exercised; that articles unlawfully obtained or possessed are being carried, or under Section 43 of the Terrorism Act 2000 that a person is a terrorist;

(b) authorised under section 60 of the Criminal Justice and Public Order Act 1994, based upon a reasonable belief that incidents involving serious violence may take place or that people are carrying dangerous instruments or offensive weapons within any locality in the police area or that it is expedient to use the powers to find such instruments or weapons that have been used in incidents of serious violence;

(c) authorised under section 44(1) of the Terrorism Act 2000 based upon a consideration that the exercise of the power is necessary for the prevention of acts of terrorism (see paragraph 2.18A), and

(d) powers to search a person who has not been arrested in the exercise of a power to search premises (see Code B paragraph 2.4).

Searches requiring reasonable grounds for suspicion

2.2 Reasonable grounds for suspicion depend on the circumstances in each case. There must be an objective basis for that suspicion based on facts, information, and/or intelligence which are relevant to the likelihood of finding an article of a certain kind or, in the case of searches under section 43 of the Terrorism Act 2000, to the likelihood that the person is a terrorist. Reasonable suspicion can never be supported on the basis of personal factors. It must rely on intelligence or information about or some specific behaviour, by the person concerned. For example, unless the police have a description of a suspect, a person's physical appearance (including any of the 'protected characteristics' set out in the Equality Act 2010 (see paragraph 1.1), or the fact that the person is known to have a previous conviction, cannot be used alone or in combination with each other, or in combination with any other factor, as the reason for searching that person. Reasonable suspicion cannot be based on generalisations or stereotypical images of certain groups or categories of people as more likely to be involved in criminal activity.

2.3 Reasonable suspicion may also exist without specific information or intelligence and on the basis of the behaviour of a person. For example, if an officer encounters someone on the street at night who is obviously trying to hide something, the officer may (depending on the other surrounding circumstances) base such suspicion on the fact that this kind of behaviour is often linked to stolen or prohibited articles being carried. Similarly, for the purposes of section 43 of the Terrorism Act 2000, suspicion that a person is a terrorist may arise from the person's behaviour at or near a location which has been identified as a potential target for terrorists.

2.4 However, reasonable suspicion should normally be linked to accurate and current intelligence or information, such as information describing an article being carried, a suspected offender, or a person who has been seen carrying a type of article known to have been stolen recently from premises in the area. Searches based on accurate and current intelligence or information are more likely to be effective. Targeting searches in a particular area at specified crime problems increases their effectiveness and minimises inconvenience to law-abiding members of the public. It also helps in justifying the use of searches both to those who are searched and to the public. This does not however prevent stop and search powers being exercised in other locations where such powers may be exercised and reasonable suspicion exists.

2.5 Searches are more likely to be effective, legitimate, and secure public confidence when reasonable suspicion is based on a range of factors. The overall use of these powers is more likely to be effective when up to date and accurate intelligence or information is communicated to officers and they are well-informed about local crime patterns.

2.6 Where there is reliable information or intelligence that members of a group or gang habitually carry knives unlawfully or weapons or controlled drugs, and wear a distinctive item of clothing or other means of identification to indicate their membership of the group or gang, that distinctive item of clothing or other means of identification may provide reasonable grounds to stop and search a person. [See *Note 9*]

2.7 A police officer may have reasonable grounds to suspect that a person is in innocent possession of a stolen or prohibited article or other item for which he or she is empowered to search. In that case the officer may stop and search the person even though there would be no power of arrest.

2.8 Under section 43(1) of the Terrorism Act 2000 a constable may stop and search a person whom the officer reasonably suspects to be a terrorist to discover whether the person is in possession of anything which may constitute evidence that the person is a terrorist. These searches may only be carried out by an officer of the same sex as the person searched (see Annex F). An authorisation under section 44(1) of the Terrorism Act 2000 allows vehicles to be stopped and searched by a constable in uniform who reasonably suspects that articles which could be used in connection with terrorism will be found in the vehicle or in anything in or on that vehicle. (See paragraph 2.18A below.)

2.9 An officer who has reasonable grounds for suspicion may detain the person concerned in order to carry out a search. Before carrying out a search the officer may ask questions about the person's behaviour or presence in circumstances which gave rise to the suspicion. As a result of questioning the detained person, the reasonable grounds for suspicion necessary to detain that person may be confirmed or, because of a satisfactory explanation, be eliminated. [See *Notes 2* and *3*] Questioning may also reveal reasonable grounds to suspect the possession of a different kind of unlawful article from that originally suspected. Reasonable grounds for suspicion however cannot be provided retrospectively by such questioning during a person's detention or by refusal to answer any questions put.

2.10 If, as a result of questioning before a search, or other circumstances which come to the attention of the officer, there cease to be reasonable grounds for suspecting that an article is being carried of a kind for which there is a power to stop and search, no search may take place. [See *Note 3*] In the absence of any other lawful power to detain, the person is free to leave at will and must be so informed.

2.11 There is no power to stop or detain a person in order to find grounds for a search. Police officers have many encounters with members of the public which do not involve detaining people against their will. If reasonable grounds for suspicion emerge during such an encounter, the officer may search the person, even though no grounds existed when the encounter began. If an officer is detaining someone for the purpose of a search, he or she should inform the person as soon as detention begins.

2.12–2.26 *****

Powers to search in the exercise of a power to search premises

2.27 The following powers to search premises also authorise the search of a person, not under arrest, who is found on the premises during the course of the search:

(a) section 139B of the Criminal Justice Act 1988 under which a constable may enter school premises and search the premises and any person on those premises for any bladed or pointed article or offensive weapon;

(b) under a warrant issued under section 23(3) of the Misuse of Drugs Act 1971 to search premises for drugs or documents but only if the warrant specifically authorises the search of persons found on the premises; and

(c) under a search warrant or order issued under paragraph 1, 3 or 11 of Schedule 5 to the Terrorism Act 2000 to search premises and any person found there for material likely to be of substantial value to a terrorist investigation.

2.28 Before the power under section 139 B of the Criminal Justice Act 1988 may be exercised, the constable must have reasonable grounds to believe that an offence under section 139A of the Criminal Justice Act 1988(having a bladed or pointed article or offensive weapon on school premises) has been or is being committed. A warrant to search premises and persons found therein may be issued under section 23(3) of the Misuse of Drugs Act 1971 if there are reasonable grounds to suspect that controlled drugs or certain documents are in the possession of a person on the premises.

2.29 The powers in paragraph 2.27 do not require prior specific grounds to suspect that the person to be searched is in possession of an item for which there is an existing power to search. However, it is still necessary to ensure that the selection and treatment of those searched under these powers is based upon objective factors connected with the search of the premises, and not upon personal prejudice.

3   Conduct of searches

3.1 All stops and searches must be carried out with courtesy, consideration and respect for the person concerned. This has a significant impact on public confidence in the police. Every reasonable effort must be made to minimise the embarrassment that a person being searched may experience. [See *Note 4*]

3.2 The co-operation of the person to be searched must be sought in every case, even if the person initially objects to the search. A forcible search may be made only if it has been established that the person is unwilling to co-operate or resists. Reasonable force may be used as a last resort if necessary to conduct a search or to detain a person or vehicle for the purposes of a search.

3.3 The length of time for which a person or vehicle may be detained must be reasonable and kept to a minimum. Where the exercise of the power requires reasonable suspicion, the thoroughness and extent of a search must depend on what is suspected of being carried, and by whom. If the suspicion relates to a particular article which is seen to be slipped into a person's pocket, then, in the absence of other grounds for suspicion or an opportunity for the article to be moved elsewhere, the search must be confined to that pocket. In the case of a small article which can readily be concealed, such as a drug, and which might be concealed anywhere on the person, a more extensive search may be necessary. In the case of searches mentioned in paragraph 2.1(b), (c), and (d), which do not require reasonable grounds for suspicion, officers may make any reasonable search to look for items for which they are empowered to search. [See *Note 5*]

3.4 The search must be carried out at or near the place where the person or vehicle was first detained. [See *Note 6*]

3.5 There is no power to require a person to remove any clothing in public other than an outer coat, jacket or gloves except under section 60AA of the Criminal Justice and Public Order Act 1994 (which empowers a constable to require a person to remove any item worn to conceal identity). [See *Notes 4* and *6*] A search in public of a person's clothing which has not been removed must be restricted to superficial examination of outer garments. This does not, however, prevent an officer from placing his or her hand inside the pockets of the outer clothing, or feeling round the inside of collars, socks and shoes if this is reasonably necessary in the circumstances to look for the object of the search or to remove and examine any item reasonably suspected to be the object of the search.

For the same reasons, subject to the restrictions on the removal of headgear, a person's hair may also be searched in public (see paragraphs 3.1 and 3.3).

3.6 Where on reasonable grounds it is considered necessary to conduct a more thorough search (e.g. by requiring a person to take off a T-shirt), this must be done out of public view, for example, in a police van unless paragraph 3.7 applies, or police station if there is one nearby. [See *Note 6*] Any search involving the removal of more than an outer coat, jacket, gloves, headgear or footwear, or any other item concealing identity, may only be made by an officer of the same sex as the person searched and may not be made in the presence of anyone of the opposite sex unless the person being searched specifically requests it. [See *Annex F Notes 4, 7* and *8*]

3.7 Searches involving exposure of intimate parts of the body must not be conducted as a routine extension of a less thorough search, simply because nothing is found in the course of the initial search. Searches involving exposure of intimate parts of the body may be carried out only at a nearby police station or other nearby location which is out of public view (but not a police vehicle). These searches must be conducted in accordance with paragraph 11 of Annex A to Code C except that an intimate search mentioned in paragraph 11(f) of Annex A to Code C may not be authorised or carried out under any stop and search powers. The other provisions of Code C do not apply to the conduct and recording of searches of persons detained at police stations in the exercise of stop and search powers. [See *Note 7*]

Steps to be taken prior to a search

3.8 Before any search of a detained person or attended vehicle takes place the officer must take reasonable steps, if not in uniform (see paragraph 3.9), to show their warrant card to the person to be searched or in charge of the vehicle to be searched and whether or not in uniform, to give that person the following information:

(a) that they are being detained for the purposes of a search;

(b) the officer's name (except in the case of enquiries linked to the investigation of terrorism, or otherwise where the officer reasonably believes that giving his or her name might put him or her in danger, in which case a warrant or other identification number shall be given) and the name of the police station to which the officer is attached;

(c) the legal search power which is being exercised; and

(d) a clear explanation of:

  (i) the object of the search in terms of the article or articles for which there is a power to search; and

  (ii) in the case of:

  • the power under section 60 of the Criminal Justice and Public Order Act 1994 (see *paragraph 2.1(b)*), the nature of the power, the authorisation and the fact that it has been given;

  • the power under section 44 of the Terrorism Act 2000, the nature of the power, the authorisation and the fact that it has been given and the grounds for suspicion; (see *paragraph 2.1(c)* and *2.18A.*)

  • all other powers requiring reasonable suspicion (see *paragraph 2.1(a)*), the grounds for that suspicion.

(e) that they are entitled to a copy of the record of the search if one is made (see section 4 below) if they ask within 3 months from the date of the search and:

  (i) if they are not arrested and taken to a police station as a result of the search and it is practicable to make the record on the spot, that immediately after the search is completed they will be given, if they request, either:

  • a copy of the record, or

  • a receipt which explains how they can obtain a copy of the full record or access to an electronic copy of the record, or

  (ii) if they are arrested and taken to a police station as a result of the search, that the record will be made at the station as part of their custody record and they will be given, if they request, a copy of their custody record which includes a record of the search as soon as practicable whilst they are at the station. [See *Note 16*]

3.9 Stops and searches under the powers mentioned in paragraphs 2.1(b), and (c) may be undertaken only by a constable in uniform.

3.10 The person should also be given information about police powers to stop and search and the individual's rights in these circumstances.

3.11 If the person to be searched, or in charge of a vehicle to be searched, does not appear to understand what is being said, or there is any doubt about the person's ability to understand English, the officer must take reasonable steps to bring information regarding the person's rights and any relevant provisions of this Code to his or her attention. If the person is deaf or cannot understand

English and is accompanied by someone, then the officer must try to establish whether that person can interpret or otherwise help the officer to give the required information.

4   Recording requirements

(a) Searches which do not result in an arrest

4.1 When an officer carries out a search in the exercise of any power to which this Code applies and the search does not result in the person searched or person in charge of the vehicle searched being arrested and taken to a police station, a record must be made of it, electronically or on paper, unless there are exceptional circumstances which make this wholly impracticable (e.g. in situations involving public disorder or when the recording officer's presence is urgently required elsewhere). If a record is to be made, the officer carrying out the search must make the record on the spot unless this is not practicable, in which case, the officer must make the record as soon as practicable after the search is completed. [See *Note 16.*]

4.2 If the record is made at the time, the person who has been searched or who is in charge of the vehicle that has been searched must be asked if they want a copy and if they do, they must be given immediately, either:

- a copy of the record, or
- a receipt which explains how they can obtain a copy of the full record or access to an electronic copy of the record.

4.2A An officer is not required to provide a copy of the full record or a receipt at the time if they are called to an incident of higher priority. [See *Note 21*]

(b) Searches which result in an arrest

4.2B If a search in the exercise of any power to which this Code applies results in a person being arrested and taken to a police station, the officer carrying out the search is responsible for ensuring that a record of the search is made as part of their custody record. The custody officer must then ensure that the person is asked if they want a copy of the record and if they do, that they are given a copy as soon as practicable. [See *Note 16*].

(c) Record of search

4.3 The record of a search must always include the following information:

- (a) A note of the self defined ethnicity, and if different, the ethnicity as perceived by the officer making the search, of the person searched or of the person in charge of the vehicle searched (as the case may be); [See *Note 18*]
- (b) The date, time and place the person or vehicle was searched [See *Note 6*];
- (c) The object of the search in terms of the article or articles for which there is a power to search;
- (d) In the case of:
  - the power under section 60 of the Criminal Justice and Public Order Act 1994 (see *paragraph 2.1(b)*), the nature of the power, the authorisation and the fact that it has been given; [See *Note 17*]
  - the power under section 44 of the Terrorism Act 2000, the nature of the power, the authorisation and the fact that it has been given and the grounds for suspicion; [see *paragraphs 2.1(c)* and *2.18A and Note 17*].
  - all other powers requiring reasonable suspicion (see *paragraph 2.1(a)*), the grounds for that suspicion.
- (e) subject to paragraph 3.8(b), the identity of the officer carrying out the search. [See *Note 15*]

4.3A For the purposes of completing the search record, there is no requirement to record the name, address and date of birth of the person searched or the person in charge of a vehicle which is searched and the person is under no obligation to provide this information.

4.4 Nothing in paragraph 4.3 requires the names of police officers to be shown on the search record or any other record required to be made under this code in the case of enquiries linked to the investigation of terrorism or otherwise where an officer reasonably believes that recording names might endanger the officers. In such cases the record must show the officers' warrant or other identification number and duty station.

4.5 A record is required for each person and each vehicle searched. However, if a person is in a vehicle and both are searched, and the object and grounds of the search are the same, only one record need be completed. If more than one person in a vehicle is searched, separate records for each search of a person must be made. If only a vehicle is searched, the self-defined ethnic background of the person in charge of the vehicle must be recorded, unless the vehicle is unattended.

4.6 The record of the grounds for making a search must, briefly but informatively, explain the reason for suspecting the person concerned, by reference to the person's behaviour and/or other circumstances.

4.7 Where officers detain an individual with a view to performing a search, but the need to search is eliminated as a result of questioning the person detained, a search should not be carried out and a record is not required. [See *paragraph 2.10, Notes 3* and *22A*]

4.8 After searching an unattended vehicle, or anything in or on it, an officer must leave a notice in it (or on it, if things on it have been searched without opening it) recording the fact that it has been searched.

4.9 The notice must include the name of the police station to which the officer concerned is attached and state where a copy of the record of the search may be obtained and how (if applicable) an electronic copy may be accessed and where any application for compensation should be directed.

4.10 The vehicle must if practicable be left secure.

4.10A–4.20 *****

5   Monitoring and supervising the use of stop and search powers

5.1 Supervising officers must monitor the use of stop and search powers and should consider in particular whether there is any evidence that they are being exercised on the basis of stereotyped images or inappropriate generalisations. Supervising officers should satisfy themselves that the practice of officers under their supervision in stopping, searching and recording is fully in accordance with this Code. Supervisors must also examine whether the records reveal any trends or patterns which give cause for concern, and if so take appropriate action to address this.

5.2 Senior officers with area or force-wide responsibilities must also monitor the broader use of stop and search powers and, where necessary, take action at the relevant level.

5.3 Supervision and monitoring must be supported by the compilation of comprehensive statistical records of stops and searches at force, area and local level. Any apparently disproportionate use of the powers by particular officers or groups of officers or in relation to specific sections of the community should be identified and investigated.

5.4 In order to promote public confidence in the use of the powers, forces in consultation with police authorities must make arrangements for the records to be scrutinised by representatives of the community, and to explain the use of the powers at a local level.

Notes for guidance

Officers exercising stop and search powers

1 This code does not affect the ability of an officer to speak to or question a person in the ordinary course of the officer's duties without detaining the person or exercising any element of compulsion. It is not the purpose of the code to prohibit such encounters between the police and the community with the co-operation of the person concerned and neither does it affect the principle that all citizens have a duty to help police officers to prevent crime and discover offenders. This is a civic rather than a legal duty; but when a police officer is trying to discover whether, or by whom, an offence has been committed he or she may question any person from whom useful information might be obtained, subject to the restrictions imposed by Code C. A person's unwillingness to reply does not alter this entitlement, but in the absence of a power to arrest, or to detain in order to search, the person is free to leave at will and cannot be compelled to remain with the officer.

2 In some circumstances preparatory questioning may be unnecessary, but in general a brief conversation or exchange will be desirable not only as a means of avoiding unsuccessful searches, but to explain the grounds for the stop/search, to gain cooperation and reduce any tension there might be surrounding the stop/search.

3 Where a person is lawfully detained for the purpose of a search, but no search in the event takes place, the detention will not thereby have been rendered unlawful.

4 Many people customarily cover their heads or faces for religious reasons – for example, Muslim women, Sikh men, Sikh or Hindu women, or Rastarfarian men or women. A police officer cannot order the removal of a head or face covering except where there is reason to believe that the item is being worn by the individual wholly or mainly for the purpose of disguising identity, not simply because it disguises identity. Where there may be religious sensitivities about ordering the removal of such an item, the officer should permit the item to be removed out of public view. Where practicable, the item should be removed in the presence of an officer of the same sex as the person and out of sight of anyone of the opposite sex.

5 A search of a person in public should be completed as soon as possible.

6 A person may be detained under a stop and search power at a place other than where the person was first detained, only if that place, be it a police station or elsewhere, is nearby. Such a place should be located within a reasonable travelling distance using whatever mode of travel (on foot or by car) is appropriate. This applies to all searches under stop and search powers, whether or not they involve the removal of clothing or exposure of intimate parts of the body (see paragraphs 3.6 and 3.7) or take place in or out of public view. It means, for example, that a search under the stop and search power in section 23 of the Misuse of Drugs Act 1971 which involves the compulsory removal of more than a person's outer coat, jacket or gloves cannot be carried out unless a place which is both nearby the place they were first detained and out of public view, is available. If a search involves exposure of intimate parts of the body and a police station is not nearby, particular care must be taken to ensure that the location is suitable in that it enables the search to be conducted in accordance with the requirements of paragraph 11 of Annex A to Code C.

7 A search in the street itself should be regarded as being in public for the purposes of paragraphs 3.6 and 3.7 above, even though it may be empty at the time a search begins. Although there is no power to require a person to do so, there is nothing to prevent an officer from asking a person voluntarily to remove more than an outer coat, jacket or gloves in public.

8 Not Used

9 Other means of identification might include jewellery, insignias, tattoos or other features which are known to identify members of the particular gang or group.

*10–23 *****

24–25 Not Used

Annexes A–C and F *****

Code B Code of Practice for Searches of Premises by Police Officers and the Seizure of Property Found by Police Officers on Persons or Premises

1   Introduction

1.1 This Code of Practice deals with police powers to:
- search premises
- seize and retain property found on premises and persons

1.1A These powers may be used to find:
- property and material relating to a crime
- wanted persons
- children who abscond from local authority accommodation where they have been remanded or committed by a court

1.2 A justice of the peace may issue a search warrant granting powers of entry, search and seizure, e.g. warrants to search for stolen property, drugs, firearms and evidence of serious offences. Police also have powers without a search warrant. The main ones provided by the Police and Criminal Evidence Act 1984 (PACE) include powers to search premises:

- to make an arrest
- after an arrest

1.3 The right to privacy and respect for personal property are key principles of the Human Rights Act 1998. Powers of entry, search and seizure should be fully and clearly justified before use because they may significantly interfere with the occupier's privacy. Officers should consider if the necessary objectives can be met by less intrusive means.

1.3A Powers to search and seize must be used fairly, responsibly, with respect for people who occupy premises being searched or are in charge of property being seized and without unlawful discrimination. The Equality Act 2010 makes it unlawful for police officers to discriminate against, harass or victimise any person on the grounds of the 'protected characteristics' of age, disability, gender reassignment, race, religion or belief, sex and sexual orientation, marriage and civil partnership, pregnancy and maternity when using their powers. When police forces are carrying out their functions they also have a duty to have regard to the need to eliminate unlawful discrimination, harassment and victimisation and to take steps to foster good relations.

1.4 In all cases, police should:

- exercise their powers courteously and with respect for persons and property
- only use reasonable force when this is considered necessary and proportionate to the circumstances

1.5 If the provisions of PACE and this Code are not observed, evidence obtained from a search may be open to question.

2 General

2.1 This Code must be readily available at all police stations for consultation by:

- police officers
- police staff
- detained persons
- members of the public

2.2 The *Notes for Guidance* included are not provisions of this Code.

2.3 This Code applies to searches of premises:

(a) by police for the purposes of an investigation into an alleged offence, with the occupier's consent, other than:
- routine scene of crime searches;
- calls to a fire or burglary made by or on behalf of an occupier or searches following the activation of fire or burglar alarms or discovery of insecure premises;
- searches when *paragraph 5.4* applies;
- bomb threat calls;

(b) under powers conferred on police officers by PACE, sections 17, 18 and 32;

(c) undertaken in pursuance of search warrants issued to and executed by constables in accordance with PACE, sections 15 and 16;

(d) subject to *paragraph 2.6*, under any other power given to police to enter premises with or without a search warrant for any purpose connected with the investigation into an alleged or suspected offence.

For the purposes of this Code, 'premises' as defined in PACE, section 23, includes any place, vehicle, vessel, aircraft, hovercraft, tent or movable structure and any offshore installation as defined in the Mineral Workings (Offshore Installations) Act 1971, section 1.

2.4–2.13 *****

3   Search warrants and production orders

(a) Before making an application

3.1 When information appears to justify an application, the officer must take reasonable steps to check the information is accurate, recent and not provided maliciously or irresponsibly. An application may not be made on the basis of information from an anonymous source if corroboration has not been sought. See *Note 3A*

3.2 The officer shall ascertain as specifically as possible the nature of the articles concerned and their location.

3.3 The officer shall make reasonable enquiries to:
- (i) establish if:
  - anything is known about the likely occupier of the premises and the nature of the premises themselves;
  - the premises have been searched previously and how recently
- (ii) obtain any other relevant information.

3.4 An application:
- (a) to a justice of the peace for a search warrant or to a circuit judge for a search warrant or production order under PACE, Schedule 1 must be supported by a signed written authority from an officer of inspector rank or above;

  Note: If the case is an urgent application to a justice of the peace and an inspector or above is not readily available, the next most senior officer on duty can give the written authority.
- (b) to a circuit judge under the Terrorism Act 2000, Schedule 5 for
  - a production order;
  - search warrant; or
  - an order requiring an explanation of material seized or produced under such a warrant or production order
  - must be supported by a signed written authority from an officer of superintendent rank or above.

3.5 Except in a case of urgency, if there is reason to believe a search might have an adverse effect on relations between the police and the community, the officer in charge shall consult the local police/community liaison officer:
- before the search; or
- in urgent cases, as soon as practicable after the search

(b) Making an application

3.6 A search warrant application must be supported in writing, specifying:
- (a) the enactment under which the application is made,
- (b) (i) whether the warrant is to authorise entry and search of:
  - one set of premises; or
  - if the application is under PACE section 8, or Schedule 1, paragraph 12, more than one set of specified premises or all premises occupied or controlled by a specified person, and
  - (ii) the premises to be searched;
- (c) the object of the search,
- (d) the grounds for the application, including, when the purpose of the proposed search is to find evidence of an alleged offence, an indication of how the evidence relates to the investigation;
- (da) where the application is under PACE section 8, or Schedule 1, paragraph 12 for a single warrant to enter and search:
  - (i) more than one set of specified premises, the officer must specify each set of premises which it is desired to enter and search

    (ii) all premises occupied or controlled by a specified person, the officer must specify;
- as many sets of premises which it is desired to enter and search as it is reasonably practicable to specify
- the person who is in occupation or control of those premises and any others which it is desired to search
- why it is necessary to search more premises than those which can be specified
- why it is not reasonably practicable to specify all the premises which it is desired to enter and search;

  (db) whether an application under PACE section 8 is for a warrant authorising entry and search on more than one occasion, and if so, the officer must state the grounds for this and whether the desired number of entries authorised is unlimited or a specified maximum;

  (e) there are no reasonable grounds to believe the material to be sought, when making application to a:

    (i) justice of the peace or a Circuit judge, consists of or includes items subject to legal privilege;

    (ii) justice of the peace, consists of or includes excluded material or special procedure material;

  (f) if applicable, a request for the warrant to authorise a person or persons to accompany the officer who executes the warrant.

3.7 A search warrant application under PACE, Schedule 1, paragraph 12(a), shall if appropriate indicate why it is believed service of notice of an application for a production order may seriously prejudice the investigation. Applications for search warrants under the Terrorism Act 2000, Schedule 5, paragraph 11 must indicate why a production order would not be appropriate.

3.8 If a search warrant application is refused, a further application may not be made for those premises unless supported by additional grounds.

Notes for guidance

3A The identity of an informant need not be disclosed when making an application, but the officer should be prepared to answer any questions the magistrate or judge may have about:
- *the accuracy of previous information from that source*
- *any other related matters*

3B The information supporting a search warrant application should be as specific as possible, particularly in relation to the articles or persons being sought and where in the premises it is suspected they may be found. The meaning of 'items subject to legal privilege', 'excluded material' and 'special procedure material' are defined by PACE, sections 10, 11 and 14 respectively.

3C Under PACE, section 16(2), a search warrant may authorise persons other than police officers to accompany the constable who executes the warrant. This includes, e.g. any suitably qualified or skilled person or an expert in a particular field whose presence is needed to help accurately identify the material sought or to advise where certain evidence is most likely to be found and how it should be dealt with. It does not give them any right to force entry, to search for or seize property but it gives them the right to be on the premises during the search without the occupier's permission.

4 *****

5 Search with consent

5.1 Subject to *paragraph 5.4*, if it is proposed to search premises with the consent of a person entitled to grant entry the consent must, if practicable, be given in writing on the Notice of Powers and Rights before the search. The officer must make any necessary enquiries to be satisfied the person is in a position to give such consent. *See Notes 5A and 5B*

5.2 Before seeking consent the officer in charge of the search shall state the purpose of the proposed search and its extent. This information must be as specific as possible, particularly regarding the articles or persons being sought and the parts of the premises to be searched. The person concerned must be clearly informed they are not obliged to consent, that any consent given can be withdrawn at any time, including before the search starts or while it is underway and anything seized may be produced in evidence. If at the time the person is not suspected of an offence, the officer shall say this when stating the purpose of the search.

5.3 An officer cannot enter and search or continue to search premises under *paragraph 5.1* if consent is given under duress or withdrawn before the search is completed.

5.4 It is unnecessary to seek consent under *paragraphs 5.1* and *5.2* if this would cause disproportionate inconvenience to the person concerned. See *Note 5C*

Notes for guidance

5A In a lodging house or similar accommodation, every reasonable effort should be made to obtain the consent of the tenant, lodger or occupier. A search should not be made solely on the basis of the landlord's consent.

5B If the intention is to search premises under the authority of a warrant or a power of entry and search without warrant, and the occupier of the premises co-operates in accordance with paragraph 6.4, there is no need to obtain written consent.

5C Paragraph 5.4 is intended to apply when it is reasonable to assume innocent occupiers would agree to, and expect, police to take the proposed action, e.g. if:

- *a suspect has fled the scene of a crime or to evade arrest and it is necessary quickly to check surrounding gardens and readily accessible places to see if the suspect is hiding*
- *police have arrested someone in the night after a pursuit and it is necessary to make a brief check of gardens along the pursuit route to see if stolen or incriminating articles have been discarded.*

6 Searching premises—general considerations

(a) Time of searches

6.1 Searches made under warrant must be made within three calendar months of the date of the warrant's issue.

6.2 Searches must be made at a reasonable hour unless this might frustrate the purpose of the search.

6.3 When the extent or complexity of a search mean it is likely to take a long time, the officer in charge of the search may consider using the seize and sift powers referred to in *section 7*.

6.3A A warrant under PACE, section 8 may authorise entry to and search of premises on more than one occasion if, on the application, the justice of the peace is satisfied that it is necessary to authorise multiple entries in order to achieve the purpose for which the warrant is issued. No premises may be entered or searched on any subsequent occasions without the prior written authority of an officer of the rank of inspector who is not involved in the investigation. All other warrants authorise entry on one occasion only.

6.3B Where a warrant under PACE section 8, or Schedule 1, paragraph 12 authorises entry to and search of all premises occupied or controlled by a specified person, no premises which are not specified in the warrant may be entered and searched without the prior written authority of an officer of the rank of inspector who is not involved in the investigation.

(b) Entry other than with consent

6.4 The officer in charge of the search shall first try to communicate with the occupier, or any other person entitled to grant access to the premises, explain the authority under which entry is sought and ask the occupier to allow entry, unless:

- (i)   the search premises are unoccupied;
- (ii) the occupier and any other person entitled to grant access are absent;
- (iii) there are reasonable grounds for believing that alerting the occupier or any other person entitled to grant access would frustrate the object of the search or endanger officers or other people.

6.5 Unless *sub-paragraph 6.4(iii)* applies, if the premises are occupied the officer, subject to *paragraph 2.9*, shall, before the search begins:

    (i)   identify him or herself, show their warrant card (if not in uniform) and state the purpose of and grounds for the search;

    (ii)   identify and introduce any person accompanying the officer on the search (such persons should carry identification for production on request) and briefly describe that person's role in the process.

6.6 Reasonable and proportionate force may be used if necessary to enter premises if the officer in charge of the search is satisfied the premises are those specified in any warrant, or in exercise of the powers described in *paragraphs 4.1* to *4.3*, and if:

    (i)   the occupier or any other person entitled to grant access has refused entry;

    (ii)   it is impossible to communicate with the occupier or any other person entitled to grant access; or

    (iii)   any of the provisions of *paragraphs 6.4* apply.

6.7, 6.8 *****

(d) Conduct of searches

6.9 Premises may be searched only to the extent necessary to achieve the purpose of the search, having regard to the size and nature of whatever is sought.

6.9A A search may not continue under:

- a warrant's authority once all the things specified in that warrant have been found;
- any other power once the object of that search has been achieved.

6.9B No search may continue once the officer in charge of the search is satisfied whatever is being sought is not on the premises. This does not prevent a further search of the same premises if additional grounds come to light supporting a further application for a search warrant or exercise or further exercise of another power. For example, when, as a result of new information, it is believed articles previously not found or additional articles are on the premises.

6.10 Searches must be conducted with due consideration for the property and privacy of the occupier and with no more disturbance than necessary. Reasonable force may be used only when necessary and proportionate because the co-operation of the occupier cannot be obtained or is insufficient for the purpose.

6.11 A friend, neighbour or other person must be allowed to witness the search if the occupier wishes unless the officer in charge of the search has reasonable grounds for believing the presence of the person asked for would seriously hinder the investigation or endanger officers or other people. A search need not be unreasonably delayed for this purpose. A record of the action taken should be made on the premises search record including the grounds for refusing the occupier's request.

6.12 A person is not required to be cautioned prior to being asked questions that are solely necessary for the purpose of furthering the proper and effective conduct of a search, see Code C, *paragraph 10.1(c)*. For example, questions to discover the occupier of specified premises, to find a key to open a locked drawer or cupboard or to otherwise seek co-operation during the search or to determine if a particular item is liable to be seized.

6.12A If questioning goes beyond what is necessary for the purpose of the exemption in Code C, the exchange is likely to constitute an interview as defined by Code C, *paragraph 11.1A* and would require the associated safeguards included in Code C, *section 10*.

(e) Leaving premises

6.13 If premises have been entered by force, before leaving the officer in charge of the search must make sure they are secure by:

- arranging for the occupier or their agent to be present
- any other appropriate means.

6.14, 6.15 *****

Notes for guidance

6A Whether compensation is appropriate depends on the circumstances in each case. Compensation for damage caused when effecting entry is unlikely to be appropriate if the search was lawful, and the force used can be shown to be reasonable, proportionate and necessary to effect entry. If the wrong premises are searched by mistake everything possible should be done at the earliest opportunity to allay any sense of grievance and there should normally be a strong presumption in favour of paying compensation.
*****

7   Seizure and retention of property

(a) Seizure

7.1 Subject to *paragraph 7.2*, an officer who is searching any person or premises under any statutory power or with the consent of the occupier may seize anything:

(a) covered by a warrant;

(b) the officer has reasonable grounds for believing is evidence of an offence or has been obtained in consequence of the commission of an offence but only if seizure is necessary to prevent the items being concealed, lost, disposed of, altered, damaged, destroyed or tampered with;

(c) covered by the powers in the Criminal Justice and Police Act 2001, Part 2 allowing an officer to seize property from persons or premises and retain it for sifting or examination elsewhere.

7.2 No item may be seized which an officer has reasonable grounds for believing to be subject to legal privilege, as defined in PACE, section 10, other than under the Criminal Justice and Police Act 2001, Part 2.

7.3–7.13 *****

(c) Retention

7.14 Subject to *paragraph 7.15*, anything seized in accordance with the above provisions may be retained only for as long as is necessary. It may be retained, among other purposes:

(i)   for use as evidence at a trial for an offence;

(ii)   to facilitate the use in any investigation or proceedings of anything to which it is inextricably linked;

(iii) for forensic examination or other investigation in connection with an offence;

(iv)   in order to establish its lawful owner when there are reasonable grounds for believing it has been stolen or obtained by the commission of an offence.

7.15 Property shall not be retained under *paragraph 7.14(i), (ii) or (iii)* if a copy or image would be sufficient.

(d) Rights of owners etc

7.16 If property is retained, the person who had custody or control of it immediately before seizure must, on request, be provided with a list or description of the property within a reasonable time.

7.17 That person or their representative must be allowed supervised access to the property to examine it or have it photographed or copied, or must be provided with a photograph or copy, in either case within a reasonable time of any request and at their own expense, unless the officer in charge of an investigation has reasonable grounds for believing this would:

(i)   prejudice the investigation of any offence or criminal proceedings; or

(ii)   lead to the commission of an offence by providing access to unlawful material such as pornography

A record of the grounds shall be made when access is denied.

8, 9 *****

Code C   Code of Practice for the Detention, Treatment and Questioning of Persons by Police Officers

1   General

1.1 All persons in custody must be dealt with expeditiously, and released as soon as the need for detention no longer applies.

1.1A A custody officer must perform the functions in this Code as soon as practicable. A custody officer will not be in breach of this Code if delay is justifiable and reasonable steps are taken to prevent unnecessary delay. The custody record shall show when a delay has occurred and the reason.

1.2 This Code of Practice must be readily available at all police stations for consultation by:

- police officers
- police staff
- detained persons
- members of the public.

1.3 The provisions of this Code:

- include the *Annexes*
- do not include the *Notes for Guidance*.

1.4 If an officer has any suspicion, or is told in good faith, that a person of any age may be mentally disordered or otherwise mentally vulnerable, in the absence of clear evidence to dispel that suspicion, the person shall be treated as such for the purposes of this Code.

1.5 If anyone appears to be under 17, they shall be treated as a juvenile for the purposes of this Code in the absence of clear evidence that they are older.

1.6 If a person appears to be blind, seriously visually impaired, deaf, unable to read or speak or has difficulty orally because of a speech impediment, they shall be treated as such for the purposes of this Code in the absence of clear evidence to the contrary.

1.7 'The appropriate adult' means, in the case of a:

(a) juvenile:

    (i)   the parent, guardian or, if the juvenile is in local authority or voluntary organisation care, or is otherwise being looked after under the Children Act 1989, a person representing that authority or organisation;

    (ii)   a social worker of a local authority;

    (iii)   failing these, some other responsible adult aged 18 or over who is not a police officer or employed by the police.

(b) person who is mentally disordered or mentally vulnerable:

    (i)   a relative, guardian or other person responsible for their care or custody;

    (ii)   someone experienced in dealing with mentally disordered or mentally vulnerable people but who is not a police officer or employed by the police;

    (iii)   failing these, some other responsible adult aged 18 or over who is not a police officer or employed by the police.

1.8 If this Code requires a person be given certain information, they do not have to be given it if at the time they are incapable of understanding what is said, are violent or may become violent or in urgent need of medical attention, but they must be given it as soon as practicable.

1.9–1.17 *****

Notes for guidance

1A Although certain sections of this Code apply specifically to people in custody at police stations, those there voluntarily to assist with an investigation should be treated with no less consideration, e.g. offered refreshments at appropriate times, and enjoy an absolute right to obtain legal advice or communicate with anyone outside the police station.

*****

2 Custody records

2.1A When a person is brought to a police station:
- under arrest;
- is arrested at the police station having attended there voluntarily; or
- attends a police station to answer bail

they should be brought before the custody officer as soon as practicable after their arrival at the station or, if appropriate, following arrest after attending the police station voluntarily. This applies to designated and non-designated police stations. A person is deemed to be 'at a police station' for these purposes if they are within the boundary of any building or enclosed yard which forms part of that police station.

2.1 A separate custody record must be opened as soon as practicable for each person brought to a police station under arrest or arrested at the station having gone there voluntarily or attending a police station in answer to street bail. All information recorded under this Code must be recorded as soon as practicable in the custody record unless otherwise specified. Any audio or video recording made in the custody area is not part of the custody record.

2.2 If any action requires the authority of an officer of a specified rank, subject to *paragraph 2.6A*, their name and rank must be noted in the custody record.

2.3 The custody officer is responsible for the custody record's accuracy and completeness and for making sure the record or copy of the record accompanies a detainee if they are transferred to another police station. The record shall show the:
- time and reason for transfer;
- time a person is released from detention.

2.4 A solicitor or appropriate adult must be permitted to consult a detainee's custody record as soon as practicable after their arrival at the station and at any other time whilst the person is detained. Arrangements for this access must be agreed with the custody officer and may not unreasonably interfere with the custody officer's duties.

2.4A When a detainee leaves police detention or is taken before a court they, their legal representative or appropriate adult shall be given, on request, a copy of the custody record as soon as practicable. This entitlement lasts for 12 months after release.

2.5 The detainee, appropriate adult or legal representative shall be permitted to inspect the original custody record after the detainee has left police detention provided they give reasonable notice of their request. Any such inspection shall be noted in the custody record.

2.6–2.7 *****

3 Initial action

(a) Detained persons—normal procedure

3.1 When a person is brought to a police station under arrest or arrested at the station having gone there voluntarily, the custody officer must make sure the person is told clearly about the following continuing rights which may be exercised at any stage during the period in custody:
(i) the right to have someone informed of their arrest as in *section 5*;
(ii) the right to consult privately with a solicitor and that free independent legal advice is available;
(iii) the right to consult these Codes of Practice.

3.2 The detainee must also be given:
- a written notice setting out:
  – the above three rights;
  – the arrangements for obtaining legal advice;
  – the right to a copy of the custody record as in *paragraph 2.4A*;
  – the caution in the terms prescribed in *section 10*.
- an additional written notice briefly setting out their entitlements while in custody.

Note: The detainee shall be asked to sign the custody record to acknowledge receipt of these notices. Any refusal must be recorded on the custody record.

3.3 A citizen of an independent Commonwealth country or a national of a foreign country, including the Republic of Ireland, must be informed as soon as practicable about their rights of communication with their High Commission, Embassy or Consulate. See *section 7*

3.4 The custody officer shall:

- record the offence(s) that the detainee has been arrested for and the reason(s) for the arrest on the custody record. See *paragraph 10.3 and Code C paragraphs 2.2 and 4.3*;
- note on the custody record any comment the detainee makes in relation to the arresting officer's account but shall not invite comment. If the arresting officer is not physically present when the detainee is brought to a police station, the arresting officer's account must be made available to the custody officer remotely or by a third party on the arresting officer's behalf. If the custody officer authorises a person's detention the detainee must be informed of the grounds as soon as practicable and before they are questioned about any offence;
- note any comment the detainee makes in respect of the decision to detain them but shall not invite comment;
- not put specific questions to the detainee regarding their involvement in any offence, nor in respect of any comments they may make in response to the arresting officer's account or the decision to place them in detention. Such an exchange is likely to constitute an interview as in *paragraph 11.1A* and require the associated safeguards in *section 11*.

See *paragraph 11.13* in respect of unsolicited comments.

3.5 The custody officer shall:

(a) ask the detainee, whether at this time, they:
   (i) would like legal advice, see *paragraph 6.5*;
   (ii) want someone informed of their detention, see *section 5*;
(b) ask the detainee to sign the custody record to confirm their decisions in respect of (a);
(c) determine whether the detainee:
   (i) is, or might be, in need of medical treatment or attention, see *section 9*;
   (ii) requires:
      - an appropriate adult;
      - help to check documentation;
      - an interpreter;
(d) record the decision in respect of (c).

3.6–3.10 *****

3.11 If video cameras are installed in the custody area, notices shall be prominently displayed showing cameras are in use. Any request to have video cameras switched off shall be refused.

3.12–3.20 *****

(c) Persons attending a police station voluntarily

3.21 Anybody attending a police station voluntarily to assist with an investigation may leave at will unless arrested. If it is decided they shall not be allowed to leave, they must be informed at once that they are under arrest and brought before the custody officer, who is responsible for making sure they are notified of their rights in the same way as other detainees. If they are not arrested but are cautioned as in *section 10*, the person who gives the caution must, at the same time, inform them they are not under arrest, they are not obliged to remain at the station but if they remain at the station they may obtain free and independent legal advice if they want. They shall be told the right to legal advice includes the right to speak with a solicitor on the telephone and be asked if they want to do so.

3.22 If a person attending the police station voluntarily asks about their entitlement to legal advice, they shall be given a copy of the notice explaining the arrangements for obtaining legal advice. See *paragraph 3.2*

3.23–3.25 *****

4 Detainee's property

(a) Action

4.1 The custody officer is responsible for:

(a) ascertaining what property a detainee:

  (i) has with them when they come to the police station, whether on:
   • arrest or re-detention on answering to bail;
   • commitment to prison custody on the order or sentence of a court;
   • lodgement at the police station with a view to their production in court from prison custody;
   • transfer from detention at another station or hospital;
   • detention under the Mental Health Act 1983, section 135 or 136;
   • remand into police custody on the authority of a court

  (ii) might have acquired for an unlawful or harmful purpose while in custody;

(b) the safekeeping of any property taken from a detainee which remains at the police station.

The custody officer may search the detainee or authorise their being searched to the extent they consider necessary, provided a search of intimate parts of the body or involving the removal of more than outer clothing is only made as in *Annex A*. A search may only be carried out by an officer of the same sex as the detainee.

4.2–4.5 *****

5 Right not to be held incommunicado

(a) Action

5.1 Any person arrested and held in custody at a police station or other premises may, on request, have one person known to them or likely to take an interest in their welfare informed at public expense of their whereabouts as soon as practicable. If the person cannot be contacted the detainee may choose up to two alternatives. If they cannot be contacted, the person in charge of detention or the investigation has discretion to allow further attempts until the information has been conveyed.

5.2 The exercise of the above right in respect of each person nominated may be delayed only in accordance with *Annex B*.

5.3 The above right may be exercised each time a detainee is taken to another police station.

5.4 The detainee may receive visits at the custody officer's discretion.

5.5 If a friend, relative or person with an interest in the detainee's welfare enquires about their whereabouts, this information shall be given if the suspect agrees and *Annex B* does not apply.

5.6 The detainee shall be given writing materials, on request, and allowed to telephone one person for a reasonable time, see *Notes 5A* and *5E*. Either or both these privileges may be denied or delayed if an officer of inspector rank or above considers sending a letter or making a telephone call may result in any of the consequences in:

  (a) Annex B paragraphs 1 and *2* and the person is detained in connection with an indictable offence;

  (b) …

Nothing in this paragraph permits the restriction or denial of the rights in *paragraphs 5.1* and *6.1*.

5.7 Before any letter or message is sent, or telephone call made, the detainee shall be informed that what they say in any letter, call or message (other than in a communication to a solicitor) may be read or listened to and may be given in evidence. A telephone call may be terminated if it is being abused. The costs can be at public expense at the custody officer's discretion.

5.7A Any delay or denial of the rights in this section should be proportionate and should last no longer than necessary.

5.8 *****

6   Right to legal advice

(a) Action

6.1 Unless *Annex B* applies, all detainees must be informed that they may at any time consult and communicate privately with a solicitor, whether in person, in writing or by telephone, and that free independent legal advice is available. See *paragraph 3.1*

6.2 Not Used

6.3 A poster advertising the right to legal advice must be prominently displayed in the charging area of every police station.

6.4 No police officer should, at any time, do or say anything with the intention of dissuading a detainee from obtaining legal advice.

6.5 The exercise of the right of access to legal advice may be delayed only as in *Annex B*. Whenever legal advice is requested, and unless *Annex B* applies, the custody officer must act without delay to secure the provision of such advice. If, on being informed or reminded of this right, the detainee declines to speak to a solicitor in person, the officer should point out that the right includes the right to speak with a solicitor on the telephone. If the detainee continues to waive this right the officer should ask them why and any reasons should be recorded on the custody record or the interview record as appropriate. Reminders of the right to legal advice must be given as in *paragraphs 3.5, 11.2, 15.4, 16.4, 2B of Annex A, 3 of Annex K* and *16.5* and Code D, *paragraphs 3.17(ii)* and *6.3*. Once it is clear a detainee does not want to speak to a solicitor in person or by telephone they should cease to be asked their reasons. See *Note 6K*

6.5A In the case of a juvenile, an appropriate adult should consider whether legal advice from a solicitor is required. If the juvenile indicates that they do not want legal advice, the appropriate adult has the right to ask for a solicitor to attend if this would be in the best interests of the person. However, the detained person cannot be forced to see the solicitor if he is adamant that he does not wish to do so.

6.6 A detainee who wants legal advice may not be interviewed or continue to be interviewed until they have received such advice unless:

   (a) *Annex B* applies, when the restriction on drawing adverse inferences from silence in *Annex C* will apply because the detainee is not allowed an opportunity to consult a solicitor; or

   (b) an officer of superintendent rank or above has reasonable grounds for believing that:
      (i)   the consequent delay might:
         • lead to interference with, or harm to, evidence connected with an offence;
         • lead to interference with, or physical harm to, other people;
         • lead to serious loss of, or damage to, property;
         • lead to alerting other people suspected of having committed an offence but
         • not yet arrested for it;
         • hinder the recovery of property obtained in consequence of the commission of an offence.
      (ii) when a solicitor, including a duty solicitor, has been contacted and has agreed to attend, awaiting their arrival would cause unreasonable delay to the process of investigation.
   Note: In these cases the restriction on drawing adverse inferences from silence in *Annex C* will apply because the detainee is not allowed an opportunity to consult a solicitor;

   (c) the solicitor the detainee has nominated or selected from a list:
      (i)   cannot be contacted;
      (ii) has previously indicated they do not wish to be contacted; or
      (iii) having been contacted, has declined to attend; and the detainee has been advised of the Duty Solicitor Scheme but has declined to ask for the duty solicitor.
   In these circumstances the interview may be started or continued without further delay provided an officer of inspector rank or above has agreed to the interview proceeding.
   Note: The restriction on drawing adverse inferences from silence in *Annex C* will not apply because the detainee is allowed an opportunity to consult the duty solicitor;

(d) the detainee changes their mind, about wanting legal advice.

In these circumstances the interview may be started or continued without delay provided that:

(i) the detainee agrees to do so, in writing or on interview record made in accordance with Code E or F; and

(ii) an officer of inspector rank or above has inquired about the detainee's reasons for their change of mind and gives authority for the interview to proceed.

Confirmation of the detainee's agreement, their change of mind, the reasons for it if given and, subject to *paragraph 2.6A*, the name of the authorising officer shall be recorded in the written interview record or the interview record made in accordance with Code E or F. Note: In these circumstances the restriction on drawing adverse inferences from silence in *Annex C* will not apply because the detainee is allowed an opportunity to consult a solicitor if they wish.

6.7 If *paragraph 6.6(b)(i)* applies, once sufficient information has been obtained to avert the risk, questioning must cease until the detainee has received legal advice unless *paragraph 6.6(a), (b)(ii), (c) or (d)* applies.

6.8 A detainee who has been permitted to consult a solicitor shall be entitled on request to have the solicitor present when they are interviewed unless one of the exceptions in *paragraph 6.6* applies.

6.9 The solicitor may only be required to leave the interview if their conduct is such that the interviewer is unable properly to put questions to the suspect.

6.10 If the interviewer considers a solicitor is acting in such a way, they will stop the interview and consult an officer not below superintendent rank, if one is readily available, and otherwise an officer not below inspector rank not connected with the investigation. After speaking to the solicitor, the officer consulted will decide if the interview should continue in the presence of that solicitor. If they decide it should not, the suspect will be given the opportunity to consult another solicitor before the interview continues and that solicitor given an opportunity to be present at the interview.

6.11 The removal of a solicitor from an interview is a serious step and, if it occurs, the officer of superintendent rank or above who took the decision will consider if the incident should be reported to the Law Society. If the decision to remove the solicitor has been taken by an officer below superintendent rank, the facts must be reported to an officer of superintendent rank or above who will similarly consider whether a report to the Law Society would be appropriate. When the solicitor concerned is a duty solicitor, the report should be both to the Law Society and to the Legal Services Commission.

6.12–6.17 *****

Notes for guidance

6A In considering if paragraph 6.6(b) applies, the officer should, if practicable, ask the solicitor for an estimate of how long it will take to come to the station and relate this to the time detention is permitted, the time of day (i.e. whether the rest period under paragraph 12.2 is imminent) and the requirements of other investigations. If the solicitor is on their way or is to set off immediately, it will not normally be appropriate to begin an interview before they arrive. If it appears necessary to begin an interview before the solicitor's arrival, they should be given an indication of how long the police would be able to wait before 6.6(b) applies so there is an opportunity to make arrangements for someone else to provide legal advice.

*6B, 6B1 *****

6B2 With effect from 21 April 2008, the contents of Notes for Guidance 6B and 6B1 above will be superseded by this paragraph in all police forces areas in England and Wales by the following. A detainee who asks for legal advice to be paid for by himself should be given an opportunity to consult a specific solicitor or another solicitor from that solicitor's firm. If this solicitor is unavailable by these means, they may choose up to two alternatives. If these attempts are unsuccessful, the custody officer has discretion to allow further attempts until a solicitor has been contacted and agrees to provide legal advice. Otherwise, publicly funded legal advice shall in the first instance be accessed by telephoning a call centre authorised by the Legal Services Commission (LSC) to deal with calls from the police station. The Defence Solicitor Call Centre will determine whether legal advice should be limited to telephone advice or whether a solicitor should attend. Legal advice will be by telephone if a detainee is:

- detained for a non-imprisonable offence,
- arrested on a bench warrant for failing to appear and being held for production before the court (except where the solicitor has clear documentary evidence available that would result in the client being released from custody),
- arrested on suspicion of driving with excess alcohol (failure to provide a specimen, driving whilst unfit/drunk in charge of a motor vehicle), or
- detained in relation to breach of police or court bail conditions.
- An attendance by a solicitor for an offence suitable for telephone advice will depend on whether limited exceptions apply, such as:
- whether the police are going to carry out an interview or an identification parade,
- whether the detainee is eligible for assistance from an appropriate adult,
- whether the detainee is unable to communicate over the telephone,
- whether the detainee alleges serious maltreatment by the police.

Apart from carrying out these duties, an officer must not advise the suspect about any particular firm of solicitors.

6C Not Used

6D A detainee has a right to free legal advice and to be represented by a solicitor. Legal advice by telephone advice may be provided in respect of those offences listed in Note for Guidance 6B1 and 6B2 above. The Defence Solicitor Call Centre will determine whether attendance is required by a solicitor. The solicitor's only role in the police station is to protect and advance the legal rights of their client. On occasions this may require the solicitor to give advice which has the effect of the client avoiding giving evidence which strengthens a prosecution case. The solicitor may intervene in order to seek clarification, challenge an improper question to their client or the manner in which it is put, advise their client not to reply to particular questions, or if they wish to give their client further legal advice. Paragraph 6.9 only applies if the solicitor's approach or conduct prevents or unreasonably obstructs proper questions being put to the suspect or the suspect's response being recorded. Examples of unacceptable conduct include answering questions on a suspect's behalf or providing written replies for the suspect to quote.

6E An officer who takes the decision to exclude a solicitor must be in a position to satisfy the court the decision was properly made. In order to do this they may need to witness what is happening.

6F If an officer of at least inspector rank considers a particular solicitor or firm of solicitors is persistently sending probationary representatives who are unsuited to provide legal advice, they should inform an officer of at least superintendent rank, who may wish to take the matter up with the Law Society.

6G Subject to the constraints of Annex B, a solicitor may advise more than one client in an investigation if they wish. Any question of a conflict of interest is for the solicitor under their professional code of conduct. If, however, waiting for a solicitor to give advice to one client may lead to unreasonable delay to the interview with another, the provisions of paragraph 6.6(b) may apply.

6H In addition to a poster in English, a poster or posters containing translations into Welsh, the main minority ethnic languages and the principal European languages should be displayed wherever they are likely to be helpful and it is practicable to do so.

6I Paragraph 6.6(d) requires the authorisation of an officer of inspector rank or above to the continuation of an interview when a detainee who wanted legal advice changes their mind. It is permissible for such authorisation to be given over the telephone, if the authorising officer is able to satisfy themselves about the reason for the detainee's change of mind and is satisfied it is proper to continue the interview in those circumstances.

6J Whenever a detainee exercises their right to legal advice by consulting or communicating with a solicitor, they must be allowed to do so in private. This right to consult or communicate in private is fundamental. The requirement for privacy is compromised because what is said or written by the *detainee or solicitor for the purpose of giving and receiving legal advice is overheard, listened to, or read by others without the informed consent of the detainee, the right will effectively have been denied. When a detainee chooses to speak to a solicitor on the telephone, they should be allowed to do so in private unless this is impractical because of the design and layout of the custody area or the location of telephones. However, the normal expectation should be that facilities will be available, unless they are being used, at all police stations to enable detainees to speak in private to a solicitor either face to face or over the telephone.*

6K   A detainee is not obliged to give reasons for declining legal advice and should not be pressed to do so.

7   Citizens of independent Commonwealth countries or foreign nationals

(a) Action

7.1 Any citizen of an independent Commonwealth country or a national of a foreign country, including the Republic of Ireland, may communicate at any time with the appropriate High Commission, Embassy or Consulate. The detainee must be informed as soon as practicable of:

- this right;
- their right, upon request, to have their High Commission, Embassy or Consulate told of their whereabouts and the grounds for their detention. Such a request should be acted upon as soon as practicable.

7.2 *****

7.3 Consular officers may visit one of their nationals in police detention to talk to them and, if required, to arrange for legal advice. Such visits shall take place out of the hearing of a police officer.

7.4 Notwithstanding the provisions of consular conventions, if the detainee is a political refugee whether for reasons of race, nationality, political opinion or religion, or is seeking political asylum, consular officers shall not be informed of the arrest of one of their nationals or given access or information about them except at the detainee's express request.

7.5 *****

8   Conditions of detention

(a) Action

8.1 So far as it is practicable, not more than one detainee should be detained in each cell.

8.2 Cells in use must be adequately heated, cleaned and ventilated. They must be adequately lit, subject to such dimming as is compatible with safety and security to allow people detained overnight to sleep. No additional restraints shall be used within a locked cell unless absolutely necessary and then only restraint equipment, approved for use in that force by the Chief Officer, which is reasonable and necessary in the circumstances having regard to the detainee's demeanour and with a view to ensuring their safety and the safety of others. If a detainee is deaf, mentally disordered or otherwise mentally vulnerable, particular care must be taken when deciding whether to use any form of approved restraints.

8.3 Blankets, mattresses, pillows and other bedding supplied shall be of a reasonable standard and in a clean and sanitary condition.

8.4 Access to toilet and washing facilities must be provided.

8.5 If it is necessary to remove a detainee's clothes for the purposes of investigation, for hygiene, health reasons or cleaning, replacement clothing of a reasonable standard of comfort and cleanliness shall be provided. A detainee may not be interviewed unless adequate clothing has been offered.

8.6 At least two light meals and one main meal should be offered in any 24 hour period. Drinks should be provided at meal times and upon reasonable request between meals. Whenever necessary, advice shall be sought from the appropriate health care professional, on medical and dietary matters. As far as practicable, meals provided shall offer a varied diet and meet any specific dietary needs or religious beliefs the detainee may have. The detainee may, at the custody officer's discretion, have meals supplied by their family or friends at their expense.

8.7 Brief outdoor exercise shall be offered daily if practicable.

8.8 A juvenile shall not be placed in a police cell unless no other secure accommodation is available and the custody officer considers it is not practicable to supervise them if they are not placed in a cell or that a cell provides more comfortable accommodation than other secure accommodation in the station. A juvenile may not be placed in a cell with a detained adult.

8.9–8.11 *****

9   Care and treatment of detained persons

(a) General

9.1 Nothing in this section prevents the police from calling the police surgeon or, if appropriate, some other health care professional, to examine a detainee for the purposes of obtaining evidence relating to any offence in which the detainee is suspected of being involved. See *Note 9A*

9.2 If a complaint is made by, or on behalf of, a detainee about their treatment since their arrest, or it comes to notice that a detainee may have been treated improperly, a report must be made as soon as practicable to an officer of inspector rank or above not connected with the investigation. If the matter concerns a possible assault or the possibility of the unnecessary or unreasonable use of force, an appropriate health care professional must also be called as soon as practicable.

9.3–9.4 *****

(b) Clinical treatment and attention

9.5 The custody officer must make sure a detainee receives appropriate clinical attention as soon as reasonably practicable if the person:

   (a) appears to be suffering from physical illness; or
   (b) is injured; or
   (c) appears to be suffering from a mental disorder; or
   (d) appears to need clinical attention.

9.5A This applies even if the detainee makes no request for clinical attention and whether or not they have already received clinical attention elsewhere. If the need for attention appears urgent, e.g. when indicated as in *Annex H*, the nearest available health care professional or an ambulance must be called immediately.

9.5B–9.17 *****

10   Cautions

(a) When a caution must be given

10.1 A person whom there are grounds to suspect of an offence, see *Note 10A*, must be cautioned before any questions about an offence, or further questions if the answers provide the grounds for suspicion, are put to them if either the suspect's answers or silence, (i.e. failure or refusal to answer or answer satisfactorily) may be given in evidence to a court in a prosecution. A person need not be cautioned if questions are for other necessary purposes, e.g.:

   (a) solely to establish their identity or ownership of any vehicle;
   (b) to obtain information in accordance with any relevant statutory requirement, see *paragraph 10.9*;
   (c) in furtherance of the proper and effective conduct of a search, e.g. to determine the need to search in the exercise of powers of stop and search or to seek cooperation while carrying out a search;
   (d) to seek verification of a written record as in *paragraph 11.13*;
   (e) Not Used

10.2 Whenever a person not under arrest is initially cautioned, or reminded they are under caution, that person must at the same time be told they are not under arrest and are free to leave if they want to. See *Note 10C*

10.3 A person who is arrested, or further arrested, must be informed at the time, or as soon as practicable thereafter, that they are under arrest and the grounds for their arrest, see *Note 10B and Code G, paragraphs 2.2 and 4.3*.

10.4 A person who is arrested, or further arrested, must also be cautioned unless:
   (a) it is impracticable to do so by reason of their condition or behaviour at the time;
   (b) they have already been cautioned immediately prior to arrest as in *paragraph 10.1*.

(b)　Terms of the cautions
   10.5 The caution which must be given on:
   (a) arrest;
   (b) all other occasions before a person is charged or informed they may be prosecuted, see *section 16*,

should, unless the restriction on drawing adverse inferences from silence applies, see *Annex C*, be in the following terms:

'You do not have to say anything. But it may harm your defence if you do not mention when questioned something which you later rely on in Court. Anything you do say may be given in evidence.'

[Where the use of the Welsh Language is appropriate, a constable may provide the caution directly in Welsh in the following terms:

'Does dim rhaid i chi ddweud dim byd. Ond gall niweidio eich amddiffyniad os na fyddwch chi'n sôn, wrth gael eich holi, am rywbeth y byddwch chi'n dibynnu arno nes ymlaen yn y Llys. Gall unrhyw beth yr ydych yn ei ddweud gael ei roi fel tystiolaeth.']

   10.6 *Annex C, paragraph 2* sets out the alternative terms of the caution to be used when the restriction on drawing adverse inferences from silence applies.

   10.7 Minor deviations from the words of any caution given in accordance with this Code do not constitute a breach of this Code, provided the sense of the relevant caution is preserved. See *Note 10D*

   10.8 After any break in questioning under caution, the person being questioned must be made aware they remain under caution. If there is any doubt the relevant caution should be given again in full when the interview resumes. See *Note 10E*

   10.9 When, despite being cautioned, a person fails to co-operate or to answer particular questions which may affect their immediate treatment, the person should be informed of any relevant consequences and that those consequences are not affected by the caution. Examples are when a person's refusal to provide:
   • their name and address when charged may make them liable to detention;
   • particulars and information in accordance with a statutory requirement, e.g. under the Road Traffic Act 1988, may amount to an offence or may make the person liable to a further arrest.
   10.10, 10.11 *****

(d)　Juveniles and persons who are mentally disordered or otherwise mentally vulnerable
   10.12 If a juvenile or a person who is mentally disordered or otherwise mentally vulnerable is cautioned in the absence of the appropriate adult, the caution must be repeated in the adult's presence.

(e)　Documentation
   10.13 A record shall be made when a caution is given under this section, either in the interviewer's pocket book or in the interview record.

Notes for guidance

10A There must be some reasonable, objective grounds for the suspicion, based on known facts or information which are relevant to the likelihood the offence has been committed and the person to be questioned committed it.

10B An arrested person must be given sufficient information to enable them to understand that they have been deprived of their liberty and the reason they have been arrested, e.g. when a person is arrested on suspicion of committing an offence they must be informed of the suspected offence's nature, when and where it was committed. The suspect must also be informed of the reason or reasons why the arrest is considered necessary. Vague or technical language should be avoided.

10C The restriction on drawing inferences from silence, see Annex C, paragraph 1, does not apply to a person who has not been detained and who therefore cannot be prevented from seeking legal advice if they want, see paragraph 3.21.

10D If it appears a person does not understand the caution, the person giving it should explain it in their own words.

10E It may be necessary to show to the court that nothing occurred during an interview break or between interviews which influenced the suspect's recorded evidence. After a break in an interview or at the beginning of a subsequent interview, the interviewing officer should summarise the reason for the break and confirm this with the suspect.
*****

11   Interviews—general

(a) Action

11.1A An interview is the questioning of a person regarding their involvement or suspected involvement in a criminal offence or offences which, under *paragraph 10.1*, must be carried out under caution. Whenever a person is interviewed they must be informed of the nature of the offence, or further offence. Procedures under the Road Traffic Act 1988, section 7 or the Transport and Works Act 1992, section 31 do not constitute interviewing for the purpose of this Code.

11.1 Following a decision to arrest a suspect, they must not be interviewed about the relevant offence except at a police station or other authorised place of detention, unless the consequent delay would be likely to:

(a) lead to:
- interference with, or harm to, evidence connected with an offence;
- interference with, or physical harm to, other people; or
- serious loss of, or damage to, property;

(b) lead to alerting other people suspected of committing an offence but not yet arrested for it; or

(c) hinder the recovery of property obtained in consequence of the commission of an offence.

Interviewing in any of these circumstances shall cease once the relevant risk has been averted or the necessary questions have been put in order to attempt to avert that risk.

11.2 Immediately prior to the commencement or re-commencement of any interview at a police station or other authorised place of detention, the interviewer should remind the suspect of their entitlement to free legal advice and that the interview can be delayed for legal advice to be obtained, unless one of the exceptions in *paragraph 6.6* applies. It is the interviewer's responsibility to make sure all reminders are recorded in the interview record.

11.3 Not Used

11.4 At the beginning of an interview the interviewer, after cautioning the suspect, *see section 10*, shall put to them any significant statement or silence which occurred in the presence and hearing of a police officer or other police staff before the start of the interview and which have not been put to the suspect in the course of a previous interview. See *Note 11A*. The interviewer shall ask the suspect whether they confirm or deny that earlier statement or silence and if they want to add anything.

11.4A A significant statement is one which appears capable of being used in evidence against the suspect, in particular a direct admission of guilt. A significant silence is a failure or refusal to answer a question or answer satisfactorily when under caution, which might, allowing for the restriction on drawing adverse inferences from silence, see *Annex C*, give rise to an inference under the Criminal Justice and Public Order Act 1994, Part III.

11.5 No interviewer may try to obtain answers or elicit a statement by the use of oppression. Except as in *paragraph 10.9*, no interviewer shall indicate, except to answer a direct question, what action will be taken by the police if the person being questioned answers questions, makes a statement or refuses to do either. If the person asks directly what action will be taken if they answer questions, make a statement or refuse to do either, the interviewer may inform them what action the police propose to take provided that action is itself proper and warranted.

11.6 The interview or further interview of a person about an offence with which that person has not been charged or for which they have not been informed they may be prosecuted, must cease when:

> (a) the officer in charge of the investigation is satisfied all the questions they consider relevant to obtaining accurate and reliable information about the offence have been put to the suspect, this includes allowing the suspect an opportunity to give an innocent explanation and asking questions to test if the explanation is accurate and reliable, e.g. to clear up ambiguities or clarify what the suspect said;
>
> (b) the officer in charge of the investigation has taken account of any other available evidence; and
>
> (c) the officer in charge of the investigation, or in the case of a detained suspect, the custody officer, see *paragraph 16.1*, reasonably believes there is sufficient evidence to provide a realistic prospect of conviction for that offence. See *Note 11B*

This paragraph does not prevent officers in revenue cases or acting under the confiscation provisions of the Criminal Justice Act 1988 or the Drug Trafficking Act 1994 from inviting suspects to complete a formal question and answer record after the interview is concluded.

(b) Interview records

11.7 (a) An accurate record must be made of each interview, whether or not the interview takes place at a police station

> (b) The record must state the place of interview, the time it begins and ends, any interview breaks and, subject to *paragraph 2.6A*, the names of all those present; and must be made on the forms provided for this purpose or in the interviewer's pocket book or in accordance with the Codes of Practice E or F;
>
> (c) Any written record must be made and completed during the interview, unless this would not be practicable or would interfere with the conduct of the interview, and must constitute either a verbatim record of what has been said or, failing this, an account of the interview which adequately and accurately summarises it.

11.8–11.14 *****

(c) Juveniles and mentally disordered or otherwise mentally vulnerable people

11.15 A juvenile or person who is mentally disordered or otherwise mentally vulnerable must not be interviewed regarding their involvement or suspected involvement in a criminal offence or offences, or asked to provide or sign a written statement under caution or record of interview, in the absence of the appropriate adult unless *paragraphs 11.1, 11.18 to 11.20 apply*. See *Note 11C*

11.16 Juveniles may only be interviewed at their place of education in exceptional circumstances and only when the principal or their nominee agrees. Every effort should be made to notify the parent(s) or other person responsible for the juvenile's welfare and the appropriate adult, if this is a different person, that the police want to interview the juvenile and reasonable time should be allowed to enable the appropriate adult to be present at the interview. If awaiting the appropriate adult would cause unreasonable delay, and unless the juvenile is suspected of an offence against the educational establishment, the principle or their nominee can act as the appropriate adult for the purposes of the interview.

11.17 If an appropriate adult is present at an interview, they shall be informed:

- they are not expected to act simply as an observer; and
- the purpose of their presence is to:
  - advise the person being interviewed;
  - observe whether the interview is being conducted properly and fairly;
  - facilitate communication with the person being interviewed.

11.18 *****

11.19 These interviews may not continue once sufficient information has been obtained to avert the consequences in *paragraph 11.1(a) to (c)*.

11.20 A record shall be made of the grounds for any decision to interview a person under *paragraph 11.18*.

Notes for guidance

11A Paragraph 11.4 does not prevent the interviewer from putting significant statements and silences to a suspect again at a later stage or a further interview.

11B The Criminal Procedure and Investigations Act 1996 Code of Practice, paragraph 3.4 states 'In conducting an investigation, the investigator should pursue all reasonable lines of enquiry, whether these point towards or away from the suspect. What is reasonable will depend on the particular circumstances.' Interviewers should keep this in mind when deciding what questions to ask in an interview.

11C Although juveniles or people who are mentally disordered or otherwise mentally vulnerable are often capable of providing reliable evidence, they may, without knowing or wishing to do so, be particularly prone in certain circumstances to provide information that may be unreliable, misleading or self-incriminating. Special care should always be taken when questioning such a person, and the appropriate adult should be involved if there is any doubt about a person's age, mental state or capacity. Because of the risk of unreliable evidence it is also important to obtain corroboration of any facts admitted whenever possible.

11D Juveniles should not be arrested at their place of education unless this is unavoidable. When a juvenile is arrested at their place of education, the principal or their nominee must be informed.

11E Significant statements described in paragraph 11.4 will always be relevant to the offence and must be recorded. When a suspect agrees to read records of interviews and other comments and sign them as correct, they should be asked to endorse the record with, e.g. 'I agree that this is a correct record of what was said' and add their signature. If the suspect does not agree with the record, the interviewer should record the details of any disagreement and ask the suspect to read these details and sign them to the effect that they accurately reflect their disagreement. Any refusal to sign should be recorded.

12   Interviews in police stations

(a) Action

12.1 If a police officer wants to interview or conduct enquiries which require the presence of a detainee, the custody officer is responsible for deciding whether to deliver the detainee into the officer's custody.

12.2 Except as below, in any period of 24 hours a detainee must be allowed a continuous period of at least 8 hours for rest, free from questioning, travel or any interruption in connection with the investigation concerned. This period should normally be at night or other appropriate time which takes account of when the detainee last slept or rested. If a detainee is arrested at a police station after going there voluntarily, the period of 24 hours runs from the time of their arrest and not the time of arrival at the police station. The period may not be interrupted or delayed, except:

    (a) when there are reasonable grounds for believing not delaying or interrupting the period would:

        (i)   involve a risk of harm to people or serious loss of, or damage to, property;

        (ii) delay unnecessarily the person's release from custody;

        (iii) otherwise prejudice the outcome of the investigation;

    (b) at the request of the detainee, their appropriate adult or legal representative;

    (c) when a delay or interruption is necessary in order to:

        (i)   comply with the legal obligations and duties arising under *section 15*;

        (ii) to take action required under *section 9* or in accordance with medical advice.

If the period is interrupted in accordance with *(a)*, a fresh period must be allowed. Interruptions under *(b)* and *(c)*, do not require a fresh period to be allowed.

12.3 *****

12.4 As far as practicable interviews shall take place in interview rooms which are adequately heated, lit and ventilated.

12.5 A suspect whose detention without charge has been authorised under PACE, because the detention is necessary for an interview to obtain evidence of the offence for which they have been arrested, may choose not to answer questions but police do not require the suspect's consent or agreement to interview them for this purpose. If a suspect takes steps to prevent themselves being questioned or further questioned, e.g. by refusing to leave their cell to go to a suitable interview room or by trying to leave the interview room, they shall be advised their consent or agreement to interview is not required. The suspect shall be cautioned as in *section 10*, and informed if they fail or refuse to co-operate, the interview may take place in the cell and that their failure or refusal to co-operate may be given in evidence. The suspect shall then be invited to co-operate and go into the interview room.

12.6 People being questioned or making statements shall not be required to stand.

12.7 Before the interview commences each interviewer shall, subject to *paragraph 2.6A*, identify themselves and any other persons present to the interviewee.

12.8 Breaks from interviewing should be made at recognised meal times or at other times that take account of when an interviewee last had a meal. Short refreshment breaks shall be provided at approximately two hour intervals, subject to the interviewer's discretion to delay a break if there are reasonable grounds for believing it would:

    (i)   involve a:
- risk of harm to people;
- serious loss of, or damage to, property;

    (ii) unnecessarily delay the detainee's release;

    (iii) otherwise prejudice the outcome of the investigation.

12.9 If during the interview a complaint is made by or on behalf of the interviewee concerning the provisions of this Code, the interviewer should:

    (i)   record it in the interview record;

    (ii) inform the custody officer, who is then responsible for dealing with it as in *section 9*.

12.10–12.14 *****

13–15 *****

16 Charging detained persons

(a) Action

16.1 When the officer in charge of the investigation reasonably believes there is sufficient evidence to provide a realistic prospect of the detainee's conviction, see *paragraph 11.6*, they shall without delay, and subject to the following qualification, inform the custody officer who will be responsible for considering whether the detainee should be charged. When a person is detained in respect of more than one offence it is permissible to delay informing the custody officer until the above conditions are satisfied in respect of all the offences, but see *paragraph 11.6*. If the detainee is a juvenile, mentally disordered or otherwise mentally vulnerable, any resulting action shall be taken in the presence of the appropriate adult if they are present at the time.

16.1A Where guidance issued by the Director of Public Prosecutions under section 37A is in force the custody officer must comply with that Guidance in deciding how to act in dealing with the detainee. See *Notes 16AA and 16AB*.

16.1B Where in compliance with the DPP's Guidance the custody officer decides that the case should be immediately referred to the CPS to make the charging decision, consultation should take place with a Crown Prosecutor as soon as is reasonably practicable. Where the Crown Prosecutor is unable to make the charging decision on the information available at that time, the detainee may be released without charge and on bail (with conditions if necessary) under section 37(7)(a). In such circumstances, the detainee should be informed that they are being released to enable the Director of Public Prosecutions to make a decision under section 37B.

16.2 When a detainee is charged with or informed they may be prosecuted for an offence, they shall, unless the restriction on drawing adverse inferences from silence applies, see *Annex C*, be cautioned as follows:

'You do not have to say anything. But it may harm your defence if you do not mention now something which you later rely on in court. Anything you do say may be given in evidence.'

[Where the use of the Welsh Language is appropriate, a constable may provide the caution directly in Welsh in the following terms:

'Does dim rhaid i chi ddweud dim byd. Ond gall niweidio eich amddiffyniad os na fyddwch chi'n sôn, wrth gael eich holi, am rywbeth y byddwch chi'n dibynnu arno nes ymlaen yn y Llys. Gall unrhyw beth yr ydych yn ei ddweud gael ei roi fel tystiolaeth.']

Annex C, paragraph 2 sets out the alternative terms of the caution to be used when the restriction on drawing adverse inferences from silence applies.

16.3 When a detainee is charged they shall be given a written notice showing particulars of the offence and, subject to *paragraph 2.6A*, the officer's name and the case reference number. As far as possible the particulars of the charge shall be stated in simple terms, but they shall also show the precise offence in law with which the detainee is charged. The notice shall begin:

'You are charged with the offence(s) shown below.' Followed by the caution.

If the detainee is a juvenile, mentally disordered or otherwise mentally vulnerable, the notice should be given to the appropriate adult.

16.4 If, after a detainee has been charged with or informed they may be prosecuted for an offence, an officer wants to tell them about any written statement or interview with another person relating to such an offence, the detainee shall either be handed a true copy of the written statement or the content of the interview record brought to their attention. Nothing shall be done to invite any reply or comment except to:

    (a) caution the detainee, *'You do not have to say anything, but anything you do say may be given in evidence.'* [Where the use of the Welsh Language is appropriate, caution the detainee in the following terms: 'Does dim rhaid i chi ddweud dim byd, ond gall unrhyw beth yr ydych yn ei ddweud gael ei roi fel tystiolaeth.']; and

    (b) remind the detainee about their right to legal advice.

16.4A If the detainee:

- cannot read, the document may be read to them
- is a juvenile, mentally disordered or otherwise mentally vulnerable, the appropriate adult shall also be given a copy, or the interview record shall be brought to their attention

16.5 A detainee may not be interviewed about an offence after they have been charged with, or informed they may be prosecuted for it, unless the interview is necessary:

- to prevent or minimise harm or loss to some other person, or the public
- to clear up an ambiguity in a previous answer or statement
- in the interests of justice for the detainee to have put to them, and have an opportunity to comment on, information concerning the offence which has come to light since they were charged or informed they might be prosecuted

Before any such interview, the interviewer shall:

    (a) caution the detainee, *'You do not have to say anything, but anything you do say may be given in evidence.'* [Where the use of the Welsh Language is appropriate, the interviewer shall caution the detainee, 'Does dim rhaid i chi ddweud dim byd, ond gall unrhyw beth yr ydych yn ei ddweud gael ei roi fel tystiolaeth.'];

    (b) remind the detainee about their right to legal advice.

16.6–16.10 *****

17   *****

Annex A   *****

Annex B   Delay in notifying arrest or allowing access to legal advice

A   Persons detained under PACE

1. The exercise of the rights in *Section 5* or *Section 6*, or both, may be delayed if the person is in police detention, as in PACE, section 118(2), in connection with an indictable offence, has not yet

been charged with an offence and an officer of superintendent rank or above, or inspector rank or above only for the rights in *Section 5*, has reasonable grounds for believing their exercise will:

    (i) lead to:
- interference with, or harm to, evidence connected with an indictable offence; or
- interference with, or physical harm to, other people; or

    (ii) lead to alerting other people suspected of having committed an indictable offence but not yet arrested for it; or

    (iii) hinder the recovery of property obtained in consequence of the commission of such an offence.

2. These rights may also be delayed if the officer has reasonable grounds to believe that:

    (i) the person detained for an indictable offence has benefited from their criminal conduct (decided in accordance with Part 2 of the Proceeds of Crime Act 2002); and

    (ii) the recovery of the value of the property constituting that benefit will be hindered by the exercise of either right.

3. Authority to delay a detainee's right to consult privately with a solicitor may be given only if the authorising officer has reasonable grounds to believe the solicitor the detainee wants to consult will, inadvertently or otherwise, pass on a message from the detainee or act in some other way which will have any of the consequences specified under *paragraph 1* or *2*. In these circumstances the detainee must be allowed to choose another solicitor.

4. If the detainee wishes to see a solicitor, access to that solicitor may not be delayed on the grounds they might advise the detainee not to answer questions or the solicitor was initially asked to attend the police station by someone else. In the latter case the detainee must be told the solicitor has come to the police station at another person's request, and must be asked to sign the custody record to signify whether they want to see the solicitor.

5. The fact the grounds for delaying notification of arrest may be satisfied does not automatically mean the grounds for delaying access to legal advice will also be satisfied.

6. These rights may be delayed only for as long as grounds exist and in no case beyond 36 hours after the relevant time as in PACE, section 41. If the grounds cease to apply within this time, the detainee must, as soon as practicable, be asked if they want to exercise either right, the custody record must be noted accordingly, and action taken in accordance with the relevant section of the Code.

7. A detained person must be permitted to consult a solicitor for a reasonable time before any court hearing.

*****

Annexes C–F ****

Code G Code of Practice for the Statutory Power of Arrest by Police Officers

1. Introduction

1.1 This Code of Practice deals with statutory power of police to arrest persons suspected of involvement in a criminal offence.

1.2 The right to liberty is a key principle of the Human Rights Act 1998. The exercise of the power of arrest represents an obvious and significant interference with that right.

1.3 The use of the power must be fully justified and officers exercising the power should consider if the necessary objectives can be met by other, less intrusive means. Arrest must never be used simply because it can be used. Absence of justification for exercising the powers of arrest may lead to challenges should the case proceed to court. When the power of arrest is exercised it is essential that it is exercised in a non-discriminatory and proportionate manner.

1.4 Section 24 of the Police and Criminal Evidence Act 1984 (as substituted by section 110 of the Serious Organised Crime and Police Act 2005) provides the statutory power of arrest. If the provisions of the Act and this Code are not observed, both the arrest and the conduct of any subsequent investigation may be open to question.

1.5 This code of practice must be readily available at all police stations for consultation by police officers and police staff, detained persons and members of the public.

1.6 The notes for guidance are not provisions of this code.

2 Elements of arrest under section 24 PACE

2.1 A lawful arrest requires two elements:

A person's involvement or suspected involvement or attempted involvement in the commission of a criminal offence;

AND

Reasonable grounds for believing that the person's arrest is necessary.

2.2 Arresting officers are required to inform the person arrested that they have been arrested, even if this fact is obvious, and of the relevant circumstances of the arrest in relation to both elements and to inform the custody officer of these on arrival at the police station. See Code C paragraph 3.4.

Involvement in the commission of an offence

2.3 A constable may arrest without warrant in relation to any offence, except for the single exception listed in Note for Guidance 1. A constable may arrest anyone:

- who is about to commit an offence or is in the act of committing an offence
- whom the officer has reasonable grounds for suspecting is about to commit an offence or to be committing an offence
- whom the officer has reasonable grounds to suspect of being guilty of an offence which he or she has reasonable grounds for suspecting has been committed
- anyone who is guilty of an offence which has been committed or anyone whom the officer has reasonable grounds for suspecting to be guilty of that offence.

Necessity criteria

2.4 The power of arrest is only exercisable if the constable has reasonable grounds for believing that it is necessary to arrest the person. The criteria for what may constitute necessity are set out in paragraph 2.9. It remains an operational decision at the discretion of the arresting officer as to:

- what action he or she may take at the point of contact with the individual;
- the necessity criterion or criteria (if any) which applies to the individual; and
- whether to arrest, report for summons, grant street bail, issue a fixed penalty notice or take any other action that is open to the officer.

2.5 In applying the criteria, the arresting officer has to be satisfied that at least one of the reasons supporting the need for arrest is satisfied.

2.6 Extending the power of arrest to all offences provides a constable with the ability to use that power to deal with any situation. However applying the necessity criteria requires the constable to examine and justify the reason or reasons why a person needs to be taken to a police station for the custody officer to decide whether the person should be placed in police detention.

2.7 The criteria below are set out in section 24 of PACE as substituted by section 110 of the Serious Organised Crime and Police Act 2005. The criteria are exhaustive. However, the circumstances that may satisfy those criteria remain a matter for the operational discretion of individual officers. Some examples are given below of what those circumstances may be.

2.8 In considering the individual circumstances, the constable must take into account the situation of the victim, the nature of the offence, the circumstances of the suspect and the needs of the investigative process.

2.9 The criteria are that the arrest is necessary:

(a) to enable the name of the person in question to be ascertained (in the case where the constable does not know, and cannot readily ascertain, the person's name, or has reasonable grounds for doubting whether a name given by the person as his name is his real name);

(b) correspondingly as regards the person's address an address is a satisfactory address for service of summons if the person will be at it for a sufficiently long period for it to be possible to serve him or her with a summons; or, that some other person at that address specified by the person will accept service of the summons on their behalf;

(c) to prevent the person in question—

    (i) causing physical injury to himself or any other person;

    (ii) suffering physical injury;

    (iii) causing loss or damage to property;

    (iv) committing an offence against public decency (only applies where members of the public going about their normal business cannot reasonably be expected to avoid the person in question); or

    (v) causing an unlawful obstruction of the highway;

(d) to protect a child or other vulnerable person from the person in question;

(e) to allow the prompt and effective investigation of the offence or of the conduct of the person in question. This may include cases such as:

    (i) Where there are reasonable grounds to believe that the person:

- has made false statements;
- has made statements which cannot be readily verified;
- has presented false evidence;
- may steal or destroy evidence;
- may make contact with co-suspects or conspirators;
- may intimidate or threaten or make contact with witnesses;
- where it is necessary to obtain evidence by questioning; or

    (ii) when considering arrest in connection with an indictable offence, there is a need to:

- enter and search any premises occupied or controlled by a person
- search the person
- prevent contact with others
- take fingerprints, footwear impressions, samples or photographs of the suspect;

    (iii) ensuring compliance with statutory drug testing requirements;

(f) to prevent any prosecution for the offence from being hindered by the disappearance of the person in question. This may arise if there are reasonable grounds for believing that

- if the person is not arrested he or she will fail to attend court
- street bail after arrest would be insufficient to deter the suspect from trying to evade prosecution.

3   Information to be given on arrest

(a) Cautions—when a caution must be given

[Note: Code G at this point replicates the material taken from Code C, paragraphs 10.1 to 10.9 (*supra*).]

    3.1–3.7 *****

4   Records of arrest

(a) General

    4.1 The arresting officer is required to record in his pocket book or by other methods used for recording information:

- the nature and circumstances of the offence leading to the arrest
- the reason or reasons why arrest was necessary
- the giving of the caution
- anything said by the person at the time of arrest

4.2 Such a record should be made at the time of the arrest unless impracticable to do. If not made at that time, the record should then be completed as soon as possible thereafter.

4.3 On arrival at the police station, the custody officer shall open the custody record (see paragraph 1.1A and section 2 of Code C). The information given by the arresting officer on the circumstances and reason or reasons for arrest shall be recorded as part of the custody record. Alternatively, a copy of the record made by the officer in accordance with *paragraph 4.1* above shall be attached as part of the custody record. See *paragraph 2.2* and *Code C paragraphs 3.4 and 10.3*.

4.4 The custody record will serve as a record of the arrest. Copies of the custody record will be provided in accordance with paragraphs 2.4 and 2.4A of Code C and access for inspection of the original record in accordance with paragraph 2.5 of Code C.

(b) Interviews and arrests

4.5 Records of interview, significant statements or silences will be treated in the same way as set out in sections 10 and 11 of Code C and in Code E (tape recording of interviews).

Notes for guidance

1 The powers of arrest for offences under sections 4(1) and 5(1) of the Criminal Law Act 1967 require that the offences to which they relate must carry a sentence fixed by law or one in which a first time offender aged 18 or over could be sentenced to 5 years or more imprisonment.

2 There must be some reasonable, objective grounds for the suspicion, based on known facts or information which are relevant to the likelihood the offence has been committed and the person to be questioned committed it.

3 An arrested person must be given sufficient information to enable them to understand they have been deprived of their liberty and the reason they have been arrested, e.g. when a person is arrested on suspicion of committing an offence they must be informed of the suspected offence's nature, when and where it was committed. The suspect must also be informed of the reason or reasons why arrest is considered necessary. Vague or technical language should be avoided.

4 Nothing in this Code requires a caution to be given or repeated when informing a person not under arrest they may be prosecuted for an offence. However, a court will not be able to draw any inferences under the Criminal Justice and Public Order Act 1994, section 34, if the person was not cautioned.

5 If it appears a person does not understand the caution, the people giving it should explain it in their own words.

6 The powers available to an officer as the result of an arrest – for example, entry and search of premises, holding a person incommunicado, setting up road blocks – are only available in respect of indictable offences and are subject to the specific requirements on authorisation as set out in the 1984 Act and relevant PACE Code of Practice.

Code H Code of Practice for the Detention, Treatment and Questioning by Police Officers of Persons under Section 41 of, and Schedule 8 to, the Terrorism Act 2000

[**Note:** This Code largely replicates the provisions of Code C except that in places it is slightly varied to allow for the possibility of longer periods of detention or to reflect that the power of arrest is only that contained in s. 41 of the Terrorism Act 2000. We have therefore included some of the general provisions of the Code before it begins to replicate Code C and s. 14, which does vary from Code C dealing, as it does, specifically with review of detention under Schedule 8 to the Terrorism Act 2000.]

1 General

1.1 This Code of Practice applies to, and only to, persons arrested under section 41 of the Terrorism Act 2000 (TACT) and detained in police custody under those provisions and Schedule 8 of the Act. References to detention under this provision that were previously included in PACE Code C–Code for the Detention, Treatment, and Questioning of Persons by Police Officers, no longer apply.

1.2 The Code ceases to apply at any point that a detainee is:

    (a) charged with an offence

    (b) released without charge, or

    (c) transferred to a prison see *section 14.5*

1.3 References to an offence in this Code include being concerned in the commission, preparation or instigation of acts of terrorism.

1.4 This Code's provisions do not apply to detention of individuals under any other terrorism legislation. This Code does not apply to people:

    (i) detained under section 5(1) of the Prevention of Terrorism Act 2005;

    (ii) detained for examination under TACT Schedule 7 and to whom the Code of Practice issued under that Act, Schedule 14, paragraph 6 applies;

    (iii) detained for searches under stop and search powers.

The provisions for the detention, treatment and questioning by police officers of persons other than those in police detention following arrest under section 41 of TACT, are set out in Code C issued under section 66(1) of the Police & Criminal Evidence Act (PACE) 1984 (PACE Code C).

1.5–1.21 *****

2–13 *****

14　Reviews and extensions of detention

(a) Reviews and extensions of detention

14.1 The powers and duties of the review officer are in the Terrorism Act 2000, Schedule 8, Part II. See *Notes 14A* and *14B*. A review officer should carry out his duties at the police station where the detainee is held, and be allowed such access to the detainee as is necessary for him to exercise those duties.

14.2 For the purposes of reviewing a person's detention, no officer shall put specific questions to the detainee:

- regarding their involvement in any offence; or
- in respect of any comments they may make:
  - when given the opportunity to make representations; or
  - in response to a decision to keep them in detention or extend the maximum period of detention.

Such an exchange could constitute an interview as in *paragraph 11.1* and would be subject to the associated safeguards in *section 11* and, in respect of a person who has been charged see *PACE Code C Section 16.8*.

14.3 If detention is necessary for longer than 48 hours, a police officer of at least superintendent rank, or a Crown Prosecutor may apply for warrants of further detention under the Terrorism Act 2000, Schedule 8, Part III.

14.4 When an application for a warrant of further or extended detention is sought under Paragraph 29 or 36 of Schedule 8, the detained person and their representative must be informed of their rights in respect of the application. These include:

    (a) the right to a written or oral notice of the warrant See Note 14G.

    (b) the right to make oral or written representations to the judicial authority about the application;

    (c) the right to be present and legally represented at the hearing of the application, unless specifically excluded by the judicial authority;

    (d) their right to free legal advice (see section 6 of this Code).

(b) Transfer of detained persons to Prison

14.5 Where a warrant is issued which authorises detention beyond a period of 14 days from the time of arrest (or if a person was being detained under TACT Schedule 7, from the time at which the examination under Schedule 7 began), the detainee must be transferred from detention in a police station to detention in a designated prison as soon as is practicable, unless:

(a) the detainee specifically requests to remain in detention at a police station and that request can be accommodated, or

(b) there are reasonable grounds to believe that transferring a person to a prison would:

    (i) significantly hinder a terrorism investigation;

    (ii) delay charging of the detainee or his release from custody; or

    (iii) otherwise prevent the investigation from being conducted diligently and expeditiously.

If any of the grounds in (b)(i) to (iii) above are relied upon, these must be presented to the judicial authority as part of the application for the warrant that would extend detention beyond a period of 14 days from the time of arrest (or if a person was being detained under TACT Schedule 7, from the time at which the examination under Schedule 7 began) See *Note 14J*.

14.6 If a person remains in detention at a police station under a warrant of further detention as described at section 14.5, they must be transferred to a prison as soon as practicable after the grounds at (b)(i) to (iii) of that section cease to apply.

14.7 Police should maintain an agreement with the National Offender Management Service (NOMS) that stipulates named prisons to which individuals may be transferred under this section. This should be made with regard to ensuring detainees are moved to the most suitable prison for the purposes of the investigation and their welfare, and should include provision for the transfer of male, female and juvenile detainees. Police should ensure that the Governor of a prison to which they intend to transfer a detainee is given reasonable notice of this. Where practicable, this should be no later than the point at which a warrant is applied for that would take the period of detention beyond 14 days.

14.8 Following a detained person's transfer to a designated prison, their detention will be governed by the terms of Schedule 8 and Prison Rules, and this Code of Practice will not apply during any period that the person remains in prison detention. The Code will once more apply if a detained person is transferred back from prison detention to police detention. In order to enable the Governor to arrange for the production of the detainee back into police custody, police should give notice to the Governor of the relevant prison as soon as possible of any decision to transfer a detainee from prison back to a police station. Any transfer between a prison and a police station should be conducted by police, and this Code will be applicable during the period of transit See *Note 14K*. A detainee should only remain in police custody having been transferred back from a prison, for as long as is necessary for the purpose of the investigation.

14.9 The investigating team and custody officer should provide as much information as necessary to enable the relevant prison authorities to provide appropriate facilities to detain an individual. This should include, but not be limited to:

    (i) medical assessments

    (ii) security and risk assessments

    (iii) details of the detained person's legal representatives

    (iv) details of any individuals from whom the detained person has requested visits, or who have requested to visit the detained person.

14.10 Where a detainee is to be transferred to prison, the custody officer should inform the detainee's legal adviser beforehand that the transfer is to take place (including the name of the prison). The custody officer should also make all reasonable attempts to inform:

- family or friends who have been informed previously of the detainee's detention; and
- the person who was initially informed of the detainee's detention as at paragraph 5.1.

(c) Documentation

14.11 It is the responsibility of the officer who gives any reminders as at *paragraph 14.4*, to ensure that these are noted in the custody record, as well any comments made by the detained person upon being told of those rights.

14.12 The grounds for, and extent of, any delay in conducting a review shall be recorded.

14.13 Any written representations shall be retained.

14.14 A record shall be made as soon as practicable about the outcome of each review or determination whether to extend the maximum detention period without charge or an application for a warrant of further detention or its extension.

14.15 Any decision not to transfer a detained person to a designated prison under paragraph 14.5, must be recorded, along with the reasons for this decision. If a request under *paragraph 14.5(a)* is not accommodated, the reasons for this should also be recorded.

Notes for guidance

14A TACT Schedule 8 Part II sets out the procedures for review of detention up to 48 hours from the time of arrest under TACT section 41 (or if a person was being detained under TACT Schedule 7, from the time at which the examination under Schedule 7 began). These include provisions for the requirement to review detention, postponing a review, grounds for continued detention, designating a review officer, representations, rights of the detained person and keeping a record. The review officer's role ends after a warrant has been issued for extension of detention under Part III of Schedule 8.

14B Section 24(1) of the Terrorism Act 2006, amended the grounds contained within the 2000 Act on which a review officer may authorise continued detention. Continued detention may be authorised if it is necessary

    (a) to obtain relevant evidence whether by questioning him or otherwise

    (b) to preserve relevant evidence

    (c) while awaiting the result of an examination or analysis of relevant evidence

    (d) for the examination or analysis of anything with a view to obtaining relevant evidence

    (e) pending a decision to apply to the Secretary of State for a deportation notice to be served on the detainee, the making of any such application, or the consideration of any such application by the Secretary of State

    (f) pending a decision to charge the detainee with an offence.

14C Applications for warrants to extend detention beyond 48 hours, may be made for periods of 7 days at a time (initially under TACT Schedule 8 paragraph 29, and extensions thereafter under TACT Schedule 8, Paragraph 36), up to a maximum period of 28 days from the time of arrest (or if a person was being detained under TACT Schedule 7, from the time at which the examination under Schedule 7 began). Applications may be made for shorter periods than 7 days, which must be specified. The judicial authority may also substitute a shorter period if he feels a period of 7 days is inappropriate.

14D Unless Note 14F applies, applications for warrants that would take the total period of detention up to 14 days or less should be made to a judicial authority, meaning a District Judge (Magistrates' Court) designated by the Lord Chancellor to hear such applications.

14E Any application for a warrant which would take the period of detention beyond 14 days from the time of arrest (or if a person was being detained under TACT Schedule 7, from the time at which the examination under Schedule 7 began), must be made to a High Court Judge.

14F If an application has been made to a High Court judge for a warrant which would take detention beyond 14 days, and the High Court judge instead issues a warrant for a period of time which would not take detention beyond 14 days, further applications for extension of detention must also be made to a High Court judge, regardless of the period of time to which they refer.

14G TACT Schedule 8 Paragraph 31 requires a notice to be given to the detained person if a warrant is sought for further detention. This must be provided before the judicial hearing of the application for that warrant and must include:

    (a) notification that the application for a warrant has been made

    (b) the time at which the application was made

    (c) the time at which the application is to be heard

    (d) the grounds on which further detention is sought

A notice must also be provided each time an application is made to extend an existing warrant.

14H An officer applying for an order under TACT Schedule 8 Paragraph 34 to withhold specified information on which he intends to rely when applying for a warrant of further detention, may make the application for the order orally or in writing. The most appropriate method of application will depend on the circumstances of the case and the need to ensure fairness to the detainee.

14I Where facilities exist, hearings relating to extension of detention under Part III of Schedule 8 may take place using video conferencing facilities provided that the requirements set out in Schedule 8 are still met. However, if the judicial authority requires the detained person to be physically present at any hearing, this should be complied with as soon as practicable. Paragraphs 33(4) to 33(9) of TACT Schedule 8 govern the relevant conduct of hearings.

14J Transfer to prison is intended to ensure that individuals who are detained for extended periods of time are held in a place designed for longer periods of detention than police stations. Prison will provide detainees with a greater range of facilities more appropriate to longer detention periods.

14K The Code will only apply as is appropriate to the conditions of detention during the period of transit. There is obviously no requirement to provide such things as bed linen or reading materials for the journey between prison and police station.

*****

Index

The Lord Rodger Essay Prize
Sponsored by Oxford University Press

The Statute Law Society ('the Society') invites applications for the Lord Rodger Essay Prize.

The Society is a charitable body, which aims to educate the legal profession and the public about the legislative process, with a view to encouraging improvements in statute law. It was founded in 1968 and has members throughout Britain, Europe and the Commonwealth.

Lord Rodger of Earlsferry SCJ was Chair of the Society from 2002 until his death in 2011. He was involved in the legislative process at various stages of his career and retained a strong interest in the making and interpretation of statute law.

In memory of Lord Rodger, the Society has established an annual essay prize worth £1,000.

◄ Essays submitted must concern one or more of the following topics:

  ➤ the legislative process,

  ➤ the use of legislation as an instrument of public policy,

  ➤ the drafting of legislation,

  ➤ the interpretation of legislation.

◄ Essays may relate to the United Kingdom and/or any other jurisdiction or jurisdictions.

◄ Essays must be written in English and must be between 5,000 and 8,000 words long, including footnotes. They must be preceded by an abstract of no more than 200 words.

◄ Essays may be submitted by anyone who is reading for an undergraduate degree at any University and in any subject; or has held their first (or only) undergraduate degree for not more than five years.

Full information about the prize including entry instructions and deadline details can be found on www.statutelawsociety.org and at www.oxfordtextbooks.co.uk/law/statutes

Please refer to the website for submission instructions, and to download an entry form.

The closing date for the essay prize is mid-September each year.

The winning essay will be chosen by a jury consisting of three members of the Council of the Society. The prize will be presented by the Chairman of the Law Society, at the Society's Annual Lord Renton Lecture in November.

The prize sum is £1,000. The winning essay will be considered for publication in the Statute Law Review, which is published by Oxford University Press, in association with the Society.